(continued from front flap)

Two framing chapters reflect on the constant flow of history as guided by the energy of form. Of the remaining nine chapters (two of which are previously unpublished), three chapters analyze important theorists: the concept of style in the work of Hippolyte Taine, expressive flux in the formalism of the art historian Heinrich Wölfflin, and stylistic energy in the work of the Marxist literary critic Jerome J. McGann.

Six critical studies sample works and periods ranging in time from the Renaissance through modernism, with close readings of passages and works by Coleridge, the neo-Latin poet Casimir Sarbiewski, Kant, Descartes, Thomas Parnell, and Mozart, and general considerations of style change in the eighteenth and nineteenth centuries. In sum, *Turning Points* presents an interdisciplinary perspective on the achievements of modern European culture that blends fine-grained examples with broad considerations of both intellectual history and trends in literary criticism.

Marshall Brown is Professor of English and Comparative Literature and Adjunct Professor of Music at the University of Washington. He is the author of Preromanticism *(Stanford, 1991).*

Turning Points

Essays in the History of
Cultural Expressions

Marshall Brown

«Turning Points»

Essays in the History of Cultural Expressions

Stanford University Press
Stanford, California   1997

JUN   2000

DELTA COLLEGE LIBRARY

PN 81 .B695 1997

Brown, Marshall, 1945-

Turning points

Stanford University Press
Stanford, California
© 1997 by the Board of Trustees of the
Leland Stanford Junior University
Printed in the United States of America

CIP data are at the end of the book

Stanford University Press publications are distributed
exclusively by Stanford University Press within the
United States, Canada, Mexico, and Central America;
they are distributed exclusively by Cambridge
University Press throughout
the rest of the world.

To Dorrit and Benedict

Preface

Turning Points collects both "theoretical" and "practical" essays on literature, philosophy, music, and art. "Cultural expressions" is my umbrella coinage for these various entities, whose similarities, as I argue, far outweigh their differences. The essays share a vision of cultural history rather different from those currently in favor. Our prevailing materialisms examine how cultural expressions are produced by or react to the conditions of their emergence. Texts, however important, come late, or last. In my book they come first, often rhetorically and always in importance. Whatever the massed force of circumstance, our cultures are shaped to a vast extent by the ideas, insights, and expressions of distinctive, individual minds. This book is devoted to examining and reflecting on the imprint of individual works on the history of culture.

To be sure, great works embody and express powerful cultural forces. Even anticanonists rarely escape some such implications, for it is hard to know how to recognize a culture if not at least in part through its expressions. But I want to say something different. Theories of embodiment and expression, of correspondence and mirroring, ultimately betray the history they claim to serve. That is the gist of the polemic that concludes "Why Style Matters." Instead, cultural expressions act in and on history to the extent that they are not of their time. Significant works are beyond their moment, underway toward a new age. Culture does not advance (or retreat either, for that matter) through being represented but through being escaped.

The negativity of texts is crucial to their historicity. What is deter-

mined and known is not in movement. That applies even to oppositional stances and texts: they embody one positivity facing another.
Where movement begins is where definition ends. That is why my
attention goes to the indefinite moments in all the works I study: to
the nonconceptual intuitions of style and of form, to misunderstanding, mistranslation, and disarticulation. History is made of the break-
throughs not into but out of time.

I am concerned first, then, with works in history. "Mozart and After"
serves as the model here, beginning with its very title: a new textual
intuition—a musical text in this case—becomes the vessel of a new sensibility through which new concepts and cultural shapes arise. Other
chapters trace the backgrounds rather than the aftereffects of such innovations. In "Kant's Misreading of Descartes," it is a conceptual background from which Kant swerves—and which, I suspect, could only
become coherently visible as a result of that swerve. In "Toward an
Archaeology of English Romanticism," it is a historical thrust out of
which a revolution in sensibility emerges. This essay is the earliest and
the most causal in its rhetoric; I am now inclined to explain less and
admire more. The last two chapters in this section focus on widespread
phenomena instead of individual texts, but they too are concerned with
the history made in shadows, intuitively, in acts of the mind rather than
those of the body. It may seem paradoxical that I should write about
periods when I profess such a belief in flux, but I would have periods
always understood as movements. These two essays posit a ground that
appears stable in retrospective view, but the figure only comes to rest
because the essay must stop somewhere.

Turning points thus are not just where significant works are found
but what the works are made of. They are divided and in motion, not
unified. Thomas Parnell's "Night-Piece on Death" (in "Deconstruction
and Enlightenment") is a test case, but always I am fascinated with
textual shifts and emergences. Heinrich Wölfflin is my inspiration here,
though like any great critic he must be read as a great writer, to see how
his rhetoric and critical practice escape the doctrines encumbering his
reputation. My essay on Jerome McGann argues that even a critic appearing to be a cultural historian is fundamentally motivated by the
history made in the texts themselves. Some readers have objected that

McGann is not as good a critic as I make him out to be. Perhaps by conventional standards they are right. But I make him out to be a different kind of critic, who brings texts alive by moments and who is not adequately judged by familiar criteria of coherence and completeness. For me, however, the greatest figure remains Hippolyte Taine, in whose work as in no other that I know the history stirring within texts becomes congruent with the history flowing without.

What I have called negativity also goes by the name error. Deconstruction is the most recently popular theory of error, and the opening essay might well be subtitled "From Deconstruction to History." Too often, deconstruction appears to subside into mere drift (*dérive* being the common French term). But the more Derrida and others argue with history, the more they acknowledge it as an inescapable factor. Error, deviance, vagrancy may be random in origin, but they become productive in effect; as Valéry writes: "No 'truth' without passion, without error" (*Oeuvres* 2: 641).

The agencies of the text's productivity are its style and its form. The notion of form as an inert drag upon expression depends on an identification of expression with content and on an individualist bias, both of which are at odds with the doctrines of many of the very critics who attack formalism. As my last chapter argues, form is the unheard melody that transcends the individual and releases singular thoughts into collective force. Valéry again sums up, with a pregnancy I can only envy: "*Writing*—being supposed to construct, as solidly and as exactly as possible, that language machine in which the release of the activated spirit is expended in conquering *real* resistances—demands that the writer become divided against himself" (1: 1205).

It remains only to say that the divisions celebrated by Taine, Wölfflin, and Valéry are also itineraries. My own book is divided by topics and approaches, but I would have the divisions be understood as its directions. I can identify at least four: from deconstruction to history, from style to form, from theory to practice, from expressed to concealed meanings. What I have not seen remains for others to point out.

For the present publication I have touched up the writing, corrected a handful of errors, and inserted a handful of references previously overlooked or subsequent to the original publication. (Unattributed translations are my own throughout; italics are reproduced as in the originals, except where noted.) The original publications and occasions are as follows.

"Errours Endlesse Traine" began as a lecture at the University of Washington and was published in *PMLA* 99 (1984): 9–25.

"Why Style Matters" is a new essay realizing an old dream. I first read Taine in 1976–77, when Gene Falk made me teach the history of criticism at the University of North Carolina, and an early sketch of my reading was the first conference paper I ever presented, under Don Marshall's tutelage, at the Society for Values in Higher Education in 1978. I picked the talk up again for a paper at the 1994 MLA, courtesy of David Bell, and Heather Dubrow gave me a needed critique of the pages on New Historicism. The paragraphs on Proudhon derive from a paper written in 1967 for Peter Demetz's realism course.

The essay on Wölfflin, another old passion I got to earlier, was published in *Critical Inquiry* 9 (1982): 379–404.

"What's in a Text?" was written for *Review* 12 (1990): 89–106.

"Deconstruction and Enlightenment," *The Eighteenth Century: Theory and Interpretation* 28 (1987): 259–64, was commissioned by Bob Markley before we were colleagues. The assignment, to say something about the eighteenth century and critical theory in around five printed pages, prompted the stylistic experiment.

"Mozart and After" started life as a footnote; I made it into an essay on the sly, in the basement of our house in Virginia. It was my second conference paper, for the American Society for Eighteenth-Century Studies in 1980. When I couldn't get it published, Doug Johnson told me why and showed me how. It comes from *Critical Inquiry* 7 (1981): 689–706.

"Kant's Misreading of Descartes," unpublished, started life as a digression to the book I still haven't written on Kant and the gothic novel. Early versions were presented at annual meetings of the MLA in 1983 and the International Association for Philosophy and Literature in 1992, and a full-length version—decked out as "Kant und Descartes—ein interkulterelles Mißverständnis?"—was given at Harald Weinrich's invitation in 1992 for the Institut für Deutsch als Fremdsprache of the University of Munich. At the last minute Marjorie Grene intervened to save me from the crudest of my errors.

Geoffrey Hartman suggested in 1967 that I write a course paper on Sarbiewski; one sentence from it survived into the essay that was published in *Comparative Literature* 30 (1978): 313–37. It had a tryout in Bill Oram's Renaissance colloquium at Smith around 1975. It was written long before I met Mona Modiano but was clearly destined for her.

"Romanticism and Enlightenment" was written in 1987 for Stuart Curran's *Cambridge Companion to British Romanticism* (Cambridge: Cambridge University Press, 1993). Versions were read at the MLA in 1988 (where Starry Schor and Jerry McGann asked memorable questions I only later learned how to answer) and in 1990 at the University of Florence, by invitation of Guido Fink. My memory also links David Simpson, the most enlightened romanticist I know, with the writing of it. It realizes another long-standing dream, to be able to publish an essay without footnotes.

"Origins of Modernism" was extracted by Charlie Altieri for the 1982 MLA and subsequently delivered as a lecture at Stanford and at the University of Southern California in 1984. The final version comes from a conference at Dartmouth organized by Steve Scher and Larry Kramer and appears in *Music and Text: Critical Inquiries*, ed. Steven Paul Scher (Cambridge: Cambridge University Press, 1992). Doug Johnson and Steve Hefling both commented coruscatingly and beneficially on an early version, Tom Bauman on the final draft. I owe the Billings reference to Karl Kroeger.

Finally, "Unheard Melodies" is dedicated, in code, to the musicians from whom my spirit draws sustenance. It was Lucy Shelton who sang the Strauss. Steve Hefling (musicologist as well as musician), John Rahn, and Tom Bauman all gave me musical advice, and Tom was kind enough to prepare the musical examples. Paul Fry pointed me toward Derrida's "Force et signification." Earlier versions were presented at the University of Colorado School of Music, the University of Northern Colorado, the University of Bologna (on the generous invitation of Giovanna Franci), and the University of Washington. It was published in a group of essays about performance, in *PMLA* 107 (1992): 465–81.

Mara Bundza did most of the burdensome task of creating computer files and converting them to a common reference system. The press readers—Paul Fry (a frequent inspiration) and another—saved me from error, showed me what I was about, and offered hope for the future.

Helen Tartar did nothing for three years, the kindest thing an editor can do on such occasions. A fellowship from the National Endowment for the Humanities provided the time to write the essay on Taine and to complete revisions of the entire manuscript, and a grant from the Graduate School and the Center for the Humanities of the University of Washington supported production of the index. Jane has stood by me since the beginning. Dorrit and Benedict have come and gone while the essays were a-writing; I dedicate this book to them, now that they have both reached an age where they can decide of their own accord not to read it.

Contents

IV. FINALE

Turning Points

Essays in the History of
Cultural Expressions

PART I

Overture

Errours Endlesse Traine

All transitions are crises.
—Goethe, *Wilhelm Meisters Lehrjahre*

WHERE DO WE GO from here? is, I suspect, a question more often asked than answered. Yet put it into the past tense, and the historian has little difficulty in telling us where we went from there. Indeed, the more up-to-date or, let us say loosely, the more structure-oriented the historian's approach, the easier the question is to answer. Mentalities, epistemes, deep structures: these overviews of where things were and where they went provide a kind of knowledge rarely vouchsafed to the actual participants.

This observation prompted me to reflect on the way a transition appears from the inside. The following pages are less a line of reasoning—in fact, they ultimately turn against the whole concept of linear reasoning—than they are a meditation; their aim is not to generate knowledge but to comprehend the mood in which we desire knowledge. The inquiry cannot proceed from facts to meanings or from initiatives to consequences, for what I wish to understand is precisely the moment when meanings are obscured and consequences still withheld. I offer instead a meditation on a series of images, all of which project and reflect emergent occasions. I want to examine not what was a turning point or crisis, as seen after the dust has settled, but what is a turning point in the turbulence of its occurrence. At such a moment deformity itself may wear the radiant guise of divine beauty, as Satan does in *Paradise Lost*: "So varied hee, and of his tortuous Train / Curl'd many a wanton wreath in sight of Eve, / To lure her Eye" (9.516–18). But innocence is equally prone to show up in the garb of evil, as Dickens's Esther Summerson does in her hour of trial, "when I laboured up colossal staircases, ever striving to reach the top, and ever turned, as I have seen a worm in garden path, by some obstruction, and labouring again" (*Bleak House*, chap. 35, p. 431).[1] At the height of frenzy, who can distinguish fidelity from betrayal, rectitude from its distortion?

> Ay: you did wish that I would make her turn.
> Sir, she can turn, and turn, and yet go on,
> And turn again; and she can weep, sir, weep;
> And she's obedient, as you say, obedient.
> Very obedient.
>
> (*Othello* 4.1.263–67)

As these examples show, the turning point is a trial or, as so many languages have it, a process. But when does the judgment come? "We have put our shoulders to the wheel, Mr. Carstone, and the wheel is going round," says the repulsive lawyer Vholes (*Bleak House*, chap. 39, p. 484). What sort of conclusions, if any, can the process have? What is on trial? These are the questions I wish to consider.

The Mill and the River

Maggie Tulliver first becomes aware of her "great temptation," if such a gradually dawning emotion may be said to have a beginning, at a ball. The revival of old loves in conflict with newly restored economic hopes for the family, the resolution to "go away, and wait" (*Mill on the Floss*, 6.9, p. 467) that is suspended by the intoxications of the moment—waltzing "is rather dizzy work," says Maggie, even just "to look on"—all combine to create a state of mind whose lability is extreme even for George Eliot. Stephen Guest—that dreamily romantic outsider who steals Maggie's affections away from Philip Wakem—looks powerfully at her, and his gaze "made Maggie's face turn towards it" (6.10, p. 470) in an instant of self-contradictory and indescribable emotion: "The hovering thought that they must and would renounce each other made this moment of mute confession more intense in its rapture" (471). The ecstasy cannot endure, of course, but neither does the vise of emotions ever loosen to the point where Maggie can determine her fate: her entire seduction and return pass as if in a dream that washes over her like the flood in which she and her brother will eventually drown. Let us observe some of the twists and turns of these crucial scenes.

The "mute confession" takes place as Stephen and Maggie are walking "unsteadily" across the conservatory. It ends when they "reached the end of the conservatory, and were obliged to pause and turn. The change of movement brought a new consciousness to Maggie: she blushed deeply, turned away her head, and drew her arm from Stephen's." Her departure leaves Stephen "dizzy" in his turn, angry, confused, irresolute, indeed hardly aware of himself or of the whirling of the dance that still goes on. "Stephen turned away, and walked backwards and forwards at the other end of the room. There was the dire necessity of going back into the dancing-room again, and he was beginning to be conscious of that" (471–72). The disturbed, instinctive pacing resumes—we feel that it has never stopped—in the next chapter (6.11), four days later in the lane before Aunt Moss's house. Stephen appears; Maggie, in her embarrassment, "turned to walk towards the gate. Stephen turned too. . . . Maggie . . . turned again to walk back." It is the dance of feeling that neither character can control ("Maggie dared not speak—dared not turn her head") and that prevails over all exercise of judgment (even the horse protests "against this frequent change of direction") until, "sliding downwards into a nightmare," they turn yet again "out of the sun into a side lane," and Stephen's passion "burst[s] out impetuously" yet again. Maggie yearns to yield herself up to his direction—if only she "need no longer beat and struggle against this current, soft and yet strong as the summer stream"—but instead she flees by "turn[ing] sharp round towards home again" (476–79).

There follows a family party (6.12) to celebrate the prospects for recovering the old mill, which would restore to the Tullivers their "full-rounded splendor" (482). The euphoria leads cousin Lucy, bright with optimism, to feel that even the stubborn Tom can be bent toward accommodation with Wakem and the forces of conscious progress. "Nothing was wanted, then, but for dear Tom . . . to turn completely round . . . and declare that he, for his part, was delighted that all the old grievances should be healed" (487). But the mills of the Lord grind too fine to leave this escape route, which is really a turn back rather than a turn ahead. Instead, as if in a dream, Maggie is carried off by Stephen on "the backward-flowing tide" (6.13, p. 496), in a dream she drifts out of bounds while time "flowed over her like a soft stream" (502), and still in a dream she wakes and repents: "Maggie was not conscious of a decision as she turned away from that gloomy averted face, and walked out of the room" (6.14, p. 513).

For Maggie consciousness comes too late to avoid a life of misery. ("Too late! it was too late," she thinks, and Stephen echoes later, "It is too late" [505, 511].) Indeed, we may wonder whether it ever comes. For by the time that she decides, after a long anguished vigil, to burn the last pleading letter from Stephen, the floodwaters have already begun to swirl around her feet, and the "great calm" that ensues lies far from the resoluteness that Bob Jakin thinks she possesses: "The whole thing had been so rapid—so dreamlike—that the threads of ordinary association were broken" (7.5, p. 552).

But does consciousness ever come on time? Are those threads of association ever secure? The one extended description of the mill that Eliot vouchsafes us confirms Maggie's susceptibility to the ravishments of power. After grinding her doll's head against the wall in a fit of anger and then "whirling around like a Pythoness" with her dog in a fit of exuberance, Maggie enters the mill.

The resolute din, the unresting motion of the great stones, giving her a dim delicious awe as at the presence of an uncontrollable force—the meal forever pouring, pouring—the fine white powder softening all surfaces, and making the very spider-nets look like a faery lacework—the sweet pure scent of the meal—all helped to make Maggie feel that the mill was a little world apart from the outside every-day life. (1.4, p. 28)

The spiders are emblems of consciousness that weave their connecting filaments all through Eliot's novels. But as the mill grinds, it denatures such connections: "She wondered if [the spiders] had any relatives outside the mill, for in that case there must be a painful difficulty in their family intercourse—a fat and floury spider, accustomed to take his fly well dusted with meal, must suffer a little at a cousin's table where the fly was *au naturel*" (28). Tom, too, is ground down at the mill, and so is his father; as the novel says at one point, "it is still possible to believe that the attorney was not more guilty toward [Mr. Tulliver], than an ingenious machine, which performs its work with much regularity, is guilty towards the rash man who, venturing too near it, is caught up by some fly-wheel or other, and suddenly converted into unexpected mince-meat" (3.7, p. 265). For Tom, consciousness comes too soon, as the rashness of premature judgment, and "the mill-like monotony" (2.7,

p. 200) of penurious labor converts it into a stupid and destructive obstinacy. But whether consciousness comes too soon or too late, the obscure violence of Eliot's turns shows that it is never adequately synchronized.

Such is the nature of time that its flow escapes knowledge. Rivers never stop changing: the Rhine was not always so mellow as now, nor—in Eliot's famous contrast—was the Rhone always so prosaic. And the Floss (archetypally named for the flux of time and perhaps also the filaments of consciousness) harbors "a kind of population out of keeping with the earth on which they live" (4.1, p. 289). If St. Ogg's is out of sync—its clocks fast, its civilization slow—that is better read as a metaphysical than as a social dilemma. Time is always out of joint, either a slow "doubtful distant hope" or "a fast-approaching dread" (3.7, p. 260), either the tedium of childhood that always wants to be grown up or the dizzy speed of romance that regrets having grown up so soon. But "the future will never join on to the past again" (6.8, p. 474), and the present is only fully experienced as the turning point when we are swept off our feet. "Life at this moment," thinks Maggie at the ball as Stephen approaches her, "seemed a keen vibrating consciousness poised above pleasure or pain," but how ironically constrained by encompassing dangers is Maggie's present moment. "This one, this last night, she might expand unrestrainedly in the warmth of the present, without those chill thoughts of the past and the future" (6.10, p. 470).

Eliot's present is never so warm as it appears to poor, deluded Maggie, but it is always thoughtless. It is thoughtless precisely because the meaning of time in its turnings lies beyond all possibility of awareness. For time—and here Eliot joins forces with one of Hegel's best-known concepts—is cunning. "That same nature has the deep cunning which hides itself under the appearance of openness, so that simple people think they can see through her quite well, and all the while she is secretly preparing a refutation of their confident prophecies" (1.5, p. 32). "Time, with ever-unrelenting purpose, still hides that secret in his own mighty, slow-beating heart" (2.2, p. 163). We can, of course, cooperate with the cunning of time. But to do so we must be cunning ourselves, like the wily Bob Jakin, a sympathetic character who disappears from the narrative for long stretches while his energetic slyness amasses a patrimony and a home. Bob lives in the present, as is signaled by his opportunism, his unfailing good nature with those around him, and above all his alert, salesmanlike volubility; to his whirl of words we may contrast the silence of the bookish schoolmaster Stelling, whose insistence on the classics may be considered a repudiation of time. But not even Bob understands the presence of the present; his cunning is, rather, that he has "perceptions more perfect than his comprehension" (3.6, p. 256). The cunning of history is that history is always made without our awareness, or at least without our comprehension.[2]

Literary art is constantly literalizing the turning point when actions outstrip comprehension. Among the countless ball scenes in nineteenth-century novels it is perhaps enough to cite the crisis at Netherfield that Elizabeth Bennet spends most of *Pride and Prejudice* trying to understand. Here is the dialogue that precedes the quarrel between her and Darcy:

"I cannot talk of books in a ball-room; my head is always full of something else."

"The *present* always occupies you in such scenes—does it?" said he, with a look of doubt.

"Yes, always," she replied, without knowing what she said, for her thoughts had wandered far from the subject. (chap. 18, p. 93)

At turning points our thoughts always wander, and the result is, as Darcy puts it, "I could wish, Miss Bennet, that you were not to sketch my character at the present moment" (chap. 18, p. 94).[3]

The Wheel and the Swing

At the turning point an old order is lost and a new one has yet to arrive: "things fall apart; the center cannot hold," as Yeats so famously described in "The Second Coming." Afterward, reflection begins, an image dawns, "a vast image out of *Spiritus Mundi*," and judgment becomes possible once again. But in the moment itself both thought and feeling die "into a dance, / An agony of trance" ("Byzantium," *Collected Poems* 244): the turning point is a suspension, a hiatus, the summer or winter solstice of the intellect.

Vertigo or reverie, the turning point comes as a point of disorientation "in which I had the fancy of our being almost as lost as a handful of passengers in a great drifting ship" (James, *The Turn of the Screw*, chap. 1, p. 22). "The stars ahead seemed to be gliding from right to left. And all was so still in the world that I heard the quiet remark, 'She's round,' passed in a tone of intense relief between two seamen" (Conrad, *The Secret Sharer* 143). The troubled decades before World War I are particularly prone to represent the turning point as an ongoing crisis—a screw like James's that turns relentlessly and will not relax or a story like Conrad's that refuses to let go its hold on the narrator—and thus to profile and anatomize the crisis. The turning point is, first of all, not merely vertigo or reverie, excessive speed or excessive languor, emotional heat or cold, but, confusingly, both at once, a turbulent flow whose speed is as inscrutable as its direction. Thus Mallarmé, writing in 1886 of the ballerina, that "unconscious revealer" who "delivers . . . the nudity of your concepts and will silently write your vision in the manner of a Sign, which she is," speaks in one paragraph both of the "vertiginous play of her pale satin shoes" and of a "reverie full, yet adequate: vaporous, clear and ample, or restrained" (*Oeuvres* 307). And second, it is more complicated than the mere submergence of thought and feeling or the temporary occultation of the subject while the flood of time cunningly prepares to reveal the Sign of the future. On the contrary, the subject remains, engaged yet detached, as the participant observer of his fate, "most alien spectator, Friend," as Mallarmé writes with the precision of a paradox. There is always a struggle both to know and to feel. In this moment feeling does not disappear but changes into an obscure passion to recognize itself: it grasps at knowledge. And knowledge does not disappear but gropes blindly toward a point of reference, the shred of evidence that will resolve the mystery: knowledge yearns for a feeling of orientation. The turning point, then, is a true dialectical moment, when each force of the soul turns toward its opposite to prepare for that passionate knowledge that will know how to steer into the future.

My next turning point occurs in a little-known novel, *Une Page d'amour*, by Emile Zola. From its graphological title on, this is an exceptionally self-conscious work, with five parts of five chapters each on the model of an ancient tragedy, and with a carefully measured and calculated dance of characters. The mechanism of the plot is set in motion by a scene in the fourth chapter, where Zola's femme fatale, the widowed Hélène Grandjean, falls or jumps off a swing and sprains her knee in the presence of her future lover, Dr. Deberle. The vertiginous activity of the mother who is recreating a childhood pleasure thus launches the tumultuous passions of the novel.

But it is the resonances of swinging, rather than the activity itelf, that are particularly germane to my theme. In French "swing" is *balançoire*, whose root verb also evokes the rocking of a cradle, the regulatory mechanism of a watch or clock, proportion and symmetry, and hanging and balancing. All these associations are activated at one point or another in the novel. However, Zola does not activate but instead leaves pervasively implicit the one meaning that cannot be excluded from this novel, so abstractly concerned with states of mind rather than with states of physical existence. For *balancer* is also a mental term meaning to hang in the balance, to weigh, to ponder.[4] The turning point is both a moment of balance and a moment of unbalance, of decision and of indecision, of determination (like the fatalistic mechanism of a clock) and of indeterminism. It is a regressive and metaleptic moment when the woman becomes a girl and gives birth to a monster. Finally it is the moment when falsehood begets knowledge and ignorance engenders insight. In the next chapter Hélène, still dreaming the vertiginous reverie of her passion, looks out from her sickroom one February morning over the fog enveloping Paris.

That had a great charm: not to know, to guess by halves, to yield to a slow initiation, with the obscure feeling that she was beginning her youth afresh.
How those novels lied! (1.5, p. 1007)

The explicit reference here is to *Ivanhoe*, which Hélène has just been reading. But in so highly wrought a novel as *Une Page d'amour* an element of self-reference is inescapable. The balance and symmetry of the work are a lie calculated to yield up a recognition: the insight that to ponder, not to know, or half to know—to weigh the right answer with the wrong—is the wintry ignorance from which passionate knowledge springs.

It is not coincidental that my vocabulary has taken on a Socratic tinge here in linking ignorance with insight. For if the mill is the figure of the material dialectic of history, the swing is the figure of the dialectic of mind perfected in the Socratic dialogues. The dialogue is, as it were, a con-versation, a turning together of minds in the replies and retorts, the turns and returns of utterance. Its gentle form appears in the roundtable discussions of the Ciceronian dialogues and their Renaissance avatars.

But I prefer to concern myself with the original and more dramatic form found in Plato and then spontaneously reinvented by Dante, the pilgrim who has lost his way and must wind along an incline, turning an ear now toward, now away from all those spirits that would bend his thoughts toward them, until he finally emerges into the ecstatic truth of the rotating stars.

Plato's Greek, unlike Latin and its derivatives, does not embed its metaphors for turning in its words for utterance and response. But we may find the metaphors buried in a more typically Socratic concern, the refutations of false opinion that are sometimes called turnings back.[5] Socrates' imaginary dialogue with a slave boy in the *Meno* distills the procedure: Socrates turns the boy back from all his beginnings until, like Dante, the boy has lost his bearings and does not know where to turn. This is the Socratric ἀπορία, or perplexity (84a–d), which Socrates describes as a "dreamlike" state (85c) in which true opinions can at last be aroused. The *Meno* uses the concept of recollection (ἀνάμνησις, which suggests a kind of backward flow of the mind) to bridge the gap between error and truth, but elsewhere Plato stresses the radical alteration that ensues on the turning point when the mind is perplexed. Thus in the *Phaedrus* he seems to have coined the term "method," or following a road, as the corrective for the pathlessness of aporia. The turning, or way (τρόπος) of the medical art, says Socrates, is identical to that of the rhetorical art (270b). In both, we need a road or method—the key word is first supplied by Phaedrus (270c)—without which our merely empirical procedures might be compared to the pathfinding of a blind man (ὥσπερ τυφλοῦ πορεία, 270d). The method—not so much the path as the ability to follow the path—is found, after a period of darkness, "suddenly, like a blaze kindled by a leaping spark" (letter 7, 341d).

In another dialogue, the *Statesman*, the Stranger relates to the young Socrates the myth that governs the dialectic conversion from pathlessness to path. He tells of a time when the universe rotated in the opposite direction from its present one under the direct impulse of Zeus; of the moment when Zeus released his hold and the universe, "in perplexities" (ἐν ἀπορίαις), was "in danger of sinking into the pathless (ἀπεῖρον) sea of unlikeness" (273d); and of the need for a terrestrial statesman to guide things into a stable path. Just as the seventh letter offers a political as well as an epistemological psychology, so here we clearly have an epistemological as well as a political myth. The moment when we swing back from subjection—whether under a dogma or a political leader—to independence is a period of turbulence when the movement of the soul and the movement of the world are no longer in alignment, a period of blindness and floundering before the new path is illumined.[6]

> When Loie Fuller's Chinese dancers enwound
> A shining web, a floating ribbon of cloth,
> It seemed that a dragon of air
> Had fallen among dancers, had whirled them round
> Or hurried them off on its own furious path;
> So the Platonic Year
> Whirls out new right and wrong.
> Whirls in the old instead;
> All men are dancers and their tread
> Goes to the barbarous clangour of a gong.
> (Yeats, "Nineteen Hundred and Nineteen,"
> *Collected Poems* 205–6)

Revolution

Just as in the Marxian view revolution is dialectic writ large, so from the very beginning, as we can now see, dialectic has always been revolution writ small. The analogy helps explain at least one major puzzle that, so far as I can see, no one has adequately addressed, namely, the origin of our modern term *revolution*. Indeed, it is not that long since Melvin J. Lasky first traced in reliable detail the semantic shift that changed *revolution* from an astronomical term with gradualist and conservative political implications to a primarily political term with connotations of violent progressivism (*Utopia and Revolution*, chaps. 5–6). But why should this shift have occurred? Lasky does not attempt an explanation. Nor does Hannah Arendt, whose anatomy of revolution comprises freedom, innovation, and violence (*On Revolution*, chap. 1) but omits what I have been suggesting is the key element—namely, aporia, or confusion. And Georges Gusdorf, who has also discussed the semantic shift, merely comments laconically, "De là une équivoque" (from whence a pun; *Principes* 415). A revolution is not so much a way people act as a way things move; as Reinhardt Koselleck argues, it has a characteristic speed that takes over as individual actors lose control of events (*Futures Past* 39–54;

see also Behler, "Die Auffassung der Revolution"; Ward, "The Forging of Orc"; Blanchot, "The Main Impropriety" 58–59; and Culler, "The Uses of *Madame Bovary*" 78). All these scholars remind us that until well into the eighteenth century the term revolution tended to be contrasted to rebellion. But they fail to realize that even the most peaceful revolution is a turning point. Like the sublime movement of the spheres, it transcends human comprehension; like any dance, it has—at least for some who live through it—its moments of confusion, vertigo, aporia. Turning has always suggested disorder and violence; indeed the Greek verb ἀνατρέπω means to overthrow politically as well as to refute dialectically. Thus, I suggest, a natural development led the astronomical term revolution to become a political term, winning out over less dialectical competing terms such as renewal, change of state, and rebellion.[7]

To illustrate the dynamics—the dialectic—of revolution while maintaining my focus on acts of the mind, I want to consider Kant. In the introduction to the second edition (1787) of the *Critique of Pure Reason*, Kant compares his "transformation" (*Umänderung*) of metaphysics to various "revolutions" in the history of science. On the purely intellectual level the sense of Kant's comparisons is entirely clear. Each of his revolutions is the sudden illumination of what had been perplexing; each one is accomplished by "the happy insight of a single man in one experiment, from which point on, the path that had to be taken could no longer be missed, and the secure course of a science was initiated and designated for all times and in infinite distances" (Bxii). Thus conceived, a revolution resembles more a coup than a civil war, more the Glorious Revolution that had been than the French Revolution that was about to be. But alongside this intellectual ideal of the revolution as an abrupt and enduring break with the past, there is even in Kant, as I want to show, a psychological sense of revolution as a dark force that drives individuals and is not driven by them. At such a turning point, not even the great master of the architectonic could be entirely in control of his structures.

The decisive psychological element, or inner sense, in dialectic as in revolution is the pace. Even Kant's preface acknowledges the swiftness with which a science is transformed after a long period of groping. But that account of revolution is undialectical; Kant writes as if error is motionless, the groping of a group of deluded scientists who get nowhere, and as if it is is simply abolished by truth, which is equally motionless, since a single individual instantaneously and permanently establishes the truth.

Kant's preface is a wish fulfillment. Nothing in the history of Kant's revolution in dialectic displays the ease of his ideal models. Certainly not the book itself: the 800-odd pages of elephantine prose did not suddenly illuminate everything to early readers such as Mendelssohn, who couldn't get through it; Garve, who reviewed it without pretending to understand it; or Herder, who responded with a vitriolic book attacking his former friend and teacher. And the rebarbative style is no mere blemish that accidentally obscures the basic clarity of Kant's revolutionary insights. (For further comments on Kant's style and for references to secondary literature, see Brown, *Preromanticism* 70–73.) On the contrary, despite his yearnings for popularity Kant repeatedly warns in letters and prefaces that his discoveries cannot be clearly or easily communicated. Indeed, the first preface to the *Critique of Pure Reason* claims that too much clarity can be detrimental. This preface seems to place difficulty and confusion on the side of truth and not, as in the later preface, on the side of error. Aporia is a permanent element of dialectical discovery; it is a part of the revolution in thought and not what the revolution eliminates. This, at least, is what Kant wrote to Mendelssohn on August 16, 1783: "From thence would begin the actual pleasure of a critique, walking around with a secure guide [*Leitfaden*] in a labyrinth, where one is lost at every instant and just as often finds the exit" (*Briefwechsel* 346). What a curious Ariadne's thread this is, seeming to lead onward but never altogether out! And what about the scholastic Mandarin in which Kant chose to write: is it not simultaneously the secure guide that lays the stable foundation for the new science and yet in itself the labyrinth that has doomed readers and editors alike to incessant perplexity? This is the dialectical moment in which error and truth, confusion and clarity, labor and delivery are inseparably mixed.

On the question of pace Kant's biography is instructive. From the moment he conceived his grand project Kant refused to be hurried: "Now long experience has taught me that insight into our projected materials can by no means be forced and hastened by effort, but instead requires rather a long time" (letter to Marcus Herz, June 7, 1771, 122). The threads of the secure guide must be spun—or, to change the metaphor, the text must be woven—slowly. Yet the illumination comes with dizzying rapidity: as early as the famous letter to Herz of February 21, 1772, in which Kant announced his great breakthrough, he was promising to be done with the first critique in three months. And when he finally wrote the work, he did so in a frenzy, "for I had brought to completion the product of a period of at least twelve years of reflection within about 4 to 5 months, as if on the wing, . . . a decision that I even now do not regret, because in the contrary case and with greater delay in order to bring in popularity, the work would presumably never have been finished" (letter to Mendelssohn, August 16, 1783, 345). The revolution in metaphysics is thus the product of unnatural slowness followed by unnatural haste. Or rather, of both at once: "I receive reproaches from all sides on account of the inactivity in which I seem to have been for a long time, and yet I have really never been more systematically and persistently occupied than in the years since you last saw me" (letter to Herz, Nov. 24, 1776, 198).

Fortunately, we have a guide for diagnosing the condition of the revolutionary dialectician. In the years following publication of the *Critique of Pure Reason*, Marcus Herz was at work on a book that, as he writes (letter to Kant, Nov. 25, 1785, 427), was originally inspired by conversations with Kant. In his *Essay on Vertigo* (*Versuch über den Schwindel*, 1786), we may learn to recognize Kant's state as verging on the pathological.[8] Herz considers that the soul, in its natural condition, alternates imperceptibly between effort and relaxation (153–54). In Herz's terms, Kant's ten years of inactivity constitute a condition of "Langerweile" (boredom), which can lead either to despair or, as it did for Kant, to that "preternaturally swift progression of ideas" which Herz designates as vertigo (154–62). The second edition of the *Critique* came in the following year. Can we interpret Kant's new preface, with its idea that timeless truths instantaneously replace timeless errors, as a defensive reaction to the book on vertigo and an attempt to sanitize the notion of speed that is central to all revolutionary dialectic?

Dialectic

I have no wish to argue that logic or dialectic is diseased. Quite the contrary, I have chosen examples to show how inescapably aporia is linked to progress. Feelings of disorientation and vertigo are a normal part of the processes of discovery; they constitute the inherently revolutionary element of dialectic, the dialectical element of revolution. An allusion to the work of Thomas Kuhn seems unavoidable here, since he has argued the most forcefully that revolution is a normal component of scientific progress. Yet I do not believe that Kuhn has adequately accounted for the dialectical aspect of revolution, that is, for the ways that the new does not appear randomly but necessarily emerges out of the dissolution of the old. For genuinely dialectical theories of emergence we may turn, not surprisingly, to philosophers after Kant.

Nietzsche, using some of the worst puns in the history of philosophy, ties together the threads I have been tracing. The passage in question is the chapter "Von den Taranteln" (Of Tarantulas) in the second part of *Also Sprach Zarathustra*. The theory is outspokenly dialectical: "And because height is needful, steps are needful, and contradiction of steps and of those who climb! Life wants to climb and in climbing to overcome itself" (359). Nietzsche here professes precisely the vertiginous component of dialectic that has been with us from Eliot's floury spiders on. The poisonous tarantulas, the dark negation in the dialectic, infect the dialectician with their venom. The resulting vertigo undermines the elegant demonstrations in the "divine . . . pugilism [*Ringkampfe*]" (359) of classical reasoning. Negation, the tarantula, makes the ring that was always a part of the arena into a wheel that racks the reasoner: "now it will avenge itself and make my soul rotate [*drehend*] as well" (357). But are confusion and confutation really the work of the negative, or do they begin with the inception of dialectic? Who, in fact, is first stretched on the wheel of dialectic, the bright intellect or the dark spiders? For Zarathustra has begun this section by threatening to do to the tarantulas what they later do to him: "Thus do I speak unto ye in a parable [*Gleichnis*] that will make your souls revolve, ye preachers of *Equality* [*Gleichheit*]" (357). Who is the preacher here, who the congregation? Who amid Nietzsche's "pathless sea of unlikeness" is the apostle of similitude? And who, we may finally wonder, is good, who evil? This last question arises, surely not accidentally, because of the jingle of the tarantulas' two expressed aims, which are both good and evil, both justice (*Gerechtigkeit*) and the wish to be revenged (*gerächt*). There is no escaping from the entanglements of thought.

If the tarantulas do symbolize dialectic, then what Nietzsche conjures up is the confusion intrinsic to dialectic. It is the confusion of the dance. For the tarantulas are not just spiders; they are also dancers. They dance the spider dance, the tarantella. They are, in German, *Tarantel-Tänzer*. Is Zarathustra also a tarantula? He describes himself as a dancer from the start of the book; indeed, only in the chapter on tarantulas does he resist the impulse to dance: "Truly, Zarathustra is no tornado or whirlwind; and if he is a dancer, still nevermore a *Tarantel-Tänzer*" (359). Yet by the end of the book his dance does become a whirlwind: "Praised be this wild good free storm spirit, which dances on swamps and afflictions as if on meadows." For the true dance is the wild dance that is the true dialectic: "Ye higher men, your worst side is: none of you has learnt to dance as one must dance—to dance over and beyond yourselves [*über euch hinweg*]" ("Vom höheren Menschen" [Of the Higher Man], part 4, sec. 20, p. 531). Dialectic is choreographed transcendence.

My discussion to this point can be considered a commentary on one of the most notorious utterances in the history of philosophy, Hegel's aphorism in the preface to the *Phenomenology of Mind*: "The true is thus the Bacchic whirl in which no member is sober." Easily forgotten, especially by those who are dizzied by Hegel's prose, is that the Bacchic revelry is not the end of the line. For Hegel calculatedly revives and revises the precise terms of the Platonic dialectic. Truth, he says, is not only the Bacchic revelry but also "transparent and simple peace." The mediator between these two aspects of truth, just as in Plato, is recollection, anamnesis: "In the *whole* of the movement, conceived as rest, that which differentiates itself in it and gives particular existence, is preserved as something that *remembers*, whose existence is the knowledge of itself" (39). Vertigo is a part of dialectic; in fact, in a sense, it is present in all parts. But this is a case where the whole is greater than its parts; in Nietzsche, as in Hegel, the Dionysian "drunken song" turns into a "Rundgesang" (canon) that produces self-transcendence and self-knowledge ("Das trunkene Lied" [The Drunken Song], part 4, sec. 12, p. 558).

Such absolute knowledge at the end of the dialectic remains, of course, a utopian horizon for Nietzsche, as for Eliot and our other storytellers and I believe for Hegel as well. The end of dialectic for Plato, as we have seen, is method—literally, the discovery of a path (*hodos*) for the truth seeker to follow. Nietzsche responds that "all goods things approach their goal crookedly" ("Of the Higher Man," sec. 17, p. 529). And Hegel likewise turns from his identification of truth as revelry and recollection to a critique of method as it had been traditionally understood, namely, as a collection of principles and procedures: "It is not difficult to recognize that the fashion of proposing a theorem, presenting reasons for it and likewise refuting its opposite with reasons, is not the form in which truth can appear. The truth is its movement in itself; but that method is the knowledge that is external to its matter" (40). The wheels of history, of knowledge, of fate never cease turning; the swing never comes to rest, except in death. Truth is not a place (*topos*) but a way, and the way is not a road (*hodos*) but a turning (*tropos*) off the deadly highroad. Truth is not a place: "The meaning of Socratics is that philosophy is *everywhere* or nowhere" (Novalis, *Schriften* 2: 545). It has no place, no time, and no path, or at least none in the sense that Plato meant or was often understood to mean. "Being begins at every instant; the ball There rolls around each Here. The center is everywhere. Crooked is the path of eternity" (Nietzsche, "Der Genesende" [The Convalescent], part 3, sec. 2, p. 463; the first phrase repeats the opening of Hegel's *Science of Logic*).

A Poem on Dancing

Whether we think of Berlioz or Ravel, of *Don Giovanni, Tannhäuser*, or *Salomé*, we all know the giddy seductiveness that dance had for the Romantic sensibility. In *Can You Forgive Her?* Trollope writes: "I dared them . . . to do their worst . . . ; I waltzed with him for half an hour. . . . I don't think, even in my maddest days, I ever kept it up as long as I did then. . . . There I was, going round and round and round with the only man for whom I ever cared two straws. It seemed as though everything had been a dream since the old days" (chap. 62, 2: 223). But was turning always so dangerous? Was there not a time when the crooked path of eternity was imaged as a perfect, unblemished circle? At court did not the dancers go in perfect, balanced order to the stately strains of the minuet or pavane, just as the heavenly bodies follow their appointed rounds to the accompaniment of the music of the spheres? Such, at least we are told, was the Renaissance vision of delight in a period when turning suggested concord rather than discord.

Yet all depends on how you read the evidence. Texts are, unfortunately, less stable than truth, and though we do find an ideal of order in the Renaissance, under scrutiny the ideal often seems to turn into a mirage, as evanescent as any other promised land. Thus, while one scholar assures us that the court masque allegorically instructs the participants in virtuous discipline,[9] the next scholar is apt to find in the proceedings all the intoxications of a heady illusion:

The world is topsy-turvy or "tottering" in a condition of rocking, as on the verge of turning over; reality is unstable or illusory, like a theatrical decor. And man too is in disequilibrium, convinced that he is never entirely what he is or seems to be, concealing his face under a mask with which he acts so well that it is no longer clear where the mask is, where the face is. (Rousset, *Circé* 28)

Should we regard Ben Jonson primarily as the master of the masque or as the inventor of the antimasque? Is his fundamental impulse directed toward a "stable, if beleaguered human center," or is it "a strain of half-repressed envy for the homeless and centrifugal spirit" (Greene, "Ben Jonson" 329, 337)?[10] Too often for comfort, Jonson's spokesman is Daedalus or Proteus (*Pleasure Reconciled to Virtue, Neptune's Triumph*), the steps are "curious knots and mazes" (*The Vision of Delight*, line 211), the meaning of the whole is withheld (*The Masque of Argus*, lines 336–37: "Still, still the auspice is so good; / We wish it were but understood"), or if some magic name serves as a guarantor of order, it belongs to a king already translated to the heavens (*News from the New World Discovered in the Moon*) or to the deity presiding over a millennial "heav'n on earth" (*The Golden Age Restored*, line 214). The allegory of the dance points to a transcendent mystery, not to a human truth.

Perhaps the most familiar Renaissance vision of cosmic order has been Sir John Davies's *Orchestra: A Poem on Dancing*, ever since E. M. Tillyard used it as a touchstone in *The Elizabethan World-View*. (*Orchestra* is cited by stanza number. The received view of the poem may be found in Tillyard, *Five Poems* 30–48, to be supplemented by Major, "The Moralization of the Dance," and by Thesiger, "*Orchestra*.") For this reason, I want to reexamine the poem in some detail. The poem is—like all truths—unfinished: more precisely, if we are to believe its editor, it was originally written as a finished poem in 113 stanzas that Davies later expanded and altered "to give the appearance of being incomplete" (Davies, *Poems* 359). Known as one of the great didactic poems of the Renaissance, it is also, as Tillyard himself acknowledges, full of fantasy, exuberant, and even "impudent" (35).

Impudent the poem certainly is. The praise of dancing is uttered by Antinous, better known as the most impertinent of the suitors of Penelope, whose reasoned objections to his speech Antinous glibly overrules three times in Davies's poem. At one point Antinous even has the impudence to compare the art of dance to the martial arts:

> For after Townes and Kingdomes founded were,
> Between great States arose well-ordered *war*,
> Wherein most perfect measure doth appeare.   (87)

It is hard to know just what Davies would have thought of this argument, which he drew, like so much of the poem, from a dialogue attributed to the Greek satirist Lucian. But it is easy to know that the argument would have disgusted Penelope, on the evidence not so much of Homer—Davies's editor doubts whether Davies had read Homer, though he was a close friend of Chapman, who translated Homer—as of a more accessible poem that must have echoed in the mind of any Renaissance reader, the first of Ovid's *Heroides*. By the end of the speech Antinous has "ravished" Penelope's "mind" if not her body (122), and the stanzas added in 1622 call the court

> So rare a worke, and of such subtilty,
> As did all eyes entangle and deceive,
> And in all mindes a strange impression leave.   (130A)

I do not think that the poem lets Antinous's praise of the orderliness of the dance stand uncorrected.

According to Tillyard, the prime value attributed to dance is its combination of motion and fixity. It would be more accurate to speak of motion without instability, or motion without end. As one critic has rightly observed, what the suitor seductively invokes is an Elizabethan never-never land of mutability without decay. (See Wilkes, "The Poetry of Sir John Davies" 287–90, and also Howarth, *The Tiger's Heart* 181–82. Howarth roundly confronts Tillyard in this chapter, entitled "Put Away the World Picture.") To be sure, one stanza, quoted by Tillyard, says that "the Earth doth stand for ever still" (51), but this stanza also acknowledges the new Copernican discoveries, and earlier Antinous has derived the name "world" from "whirl'd" (34) and has told about the dance of the fixed stars ("Fixt they are nam'd, but with a name untrue," 35). One climax does speak of the firm and visible order of the dance:

> Concords true picture shineth in thys Art
> Where divers men and women ranked be,
> And every one doth daunce a severall part,
> Yet all as one, in measure doe agree,
> Observing perfect uniformitie:
> All turne together, all together trace,
> And all together honor and embrace.   (110)

Yet the end of the poem insists that love is a "Maze" where footsteps are traced by "Blindness it selfe" (116) and that Penelope's ecstatic concluding vision is a "strange-eye-dazeling-admirable sight" (122).

Antinous speaks in disguise (7); his motive is love, an emotion that he, Penelope, and the narrator all term "cunning" (6, 53, 98, 105); his oration dances teasingly around its main target, which is the capture of Penelope's heart. Given such inconsistent and unreliable praise, we cannot fairly attribute fixity to the dance.

More than either motion or fixity, the dance signifies to Antinous proportion and balance. He invokes the technical balance of music with movement, the social balance of man with woman, the allegorical balance of the dance with the virtues that dance symbolizes. We have already seen numerous times how suspect and vertiginous notions of balance can be –the swing of Zola, the flywheel of the *Statesman*, the "tottering" world of the French baroque. And here, of course, Antinous's purpose is not to convince Penelope rationally but to bowl her over with the force of his eloquence. At this he may be judged to succeed, for at the end Penelope "Faine would have praised the state and pulchritude, / But she was stroken dumbe with wonder quite" (122). Instead of leading to ordered fixity, Antinous's cunning leads to subversion that wears the guise of order. Each of the balances he evokes becomes unbalanced in its turn. Thus, the technical balance seems perfect: "Where *Time the measure of all moving is*; / And Dauncing is a moving all in measure" (23). And yet Antinous immediately stresses the difference, his purpose being to insinuate an erotic note by portraying dance as the younger and thus as a "lustie youth" (25):

> Now if you doe resemble that to this
> And think both one, I think you think amis:
> But if you judge them Twins, together got,
> And Time first borne, your judgment erreth not.   (23)[11]

The social balance likewise turns slippery, as Antinous first cites the sex-changing examples of Caeneus and Tiresias (82–83) and later hints that wives sometimes get "the upper hand" of their husbands (112). This is not merely impudent but shameless.

The poem actually describes two kinds of dance. When "men more civill grew," they learned the true dance of morality and balance:

> With such faire order and proportion trew
> And correspondence every way the same,
> That no fault finding eye did ever blame.   (65)

But Antinous slips this dance into his discourse only to slip it out again. Not only were Atlas and Prometheus unable to "find such measures in the skies" (66), but also Antinous makes this poor dance sound most unappealing: "Yet all the feete whereon these measures goe, / Are onely Spondeis, solemne, grave, and sloe" (66). "Spondeis" could plausibly be etymologized as "married" feet. They are the true twins among meters, since arsis and thesis (upbeat and downbeat) are identical in the spondee. But who wants to dance with two left feet, so to speak? This kind of dance is prosaic at best, for spondees do not conform to the rule governing poetry that "all is mard if she one foote misplace" (93). Indeed, Antinous spends the rest of the poem describing the other sort of dance, the dance of nature that love teaches, a less perfectly balanced, gayer, lustier sort of dance, composed of "*rounds* and *winding Heyes*" (64).

Need it be said that dance is a rhetoric, not a logic, of action? It is "Rhetorick whose state the clouds doth reach" (92), thus introducing the poem's cosmic element. (The next section of this chapter will pursue the clouds of rhetoric further.) For rhetoric, not the more precise art of poetry, exemplifies the richly erotic movements of the dance:

> For Rhetorick clothing speech in rich aray
> In looser numbers teacheth her to range,
> With twentie tropes, and turnings every way,
> And various figures, and licentious change.   (93)

Incessant and exuberant punning clearly marks Antinous as a rhetorician, ever alert to the body of words and eager to twin in illegitimate fashion sound with sound, making use of echo effects (which come "after time") and of the "tricks and turnings of the aire" (44–45). Love is Antinous's ultimate value, and love too is a rhetorician, that is, a speaker who throws listeners off balance.

> Then first of all, hee doth demonstrate plaine
> The motions seaven that are in nature found,
> Whereof, a thousand brawles he doth compound,
> And ever with a turne they must conclude.   (62)[12]

For the purpose of my argument it is sufficient to have shown that turning and dancing were never fully imaged as a principle of order, even at the height of the Elizabethan world view. But I would be tempted to go a step further and allegorize the poem in the punning spirit in which it is written. The question is why Davies lit on Antinous as his spokesman. At the end, as a poem on dancing ought, *Orchestra* does seem to pair up Antinous and Penelope as he ravishes her mind with the aid of a magic mirror donated by Love. Tillyard reads the episode as a true pairing, a triumph of platonic love. Yet surely this is as improper a linkage as all the other twinnings of the poem, such as the twinning of poetry and rhetoric or of civil and erotic dance. Throughout the poem Penelope is associated with mind, with thought, with "reasons eye" (26).[13] Antinous, by contrast, is always the persuader, the rhetorician. Is he not therefore to be understood as the *anti-nous*, the anti-mind? Antinous is the spirit of the flesh, the life force that compels reason to remain in motion and continually to unweave the fabric of thought the mind has woven.

According to Jean Rousset, time "is engaged and rendered sensible in the [baroque] work, whereas the classic artist tends to eliminate time" (*Circé* 232).[14] This view of classicism is an idealist illusion. Time never stops; the world never ceases turning; not even the truths of reason endure forever. In a stanza added some 25 years after the original publication, Davies compares Penelope to a silkworm (130A). The comparison is either highly artful or, more likely, highly negligent, for silkworms do not weave but spin. In truth Penelope is one more of our spiders of reason, in danger of being caught, like Maggie Tulliver, in a web of her own making.

Turn Against Turn

Where do we go from here? A purely negative conclusion can hardly satisfy, yet the sense of this whole meditation has been that every point is a turning point. There is no crisis for Maggie Tulliver, no "great temptation," at least no conventional seduction. Maggie is fallen from the start, born an outsider to her society, too dizzy even to attempt joining the dance. The Greek for judgment or decision is *krisis*. Every point of judgment is a point of peril; every moment of balance a moment of unbalance. There is no right way, no end of knowledge, no truth to be unveiled. Indeed, of the texts discussed, only the second preface to the *Critique of Pure Reason* has even claimed that truth may take the form of a revelation, and that text proved a veiling of the labyrinthine truth of the *Critique*.

Alas, we cannot even receive the consolation of having discovered this melancholy condition, for Jacques Derrida ("Facteur de la vérité," "Tympan") and others have been sending us dead letters revealing the undiscoverability of truth for some years now, pounding the message into the curved drums of our middle ear. And of course Derrida did not discover this truth—if it is a truth—either; quite the contrary, he has labored to convince us that his is the oldest news known to Western civilization. Thus, my own title comes from Spenser, who tells us at the outset of *The Faerie Queene* that there is no escape from error: "So many paths, so many turnings seene, / That which of them to take in diuerse doubt they been" (1.1.10). Must we then be content to subscribe our names to the twisted line of denouncers of the truth? Or can we convert their insights to use? Is it conceivable to turn against turn?[15]

The end of Spenser's endless poem tries to do just that and nearly succeeds. Mutability, it will be remembered, claims dominion in her great peroration.

> Then, since within this wide great *Vniuerse*
> Nothing doth firme and permanent appeare,
> But all things tost and turned by transuerse:
> What then should let, but I aloft should reare
> My Trophee, and from all, the triumph beare?   (7.7.56)

Mutability loses the battle when Nature rules against her. Things

> by their change their being doe dilate:
> And turning to themselves at length againe,
> Doe worke their own perfection so by fate:
> Then ouer them Change doth not rule and raigne;
> But they raigne ouer Change, and doe their states maintaine.
>
> (7.7.58)

Yet, though we know that Nature wins the battle, we cannot be sure she wins the war.[16] Our uncertainty relates in part to the origin of the episode, which is obscure both extratextually (we cannot know how it was to fit into the scheme of the epic) and intratextually, since the first of its two cantos asserts the absolute stability of the legendary records, whereas the second asserts their absolute inaccessibility.[17] But above all it is the end that is not clearly in sight. In appearance the decision goes against Mutability. But in fact does not Nature's judgment—"And thee content thus to be rul'd by me" (st. 59)—grant what Mutability had claimed, namely, "the rule of all, all being rul'd by you" (st. 56)? What about Nature's exhortation—"Cease therefore daughter further to aspire" (st. 59)—does this mean that Mutability should not aspire at all or that she should not aspire beyond what she has already claimed? And what are we to make of Nature's sudden disappearance in the last line, just after she has awarded herself the rule of the universe? Nature's judgment sets "all things" over change; does this mean that she is subjecting Mutability to constancy, or does it mean that she is acceding to Mutability's demand by rearing things aloft and making them the trophy of Mutability?

"Trophy," like "universe" and "transverse," is yet another turning word; more specifically, a trophy fixes and consecrates a turn. "But time shall come that all shall changed bee, / And from thenceforth, none no more change shall see" (st. 59). These are Nature's last words against Mutability. But do they not constitute precisely a trophy of Mutability, a turn that is eternized? In equating the triumph of life with the triumph of death, Nature is endorsing the claims of Mutability. Alas, it does not prove so easy to turn against turn. In passing I note further that the scene on Arlo Hill is overcast—stanza 7 alludes to the episode on Mount Thabor in which the disciples hear a voice out of a cloud—and the obscurity of the judgment may reflect the obscurity of the weather. And since this is Spenser, who cannot resist a pun, perhaps we could suggest that Nature's declaration that things "raigne over Change" (st. 58) is no more than a passing shower that evaporates to make way for the greater light of "the great Sabbaoth God" (7.8.2). Perhaps this is reading too much naturalism into Spenser's Nature; it is true, in any event, that the outcome remains disappointingly cloudy. At the end of *The Clouds*, the child beats the parent—which is, of course, the central metaphor for revolution right through the *Communist Manifesto*—and perhaps the child does the same in the Mutability Cantos.[18]

One other sadly cloudy trophy will claim attention before my argument winds to a close. The ode tradition constitutes the most systematic literary exploration of turns. And given the critical popularity of Keats's "To Autumn," with its exaltation of steadiness and gradualism, we might remember that the poem is followed in order of publication by "Ode on Melancholy," which Keats intended for the conclusion of his 1820 *Poems*. "Melancholy" is a poem of memory and of the power of the past over the present. The final version opens with the line "No, no, go not to Lethe, neither twist"; the deletion of Keats's original first stanza has thus left the ode to begin with a fervent turn against turn. Written in May 1819, "Melancholy" is one of those spring songs so cavalierly dismissed by "Autumn," but it retorts with an even ruder treatment of the fruits of the harvest when it urges us to "burst Joy's grape." By his placement of the poem Keats reminds us that we cannot escape from spring, which means life but also, alas, the revolutions of the life cycle: the poem's figures of turning include the rainbow of new life, the "globéd peonies" of summer's perfection, and winter's "rosary of yewberries." However muted by the April shower, the poem's contents originate in the tropic zone of human passions, and even if wolfsbane is not twisted into poisonous wine, nevertheless "aching Pleasure" will turn "to Poison while the beemouth sips." Melancholy's cloudy trophies are turnings after all. (Cf. the turns and clouds of Keats's "Ode on Indolence," which Patricia Parker identifies as Spenserian motifs in *Inescapable Romance* 168–69.)

"Autumn" offered a myth of continuity; "Melancholy" now appears as but one more in our long list of deconstructions of that myth. Yet the deconstruction is performed here in the service of a different kind of permanence, of an unforgetting, an anti-Lethe, an *a-letheia*, a truth. "And be among her cloudy trophies hung," reads the last line. The verb "be hung" is a curious substitute for the normal "hang," which we find, for instance, when Shakespeare's melancholy Orlando makes an offering to his nocturnal goddess: "Hang there, my verse, in witness of my love" (*As You Like It*, 3.2.1). "*Be* . . . hung": the victory of Keats's Mutability, of "Beauty that must die," turns into a consecration of being rather than a triumph of death.

The melancholy train of error has no terminus named "truth." But as Keats shows us, the truth that does not lie ahead of us may, under a different name, lie behind, in the melancholy of recollection. If I were to offer a summary justification of the deep warmth of Keats and Eliot or the high spirits of Nietzsche and Hegel, I would do it by saying that something which we might call knowledge survives the demise of truth. The Greek word for knowing is *oida*, the perfect tense of the verb meaning to see. Knowledge results from a kind of vision, more specifically a pro-vision, a looking out. What I have seen and retained so that I still see it, that is my knowledge. Put in the simplest terms, knowledge pertains to process, truth to product. And human experience is always in process, a trajectory toward an unknown goal. That goal constitutes the truth of structural historians, but it is a reification that only exists outside of time. The melancholy fact is that our living knowledge abides in a fragile temporality, with a continuity of past and present that is always subject to being ruptured in the future. But a compensatory consolation is that such pro-visional knowledge can be faithful to the directions of real experience in a way that a timeless or structural truth cannot.[19]

The moment of disorientation, the moment of turn against turn, is also the moment of openness to real possibility. Thus it is, in the sense that I mean, the moment of knowledge. One commentator on Milton has put what he calls "the story of the tree of knowledge and of death and sin" in these terms: "The moment of turning, when motion in one direction is arrested and motion in the opposite direction is about to begin, is the still point at which the present is captured and alternatives are real" (Brisman, *Milton's Poetry* 61). To be sure, Brisman evokes only one of our figures for turning, the swing, and not the mill or the whirling dance. But in fact the dialectical sense of an ever-changing, ever-provisional, and therefore ever-present knowledge is the same in all figures. We might turn to one of Yeats's greatest poems of encounter with reality for a last reminder of the dialectical character of knowledge. It is the poem where Yeats asks, "How can we know the dancer from the dance?" (*Collected Poems* 214). The context is cosmic, and the attitude toward human acquisition of ultimate truths is correspondingly elegiac: "Among School Children" is a Keatsian poem about aging, full of the cloudy trophies of a visionary mutability, with elements of the last stanza deriving from Keats's "Ode on Melancholy," from "Ode on a Grecian Urn," and from the third stanza of "Ode to a Nightingale." Yeats's concluding question is correspondingly and profoundly dialectical, for it asks both about recognition (how is the dancer shown through the dance?) and about differentiation (how can we distinguish the dancer from the dance, body from soul?).[20] Knowledge of unity becomes one with knowledge of separation; the capture of the present makes alternatives real. Yet for Yeats the uncertainty or, rather, the negative capability of knowledge is finally not melancholy at all, but a "brightening glance," alert and forward-looking. It is the human intellect stepping westward into its destiny.[21]

Let me return to my original reflections. I want to suggest in conclusion that we can provide ourselves with history; we can give our truths that visionary and provisional character which stamps them as knowledge. We need only remember that the form of history is movement, not just at obvious flash points but, for those who experience it, at all points. History, as we know (experience) it, is under way toward the truths at which it never finally arrives. Historical actors are always, knowingly or (more usually) unknowingly, turning events and struggling against the counterturns of others. The historian's question of truth—"Where did we go?"—is asked of results, not of movement. It is, grammatically, in the wrong aspect. For to know, to have seen, is an ongoing and evolving condition, and the historian who wants to know must ask the question in the tense of evolution—or of revolution—which in English is the progressive tense: "Where were we going?" The structures or truths of history are not actualized in experience; they are that toward which experience points, tangents to the wheel of events.[22] We write a genuinely dialectical history when we remember that every event functions historically as a pointer, as a direction, and not as an embodied truth.[23]

Unterwegs zur Geschichte might be the motto of a study that takes movement rather than accomplishment as its fundamental category. The one in the middle, as Pope says, is "Sole judge of truth, in endless errour hurled"; truth is the regulative ideal, but turbulent movement is the reality. And the redemption of that turbulent movement comes neither from determinations of truth nor from deconstructive denials of truth but from a different, more provisional and humane kind of insight. Historical knowledge, as we are all too prone to forget, concerns truth in movement, a constant interplay of intentions and originations, and not mere results; it deals with impulses rather than with impacts. The remedy for the anxieties of "Errours endlesse traine" is perhaps to be found less easily in Spenser's conclusion in which nothing is concluded than in the lovely Wordsworth poem "Stepping Westward," to which I alluded in my last paragraph:

> and while my eye
> Was fixed upon the glowing Sky,
> The echo of the voice enwrought
> A human sweetness with the thought
> Of travelling through the world that lay
> Before me in my endless way.
>   (*Poetical Works* 3: 76)

Escapable Romance

Parker has argued, on the basis of texts ranging from Ariosto through Stevens, that romance is inescapable. If nomen is numen, she shows us that the numinous, in turn, is not far from the nubilous.

THE PLEASURES OF MERELY CIRCULATING

> The garden flew round with the angel,
> The angel flew round with the clouds,
> And the clouds flew round and the clouds flew round
> And the clouds flew round with the clouds.
>   (Stevens, *Collected Poems* 149)

But how can we convert such an experience or insight to use? The romance perspective is liable at the end merely "To have squeezed the universe into a ball / To roll it toward some overwhelming question" (T. S. Eliot, "The Love Song of J. Alfred Prufrock," lines 92–93). Is there any truth at the end of the street or at the end of time? More colloquially put, is there anything in our heads? Has there ever been, since we descended from the animals? Or is revolution the permanent dark mystery with no solution, the anguishing sound of all experience? What can we make of the uncertainty of origins, the swerve (Bloom) or turbulent flow (Serres) of descent?

> Is there any secret in skulls,
> The cattle skulls in the woods?
> Do the drummers in black hoods
> Rumble anything out of their drums?
>
> Mrs. Anderson's Swedish baby
> Might well have been German or Spanish . . .

For an expression of faith that there is more to life than these errancies and this gibberish, we may well listen to the conclusion of the Stevens poem that I have been quoting. For in a marvelously light way, free from all anxieties, Stevens urges us to turn away from the cloudy symbols of romance and toward our cultural situation and its specific processes. I could gloss Stevens's final lines with Gadamer's comment on the great philosopher of classical Athens: "It appears that it is *the* human task to constantly be limiting the measureless [i.e., the *apeiron*] with measure" (*Dialogue and Dialectic* 155).

> Yet that things go round and again go round
> Has rather a classical sound.

PART II

Critics

CHAPTER 1

Why Style Matters
The Lessons of Taine's *History of English Literature*

WITHOUT SEEKING ULTIMATES, I will open by stating my firm persuasion that Hippolyte Taine's *History of English Literature* was among the greatest works of literary criticism of its century and remains among the greatest of literary histories. Brilliant in conception, organization, and expression, it should be enjoyed as a work of art portraying the panorama of a nation. But its importance is not merely historical and aesthetic. Properly understood, it communicates a distinctive and powerful vision of the cultural function of literature, with a message perhaps more timely now than in its own day. Even a few years ago the sociological cast of his work represented an obstacle to understanding; it was then possible to write of "literary people who are angered by Taine's manner of using literature as a means of understanding an age or a nation rather than as an end in itself."[1] Most literary criticism was trying to break away from the threesome he popularized—race, moment, and milieu. Now, however, they are again objects of scrutiny; in the era of *Black Athena* and *Borderlands* it should seem natural to reexamine the European male who popularized these topics. His masterpiece has become worth not just reading, but debating.

For generations the introduction to Taine's masterpiece, the *History of English Literature*, was a touchstone, more seminal than anything by Matthew Arnold, more passionately controversial than any text of Nietzsche. Its cosmopolitan esteem for other cultures aided advanced thinkers in the nationalist years between the Franco-Prussian War and World War I; its fatalist rhetoric, abetted by the grim defeatism of Taine's later history of the French Revolution, irritated and provoked progressives in the years between the world wars. Subsequently, the cultural Darwinism with which Taine's name is linked has seemed more and more distant, and his text has dropped out of syllabi and anthologies. Like many great minds, he was traduced by his closest disciples—Zola and Brunetière above all. The slogans of a colorful writer were shorn of their contexts; the conclusions of a profoundly learned scholar lost their nuances and qualifications. Increasingly, for those who knew only his anthology pieces or digests of his writings, he fell into line, until he fell by the wayside, leaving little more than tags that no one should take seriously.

The task of resuscitating Taine, then, is threefold. My first section revives the once-familiar image. The second section scrutinizes its inadequacies, particularly with respect to the notorious triad of determinants and to the determinism that is attached to them. The third and fourth sections together concern the core of Taine's achievement, the vision of history and the role of style in propelling historical movement and cultural change. Because Taine is so little and for the most part so inaccurately read, I have written expansively in order to give a feel for his manner and to ground fully conclusions that have escaped many readers, however inescapable they appear to me. Throughout the analysis I have also made an effort to position Taine precisely in relation to thinkers he drew upon, lived among, and was succeeded by. A final section presents the case for Taine as our contemporary—a thinker capable of intervening productively in present-day disciplinary debates. He should be attended to at length and read in depth, I shall be arguing, because he is the person who gets right what New Historicists characteristically get wrong.

I

An independent writer having only occasional affiliations with institutions of higher learning, Taine (1828–93) left an astonishing body of work. Before he was 30 he had published *Voyage aux Pyrénées* (1855), featuring landscapes and legends; the prize-winning, oratorically mannered *Essai sur Tite Live* (1856); and the controversial polemic against French academic philosophy known under a later title as *Les Philosophes classiques du XIXᵉ siècle en France* (1857).[2] By 1870 Taine had published three multivolume works: his *History of English Literature* (1863, with a supplementary volume on six contemporary authors in 1867); five sets of lectures on the aesthetics of the visual arts and on the art of Italy, the Netherlands, and Greece, eventually collected as *Philosophie de l'art* (1880); and a massive and tedious psychological treatise, *De l'intelligence* (1870). Further books from this period included Taine's longest and most brilliant single-author study, *La Fontaine et ses fables* (1860, based on his 1853 French dissertation); the long *Voyage en Italie* (1866), with panoramic descriptions of the society and the art of the country; a set of sketches of Parisian life, *Notes sur Paris: Vie et opinions de Frédéric-Thomas Graindorge* (1857); and two volumes of collected essays (1858, 1865, containing important essays on Plato and Xenophon and on numerous French writers of the seventeenth and nineteenth centuries, and eventually supplemented by a third, posthumous volume). Apart from *Notes sur l'Angleterre* (1872), the rest of his life was devoted to *Les Origines de la France contemporaine*, of which the history of the Revolution in six large (or twelve moderate) volumes was completed. A fragmentary autobiographical novel, *Etienne Mayran*, was published in 1909 (in book form in 1910); a projected book on the theory of the will was never written. Never a focus for writing was Taine's intensive study of Hegel, without whom his vision of history would have been unthinkable.

So prodigious a writer must have had a system. I will begin by laying out Taine's system, before turning it over to find his genius. Taine sought out the regularities beneath the multiplicity of experience. He began at the level of the individual. A writer, artist, or thinker may produce many works throughout his career, but a single impulse gives rise to all.[3] Taine was fond of organic similes: works are like the leaves and branches of a common trunk. "The whole corpus arises from a main root; a dominant, primitive sensation sprouts and endlessly ramifies the complicated vegetation of effects" (*Philosophie de l'art* 458). Criticism, this passage continues, cannot "untangle" all the effects; it must rise above the details in order to encompass essences.

The task, then, is to characterize the fundamental impulse and to illustrate its operations. The cultural field resembles a landscape—one of Taine's landscapes, at any rate—and the critic must try to locate the central vantage from which the pattern of the whole can best be surveyed. Criticism becomes an exercise in perspective, sifting creative output for the principal, foreground works or the heartwood, the proliferating middle ground, and the inevitable profusion of trivial or ephemeral leaves at the periphery. The critic joins taste and judgment to discern what matters in a body of work—what endures, what fructifies. In the *History of English Literature*, where Taine could not confine himself to what he innately liked, he often clears deadwood away in order to find the living core. Thus, in the chapter on Joseph Addison, Taine suffers through the sterile verse, the pallid moral essays (his judgments, not mine, of course), and the conventionally prescriptive aesthetic writings, until he finds the warm humor characters and the gently radiant descriptions of visionary nature that are the "epitome of all Addison's characteristics" (2: 147/3: 419).* Except in the worst of the polemic against French philosophy, he invariably balances criticism against praise, and the best parts of a work are always judged the most characteristic. One reason Taine gives for choosing English literature as his subject is its nearly continuous strength; he may have to survive the tedious poets of the fifteenth century, "whom we only read because we must accept history from every quarter, even from imbeciles" (1: 163/ 1: 221), but even among the weeds there are always flowers. After so many Gowers you are sure to find at least a Skelton, after so many Priors a Pope.

So long as Taine focuses on individuals, his method seems tempered with imagination and predicated on a core of human sympathy and warmth. Here Taine is an impressionist before he is a systematist, a psychologist before a botanist. "Every painter, poet, novelist of unusual lucidity should be interrogated and observed in depth by a psychologist friend" (*De l'intelligence* 1: 13–14). The travel books are an essential part of his oeuvre because they let the spontaneous feelings of the man unfold. "I write down my impression just as it is and on the spot, and I do not write until I have an impression"; "since you like frank impressions, I will give you the succession and the diversity of mine" (*Italie* 1: 119, 169). In studying authors Taine regularly begins with a biography, and not infrequently (as with Pope and Wordsworth) a luridly drawn one: the man precedes and explains the work. "Faculté maîtresse" may sound dry, but Taine also calls it a passion. "If you deprive facts of the

* Citations from the *History of English Literature* are given in the form (2: 147/3: 419). Volume(s) and page(s) before the slash refer to the English translation, those that follow to the French. Translations are modified where necessary.

original passion that calls them forth and of the color that illuminates them to the senses, they do not enter the mind either pure or whole. Let us then change abstractions and reasoning into emotions and into images. May history, like nature, touch the heart and the senses at the same time as the intelligence. . . . Science becomes art" (*Essai sur Tite Live* 190). The side of Taine that loves the sketches of Rubens above all other painting (see *Italie* 1: 198 and *Philosophie de l'art* 244–49) is a connoisseur of vivid and immediate images. At this level his system would appear to be merely a more focused application of Sainte-Beuve's sensibility.

But Taine was never content with the individualism of pure feeling. Having begun with art, he must always be converting it back into science. Even Sainte-Beuve, in Taine's eyes, was covertly a systematizer: "He imported into moral history the procedures of natural history" ("Sainte-Beuve," *Derniers essais* 96). Psychology rarely means for Taine what it commonly means for us, the insightful understanding of the emotions of the soul. Instead, it is the queen of the sciences. "Just as at bottom astronomy is a mechanical and physiology a chemical problem, so history at bottom is a psychological problem." "When you have observed and noted in man one, two, three, then a multitude of sensations, does . . . your knowledge appear complete? Is a book of observations a psychology? It is no psychology" (1: 24, 8 / 1: xlv, xv). To be sure, Taine's treatise on psychology—the book he felt most affection for, the only major project not prompted by an occasion or a commission—does concern itself with the buried wellsprings of personality. But the unconscious for Taine proves to be a peculiarly abstract and desiccated realm: it is the "moral event" that is "signified" by the "physical world," which, in turn, "is reduced to a system of signs" (*De l'intelligence* 1: 331). The inner truth of character is the cause of the appearances of character, the law of its manifestations. Outer and inner prove equivalent; each reduces to the other in a common, generative necessity. In this mood, Taine is a genetic structuralist, but bereft of Jean Piaget's exploratory sensibility. "Given any pair whatever of any data whatever; so soon as they are effectively linked, there is a reason, a *because*, an intermediary that explains, demonstrates, and necessitates their connection" (*De l'intelligence* 2: 441). The study of individual character is merely an example of science in general; really, there are no individuals—and hence no faculties, no passions, no characters—but only data and their laws.[4]

Consequently, the study of individuals appears to be only a passing illusion. Yes, Taine wrote detailed studies of many great authors, painters, historians, and philosophers. But in truth these individuals are merely indicators of the unity and the law of much greater and more lasting collectivities. The *History of English Literature* is less a portrait of individuals than a panorama of eras and, ultimately, a depiction of the English nation as it has endured from the dawn of history. The book's second sentence already points the way: "A work of literature is not a mere play of imagination, the isolated caprice of a heated brain, but a copy of the surrounding manners and the sign of a state of mind" (1: 1 [but poorly translated] / 1: iii). Taine's novel remained a meager torso, and it is striking how bereft of identifiable figures many of his books are. Thus, while *Notes sur l'Angleterre* reports many conversations—England being the land of particular existences as well as the subject of the masterpiece I will later rescue from the picture I am now painting—in the more than 800 pages of the *Voyage en Italie* only a few puppet-like individuals flicker briefly into view at the opening of volume 2 ("Pérouse et Assise"). Otherwise, even in "La Société," there is only a "digest of fifty or sixty conversations" (1: 317), quoting but a single, stereotypical, reinvented political debate (1: 377–81). Even more striking is the history of the Revolution, a grim sociological study obviously intended to counterbalance the vivid poetry of the two great historians whom Taine admired but also warned against, Carlyle and Michelet.[5] The Revolution could hardly be written without its leaders, but they (and even Voltaire and the *philosophes*) become the impotent vehicles of positions and groups, and the greatest events themselves fade into a subordinate clause.[6] Taine calls the Terror an example of "forces devoid of intelligence" (*La Révolution* 1: 345), and the phrase could apply to virtually the entire story he tells.

Trees are rooted in soil, and the soil rests on bedrock. More resonant even than the botanical metaphors that evoke the life force of individuals are geological metaphors reflecting the impersonal workings of nature. "When we wish to construct a man, we must dig down to the man's foundation; that is, we must define to ourselves the structure of his bodily machine and the primitive gait of his mind" (1: 329 / 2: 110); "the fundamental faculty, . . . buried but present, [is] like one of those deep and primeval rocks, which, lying far inland, give to all undulations [*accidents*] of the soil a basis and a support" (2: 72 / 3: 277). Even intelligence is not so much human intelligence as abstract intelligibility.

Taine's fondness for grand landscapes (such as the Dickensian view of England that opens the first chapter of the history) bespeaks a desire not to write a history of literature or indeed of human affairs but to tell the story of the earth itself. The *History of English Literature* is a book about the English—and ultimately about the land of England.

The psychological reduction of creativity to a master passion is thus only a halfway house. Psychology gets reduced in its turn. For "the question of origins is no more mysterious than that of characters" (*De l'intelligence* 2: 440). There is no force, there are only forces. The greatest among us discover or voice them; the rest merely represent them and carry them out. As character unites the traits of an individual—as it is the substance of which they are the signs—so the many characters that constitute a nation are in turn united. The forces constituting their unifying origin are the grand trinity I have already named—race, milieu, and moment. To be sure, not every mote and speck of dust can be fully explained, but everything that matters can, and the explanation invariably lies in these three factors.

Indeed, the more salient a characteristic, the more fully and convincingly it shows its causal origin, which is its meaning, the bedrock of which it is the sign or the trace. Hence the notorious slogan (to which I shall return), "Vice and virtue are products, like vitriol and sugar" (1: 8 / 1: xv). They are products of their time, their environment, and their race. Everything that matters is determined in the same way, by the same factors, in manifestation of a common essence of the individual, of his time, of his nation, and finally of humanity, or intelligence, or nature in general. Freedom is an illusion. The cosmic perspective may be exhilarating, as in the Spinozist paean that concludes *Les Philosophes classiques*. But before the immensity of nature individuals shrink into insignificance, and after the eternal order is established, human endeavors can do little but mar it. Taine's pessimism was notorious; he had a bleak and frequently reiterated view of outcomes and endings. Ben Jonson's death appears as one among many such: "Thus almost always, sadly and miserably is dragged out and ends the last act of the human comedy. After so many years, after so many sustained efforts, amid so much glory and genius, we find a poor shattered body, drivelling and suffering between a servant and a priest" (1: 325 / 2: 103). Perhaps Taine let the *Origines de la France contemporaine* displace his projected *Traité de la volonté* because he had everything to say about origins and nothing about will.

For the moment I will leave open the meaning of the terms race, milieu, and moment. But from everything I have said about the thrust of Taine's thought, it should be clear that the three causal determinants are not equal in value. One—race—is the bedrock, fixed, general, and unchanging like the soil. The other two are local, contingent, or transient. One determines the essence, the others modify it. "In all things, there are *superficies* [des *dessus*]—more or less external, accidental and temporary, changing, consequently of lesser importance—and a *foundation* [un *dessous* fondamental]—stable and solid, hence of greater importance. . . . [The followers of Poussin] instinctively sought locales where steep mountains display the earth's skeleton, and where man feels himself not in a backyard but on a planet" ("Edouard Bertin," *Derniers essais* 347, Taine's emphasis). If we dig deep enough, we will strip away the surface layers and arrive finally at the one thing that is the root of all.

And so, finally, the term *history* unmasks itself as a deception. Just as there is no history in the *Voyage aux Pyrénées*, but only magnificent mountains and valleys and sordid tales and legends, so there is none in the *History* and in the *Origines de la France contemporaine*. The Revolution neither established liberty nor crushed human dignity; it merely repeated all the bureaucratic follies of the old regime, with greater outbursts of violence. Historians don't write history, they paint mankind, whether like the colorfully emotive Dutch painters or like the colorlessly energetic Greek sculptors. The end of historical study is the end of history. "In advance, and without its knowledge, each generation carries within itself its future and its history; to this one, well before the end, one might have foretold its destiny" (*L'Ancien régime* 2: 315). Hence, the *History of English Literature* originally concluded with a portrait of England:

Having reached the limits of this long review, we can now embrace in one prospect the aggregate of English civilization: everything is connected there: a few powers and a few primitive circumstances have produced the rest, and we have only to pursue their continuous action in order to comprehend the nation and its history, its past and its present. At the beginning, and furthest removed in the region of causes, comes the race. . . . This is the primitive stock: of its substance and innate properties is to spring almost the whole future growth. (2: 395 / 4: 424–25)

Once you have read the *History of English Literature,* you will never need to read it again.

II

That would be a pity, because it's a wonderful book. I know no work of scholarship to equal it in the combination of visionary sweep with coherent, meticulous immersion in its subject matter.

The previous section in effect reproduces the common view of Taine, both among his followers and through subsequent generations. In one form or another it can be found in countless books, essays, anthologies, and handbooks. An important recent example is the chapter in René Wellek's *History of Modern Criticism,* which echoes all the commonplaces and says almost nothing of why Taine is more than a fossil. The elements of this picture are all true, but they are only a part of the truth. They reflect the system but ignore the critic.

There is no shortage of signs pointing beyond the picture of Taine as a scientific determinist and a philosophical pessimist. He was not slow to protest explicitly against such one-sided readings.[7] Though he had a method (amid his veneration, Zola short-sightedly complained that it was too much of a method), Taine inveighed ceaselessly against the slaves of method, Rousseau and his revolutionary followers above all.[8] If we trust him as a writer, then we should seek a counterbalancing side to his achievement. But, indeed, we shouldn't trust him as a writer—or consequently take him at his word—when he formulates doctrine. For Taine always wrote for effect. His most memorable and most widely remembered utterances are calculated exaggerations; it is a mistake to consider his prefaces and programmatic declarations as the core of his vast achievement.[9] Rather, by his own lights they should be regarded as the sprouts of an indwelling sap or the traces of a bedrock that is to be sought beneath or within the proliferating texts.

What, first of all, can be intended by the three determinants: race, milieu, and moment? More ink has been spilled over these terms than about anything else in Taine, for nothing is really simple about them.

Race appears dangerously circular—in Taine's usage as in the present day. Race, for him, is the permanent, unchanging core. It is what remains unaccounted and mysterious when everything that has a manifest origin has been removed—a kind of residual essence, contingent surface mystically transmuted into depth. If a feature has no visible cause, then it must be racial; conversely, if it is racial, then it is inherent. By such logic, race becomes a vanishing mediator that redescribes what is least understood as that which is most true, without otherwise affecting its nature. It defines without explaining.

Milieu, on first, crude approximation, looks like a middle ground; in contrast to the everchanging moment, milieu varies slowly and produces deep, abiding effects. But if that were its character, then milieu would occupy only a vague and ill-defined terrain. It would differ quantitatively from moment by virtue of its pace, and as it approaches the permanence of landscape or climate (the quintessential milieux) it would likewise differ only quantitatively from race. In the distant past, to be sure, races traveled: you can really distinguish race from milieu when you see how the Norman character was modified when it descended into Normandy or when it swept into England. But in fact *Völkerwanderung* is not otherwise Taine's subject, and it becomes increasingly difficult to distinguish the Englishman from his milieu. Hence, milieu spoils the system: race is bound to place, moment changes with time, while milieu unsteadily absorbs whatever does not quite fit.

On closer examination, however, perhaps milieu is the system. Milieu suggests harmonious, meaningful correspondence, leaving to one side the imponderable givens of race, to the other the unseizable vagaries of the moment: "If great art and its milieu are contemporaneous, it is not that they are assembled by chance, it is that the second sketches, develops, ripens, spoils and dissolves the first along with itself, amid the accidents of the grand hubbub of humanity and the unforeseen sallies of personal originality" (*Philosophie de l'art* 168). So perhaps it is race that spoils the system: locality and time provide the external causal nexus, with race as the name for internal factors lacking visible explanation. Or, finally, perhaps moment is the spoiler: race and milieu constitute internal and external influences, and the rest is made up of the fleeting and unpredictable contingencies of the moment. "Two natures, one innate, the other acquired, constitute all the springs of . . . conduct," even though "at first sight it seems as if accidents or circumstances will govern their pace, their fall, and their success" (2: 398 / 4: 429). Taine simply offers too much facility for a rigorous, uniform system.[10]

As if that were not enough, examine the psychology. Virtue and vice may in some sense be products like vitriol and sugar—but only in their "chemical" nature, not in their historical existence. In a conceptual framework such as an introduction it may be helpful to see how vice and virtue are constituted. Yet even vitriol and sugar require a confluence of circumstances—suitable growing weather, an economic framework of production and distribution, and above all a will toward a desired result—if they are actually to be produced. The causal framework is not the only perspective on human life as experienced through time. For a naturalist such as Balzac (as Taine says in his long essay on the novelist), "virtue is a product, like wine or vinegar," but it is not one for a moralist such as Corneille. Ultimately the logic of Balzac's vision makes virtue "nothing but a usurious secured loan. It is Balzac's ugliest idea" ("Balzac," *Nouveaux essais* 60–61). Here Taine condemns the very determinism that he flaunts in introducing the *History of English Literature*. Determinism is only one side of Taine's vision; it is often the side he turns outward to capture the imagination of others, but not the side that captures his own most personal vision.

Indeed, before taking any of Taine's generalizations at face value, we must acknowledge that he had more than one face. In *Etienne Mayran* we find the conscious portrayal of the divided personality that was Taine, at once scientist and poet, prize scholar yet, when provoked, dashing pugilist. The novel fragment alternates analytical passages with landscapes and other portrayals of exalted emotion. In his introduction to the novel Paul Bourget quotes a notebook entry from 1862 (just when Taine was hardest at work on the *History of English Literature*): "My fundamental idea has been to reproduce the emotion, the passion peculiar to the man being described, and beyond that to lay out one by one all the steps of logical generation: in short, to paint him in the manner of artists, and, at the same time, to reconstruct him in the manner of reasoners" (*Etienne Mayran* 8). Of these two options, the reasoning manner is what Taine has been known for. The reasoning, however, turns out to be simplistic, arbitrary, and chaotic—good for sloganeering and partisanship, but not enduringly persuasive as scientific explanation. To be sure, I will have more to say about Taine's analytical gifts, with a different and more sympathetic way to understand his methods. But his astonishing passion and energy came from the magic of immediate contact with other souls, not from the sovereign command of meticulously disposed information.

The entire page came back, and seeing it thus unfold in his mind without needing to strain, he *felt* it, and he seemed to be hearing, not written words, but uttered speech. The book had a voice, and this voice reached his ears. "Now it is no longer my tables that I shall be studying, it is that book there; what a remarkable book!" . . . For the first time, he was touched by a thing proportioned to his mind, and that was *alive* for him. The rigid barrier that separates the books of men and the intelligences of children had given way at one point. (*Etienne Mayran* 204–5)

Such is the climax of Taine's fictional self-portrait, in the last and longest completed chapter, "Premières idées." The ecstasy was to be followed by a renewal of discipline, but Taine's heart was not in it; the next chapter (and the book) breaks off after barely a page. There are two sides to Taine's nature, as there are two sides to vice and virtue: you can know moral qualities, or you can be possessed by them. Ultimately you cannot really separate knowledge from possession. Still, what matters most is not the timelessness of science, but the feeling contact with life.[11]

Taine the vitalist. In reading Taine's more personal writings I find myself constantly thinking of Henri Bergson.[12] Everywhere, tirelessly, what captivates this man, who was himself a force of nature, is the driving energy of life. Products that can be known—even moral products such as vice and virtue—are not the vital source:

Neither the vices nor the virtues of man are his nature. . . . Our true essence consists in the causes of our good or bad qualities, and these causes are discovered in the temperament, the species and degree of imagination, the amount and velocity of attention, the magnitude and direction of primitive passions. A character is a force, like weight or steam. . . . It is therefore to ignore man, to reduce him, as Thackeray and English literature generally do, to an aggregate of virtues and vices; it is to lose sight in him of all but the exterior and social side. (2: 511 / 5: 142–43)

We study history, above all, in order to revive the lost art of the past. For a man so often accused of imposing scientific norms on artistic works, Taine leaves no doubt of his attachment to the irreproducible human individuality that they contain: "If some words are dry, like philosophical terms and like figures, others are alive like the vibrations of a violin or the tones of a painting" (*La Fontaine* 288). In his treatment of one author after another Taine extols the character portrayal; the role of literature is to bring people to life on the page. Hence his noteworthy and influential admiration for Stendhal, whose characters "are complex, multiple, particular and original like those of living beings; . . . they draw us far from our stale habits, from our mechanical life. . . . It is the spectacle of force, and force is the source of true beauty" ("Stendhal," *Nouveaux essais* 238–39). And the same is true of painting as of writing. "To paint living flesh is the supreme difficulty of art, for life is a profound, infinite thing" (*Philosophie de l'art* 501). The *Voyage aux Pyrénées* even contains a long paean to the life of rocks and to the mountains that people the earth, changing with a pace and a force that dwarf the insignificant flutterings of humanity (226–32).

But if even stones live, it is water that fascinates Taine above all. Water is his master metaphor, flowing and circulating life in all things. The definitive version of his first book opens with a prospect on a river, where "it seems that . . . the water lives and feels" (*Pyrénées* 4). The journey to England passes through a kind of landless baptism (*Notes sur l'Angleterre* 1–3; the paragraph headings—the only ones in the book—are "June 1862, at sea," and the curious "In the Thames"). In its definitive version even the book on La Fontaine (the writer's very name must have been captivating) opens, implausibly enough, with a water journey from the North Sea up the Rhine into France. And the *History of English Literature* starts with a long eulogy of English waters (1: 29–32/1: 2–6), which the original closing chapter renews (2: 403–6/438–43). Taine's waters are remarkable for their variety: the circulation of British commerce (2: 410–11/4: 449–51), the percolating terrain where the Dutch painters lived (*Philosophie de l'art* 184–88), the miracle of Venice (*Italie* 1: 290–91), the ripples that are "the only living thing" at night on the Lago Maggiore (*Italie* 1: 433), the gushing spring of Guido Reni's talent (*Italie* 2: 198), and, overwhelming all, the torrential force of the French Revolution. Even rocks are etched by water, or are residues left by water, or channels for water, a symbiosis without which rocks would be mere geometry and not the signs of authentic life. Man "is like a water" (*Italie* 1: 335); "the human spirit flows with events like a river" ("Mme de La Fayette," *Essais* 256); in its perfection "life flows, broad and measured, like a fine river" (*Philosophie de l'art* 428). While Taine was working on his *History of English Literature*, Michelet wrote a book on the sea (*La Mer*, 1861); his waters are a cauldron, a powerful engine, with a titanic circulation, the nourishing matrix of countless fascinating creatures and phenomena. But they are not, like Taine's, alive with any life of their own except for what scientific instruments discover in the currents of the globe. They teem with life, but it is Taine's waters that live.

Consequently, we must reverse the usual picture of Taine. He is not a determinist; or rather, to use the vocabulary that Zola favored, he is a determinist but not a fatalist. Even though it is closed in the past, history is open to the future: Taine willingly identifies causes but refuses to predict effects. Even so pivotal a poem as *Paradise Lost* is "not of its century" but rather a product of situation and opportunity alike, "the chance of a revolution," "the chance of a throne preserved, then re-established," "the force of his intellect," "the force of his enthusiasm" (1: 540, 555 / 2: 488, 515). To be sure, in the grand retrospect of Taine's original conclusion all falls into place. But in the supplementary volume, with its six chapters on the most notable figures of the present, the introduction avers that nothing can be securely foretold about the future course of events. There will be a pattern, but it will be composed from the inventions of the great thinkers and writers, and it cannot be traced until it has happened. Not even the men can be known truly during their lifetimes: "Unfortunately Dickens is still alive, and refutes the biographies made of him" (2: 430 / 5: 4). Events end as knowable history, but they begin with spontaneity and originality. In his last decades Taine lost his vision of human accomplishment; what makes the *Origines de la France contemporaine* so dreary is the concentration on origins and the bleak denial of individual initiative. But in the *History of English Literature* he manages the feat of balancing historical comprehensibility with personal invention.[13]

Taine's fusion of a backward-looking necessity and a forward-looking freedom is soundly Hegelian. As Taine was often caricatured as an objective, scientific determinist, so Hegel as a subjective determinist claiming that history finds its fulfillment with Napoleon. But Hegel's teleology is no more fatalistic than Taine's. His present is indeed the culmination of history, but that is because, looking back, the present always seems to be the goal. When in his lectures on the philosophy of history Hegel concludes, teleologically, that "the present form of spirit comprehends all earlier stages in itself," he does not restrict the meaning of present to his own time, but implicitly extends it to any present that reflects on its past. In truth spirit is timeless and ever present, always capable of being revealed through historical consciousness, for "what spirit is, it has always been." But while hindsight shows the present always spiritualized—fully rational and joyously perfect—in its unfolding it is tragically vulnerable. Like the phoenix, spirit must die; like the family of Zeus, it must consume its matter and be consumed in turn in order to be reborn. This "bitter potion" of determination and indeterminacy, of an unending cycle of foretold fulfillment and unforetold change, is what we can expect in the future, however cunningly rational the past inevitably appears (*Werke* 12: 104–5). While the negative and destructive sides of free, individual force figure more prominently in Hegel, a lurking suspicion of originality surfaces at times in Taine, for instance in his grim admiration of Swift: "What truth and force! . . . His originality is entire, and his genius creative; he surpasses his classical and timid age; he tyrannizes over form, breaks it, dare[s] utter anything, spares himself no strong word" (2: 174 / 4: 49–50). The passages in Taine where everything sounds totalized and foretold in the ageless and inescapable constancies of race are not his last word. Despite the panoramic retrospects collapsing history into a spatialized simultaneity, his vitalist dialectic reconciles comprehension with the onward flow of time.[14]

Comprehension is a key term: "If it is beautiful to paint a personage, it is perhaps interesting to make him *understood*" (preface [1858], *Essais* vii). Taine explores historical causation not with the scientific aim of producing or reproducing events, but with the hermeneutic one of understanding them. He clarifies his principles in the new preface to his essays, published in 1866, while he was at work on the supplementary volume to the *History of English Literature*. Claiming for himself only a retrospective system of explanation and not a prospective method of construction, he insists that his goal is a psychological analysis to reveal the structural node of an individual personality or the spirit of an age. Those who accuse such an explanatory system of inhumanity overlook

that the fundamental aptitudes and penchants of a soul belong to it, that those that it takes from the general situation or the national character are or become first off personal, that when it acts through them, it does so according to itself, by its own force, spontaneously, with complete initiative, with entire responsibility, and that the analytical artifice by which we distinguish its principal motors and gears and the ensuing distribution of its primitive movement, does not prevent the whole, which is itself, from drawing from within its impetus and its direction, that is, its energy and its effort. (*Essais* xxiii)

The more we penetrate the forces animating societies, the more we appreciate the individuals that mobilize those forces.

Taine is misconstrued as a fatalist when his notion of causes is taken in too strong a sense. The causes he alleges are factors that promote a result rather than determinants that precipitate it. He found the distinction worked out in John Stuart Mill, and he explains it in his study of the philosopher, where he reinterprets Mill's method of induction as a system of abstraction:

A fact, or a series of facts, can always be resolved into its components. It is this decomposition that is required when we ask what is the nature of an object. It is these components we look for when we wish to penetrate into the interior of a being. These we designate under the names of forces, causes, laws, essences, primitive properties. They are not new facts added to the first, but a portion or extract from them; they are contained in the first, they have not anything different from the facts themselves. When we discover them, we do not pass from one datum to another, but from the same to the same. (2: 646 / 5: 398)

There is no opposition or incompatibility between freedom and necessity, any more than there is between experiment and analysis, pragmatics and speculation, or English facts and German laws. It falls to the Frenchman (Taine concludes) to combine these two perspectives in a temperate and universal vision that accommodates them both.

Taine's *History of English Literature* is one of the nineteenth century's grandest attempts to reconcile the particularism of a Hogarth, a Scott, or a Mill with the rigorism of a Luther, a Dürer, or a Kant. In its representation of historical forces, it answers Michelet's mystic populism with a differentiated narrative where group tendency and individual accomplishment operate in constant interchange. Nationality is a spirit not freighted with compulsory nationalism, a continuing process rather than a universal idea. From François Guizot, to whom the *History of English Literature* is dedicated, Taine draws the ideal of civilization, but for him civilization is itself an evolving notion quite different from Guizot's "general and definitive fact, the culmination and summary of all the others" (Guizot, *Cours* 8).[15] Even at his most pessimistic Taine is free of the disenchanted antinaturalism of his close friend Ernest Renan; Taine's account of Shakespeare's bourgeois self-sufficiency is one implicit refutation among many of Renan's maxim that civilization is a creation of the aristocracy. Whereas the *Origines de la France contemporaine* indicts one nation's well-intentioned debacle, the *History of English Literature* chronicles another's often errant successes. The arts of a nation reveal its character and genius; they forge the possibilities of what it can imagine and accomplish. In our individualist era the notion of national identity can come to seem almost oxymoronic. (That is, indeed, the unstated presupposition of Benedict Anderson's influential *Imagined Communities*.) But artistic voices raised for the people restore the balance between the centralizing lethargy of race and the unstable opportunism of the momentary. The individual imagination, in Taine's view, does not produce the community but expands it, as the community does not command but does enable the imagination. The arts are the active expression of its will not just to be but to live.

Thus, the vitalism resurfaces as the other, less familiar, half of Taine's divided sensibility. On the one hand, as we have seen, his scientific determinism drove to the solid bedrock of timeless, essential abstractions: "Nature is, in reality, a tapestry, of which we only see the reverse; this is why we try to turn it" (2: 653 / 5: 409). Hence, he praises Macaulay for his penetration of the logic of events. "He had a most lively consciousness of causes; and causes unite facts. By them, scattered events are assembled into a single event" (2: 540 / 5: 201). To know causes is to secure the comprehensive grasp that makes them comprehensible; a unified vision is what makes understanding possible. On the other hand, in their most uncompromisingly fatalist form, abstractions clash irreconcilably against the pure contingency of random facts. When we seek the ultimate truths hidden under nature's tapestry, "we are outflanked on all sides by the infinity of time and space. . . . Chance is at the end of all our knowledge" (2: 655 / 5: 412). The ultimate in causes is an illimitable multiplicity of causes. Taine concedes as much only two pages after praising Macaulay's power of unification. "It is not enough to see causes; we must also see many. Every event has a multitude of them. . . . An incomparable advocate, [Macaulay] pleads an infinite number of causes" (2: 542 / 5: 202–4). Demands that are too positive subvert themselves in the end. It is not in experimental, materialist absolutism that man will find human truths, but in the psychology of human experience.

Taine's other great philosophical master was Spinoza. Spinoza taught him many of the same divided lessons about historical evaluation that Hegel taught him about historical understanding. From Spinoza, Taine draws not only the conventional determinist clichés, but likewise the recognition of how human consciousness encounters determinism. While material forces may steer the world, our engagement with the world occurs on a different plane—not in the absolutes of science and truth, but in affect and judgment. In the fifth and final book of Spinoza's *Ethics* the mastery of emotions through their conversion into clear and distinct ideas becomes the endless task of human reason. But the reality with which we deal as conscious beings continues to lie in the vague and fluctuating terrain of the passions, which are the subject of the fourth book. Because feelings precede knowledge, they shape our conscious experience more immediately than do the ultimate truths of nature. Fundamental for Taine's Spinozism is an axiom of *Ethics*, book 4: "Whatsoever thing be given, there is something stronger whereby it can be destroyed" (*Works* 2: 191). Precisely because everything is necessarily subject to something else, we can never actually get to the bottom of anything. Consequently, the material foundations of the world lie only with its founder. "Deus sive natura": natural forces exceed our power of control, to be sure, but also lie outside the finite realm of our existence. A human science deals with the human face of things, hence with what we now would call psychology rather than ontology. Just like Taine's supposed Darwinism, Spinoza's geometrical method works with stable axioms and postulates, but its object is the unstable intermediate terrain of humanity.

Taine footnotes the axiom to *Ethics*, book 4, at a crucial moment in the fifth section of the introduction to the *History of English Literature*. Earlier, better-known sections discuss quasi-paleontological or geological excavations for fixed, original truths:

There is an inner cause. . . . This itself comes from another more general cause. . . . This second idea in its turn depends upon a third still more general. . . . That is the master idea. . . . Here we track the root of man, . . . race itself. . . . There the search is at an end; we have arrived at a primitive disposition. . . . Here lie the grand causes, for they are the universal and permanent causes, present at every moment and in every case, everywhere and always acting indestructible, and in the end infallibly supreme. (1: 8–9 / 1: xv–xvii)

The rhetorical inundation appears uncontrollable. But then the focus shifts, as the other, more tempered side of Taine comes to the fore. "The vastness of the distance lets us but half perceive—and by a doubtful light—the origin of species,"[16] he writes in the fifth section. Essences may have ultimate explanations, but the universal ocean is too immense for us. Better to look for the indications where they gather in surveyable if provisional aggregates. Taine avoids terming these aggregates causes, for—as the imagery and the footnote to Spinoza both make clear—he is no longer thinking of the unshakable first causes with which his reputation is wrongly associated. The paragraph concludes: "Such is the first and richest source of these master faculties from which historical events take their rise; and one sees at the outset that if it be powerful, it is because this is no simple spring [punning on the French "source"], but a kind of lake, a deep reservoir wherein other springs have, for a multitude of centuries, discharged their several streams" (1: 14 / 1: xxvi). Taine's compromise learns to have it both ways: his lake is a source, yet not a source (spring) but a receptacle. Such imagery is appropriate to the logic derived from Mill; the understanding and judgment that Taine seeks are collective abstractions that pool or distill general, moral verities. In one perspective virtue and vice may be natural products, but the Spinozistic challenge is to resist and correct that perspective with the aid of human reason.

History is thus Taine's alternative to science. For, as his sentence about the origin of species continues, "the events of history sufficiently illumine the events anterior to history, to explain the almost immovable steadfastness of the primordial marks [caractères]" (1: 13 / 1: xxiv–xxv). In the Darwinian perspective, even race, though "almost immovable," is not a true absolute, but rather the outer bound of historical comprehension. Indeed, the History of English Literature opens with the migrations of the tribes that shaped the English character at the dawn of history. Of all the civilizations that Taine loved, the English appealed the most to him because of the evolving continuity of its culture, fostered by its cool, damp, settled climate. England produces strong, steady, earthy characters—at one extreme the "sympathetic genius" of a Shakespeare that becomes "a sort of abstract [abrégé] of the universe" (1: 366 / 2: 178), at the other the icy firmness into which Byron congeals Goethe's all too "flowing water" (2: 305 [a remarkable page] / 4: 387). So stable an environment allows for the powerful unfolding of the essential forces of civilization. Taine developed a horror of sudden revolution, but he continued to admire change, and his book contains numerous paeans to the quietly epochal shifts that have allowed England to adapt to circumstance without either destroying or being destroyed. The steady progress of history is the vital expression of the characters that live in it. Without stability there is no character and hence only the fearsome turmoil of the Year III of the Revolution. But without history there is no life—and that would be a transcendental condition inhuman and unearthly.

III

The debates about Taine, when he has been debated, have focused on the forces driving history: the causal or (as I have argued) explanatory determinants of events and texts. To move beyond these debates, we can turn from the forces to the object itself. Through race, milieu, and moment we can comprehend history, but what is the thing we are comprehending? Here I will introduce another triad, never formalized or expressly articulated by Taine but fundamental to his motivation. As an object of study history has for Taine three elements: the past, time, and the ideal in history. I propose to move toward the substance of Taine's achievement by surveying each of these in a widening circle.

The past. The past is the not-present. The past must be recovered if it is to be studied. Since we know men through "present, personal, direct, and sensible observation," our knowledge of the past must be "always incomplete." Still, we must do what we can to compensate (*suppléer*) the deficiency. The "first step in history" is to "make the past present" (1: 4 / 1: 9). Without that, it remains a fossil embedded in an unexcavated rock. Taine must have seen the evocations of this aspect of history writing in the much-admired Macaulay. It is the imaginative and poetic side of history: "To make the past present, to bring the distant near, to place us in the society of a great man or on the eminence which overlooks the field of a mighty battle . . . , these parts of the duty, which properly belongs to the historian, have been appropriated by the historical novelist" ("Hallam," in Macaulay's *Essays* 1: 111–12). By the novelist or, indeed, even by the poet: "No sooner are [Milton's words] pronounced than the past is present and the distant near" ("Milton," *Essays* 1: 12). Taine himself revives the past with his colorful descriptive passages, sometimes in the present tense, with his prosopopoeias, and with the sharply etched metaphors that render phenomena from the past in familiar natural or experiential terms.[17] He peppers his studies with comparisons between earlier and later or between foreign and French authors to help reduce the differences of time and space: an Anglo-Saxon funeral song sounds like Jeremy Taylor, Caedmon speaks like Milton, John Fortescue is the fifteenth-century Locke, Shakespeare's sonnets are at times worthy of Heine (!), La Bruyère foreshadows Balzac's realism, La Fontaine's power of evocation is like Musset's. To this extent Taine's practice offers a classic instance of what Collingwood (followed by Gadamer) was to claim as the historian's duty: "The gulf of time between the historian and his object must be bridged" (*The Idea of History* 304).

But if *Horizontverschmelzung* is the start of history, it is not the end. The past that is made present is no longer the past. (Gadamer, for whom history is merely a salient example of more diffuse hermeneutic concerns, does not acknowledge this limitation.) Hence, as Macaulay called for history as picture or as sculpture to be balanced by history as map or as anatomy ("Hallam" 112–13), so Taine urges a "second step" beyond evocation into excavation and analysis (1: 4, 7 / 1: ix, xiv). It is no longer a matter of bringing the past into the present, but conversely of entering the past: the historian is now "present at the drama which was enacted" (1: 5 / 1: xi). The historian submerges his sympathetic, novelistic force beneath his scientific ambitions to know his material in its irreducible inner core.

Though articulated early in the introduction, the scientific aim of history comes to the fore only rarely in Taine's writing. There are a few moments in the *History of English Literature* where he lapses into the past tense as he confronts the genuine alienness of, say, seventeenth-century religious polemic or of Hobbesian and Restoration materialism. And the essays on seventeenth-century France occasionally defer to its remote sensibility. "This style and these sentiments are so remote from ours that we understand them with difficulty. . . . We must neither denigrate nor imitate, but invent and understand. History must be respectful and art must be original" ("Madame de la Fayette," *Essais* 255). Taine is capable of forcing himself to accept what he instinctively rejects. "I even dare to go further, and I transport myself among the habits of the seventeenth century. . . . Each art and each century cloaks truth in a form that beautifies and alters it; each century and each art have the right to cloak the truth thus" ("Racine," *Nouveaux essais* 121). But such detachment is truly exceptional in his writing—and reluctantly professed at that. Even Macaulay's passions were too rationalized for Taine's taste: "He is not a genuine artist: when he draws a picture, he is always dreaming of proving something" (2: 624 / 5: 223).

For just as the drive to ultimate sources and unifying totalities is checked by Taine's humanistic vitalism, so too a self-suppressing immersion in the past yields to the urgent desire to establish a relationship. The past should no more be left in its fossil state than conjured up as a kind of paler present. It cannot be fixed at one pole or at the other. Rather, the past is like flowing water, like the circulation of mists, like the stream-fed lakes and the lake-fed streams. Even at the very moment when Taine is professing a geological model of the past as "great rocks deep-seated in the ground," he will also speak of "the continuous development and the ever-changing succession of the emotions and conceptions out of which the text has sprung" (1: 5–6 / 1: xi). The object not of charted knowledge but of nuanced understanding, the past must neither be fixed in alienness nor allowed to lapse into repetitive familiarity. For its essence is precisely to be in movement. At the heart of the era of positivism, the first great achievement of Taine's history is to have overthrown the conception of the past as fact.

Time. It might seem self-evident to take time as the founding category of history. Surely it was not without shock value when structuralist historiography from Febvre to Braudel and the early Foucault claimed to overthrow Taine's legacy and to transcend time's explanatory mediations.[18] However, Friedrich Meinecke long ago showed how arduous a process it was before growth and change became enshrined—not so long before Taine's day—as the basic focus for history. Even then, the conception of time was not yet altogether what Taine made of it. For time functions in nineteenth-century narrative representations as a regulative ideal; it is the force that is always moving onward, beneath the surface of events. What happens, then, is not part of time, but rather an interruption of time. History consequently is riven between the poles of flow and event. "Consider it well, the Event," writes Carlyle, "is it not, in all cases, some disruption, some solution of continuity?" (*French Revolution* 23). Time in this sense is not part of history but its horizon and outer bound. "But, on the whole, does not TIME envelop this present National Convention . . . ? Time surely, and also Eternity" (*French Revolution* 530). Consequently, we are but "a Phantasm-Reality born of Time . . . ; flitting ever backwards now on the tide of Time" (*French Revolution* 387). Carlyle is extreme, to be sure, but in these matters extreme in his lucidity, and a powerful stimulus for Taine as well.

The reconciliation of duration with change was a central problem for nineteenth-century fictional and historical narrative alike. Here, for instance, is what Georges Poulet concludes concerning the "moment" in Michelet. "On the one hand, the instant that he celebrates is the creator of the future, a flash of eternity, annihilating duration. On the other, it is prepared by a confluence of forces. So that this moment is at once *ultra-* and *extra-*historical. It is an apex of history, which comes to pass in a moment where the being that sees it, sees at the same time and all of a sudden history destroyed and history rebegun" (*Mesure de l'instant* 269).[19] It was one thing to make history temporal at bottom (rather than, say, moral and exemplary); it was quite another to make time part of history.

Taine's simplest solution to the polarization of events and time is to write histories without events. Thus, there is *Les Origines de la France contemporaine*, burdened by its crowds and mass forces and, as I have said, tragically occluding events from its history. But the *History of English Literature* is lightened by its freedom from events. England was of course favored in that its revolutions—with one exception that was not productive of great writing[20]—were peaceful and mostly intellectual or (in the broad sense) social rather than political. The flow of history was steadier there than in France. But Taine does much to sustain the flow. Dates, for one, are refreshingly scarce, and the disposition of the history works to reinforce a developing continuity. The *History of English Literature* is the masterpiece of a writer, all of whose writing is unsurpassed, in my reading experience, in organizational lucidity. Time progresses, but effortlessly. Seven of the original nineteen chapters (before the supplement on modern writers) concern individual authors, with the presentation sweeping effortlessly from the dynamic historical background into the life and works of the writer who shapes and advances the movement of civilization. The other twelve concern periods but remain unobsessed with chronology as they trace influences and developments. That is to say that Taine reinterprets periods as movements. Ideas and forms of expression are in continual flux, and within his always steady outline he masters the art of transition. Ends of chapters, above all, gather energy. Consolidation in Taine is tidal, not glacial, nor, except for 1789 (concluding the chapter about 1688, called "The Revolution"), volcanic.

We must, then, return to the three determinants—race, milieu, moment. If the first, scientific and geological model for Taine's theory points toward the permanence of race as the final explanatory ground, the revised, temporal and hydrologic model seeks elsewhere. It finds time operating not just through the determinants but within them. For moment in Taine is not just circumstance; it is movement, momentum. It is called "vitesse acquise" (acquired speed) in French and given the hybrid translation "acquired momentum."[21] To race we attribute the constant factors located within the person, to milieu the factors without. What these do not fix is what changes and thus what lives, and that is moment. Moment, or momentum, or speed, in this sense, cannot be dead, passive, or reactive, because then it would be race or milieu. Rather, moment is the spontaneity of active energies generated by individuals.

Most frequently, Taine specifies moment as developmental stage, particularly in the introduction, where he so consistently works to channel his vitalism into a system. The succession of "buds, flowers, fruits, seed-vessels" seems to provide a "law" that models the birth, maturing, and decadence of a movement or an epoch (1: 16–17 / 1: xxx–xxxi). This organic model is applied throughout the history, where Taine often writes eloquently about the gathering or waning energies of civilization. In the *Philosophie de l'art* a classicizing bent tends to normalize the model, so that perfection is found in the harmonious middle: "That is the moment when an art flourishes; previously it was a seed; a little later, it has faded. At this instant, the convergence of effects is complete, and an admirable harmony internally balances the characters, the style and the action. This moment is found in Greece in the time of Sophocles" (448). In such a passage moment is indeed passive; it measures value and is left behind as the organism follows the predetermined path of its race and its milieu.

But a different and more generous spirit animates much of the best of Taine. Resisting the inclination toward systematic norms, the introduction again retreats: "The magnitude and direction cannot be valued or computed" in "moral problems" as it can in "physical ones." "This quantity is not measurable like . . . pressure or . . . weight. We cannot define it in an exact or approximate formula; we cannot have more, or give more, in respect of it, than a literary impression" (1: 17 / 1: xxxii). The true emphasis lies not on position within set coordinates but on the animation moving from one position to the next. Different moments— different stages of life—are distinguished less by different degrees of perfection than by their different speeds. Each stage has its characteristic pace, and that above all is what is meant by its moment, its *vitesse acquise*. Even in the *Philosophie de l'art* Taine says so, though with a hard, stony metaphor. "Time scratches and digs at us, like a man with a pickaxe, and thus displays our moral geology; under its efforts, our superimposed layers depart one by one, *some more swiftly, and others more slowly*" (390, my emphasis).

The truth of moment is that we carry our determinants within us; as we are moved, so we move. The speed and the momentum vary with the age and the individual; what does not vary is that side by side with race and milieu runs the ever-changing current that defines humanity. Life is not a mechanical field of levers and pulleys but a dynamic universe of velocities and impulses encountering inertial drags and resistances. Nothing can be calculated or fixed. "Change a virtue in its milieu, and it becomes a vice; change a vice in its milieu, and it becomes a virtue. . . . Our true essence consists in the causes of our good or bad qualities, and these causes are discovered in the temperament, the species and degree of imagination, the amount and velocity of attention, the magnitude and direction of primitive passions. A character is a force, like gravity, weight, or steam" (2: 510–11 / 5: 142–43). If vice and virtue are products like vitriol and sugar, so be it; but Taine's deepest interest lies in understanding the productive forces and not merely the reagents and reaction conditions—race and moment—that some celestial manufacturer can then learn how to vary or to change.

The ferment of England as milieu surmounts the inertia of England as ground and as race. England is not a classicizing civilization that culminates in perfectly poised and harmonious forms. Rather, as in any arena of vitality and flux, everything is in movement. There still are swells and troughs, but no apexes or dead points. The youthful profusion of the Elizabethan stage or the twilight exquisiteness of Pope and Tennyson have a value that might be surpassed but that cannot be replaced (1: 169; 2: 262, 660/2: 6–7; 4: 199–200; 5: 421). No single standard will hold. "The pretention to judge all styles according to a single rule is as outrageous as the intention to reduce all spirits to a single mold and to reconstruct all centuries on a single plan" ("Balzac," *Nouveaux essais* 40). For indeed civilization never rests, neither on the heights nor in the abyss. The time of history knows no events because it needs none; it is always moving forward, without depending on external impulse. There are no fixed points, only transitions.

Thus, it is not the moments of classical perfection that truly enchant Taine, but the moments of passage. And they are ubiquitous—so much so that to call them moments is a misnomer. Impressionistically throughout the *Voyage en Italie* and systematically in the *History of English Literature*, he captures the flux of careers and of eras as devotedly as any critic I know. "In all times and in all countries"—everywhere, always—"what calls forth works of art is a certain complex and mixed state that is encountered in a soul located between two epochs and divided between two orders of feeling; a taste for greatness is being replaced by a taste for the agreeable; but, in passing from one to the other, the soul unites both" (*Italie* 2: 320). The poetry and art that Taine loves above all are those located not at the height of their period, but between times, like the poet Milton: "Placed, as it happened, between two ages, he participates in their two characters, as a stream which, flowing between two different soils, is tinged by their two hues" (1: 556/2: 516). Like the Sistine Chapel, in one of Taine's great set pieces, the masterpiece of a time when "man is . . . in a state of passage and leaving the Middle Ages in order to enter the modern age; or rather the two ages are at their confluence" (*Italie* 1: 215). Like Rubens, in whose characters "the present . . . is impregnated by the past and pregnant with the future" (*Philosophie de l'art* 247—an exceptional moment in this book). Like the valedictory vision of the Simplon pass at the end of the long *Voyage en Italie*: "This is the boundary of two regions, and it seems as if it is the boundary of two worlds; the dazzling summits blend with the whiteness of the clouds, so that one no longer knows where the earth ends and where the heaven begins" (2: 437). Or, indeed, like all moments of greatness: "That is why the fleeting and precious flower is found only at the confluence of two ages, . . . at the moment in which man . . . begins to rest. . . . Sooner, it would have been too early . . . ; a bit later, it would be too late. . . . Between the two is found a unique moment . . . in which men . . . relax their outstretched will to rejoice magnificently their spirit and their senses" (*Italie* 2: 320–21). A moment? Perhaps. But there are no moments, only expanses of flowing time. So let me restore and italicize a crucial phrase omitted from the abridged quotation: "a unique moment, *longer or shorter*, according as the transformation of the soul is more or less prompt." Periods, not moments, of passage are the special times of human achievement.

How unique are these passages? Gradual, steady, quiet change is as much Taine's subject as it is George Eliot's or Trollope's. Time works within his history because there is no moment without change and consequently none that initiates change. Beginnings thrill him, as in the ecstatic pages on Nicholas of Pisa (*Italie* 2: 52–54), but they come as stealthily as the dawn, which is his invariable figure for beginnings (thus, *Italie* 2: 433). And everywhere there is quiet, unperceived change, with no manifest impulse. Taine's skill at marshaling evidence and tracing the currents is such that it is difficult to describe an instance (they don't break down into instances) and unfair to highlight an example (for how can there be an example of a uniform substance, as if a drop of water could be an example of a stream?). Still, here is one among so many, so that there can be no mistaking. "Such were the ornate and polished manners which gradually pierce through debauchery and assume the ascendant. Insensibly the current grows clearer, and marks out its course like a stream, which forcibly entering a new bed, splashes about at first in a tempest of slime, then pushes forward its still muddy waters, which are purified little by little. These debauchees try to be men of the world, and sometimes succeed in it" (1: 606 / 3: 81).

The ideal in history. Images of constant flux, however, problematize human effort. What role do men play in the insensible and irresistible stream of history? The answer of the history of the Revolution is, in effect, none. In the maelstrom of "forces devoid of intelligence" (*La Révolution* 1: 345), "the revolutionary malady"—an "epidemic and contagious" disease (2: 313)—poisons even the rare individuals who surface from the swarm of names. A Marat swims with the deluge, a Danton steers briefly to no real avail, even the great Napoleon finally drowns of his own superabundant motion. Civilization turns out to be mere costume, as the innate bestiality of man comes to the fore: "All the clothing woven for him by the centuries and placed on his shoulders by civilization, the last remnants of human apparel, falls to earth; only the primitive animal remains" (3: 267). Taine's Revolution is a zoo—a Darwinian cosmos where tigers and gorillas, dogs, sheep, locusts, and countless other species follow their instincts to the bitter end. Its lesson, as Taine drew it in writing of the great novelist of the Revolution, is that "Social history is but the prolongation of natural history" ("Balzac," *Nouveaux essais* 40).

When Taine is in this cynical mood, ideas do not seem any more effective than deeds: "A doctrine only becomes active in becoming blind" (*L'Ancien régime* 2: 12). Force and mass determine what can be done or, for the writer, what can be said: "Art varies when the audience varies. . . . No one has the right to impose his pleasure and his nature on another" ("Balzac" 39). Realism thus became a watchword for Taine, as for all the advanced writers of his time. The artist in the modern spirit reproduces reality, and his value lies in extensive variety and intensive precision. He does not actually *do* anything; rather, he serves as the vehicle for the physical world to be itself to the fullest.[22] Fixed in stone, the life of the past survives into the present: "Donatello dares to risk the whole truth, the coarse details that can seem homely [*disgracieux*] to the vulgar, the frank imitation of the real individual with his own traits and the traces of his craft, and we see . . . a fragment of living humanity which, torn alive from his century, by his originality and his energy prolongs his century's life to us" (*Italie* 2: 234). Such an art can capture and preserve life. But how can it be said to live? "If you insist on photography, you become obscure and boring" (*La Fontaine* 256). Photography can be a "useful auxiliary," but "if exact imitation were the supreme goal of art," then the highest achievement would be "a shorthand transcript of trials at the court of assizes" (*Philosophie de l'art* 26). The art that is of its time may capture its time, may reflect it, may preserve it. But no such aesthetic can satisfy a need for art (or human action in general) to make, shape, or lead its time.

At the time Taine was writing, the figure around whom debates concerning the destiny of art coalesced was the great social philosopher (and exponent of realism) Pierre-Joseph Proudhon.[23] Inevitably, any publication entitled *De l'idéal dans l'art* (as was the last part of Taine's philosophy of art) would have been seen as a riposte to Proudhon and to his realist sympathizers. Indeed, in the same year Taine satirized photographic realism as shorthand reporting, a notorious passage in Proudhon's posthumous *Du principe de l'art et de sa destination sociale* instanced a photograph of a side of beef as the first level of art (29–30). But the opposition is not simple, for Proudhon was an idealist in morality and family values, and Taine was a democrat (of sorts) with great admiration for realist art, especially in earlier periods when realism marked a historical advance.[24] One explanation for the enthusiasm of Taine's early auditors and readers may be that he made sense out of the inconsistencies in the aesthetic theories around him; at any rate a summary of Proudhon's shifting aesthetic tenets will illuminate the specificity of Taine's achievement.

Proudhon's career manifests contemporary perplexities about the value of art. He had begun by scorning art in the name of reality: "The golden age of what is called purely literature has passed for ever" (*Correspondance* 1: 182). "The interest of novels disappears before the attractions of reality" (*Carnets* 1: 379). In print such condemnations climaxed in vitriolic attacks on art in the late 1840's, both in the famous *Système des contradictions économiques, ou philosophie de la misère* of 1846 that Karl Marx attacked and in the 1848 essay, "Ce que la Révolution doit à la littérature" (collected in *Idées révolutionnaires*, 1849), which lashes out at artists as sycophants to all those with power. But the Platonic attack on artistic hypocrisy leaves room for a neo-Platonic defense of true artistic insight. Two developments in Proudhon's writing of the 1850's typify the theory of realism in the Second Empire. First, Proudhon increasingly acknowledges that art can have other bases than prettification: "The image of vice, like that of virtue, is as much part of the domain of painting as of poetry" (*Philosophie du progrès* 99). Art is not decorative beauty opposed to the real, but moral beauty within the real, so that it can legitimately aim at reaching and ennobling all the people. "All of us, so long as we live, are artists, and the job of all is to erect in our persons, in our bodies and in our souls, a statue to beauty" (98). Second, Proudhon consequently develops a radical aesthetic populism. Mere utilitarianism "would have photographs, not painters," but "an artistic, flexible, living word belongs only to a free being" (*De la justice dans la Révolution* 3: 583). Art belongs to and liberates everyone equally.

Hence, as Proudhon writes in *Du principe de l'art* not three pages after faintly praising the realist photograph of the side of beef, "Art is nothing except by the ideal, has value only by the ideal; if it is confined to a simple imitation of nature, it would be well advised to bow out" (32). The resounding prophet of real life turns into an equally resounding apostle of transvaluing reality. Proudhon's late book on copyright hymns the "all but sacred" mission of the artist to reform and redeem his society: "He is the eternal prophet of divine things, . . . working . . . toward the exaltation of humanity" (*Les Majorats littéraires* 134). The artist speaks both to and for the people; he is "the interpreter of collective reason, of what is most inward in the life of the people, and of which they do not have a clear and formal awareness. . . . In a word he must be a prophet, he must speak the future, he must enlighten his contemporaries with his inspired utterance" (*De la justice dans la Révolution* 3: 417). Realism has mutated into the belief that art and the artist were powerful enough to transmute even reality, and that they must not be allowed to deflect us with any less vital interests.

The constant throughout these vagaries is the opposition between the real and the ideal. Whether denigrating art for its false glitter or extolling it for its power to transform the prose of the world, Proudhon maintains an unyielding two-valued logic that forces a choice between them. If the artist falls to the aristocrats or the bourgeoisie, he becomes a renegade to humanity. If not, he is a savior. Either way, the artist stands outside the society whose spokesman he should be. His mode remains ecstatic; his mission a conversion of the heathen; his action an elevation beyond the plane of ordinary existence. The future that he proclaims is a utopian eternity of unchanging goodness. Absolute sympathy for purified humanity must somehow join absolute judgment on social degradation. Yet the more fully the poet is clothed in a prophet's garb, the less suitable he seems as a mediator. He cannot both preach from without and work from within. Proudhon's exalted extremism was echoed by a generation, most famously in the well-known lines of Baudelaire:

> Viens-tu du ciel profond ou sors-tu de l'abîme,
> O Beauté! ton regard, infernal et divin,
> Verse confusément le bienfait et le crime.
>
> ("Hymne à la Beauté," 1860)[25]

So resounding an appeal cannot control its effects. That is a dilemma that equally confronted the Parnassian exponents of art for art's sake, the socially conscious realists, and the satanists, all of whom mingle confusingly in the cultural landscape of the period.[26] The haunted realist's godlike artist, as Flaubert envisioned him around the same time, would have no truck with his creation.

After an early flirtation with realist denigration of art, in an unpublished essay "Du style," Taine moved toward a reconciliation of realism with idealism.[27] If, as I have illustrated, he quickly became disillusioned with mimetic realism, he avoided his generation's temptations to veer to the opposite extreme. Rather, his vitalism responds to the quandaries of mid-century aestheticism. Taine's artist works on society, but from within, as a part of the social process. To be sure, he is then never perfect—neither a saint nor a prophet. On the other hand, the means of his influence become comprehensible without resort to religious or mystical enthusiasm. His effect is historical, not transcendental. The role and the possibilities of art gain in nuance: different expressions have valid functions in different societies and ages (different races and milieux), and the strength of the artistic intervention or the degree of its opposition to the social flux likewise varies according to the moment of historical inertia. In his capacity as the mediator of cultural evolution the artist can both speak for his time and advance his cause, without self-contradiction. Proudhon's artist prophesies a future that is all but eschatological; Taine's artist, along with bringing our past near to us, likewise brings the future near to his contemporaries. The representative artist lives, for Taine, between eras because he makes eras happen; the currents of time flow through him and his labor.

Consequently, the artist becomes essential not to the mystical transfiguration of society, but to its very existence. The nadir of the Revolution, grimly highlighted at the end of a long chapter, is the murder of a poet, André Chénier, by illiterate scum.

"The Republic [the judge says to the doomed Lavoisier] needs no scientists." It has equally little need for poets, and the first poet of the era, the delicate and superior artist who reopened the springs of antiquity, who opens modern ones as well, André Chénier, is guillotined; we have in the original the handwritten transcript of his interrogation, a veritable masterpiece of barbarian gibberish; it should be transcribed whole with "its turpitudes of sense and of orthography." Read it, if you want to see a man of genius delivered up to beasts, to coarse, choleric, and despotic beasts, who hear nothing, who comprehend nothing, who do not even understand ordinary words, who stumble over their own malentendus and who, in aping intelligence, wallow in asininity.—The overturn is complete: subject to the revolutionary government, France resembles a human creature who has been forced to walk on her head and to think with her feet. (*La Révolution* 3: 459–60)

No passage in Taine's writing more powerfully communicates his creed that the power of art sustains civilization. If history is the ever-flowing current passing between past and present, art is its channel. The country that murders its poets murders itself.

Striking and characteristic in Taine's narration of Chénier's murder is the association of barbarism, bestiality, and babble. Civilization, intelligence, and linguistic expression are intimately linked; what kills one kills all three. If Proudhon's artist saves humanity through the content of his message, Taine's furthers history through his form. To understand the mediations at the heart of Taine's vision, we must therefore turn to his virtually unrecognized master concept, which is that of style.[28]

IV

The artist in words, to be sure, acts directly only on words; his immediate creation is new writing. But the new writing then mediates new ways of thinking and new social constellations. He achieves a style, and the style achieves the rest. The *Philosophie de l'art* starts with the axiom that "every artist has his style" (12). When the writer is in control of his words, "the style is like a torch . . . passed in succession before each part of a large canvas. . . . By this power, imagination reproduces and replaces sight; the imagination takes the place of the object; the phrase gives presence to the thing that is not there" (*La Fontaine* 289–90). Life-preserving and life-giving, style is the vehicle through which culture enters history. "A geometer has no style" because he needs none, since he seeks the "pure light" of "universal truth" (*La Fontaine* 324). Conversely, historical degeneration correlates with a loss of style: the Revolution descends to Jacobin illiteracy (*La Révolution* 2: 264: "Social condition and degree of culture are often indicated by orthography"), to the darkness of cliché and "rude familiarity" in which "there is but one tone, one style, one language" (117), and downward to the degraded rant of Saint-Just (3: 245: "He laughs no more, he kills, but with what arguments and in what a style!" and on for three pages). To have a style is to participate in the progress of civilization; to have none is to be exempted, excluded, or corrupted.

Where Taine's interest in style is acknowledged at all, it is normally in dismissive terms such as these: "He frequently deals with style, but rarely for its own sake, his purpose usually being to illustrate through it changing modes of thought" (Weinstein, *Hippolyte Taine* 99). Indeed, Taine does repeatedly claim that human expression reflects human history: "With a sincere writer, doctrines foretell the style"; "such and such a subject demands such and such a style" (1: 521, 539 / 2: 450–51, 486). The "spirit" of an age (a very common expression in Taine), the "dominant form of thought," is at the same time "the sway of [its] style," and in return "the possession of this style [by the writers of the age] is . . . universal" (2: 246 / 4: 173–74, specifically about the classical style). Hence, at every level Taine looks for what represents the whole: "Art is the resumé of life"; "everywhere art and spirit meet; for that reason the first expresses the second and the second produces the first" (*Italie* 1: 136, 177). What applies to an age applies to an author: "Let us then look for the man, and in his style. The style explains the work; whilst showing the principal features of the genius, it proclaims the rest" (1: 370 / 2: 184). And what applies to an author applies to every line or word that he writes, at least when he is truly himself: "At every instant, in a word, in a gesture, in an imaginative sally, in an unbuttoned reflection, in a turn of phrase, a reminder and an indication that will show you the whole interior, the whole past, the whole future of a character" (Shakespeare's greatness, as summarized in *Philosophie de l'art* 440). Style does more than transmit the spirit of earlier ages and creators; it brings the past to life.

Even Taine's most routine adoptions of the language of reflection thus entail more than mere copy or illustration of the dominant present: a style that conveys the inside, past, and future of things reflects rather after the manner of a mind than after that of a mirror. Style transcribes what cannot otherwise be seen: "The principal service that literary writings render the historian is to put *extinct sentiments* before his eyes," to wit, "the spring of moral action" and "the soul" of history ("Renaud de Montauban," *Nouveaux essais* 327). And its representations arise from and serve thought: "The difference of [Xenophon's] style and of our own will mark, better than any commentary, the difference of the two civilizations" ("Xénophon," *Essais* 151).[29] Taine's countless discussions and evocations of style invariably presuppose its mission to the perceiver's present and even (as in a "presentment") to the future. "The mode of conception in a man governs the mode of thought. . . . When the mind [*l'esprit*], with rapt attention, penetrates the minute details of a precise image, joy and grief shake the whole man. . . . This impassioned style is extremely potent" (Dickens; 2: 442 / 5: 27–28). Even in his most realist utterances, Taine is capable of being seized by the power of style to govern sensibility.

As there should be no question of Taine's devotion to style, so there can be none of what he means by it. He routinely scrutinizes the characteristic sentence structure of authors, their diction, their versification and paragraphing, their imagery, their plot organization. *Explication de texte* is his métier, supported by wide reading that develops confidence in the representative nature of the passages selected. Here is one instance among countless others, giving a vivid picture even in the case of an author Taine disliked: "[Pope's Eloisa] puts ornaments in every line. . . . Now it is a happy image, filling up a whole phrase; now a series of verses, full of symmetrical contrasts; two ordinary words set in relief by strange conjunction; an imitative rhythm completing the impression of the mind by the emotion of the senses; the most elegant comparisons and the most picturesque epithets; the closest style and the most ornate" (2: 256 / 4: 189).[30] With works of visual art, similarly, Taine brings formal dimensions to the fore: "A painting is a colored surface, in which the various tones and the various degrees of light are distributed with a certain choice; there is its intimate being" (*Philosophie de l'art* 453). For these are the aspects through which artistic works communicate the spirit of their age. Typically, Taine will move from style to characters, as in the once-famous chapters on Shakespeare and Dickens. But characters themselves have for Taine a function that is more ideological than psychological, like Milton's Adam and Eve, "an English household, two reasoners of the period," who make of the epic "a political poem" (1: 541, 543 / 2: 489, 494). Indeed, "every literature," as Taine writes in summing up Thackeray's characters, "is a definition of man" (2: 509 / 5: 141). Viewed in this way, character is the apex of style, where spirit of the age and language of the text are fused.

The last chapter of the *Philosophie de l'art* relates the "force" or "expressive power" (436, 454) of a work to the cooperation of all the levels of artistic expression, in what Taine terms "the convergence of effects." Such formulations reveal the affinities between Taine and twentieth-century structuralism.[31] While he registers disparities and interferences, his primary interest lies in the higher-order regularities of a work, an author, and a period. Yet clearly he does not accord the same primacy to the synchronic as Ferdinand de Saussure or Claude Lévi-Strauss. It is not the static uniformity of unconscious conception that is envisaged, as Lévi-Strauss does in his call "to eliminate . . . historical process and . . . conscious thought" ("History and Anthropology" 23). Rather, as with the living waters of England, there is a mutual, circulating influence in which style and conception continuously regulate and shape one another. At one moment the expression will appear to be merely the surface manifestation; the true "insides" (*dessous*, italicized by Taine) consist of "the bodily temperament, the original or acquired aptitudes and tendencies, the complicated vegetation of distant or recent ideas and habits, the whole sap of human nature [which] has contributed to produce the actions and words that are its ultimate offshoot [*jet terminal*]" (*Philosophie de l'art* 441). But then Taine will reverse the valuation, making primary what seemed derivative: "There remains a last element, style. In truth, it is the only visible one; the two others [characters; situations and events] are merely its *insides*; it clothes them and is alone found on the surface.—A book is nothing but a succession of sentences that the author pronounces or has his personages pronounce. . . . This, then, is a third element of higher importance" (443–44). Here, where the imagery changes from botany to culture and where determinist natural history thus appears to yield to the vitalist history of civilization—here, where "art is higher than nature"—"each form of style determines a state of mind" (444–45). Style takes over as a force not merely expressing but guiding the inside of man in his historical expression.

Everywhere in Taine there is this dynamic of style. In bringing forth or advancing thoughts and intuitions, expression also moves them forward. By expressing, it creates possibilities for expression. It is style that performs the work of culture. The history of civilization is a history of art which is in turn a history of style for the very reason that, simply put, *style is history*. All the rest is mere events. And it is abundantly clear, from the historical passages in the *History of English Literature*—above all concerning medieval *Völkerwanderungen*—and certainly from the history of the Revolution, that events can only consolidate and affirm the ahistorical constancies of the race. To say that race and style are the two poles of human experience—the former negative, passive, determinist, the latter positive, active, and creative—is to reach the heart of Taine's vision.

Taine's first published book was a study of a historian, the *Essai sur Tite Live*. It is divided into two parts of equal length, first "History Considered as a Science," then "History Considered as an Art." One chapter of the second part concerns Livy's style in particular. But it is the culmination of its first chapter, "Of the Art in History," that forms Taine's earliest great statement of faith. "For," he writes at the climax, "in what does style consist, if not in the author's share in the narration, in the emotions that it arouses in him, in the passionate accents, the varied tones, the agitations of the soul manifested in the choice of words and expressions, the sound and the symmetry of the sentences?" The science of history, according to this book, begins with criticism of the sources and aims at reconstructing the past in its authentic pastness. But the art of history brings that pastness alive. Style gives form, order, and consequently meaning to science's raw assemblages of fact. Style is intelligence, "because the art of writing is only the art of thinking, and, in order to speak well, one need only have thought much" (193).

The *Essai sur Tite Live* is about a historian but is not really a work of history. It is still too caught up in a Spinozist exhilaration at perfect, rational orders. The ambition to capture the Academy's prize by sheer force of intellect—an ambition equivocally depicted in chapter 7 of *Etienne Mayran*, "The Test"—seduces Taine into a desire to explain and also to judge everything as the operation of unchanging laws of the intellect. In subsequent books the work of style and thought becomes more differentiated, more subtle, and thus more powerful as well. It transforms whatever it expresses. Hence the greatest creators do not just happen to fall between epochs; it is their works that make the epochal changes constituting history. Earlier I quoted the opening of the last paragraph of Taine's Milton chapter: "Placed, as it happened [*par le hasard*], between two ages . . ." But there is more than happenstance to make Milton the significant figure of the transition. He worked to fuse the two ages: "He employed the one in the service of the other, and displayed the old inspiration in the service of new subjects." And that work, as Taine describes it, seems at once severely truthful and prophetic: "This style and these ideas are monuments of history: they concentrate, recall, or anticipate the past and the future; and in the limits of a single work are found the events and the feelings of several centuries and of a whole nation" (1: 556/2: 516–17). Milton makes it possible to conceive the future, to imagine the movement of the past into the future, and thus he opens the way for the future to happen.

I have glossed the Milton passage somewhat freely. It is a striking expression of the imaginative presence of history in literature, but perhaps not so unambiguous a celebration of the historical power of literature as I have made out. However, as one of a series, its intent seems to me beyond question. In the aggregate, it is clear that style does not simply represent or participate in the progress of civilization, but in fact makes that change happen. Chaucer's artistry is another instance, at an earlier stage. He was the first writer in England to develop a self-conscious awareness of his place in history. At his best—and his inconsistency is part of Taine's story—his skill at disposing events and reflecting on them prepares the ground for the human mastery over events that constituted the Renaissance. His writing gives men power—not yet confident, controlled power, but at least the image of where that power might lie. Thus, it starts freeing men from the shackles of scholasticism. In the case of a newcomer such as Chaucer the achievement is less certain than was Milton's; more certain, on the other hand, is that his texts were responsible for what achievement there was. Here are some distinctive fragments from the center of the remarkable chapter, representing at least the generalizations, shorn of most of the fabric of observation that supports them:

Such is the reflection which begins to dawn, such the high art. . . . The poem is no longer, as in contemporary literature, a mere procession, but a painting in which the contrasts are arranged, the attitudes chosen, the *ensemble* calculated, so that life is invigorated. . . . Weigh the value of this *ensemble*. Is it a dream or not, in its maturity or infancy? The whole future is before us. . . . Here for the first time appears a superiority of mind, which at the instant of conception suddenly halts, rises above itself, passes judgment, and says to itself, "This phrase tells the same thing as the last—remove it; these two ideas are disjointed—bind them together; this description is feeble—reconsider it." When a man can speak thus he has an idea, not learned in the schools, but personal and practical, of the human mind, its process and needs, and of things also, their composition and combinations; he has a style, that is, he is capable of making everything understood and seen by the human mind. . . . He is capable, as Chaucer was, of seeking out in the old common forest of the middle ages, stories and legends, to replant them in his own soil, and make them send out new shoots. . . . At the distance of a century and a half, he has affinity with the poets of Elizabeth. . . . Affinity merely. He advanced a few steps beyond the threshold of this art, but he paused at the end of the vestibule. (1: 154–56 / 1: 214–17)

The Chaucer passage is revealing in another way: style is the form or garb of thought. The *Essai sur Tite Live* makes style sound secondary to thought, as initially does the last chapter of the *Philosophie de l'art*. But the reversal in that chapter reflects a crucial development in Taine's conception, where style becomes formative rather than formed. Thought follows the course laid out by the style or form of expression. But if it is through a style that thought becomes possible, then the style itself cannot be the product of thought, at least not in any ordinary sense. Rather, style is the threshold or dawn of thought. Primitive shapelessness is thoughtless; with style, consciousness appears, as it did in Chaucer. Hence style is the birth of consciousness, the becoming-conscious of consciousness; or, more simply put, style is equivalent to self-consciousness. One knows oneself in the manner of one's thought. Style itself is then a borderline or transition, from nature to civilization and from stupor to awareness. The border (or "end of the vestibule," as the Chaucer passage calls it) is a shadowy realm, half-awake but not yet fully conscious. As such, it is naturally the realm of art, where the inspired artist, always a historical threshold figure, sees and does more than he knows.

A new style advances civilization—gropingly at first, until successor figures explore and refine its accomplishments. Eras thus have their stages or moments: the inconspicuous yet increasingly confident young dawn of new conceptions, the striding maturity, the ornate and subtle twilight, each with its own characteristic unfolding and pace. Historical development is semi-conscious; true progress is never imposed. It creeps over the age and even over the artist who is first responsible, never sudden, always gradual. It can happen over a span of nearly anonymous creations, as it did at the birth of the Renaissance: "Insensibly the growth becomes complete, and at the end of the century all was changed. A new, strange, overloaded style has formed . . . , so suitable to the spirit of the age, that we meet with it throughout Europe" (1: 193/ 1: 277–78). It can also happen in specific, individual models, like Dryden's few poetic masterpieces. Here, surrounding a splendidly detailed synopsis and evocation of the characteristics of Dryden's style and imagery, are the generalizations that again reveal Taine's fundamental conception: "In these three poems . . . a new career is opened; man has the whole world resubjected to his thought; the change in his thought has changed all the aspects, and everything assumes a new form in his transformed mind. His task is to explain and to prove; this, in short, is the classical style, and this is the style of Dryden" (2: 47–48 / 3: 236–38). And it can even arrive in single flashes of intuition, as with Robert Burns: "Now and then, driving his plough, he lighted on genuine verses, verses such as Heine and Alfred de Musset have made in our own days. In those few words, combined after a new fashion, there was a revolution. Two hundred new verses sufficed. The human mind turned on its hinges, and so did civil society" (2: 282/4: 231).[32]

In portraying the accomplishments of style Taine does not even shy away from the dangerous word *revolution*; indeed, he features it repeatedly. For the curative to the kind of style-destroying revolution that occurred tragically in France is not stagnation and regression—which occur at the ends of eras and actually precipitate revolutions—but the reformed thinking that a successful new style brings with it. Not all styles succeed, to be sure. The style of the *philosophes*, notably, was so full of "multiple precautions," so "insensible" in its transitions, leading its readers to advance so "involuntarily," that it missed out on the true course. Its "excess indicates a lacuna"; "the obligation always to speak well interfered with saying everything needful"; the "personages are only half real." "There is then an original defect in the classical spirit," which might not be so bad, "if we did not know that all this ends in practical and terrible effects." For "when the Revolution comes, the retrenchment will be all the greater" (*L'Ancien régime* 1: 302–15). Revolution is the punishment for stylistic failure, for a refusal to advance or an advance so hedged in that it amounts to a blind refusal.

That, however, is France. Except during the Interregnum, England successfully negotiated its transitions, with reformations in thought that permitted it to cope conceptually and practically with changes in society.[33] Revolution in England characteristically takes place in the mind, not the body, and is progressive rather than destructive. A dozen or more noble passages in the *History of English Literature* extol this greatest historical accomplishment of English civilization. At the end of the Mill chapter there is, for instance, a lengthy vision of a rich autumn landscape whose organic growth reconciles steadfastness and innovation. Taine sees

enormous trees, four centuries old, extended in regular lines; and I found in them a new trace of that practical good sense which has accomplished revolutions without committing ravages; which, while improving everything, has overthrown nothing; which has preserved both its trees and its constitution, which has lopped off the dead branches without levelling the trunk; which alone, in our days, among all nations, is in the enjoyment not only of the present, but of the past. (2: 658 / 5: 418)

Steering between the poles of Experience and Abstraction (Taine's names in this chapter for empiricism and dogmatism), England has avoided their respective blindnesses to the future and to the past. Revolution becomes a common stylistic project, intuited, felt, conceived, shaped, and implemented first by the artists and through them by society as a whole.

English revolutions are the achievement, collective or individual, of speakers and writers; they are promulgated in public forums like the pulpit, diffused through shared practices like the art of conversation in the public culture promoted by Addison (an argument that did not have to wait on Jürgen Habermas to be made), or disseminated in the publications of the great and popular poets. The best revolutions come "slowly, by degrees," like the "moral revolution" after 1688 (2: 58 / 3: 255, the start of the chapter called "The Revolution"). Or even "by a side door," like the Reformation, "for great revolutions are not introduced by court intrigues and official sleight of hand, but by social conditions and popular instincts" (1: 483 / 2: 301). "A revolution," Taine writes at yet another moment, "is but the birth of a great sentiment" (2: 599 / 5: 313). That one, deep-seated change changes all.[34]

Because style is a cultural system and a structure of expression, style change appears in the guise of structural transformation. Alert to systematic interrelationships, Taine is partial to the image of a pivot on which the whole mechanism of society turns: "The central pivot of the vast wheel on which human affairs move must be displaced one notch, that all may move with its motion. At this moment the pivot was moved, and thus a revolution of the great wheel begins" (1: 265 / 1: 402; for another instance see the passage about Burns, four paragraphs back). Such imagery bears an important relationship to Saussure's famous comparison of language to a game of chess: "A certain move can revolutionize the whole game and even affect pieces that are not directly involved" (*Course* 89). But the differences from twentieth-century structuralism are as significant as the similarities. Change, as Saussure describes, is deeply meaningless—abrupt, disruptive, entirely external, and even antithetical to the systems through which meaning is constituted and expressed: "The change effected belongs to neither state: only states matter." Consequently, change has no past ("the route used in arriving there makes no difference") and at best a very uncertain future ("it is impossible for the player to foresee exactly the extent of the effect"). As his editors comment, change "is outside the system, for the system is never observed in its evolution" (*Course* 143, note). The motor may even be simply error (Burger, "Phonématique et diachronie" 230). Saussurian structuralism, as Piaget finely observed, deprives structure of value in depriving it of history (*Structuralism* 79–80). Taine's machine produces value—designated moral or scientific "truth"—as his trees produce limbs and fruit; Saussure's chess game produces nothing.

At the cost of some reiteration, I want to dwell for a few paragraphs on the mechanisms of history. I do so partly to create the opportunity for quoting further representative passages (though by no means all such), in the hope of persuading readers how consistent and unmistakably present are the themes I have been discussing. But I do it chiefly in order to build up the case that Taine's two-sidedness is not merely accidental. Hitherto I have written of ways in which Taine appears divided between falsity and truth—an apparent determinist who in reality is a vitalist. I now wish to show that his view makes contradiction fundamental to human experience and expression. Smooth change and quiet revolutions, yes, but not for all that without contrast and opposition.

True, history is not the product of individual volition. Not even Napoleon, though Taine calls him a towering political artist and a sculptor of living flesh, could alter civilization by design. In the period when France was suffering its cataclysm, the English romantic school "had violently broken with tradition"; its Jacobin-leaning poets "labored to destroy the great aristocratical and oratorical style" and "proposed to replace studied phrases and lofty vocabulary by natural tones and plebeian words" (2: 314–15/4: 286–87). The works of these writers do not much please Taine; he disapproves of the literalist exoticism of the historical poetry, of Scott's pedantry and his "pasty and emphatic style" (2: 325/4: 304), and of the hectoring philosophic verse.[35] Nevertheless, England works its magic even at this most dangerous passage: "Under their multiplied efforts, and by their involuntary concert, the idea of the beautiful is changed, and other ideas change by contagion. . . . The old edifice totters, and the Revolution enters, not by a sudden inundation, as in France, but by slow infiltration" (2: 341–42/4: 330–31). For 50 years, Taine concludes, all great writers have been "bent, some with more of eagerness, others with more of distrust, in welcoming or giving entrance to the growing tide of modern democracy and philosophy in constitution and church, without doing damage, and gradually so as to destroy nothing, and to make everything bear fruit" (2: 343/4: 333). The long revolution is the genuine one.

Still, history is neither willful nor random. It may be that "the circumstances that are encountered finish the natural revolution" (1: 600/ 3: 70), but they do not propel it. "Great and efficacious [ideas] do not come at will and by chance, by the effort of an individual, or by an accidental encounter" (1: 264/1: 401). And when it comes to the destiny of the great races, "chance has no influence over events so vast" (2: 398/ 4: 429). Even though prediction is impossible, the retrospective teleology whose law Mill formulated guarantees the meaningfulness of organic historical development.

Following Mill, Taine succeeds in having everything about history both ways. It both is and is not purposive; it both is and is not shaped by individual creativity; its transformations both are and are not radical or revolutionary; its constancies both are and are not fated. Yet whatever the impression such a summary gives, it is hard to imagine a book more masterfully controlled and less confused than Taine's, or more consistent in its unfolding and in its methods. The contradictions are fundamental to the system. For the spirit of the book is deeply if unostentatiously dialectical. That above all is missed by the vulgar view of Taine as a narrowly Darwinian dogmatist. In its systematic and explanatory character it resembles a hierarchical, Kantian dialectic, divided between the flux of empirical facts and the constant, regulatory, transcendental, or phantasmic truths of race (pseudo-material causality) and morality (pseudo-ideal purpose). The process and the hermeneutic texture, however, are more Hegelian.

Taine's history spirals ever onward, with a constant interchange of powers and directions, none of which remains for long the ground of the others; "After all, man is ever his own master and his own slave" (2: 398 / 4: 429). The original last page of the book expresses a faith in the stability of nations, but even there the faith is hedged around by the onward march of history. The English race suffered "a violent perturbation" with the Norman Conquest and subsequently "various oscillations," but we are on a more even keel "now that great historic violences . . . have become almost impracticable." (As if that proclamation of the end of history were not belied by the French Revolution and by the impending upheavals of 1870 that were to impel Taine to study the Revolution; as if the general unpredictability of the future were not one of Taine's themes.) But the book then ends on a note of fundamental change, not of stability: "We know that positive discoveries go on increasing day by day, that they will increase daily more and more, that from object to object they reach the most lofty, that their useful application and their philosophical consequences are ceaselessly unfolded; in short, that their universal encroachment will at last comprise the whole human mind." There is, it seems, a perspective even beyond race or nationality, an absolute knowledge from whose vantage any human structures appear merely historical. But that perspective is given to us only as the eternal power of the negative to resist all premature fixities, which is to say, all fixities whatsoever:

From this body of invading truths springs in addition an original conception of the good and the useful, and, moreover, a new idea of state and church, art and industry, philosophy and religion. This has its power, as the old idea had; it is scientific, if the other was national; it is supported on proved facts, if the other was upon established things. Already their opposition is being manifested; already their results begin; and we may affirm beforehand, that the proximate condition of English civilization will depend upon their divergence and their accord. (2: 425–26 / 4: 473–75)

The contradictions upon which Taine's history rests are the work of the never-ending dialectic of history. Opposition, divergence, and accord are the last words that Taine originally bequeathed to the readers of his history.[36]

From the pervasive dialectic arises the strangest and most wonderful characteristic of artistic style. Gradualist, half-conscious, diffusive, the last thing that the artist can be is imperious. The man with a new vision is not a monomaniac (like Napoleon) who imposes his will upon others. Nor, more surprisingly given his intellectual pedigree, does Taine ever portray the artist in the guise of a Kantian genius who spontaneously gives laws to nature. For laws are not where Taine's interest lies; it lies in change. In touch with the most profound nineteenth-century conception of organic life, Taine regards organisms not as beings that can reproduce themselves but as beings that can differ from themselves. They do not settle into a rock-solid unity such as "agreement" might betoken, but rather into the harmonious concord or working together of different functions. And if they are to live, they must produce further differences, which are their most genuine offspring.

No creator could consciously fashion a genuine style. For conscious fashioning proceeds according to a ruling idea. It aims at uniformity. But styles are not ideas, and they are productive of antitheses, not of agreements. This is a theme that Foucault has formulated pregnantly for our time: "Contradiction . . . functions throughout discourse, as the principle of its historicity" (*The Archaeology of Knowledge* 151). But Taine formulated it a century earlier: "When a form of mind comes to light, it . . . enters simultaneously the two opposite camps, and seems to undo with one hand what it has made with the other. If it is, as it was formerly, the oratorical style, we find it at the same time in the service of cynical misanthropy, and in that of decorous humanity, in Swift and in Addison. If it is, as now, the philosophical spirit, it produces at once conservative preachings and socialistic utopias, Wordsworth and Shelley" (2: 337 / 4: 322). The greatest genius of all time, Shakespeare, is ipso facto the most fertile in contradictions; that is how Taine introduces him and how he regularly praises Shakespeare's unequaled capability as a dramatist. But self-contradiction is likewise characteristic of Milton, who "refused to be a priest from the same feelings that he had wished it" (1: 502 / 2: 417); of Puritanism, which, by unleashing the forces of the Restoration, "brought on an orgie" (1: 559 / 3: 5); of the "two currents" of "modern man, impelled by two sentiments, one democratic, the other philosophic, . . . at once generous and rebellious" (2: 289 / 4: 242). The deepest reason why the great artists are always found between two ages is not just that their work initiates changes, but that all true change proceeds by way of contrast and contradiction. The most authentic creators are not the most unified but the most divided.

Divided, but not at war. That is the meaning of the term "accord," which is so much richer than mere agreement. The richest art of all, for Taine, is the art of accord. And that art, which he himself practiced for enjoyment throughout his life, is music. Perhaps there was in Taine something of the music teacher of chapter 5 of *Etienne Mayran*, capable of conceptualizing technique and of training fluent players, but frustratedly incapable of communicating the spirit that he feels so intensely. At any rate, on the few occasions when Taine speaks of music, he does so with a rare intensity. In one place only there is an extended, uniquely rapturous description of a Beethoven soirée (*Notes sur Paris* 322–33).[37] And a long climactic paragraph in the lectures "Of the Nature of the Work of Art" concerns music as the quintessential art of the nineteenth century. Devoid of representational features, music is free to be pure style. It is, in consequence, the ultimate in contradiction, for, "on the one hand," it is a cry from the heart, "the direct, natural, and complete expression of passion" that "instantaneously arouses our involuntary sympathy," while, "on the other hand," it is a pure formalism of "relations of sounds imitating no living form" (*Philosophie de l'art* 77).

Pure formalism—that is another scapegoat of much of the most recent aesthetic and critical thinking. But, like style, formalism does not mean to Taine what it means to its present-day detractors. It is exempt neither from significance nor from history. Rather, its formalism, its stylistic purity, frees music into—not from—the historical expression of everything that is of deepest concern to humanity.[38] Resembling "the dreams of an incorporeal soul, [music] is more fitting than any other art to express the floating thoughts, the formless dreams, the desires without an object or a limit, the painful and grandiose confusion of a troubled heart that aspires to everything and attaches itself to nothing." Intimate, yes, but why do I say historical? Because Taine concludes the peroration by invoking the public destiny of music's private dreams: "That is why, with the agitations, the discontents and the hopes of modern democracy, it has come forth from its native lands to spread all across Europe; and today you see the most complicated symphonies attract crowds, in this France where our national music was hitherto limited to the vaudeville and the chanson" (*Philosophie de l'art* 77). In music, style fulfills its mission to shape, indeed to *be* the historical destiny of civilization, private and public, with all its essential contradictions. The dialectic distills not into a static essence, but into a living spirit. The impure examples of style at work—soiled, as it were, by words or pictures—are more approachable for being more local and limited. Shakespeare is the grandest and the hardest, a man of pure imagination, "shocking to all French habits of analysis and of logic," "one of those delicate souls which, like a perfect instrument of music, vibrate of themselves at the slightest touch" (1: 357, 365 / 2: 164, 177). Yet beyond even Shakespeare lies the magical accord of music, harmonies compounded of differences, which in their unspeakable purity engage all the antithetical forces of human existence.

Style incorporates the contradictory factors that constitute the historical dialectic: it is personal and social, mental and embodied, expressive and formal, revolutionary and incremental. While an isolated action or utterance is attached to a moment without temporal depth, a work of art draws on the resources of the past and advances the interests of the future. Music, as the most rarified and stylized form of expression, is at once the most powerful and the most impalpable. All others are necessarily imperfect in comparison. Consequently, they appear at least partly willful, unpredictable, or random—though retrospective, explanatory abstraction succeeds in putting everything in its place and generating the appearance of determinism. These paradoxes of artistic achievement are essential to the destiny of race (or nation) that remains constant to the character it is always in the process of discovering. The national character is not "the caprice of an artist or the chance of the moment." A series of chances steers it: "The chance of a victorious invasion," "the chance of an insular position," "the chance of an old hostility to Rome," and the like combine to form "dispositions" that in turn are corrected when a writer (Dickens in this case) "moves his reader in the most inner depths, and becomes the master of all hearts" (2: 464–65 / 5: 65–66). Style is, in its fundamental character, a happily mixed blessing.

V

It remains now to position Taine's dynamic of style with respect to other conceptions. Before the eighteenth century style was the point of inter-section of the aesthetic and the ethical. Adjusting the form of speech to the form of thought led to a fit for which the name was decorum. The choice of a style or form—high, middle, or low, Ciceronian or Senecan, and so forth—was also a choice of personal stance. Style was the individual's manner of engagement with the world.[39] Style in this older sense is descriptive, not normative. Everything has a style of one sort or another. While the value (but more often the decorum or suitability) of a particular stylistic choice could be debated, it would not be meaningful to ask whether style as such has a value. Only at the very end of the eighteenth century did the normative terms "stylish" and "styleless" enter the language, and apparently the normative uses of the noun as well.[40]

In Buffon's famous dictum that style is "l'homme même," style acquires a new status. The qualities of style evoked in Buffon's inaugural discourse for the Académie Française are numerous, but all relate to its character as a transcendental absolute. Higher than mere facility of speech, style is a mysterious, distilled, almost transcendental quality. "It is nothing but order and movement" (*Oeuvres* 500b): though the categories of *taxis* and *dynamis* could come straight out of the Renaissance, the limiting "nothing but" frees style from its earthly entanglements. Its material is ideas, not words or imitation of things; its atmosphere is "luminous" (502a) but not dazzling; its ethos is "good faith with oneself" (503a). Thus, it demands unity (the chief characteristic distinguishing men from animals, as Buffon says in "Le Lion" 378a and elsewhere) but remains indefinable; it can be taught only by example, not by precept. Buffon's examples are the great men of history, much of philosophy, poetry always. The oration concludes with praise of the king (as the source of illumination), of the Immortals in the Académie, of France, and, obligatorily, of Buffon's deceased predecessor. While itemizing many characteristics of style and numerous goals such as truth, wholeness, Being, and eternity, Buffon isolates it from all questions of substance or morality. In its unifying and ennobling force, style is constitutive of true humanity—"man himself, . . . the truth that is enduring and even eternal" (503b), to continue the normally truncated passage. But style then becomes a concept so nebulous that it vanishes into the Empyrean.

The next two centuries have insistently taken apart what Buffon so eloquently put together.[41] From his universal absolute, different thinkers absolutize various particulars. In Goethe's distinction of style from simple imitation and from mannerism (in the essay "Simple Imitation, Manner, Style"), and likewise in Nietzsche's equation of style with culture in contrast to bourgeois philistinism (*Bildungsphilistertum*, in the first of the *Untimely Meditations*), style becomes a high ideal, accessible only to the chosen few. In the nineteenth century style is equated with beauty (both Louis Juglar, *Le Style dans les arts* 89–94, and Gilles-Gaston Granger, *Essai d'une philosophie du style* 208, attribute this notion to the architect Eugène-Emmanuel Viollet-le-Duc); among symbolists and imagists such as Remy de Gourmont and J. Middleton Murry, style is exalted as contentless purity of vision. For Proust, too, "style for the writer . . . is a question not of technique but of vision. It is the revelation, which would be impossible by direct and conscious means, of the qualitative difference that there is in the manner whereby the world appears to us, a difference which, were it not for art, would remain the eternal secret of each of us. Through art alone can we go outside ourselves, know what another sees of this universe which is not the same as our own" (*A la recherche* 3: 895). Others personalize style in less exalted ways by treating it as linguistic usage (as, say, in William Wimsatt's *Prose Style of Samuel Johnson*), as ornament, or as individual quirk (as in Wolfgang Kayser, "Der Stilbegriff"). Thinkers resistant to cults of personality, on the other hand, have often condemned style as irresponsibility (Roland Barthes being a notable recent example) or exalted bad style for its rugged honesty.[42] Wanting to have it both ways, finally, Walter Pater subordinates style in the course of trying to exalt it. He links style to soul, but he is opposed to ornament, in favor of austere truth, and given to images of hardness: thus, he speaks of Flaubert's "phrase so large and so precise at the same time, hard as bronze, in service to the more perfect adaptation of words to their matter" ("Style" 33). His criticism of "surplusage" is consonant with Herbert Spencer's contemporaneous advocacy of economy, as style becomes an instrumental value in the service of ethical absolutes. For none of these thinkers is style, as it is for Taine, both representative and ideal, imaginative and historical.[43]

Inevitably, changes in taste, the growth of specialized knowledge, and the emergence of new objects and forms of attention all will lead today's readers to critical judgments different from Taine's.[44] Yet the kind of analysis and synthesis he practiced retains a value that is more than merely historical. In my concluding pages I wish to argue that a study of Taine's methods can suggest a way out of certain impasses of contemporary criticism. Indeed, in some ways Taine's contemporary relevance may be greater than his historical importance. For it is a curious fact that his admirers and his detractors alike grievously misrepresented Taine, to the point of ignoring what is expressly pivotal in his writing. They may perhaps be excused by the impression created by Taine's last, longest, and for them most recent work, the history of the Revolution. But it seems clear that his great achievement remains unassimilated. In studies of style he represents a road not only distinctive, as I have just suggested, but never again taken with his kind of commitment.[45]

What is called New Historicism has compelled reconsideration of the historical dynamic of literature. New Historicists diverge radically, of course, in their conceptions of textual individuality and textual agency. But there is general consensus that powerful currents flow into and through representative texts (and text-like artifacts and practices) and that these texts in turn powerfully further social and historical processes. After decades of avoidance, Taine's triad of race, milieu, and moment is rarely far from the surface of New Historicist writing. (Race is often replaced by nation; perhaps even more often the two are played off against one another.) Yet for all the power exerted—or exuded—by society and by social texts in these critics' descriptions, the dynamic falls short of a dialectic. In the fascination with the power of texts to shape and to express, their power to effect change is slighted. Because it replaces a one-sided progressivism with an even less fortunate, self-regarding teleology, the recent critical fashion of renaming the Renaissance as the early modern period signals the deficient historicism in much of what currently passes for materialist enquiry.[46] The limitations are encapsulated in one of Stephen Greenblatt's epigrams (highlighted by citation out of its deceptively cushioning context): "If I wanted to hear the voice of the other, I had to hear my own voice" (*Shakespearian Negotiations* 20). It will be my closing contention that New Historicists, above all, can profit much from hearing the voice of Taine.

Greenblatt's work is the best case in point, not so much on account of its originating influence as because of his self-aware fascination with individual authors. A professed dialectician, Greenblatt if anyone should be alert to interchanges between individual and social expressions. Indeed, the title of his programmatic essay (and subtitle of the book), "The Circulation of Social Energy" (*Shakespearian Negotiations* 1–20), suggests the same sort of fluid vitalism that Taine so fully develops. But Greenblatt's circulation is economic, not hydraulic, and it produces neither fruit nor (as in Marx) capital, but only "simulations" (1). Negotiation is linked with exchange, contest, conflict. It is, however, "absolute play" (a phrase used in titling the Marlow chapter in *Renaissance Self-Fashioning*), marked by repeated denials of movement: "there is no escape from contingency"; "there is no originary moment, no pure act of untrammeled creation"; "there is very little pure invention in culture," but only many "modes [that] are continually renegotiated," in "a sustained collective improvisation" (*Shakespearian Negotiations* 3, 6, 13, 8, 14). The demand for absolutes or "pure" states sets a standard for historical outcomes as definitive ends, without which no result is acknowledged: either there is victory or there is running in place. The alternatives are power and subversion, the circulation is only the mutual reinforcement of the two poles ("the subversiveness is the very product of that power and furthers its ends," 30), and self-fashioning becomes inseparable from submission (*Renaissance Self-Fashioning* 9). Such rigid categories undermine any possible self-transforming process. Dialectic turns out to be equivalent to *aporia*.[47]

Hence, I do not think it is merely coincidental that the word "style" is all but absent from Greenblatt's writing.[48] For style names the individual's differential engagement with cultural norms, or else the individual's self-transformation into a real or potential norm. Even in its simplest designations, style is an impure invention or a mongrel act of trammeled creativity—exactly the sort of complex, partial cultural action that Greenblatt's polarizations devalue. In what may be his most forthright theoretical pronouncement on the activity of the literary critic, Greenblatt has advocated a "daylight method of interpretation" ("Loudun and London" 343) that could bring to light the cultural negotiations producing the aesthetic and social construct known as the theater. If the light imagery is reminiscent of Auerbach (see note 45), so is the problematic sense of historical action. The negotiation, in this image, is all backstage. What enters the public sphere has already lost its potential and been abandoned to a role as mere product or reflector. And the interpreter, as light-bringer, remains comparably passive. If only all could be revealed. If only things could speak for themselves, without style or other such entanglements that sully their pure visibility. Greenblatt's power as a critic resides in his resourceful and relentless demonstration of the impossibility of his aims. From Taine one can learn how the shadows are not a pathology but the very process of living.[49]

When more or less closely related studies do acknowledge style, the results are not much happier. Jonathan Goldberg's *James I and the Politics of Literature*, for instance, includes a section titled "The Style of Gods" (28–54). The source for the phrase is a line by James in which style means label or title: "God gives not Kings the stile of *Gods* in vain" (26). During his discussion, Goldberg corrodes the phrase so that "style" bends toward its more common meaning, as when he calls "textual transformations into enduring Roman images," "the style of gods and of royal representation" (42). But the powerless inertness of the earlier sense hovers over the text: "The coins and medals preserve, commemorate, and memorialize the style of power and translate it into the vital economy of real life" (46). "Style here . . . is content" (47). Expression intrinsically corrupts, governed by "the sustaining contradictions by which power is represented" (5). Cultural products have an overwhelming past, an earnest present, and no future. A richer valuation of the expressive dynamic of style, inspired by Taine, could model a different lesson— that the "infinite regress" (affecting "absolute power," "real power," and "represented power" alike [12]) is not a defect to be contrasted to the real and the vital, but rather the imperfection making thought and expression human.

One of the most acute critiques of New Historicism, mounted as it were from within, is found in Richard Halpern's *The Poetics of Primitive Accumulation*. Objecting that "the new historicism dissolves [questions of epochal transition] into empiricisms or pragmatisms" (13), Halpern endeavors to recapture from Marx a historical dynamic hollowed out by Foucault and his followers. His primitive accumulation is the materialist counterpart to Taine's idealist emergence or dawning. But even Halpern, I believe, succumbs to the lure of categories too pure and demanding for instantiation. It is not just that his chapter on education, "A Mint of Phrases: Ideology and Style Production in Tudor England" (19–60), regards styles as conformations instilled by pedagogical technologies.

Nor is it even that he remains mystified by the genuinely profound problem he unearths—namely, how such an educational system could have fostered poets. It is, rather, that he acknowledges no mediation between (nor any alternates to) subjection and lawlessness. In the language of Gilles Deleuze and Félix Guattari he writes: "Style was the sign that textual decoding had ultimately been unified and reterritorialized and could now be inserted into a system of regular differences. . . . It is clear the role of style is to reunify and homogenize the text, to recode its imaginative anarchy while guarding against sudden power surges of *energeia*" (56). In irreconcilable contrast to the uniformity of style is poetic imagination, which "implied a desire whose workings were more fully opaque and unpredictable, more resistant to attempts at rational or instrumental control . . . , an outlaw factor [whose] autonomy and automatism . . . resisted instrumental control and thus threw a shadow on humanist optimism" (56–57). Halpern's imagery in these sentences intones a curious logic: they presume that a system of regular differences is likewise a homogenization, that resistance to control is outlawry, and that shadows are opaque. The later chapters on individual writers and works do not liberate expression from this bind. Signally, the concluding analysis of *King Lear*—named *"Historica Passio"* from a phrase (presumed to be a typo) that equates history with hysteria—leaves society "reconstitute[d] through destruction" (269). The conflictual logic operates throughout, on a deconstructive ground resembling that of Greenblatt and the others whom Halpern means to be revising. The interesting analysis of penmanship as both a discipline and a skill can serve as a last example: "The ideological force of writing is the specific pressure that its virtual regimes can exert . . . either to reinforce or to oppose the reproduction of the social order." No middle ground between reproduction and destruction is envisioned, even in such a case as this, where "the pressure is neither especially great nor particularly focused" (84). No wonder primitive accumulation turns out to be a myth. Studies of this sort—enormously fertile in observing, questioning, and critiquing—fall short when it comes to constructing an alternative vision. What they consign to the dustbin of history is, finally, history itself.

Even Richard Helgerson's *Forms of Nationhood*, a more dialectical and consequently more historical work than those I have just discussed, falls prey to the same polarizing tendency. Helgerson studies the passage "through self-alienation" "to an acceptable national self" (243). Yet throughout the book (and even in the opening chapter on the apparently stylistic issue of versification) agency tends to grow "depersonalize[d]" (220—and see the skittishness about agency on 215); negation is a "dark other" (212), something "powerful and powerfully disruptive" (170) that "upend[s]" authorial intentions, even Helgerson's own (9). Defining general issues requires a distanced view (72) and a "superficial regard" (54) resistant to close reading (which Helgerson sees rather as an "institutional" imperative than as a personal engagement, 311 n. 55). Hence, the decisive texts are those in which the strongest authorial resistance is conquered by the most powerful historical current. History is inherently, if abstractly, imperialist, imposing its "misnamings" through "powerfully hidden . . . material and textual forces," in a world where no true namings are conceivable (190–91). Helgerson had previously written the ironically titled *Elizabethan Prodigals* and *Self-Crowned Laureates*; in *Forms of Nationhood*, with its national self and depersonalized agents, it is not surprising that no chapter or section titles bear the name of an individual and that the word "style" appears, so far as I have noted, only once, in a quotation (35).

Halpern alludes disparagingly but not inappropriately to Hegel with a "capital H" (2). For the operational tool neglected by the works I have been discussing is indeed a Hegelian one. They all lack a concept of determinate negation.[50] A contradiction that advances an alternative rather than a conflict, a negotiation that is not primarily a contest, an other that is neither alien nor dead—positions like these remain uncharted by the critics I have discussed. At best their stark contrasts employ only the more primitive form that Hegel calls general negation. General negation is the subject of the famous chapter of the *Phänomenologie des Geistes* on master and servant; it is the moment of arrest opposing selfhood and world, or knowledge and action. Whenever we stop thinking and start doing, or confront our consciousness with an actual object, we engage in a general negation. It is a jolt of reality, accompanied by anxiety or fear, that tests, corrects, and validates what we think we know or what we think we have done. It remains general, however, because it entails a holistic movement from one plane of existence to a different plane, as being is tested by life, or form by content, and vice versa.

Determinate negation, by contrast, is the passage from the abstract "thing" (*Ding*) to the intentional object that Hegel calls "the matter it-self" (*die Sache selbst*), and from consciousness to individuality. Whereas general negations teach conscious beings their limits and impose form on recalcitrant materiality, determinate negations begin with already identified things and shape them to particular purposes. They are "neg-ativity as quality" (*Phänomenologie* 289) rather than as contradiction; they foreground facets of the thing in order to bring it into relationship with a particular will. General negation, says Hegel, imputes "absolute difference" such as good versus bad (289), whereas determinate nega-tion modalizes things in terms of their correspondence to particularities of wish, interest, and fortune (*Mögen, Interesse, Glück*, 296). The logic of determinate negation can be wishful in its claims for the suitability of particular judgments: instinctive animal purposiveness does not really understand what it is doing, frank acknowledgment (*Ehrlichkeit*) de-ceives itself about the stability of matter's adjustment to mind, and high-toned moralism such as Antigone's tragic self-sacrifice condemns itself in the attempt to return the individual will to a universal destiny. But when determinate negation fails, the problem lies in a faulty adjustment of conscious intention to particular circumstances, not in general quan-daries about finding stable names for unstable things or articulated categories for fluid perceptions. Lacking the appropriate category, Hel-gerson figures negation either as a "signifying absence" (71) or as a heuristic comparison and contrast, where "similar questions" give "in-terestingly different" answers, while other oppositions can generate "suddenly changing" evaluations of the same term (154). Using such logic criticism either falls back into the old view that the Renaissance self was infinitely flexible or ahead into the new one that it is a hollow shell of impersonation.[51] But no positive, stable core remains. There are no beginnings, only resistances.

What such studies lack is what Taine has to offer. *Style*, as he presents it, *is precisely the ideal form of determinate negation*. A better dialectician than any I have just cited, Fredric Jameson, in fact invokes the concept of determinate negation in his analysis of Wyndham Lewis's style (*Fables of Aggression* 30). He puts the matter most simply and effectively in his first book, on Sartre's style: "Where there is no possibility of doing something in different ways, there is no possibility of a style" (*Sartre* 41). And his general discussion of style in *Marxism and Form* comes close to the spirit of analysis for which Taine provides the finest exemplar. "To define style," he writes, "as language which deliberately calls attention to itself . . . is to reassert, as over against stylistics, the profoundly historical nature of the phenomenon" (335). It remains only to be said that if style is "profoundly" historical, that is because history is begotten within the depths of the stylistic imagination.

Style as such cannot ever be defined conceptually because it constitutes the movement between concepts. It is the personal element in a collective discourse, the public stance of private expression, the alterity within the present, and the coherence within change. We locate as style whatever remains outside of the conceptual determinants of an utterance. To be style, however, it must be identified: it is a specific inflection and a specifiable qualifier. It is not content but what relativizes content— ornament, or trope, or mode, or ethos. But to be distinguished as style, it must be regarded in a determinate relationship to content. Hence, style is "at once the writer's internalized knowledge and what in it can be captured in a formal theory" (Banfield, *Unspeakable Sentences* 14). Neither empty form nor unanchored invention, it is what Jerome J. McGann calls "the refusal of . . . refusal" and, invoking Hegel, "the negation of the negation" (*Black Riders* 34, 56).[52] In Taine's most profound insight, style generates antitheses because style is the perpetual dialectical unrest that makes works alive and productive. That construction of the experience of time is what we stand to recover in rereading Taine's grand enterprise.

CHAPTER 2

The Classic Is the Baroque
On the Principle of Wölfflin's Art History

HEINRICH WÖLFFLIN belonged to a large and distinguished generation of art historians and aestheticians.[1]* At the height of his career, he appeared to be merely *unus inter pares*, not *primus* or *unicus*. Since his time, the names of his contemporaries have mostly faded into semiobscurity or fallen into oblivion, while Wölfflin's works continue to be readily available and widely read. He has become what no one can be in his own time: a classic. Yet in the continuing stream of critical commentary, it is difficult to find any wholehearted praise except in the writings of Wölfflin's own students. And even among the students who experienced the magic of Wölfflin's presence, some dissenting voices have arisen, such as that of Frederick Antal, who wrote in 1949, "Wölfflin's very lucid, formal analyses, behind which there is an undisguised bias in favour of the classicist Cinquecento composition, reduced the wealth of historical evaluation to a few fundamental categories, a few typical schemes" (Antal, "Remarks" 49).[2] Wölfflin's classically clear and modest work often serves today as provocation rather than inspiration or else seems to be on the point of dissolving into insipidity, as E. H. Gombrich claimed in his well-known attack: "I remember the high hopes with which I went to Berlin University and the impression Wölfflin's personality made on me, the tall Swiss with beautiful blue eyes and a firm and self-assured manner of delivery that held the *auditorium*

---

* All references to Wölfflin's works will be included in the text, abbreviated as follows: *CA* = *Classic Art*; *Dürer* = *The Art of Albrecht Dürer*; *Ged* = *Gedanken zur Kunstgeschichte*; *KS* = *Kleine Schriften*; *PAH* = *Principles of Art History*; *RB* = *Renaissance and Baroque*; *SFA* = *The Sense of Form in Art*.

maximum spellbound. I confess that the spell did not work on me for very long" (Gombrich, *Norm and Form* 92).

Some paradoxical quality has evidently kept Wölfflin's writings alive while concealing the nature of their vitality from his commentators. In his eloquent memoir, *Zu Heinrich Wölfflin's Gedächtnis*, Fritz Strich tells us that Wölfflin was not an easy man to know, and this is just as true of his works, which are likewise animated by unsuspected conflicts and dynamisms. Far from "exclud[ing] the possibility of the coexistence of several modes of vision in a single period or an individual work," as W. Eugene Kleinbauer claims, Wölfflin's real message is that the history of art is an unremitting struggle for expression (Kleinbauer, *Modern Perspectives* 28). Those who criticize Wölfflin's apparent oversimplifications almost invariably do so in the service of convictions about the complexity and difficulty of style formation that they have unwittingly learned from him. I hope to show that the hidden power of those insights accounts for the continued importance of Wölfflin's works to contemporary critical theory.

Before analyzing Wölfflin's masterpiece, *Principles of Art History*, I would like to discuss two general issues. The first is the nature of Wölfflin's categories. It is essential to recognize that Wölfflin considered himself a morphologist and not a taxonomist of art. Morphology as Wölfflin practices it, in the spirit of his predecessor Johann Wolfgang von Goethe and his contemporary Max Weber, is not the study of forms but of forming powers. The taxonomist multiplies categories in order to establish a stable stratification of reality. Ideally, all taxonomic types are pure; deviation from type creates a new type or a monster. We denominate biological types in Latin, as if the dead language guaranteed their freedom from change, and in fact Carolus Linnaeus, who founded modern biological taxonomy, was one of the last rigid scientific "fixists." The charge of inflexibility often leveled against Wölfflin's categories properly applies only to taxonomic typologies, and a taxonomy that consisted of ony two genera and five species would be negligible indeed. But a morphologist's categories are limited by design. His universe consists not of numerous separate classes but of a continuum of individuals related through principles of formation and transformation. As Goethe says, "Here we do not inquire after causes but after conditions under which phenomena appear; we view and accept their consistent sequence, their eternal return in a thousand different circumstances, their uniformity and variability; we recognize their definiteness and redetermine it through the human spirit" (Goethe, "Erfahrung and Wissenschaft," *Werke* 18: 95–96). This sense for the pullulation of things is fundamental to Wölfflin, as to any true morphologist.

My second general consideration concerns the relationship of morphology to Wölfflin's philosophy of history. Whereas his great contemporary Alois Riegl was committed to a progressivist view of history, Wölfflin subscribed to a cyclical view derived from biological morphology, with its circular succession of seed, stalk, leaf, flower, fruit, seed. "Style unravels, fades out, or however one wishes to express it. The image of the blooming and fading of a flower presents itself as the guiding perspective of this theory" (*RB* 74). Yet this theory is weakly supported in Wölfflin's writings, which obsessively focus on a single transformation, that from the mature flowering of the classic to the late style of the baroque, which is initially seen as classicism gone to seed and in later writings as the fruit of classicism. Of the process of rebirth and renewal, Wölfflin's entire corpus contains no account more specific than this one of Albrecht Dürer: "His historic deed was to have broken through to a new attitude and a new perception. No one will be able to say where he got the strength to do so. Even if the whole network were visible and we could see what influences he came under we still would not find an answer because genius cannot be explained by an addition of influences" (*Dürer* 41–42).[3] Wölfflin's commitment to historical circularity thus seems empirically superfluous and can only be explained on an emotional level: it marks a refusal to admit the possibility of either an end point or a simple directionality in the historical process. As static as Wölfflin's view of history appears in the hands both of his critics and of imitators such as Strich and Marcel Raymond, history never stops for Wölfflin himself. Form for Wölfflin always needs to be energized, under way; his sense of the will to form is even more dynamic than that of Riegl, who coined the term *Formwollen*. It remains to be shown how this concealed Romantic vitalism governs *Principles of Art History*; like most aspects of Wölfflin's Romanticism, it is fully explicit only in his dissertation, *Prolegomena to a Psychology of Architecture*, which announces outright the maxim "Form is act" (*Form ist Tat*; *KS* 39).

A balanced, objective, or "classic" description of *Principles of Art His-*

tory might begin as follows. The book is an account of the main trends in Western art in the sixteenth and seventeenth centuries. Its purpose is to return art history "to the objects themselves" by considering them strictly as formal structures, without reference to what they represent or express. By a kind of phenomenological reduction, Wölfflin aspires to a scientific presentation freed from subjectivity, an "art history without names" (*Kunstgeschichte ohne Namen*) as he termed it in a famous slogan.[4] The resulting book is a careful and subtle interweaving of many strands. Wölfflin develops his well-known set of five paired categories to distinguish Renaissance from baroque (linear vs. painterly, plane vs. recession, closed vs. open form, multiplicity vs. unity, clearness vs. unclearness) and examines their ramifications with respect not only to periods but also to national differences and to the various genres and subgenres of the major and minor visual arts. The book is thus remarkably comprehensive, even while restrained and selective in presentation.

The aims and virtues of *Principles of Art History*, on this account, are entirely those of classicism. The book can be readily tested by its own categories. Its careful discriminations mark it as clear and linear; its comprehensiveness is that of classic closed forms; its articulation into separate units and subunits displays the multiplicity of classic structures. The overall objectivity of presentation is itself a classicizing trait, for, as Wölfflin says, classicism "represents things as they are," while the baroque represents them "as they seem to be," even though this appearance "never coincides with the form of the object" (*PAH* 20). It is true that Wölfflin intended *Principles of Art History* in part as a defense of baroque art; indeed, he takes to task those who read his predecessor Adolf von Hildebrand as a one-sided exponent of classicism. Yet Wölfflin's defense of the baroque seems curiously backhanded, for he spurns the flamboyance of mannerism and regularly praises the most restrained and orderly manifestations of seicento art. Only these latter, he insists, are the baroque in its pure form; mannerist art is actually a transitional form. In Wölfflin's hands, the true baroque becomes nothing other than a delicate variation on the classic, "indicated by very slight means," "by quite trivial projections," "the gentle flicker of a façade in which the projections are hardly noticeable" (*PAH* 112, 122, 65). This assimilation of baroque to classic might seem to be baroque trickery on Wölfflin's part, a kind of logical trompe l'oeil, were he not so astonishingly direct, so classically naive in his acknowledgment: "The word classic here denotes no judgment of value, for baroque has its classicism too" (*PAH* 14)!

Wölfflin's praise of the baroque in fact belongs to the classicizing presentational strategy; it gives the book a flexible balance, unlike the structured imbalance that characterizes the baroque. Bilateral symmetry is a classic virtue, and hence it is the classicizing historian who says, "The occidental development of modern times cannot simply be reduced to a curve with rise, height, and decline: it has two culminating points" (*PAH* 14). Like every other book, *Principles of Art History* had to be narrated in one-dimensional fashion, with a beginning, a middle, and an end, but its symmetries and interweaving of motifs are designed to cancel the temporal directionality of presentation. The book exhibits what has come to be called spatial form, a static quality that is clearly to be associated with classicism and that leads to some subtle compositional effects.

Each of the five main chapters, for instance, moves from painting to architecture. (The earlier chapters include other headings as well, but these drop out as the structural symmetries grow more evident.) And the movement within the chapters is duplicated by the book as a whole, which begins with a distinction (linear / painterly) that is native to painting and progresses toward distinctions that are naturally architectural.[5] This overall sweep from painting to architecture entails a shift in values, for painting inevitably comes to be associated with the painterly or the art of the baroque (specifically in *RB* 29), while architecture is preeminently a classic art: "The Cinquecento conceived everything *sub specie architecturae*" (*CA* 286; see also *PAH* 139 and *SFA* 87). The organization of the book thus betrays a quietly polemical intent. But what is the direction of the polemic? Are we to take the movement toward architecture as a return from the baroque back to Wölfflin's true base in classicism? Or do we perhaps read the book under the aegis of what has been termed the "primacy effect" (see Sternberg, *Temporal Modes*, chaps. 4–5), so that each chapter appears to be governed by the example of painting and thus to subsume the architectural or classic under the painterly or baroque? The most startling aspect of the book's classicizing balance is indeed that it perfectly balances praise of classicism with praise of the alternative to classicism.

It quickly becomes evident that this "classic" reading of Wölfflin is self-limiting. In the first place, the objectivity of the morphological approach is a mask. For Wölfflin as for Weber, value-freedom is itself a value and disinterestedness a polemical stance.[6] There is a forcefulness within his lucidity that Wölfflin's interpreters have tended to repress, as when Wölfflin attributes classic beauty to "figures energetically [posing] in the plane, so that the stratum of space looks uniformly living in all its parts" (PAH 76).[7] Moreover, the value-free value that Wölfflin inculcates is itself ambiguous, for the classicism or objectivity of the classicist impels him to admire that which is anticlassic—or, more specifically, classic forms of anticlassicism—along with classicism itself. In the current parlance of criticism, Principles of Art History might be termed a deconstructive machine that repeatedly entraps the impartial reader into a value system and then turns around to problematize that system. It is no wonder that most of those who write about Wölfflin express mystification, frustration, or anger. But this dilemma becomes benign once it is recognized that deconstruction is not an end in itself; it is a highly flexible mode that leads to a reorientation, not a destruction, of perspectives.[8] Wölfflin's paradoxes do not undermine classicism; rather, they redefine and reinterpret it, provided only that we are sufficiently attentive to his specific procedures.

Wölfflin begins with a principle of bilateral symmetry. But my analysis has shown an unsuspected or overlooked dimension to classic symmetry: the balance of a thing not against itself but against its opposite, right against left, classic against baroque. "There is symmetry and symmetry," writes Wölfflin. "Not until Leonardo's Last Supper, by the . . . contrasted handling of the groups to right and left, did the symmetrical form first become living" (PAH 128).[9] It is true that the distinction between the balanced unbalance of classicism and the unbalanced balance of the baroque is as minimal as all other differences between the classic proper and the classic or pure type of the baroque. "The baroque, however, consciously emphasizes one side, and thus, since the really unbalanced is no longer art, creates the relation of oscillating balance. . . . Always, often with quite unobtrusive devices, the balance of the picture is upset" (PAH 130, my italics). The troubling thought arises here that Principles of Art History might in fact be an example of baroque historiography, dedicated not to a symmetrical contrast of classic and baroque but rather to creating an oscillating balance of sympathy between them. (Michael Ann Holly has pursued this suggestion in "Wölfflin and the Imagining of the Baroque.") Where, in fact, can we draw the line between classic and baroque? Does anything ultimately distinguish the one-sidedness of the baroque—which isn't really unbalance—from that of a classic picture where "the figures are moved to one side without the balance being upset" (*PAH* 143)? Could the whole point of Wölfflin's book be that the classic and the baroque are identical?

Hardly that. The distinction between baroque and classic must be upheld if the principle of bilateral symmetry is to have any meaning. Yet Wölfflin maintains a difficult, Hegelian logic which regards contrast as a form of mutual dependence. Polar definitions of style in the tradition of Schiller were ubiquitous during Wölfflin's formative and creative years, but Wölfflin was alone in the generation after Nietzsche in understanding how each style necessarily implies the antithetical style as a negative self-image.[10] The full importance of this logic will become clear later; for now it is enough to see why the proponent of classicism who is constantly metamorphosing into a proponent of the opposite of classicism embodies the classic spirit. That spirit of self-definition through self-contradiction animates Wölfflin's account of classicism, with its "relation between energy and repose which we feel to be an enduring state," and it equally animates his account of the baroque, where "the a-tectonic always mirrors itself in the tradition of the tectonic" (*PAH* 152). The classicism of *Principles of Art History* is a form of negative capability; it has no other principle of identity than that of identity with the opposite. When the classicist looks in the mirror, he always see a reversed or mirror image. The identity of same with same, the principle of mimesis—never a positive notion in *Principles of Art History*—is invariably associated by Wölfflin with the so-called primitives of the fifteenth century. What the classicist sees in the mirror is a transformation, not a transcription; his mirrorings are speculations, detached, idealizing counterparts of the world around him. The classicist's objectivity is a reflective mode, antithetical both in its internal structuring and in its external relationship to the world.

The paradoxical logic of identity gives rise to well-known problems of definition: the troublesome overlap of the terms "painterly" and "painting" as well as the often-alleged possibility of reducing Wölfflin's five paired categories to Riegl's single pair, optic and haptic.[11] The same framework explains the numerous rhetorical excesses that seem to tarnish the classicism of *Principles of Art History*. In a classic painting by Joachim Patenir, "the tree is thoroughly felt in its relation to the picture edge, from which it draws strength just as, on the other hand, it establishes the close of the picture"; in a baroque Rembrandt, "the unity . . . lies in the absolutely compelling coherence of the movement of the whole" (*PAH* 144, 171). Such effusive writing is by no means rare in *Principles of Art History* and reflects Wölfflin's intuition that cool classicism is inseparable from its warmer opposite.

The impurity of *Principles of Art History*, on this view, is part of its strength. However, at least one major art historian, Gombrich, has expressed a decided preference for Wölfflin's earlier book, *Classic Art*, and the grounds for his preference are evident: *Classic Art* is less emotive and more consistently formalistic, as well as simpler in structure, than its successor. Gombrich's preference suggests a schematization of Wölfflin's four major surveys of Renaissance art in which *Renaissance and Baroque* (written in a staccato telegraph style) illustrates the undisciplined genius of the primitive, *Classic Art* the economy of the classic, *Principles of Art History* the intricacy of the baroque, and the effusively generalizing *Sense of Form in Art* the mechanical formalism of rococo decadence. There are two pillars in Wölfflin's achievement, and they confront us with a critical choice. Which is the true model, the analytical classicism of *Classic Art* or the expressive (baroque) classicism of *Principles of Art History*?

Wölfflin's answer to this question is unambiguous. Greatly as he was influenced by the formalistic theories of "pure visibility" found in the writings of Conrad Fiedler and Adolf von Hildebrand, he never treated them as more than a way station in formulating a true understanding of the artistic process.[12] The last sentence of *Classic Art* is perhaps sufficient evidence: "We have no desire to advocate a formalist type of art criticism: it is indeed the function of light to make the diamond sparkle" (*CA* 288)—as is the equally decisive opening sally of a review of Riegl's *Entstehung der Barockkunst in Rom*: "That art history is primarily concerned with seeing does not mean that thinking must be shunned" (356). Formalism is not the thing itself but the foil against which the thing appears. Forms as such are dead, and the mechanical production of forms is always, for Wölfflin, a sign of decadence. In order to come alive, the form must be broken, the spatial symmetry must be violated by a univocal and temporal element, the stable patterning must be marked by a moment of will or intentionality. We have already seen that classic symmetry cannot exist for Wölfflin without incorporating a contrast—at least the contrast of right and left—that prevents the symmetry from collapsing into unity. But beyond this, symmetry also cannot exist—or cannot come alive—except in the presence of asymmetry. Put in the most elementary terms, classicism cannot exist without the baroque.

The principle of contrast, in this more radical form, is one of the constants of Wölfflin's work. Where all conforms to a single code, there is compulsion, not free expression, and therefore only primitive or decadent art. "This classic plane looks quite different from the primitive plane, not only because the relation of the parts is more deeply felt [another example of the baroque or expressive prose of *Principles of Art History* that makes its predominant classicism perceptible], but because it is interspersed with contrasting motives. Only by the foreshortened motives leading into the pictures does the character of what is extended and united in the plane reach its full significance" (*PAH* 101). What applies to the intentionality of mature classicism also applies, of course, to the intentionality of mature (or classic) baroque. "The baroque arranges the figures in rows, orders them in niches: it has the greatest interest in insisting upon a spatial orientation. Only in the plane, in the negation of the plane, does recession become palpable" (*PAH* 108; see also *Dürer* 234 and *SFA* 89). The most extreme and decisive formulations of this notion, as well as many of his others, may be found in Wölfflin's dissertation; here he claims—against the authority of the source he cites—that symmetrical arrangements, as in Greek temples, always have an odd number of parts. Without an asymmetrical central element, there can be no symmetry. "We use a symmetrical articulation of uneven division for everything self-contained, since when the middle is stressed, and unlike the parts, it stands for just this inner cohesion" (*KS* 34–35; see also *SFA* 92).

The whole purpose of classic symmetries can be seen as that of concentrating the energy in the center of the work. Classicism began when the dynamism of the center was discovered, as will be seen when I restore a phrase omitted from an earlier quotation: "Not until Leonardo's *Last Supper, by the isolation of the one central figure* and the contrasted handling of the groups to right and left, did the symmetrical form first become living" (*PAH* 128, my italics). In this respect, as in all others, it must be added, the difference between classic and baroque is minimal. "It is a natural result of the facts here given that the baroque façade will tend to emphasize individual parts, at first in the sense of a dominating central motive" (*PAH* 189). Even in works of the purest (most symmetrical) classicism, Wölfflin's interpretive eye regularly gravitates toward the expressive center of the picture. "The whole picture is so planned that the central figure has no counterpart but only favourable contrasts. . . . She [Raphael's *Sistine Madonna*] is the norm, the others are variations from it which yet seem ordered by some hidden law" (*CA* 134).

Where the center is unmarked, Wölfflin can arbitrarily displace its life-giving force. He says of Barend van Orley's *Rest on the Flight*: "Naturally, much depends on the tree. It does not stand in the middle, but for all that, we perceive very clearly where the middle lies: the trunk is no mathematical vertical, but we feel that it is related to the line of the picture frame: the whole growth goes into the picture space" (*PAH* 143). The greater the displacement, the greater the violence attributed to the energizing function that must be present. For example, in Raphael's *Death of Ananias* the center retains a power of a life-denying sort, while the energy of life is wrenched into a different position. Wölfflin's emotional response to this high-classic work is nearly indistinguishable from his response to baroque art.

The people nearest him recoil in horror, and the circle of these foreground figures [who, incidentally, make Ananias into a kind of surrogate center] is so constructed that Ananias, in collapsing backward, tears a hole in the composition which is visible even at a distance, and this shows why everything else in the picture is so rigidly ordered: for this one asymmetry is the more powerfully reinforced by it. Like a thunderbolt, the judgement has torn the ranks apart and struck down its victim. . . . The eye is led directly to the centre, where St. Peter stands, a minatory arm outstretched, yet it is not an excited gesture and Peter does not fulminate: he merely pronounces the judgement of God. The Apostles themselves remain calm and unaffected by the occurrence. (*CA* 114)

Wölfflin's classicism is a structure that channels expressive energies. His categories are not taxonomies of dead or unchanging species but a morphology of living forms. His analyses, to be sure, are formalistic or objective, but his is a sophisticated objectivity rather than a primitive one: that is, in terms of the principle of contrasts, Wölfflin's objectivity is inseparable from subjectivity. He dissects not to murder but to bring to life. The three analyses from which I have just quoted all typify his procedure: he regularly allegorizes because every significant structure is also a signifying structure. Intentionality must be present; there is no mature form without a will to form. To find the expressive center of a work is to make the leap from structure into meaning, for at the center is not a mere pattern but an eloquent, unquenchable human voice.

The fundamentally baroque aspect of Wölfflin's thought is thus that his categories are anthropological and affective. They work as analytical categories because they work as human categories. This is the assumption behind the title of Wölfflin's *Prolegomena to a Psychology of Architecture*, and it is repeatedly stressed throughout that work. "We impose the image of ourselves on all appearances." *"Our bodily organization is the form in which we grasp everything corporeal"* (KS 16, 21). Though Wölfflin uses the term "form" here, its meaning is antithetical to the formalism of Fiedler and Hildebrand (see in particular Hildebrand's posthumously published essay "Über das Vorstellen"); the sequel shows unmistakably Wölfflin's affinity with the philosophy of "empathy" (*Einfühlung*) developed by followers of the Romantic philosopher Johann Friedrich Herbart. "Cubes are clumsy—good-natured—dumb"; windows are eyes that " 'spiritualize' the structure"; "the pillar knows exactly what it has to carry and acts accordingly." Buildings are living beings and they speak to us with the voice of their age: "What a people has on its mind it speaks out in every case" (KS 31, 38, 42, 47). Underneath form lies feeling, and the primacy of the body lies in its role as the medium for understanding and communicating human emotions. Or, as Theodor Lipps writes in his introduction to logic, in a sentence that might have been written by Wölfflin himself: "We do not learn the form of the human body from considering the clothed body; rather everyone knows on the contrary that the forms and folds of drapery can only become comprehensible from a knowledge of the body."[13]

Principles of Art History is far more mature and restrained than the dissertation, but the anthropological basis has only been concealed in the later work, not eliminated. Wölfflin still begins by calling himself a "psychologist of style," and the psychological dimension of the categories remains implicit in his imagery, though not always explicit in his analytical terminology. Indeed, for purely analytical purposes, the categories have often seemed dubious. The distinctions between opposing pairs only become clear when the categories are translated into their psychological equivalents, for their true function is to identify the expressivity, not the patterning, of the work of art. In recognizing that the categories are both sign and significance, we are driven back once again to that nagging question, where *is* the boundary between form and meaning, classic and baroque, north and south?

The first chapter of *Principles of Art History*, "Linear and Painterly," is preliminary to the whole; it is the longest and has the broadest coverage of genres as well as the only "general," nongeneric subchapter. Its categories, likewise, translate into the most general terms: the linear "represents things as they are," the baroque represents them "as they seem to be" (*PAH* 20). The linear style, in other words, is objective, the baroque subjective. Initially this clarification seems to give priority to the linear, for in classicism the image coincides with the form of the object, whereas the baroque is a "system of form-alienated signs" and is thus based on a negation (*PAH* 44). A second and more obviously anthropological rendition of the categories takes this apparently evaluative system and moves toward restoring its objectivity and classic balance. According to this rendition, the linear "appeals to the sense of touch" as well as to the eye, whereas the painterly "appeals only to the eye." This still seems to attribute greater breadth to the linear style, but the painterly compensates with possibilities unavailable to the linear, for "the painterly style alone knows a beauty of the incorporeal." In terms of subject matter, the linear style is more comprehensive: it can represent the sensations of both senses. But, curiously, in terms of the perceiving subject, it is the baroque or painterly experience that seems the richer: "And if we can say that in the linear style the hand has felt out the corporeal world essentially according to its plastic content, the eye in the painterly stage has become sensitive to the most various textures, and it is no contradiction if even here the visual sense seems nourished by the tactile sense— that other tactile sense which relishes the kind of surface, the different skin of things" (*PAH* 21, 27).

At the end of the chapter, Wölfflin acknowledges what is implicit in the greater sensual richness attributed to the second, baroque sense of the tactile: the anthropological pressure of these categories pushes us away from the linear and toward the painterly. "We are always prone to take things in a still more painterly way than they are meant to be taken, even to force the definitely linear, if it is at all possible, into the painterly" (PAH 71). The apparent reversal of evaluation in this chapter becomes comprehensible if we realize just how broadly anthropological this first pair of categories is. The linear or objective hand feels out the "plastic content" of things, while the painterly or subjective hand "relishes" their "skin": the difference in rhetorical intensity between these two descriptions shows clearly how objective and subjective become tantamount respectively to the simple absence or presence of human subjectivity. Here lies the ultimate significance of the first pair of categories: the linear, pure formalism of classicism is that which excludes us; the painterly system of "form-alienated signs" is that toward which the human subject gravitates by its very nature.

The next paired categories, plane and recession, are equivalent in psychological terms to rest and movement. Wölfflin is explicit about the significance of the baroque forms. "The beauty of recession," he says at one point, "is always combined with an impression of movement," and later he repeats that "recession speaks most intensely when it can reveal itself as movement" (PAH 76, 94). He is not so explicit with reference to classic art, but numerous references to "quiet plane-form" in Raphael, to the "unprecedented repose and lucidity" of Joachim Patenir's planar landscape, to the "atmosphere of quiet plane sequence" in Quentin Massys, and the like render unmistakable the association of the classic plane with a state of rest (PAH 79, 82, 90). Wölfflin's discussion of an interior by Pieter Janssens in the following chapter reveals the inherent subjectivity of his approach; he shows that the painting is entirely recessional and atectonic in its formal arrangement, yet he concludes by attributing a classic repose to it. "For all its intersections and discrepancies, however, the picture does not look limitless. The space enclosed apparently haphazard is still quite at rest in itself" (PAH 133). Here it is evident that the psychological interpretation takes precedence over the formal analysis. Closure and planar structure are ultimately feeling-states, and the decision to declare the painting closed depends on the decision about the feeling it communicates.

Wölfflin is again quite explicit about the feelings communicated by

closed and open form respectively: "The a-tectonic style does not fall
into lawlessness, but the order on which it is based is so much freer that
we may well speak of a general contrast of law and freedom." "In the
former case, the vital nerve in every effect is the inevitability of the
organisation, absolute immutability. In the latter, art plays with the sem-
blance of the lawless" (*PAH* 134, 149). Again the prevalence of affective
over analytical motives is self-evident: the baroque style differs from
the classic not because it *is* lawless but because it gives the effect of
lawlessness.

In the chapter on multiplicity and unity, the affective or anthropological motifs are both more complex and more interesting. Wölfflin's initial
distinction is between "the articulated system of forms of classic art and
the (endless) flow of the baroque" (*PAH* 158). Imagery of fluidity pervades the chapter, for water, according to Wölfflin, "was the period's
favourite element" (*RB* 154). "Now, and now only," he says, "the greatness of the sea could find its representation" (*PAH* 178), and as if to
inculcate this affinity he places the reproduction of a baroque seascape
by Jan van Goyen at the head of the introduction to the book and a
riverscape by Pieter Breughel at the head of this chapter even though
neither painting is discussed where it is reproduced. In fact it is worth
observing that Wölfflin does not discuss any water paintings in this
chapter, though of course he does so elsewhere. Where fluidity becomes
the meaning of his category, it is absent from the contents of the paintings. Wölfflin's procedure, as I have argued, is both objectively analytical and subjectively interpretive, and in this chapter he seems careful to
preserve the distance between the forms he describes and the significances he reveals. Were he to treat water paintings here, he would obscure the fact that his analyses are always the prelude to translations.

Though he conceals the fact, Wölfflin has here effected a translation of
the baroque into itself, of water painting (and fountain architecture) into
fluidity. Baroque art has declared its true meaning, which is to be an art
of flux—of time and, throughout this chapter, of momentariness. Suddenly here the baroque comes into its own, with a surprising reversal in
Wölfflin's categories. Until now he has associated the baroque with
lawlessness and confusion, and classicism with the unifying force of
symmetrical organization around a center. Unity is repose—the equation had been made explicitly in the discussion in *Classic Art* of Michel-

angelo's Medici *Madonna* (see 194)—and early in *Principles of Art History* Wölfflin seems to say that the unification achieved in Leonardo's *Last Supper* was later lost in Tiepolo's version.[14] As Wölfflin says in the first sentence of chapter 4, "The principle of closed form of itself presumes the conception of the picture as a unity." But as the baroque now comes into its own, it appears that the unity of classicism is an illusory, "multiple unity," whereas the true or "unified unity" actually pertains to the baroque. It is the usurping baroque, rather than the deposed classic, that now has "a dominating central motive." And so Wölfflin returns in this chapter to the two *Last Suppers* in order to rescind his earlier position. He still claims that Leonardo's painting is unified, but he offers Tiepolo's version to illustrate the "possibility of surpassing this unity" (*PAH* 189, 174). In becoming itself, baroque art has overthrown classicism.

As throughout *Principles of Art History*, the difference here between classic and baroque with respect to the question of flow is minimal; specifically, in Leonardo "a definite moment is seized for representation," while Tiepolo features "a more acute concentration on the momentary." Once again analytical categories fail us here. But that is because Wölfflin's true impulse is anthropological (or affective, or baroque), and at this point in the book voice supervenes on the motif of flux as a second and more anthropological motif. In terms of voice classic and baroque are as distinct as night and day. It is in this chapter, it will be remembered, that content and meaning coincide—as they never do in classicism, where instead form and meaning coincide—so as to reveal the true significance of the baroque as flux. The baroque at last *speaks out*. Though "it is a pity Tiepolo has no more to say to us," even he "speaks with double energy throughout the whole picture" (*PAH* 174).

The unity of classicism is an articulated unity, a rhythm or harmony, as Wölfflin constantly repeats. But anthropologically it is a silent articulation. Indeed, Wölfflin elsewhere tells us that "Leonardo was the first to venture" "to make the silence following speech the motive of the principal figure" (*CA* 27). He touches on this theme again in describing Leonardo in chapter 4 of *Principles of Art History*, where he contrasts the absence of voice in the classic with the presence of voice in the baroque, which could be described as articulate articulation or, in Wölfflin's phrase, "unified unity." (There is a clear though distant echo here of a Romantic motif, Friedrich Schlegel's oft repeated definition of Romantic—anticlassic—poetry as "the poetry of poetry.") In the baroque, "places of most speaking form emerge from a groundwork of mute or less speaking form"; "the babel of voices here rises to intelligible speech"; the older versions of the Susanna story concern how "the elders watch their victim from afar," while the baroque version concentrates on the enemy "whispering his lascivious words into her ear"— such motifs are rife in this chapter (*PAH* 164, 172, 175).

Particularly subtle is Wölfflin's play on the word "accent." Accent is first of all a painterly technique: "a single colour can stand out as a solitary accent." But the single-color accent is part of a whole expressional system, a "new economy of spiritual accents," accents that can, for instance, "re-echo in the 'topographical diagonal' of Van Goyen's dune landscapes." And so accent is not just a technique but a technique that for once coincides with its affective meaning, for "the liveliest expressional accent" is equivalent to "intelligible speech" (*PAH* 165, 171, 175, 172). Classicism gives us the background rhythm and harmony; the melodic flow and expressive accent of the leading voice are added by the baroque. Or is this not a type of presence that is demanded within the very heart of the structured absence that is classicism? For one of the glories of sixteenth-century art is Michelangelo's crowning, though alas unfinished, masterpiece, the Medici Chapel. What makes this room so splendid is the accents, the "violations of the expected," the "dissonances," the "shift of emphasis" to the side niches; as a result "there is no other room in the whole world where sculpture speaks with such force" (*CA* 186, 188). It seemed that chapter 4 of *Principles of Art History* had at last established a decisive difference between classic and baroque, but again the distinction is no more than a trick, capable of dissolving at a wave of the interpreter's wand.

Wölfflin returns in chapter 5 to a very general anthropological motif that is decisive for his reevaluation of art history. He comes back to Leonardo and Tiepolo yet once more in order to say that "the clarity of renaissance art must have seemed lifeless to this generation." And if it seemed so to them, it also seems so to us, for later on the same page, in connection with a painting by Joos van Cleve, Wölfflin drops the modal qualifier and says that the coloration "is not a homogeneous living element"—and that despite the fact that color is van Cleve's great achievement and "orders the whole" (*PAH* 208). Classicism is an art of the dead, to be set beside the baroque, which gives, "primarily" or in fact "only" (this is Wölfflin's self-correction), "the form of the living." In the baroque, "the body breathes" (*PAH* 232, 229).

On the one side, we have absence, rest, law, silence, death; on the other, presence, movement, freedom, voice, life. It could hardly be clearer that in affective terms Wölfflin's sympathies are entirely with the baroque; indeed, in his first book he even writes of "the affinity that our age in particular bears to the Italian baroque" (*RB* 87). Over and over again we have seen how classic works triumph by breaking out into the values of the baroque, into energy, speech, life. This subsurface energy is ever present in the masterpieces of classicism. To the baroque (read: the German spirit), "the clarity of renaissance art" (read: Italy) "must have seemed lifeless." But it is not lifeless, or at least it can be brought to life. This was Wölfflin's mission, to translate, allegorize, and humanize classicism so as to bring back to life what age and distance had rendered sterile and artificial. It is only if we treat him as an advocate not of the classic forms of baroque art but of the baroque element hidden at the heart of classicism that we can understand why he devoted two books entirely to Renaissance art—*Classic Art* and *The Art of Albrecht Dürer*—but none entirely to the seventeenth century. It was about classicism that he had something passionately new to say. The young Gombrich missed the baroque urgency in that tall, blue-eyed Swiss, but it emerges luminously throughout Strich's memoir: "When I again . . . think of the twitching and the lightning around his eyes, of his restlessness and impenetrable reserve, of his speaking style, this never overloaded, never overbalancing, measured and rhythmic style that struggled upwards toward the light out of deep shafts and layers, then do I understand that classic art indeed brought him release, but release into the very thing that he himself was not" (Strich, *Zu Heinrich Wölfflin's Gedächtnis* 34–35).

Down deep this classic taxonomist is really a baroque morphologist. His forms are never stable but always shadings and accents. "Everything is transition," he tells us early and late (*PAH* 22, 183, 227). "We should need a thousand words to denote all the transitions. It is throughout a question of relative judgments. Compared with one style, the next can be called painterly" (*PAH* 30). Such statements, prominent though they are, seem to contradict the broad canvas over which the book is articulated, but close reading has shown us how invariably the clear-cut differences dissolve in favor of a living energy that permeates the whole.

A deeply buried polemical intention can be recovered here. It is possible to recognize as Wölfflin's unnamed antagonist his revered teacher Jacob Burckhardt. In *The Civilization of the Renaissance in Italy*, Burckhardt had created an intricately composed and moving panorama of a world of spectacle that could change only to decay. History is an aesthetic pageant that turns to action at its peril, and the classical world is defined conjointly by its changeless purity and by its remoteness. This is an old tradition in German thought that acquires in Burckhardt the political dimension of a deeply felt quietism: the remoteness of history in the past is echoed by the individual's remoteness from history in the present.[15] Against this are to be placed Wölfflin's images of the growth of a remote style into a familiar one, of south into north, and of death into life. History is movement, in a constant interpenetration of forces and motifs.

The vitalism that separates Wölfflin from Burckhardt links him to two other great contemporaries. Behind his account of the birth of the baroque out of the spirit of music can be recognized the impact of his other great compatriot, Nietzsche, with his similarly shifty dialectic of the Apollonian and the Dionysian. And I think that another influence can be discerned as well. At the end of *Classic Art*, Wölfflin argues against Hippolyte Taine, but this is as deceptive as his apparent alignment with Burckhardt.[16] In fact, *Principles of Art History* is concerned with the relation of "personal style" to "*the style of the school, the country, the race*" (*PAH* 6), a triad of factors discernibly derived from Taine's moment, milieu, and race. Wölfflin rejected a tendency in Taine toward a mechanicalism "which attempts to interpret every style as an expression of the prevailing mood of the age" (*CA* 287). But he would also have found in the historian of English literature the century's greatest psychologist of style, concerned, precisely like Wölfflin, to show that works of art have a "double root," in form as well as in content. As the preceding chapter has shown, Taine, like Wölfflin, conceived of history as movement rather than (like Burckhardt) as spectacle, and as the source rather than the antidote of the modern. Taine also would have appealed to Wölfflin as a writer concerned to balance the traditional twin aims of the historian, the "baroque" or animating aim of making the past present and the "classic" aim of preserving the pastness of the past. This delicate balance is at the heart of Wölfflin's dialectic.

There cannot be a dialectic without differences. Yet so far, wherever we have approached Wölfflin, the line between baroque and classic has dissolved. I have just suggested that Wölfflin's thought was shaped in response to some of the great historians of the nineteenth century, but Wölfflin is still liable to seem an outright failure as a historian. Even if we discount as an aberration Wölfflin's cyclical view of development, his "history of the development of occidental seeing" appears to issue in chaos rather than system (*PAH* 12). First, he insists that there is no connection between classic and baroque and that no evaluative comparison of them is possible. "Baroque . . . is neither a rise nor a decline from classic, but a totally different art. The occidental development of modern times cannot simply be reduced to a curve with rise, height, and decline: it has two culminating points." "It is not a difference of quality if the baroque departed from the ideals of the age of Dürer and Raphael, but, as we have said, a different attitude to the world" (*PAH* 14, 16). Second, he stresses the irreversible logic of the historical curve that leads from classic to baroque and never in the other direction. "The transition from tangible, plastic, to purely visual, painterly perception follows a natural logic, and could not be reversed," a logic, be it said, that begins with a rise from the primitives and ends with a decline into the rococo (*PAH* 17). Third, from whatever conventionalities of diction or strategies of rehabilitation, a rhetoric of historical progress is often on the horizon; wittingly or unwittingly, Wölfflin often speaks of the "advancing" of art, of an "enhancement of interest" in the baroque, of the development of taste, of a "gain" that results when the baroque "avoids classic frontality" (*PAH* 196, 223). And fourth, as we have seen, Wölfflin repeatedly insists on denying the historical dualism that he has insisted on establishing: "As regards chronology, the facts cannot, of course, be mastered with two concepts" (*PAH* 67). The baroque is at once the opposite of the classic and identical to it, later and simultaneous, cancellation and fulfillment.

The explanation of this historiographical muddle—which points to the core of Wölfflin's achievement—is both unmistakably implicit and, at one key point, inescapably explicit. Classic art is absent, silent, static,

or even dead; baroque is present, vocal, and alive. The difference between classic and baroque that rationalizes Wölfflin's system and that
establishes at once their radical opposition and their total identity is
quite simply this: that *the classic does not exist*. It never existed and can
never have existed, for when the classic comes into existence or manifests itself, it does so in the form of existence, which is the baroque. The
classic *is* the baroque. This is not a speculative judgment about Wölfflin.
It is precisely what he says, if not about all of classic art, at least about
the most classic form of classicism, the art that forms the subject of
Classic Art. The passage from the introduction to *Classic Art* is long but
worth quoting in full for its pathetic and rhetorically moving insistence
on the irredeemable nonexistence of the classic.

It is not easy to obtain a general view of this period. However well-known to us
from youth onwards these masterpieces may be through engravings and repro-
ductions of every kind, only slowly does a consistent and living picture form
itself of the world which bore these fruits. It is different with the Quattrocento.
In Florence the fifteenth century still stands before our eyes like a living thing.
True, much of it is lost, many things have been taken from their natural setting
and put into the prison-like custody of museums but there still remain enough
places to recreate for us a vivid impression of the life of those days. The Cinquecento is preserved more fragmentarily and, moreover, did not reach a complete
development. In Florence one has the feeling that the broad substructure of the
Quattrocento lacks the crown of final achievement because one cannot properly
see the completion of the development. I do not mean that this is because of the
export of panel pictures out of the country, so that, for example, there is practically nothing by Leonardo left in Italy, but because, from the beginning, the
forces squander themselves. Leonardo's *Last Supper*, which is an essentially
Florentine work, is in Milan; Michelangelo became half Roman and Raphael
entirely so. Of their great Roman works, the Sistine ceiling is an absurdity, a
torment to the artist and the spectator alike, and Raphael had to paint some of
his Vatican pictures in sections on walls where one can never see them properly.
So one is left wondering how much ever came to anything, how much out of
those short, few, peak years remained only as a project or fell victim to early
destruction. Leonardo's *Last Supper* itself is only a wreck; his great battle-piece,
commissioned for Florence, was never finished and even the cartoon is lost.
Michelangelo's *Bathing Soldiers* shared the same fate, while the Julius Tomb remained unexecuted save for a few single figures, and the facade of San Lorenzo,
which was to have displayed the full splendour of Tuscan architecture and
sculpture, remained no more than a project on paper. The Medici Chapel only
counts as a partial substitute, for it already stands on the verge of Baroque.

Classic art has left no monument in the great style, where architecture and sculpture are blended together for the full expression of the artist's concept, and the greatest architectural commission on which all the artistic forces of the age were concentrated—St. Peter's in Rome—was, finally, not allowed to become a monument of the High Renaissance.

One can compare classic art with the ruins of a building, nearly, but never quite, finished, the original form of which must be reconstructed from far-scattered fragments and incomplete accounts, and it is perhaps not wrong to say that in the whole history of Italian art no epoch is less known than the Golden Age. (CA xvii–xviii)

Wölfflin's sensibility is thus dominated by a pathos of which hints can be found even in Burckhardt, who writes at one point in the *Cicerone*, "Naturally the best and grandest projects also remained unconsummated in the full flowering of the renaissance" (Burckhardt, *Gesammelte Werke* 9: 144). That classicism is a mirage—a necessary illusion or, more technically, a regulative ideal—is one of the profound discoveries of that branch of Romanticism curiously known as German classicism. For Schiller, for Goethe, for Humboldt, the classical is a figure of desire, an Arcadia well lost and never to be recaptured. It is no coincidence that Faust's road to the classical world is guarded by Sphinxes; for when the classical comes to life it always does so in a belated baroque language of turmoil and self-division:

> Exalted much and much disparaged, Helena,
> I leave behind the strand where first we came ashore,
> Still in a stupor from the nimble tilt and pitch
> Of rolling seas that brought us from the Phrygian plain.
> (Goethe, *Faust*, lines 8488–91)[17]

Wölfflin's logic is uncompromising: if art is a human expression subject to the flow of history, then it can never have been ideally pure or timeless. Yet he makes this rigorous logic seem natural and inevitable by subordinating it to the directness of ocular demonstration. His greatness thus rests, in the most literal sense, on a visionary power. Wölfflin's vision of classicism elided places him in one of the main lines of modern thought, a line whose empirical richness is in danger of being obscured when its insights are reduced to the formula, "the destruction of metaphysics."

It may seem a long way from *Principles of Art History* to proofs of the existence of God. Yet the classic serves as a god term for Wölfflin, and the secret kernel sentence of his writings, the classic is the baroque, is in a sense an assertion concerning the existence of a creative essence. To realize the implications of Wölfflin's writings, we need to understand the background and grammar of that kernel sentence. And nowhere—at least nowhere in the tradition out of which Wölfflin came—has the grammar of being been so extensively scrutinized as in connection with the ontological proof of the existence of God.

God is defined as the most perfect being; but to exist is better than not to exist, so by definition God possesses existence. So, in a simple form, runs the proof. God existing is better than and hence different from God merely imagined. One of the most famous sections of Kant's *Critique of Pure Reason* refutes this argument. Kant argues that being is not a predicate or, to be more specific, not a determinant. One hundred talers in my pocket is no greater a sum than 100 talers in my imagination, and God existing is no greater than God merely conceived. Existence does not change—and hence does not improve—the nature of the deity. God is God.

Paraphrased in this crude way, Kant's argument sounds like a denial of the distinction between essence and existence, and on this ground it has been repeatedly assailed (see, for instance, Wood, *Kant's Rational Theology* 104–9). The predicate, he seems to say, adds nothing to the subject and thus is empty. Being is no different from nonbeing. God is not God. But Kant's true contention is not that being is an empty notion but rather that being is unanalyzable. He denies only that we can know what existence entails. The refutation is concerned not with God's existence but with our conception of God's existence; hence God is mysterious, or, as Kant writes in a posthumous fragment, "Real being is the first absolute concept—completely heterogeneous (*but not even that*) with nothing: thus not o + a = a" (Kant, *Gesammelte Schriften* 28: 957). What this adds up to is an incipient recognition on Kant's part that being, identity, and truth are dialectical concepts, problems and not answers, tokens of an incalculable difference.[18]

Hegel's numerous commentaries on Kant's refutation—four in the *Science of Logic* alone and four more in various series of lectures on religion—all concern the dialectics of being. Kant's refutation, as Hegel says, only deals with the subjective stage of being-for-us, not the objective stage of being in and for itself. In itself being is changeless and therefore empty: *"Pure being* and pure *nothing* are, therefore, the same" (*Science of Logic* 82). And for us, being is pure evanescence and hence again empty:

The difficulty of finding *being* in the Notion as such and equally in the Notion of God, becomes insuperable when the being is supposed to be that which obtains *in the context of outer experience* or *in the form of sensuous perception, like the hundred* [*talers*] *in my finances,* something to be grasped with the hand, not with the mind, something visible essentially to the outer, not to the inner eye; in other words, when that being which things possess as sensuous temporal and perishable, is given the name of reality or truth. (*Science of Logic* 707)

But through the contrast between these two inessential modes of being, a third mode is generated in which being is assimilated to becoming. God is that purity in existence which points beyond pure existence, destroyer and preserver at once. Hegel is always at his most lucid when commenting on Kant, and despite his inveterate abstractness the ideas here are straightforward:

Existence, then, is not to be taken here as a *predicate* or as a *determination* of essence, the proposition of which would run: essence exists, or *has* existence; on the contrary, essence has passed over into Existence; Existence is essence's absolute emptying of itself or self-alienation, nor has it remained behind on the further side of it. The proposition should therefore run: essence is Existence; it is not distinct from its Existence. Essence has *passed over* into Existence in so far as essence as ground no longer distinguishes itself from itself as the grounded, or in so far as this ground has sublated itself. But this negation is equally essentially its position, or absolutely positive continuity with itself, its identity-with-self achieved in its negation. (483)[19]

Hegel stresses that this is the logic of the concept in general, of which the logic of the concept of God is only an important instance. Hegel's logic is precisely that of Wölfflin's art history as well. The baroque is the fulfillment of the classic. But it is a fulfillment in the sense of a crossing over—from essence into existence, from death into life—and hence the absolute negation of the classic. Finally, it is the condition of the possibility of classic being, determining the classic as the ever remote, alien ground of existence. This eternal mutation of classic into baroque, without which neither classic nor baroque could exist, is the logic of history—this, and not, in particular, some reverse pendulum swing from baroque existence toward classic essence, such as Strich argues for at the end of his memoir and tries to document in his studies of German classicism and German Romanticism.

History is also moving toward the baroque and away from the classic. This means that each age serves as the baroque to some earlier age and as the classic to some later one. The Romanesque can be viewed as the classic of the Gothic, the late-Gothic primitives as the silent ground underlying the expressivity to be found in sixteenth-century art, the Florentine cinquecento as the classic of a certain tall, blue-eyed Swiss.[20] And in turn history is recapitulated in each individual work of art, for each must have two faces if all do. We may take it as a second hidden kernel sentence of Wölfflin's writings that *every artwork is both classic and baroque*, classic in its essence and baroque in its existence, classic in its formal perfection and baroque in its expressivity. Indeed, form and expression are inseparable, if dialectical, complements. No matter how much form strikes us as permanently valid, it is also always something that has been created; it is both a mode of stability and a mode of beginning or initiation and cannot be the one without being the other. "Of course, in the strictest sense of the word, there is nothing 'finished': all historical material is subject to continual transformation; but we must make up our minds to establish the distinctions at a fruitful point, and there to let them speak as contrasts, if we are not to let the whole development slip through our fingers" (*PAH* 14).

By virtue of the very intensity of its commitment to formalism, Wölfflin's work thus becomes—or rather remains what his earliest writing most obviously is—the antithesis of a pure formalism. He is concerned with locating fruitful points within history, as if the continual flux of history were not fruitful enough for the imagination of any scholar. This is no mere typology, no impoverished study of artistic structures, but one of our most powerfully and concretely realized theories of the aesthetics of artistic production. To be sure, Wölfflin is less concerned than Riegl—though by no means unconcerned—with the material and technical conditions of production. Yet, though Louis Althusser has contended that Marxism is not a formalism, Wölfflin's formalism is still, if I may use names loosely for a moment, a rarefied or Hegelian brand of Marxism.

That an art history without names should at the same time amount to an aesthetics of production should no longer startle us. We have grown used to answering the question "What is an author?" with Michel Foucault's response, "What matter who's speaking?" "Art is a work not of man but of that which produces it (and this producer is not a subject centered in its creation, it is an element in a situation or a system)." This is not Wölfflin, of course—though it almost could be—but a contemporary Frenchman, Pierre Macherey (*Pour une théorie* 84). Nor, obviously, is this rejoinder Wölfflin, though again the sentiments move in territory that Wölfflin staked out:

A text puts texts in relation to one another and not an author and a reader assimilated to some referents: here the language-text is in such relation to the emitter of the text that his person, his life-his death, his biography, are indifferent: the emitter is present in the text by his very absence, but [here at last is the critique of Macherey] *it is not the disappearance of the subject that is manifested in the text, it is the disappearance of the nondialectical opposition subject-object*, and it is through this dialectic at work that the text performs its slippage.[21]

Finally, we have neither Wölfflin nor a French critic but Hegel, commenting once more on creators and on the Creator:

No man is satisfied with his mere selfhood; self is active, and this activity is to objectify the self, to give it reality, existence. In a further, more concrete specification, this activity of the concept is instinct. Every satisfaction is this process of suspending subjectivity and of positing this inner, this subjective quality equally as something external, objective, real, of producing the unity of the merely subjective and the merely objective, of stripping them of their onesidedness. (*Werke* 17: 526, from the 1827 revision of the *Lectures on the Philosophy of Religion*)

This is, to be sure, far from the only place where modern polemics sound like nothing more than a series of footnotes to Hegel. And that is why I should like to return to Wölfflin, whose research, lying almost precisely halfway between the abstract speculations of the philosopher and the equally abstract debates of the critics, gives these abstractions a concrete meaning.

Works of art participate in history because they make history. They make history—as Macherey also argues, using, like Wölfflin, an insistently bivalent logic—because they are intrinsically in flux. "Form is act" because artistic shaping both grows out of and reflects the labor of creation. This insight into the artistic process, and not the mere formalism of the product, is the true link between Wölfflin and the school of

Fiedler and Hildebrand, and it inspires the fascination with the physical aspects of graphic technique that so distinguishes *The Art of Albrecht Dürer*. Each work of art moves toward its center—what we feel, not necessarily what we measure, as its center (and here the debates about the vanishing point in *Las Meninas* can be reopened)[22]—where the expressive, existential force (*Kraft*) is concentrated that carries it beyond a merely inertial objectification (*Stoff*) of essence. This internal movement of the work is the "rhythm" that Wölfflin often evokes and that in appreciative art criticism so often degenerates into a merely formal category. But Wölfflin's own five paired categories of the understanding are tools for interpreting the meaning of the artistic act and never a merely formal or analytic apparatus. There is no magic about the number five; we may feel that more or fewer would be preferable. But I know of no author who endeavors so consistently and directly to explore the *work* performed by what all Western languages agree in calling the work of art.

CHAPTER 3

What's in a Text?

FOR AT LEAST a decade, from, say, 1965 to 1975, Romantic studies were the cutting edge of literary criticism in this country. The mantle has since passed to the Renaissance, and to nineteenth-century fiction. If Romanticism also continued through the 1980's to influence directions of thought generally, that was mostly due to two very different thinkers, Paul de Man and Jerome J. McGann. McGann's project of self-definition is contained in a central suite of volumes beginning with *The Romantic Ideology* (*RI*) and *A Critique of Modern Textual Criticism* (*CMTC*), both published in 1983, and continued with *The Beauty of Inflections* (*BI*, 1985), *Social Values and Poetic Acts* (*SV*, 1988), and *Towards a Literature of Knowledge* (*TLK*, 1989). (Also cited are *Black Riders* [*BR*, 1993] and the collection edited by McGann, *Textual Criticism and Literary Interpretation* [*TCLI*, 1985].) In them we can see the maturity of a Marxist critical orientation quite distinct from the cultural studies of a Fredric Jameson or an Edward Said. The following pages attempt to determine the essence of McGann's many seminal contributions.

That is not easy to do, for McGann's work resists summation. His principles of active, engaged writing demand an adjustment and response to varied situations and contexts. The centered self and the interpreter's self-analysis are not for him. Even his first book, *Fiery Dust* (1968), though a composed study of Byron's self-fashioning, "deliberately cultivate[s] a variety of critical approaches" (viii); *Swinburne* (1972) is an elegant, multiperspectival critical dialogue; *Don Juan in Context* (1976) programmatically proliferates contexts; and the subsequent critical books all have been in effect collections of essays, with increasingly frequent and resourceful recourse to dialogue forms.[1] The range in *Social Values* is particularly daunting. In support of general theoretical reflection of a kind he has seldom previously undertaken, McGann adds to his staple nineteenth-century repertoire (here represented chiefly by Blake, Kant, and Arnold) the Bible, the Greeks (Herodotus, Aeschylus, Plato), Pound and contemporary poets, and even *Ulysses*. *Social Values* and *The Beauty of Inflections* encompass extended close readings of poems in the context of contemporary history and social currents (among them a particularly impressive revaluation of *The Charge of the Light Brigade*); suggestions for new approaches to familiar poems (including the well-known essays on Keats and on the historically layered textual presentation of *The Rime of the Ancient Mariner*); career surveys of canonical and neglected authors (George Crabbe, Christina Rossetti, and a rich overview of the interpenetration of life and history in Byron's poems, followed in recent years by a series of exhilarating essays on women poets of the nineteenth and twentieth centuries); textual and bibliographical essays (including a fine one on the intellectual currents behind the format of Blake's *Book of Urizen*); a thematic essay ("Rome and Its Romantic Significance," which deals persuasively with Goethe, Mme. de Staël, and Stendhal, along with Byron); critical accounts of other theorists (Cleanth Brooks, de Man, J. Hillis Miller, Stanley Fish, M. M. Bakhtin, Jürgen Habermas); defenses of poetry; and even a brief set of aphorisms ("Theses on the Philosophy of Criticism," *BI* 343–44).

Questions and concerns overlap and diverge to project a mind ever alert to opportunities (as well as to what prior critics have said), never closed in upon itself. The doctrinal center lies in Marxism, but the spirit—the capaciousness, the generous response, the claims for the preeminence of literature as a vehicle for distilling and communicating social forces, the sense of the past as a varied resource that can guide the present toward the future, the rejection of disengaged hermeneutics, and even the love-hate relationship toward reductive proverbs and inevitably premature totalizations (see *SV* 105–6)—seems to me closer to Goethe. Militant humanists both, Goethe and Marx have much in common—as do Goethe and Byron—but not enough to make Marxist doctrine and Goethean spirit easily reconcilable.[2] McGann encourages us to seek out the identifying divisions, or "rifts," in poets and critics alike: "The entire *work* is never equal to itself—it is always 'incommensurate' "

(*TLK* x). It is the split between Marxism and Goethean humanisms that, for me, gives his work its distinctive profile and makes it hardest to sum up.

Contradictions energize. McGann values history for its contrasts: we need to salvage the past as ballast to the present. Poetry presents tensions, and does so "as a challenge . . . and not simply as a picture to be observed" (*SV* 9). Under poetic totalizations, he contends, lie the incommensurate particulars that "in fact *make (and/or have made) a difference*" (*SV* 128). Consequently, "sociohistorical criticism . . . holds that art imitates not merely the 'fact' and the 'ideal,' but also the dynamic relation which operates between the two . . . [and it] both assumes and seeks to display the *determinate* character of this dynamic relation" (*SV* 128).

McGann is too committed to change to be comfortable reducing his beliefs to formulas.[3] That is surely why he elsewhere avoids the propositional mode that prevails in much of *Social Values* and why his theorizing can seem frustrating. His energy and Byronic flexibility seem to entail a certain slippage in the terms. By lining up the right excerpts, you can make McGann seem to be chasing his own tail. "Of all forms of communication, the poetic alone entails the *whole* of what is true" (*SV* 92). That whole is not a Wordsworthian intuition, or "spot of time," but rather a Poundian compendium (*SV* 52). Totalization must not be idealized, as it is in the aesthetics of Kant and Coleridge, for "any great historical product . . . is a work of transhistorical rather than so-called universal significance" (*BI* 187). Hence McGann experiments in one essay with the notion of a "Mastercode" or "general fact" of a "political and social" nature (*SV* 75) that "define[s] the poem's communication system" and "establish[es] the poem's particular set of sociohistorical interests and engagements" (*SV* 77). A typically tactical formulation (the essay's full title is "Poetic Ideology and Nonnormative Truth: To the Marxists"), McGann's version of a Mastercode can serve as an alternative to the "master code" (a "theme or 'inner essence,'" a "hidden master narrative") that Jameson reluctantly rejects (*The Political Unconscious* 28). From totalizing or at least transhistorical, the Mastercode thus migrates toward the poem's particular situation—its spot of time— such as (here) the moment of composition of Juvenal's satires. "The *whole* of what is true" has shed its extensive, "transhistorical . . . significance" to acquire a punctual intensity.

McGann's turn from totality to particularity reproduces a discussion that finds Platonic truth to be not Ideas but "a pursuit and an eventuality" (*SV* 28). Ideology—if I set the accents right on some evasive passages—is not just the "permanent and originary meaning" that the Bible "struggle[s]" to "deploy" (*SV* 57), but also "a matrix of historical particularities" on behalf of which Tennyson undertakes "a quest and polemic" (*BI* 182), consequently a kind of "performativity" that "poetic performativity overtakes" as it "strives to thicken and realize the entire communicative field" (*SV* 91), and thus at its nether end the fugitive "illusions" and "ghostly shapes" that literature "dispel[s]" (*SV* 107). What matters throughout is not the position but the resistance to fixity. So, finally, "meaning in poetry is neither the ideology of the poem nor the ideology of the critic; it is the process in which those ideologies have found their existence and expression" (*BI* 10).

Such prose neither can nor wants to stand still. The occasional declarative passages are both inert and disorienting:

This emphasis upon the determinate *is* fundamental if "what is" *is* to stand in a natural or scientific relation to "what should be." But because knowledge *is* a project rather than a possession, it falls short of a complete grasp of its objects. The determinate relation between "what is" and "what should be" *is* what Shelley had in mind when he spoke of "something longed for, never seen." The determinate *is*—in the alternative sense of that word—what exists by acts of determination. Knowledge as a project *is* knowledge grounded in a platonic Eros, which *is* in the end both determined and determinative, in every sense of those two terms. Kant's "categorical imperative" *is* an analogous concept, though it seems to me that subsequent readers of Kant have misleadingly emphasized the categorical rather than the imperative salient in his thought.[4]

Yet even passages intended to declare settled convictions enact the slippage they are meant to propound. We see in them what McGann terms the hermeneutic pseudo-dialectic of object and subject (or of Realism and Romanticism), whose hegemony screens out the "third world" of the voiceless and the invisible (*SV* 63–64), and we are driven to intuit in "literary work (poetry and philology)" "a network constructed to maximize contradictions and incommensurability, . . . mark[ing] an antithesis to forms of normativity and dominance" (*SV* 55–56). De Man's work is for him the chief case in point: by pitting nature against mind in order to argue that the poetic is the only realm where the two fuse, de Man (in McGann's account) erects a false dichotomy, leading to a false reconciliation that hides the way literature "deploy[s] value" as "a concrete social institution" (*SV* 102–3). Standing Hegel on his feet, McGann argues against merely conceptual resolutions that subsume "facts" under "interpretations," and in favor of human experience as "*events*— specific and worlded engagements in which meaning is rendered and used" (*SV* 72). A literary work is "a dynamic event in human experience"; poems are "structures of social energy" (*BI* 108, 128).

*   *   *

It's a game of both ends against the middle. That doesn't always appear in the formulations as such, for not infrequently the treatment of tension or contradiction can verge on Cleanth Brooks's cohesive irony or on Coleridge's symbolic "translucence of the Special in the Individual or of the General in the Especial or of the Universal in the General" (Coleridge, *Statesman's Manual* 30). But the logic of the argument, reinforced by the slipperiness (or dynamic urgency, or temporality) of the terms, saves McGann from the placid center and underwrites his claim that literature is "performative," not "representational" (*SV* viii). "The Israel of Genesis is an island in a greater world, and the more it insists that it is the center of that world, the more it gives us glimpses of the actual, the whole, the objective truth. . . . Literary work is the art of multiplicities and minute particulars, the science of *un*buildings: one law for the lion and the ox *is* oppression" (*SV* 230). He prefers unpredictable debate to security and determination.

McGann drives, then, in two directions. One is toward a broadening reflection on what he likes to call "the meanings of the meanings." The other is toward an ever more precise account of texts, their production, and the factors that condition composition and publication. Arguing against New Critics and their poststructuralist avatars, McGann insists that a "work" is more than a "text," for he is interested both in the work that poems accomplish and in the work that goes into generating them. Ideology critique and textual criticism are convenient names for the two directions; future and past are the vectors that he wants to rescue from the stasis of momentary or eternal presence. (One section of *Social Values* is called "Literature and the Future of History." It includes the visionary teleology of "The Third World of Criticism," which contends that "in writing what amounts to an imaginative history of the present, every poem thereby constructs a past and a set of possible futures" [*SV* 229], encompassing insights into events after its composition.) The unacceptable alternative, he writes in his conclusion, would be to imagine literature "as occupying a world elsewhere, . . . a 'poetic' space redeemed from time and the agencies of loss" (*SV* 246). Even Genesis shows us— not through its doctrines, to be sure, but through the meanings of its meanings—that we must "relinquish an imperial imagination."

* * *

> Three times the concentred self takes hold, three times
> The thrice concentred self, having possessed

> The object, grips it in savage scrutiny,
> Once to make captive, once to subjugate
> Or yield to subjugation, once to proclaim
> The meaning of the capture, this hard prize,
> Fully made, fully apparent, fully found.
>   (Wallace Stevens, *Credences of Summer*, lines 99–105)

It is suspicious that *The Beauty of Inflections* takes its title from that great visionary of the central imagination, Wallace Stevens. Decentering poetry may be harder than McGann dreams. Between meanings and the meaning of meanings, between textual criticism and the critique thereof, lies at best a very fine line. The more we scrutinize McGann's two moments, the ideological and the material, the more we realize that their core is textual after all. This is not to go back on his achievements: McGann's writings make it impossible to return to the negative idealizations of "the poem itself" or to confuse Stevens's problematic *Credences of Summer* with a positive creed. But it remains important to reaffirm the dialectical productivity of poetry in creating the possibility of the very critique that McGann undertakes.

What's in a poem? McGann argued lucidly in *A Critique of Modern Textual Criticism* that poems are not isolated products of the solitary imagination. Conditions of production and reception are both fundamental to what Habermas calls the communicative act. Scholars should abandon the notion that the author's manuscript, prior to editorial intervention, preserves the purest and truest state of a work, for "the fully authoritative text is always one that has been socially produced" (*CMTC* 75).[5] Hence "the study of texts is fundamental and primary" (*SV* 99) in order "to restore the connection . . . between 'intrinsic' and 'extrinsic' literary investigations, between hermeneutics and scholarship, *verstehen* and *erklären*" (*SV* 16). In the conjoint critique of de Man and Fish (*SV* 95–114), both are taken to propound self-enclosed systems, the former's exclusively intrinsic, the latter's exclusively extrinsic. Restoring connections means testing the poem's opening to the world. "The set of ideological formations imbedded in the poem at its historical inception will always remain part of the work's fixed dialectical pole with which the moving pole of the reader interacts" (*RI* 157).

The nature of the work's embedding needs to be interrogated here, together with the curious fixity of the dialectical pole. What puts meaning into the poem? The long Keats essay in *Social Values* relates textual variants to the specific media of publication of several poems as elements of Keats's communicative situation. It argues that to know what Keats meant we must know what was meant by those who designed and published his books and the journals where his poems appeared, and it has been rightly influential in counteracting both the intrinsic philosophical allegories of critics of consciousness such as Earl Wasserman and Geoffrey Hartman and the extrinsic social and class allegories of critics such as Walter Benjamin and Terry Eagleton. But in the case of someone like Keats, how do we distinguish significant choice from contingent opportunity? Did Keats intend the publishing options which he used? To what extent are they part of the meaning of his meaning? The essay has been emphatically attacked for neglecting to face these questions (see Paul Fry, "History, Existence, and 'To Autumn'"). But it does face them implicitly, for Donne's metaphor of fixed and moving poles suggests where McGann will be seen to stand: the energy to encompass and circumscribe its worldly engagements comes from the work, not from the world.

In a notable essay inspired and praised by McGann, Marjorie Levinson has claimed that " 'Tintern Abbey' finally represents mind . . . as a barricade to resist the violence of historical change and contradiction" (*Wordsworth's Great Period Poems* 53). How does the moving, extrinsic, worldly pole get attached to the fixed dialectical pole (the resistive barricade) of the text? To a large degree by conjectural inference: Levinson's essay bristles with such formulations as "to a man of Wordsworth's experience and inclination, Tintern Abbey would have represented"

(32), "a poet given to historical perspectives could not but remark" (32), "he must have felt" (34), "the spoiled ruin would have figured" (35), and "surely" (36). The moving pole of the reader, indeed. Yet Levinson shows the spirit of McGann when she rescues the argument from circularity by means of a textual sensitivity that, from within the poems, "bring[s] out . . . the aura of the enclosure in Wordsworth's authorial ideology" (33). The meanings of the meanings are the authorial ideology as its aura reaches out beyond the letter of the text.

The fixed pole of authorial ideology is the firm foot of McGann's readings, as of Levinson's. As "a social event," "every poem" may well entail a "dialectical relation" between intention ("the author's expressed decisions and purposes") and reception ("the critical reactions of the poem's various readers") (BI 24). Yet our access to "the aesthetic domain which Cockney verse attempted to conquer" is "not merely the abstract *characteristics*, but the felt *qualities* of its poetic structure" (BI 28). The word that really should have been emphasized here is "felt." Textual intuitions govern our adjustments of text to context—ours and even McGann's. Thus, in the midst of contending that we need to consider the different publication formats of *Don Juan* in order to appreciate the poem's significance, he says, "The fact that Byron's *Don Juan* should have called out these two sorts of edition is one sign of its creative power" (BI 121). The text's power, in other words, precedes the editions and channels their impact.

In the Mastercodes essay, McGann insists that reception defines the crucial extrinsic code, which must not be neglected: "That initial documentary situation highlights, by its concrete and positive differentials, the fact that later texts are equally marked, at the level of production, by specific ideological interests" (SV 83). Yet it turns out that the "horizon of critical values" is never out of sight; "In fact, *of course*, the poem *always has* been read within that context" (SV 85; McGann emphasizes only "has"). In repeatedly denouncing "the modern fashion of referring to poems as 'texts' " (BI 121), precisely in order to draw attention to their "many different textual constitutions" (BI 121), McGann commits a telltale terminological contamination. Much as he would like to pit intrinsic factors against extrinsic ones, the crucial dialectic remains intratextual.[6] What's in the poem is what's in the text, either as meaning, or as implication, aura, the meaning of the meaning. Reception history paves the way toward "a 'close' linguistic reading" through which "the poem's more localized and particular details might be reimagined" ("Literary History" 232). Situations may exist where the textual constitutions and the reception history of a poem contribute essential meanings at odds with the text, but I don't think that McGann ever exhibits any. Indeed, I don't think that, deep down, he even *wants* to.[7]

The fate of polarities in McGann is to be undermined. That's what gives them (like his prose) their flux and their energy. By his own yardstick, he becomes a critical thinker at the moment when his categories suspect themselves. I will examine a strong essay where the reversal is explicit, and then, approaching my conclusion, a weak essay where it is shunned. (The weaker, by the way, is the more self-revealing.) Explicit dialectic guards appearances, and the polarized categories that are transcended nevertheless remain as apparitional—the term is McGann's—structures with an illusion of substance. Hence the strong essay is incomplete, whereas the tottering categories of the weak essay provoke more forthright response. McGann is an artist of what the Italian philosopher Gianni Vattimo has come to call "weak thought." Like some of the authors he most admires, such as Herodotus and Montaigne, his writing is more than the sum of its parts, more suggestive by moments than rhetorically complete. And its true character lies in the confrontations that it evades. Thus it will take me back, at the last, to Stevens and to Goethe—and to Wordsworth.

* * *

"Some Forms of Critical Discourse" (*SV* 132–51) embodies McGann's yearnings for discontinuity. Taking off from an essay by Hayden White, McGann proposes some alternatives to the essay form that prevails among literary critics. (McGann characterizes the form he is questioning—since the text matters here—"as a lecture or, more normatively, as an essay or monograph" [*SV* 135]. His book in fact contains six lectures— the first five numbered chapters and the last—surrounding five "more detailed and scholastically rigorous" chapters that "execute shifts in the formal continuities of the book" [*SV* ix].) Essays are narrative and hermeneutic, and hence discourage "true criticism," which "entails a self-conscious response to certain social and historical factors" (*SV* 149). By disrupting the link of mind to mind, we can rupture the illusory timelessness of poetic truth so as to gain a fuller appreciation of poetic acts.

Here we have to undertake some textual criticism. When the essay (and it is an essay) was originally published, McGann identified four "nonnarrative forms." These are the hypothetical, the practical or injunctive, the array, and the dialectic, and they are exemplified respectively by the scientific paper, by "a book like Euclid's *Elements*, or any cookbook," by the bibliography (McGann's substitute for the historical annals that White discusses), and by Montaigne's—yes—essays.[8] Now, it is virtually a reflex of modern critical rhetoric that any of these forms actually ought to be decoded narratively.[9] I suspect that is the reason why McGann drops reference to the first two forms in the *Social Values* text. Deep down, he knows that what matters is the internal workings of the particular text, not the external format. Formal nonnarrativity is merely an appearance; what really counts is the spirit within: "The *apparition* of such forms is not, however, a guarantee that the discourse will in fact be critical, only that it will exhibit the form of criticism."[10] Almost at the end, then, McGann adduces an "essay" of Hartman's, "The Interpreter: A Self-Analysis," as an almost successful critical and dialogic project. The essay's failure may be that it is "formally narrativized" as McGann claims (*SV* 150), but more likely the failure is rhetorical, as his footnoted evidence demonstrates (*SV* 262 n. 16). After all, the same "fundamental question . . . must [be] put to every form of ideological discourse," namely, "How much genuine self-criticism does a scholar's or an ideologue's work seek after and encourage?" (*SV* 150). First and last, it is the spirit and the "scholarly climate" (*SV* 151) that matter, and the forms are at most only conducive to the true aims. Formalism is not ideological criticism, and the revised version that appears in *Social Values* retreats in full self-awareness from the formalist illusion that seems to have prompted the essay initially.[11]

"Some Forms of Critical Discourse" ends by "speculat[ing] on the possibility that a critical edition . . . is now being assembled somewhere which will induce a major shift in scholarly understanding" (*SV* 151). Two essays later comes the opportunity which that conclusion had seemed to forecast. "*Ulysses* as a Postmodern Work" (*SV* 173–94) reviews the new critical edition of Joyce's novel by Hans Walter Gabler. Here McGann erects the editor into a hero much as earlier textual critics idealize the author. The modernist *Ulysses*, he tells us, was a private and elitist work, "finished and monumental," "a limited edition and supported by subscriptions of the literati."[12] The postmodern *Ulysses* is a technological book and a process text. The editor's job is to lay bare the productive forces by determining the various layers of the text. Following several Continental precedents—McGann mentions editions of Friedrich Hölderlin, Kafka, Flaubert, Friedrich Klopstock, and Proust—Gabler has produced the first such edition in English.

To my mind this is the weakest of all McGann's essays, partly because the information is defective. The notion of Klopstock—the arch-sentimental author of the mid-eighteenth century biblical epic, *Der Messias*—as postmodernist poet is untenable. And the prescription for *Ulysses* combines two ideals, (hydrologic) flux and (geologic) layering, whose compatibility is open to serious question. In particular, the notorious Frankfurt edition of Hölderlin, which aroused a storm of public debate on the politics of editing, is precisely an attempt to produce an image of continual change in order to counter the layered text (based on a notion of determinate compositional process in stages) in the monumental Stuttgart edition that preceded it. Elsewhere McGann says that we live amid "an indeterminate flux of conflicted and competing possibilities" (*SV* 246). Here, by contrast, he claims that the number of forms of a given text "will always be a small number *in actual fact*" (*SV* 182) and that "unstable 'texts'—texts that are 'in process' or 'indeterminate'— always appear in material forms that are as determinate as the most 'stable' text one might want or imagine" (*SV* 186). Popular ballads are a counterinstance to the first claim, Verdi's operas to the second.[13] As so often in McGann, the polarities—modern versus postmodern, stable versus indeterminate—won't work. Where poetic movement is the concern, textual fixation comes to seem a regression, or a bulwark.

A bulwark against what? I find it curious that in listing Continental predecessors and in calling Gabler's *Ulysses* "the first English-language work to illustrate these new European lines" (*SV* 186), McGann neglects a well-established project closer to home, the Cornell Wordsworth edition. The omission is not in itself a statement, since McGann is a known admirer of the Cornell text. But it calls attention to his general slighting of Wordsworth, and that is significant. Chapter 8 of *The Romantic Ideology* presents Wordsworth as a representative of Romantic evasion and false consciousness. "Wordsworth's poetry elides history," he writes, as if the three poems discussed (*The Ruined Cottage, Tintern Abbey*, and the Immortality Ode) represented all that Wordsworth had to say (*RI* 91).[14]

Wordsworth also figures in the conclusion to *The Beauty of Inflections* as the exemplar of Romantic displacement (McGann's term for sublimation, viewed negatively), to be admired for the "resistances . . . dissatisfactions and yearnings" (*BI* 337) that hedge in his utopian individualism and psychologism. Another essay depreciates Wordsworth in order to praise Crabbe. Quantitatively, McGann's selections display an overwhelming preference for narrative poetry—for ballads or ballad-like lyrics. Lyric and reflective moments—the Wordsworthian inwardness—are kept on the margins or out of sight.

To read Wordsworthian displacement "as an invitation to substitute interiorized spiritual values for social ones is, in my view, a travesty of Wordsworth's work" (*BI* 340). I agree with the judgment here, but not with the terms. How does one distinguish interiorized spiritual values from social ones? Is not the lesson that we should draw from McGann's searchingly honest investigations that social values *are* spiritual, that the interior and the exterior are connected, that interpretation *is* critique, that reaction is a form of action, that thinkers are laborers, and that works work? The maker of the phrase, "the beauty of inflections," made other phrases that link up with it: "There is nothing beautiful in life except life." "It is life that we are trying to get at in poetry." "Art, broadly, is the form of life or the sound or color of life. Considered as form (in the abstract) it is often indistinguishable from life itself" (Stevens, "Adagia," 162, 158). McGann likes to present himself in an antithetical or polemical Blakean stance. But the separation of life from thought, or of the narrative from the reflective, is an unreflected abstraction. It is the ideological moment exposed through McGann's endeavors.[15]

Stanley Fish and others have argued that theories have no consequences.[16] That holds for abstract theories and intended consequences. A case in point would be "The Anachronism of George Crabbe" in *The Beauty of Inflections* 294–312. Here McGann describes the formal characteristics of Crabbe's poetry, which is additive, nontotalizing, nonredemptive, empiricist, and scientific—thereby, he contends, challenging idealist illusions that the Romantics share with the Augustans. To see that the conclusions do not follow simply from the abstract pattern, you need only consider John Clare, to whom all of these terms apply equally well, but who was an extreme Wordsworthian individualist.

Forms indeed do not have a life of their own, apart from the spirit that lives in their concrete embodiments. While consequences are all about us, they arise from complex insights, not from mere categories or denominations. In a writer such as Blake, absence "rises up before us . . . as objectivity and otherness" (*TLK* 36); without confidently knowing what we see, we can still advance toward knowledge through imagining what we do not see. The projected equivalence of literature and knowledge arises from literature's special power to subvert theories. Texts retain a richness always in advance of our invariably partial truths.

Despite itself, and through its failure to confront adequately the Romantic poet who should be central to it, McGann's work reveals the binding of form and content, substance and style, (hermeneutic) meaning and (ideological) meaning of meaning. Those interpenetrations are the Goethean essence of the totalizing ideal that McGann can never bring himself to renounce. He presents it in Lukácsian-sounding formulations such as "the critical ideal must be a totalizing one, for literary 'works' *continue* to live and move and have their being" (*SV* 125). But the polemical "must be" proves in practice to be an empathic "is"—a universal fact of our relation to the world:

For merely eyeing a thing is no help. Every look turns into a consideration, every consideration into a contemplation, every contemplation into a connection, and so it can be said that we always theorize with every attentive glance at the world. But to do and undertake this with consciousness, with self-knowledge, with freedom, and, to use a daring expression, with irony requires such a skill, if the abstraction that we fear is to become harmless and the desired result is to be alive and useful. (Goethe, *Zur Farbenlehre*, "Vorwort," *Werke* 21: 15)

Scratch the dialectician and you find the harmonizer. In Hugh Kenner's *The Pound Era*, "expository form . . . rhyme[s] with the complexities of its subjects" (*SV* ix). Arnold's "Sohrab and Rustum" is "a polyglottal text moaning round with many voices" (*SV* 89), but the effect is more a polyphony than a cacophony: "Arnold's book [*Poems* 1853] says one thing *and* (not *but*) means another" (*SV* 86). There is a "consonance between [Allen Tate's] interpretation of the Dickinson poem and his ignorance of its textual problems" (*BI* 130). "Tennyson's verse style and form exhibit a genuine congruence and symmetry with his methods of production" (*BI* 178). It is not by chance that one of the most brilliant of the essays demonstrates homologies among Don Juan's life, Byron's life, and the history of the French Revolution. Like the Kant whom he criticizes, McGann finally has a correspondence notion of truth: "That the poem should have been transmitted and finally published in this way is in perfect keeping with every other aspect of its text and context" (*BI* 101).

And in practice, the text remains *primus inter pares*. For, scratch the ideologist and you find the stylistician. If for McGann "the poem is a social act" (*BI* 21), it acts *as a poem*, and that means verbally, or, in the most extended of McGann's notions of the terms, as a text. That isn't always what McGann says, but I don't think he speaks clearly, consistently, or in his own best interest when he asserts that "it is not 'texts' which act in the world, it is the men and women who formulate and deploy those texts and who have assented to the textualization of their lives" (*SV* 16). For many of his greatest triumphs as a commentator are actually with words. His mastery lies in both the knowledge of and the feeling for words, inseparably mixed: the knowledge that Dickinson's plural "Horses Heads" indicates a funeral procession, not a bridal journey; the feel for the resonance of the word "world-wind" in a variant text of Keats's Paolo and Francesca sonnet; the knowing grasp of iconographic connotation in the wonderful reading of *The Charge of the Light Brigade*; the stylistic intuition to recognize that "bassoon" and "lighthouse" are anachronistically modern terms in *The Rime of the Ancient Mariner*—the crucial detail in McGann's historicizing account of that poem. Because he knows how saturated our languages are with meanings, with social values, and with history, McGann regularly and powerfully makes the totality of poetic acts depend on such punctual responses.

Like virtually all the poets with whom he has identified himself particularly, McGann is a connoisseur. His admiration goes out to the living world of incommensurates that are found on the textured surface of things. He is a great connoisseur because his tact is controlled by vast and exact knowledge and empowered by ideological sophistication. He knows how to make the precise details that act on him count for us as well. As editor and as critic, he takes his mission to be saving the past. Distinctions and recognitions go hand in hand as we channel past energies toward the future. "Thus," concludes the most theoretical of the essays in the earlier book, "in our differences do we learn about, and create, a community" (*BI* 132). On the one hand, as McGann has written more recently, the contexts in which we operate are entailed on us historically: "For human beings, to enter the world is to enter language—a world that is always-changing but ever-determinate and concrete, and a world no *one* ever made or could have made" (*BR* 140). Yet on the other hand the life world is one crucially begotten by our poets: "It is a (social) world made by (and discovered as) language, through unceasing acts of textual intercourse" (*BR* 140). Unlike the Renaissance New Historicists whom I discuss at the end of my chapter on Taine, McGann (together with Levinson, David Simpson, and a host of younger Romanticists) finds the resources to save the power of the word. What's in a text is the social activism of its temporality.

PART III

Texts and Periods

CHAPTER 4

Deconstruction and Enlightenment

Whither wander you?
  —Shakespeare, *A Midsummer Night's Dream*

Whither wander we (*Kuda zh nam plyt'*)?
  —Pushkin, *Osen'*

ROMANTICISTS HAVE BEEN the main disseminators of the various French theoretical modes in this country. American scholars consequently tend to link the two, as Jerome Christensen has done with deconstruction in an essay subtitled "The Apostasy of Criticism": "The deconstructive method makes a neat fit with the Coleridgean text—a fit so neat as to suggest a propriety for deconstruction in Coleridge" (771). This Romantic-deconstructive organism is our apostasy: "The critic is always the author of the text he reads . . . : this state of affairs is not necessarily so, but it has ever been so since Coleridge." Christensen, the critic, authored this text (781); Coleridge as the arch-deconstructor is a typically American rewriting of history.

First, a reminder. Jacques Derrida made his reputation with a book on Rousseau. Gilles Deleuze began with books on Kant, Hume, and Spinoza. Michel Foucault's thesis was on Kant, Michel Serres's on Leibniz. Roland Barthes's renown dates from his book on Racine—a neoclassicist, marginally an Enlightenment figure, certainly no Romantic. One could go back, to Claude Lévi-Strauss's debt to Rousseau, to Gaston Bachelard's beginnings as a critic of eighteenth-century science. And one could extend the list: Kant is seminal for Jacques Lacan and Jean-François Lyotard, Casanova for François Roustang. Kant and Rousseau straddle the eras but hardly the centuries; the impulse for all these theorists comes from Enlightenment and eighteenth-century authors.

Second, a reflection. To apply an Enlightenment model to a Romantic text is hard work. Most American deconstructionists—Geoffrey Hartman is the notable exception—work hard, even laboriously, at disrupting their exemplary texts. A favorite term is aporia, the pathlessness of a self-canceling argument. Reason against reason. Serious business; exhilarating, heady, even dizzy stuff.[1]

Eighteenth-century texts, large or small, are loose and baggy. They meander of their own accord, succeeding at picaresque expansiveness, failing at tragic concentration. Deconstruction comes naturally to them. Too easily, in fact. Many areas of eighteenth-century criticism are still caught up in the hard task of trying to structure them, logically, organically. I propose that we unbend. We may remember some things about the eighteenth century that we had forgotten, and learn some things about critical theory at the same time.

Third, an example. One doesn't prove anything, but it's all I have space for. Not even for one: there's so much to say about how Thomas Parnell's *A Night-Piece on Death* undoes its premises. Illogic is ubiquitous—if we are taken in by Pope's "Whatever is, is right," we are destined to be taken aback by another, equally memorable locus, "What's wrong is wrong, wherever it be done" (Pope, *Sober Advice from Horace* 78)—the trick is to find what is born of reason's collapse. *A Night-Piece on Death*, like so many texts, "is a falling away from itself that is a reading of itself, falling to know its constitution, falling to know the course of its descent—a narcissism providentially flawed by the apostasis that motivates a theoretically endless tracking." Christensen says this of the margins that unravel the *Biographia Literaria* (777), but Parnell says it too, plain as day, at the climax of *A Hymn on Contentment:*

> Go search among your idle Dreams [narcissism],
> Your busie or your vain Extreams [falling away from itself];
> And find a *Life* of equal Bliss [providentially flawed apostasis,
>   unless you can live up to your dreams],
> Or own the *next* begun in *this* [theoretically endless tracking].

Not convincing? You think celestial wisdom calms Parnell's mind too easily?

Easy does it. Tetrameters jog so nicely. That "or own" could be a consequence (own = acknowledge), or it could be a threat (own = confess). Not to worry. Tetrameters offer "a readier Path" (*Night-Piece*, like all unidentified quotes), a fallen wisdom ("Where Wisdom's surely taught *below*"—"surely," is that for certain?), adapted to night's dim vision, a "blinded insight" (Christensen 778; Parnell has, "That Steeple guides thy doubtful sight"). Colloquy leads to conviction, with the tune called by internal and external voices, bells, even croaks. But salvation can't be colloquial. The style can't free itself from quiet tropes, figures, sound effects, heightenings (note the Latinism "aspire"). The "deep . . . Sky," the "nether Crescent," "the spangled Show [that] / Descends to meet our Eyes below"—everything heaves and swells with a bad faith that looks up indirectly or with a pretense of looking down. Fuzzy is about the best you could say of Parnell's dialectic. The first two paragraphs contrast as indoors to outdoors, sky to earth, artificial to natural illumination. But what's the difference? One is "blue," the other "Azure." One light trembles, the other gleams lividly. One is "endless View," the other "from the View retire[s]." Surely, "surely," treading the path of death is not the clearest road to go. Is it, indeed, the path of death, or "the path of death"—the experience of death itself ("Death's but a Path that must be trod"—but is this utterance, or imaginary utterance, the content of the wisdom, or just the way to get there?), or a guided tour of the premises ("And think, as softly-sad you tread / Above the venerable Dead")? Confusion heaped on confusion. A "crumbled Ground" for "glancing Thought," if ever there was. Revelation comes—is that really how Parnell thinks "Wisdom's . . . taught *below*"?—but it doesn't help much. "The bursting earth unveils"—what?—"the Shades." "I hear a *Voice*," he says . . . "Methinks." Surely, "surely," this hesitancy isn't how wisdom teaches, even "from among the Bones."

So you get nowhere? Not quite. Not at all. By the end, Parnell is standing on his head, looking up at the earth ("tow'r away") instead of down at the sky. From the scholastic prison he turned to nightlife; now from the earthly prison (whose "Lamps" are stars, both like and unlike the beginning) he turns to "the Blaze of Day." Those sour scholastic books "widely stray," but, now, "See the glad Scene unfolding wide." How did we get here?

How did we get here? That's the question to be asked by a speculative criticism. Logic abandons us, but something takes us along. Parnell's flow starts punningly, with "pore" and "dies" (i.e., dyes), gingerly with "glide," but soon water is all about him. Flow is an advantage tetrameters possess over pentameters, so much more inclined to turn back on themselves. But then flow swells into a tempest vexing Parnell's decreation, "the rough Rage of swelling Seas." Flux becomes the realm of death, "flowing sable Stoles, / Deep pendant Cypress." And of release: "Spring forth to greet the glitt'ring Sun."

The image washes out the conceptual ground until "earth" seems a waste ("A few, and evil Years"). Yet isn't that natural for a cemetery, a "Charnel House" bathed "with Dew"? *Night-Thoughts* will do, so will *The Grave*, but *A Night-Piece on Death* is too much of a bad thing, one darkness canceling out the other. So, from out the logical collapse, the image takes charge, transforming itself as it goes. Self-identity, Johann Gottlieb Fichte's *A = A*, is the enabling fiction of Romanticism; from Parnell, by contrast, we get a moving picture. To "mingle with the Blaze of Day" is to experience aporia as consolation—none too easy a liberation after all. Deconstruction and the other poststructuralisms—for us modes melt together, mingling in the blaze from the East, that at a nearer, Parisian view, seems irreconcilable—are change, flow, overthrow. Deconstruction is death, is life, is history. It is the most natural, colloquial substratum of thought, not to be wondered at, though the Romantics bravely tried to face it down, packing history away in their spots of time and their Grecian urns. Theirs is the apostasy from, not of, deconstruction, and deconstruction takes its revenge on them in American criticism, appearing as a *Triumph of Life* that is also an *Arrêt de mort*. (Those are the joint pre-texts for Derrida's 1979 American essay, only belatedly [1986] published in French, "Living On: Border Lines.")

Living on is Derrida's one great theme, together with the diverse images that make living on possible when logic is dethroned. And death is the ground of living on: "It is thus the relation to *my death* (to my disappearance in general) which is hidden in this determination of being as presence, ideality, absolute possibility of repetition. The possibility of the sign is this relation to death. . . . *I am* thus means at the origin *I am mortal*" (*La Voix* 60–61, and see 44, 108, 114). Derrida says it thus early; he reiterates it in *Glas*; he bases his nuclear criticism on it, and much else besides (92b).[2] "They pierce my thickets, through my grot they glide" (Pope): here already deconstruction is joined to flow, with the heavy and complex dose of sexuality that the French teach us to recognize. That looks like the enemy, but it's all part of "this long disease, my life." It's not a cavalier acceptance of mortality that Derrida is after, but still it's less traumatic than the presumed Romantic timelessness, "the trance of literature" (Christensen, 784). Foucault talks more about death than

Derrida, and not all that differently at the moments when he remembers that discourse is discursive, flow and not stasis.

The issue, at the last, is the Enlightenment of death. That's an ambiguous phrase, one way of specifying the end of Enlightenment, but not in any event its undoing, which comes later, with the Romantic death of Enlightenment. For Romanticists deconstruction is a spiritual pugilism that topples claims of authority.

> Die abgestorbne Eiche steht im Sturm
> Doch die gesunde stürzt er schmetternd nieder,
> Weil er in ihre Krone greifen kann.
> (Kleist, *Penthesilea* 3041–43)

Less imperious, enlightened deconstruction takes the part of the uncrowned oak. Its activity is hermeneutic rather than critical: it uncovers and teaches the ruses by means of which death survives after all.[3] Let us not encounter as an adversary what should come to us in a spirit of consolation. The same knell tolls in Derrida as in the enlightened graveyard, calling to reckoning the currents that link death and life, the past and the present. Indulge me if I dub their affinity with the exemplary appellation of . . . par-knell.

A NIGHT-PIECE ON DEATH

By the blue Tapers trembling Light,
No more I waste the wakeful Night,
Intent with endless view to pore
The Schoolmen and the Sages o'er:
Their Books from Wisdom widely stray,
Or point at best the longest Way.
I'll seek a readier Path, and go
Where Wisdom's surely taught *below.*

How deep yon Azure dies the Sky!
Where Orbs of Gold unnumber'd lye,
While thro' their Ranks in silver pride
The nether Crescent seems to glide.
The slumb'ring Breeze forgets to breathe,
The Lake is smooth and clear beneath,
Where once again the spangled Show
Descends to meet our Eyes below.
The Grounds which on the right aspire,
In dimness from the View retire:
The Left presents a Place of Graves,
Whose Wall the silent Water laves.
That Steeple guides thy doubtful sight
Among the livid gleams of Night.
There pass with melancholy State,
By all the solemn Heaps of Fate,
And think, as softly-sad you tread
Above the venerable Dead,
Time was, like thee they Life possest,
And Time shall be, that thou shalt Rest.

Those Graves, with bending Osier bound,
That nameless heave the crumbled Ground,
Quick to the glancing Thought disclose
Where *Toil* and *Poverty* repose.

The flat smooth Stones that bear a Name,
The Chissels slender help to Fame,
(Which e'er our Sett of Friends decay
Their frequent Steps may wear away.)
A *middle Race* of Mortals own,
Men, half ambitious, all unknown.

The Marble Tombs that rise on high,
Whose Dead in vaulted Arches lye,
Whose Pillars swell with sculptur'd Stones,
Arms, Angels, Epitaphs and Bones,
These (all the poor Remains of State)
Adorn the *Rich*, or praise the *Great*;
Who while on Earth in Fame they live,
Are sensless of the Fame they give.

Ha! while I gaze, pale *Cynthia* fades,
The bursting Earth unveils the Shades!
All slow, and wan, and wrap'd with Shrouds,
They rise in visionary Crouds,
And all with sober Accent cry,
Think, Mortal, what it is to dye.

Now from yon black and fun'ral Yew,
That bathes the Charnel House with Dew,
Methinks I hear a *Voice* begin;
(Ye Ravens, cease your croaking Din,
Ye tolling Clocks, no Time resound
O'er the long Lake and midnight Ground)
It sends a Peal of hollow Groans,
Thus speaking from among the Bones.

When Men my Scythe and Darts supply,
How great a *King* of *Fears* am I!
They view me like the last of Things:
They make, and then they dread, my Stings.
Fools! if you less provok'd your Fears,
No more my Spectre-Form appears.
Death's but a Path that must be trod,
If Man wou'd ever pass to God:
A Port of Calms, a State of Ease
From the rough Rage of swelling Seas.

Why then thy flowing sable Stoles,
Deep pendent Cypress, mourning Poles,
Loose Scarfs to fall athwart thy Weeds,
Long Palls, drawn Herses, cover'd Steeds,
And Plumes of black, that as they tread,
Nod o'er the 'Scutcheons of the Dead?

Nor can the parted Body know,
Nor wants the Soul, these Forms of Woe:
As men who long in Prison dwell,
With Lamps that glimmer round the Cell,
When e'er their suffering Years are run,
Spring forth to greet the glitt'ring Sun:
Such Joy, tho' far transcending Sense,

Have pious Souls at parting hence.
On Earth, and in the Body plac't,
A few, and evil Years, they wast:
But when their Chains are cast aside,
See the glad Scene unfolding wide,
Clap the glad Wing and tow'r away,
And mingle with the Blaze of Day.

CHAPTER 5

Mozart and After

The Revolution in Musical Consciousness

THE 1780'S WERE MARKED not only by political revolution but also by Kant's "second Copernican revolution" in philosophy and by the beginnings of a revolutionary change in literary style.[1] In at least one characteristic aspect, the origins of the musical style that we know as Romantic are to be found in the same decade and can be analyzed in exactly the same terms.

Kant's revolution was initiated by a new concept of the nature of consciousness. As the first readers of the *Critique of Pure Reason* (1781) immediately appreciated, Kant's starting point was a reversal of priorities. In the then-dominant tradition of Locke, consciousness was held to follow on perception. The mind begins empty, as a tabula rasa; it fills itself by attending to sensations which reach it from the external world. Consciousness, for Locke, is not awareness of self; instead, it is taking cognizance of what lies outside the mind. Indeed, before the 1780's it was not even possible to say, simply, "I am conscious" but only, "I am conscious of *x*." Kant began by exchanging the positions of consciousness and sensation. In his system consciousness precedes sensation, and he argues that meaningful sensations are possible only if a well-defined consciousness already exists to perceive them. Logically speaking, we must be aware of ourselves before we can become aware of anything outside us; we must be conscious in general before we become conscious of anything in particular; we must be conscious of ourselves internally—and for Kant that means in time—before we can become conscious of any objects or orientations in space. The details of this part of Kant's system are, of course, vastly more complex, but for the present analysis these elements suffice: Kant posits an indefinite, infolded, temporal self-consciousness which determines the forms (or "categories") of perception prior to any particular, structured, external acts of perception.

Literary Romanticism likewise began by isolating or discovering a state of pure undifferentiated self-consciousness. Certain well-known texts from the 1780's, often imitated and enormously influential, depict an unformed sense of self, cut off from external perceptions and entirely comparable to Kantian self-consciousness. Kant considers such a state merely a logical possibility, but these texts and their later offshoots treat it as an empirical state that can be really experienced and therefore concretely described. The fifth of Rousseau's *Reveries of a Solitary Wanderer* (1782) contains perhaps the most famous early description of the experiential origin of this "feeling of existence stripped of any other sentiment":

The noise of the waves and the agitation of the water fastening my senses and chasing all other agitation from my soul plunged it into a delicious reverie where night often surprised me without my being aware of it. The ebb and flow of this water, its noise, continuous but swelling by intervals, striking without respite my ear and my eyes substituted for the internal movements which the reverie extinguished in me and sufficed to make me feel my existence with pleasure, without taking the trouble to think. (*Oeuvres* 1: 1045)

Nothing is heard or seen in this state except an ongoing rhythmic pulse, flickering in intensity and lacking any more definite shape. Time is felt but not measured, and no effort of thought imposes an order, a center, or a meaning on the flow of sensations. Such is a general picture of a state of mind that may be called by various names: pure or primitive consciousness, preconsciousness, reverie, daydream, or ecstasy. With some variation, such states were also described, for the most part independently and without mutual influence, by a number of other leading writers of the decade, including the philosopher Thomas Reid and the poet William Cowper in England, the novelist Jacques-Henri Bernardin de Saint-Pierre in France, and the prose writer Wilhelm Heinse and the young poet Goethe in Germany.

What emerges in both the literature and the music of the 1780's is not only a new type of experience but also a new conception of form. No longer does consciousness begin with external perception or artistic form with inherited convention; now the basic structural orientation is generated from within, from the flow of time. As we read in an early review of Beethoven's Choral Fantasia, such a form is "the monologue of the artist, the pure expression of his own, personal feelings, whereas his relation to set forms—opera, oratorio, etc.—is a dialogue in which he can only deliver what is occasioned by the given forms."[2] Rather than beginning with an unmistakable tonic chord or a forthright statement of the principal theme or subject, musical reveries of this type proceed gradually from dark confusion to clarity and reason. Normally characterized by an audible pulse but no clearly articulated meter, and often characterized by an absence of clear tonal focus as well, they generate the fundamental organizing categories of the piece while seeming to lack a clear organization of their own. The opening bars of Beethoven's Ninth Symphony are a classic example. Some further excerpts from the review of the Choral Fantasia will illustrate how this principle of structure was perceived after it had become somewhat familiar:

This Fantasia opens . . . not without chaotic confusion which causes the listener at first to fear that the spirit [*der Geist*] might lose itself in self-absorption and, wholly dissipated, never emerge into daylight. This can be imagined as the preface to the career of the artist's life. Pictures and dreams chase and pursue one another, lose themselves in the tightly woven choreography, and the development remains latent—self-consciousness still seems to be lacking. . . . A brief allegro, destined merely as a cadence and transition to the succeeding chorus, closes the Fantasia, which now proceeds to actual words—as the genius which has now arrived at self-consciousness hastens to display itself in the utmost clarity. (78–79)

Reveries such as I have been describing are rare and pioneering innovations in the 1780's and become increasingly common thereafter. Furthermore, the condition of reverie came more and more to be described for its own sake rather than as the prelude to some ordinary, waking consciousness. By the middle of the nineteenth century, many independent "moodpieces" were written which were not subordinated to any larger structure. In literature the prose poems of Thomas de Quincey, Charles Baudelaire, and Louis Bertrand come to mind, the poems of Eduard Mörike and Annette von Droste-Hülshoff, or the dream sequences in the fiction of Emily Brontë, Nathaniel Hawthorne, and Charles Dickens. In music the moodpiece first reaches independent status in Beethoven's

Bagatelles and in Schubert's late songs, and after Schumann and Chopin it is ubiquitous. Before turning to Mozart and the origins of this phenomenon, I would like to review some later examples in order to ascertain the technical musical equivalents of the preconscious reverie and to illustrate the various means available to reach definably similar effects.

Since the presence of a text helps to validate the correspondence of musical and literary forms, I begin my characterization of musical reverie with a song, Schumann's setting of Lynkeus's song from Goethe's *Faust* (Example 1). Lynkeus is a dreamlike character in a dream vision, an alien survivor from antiquity in the medieval world. Though in theory a watchman, in practice he is completely self-involved, seeing (as the text tells us) only what he wishes to see and what is eternal and not the destructive events actually occurring around him while he sings. Since he sings offstage, the song may well be called the disembodied reverie of a timeless, "pure" consciousness. The musical expression corresponding to Lynkeus's text is marked by the following devices, among others. The first half of the melody is a repeated phrase played without harmonization. The piano plays the melody in treble and bass, two octaves apart, its hollow sonorities underlining the absence of harmonic definition. In addition, every note of the scale is sounded before the middle of bar 3 except the leading tone A, which is the crucial note for defining the key. The continuation of the melody is harmonized but cadences strongly in the wrong key, F instead of B-flat. The song also cadences in G minor and C minor and crashes into a deceptive cadence on the first inversion of the D-minor triad. Finally the vocal line comes to rest on the tonic, and the piano postlude has two further cadences that also reach the tonic but by plagal progressions so weak they undermine the tonic effect. What this amounts to, in less technical language, is that Schumann characterizes the dreamlike Lynkeus by means of notably drifting tonality. The rhythmic impulse is likewise weak: the dominant rhythm is a monotonously lilting dotted figure, with the piano initially reinforcing the offbeats with extra notes (and thus weakening the impulse). Thus the rhythm, like the harmonization, is unsettled, constantly in motion, and shapeless, a flowing duration without direction or dramatic intensity.

Schumann is not alone in furnishing a programmatic text to accompany his musical reverie. A more famous and almost equally decisive example is the prelude to Wagner's *Rheingold*. For 136 bars Wagner

Example 1. Lied Lynkeus des Türmers, by Robert Schumann.

sustains an unvaried E-flat-major chord, devoid of either harmonic or melodic development. The tonality and meter are determinate, but only passively; there is nothing external to the central root chord and simple rhythmic pulsation. One critic has described this moment of fluid inwardness before the action begins as "timeless" music, an "account of the origins of consciousness" (Donington, *Wagner's "Ring"* 38, 36). But Wagner's own well-known description of the inspiration for the prelude is, if possible, even more to the point.

I sank into a kind of somnambulistic state in which I suddenly received the sensation of submerging under a powerful current of water. I soon imagined the rustling of the water in the musical sound of an E-flat-major chord breaking in waves of continual arpeggios; these appeared as melodic figurations of increasing importance, but with no change in the pure E-flat-major triad, whose endurance seemed to attribute an infinite significance to the element in which I was submerged. . . . I quickly comprehended just what my situation was: the current of life should flow toward me from within, not from without. (*Mein Leben, Schriften* 15: 68)

Throughout the nineteenth century, harmonic and rhythmic vagueness reflect the generation of form from within rather than its imposition from without. And where a program can be attributed to these musical techniques, it is associated with dreamy or abnormal states of mind. It can be the "wave of passions" pouring over the opium dreamer at the opening of Berlioz's *Symphonie fantastique*. It can be the momentary anxiety—marked *beklemmt* ("anxious" or "short of breath")—when the first violin finds itself playing in a different key and meter from the other instruments in the cavatina of Beethoven's Quartet, opus 130. Alternatively, it can be the pure ethereal bliss of the "holy song of thanksgiving of one recovered from illness" in his A-Minor Quartet, opus 132. In this quartet extreme slowness renders the beat almost inaudible, and the unusual Lydian mode (whose scale is that of C major but whose tonic is F) frustrates the ordinary sense of key, until the convalescent moves toward normal activity in the harmonically clear and metrically forceful sections marked *neue Kraft fühlend* ("feeling new force").

Such explicit programmatic associations justify attributing to other works equally specific but implicit correspondences of musical and psychological structures. Thus Edward Cone has associated the tantalizing

Example 2. Schumann Piano Quartet, Andante, beginning (left) and end (right).

harmonic mysteries of Brahms's Intermezzo, opus 118, no. 1, with the characteristic atmosphere of detective stories ("Three Ways of Reading"). By late in the century, the spontaneous, inward, and variable pulse of reverie becomes the norm rather than the exception, just as the three-volume novel comes to be an art of natural time in authors as disparate as Adalbert Stifter and Anthony Trollope, just as a self-absorbed timelessness becomes the characteristic stance in painting from Courbet onward, and, finally, just as the inner sense which is the ground of consciousness for Kant is generalized into the all-embracing *temps vécu* of Henri Bergson.

Before returning to the sources of these musical gestures in Mozart, I would like to discuss one final Romantic reverie, the exquisite slow movement of Schumann's Piano Quartet, which distills many of the elements I have been describing (Example 2). The key, B-flat major, is unambiguous, but the mood remains dreamy because of the unceasing yet unemphatic rhythmic pulse. The instruments enter in midtheme, as if discovering a subsisting flow, and the unbroken quarter-note pulse is maintained by dovetailing: each statement of the theme begins before the previous statement has concluded. The overlapping is reinforced for most of the movement (including the middle section) by canonic treatment of the theme. The theme itself proceeds by stepwise motion, but its simple directionality is undermined by displacements in register: up a seventh in the middle of descents, down a seventh in the middle of ascents. The opening also features a subtle rhythmic effect. The violin and viola play accompaniment notes on the third beat of each bar. The viola plays a quarter note, the violin a quarter preceded by a grace note. The violin's grace note is the same pitch as the viola's note. The result is that the note is heard twice, an instant apart, in slightly differing timbres. There is a minute eddy in the pulse; the meter is regular, continuous, yet not rigidly rationalized.

These are some of the devices that give the movement its dreamy quality. The movement is especially noteworthy, however, for the clarification at the end, as if a preconscious state were yielding to a conscious one. The canon is over, and the final statement of the theme is simple, without overlapping. The rhythmic eddy gives way early in the movement to syncopations, a more measurable kind of turbulence; at the end only a residual swaying remains in the notes, two bars long, which the violin and viola shift in turn, one instrument at the beginning of each bar. Alternation is now made to work in support of the meter rather than against it. Then, suddenly, the last eight bars of the movement replace the archaic arioso mode by rapid scales in contrary motion in the style of Beethoven: music history has come alive along with the unexpected animation. And under the whole, as the ground above which this clarification and awakening occur, the cello holds a tonic pedal tone, B-flat, for thirteen measures. This note is remarkable, for it requires tuning the lowest string down from C to B-flat just before entering. Thus the cellist plays a note which, ordinarily, does not exist, an ethereal fundamental whose entry into musical reality initiates the striking *prise de conscience* with which the reverie concludes.

Customarily only small, independent musical forms are identified as reveries, but this obscures both their function and their origins. There is a tendency to see in these small pieces only a negative or ironic import—a denial of classical norms—and to trace them back to Beethoven's Bagatelles, relatively minor pieces whose small notoriety in no way corresponds to the impact claimed for them.[3] Such a view renders a positive account of the musical reverie unfeasible: it becomes impossible to say convincingly what composers of reveries were trying to do or what models they were trying to implement. The historical picture immediately becomes clearer if we view the reverie as a musical gesture rather than as a form: a harmonic and metric uncertainty or openness which may occur in a passing episode, introduce a movement, or shape a whole piece. The function of the reverie is not simply to loosen classical bonds but to explore a whole range of formal possibilities unknown to classical experience. Historically the reverie emerged from within classical form and only gradually emancipated itself. I chose the slow movement of the Schumann Piano Quartet for analysis partly because it shows the reverie at a moment of transition. A typical extended Schumann *Träumerei* closed off by a classicizing conclusion, it is a nearly independent reverie that demonstrates the emergence of Romantic small forms out of the late-classical introduction.

Versions of the metric and harmonic inwardness of the Romantic reverie can be found in many classical-period introductions. Even a relatively simple introduction like that to Beethoven's First Symphony illustrates the form: it begins in the wrong key, juxtaposing long-held wind chords with the instantaneous sound of string pizzicatos, and only gradually works around to the C-major tonic key and develops an audible metric definition. It was Mozart, however, who composed the introductory reverie that had by far the greatest influence and renown: the introduction to the so-called *Dissonance* Quartet in C Major (K. 465) of 1785 (Example 3). An object of controversy almost from its composition, so puzzling harmonically and metrically that the powerful academician François-Joseph Fétis was led to propose a notorious correction in 1829, this piece exhibits the precise preromantic characteristics of the gradual emergence of form out of the preconscious, indistinct, throbbing pulse of time. Indeed, the authoritative Mozart biographer, Hermann Abert, has compared the quartet to "the picture of a mind weighed down by gloomy forebodings and striving to master its spiritual oppression." "In the introduction," he continues, "this process does not leave the stage of unconsciousness. Only in the allegro does the composer open his eyes, so to speak, and pursue the battle consciously" (*Mozart* 2: 145–46).[4] Among the numerous compositions directly inspired by this quartet was the musical depiction of chaos at the beginning of Haydn's *Creation*. I would now like to describe the gradual emergence of conscious form out of chaos in the *Dissonance* Quartet itself by examining in closer detail the meter, tonality, sonority, and genre of its introduction.

Meter. The introduction opens quietly, with an eighth-note pulse in the cello alone. The other instruments enter in canonical imitation on different beats. Thus, no beat is established as the principal one; there is a sense of time but no definite audible organization of the bar.[5] The ongoing regular pulse is subject to a further, almost painful disorientation in the middle of the introduction (bars 13–15). Here the two violins and the cello have imitative descending chromatic runs; the metric values are highly irregular, with each part showing a different distribution of long, medium, and short notes, an aural confusion compounded by uncomfortable harmonic intervals (seconds and parallel fourths). At the end (bars 19–22), rhythmic irregularity is systematized and thus brought a step closer to regularity: the violins play in ¾ meter, with an accent marked at the bar line, while the lower instruments play in what sounds like a displaced ⅝, with an accent marked in the middle of the written bar and no note coinciding with the bar line. Thus, the stages leading to

Example 3. Mozart Dissonance Quartet, introduction.

the allegro are (1) empty pulse, (2) confused meter, and (3) polyrhythm, with two distinct meters in conflict. The common time of the allegro at last resolves the conflict: it divides both bar and beat into two parts and sublimates the asymmetrical triple rhythms into the three-note upbeats which are prominent throughout the first subject.

Tonality. The irregular harmonies and cross-relations that give the quartet its name are so obvious as not to need analysis here. I would point only to the gradual clarification of the tonality. Charles Rosen has claimed that features such as the Neapolitan D-flat in bar 5 and the E-naturals of bars 7–9 render the C-major tonality unambiguous almost from the very beginning of the piece (*Classical Style* 186, amplified in conversation). But the implicit tonality only becomes fully explicit from bar 13, where the dominant-seventh chord prevails. And throughout the middle of the introduction, the mode grows less certain: in bars 9–18 no less than fourteen E-flats are heard as opposed to only three passing Es. Only in the closing bars (19–22) does E-flat give way to E-natural (accented in the viola part). In addition, C-sharps are now heard in both violin parts and repeatedly, with accents, in the cello part; the sharps give these bars a strongly dominant coloration and a predominantly rising movement, correcting the subdominant coloration and downward movement of the middle section.[6] To be sure, minor episodes are not uncommon in classical-period introductions, but most often they fall between clearly demarcated, harmonically stable major-key areas. The introduction to the *Dissonance* Quartet is innovative in that it moves from harmonic obscurity through the harmonic instability of the C-minor episode and establishes the ultimate C-major tonality only after a struggle (the emphatic repetitions in bars 19–22).

Sonority. The opening cello note is unprecedented and cannily chosen. It is the C below middle C, the first harmonic on the cello's lowest string. The note may be played as a harmonic on the C string (a fingering given in some editions) or as a stopped note on the G string; in the latter case, the harmonic will still be present, vibrating sympathetically. Either alternative yields approximately the same effect: the continuous resonance of the C string helps attenuate the softly pulsating rhythm, while a "hollow" sound results from the harmonic whose fundamental tone is lacking. Thus, the quartet opens with an absent foundation, an ethereal effect symmetrical to that of the Schumann Piano Quartet, where a normally unheard fundamental becomes audible at the end.[7] The allegro supplies what is lacking in the sonority, just as it does in the meter and the tonality. The first compensation is indirect: the cello is silent during the first statement of the opening theme while the bass is supplied by repeated middle Cs on the viola. This note is analogous to the opening cello note since it is an octave above the viola's lowest string, but on a different instrument and at a different speed the articulation sounds precise and well supported rather than ethereal. The cello's fundamental open C is heard six times later in the movement at key points: as the very first note in the cello part and twice when the recapitulation begins; accented at the start of the bridge passage to the second subject (that is, as a send-off to the tonic before the customary modulation into the dominant); at the beginning of the dramatic bridge to the coda; and as the very last note in the part.

Genre. The gradual awakening that opens the *Dissonance* Quartet is all the more striking for being found in a string quartet, for this had become the most intimate of the musical genres. Whereas introductory fanfares and (slightly later) slow introductions were common in symphonic music as a means of alerting the audience and publicly announcing the tonality, they were rare in quartets, where the key signature is the only announcement needed. A slow introduction in a quartet thus would tend to have the opposite expressive function from one in a symphony: in the symphony the introduction makes a declaration (to the audience); in the quartet it serves to suspend or question a declaration which has already been made (to the players). The symphonic introduction is extroverted; the quartet introduction introverted. These are only generalizations, of course, and need to be tested in each individual case, but in fact no other quartet by Mozart has a comparable slow introduction (the early K. 171 has a slow-fast-slow overture form in the first movement), only one later Haydn quartet has such an introduction, and among Beethoven's quartets none has it before the ninth (opus 59, no. 3), a work in C major whose form derives in this respect from Mozart's example.[8] Thus, Mozart's unique slow introduction calls the genre into question, just as it does the tonality. The form is not given from without by conventional fiat but is engendered uniquely from within. And if this change first occurs in the most intimate of musical forms, it corresponds precisely to the revolutionary innovations of Rousseau's political theory and of Kant's philosophy, according to which social cohesion and universal truths likewise must be regenerated on the basis of the priority of the individual. The welding of four throbbing adagio voices into a harmonious allegro is Mozart's social contract.

The other essentially private musical genre is the solo keyboard sonata. None of Mozart's piano sonatas was written with a slow introduction. But a few months after the C-Major Quartet, as an afterthought, Mozart wrote a long Fantasia (K. 475) to preface the C-Minor Sonata (K. 457): this Fantasia is the other famous Mozartean example of the structural revolution I have been analyzing (Example 4). It is, as Rosen writes, "truly abnormal by classical standards," not lacking in large-scale tonal patterns but so restless that it frustrates the desire for audible tonal focus at almost every point (*Classical Style* 92). The opening four bars, indeed, are almost note for note a simplified (and hence even more ambiguous) harmonic sketch of the opening four bars of the quartet. In the remainder of the piece, the sustained harmonic turbulence is generally associated with falling movements (as is also the case in the *Dissonance* Quartet). The Fantasia develops increasingly into a combat of rising and falling movements, until at the end the tonal clarification is accompanied by the final triumph of ascending figures, as the left hand plays the only two measured ascending chromatic scales in the piece (bars 3–4 from the end) and then (rather as in the Schumann Piano Quartet) the tonic scale is heard, a loud, three-octave C-minor scale in the right hand, in the very last bar.[9]

Ambiguity or uncertainty is common in the opening of major compositions of the 1780's and even more so in Haydn's introductions in the 1790's. The two works I have discussed are, in one sense, different only in degree, not in kind. The intensification of a common gesture does, however, ultimately amount to a difference in kind: instead of confiding wit, there is a feeling of disembodied distance; instead of dramatic expectancy, there is the self-sufficiency of a slow, seemingly directionless flow.[10] The hypothesis that these two works were felt to have initiated something new is corroborated by the fact that for a long time the preponderance of compositions opening with a chaotic or dreamlike introduction were also in the key of C: the list includes Haydn's *Creation*; Beethoven's First and Fifth Symphonies, *Coriolanus* Overture, Choral Fantasia, Quartet, opus 59, no. 3, and Piano Sonata, opus 111;

FANTASIA.

Example 4. Mozart Fantasia (K. 475).

Schubert's Fourth Symphony and his song "Die Stadt"; and Berlioz's *Symphonie fantastique*.[11] The series of avatars and variants ends, perhaps, with Brahms's First Symphony. Like Mozart's *Dissonance* Quartet (and Berlioz's *Symphonie fantastique*), Brahms's work opens with an eighth-note pulse on a single tone. But unlike Mozart's ghostly solo cello, the pulse (three octaves, forte and pesante, simultaneously in contrabassoon, string bass, and tympany) gives a powerful foundation to a crashing four-octave C sustained by the rest of the orchestra and then to predominantly rising progressions, somewhat chromatic but completely unambiguous in key. Brahms's symphony is a refutation of Mozart's budding Romanticism, a return to an uncompromisingly classic stance.

We do not ordinarily think of Mozart as a revolutionary composer but rather as a "pure" classical genius, affiliated stylistically with Haydn. In the later nineteenth century, he was often compared with Raphael or with the "naive" Goethe.[12] But in his own day—when he was sometimes compared with Friedrich Klopstock, the first titanic innovator in modern German letters—and for almost two generations thereafter, the standard view was quite the reverse. Until the time of Schumann or even until Otto Jahn's standard biography (1856), Mozart was viewed as a dark and demonic figure. He was often assimilated to his own Don Giovanni, as in Hoffmann's famous "Don Juan," or else associated with the dark specter of the *Requiem* in contrast to the clear brightness of Papa Haydn, as may be seen in Hoffmann's essay "Beethovens Instrumentalmusik" and Pushkin's marvelous playlet *Mozart and Salieri*. Yet at the same time, the early biographical materials all portray him as withdrawn, innocent, childlike, and helpless in worldly matters.[13] This aspect of his image also needs to be taken seriously, for the Mozartean revolution did not proceed with the flamboyance of a Beethoven. It was a quiet, inward revolution, a new way of thinking or, yet, of dreaming in musical forms, a mood of intense self-absorption that is favored even in the operas—in lyrical pauses such as Tamino's "Dies Bildnis ist bezaubernd schön" in *The Magic Flute* or Cherubino's "Non so più cosa son, cosa faccio" in *The Marriage of Figaro*—but that is particularly developed in the more private musical genres. With this revolutionary self-absorption, we have moved again into the sphere of the hermit of the Ile de Saint-Pierre and the hermit of Königsberg.

There can be no question, of course, of any "influence" of Rousseau's or Kant's ideas on Mozart's musical structures. While I have used various loosely synonymous nonmusical terms—reverie, dream, unconscious, ethereal, and so on—the analysis could proceed on a non-metaphorical, strictly technical basis. Indeed, much of it has. I should therefore clarify why I have superimposed a philosophical and literary layer on the musical analysis, even at the risk of giving the false impression that I wished to make the history of music dependent upon the history of ideas.

My answer lies, first of all, in the contention—in which I follow chiefly Michel Foucault, though with qualifications—that at every period in history a subterranean network of constraints governs the organization of human thought. Different fields develop and change in parallel not because they affect one another but because the infrastructures of mental activity affect all of them. In this respect, the relationship of music and philosophy is no different from the relationship of literature and philosophy. The infrastructure is the precondition of thought and is by definition unconscious and unarticulated. Because it lies outside the limits of the individual disciplines, it cannot really be formulated within any of them. Hence arises the necessity of comparative study. The infrastructure comes to light at the juncture of independent fields. In the present case, it is accurate to say that music and philosophy mutually illuminate one another precisely because they are such different media; where they coincide lie the true invariants of eighteenth-century thought.

Beyond these general considerations, applicable to all comparisons, is the special challenge of understanding a nonverbal medium such as music. Here the problem, so insistently raised in the work of Leonard Meyer, is the expressivity of musical gestures: what they mean, what their purpose is, or what they communicate. The relationship of musical (or literary or philosophical) forms to the intuitive presuppositions of thought is that of a manifest superstructure to a concealed depth: we may conceive the surface forms as representations or signs of their hidden presuppositions. The concrete manifestations *express* their latent presuppositions; they *signify* the unconscious systems in which they are rooted. To *understand* expressive forms in this sense is thus to describe the mediations between conscious superstructure and unconscious infrastructure; hence, as Claude Lévi-Strauss has said in an important justification of his own structuralist enterprise, this kind of understanding "is first of all psychology" (*Savage Mind* 131). The explanatory process leads from the musical surface to that aspect of the mental system (that "state of mind") which it represents, in this case the reverie of nascent, disembodied self-consciousness.

The Marxian terminology of infra- and superstructures seems unwieldy, but its very remoteness from the objects of study is actually an advantage: it calls our attention to the fact that all of our processes of understanding involve a movement out of one system into another. Explanation is always an abstraction or, what amounts to the same thing, a metaphor. This is just as true of the explanation of verbal media (poetry or philosophy) as of nonverbal media. It is equally daring to assign a reason for a development in the history of ideas or to declare what a poem expresses as to attribute a meaning to musical forms. The only difference is that in the earlier cases the process of abstraction is easily concealed, since words are being substituted for other words, whereas the abstraction in explanations of music is patent.

The special challenge of analyzing a nonverbal medium, then, is to recognize that no special challenge is involved. All explanation is transference or metaphor (nothing much different is meant when certain literary critics contend that all reading is misreading), for understanding depends on finding a convincing mediation between what is actually present in the text and something that, in an important sense, is not so present. Explanation never remains within the charmed circle of what is to be explained; the essential thing is to find mediations that are sufficiently precise and well articulated. Whether mine are, I leave to my examples to show; but I would repeat that my analysis has not been an application of philosophical terms to musical problems. On the contrary, the guiding terms of the analysis, disorientation and undirected pulse, surface only in Rousseau's *Reveries*, a "marginal" text by an "interdisciplinary" author who was as seriously involved in the study of music as in the study of philosophy. Indeed, it would be more accurate to say that the present essay applies musical terms to the clarification of a philosophical problem. Perhaps it would be even better to remain close to Lévi-Strauss's view and say that if music is fundamentally an expression of emotions, then my analysis may contribute toward laying bare the emotional and psychological foundations of the Romantic consciousness.

CHAPTER 6

Kant's Misreading of Descartes

KANT'S TREATMENT OF Descartes in the *Critique of Pure Reason* is notably obtuse. Descartes's systematic doubt is a kind of spiritual exercise establishing the *cogito* as a theoretical and a practical maxim. In response, Kant contends that both thought (*cogito*) and personal identity (*ego*) should be taken in some sort of intuitive and transcendental sense as entities that precede experience. Empirical reality is reduced to secondary status as the mere "condition of the application" of a dictum whose truth is "pure[ly] intellectual," with an immediacy that does not even require an act of reasoning to ground it. At one stroke, both empiricism and rationalism, as Descartes combined them, are swept under the rug, in a forbiddingly abstract dismissal. (The entire paragraph in question is quoted below.)

Short of ignoring the difficulty, we must try to account for the confusion. Steven C. Patten argues that Descartes is at fault: he singles out inconsistent statements about whether perceptions are always self-conscious. Kant's dismissal then appears as a mere reflection of Descartes's inadequacies. Alberto Rouges and Vicente Quintero both maintain that the problem is Kant's. The former claims that Kant mistook Descartes's pure consciousness for an empirical consciousness, as if Descartes were truly a Kantian all along; the latter claims that Kant mistook his own idealism for an empirical realism and was, in effect, a failed Cartesian. Ferdinand Alquié exonerates both Descartes and Kant from blame. In his view, Leibniz is the true villain, and "Kant contends only with a deformed Cartesianism" (Alquié, "Lecture cartésienne" 151). Or maybe neither philosopher can be credited with a true grasp of the issues: "Kant and Descartes alike committed the error of failing to see the relation in which the initial 'cogito'—or its more precise form as a synthesis a priori in the *Ich denke*—stood with the eternal problem of being" (Barié, "Du 'cogito' cartésien" 217). But perhaps, as I shall be arguing, such confusions about where the confusion lies point to a deeper difficulty of comprehension. We don't know who is at fault because language will not formulate what needs to be said.

My thesis in this essay will be double. First, Kant's misreading of Descartes is not a mistake but a swerve in the history of thought. It registers a change in the way problems can be formulated. Second, Descartes offers the proper subject for communicating this transformation because Kant in truth is responding to a swerve of Descartes's own. Descartes's writing matters precisely because it reflects a struggle to advance beyond his conceptions. The issue is not that Descartes had thoughts he would not or could not write, but that he wrote things that he could not yet think and that Kant's new language finally enabled Kant to think for him. Similarly, the brevity of Kant's critique foregrounds the impossibility of his ever communicating with Descartes. It is more direct and more honest than any attempt to bridge the gap between them. Heidegger says that "Nietzsche's misunderstanding of the Cartesian sentence [*Satz*—the translators write "principle"] is even necessary, for a number of metaphysical reasons" (*Nietzsche* 4: 104), and I shall be arguing the same about Kant. My analysis is directed at showing why Kant and Descartes could say no more on the very subjects they have in common.

A weaker version of my argument maintains that Descartes's ideas were in advance of the late scholastic language to which he resorted. The view that Descartes meant more than he said is perhaps best known from Heidegger: "Through his many efforts to make what was new in his grounding of metaphysics intelligible to his contemporaries by responding to their doubts, Descartes was forced to discourse at the already prevailing level and so to explain his fundamental position superficially, that is, always inappropriately, a contingency that threatens *every essential thinking*" (*Nietzsche* 4: 118).[1] Zeno Vendler argues along similar lines with an eye to Kant: "[Descartes] really speaks, or *should* speak, not of the will but of the self. . . . Yet, for obvious religious reasons, he never had the courage to . . . abandon the doctrine of the soul as a 'substance' interacting with other substances in the world. That final step remained for Kant to take" (Vendler, "Descartes' Res Cogitans" 170, his italics). Arguments such as these presuppose our ability to seize thoughts that lie beyond language—beyond the language of the philosopher whose thoughts they should have been, or else beyond all language. The philosopher's inability to complete his system becomes a mark of its pregnancy.

The notion of a truth that transcends its particular formulations accords with the tendency of most philosophical scholarship at present, and especially in English, namely, to rework and reorder a philosopher's arguments so as to uncover their fundamental logic. Oriented toward philosophical problems rather than philosophical writing, such an approach presupposes common issues discussable in a common vocabulary. It honors one of the traditional canons of hermeneutics—to understand authors better than they understand themselves—at the expense of another: to understand authors at their own level, or, as Friedrich Schlegel phrases it, to be just as smart, and just as dumb as the author.[2] As if philosophers might communicate despite themselves, those who expand Descartes's retrograde formulations or Kant's cryptic utterances about him often obscure essential differences by failing to investigate the force of the writing.[3]

More "literary" studies typically take the opposite tack by positing the equivalence of language and idea. One knows philosophers by knowing their language: "Philosophy does not preexist speech, but exists in and through it. The one does not transcend the other, and the philosophical signified and its textual signifier are one and the same" (Romanowski, L'Illusion chez Descartes 176). In its attention to systems and their expression, however, the equation of utterance with thought obscures the dynamism of struggle and advance. Even if it is difficult to accept the notion that thoughts can somehow be superior to the words that clothe them, there remains a force (at least the force of tradition) to the historical commonplace that the great philosophers were in advance of their times. Logical reconstruction of systems of ideas and hermeneutic reconstruction of textual systems represent alternative structuralisms; the stylistic approach does not so much refute the logical approach as confront it in an unresolved standoff.

An enduring legacy of deconstruction is its critique of such structuralisms. Texts can no more be tailored to the implicit thoughts than can thoughts to the explicit texts. What both approaches lack is a sufficiently rich concept of intentionality. Derrida's first book, *La Voix et le phénomène* (Speech and Phenomenon), critiques the psychologized intentionalism in Husserl that covertly reassimilates language to thought and thus impoverishes both. Derrida's theory here and his practice throughout his career show the persistence of intentions that outpace formation. The point of breakthrough does occur where language and thought are out of alignment, but not because the thoughts are somehow better formed than the words. Rather, philosophers enter history when they simultaneously say more than they can think and mean more than they can say. The strength of a philosophical system resides in its passionate desire or longing for a new idea, a kind of nostalgia for the future of the intellectual world. My essay, consequently, speculates on the Cartesian beyond.

The issue, then, is an epochal change in philosophical language. Just approaching the threshold of the new, and torn between an immature French and an overripe Latin, Descartes's language forecasts intuitions that he is not prepared to conceive. Three kinds of philological analysis form the kernel of my exposition. The first two are concrete: textual observations concerning Descartes's *ego* and semantic ones concerning the meaning of the verb *cogito*. The third is speculative and stylistic, concerning the imaginative valence of the wax that Descartes takes for an example of corporeal substance in the second part of the *Meditations*. The first two kinds fix Descartes in his roots, the third frees him into his dreams.

However much I may attempt to hedge the kernels around with supporting evidence, there will seem to be a radical discontinuity in my argument, as indeed there always is between past and future. Nevertheless, it is important to acknowledge the fundamental kinship of the apparently disparate kinds of philology—the determinate and the intuitive, the grammatical and the stylistic, the scholarly and the critical. For, on the one hand, the determination of the meaning of a word such as *ego* or *cogito* must depend on our ability to imagine how potential nuances of tone might liberate it under the influence of a second language, a resource of thought, or a stray inspiration. And, on the other hand, the identification of an imagistic resonance must equally depend on our ability to situate that resonance firmly within the thrust of the author's thinking (or, in an impersonal formulation, within the dimensions of the textual practice). In between, where meaning is free and style controlled, one can speak of choices, decisions, opportunities, experiments, successes and mistakes, felicities and infelicities. But at the ends of the spectrum with which this essay is concerned, a kind of linguistic fatalism operates. There, authors cannot help but betray themselves, violating conscious thoughts while revealing the swerves or errancies of their true inspiration. Better than any hermeneutic aids to reflection, Kant's helplessness captures the nuances of such self-betrayal in Descartes.

* * *

The most imposing and least intelligible of Kant's comments on Descartes is contained in a note to the second version of the paralogisms of pure reason (*Kritik der reinen Vernunft* B422–23). It reads as follows.

Das Ich denke ist, wie schon gesagt, ein empirischer Satz, und hält den Satz, Ich existiere, in sich. Ich kann aber nicht sagen: alles, was denkt, existiert; denn da würde die Eigenschaft des Denkens alle Wesen, die sie besitzen, zu notwendigen Wesen machen. Daher kann meine Existenz auch nicht aus dem Satze, Ich denke, als gefolgert angesehen werden, wie Cartesius dafür hielt (weil sonst der Obersatz: alles, was denkt, existiert, vorausgehen müßte), sondern ist mit ihm identisch. Er drückt eine unbestimmte empirische Anschauung, d. i. Wahrnehmung, aus (mithin beweiset er doch, daß schon Empfindung, die folglich zur Sinnlichkeit gehört, diesem Existenzialsatz zum Grunde liege), geht aber vor der Erfahrung vorher, die das Objekt der Wahrnehmung durch die Kategorie in Ansehung der Zeit bestimmen soll, und die Existenz ist hier noch keine Kategorie, als welche nicht auf ein unbestimmt gegebenes Objekt, sondern nur ein solches, davon man einen Begriff hat, und wovon man wissen will, ob es auch außer diesem Begriffe gesetzt sei, oder nicht, Beziehung hat. Eine unbestimmte Wahrnehmung bedeutet hier nur etwas Reales, das gegeben worden, und zwar nur zum Denken überhaupt, also nicht als Erscheinung, auch nicht als Sache an sich selbst (Noumenon), sondern als etwas, was in der Tat existiert, und in dem Satze, ich denke, als ein solches bezeichnet wird. Denn es ist zu merken, daß, wenn ich den Satz: ich denke, einen empirischen Satz genannt habe, ich dadurch nicht sagen will, das I c h in diesem Satze sei empirische Vorstellung; vielmehr ist sie rein intellektuell, weil sie zum Denken überhaupt gehört. Allein ohne irgend eine empirische Vorstellung, die den Stoff zum Denken abgibt, würde der Actus, Ich denke, doch nicht stattfinden, und das Empirische ist nur die Bedingung der Anwendung, oder des Gebrauchs des reinen intellektuellen Vermögens.

The "I think" is, as already stated, an empirical sentence, and contains within itself the sentence "I exist." But I cannot say "everything which thinks, exists." For in that case the property of thought would render all beings which possess it necessary beings. My existence cannot, therefore, be regarded as inferred from the sentence "I think," as Descartes contended—because otherwise it would have to be preceded by the major premise "Everything which thinks, exists"— but is identical with it. The "I think" expresses an indeterminate empirical intuition, *i.e.* perception (and thus shows that sensation, which as such belongs to sensibility, lies at the basis of this existential sentence). But the "I think" precedes the experience which is required to determine the object of perception through the category in respect of time; and existence here [referred to] is not a category. The category as such does not apply to an indeterminately given object but only to one of which we have a concept and about which we seek to know whether it does or does not exist [*gesetzt sei*] outside the concept. An indeterminate perception here signifies only something real that is given, given indeed to thought in general, and so not as appearance, nor as thing in itself (*noumenon*), but as something which actually exists, and which in the sentence, "I think," is denoted as such. For it must be observed, that when I have called the sentence, "I think," an empirical sentence, I do not mean to say thereby, that the "I" in this sentence is an empirical representation. On the contrary, it is purely intellectual, because belonging to thought in general. Without some empirical representation to supply the material for thought, the *actus*, "I think," would not, indeeed, take place; but the empirical is only the condition of the application, or of the employment, of the pure intellectual faculty.[4]

Ego

The confusions in this passage begin at Descartes's name, which appears at the point where Kant challenges the status of the *cogito*. It is uncertain which verb the "because" clause modifies and consequently it is unclear whether Kant thinks Descartes believed in an implied major premise. If so, Kant was wrong, since Descartes's discussions in the *Meditations* repeatedly deny the presupposition of a distinct major premise. It could also be wrong to claim that Descartes regarded the *cogito* as a deduction, though here the uncertainty lies in Descartes's texts: it remains a matter of debate whether his *therefore* (*ergo, donc*) is meant to signal a consequence or a clarification. (For a good analysis, see Bernard Williams, *Descartes* 88–90.) Textual confusions in both authors thus lie behind Kant's description of "an indeterminate empirical intuition, *i.e.* perception": whatever the psychology of the *cogito* may be, its logic is vague.

Too much cannot depend on it; consequently Kant concludes his note by relegating the *cogito* to an accessory status, as he had done even more decisively in the first version of the paralogisms, where he called the *cogito* "the form of apperception, which *attaches to* [*anhängt*; Kemp Smith translates "belongs to"] and precedes every experience" (A354, my emphasis). Kant acknowledges the *cogito* as a first principle, but a principle of something else, namely of experience. It is obscurely there, but Kant refrains from saying that we must be conscious of our consciousness. Rather: "It must be *possible* for the 'I think' to accompany all my representations" (B131, Kant's emphasis, omitted by Kemp Smith). Descartes, of course, had explicitly identified "I think" as the shiningly clear and distinct idea that grounds the possibilities of knowledge. Even as he aims to be faithful to the obscure truth of the Cartesian *cogito*, Kant thus deviates massively from Descartes's stated intentions. I shall be arguing that his instincts in doing so are better than either he or Descartes could have recognized.

Kant's note starts by calling "ich denke" a "Satz," which derives from the verb *setzen* and connotes something settled, either a sentence or a theorem. But he concludes unsettlingly by calling the *cogito* an "act." Descartes's *Discourse* calls the *cogito* a "vérité." The Latin translation, whose departure from the French is surely authorized, calls it a pronouncement (*pronuntiatum*), and that word reappears to designate the statement "ego sum, ego existo," in the Second Meditation, where it is translated with the French term *proposition*. No word available to Kant (neither *Satz* nor *Äußerung* nor *Behauptung* nor *Verkündigung*) could quite capture the existential, here-and-now quality of *pronuntiatum*; nor for that matter could any French word. Yet, paradoxically, its spontaneity is lost in being conceptually captured and thus better preserved in Kant's terminological fluctuations. Rather than an eternal truth, it is a living gesture, not stable, but forever repeated and renewed: "Statuendum [est] hoc pronuntiatum, *Ego sum, ego existo*, quoties a me profertur, vel mente concipitur, necessario esse verum" (It is to be taken as settled that this pronouncement, "I am, I exist," every time it is uttered by me or conceived in my mind, is necessarily true; *Oeuvres* 7: 25).[5]

Cogito and its correlatives in other deductions (*dubito, sum*) are not the true founding moment of Cartesianism. Descartes's truth lies in the exact wording of his Latin. Though "*Cogito ergo sum*" (thus, in quotes) is the title of Hartmut Brands's valuable but tendentious collection of materials on my topic, I do not believe that it is, in this form, an authentically Cartesian phrase. Descartes seems to have written it only once, in a letter (Jan. 1642 to Regius; *Correspondance* 5: 133), where he quotes it from an attack on him. The phrase "cogito ergo sum" appears in two other passages in Descartes's works, in the conversations recorded by Burman and again in the posthumous Latin translation of the *Recherche de la vérité*. But the phrase apparently never occurs as Descartes's own. Rather, in the second Responses to the *Meditations* and the *Principles of Philosophy*, as well as in the authorized Latin translation of the *Discourse on Method*, the phrase that appears is this: "Ego cogito, ergo sum." The *I* comes first, not just in French, where it is grammatically required, but equally in Latin, where it is optional. It initiates Descartes's statements of principle.

A pronouncement must be pronounced. Before Descartes could say "think," or "doubt," or "am," he had to say "I." That word, or that intuition of self, is his true starting point. In the first version of the paralogisms Kant reduces "I think" to "*I simply am*" and finally to "this representation, 'I'" (A354–55).[6] Descartes never acknowledges such a reduction. Yet that concealed self-assertion is the true origin of Cartesianism—true as assertion, and equally true in the concealment whose veil Kant lifts—an assertion that Descartes did not know how to assert, a pronouncement masquerading as a truth.

What is Descartes's *I*? Kant rightly calls it indistinct, even though Descartes insists that the *cogito* is a clear and evident pronouncement. And, echoed by Heidegger, Kant calls it an intuition, a representation, and simple being, all of which it would be if Descartes knew how to imagine it so. Heidegger turns the *cogito* into Kant's implicit, intuitive "ich denke" when he writes, "We can most pointedly express what the *ergo* is supposed to say if we leave it aside, and furthermore if we remove the emphasis on "I" in the word *ego*, because the first-person pronoun [*das Ichhafte*] is not essential here" (*Nietzsche* 4: 113). But Descartes lacks the kind of implicit, essential ground, the subjacent "subject in the subject" (4: 114) that would free him from saying *I*. He designates himself in lieu of feeling or knowing himself inwardly.

By saying that Descartes lacks a substantive subjectivity, I both do and do not mean to accuse him of a deficiency that Kant cures. It is all too easy to write the history of philosophy on the Whig system, as a series of errors righted and ignorances satisfied. Yet for Descartes the absence of a notion of personal essence constitutes the strength and solidity of his system. By comparing French and Latin texts we can see that Cartesianism regularly equates "who I am" with "what I am," that is, the personal being with the knowable quantity.[7] To this extent there is not even a problem of personal identity in Descartes, as Locke was to formulate it, because there is no possibility of conceiving the subsistence of a personal essence beneath experience. To designate such a subsistence he had a name both grander and more mysterious, in which he firmly believed and which he refused to quarrel with or to doubt. That name was, of course, God. Nevertheless, at an unconscious level, Descartes is driven toward yearning for a terrestrial essence, something that might resemble a thinking stone.[8] That yearning, though it acknowledges a lack, is the opposite of a weakness; it marks the point where his philosophy imagines a future.

All Descartes scholars know the philosopher's self-portraits. One is the polysemous motto that he reports in a letter to Mersenne of April 1634, "Bene vixit, bene qui latuit" (most literally: "He has lived well who has remained well hidden"). Another is the early notebook jotting, "Vt comoedi, moniti ne in fronte appareat pudor, personam induunt: sic ego, hoc mundi theatrum conscensurus, in quo hactenus spectator exstiti, larvatus prodeo" (As actors, wary lest shame appear on their face, put on a mask: thus I, preparing to ascend the theater of the world, where I have hitherto been a spectator, step forth masked; 10: 213). It appears that, having something to hide, Descartes hid himself, for, says another letter to Mersenne, "I am ashamed to speak of myself" (Jan. 1630; *Correspondance* 1: 112). Yet his voluminous discussions of his own ideas and his sometimes testy, occasionally even violent responses to others do not evidence any genuine bashfulness, and in the last part of the *Discourse on Method* (which was, to be sure, published anonymously), he tells us that "I have never sought to hide my actions like crimes, nor have I used many precautions to be unknown" (*Oeuvres* 6: 76). The conflicting evidence suggests that no uniform decoding of Descartes's fugitive personality will be satisfactory.[9]

Descartes's essence remains hidden and difficult to talk about because it doesn't exist. In the motto it is possible to emphasize the adverbs that are syntactically foregrounded: "Effective hiding makes a good life."[10] In the notebook passage it is customary to infer negative connotations from "larvatus," but it is at least equally possible to infer positive ones from mounting a stage. Putting on a *persona* may be hiding, but it may also imply becoming a person: until you put on a mask, you are not a real, living creature but only an external spectator. Another passage in the same notebook unquestionably denigrates masks, but it refers to masked objects of knowledge ("Larvatae nunc scientiae sunt: quae, larvis sublatis, pulcherrimae apparerent" [The sciences are now masked: which, with the masks removed, will appear most beauteous]; 10: 215). The situation is, at the least, less clear with respect to masked persons. The biographer Adrien Baillet reports that Descartes, on a journey perhaps a year or two after the notebook entry, heard some bandits talking in Dutch to plan a murderous attack. He saved himself, we are told, by brave theatrics.[11] In a dangerous situation, energetic deception is the only possible salvation for the ego. But indeed, no clear line can be drawn between concealment, deception, self-fashioning, and self-presentation. Both *Satz* and *actus*, the self is posited through its actions and its pronouncements. Nothing distinct precedes and grounds them, or needs to.

The absence of a substantial self makes Descartes conducive to fine deconstructive readings, such as those of Derrida, of Bernard Bass and Armand Zaloszyc, and, best of all, of Jean-Luc Nancy. Yet all except the first of these ultimately err, as does Heidegger, by treating the absence of self as a deprivation (madness, vertigo, or spasm). For a deprivation would presuppose a possible presence—some residual ideal of self that undermines deconstructive skepticism.[12] But Descartes can imagine no other self than the person saying "I" at this very moment.[13] There is perhaps no philosopher who repeats himself so much as Descartes, and none who says "I" so often. The self exists precisely as its momentary acts of consciousness. Descartes's philosophy is his identity; there is no other.

Cogito

It might seem factitious to wonder what Descartes was thinking when he said "ego cogito."[14] He provides, after all, numerous lists of the modalities of consciousness that are comprised under the rubric "thought," including doubting, willing, and feeling. Descartes might, it seems, have been thinking almost anything. Nevertheless, there is a limit to the *cogito*. The very proliferation of the faculties of mind shows us at least that Descartes was surely thinking *something*. His thought was always underway somewhere, directed toward an object. Descartes even coins the phrase "cogitative acts" as a periphrastic definition of thought (7: 176; *Responses to Objections* 3.2). Thought is Descartes's bridge to action. As he says in the second sentence of the *Meditations*, "I have delayed so long that henceforth I should be at fault if I were to consume in deliberation what time remains for acting" (7: 17).

As a generalization, then, it may be said that Descartes's thought and even his doubt formed part of a system of clear, fundamentally confident affirmation.[15] In all its modalities Cartesian thought is an assertion; it brings him into contact with the world.[16] Descartes was incapable of staying home and daydreaming. Not even his nighttime dreams exhibit the blurred obscurity of romantic reverie: "For whence do we know that the thoughts that come in dreams are more false than others, seeing that often they are no less lifelike and definite?" (*Discourse* 4; *Oeuvres* 6: 38). Let us give its full significance to the last word in the Latin formulation: "Ego cogito, ergo sum, sive existo." Thinking is being in the form of ex-isting, standing forth. Descartes's vocation, just the reverse of Kant's, led out into worldly activity.[17]

We can be sure of one thing about the contents of Descartes's thought: when he said "ego cogito," he was not merely apprehending himself in a gesture of simple self-consciousness. The verb *cogito* derives from *cogo* and refers to a bringing together of ideas in the mind; its object is always a judgment or else a thing mentally constructed, never that less than a thing which is the self. By this I do not mean to exclude the possibility that he might single out for attention some part or aspect of himself, or else, as Robert Champigny intriguingly argues, the category of "selfness." But Cartesian thought is transitive as well as active. It cannot be taken as a reflexive middle voice or an action with a purely internal object. Thus, it cannot bear any resemblance to Kant's pure consciousness.[18] The scholar who paraphrases the Second Meditation in these terms—"But even if I thinking should reach no object, if I grow uncertain and just merely think, still *I* think"[19]—is importing an alien conception into the Cartesian world.

The structure of the pronouncement "ego cogito, ergo sum" likewise forbids any interpretation that refers *cogito* to pure self-consciousness. Descartes tells us that the pronouncement is not a syllogism. He is not deriving existence from thought; he is deriving the knowledge that I exist from the knowledge that I think. It is a confirmation, not a discovery: "I exist" draws out the meaning of "I think." This seems to me clear from the Latin, which is not two independent clauses as the French necessarily is. "Ego . . . cogito, ergo sum"; we might translate, "I think, thus am," "I think, therefore, in other words, I am (namely, a thinking thing)." *Sum* explains or generalizes *cogito*; the first term of the judgment is contained within the second term. But if being encompasses thinking, then thinking cannot encompass being; "I think my being (or: I think that I am, or I think that I think), therefore I am" contains the one complement for *cogito* that for Descartes is not possible.[20] And this is precisely the possibility that Kant finally liberates.

We need to ask why thought enjoys a privileged position in Descartes's classification of mental activities. To be sure, he does explain both in the responses to Gassendi and in the *Principles* why philosophy cannot begin with a physical formula such as "I walk, therefore I am." But no such logic prevented him from arguing "ego sentio, ergo sum"— "I feel, therefore I am (a sentient being)." An underlying anthropology is presupposed that puts thought over sensation.[21] The psychological hierarchy begins to break down in the school of sensibility, and Kant (along with other writers of the 1780's) finally though silently overthrows it.[22] I could formulate my thesis about the relationship of Kant to Descartes in these terms: Kant represses thought as cogitation in order to open up a space for thought as intuitive self-presence.[23] But in order to understand this thesis, which in itself is hardly more than a slogan, we have to consider further the temporality of thought in Descartes.

Strictly speaking, Descartes's arguments do not privilege thought, but thought and doubt together: the pronouncement "ego dubito, ergo sum" is at least as important for him as the pronouncement "ego cogito, ergo sum." This fact has no influence on his anthropology; the anthropological implication of "ego dubito, ergo sum" remains "sum res cogitans," not "sum res dubitans" (see *Recherche de la vérité*; 10: 521–22). But in return the addition of the argument from doubt should remind us of a crucial aspect of Descartes's ontology, an aspect that is well known but seemingly not often enough related to the *cogito*. For what distinguishes *cogito* and *dubito* from all other types of mental activity that Descartes itemizes is their grammatical form: both are iterative verbs.[24] (A third iterative verb, *pensitare*, appears at the climax of the Second Meditation: "Adeo ut, omnibus satis superque pensitatis, denique statuendum sit hoc pronuntiatum, *Ego sum, ego existo*, quoties a me profertur, vel mente concipitur, necessario esse verum"; 7: 25). Mental life, for Descartes, exists primarily in the mode of repetition, not that of duration. What Kant makes us forget is that Cartesian thought is a worldly activity and subject to the same temporal fragmentation as corporeal existence. The continuity of mind is just as problematic as the continuity of body, except to the extent that it is sustained by God's continuous creation; as Wahl suggests (in a rhetorical question), "this continuous creation is a sort of myth maintained by Descartes in the center of his philosophy in order to signify the omnipotence of God and the independence of instants" (*Du rôle de l'idée de l'instant* 19). A thought is an act, not a substance; it lasts but an instant.[25]

Remanet Cera

Where in experience is substance to be found? Does it have no more body than a piece of wax in the sun? Being, for Descartes, remains the incomprehensible mystery of an essential existence outside of time. *Sum* functions as an empty predicate; it requires a complement or a clarification in order to have meaning: "sum, sive existo," "sum res cogitans." Even when reasoning of God, Descartes is concerned with His existence rather than His being. Even God "est ou existe" (*Discourse* 4; 6: 36) not outside of time, but in the fullness of time, as the sum of all its moments: necessary existence is the same as existing always (*Meditations* 5; 7: 65: "ut semper existat").[26] Descartes's fundamental intuition, then, is an instinctive nominalism. Though the *cogito* functions logically as an analytical truth to be unfolded, psychologically it is implicitly couched in the mode of limitation: not that thought is sufficient to ground being but that being is in truth no more than its thoughts. Nothing transcends the moment of its conception.

This reduction has evident advantages for science. All things become countable, measurable, comparable, and thus knowable in the medium of thought. But what about the costs? To us they are evident in the pathos of *L'Homme*, where man is all too easily reduced to a knowable machine. The doctrine of continuous creation precludes any doctrine of Creation, that is, of a beginning or boundary of time (see on this Gilson's commentary, pp. 390–92). The primitive or original of things is a chaos, not in the Greek sense of a "yawning void" or abyss of non-being, nor in the deconstructive sense of Nancy's vertiginous chaogito, but rather in the sense of a congeries of the not yet organized building blocks of our universe. That chaos, which is discussed in chapter 6 of *Le Monde* (11: 34–35), is evoked in the famous passage of the Second Meditation where Descartes looks out the window and sees not "men crossing in the street," but only "hats and coats under which automata might be hiding." Creation here requires no more than the conscious recognition of the order and meaning of our perceptions: things are constituted by the judgments (or thoughts) inseparably attached to sensation.

Can we not, however, sense a worry that the thoughts might be dreams and the reality mere hallucination? *Bene vixit, bene qui latuit.* But suppose that what hides is not alive. The translator is explicit in his fear of ghosts: "Que vois-je de cette fenêtre sinon des chapeaux et des manteaux, qui peuvent couvrir des spectres ou des hommes feints qui ne se remuent que par ressorts, mais je juge que ce sont de vrais hommes" (9: 25). Still, in some respects Descartes's own text is the more worrisome: "Quid autem video praeter pileos & vestes, sub quibus latere possent automata? Sed judico homines esse" (7: 32). The translator makes the men true and emphasizes the unreality of the primitive perceptions, though conceivably the clothes can be covering ghosts. But for Descartes himself the men are merely inferential, and automata—the subjects of the verb, rather than the objects as in the French—can indeed lurk under them. Science benefits from the *cogito*, but what becomes of soul and of substance? The best things in life are the best hidden.

The unstated question haunting the Second Meditation is this: if being is no more than thought, then what is a thing? The problem of substances becomes, at a subliminal level, a nostalgia for what, in a world of reiterated thoughts, lies beyond repetition and therefore beyond thought, or in short, for a being outside of existence. Stanley Cavell puts it this way : "The hyperbolical [doubt] is a turn to emptiness (sometimes I say a craving for nothingness), a wish to exist outside language games—not so much as it were beyond language, perhaps, as before it. Both excess and emptiness express the human wish to escape the human—the desire for the inhuman, or the demonic" ("Naughty Orators" 363–64). The true thing ("res vera," 7: 27) is, in truth ("revera," 7: 32) but an object of thought (cf. *reor*, I think), a creature of reason (*ratio* comes from the past participle of *reor*). You may repeat your search for the real thing, the substratum of thought forever, but you seek the thing in vain ("frustra re-petere," 7: 27). The example of the wax reminds us that some unaccounted residue remains of the thing itself, distinct from all its perceived metamorphoses. "Remanetne adhuc eadem cera? Remanere fatendum est. . . . Remanet cera" (7: 30). Yet the example moves toward showing that the thing itself, "nude," the mere thing, is in truth less than the mind that conceives it (7: 32). It exists only in the domain of error ("quamvis adhuc error in judicio meo esse possit," 7: 32): for Descartes, as opposed to Kant, the naked is not the pure.

Indeed, when Descartes chooses a bodily "thing" to be his example proving that the mind is a thinking thing, the example also reflects the mind's propensity to "wander" beyond "the limits of truth" ("gaudet aberrare mens mea, necdum se patitur intra veritatis limites cohiberi," 7: 29).[27] No wonder, then, that the same nominalism that reduces thought to the sum of thoughts also reduces substance to a shadowy thing. And no wonder if the thing that surfaces from the wandering error of the mind is further reduced to a syllable wandering through a text. On a single page (7: 30) we can find as traces of the subsisting thing the hope for a reduction to order ("*reductis*," "*regi*") and the search ("*requiri*") for some residue ("*reliquiae*") that might be retained ("*retinet*"). The very insubstantial substance that provides Descartes's erroneous example of a real thing has a name (*cera*) that in the French pronunciation (/sera/) is little more than an anagram for the thing (*res*) that it would be and an echo of the cipher (*zero*) that it is. Here, in the depths of one of Descartes's most crucial and most obscure passages, we can hear his language subliminally protesting against the limits of his power of formulation, reaching out toward a reality that might become more than an assemblage of discrete thoughts.[28]

As early as his dissertation (1770), Kant criticized reductions of time and space to moments and points: "Each portion of time whatsoever is thus time, and the simples that are in time, namely *moments*, are not parts of it, but boundaries, between which time lies" (*De mundi sensibilis*

A15).[29] Objects and actions, insofar as they are bounded and particular, *occupy* a space and time of which they are not actually part. Outside these particular sensations and experiences lie a space and time without internal boundaries or demarcations. The mind or consciousness is cognate with these pure, unbounded forms of perception. In particular, the time of thought or consciousness is not a moment but an indefinite extent. Time becomes a correlative of space, long before the refutation of Berkeley in the second edition of the *Critique of Pure Reason*; it is the inner space in which our experiences become continuous and therefore comparable with one another. What matters is expanse and flow, not measure.

When we say that Kant's system is transcendental, we mean that it circumscribes the limits that constitute empirical reality. In their transcendental use words such as *time* or *consciousness* suppress the discrete, quantitative connotations of prior usage and acquire new, qualitative meanings. They become an indistinct feeling (say, of orientation or of personal identity) that precedes any possible, limited application. In these terms Kant's obscure critique of Descartes becomes comprehensible as the creation of a new conception through the willful suppression of the old.

Kant misunderstands Descartes—he *must* misunderstand Descartes—by misreading an empirical intuition as a transcendental syllogism: "The 'I think' is, as already stated, an empirical sentence, and contains within itself the sentence, 'I exist.'" But Descartes never said, "Cogito, ergo existo," but rather "Ego cogito, ergo sum (sive existo)." Kant's criticism is only possible if the difference between particular existence at this moment or these moments and existence in general (being, or necessary existence) has been effaced. He wanders furthest from Descartes not in the contents of his critique but in the vocabulary that gives it its transcendental coloration. The words *indefinite, pure, in general*, with which Kant strews his note, are, to Descartes, neither thinkable nor writable. Though Descartes inhabits "shadows" (*Discourse* 2; 6: 16: "dans les ténèbres"; Latin 6: 547: "noctu et in tenebris"), the shadows presume at least a little light, perhaps from his stove, and he marches, however circumspectly, toward the brightness. There are no fundamentally hidden recesses, no inscrutable labyrinths, no prudential authorial reserves.[30]

The Kantian self consists of a collection of pure, transcendental intuitions, such as time, that lie between, around, outside of all its empirical experiences. The problem of personal identity has been circumvented. Selfhood is not subject to the whims of empirical memory, as in Locke; our dreams are part of our self because they exist in temporal continuity with our waking existence, even though in our dreams we may not remember who we are. Selfhood is also not the fiction of a subsisting intelligence as in Hume; consequently, we remain the same person even when we go mad and lose the power to shape our life. But what this "something" is, this third thing (neither phenomenon nor noumenon) designated by the sentence, "I think"—that we cannot further say. It is an abstract existence, a space of possibility, beyond any conceivable specification. The purity of the transcendental ego depends on its intangibility. Both Descartes and Kant utter the sentence *ego sum* (or "ich bin einfach") as a founding gesture, but for the former it is the predicate, for the latter the subject that remains empty, opening onto mysterious potentialities.

Elaborating those potentialities must be the task of other accounts of Descartes's materialism and Kant's idealism. This chapter is directed toward their origins. Concepts and systems take their rise from the places where the language fails in clarity and in comprehension. Even Kant and Descartes, two of the least graceful writers of philosophical prose, elicit the conceptual power of their language from out of its nodes of silence. Kant misunderstands Descartes in virtue of a precise grasp of what Descartes would have had to say if he spoke Kant's language. The precision of the misunderstanding is reflected in the many commentators who assimilate the two philosophers to one another. Such affinities will always be felt where doctrine responds to doctrine, even in correction or disagreement. But the greatest thinkers, like the greatest poets, find their imaginations rooted in the mysteries of their language. Mind calls out to mind, but from the solitude of words, migrating through the vacancy of the ages.

CHAPTER 7

Toward an Archaeology of English Romanticism

Coleridge and Sarbiewski

GREAT WORKS OF literature conceal their origins: they are great because they solve stylistic problems, not because they raise them. Often, therefore, vital poetic issues surface not in the mature works of major authors but in less polished and more truly problematic minor works. The historical dialectic of styles is most directly expressed in such partial successes, rather than in masterpieces or in outright failures. If it is true of history, as Michel Foucault has said of discourse, that it is "the path from one contradiction to another," then these works are the points of articulation. And if to analyze history (Foucault again says discourse) is "to hide and reveal contradictions," then the historian's task is clearly indicated: to study them against the receding background to which they respond and in the light of the nascent works toward which they point (*Archaeology of Knowledge* 151). They will be the historian's poetic crossings, the signposts of literary history.

The poem at the center of the present chapter, Coleridge's "Ad Lyram," is translated from a Latin ode by Matthew Casimir Sarbiewski, among the most widely read of all neo-Latin poets and then still famous as the "divine Casimire" and the "Polish Horace." As a translation Coleridge's poem conveniently defines the specific context from which it emerges. The works of Sarbiewski present the problems and the prior English translations anticipate the Romantic solution whose stylistic intention is most clearly visible in Coleridge's exploratory translation.

IMITATION

The solemn-breathing air is ended—
　　Cease, O Lyre! thy kindred lay!

From the Poplar branch suspended,
    Glitter to the eye of Day!

On thy wires hov'ring, dying,
    Softly sighs the summer wind:
I will slumber, careless lying,
    By yon *waterfall* reclin'd.

In the forest hollow-roaring,
    Hark! I hear a deep'ning sound—
Clouds rise thick with heavy louring!
    See! th'horizon blackens round!

Parent of the soothing measure,
    Let me seize thy wetted string!
Swiftly flies the flatterer, Pleasure,
    Headlong, ever on the wing.

The following advertisement was prefixed to the original publication, and the Latin text was added.

If we except Lucretius and Statius, I know not of any Latin poet, ancient or modern, who has equalled Casimir in boldness of conception, opulence of fancy, or beauty of versification. The ODES of this illustrious Jesuit were translated into English about one hundred and fifty years ago, by a Thomas Hill, I think. I never saw the translation. A few of the ODES have been translated in a very animated manner by Watts. I have subjoined the third ode of the second book, which, with the exception of the first line, is an effusion of exquisite elegance. In the imitation attempted, I am sensible that I have destroyed the *effect of suddenness*, by translating into two stanzas what is one in the original.

AD LYRAM

Sonora buxi Filia sutilis,
Pendebis alta, Barbite, populo,
    Dum ridet aer, et supinas
        Solicitat levis aura frondes:

Te sibilantis lenior halitus
Perflabit Euri: me juvet interim
    Collum reclinasse, et virenti
        Sic temere jacuisse ripa.

Eheu! serenum quae nebulae tegunt
Repente caelum! quis sonus imbrium!
    Surgamus! heu semper fugaci
        Gaudia praeteritura passu.[1]

Sonorous daughter of sewn boxwood, o Lyre, thou wilt hang from the tall poplar, so long as the air smiles and a gentle breeze stirs the reclining boughs: through thee the gentler breath of the whistling east wind will blow: meanwhile I shall enjoy having reclined my head, and thus perchance having lain on the green bank. Alas! what clouds suddenly cover the clear sky! what a sound of showers! Let us rise! alas joys will always pass by with a fleeting step.

"The influence of [the Aeolian harp] upon the heart is truly pleasing," wrote one Charles Bucke around 1808: "it disposes the mind to solemn, tender and pathetic emotion, and, winning upon the imagination, strikes the heart with its simplicity, and leaves it resting in all the pure delights of a pleasing melancholy" (quoted in Bloomfield, *Remains* 1: 126–27). Coleridge's poem certainly aspires to a wistful Aeolian simplicity, and for that very reason it remains difficult to analyze. But we can take his advertisement as an initial guide to the hidden and revealed contradictions in the translation and to the necessary preparations and conditions for Coleridge's achievement. Three signal departures from Sarbiewski can be identified; in each case the English retains a trace of the original orientation as a token of the change in perspective and as a link to the past. First, there is the "opulence" and "exquisite elegance" of the Latin—such as its precious refinement of temporal and modal relationships—from which Coleridge derives only one hint of jewel-like "glitter" and one elegantly metaphorical usage, the delicate "wires" of the lyre. Second, where Sarbiewski, in the first stanza, portrays the lyre as a "daughter" of nature, Coleridge's last stanza views it as the "parent" of a humanized "measure." Gone is the natural filiation of art, though even Coleridge's lyre remains mysteriously "akin" to the air. Finally, Coleridge claims to have suppressed the original "effect of suddenness," though again the conventionally epiphanic "hark" and "see" preserve a residue of that "crash of onset" ("Fears in Solitude," line 37) with which Coleridge's poems so often flirt.

Each of these changes identifies and responds to a significant contradiction in the tradition and thus defines an element of the poem's originality. Coleridge's reservations about Sarbiewski's opening line help to pinpoint two of the contradictions. To begin with, elegant, elaborately decorative language is liable to be mere show, tinsel masquerading as substance. The first line in particular, with its all too prominent phonetic patterning and its empty mythological display, is "sonorous" and flamboyant rather than exquisite. Moreover, the dangers of excess display are not only stylistic. Sarbiewski's moral, with its shift from "I" to "we" ("surgamus"), claims to be universal. But his language is too well-knit ("sutilis"), his setting too artfully contrived, his casual "thus perchance" ("sic temere") too coyly casual—and his Latin too learned—for this to seem anything but a fashionable *bergerade*, a spoiled picnic of no general moral significance. Coleridge's simplicity, then, is an attempt to replace the false subtlety of overelaboration with a true subtlety of implication.

The second problem is that of art and nature. As the "daughter of boxwood," the lyre is a natural object. Yet even for Sarbiewski the lyre is a human artifact: it is *his* lyre ("Ad suam testudinem" is the title in the editions), and it regularly appears as a symbol for his poetry (cf. esp. *Odes* 3.32 and 4.26). Poetry is a product of human language, not of nature. Indeed, poetry is an especially artificial type of language: it uses the learned Latin instead of Sarbiewski's native Polish, the learned word "barbitos" instead of the natural "lyra" (Coleridge significantly substitutes "lyra" in the title for the original, figurative "testudo" [literally a tortoise-shell]), the learned feminine gender of "barbitos" instead of the "natural" masculine (*Od.* 4.26.11–12), the circumlocution "daughter of the box" instead of the natural "lyre," and so forth. Moreover, the artifice is inevitable. If art is to read a human significance in a natural occurrence, then it must see nature in human terms; if Sarbiewski wishes to have nature minister a moral lesson, then he must personify nature as the minister. From the romantic perspective, the language of art—indeed all language, though that is not the issue here—is not inherently natural, but rather human and, so to speak, artificial.[2] Coleridge's simplicity is an attempt to replace a histrionic pretense of naturalism with a true directness of refined human speech.

But what about the third problem? Why suppress the effect of suddenness? And what replaces—or rather transcends—it in Coleridge's poem? This is the most fundamental and difficult question. To approach it, I should like to examine Sarbiewski's poetry in more detail and in particular to study the problem of the continuity of his poetic voice.

*   *   *

Compounded of precious gems, flashing lights, sparkling waters, and surprising conceits, Sarbiewski's odes are anything but reticent.[3] Their poet seeks rare words ("illimis," "regemo"), coins resonant phrases ("formidolosos quadrupedantum onagrorum hiatus"), and competes with his poetic antecedents (as with the more than sesquipedalian word "superstitiosioris"). It is undoubtedly such vocal pyrotechnics which led Edward Young to praise Sarbiewski for his "ready wit and happy fire" ("An Essay on Lyric Poetry," *Works* 332). Yet the odes are wooden and without music. Extremely derivative—virtually a Horatian cento—and written in a foreign language, they are mechanical in their treatment of a limited repertoire of stanza forms, with an arbitrary placement of pauses and no regard for normal stress patterns.[4] Showy but graceless, the Latin of the odes is strictly a learned and written language.

The odes thus embody a contradiction: a will to vocal display combined with a failure of the voice. Sarbiewski's primary commitments were, indeed, not to poetry, but to the service of God, the glory of his countrymen, and the defeat of the infidels. He views poetry as imitation, a fundamentally redundant and empty activity regularly associated with the vocabulary of repetition: "iterare," "geminare," and a whole series of "re-" compounds. Properly, the poet's voice is merely a preparation for the warrior's silent action: "Many are we who can speak great things; arduous enterprises call on few."[5] Though a spokesman and a prophet, Sarbiewski's poet calls for an end to the lazy luxury of speech, notably in the last ode in book 3, a farewell to poetry which concludes the first edition of the odes and which stands in polemical contrast to Horace's similarly placed, proud, "Exegi monumentum aere perennius." Hence, a conflict arises between religious and national allegiance and poetic calling, between duty and reflection, conscience and voice.

Poetic narrative is weak and effeminate, a mere surrogate for true life: "In vain by the November hearth do we tell of the wars fought beneath the Rhaetian Alps; in vain do we recount the Gelonian standards carried backwards in retreat: unless we ourselves dare to grasp Norican swords."[6] Though the odes refer rather often to narration, they contain little actual narrative, and most of it is "concealed" in some fashion by being purely imaginary, for instance, or by encapsulation in a simile or a fictional inserted story ("fabula": *Odes* 2.17.21). At its worst—as in the following excerpt from an extended imaginary narration describing the future recovery of the lush, pastoral Greek landscape—narrative degenerates into a flamboyant play with sound effects:

Est, quem comantûm gratia montium,
Aut floridorum tangit amoenior
  Vultus Viretorum?

(*Odes* 1.12.41–43)

At best, the achievement of narrative is not a creation, but a mere recreation,[7] a bad luxury purchased at a mortal cost. An exception is made only for those actions which cannot be suspected of indulgence and sloth: unconcealed narrative in the odes concerns chiefly heroic action, death, and natural catastrophe. Thus, the only conceivable modes of being are stasis (absence of narrative, pastoral reduced to gemlike hardness) and disruption,[8] and the only people are those with whom we live in harmony and the bellicose Others (Protestants and Muslims) whose very existence presents a dire threat. Predictably, this threat predominates over the illusion of peaceful harmony, just as action predominates over hollow leisure and silence over the tinkle of verse. The whole complex of values is illustrated by Sarbiewski's idiosyncratic version of the mutability theme: in his poetry time completely effaces the inauthentic, vocal, poetic order of nature, and mutability consequently is a silent and exclusively human spectacle: "Whatever a human hand has joined a human hand will tear asunder." "And I, who yesterday was beheld by many peoples not without silent joy, tomorrow shall behold the substitute tragedy from among the crowd."[9]

In order to make the ode speak, Coleridge must attempt first of all to find a compromise between the irreconcilable poles of narrative: immobility and destruction. If the language of poetry is not to be as dead as Sarbiewski's Latin, it must produce a model for a kind of change which is not destructive. It must, in sum, learn to trace a development while suppressing the shock—the "effect of suddenness"—that always accompanies development in Sarbiewski.

But the problem of voice in Sarbiewski is even more complex, for he spurns natural space along with the natural temporal continuum. The "golden profusion" of "pleasant meadows" is a deceitful illusion, and one ode reminds us that Jason had to "wound" the land "with the iron teeth of the Chalybes" before he could harvest "the deciduous manes of gold."[10] Never more than a place for temporary recuperation and dissipation of sorrow (*Odes* 3.5, "Si quae juvabit dicere saucium," again associating natural peace with a wound), nature appears more characteristically as the place in which God is silent and hidden from man: "O what region detains you in silent repose, O Jesus? What spot begrudges you to me with blind shadows or thick foliage?"[11] Indeed, Sarbiewski rarely turns his attention to nature, and then never as a real object of description but always as an unreal allegorical construct or typological prefiguration (as in *Odes* 2.13, the night sky as a figure of the absent Virgin).

There is, in effect, no world for him to describe; his speech is invariably either reflexive or empty. Where description is in order, as in *Odes* 2.12, whose subtitle is "Describit pacis commoda" [describes the comforts of peace], the incantatory excitement of the verse attempts to compensate for the absence of true vision and significant description. Instead of actually portraying the advantages of a future state of peace, the poem gives only a feeble and derivative evocation of the ceremony of triumph by the victors, with a false urgency of repetition and a false luxuriance of sound.

> Ite, Rhaetaeis sociae triumphis,
> Ite delectos religate flores,
> Ite, Virtutes: iterate nexis
>   Serta tropaeis.
>
> Te Ceres flavis redimita culmis,
> Magne pacati Moderator orbis,
> Te Jovis quercus, & Apollinaris
>   Umbra corymbi,
>
> Te volunt lauri.[12]

The emptiness of such an external world casts doubt on the authenticity of vision. The poet is a prophet, but does he see the things of which he speaks?[13] The answer is clearly no; prophecy remains intransitive. All the odes, for example, have an addressee, save one: "The Prophecy of Noah" (4.27) is the most self-consciously prophetic but also the least transitive. The omission of the addressee here indicates a general plight: Sarbiewski everywhere mistrusts his vision: "And, *Lycus*, is there anything which we discern? Or does our sight err (through the foolish lids) and the glass of the eye lie? Or is it the tale of a long sleep which is being drawn out?"[14] The odes are full of prophecies, but it is significant that the prophetic formulae are always the most cautious imaginable: "videor videre," "videor audire," "aut vidi, aut vidisse putavi" (I seem to see, I seem to hear, either I saw or I thought I saw).

Again there is a fundamental contradiction, a will to vision combined with a failure of vision. The odes contain an abundance of introspective moral reflection, but there is no revelation of an outside reality, no epiphany. Even the formulae of epiphany are absent: the Christian "ecce" does not appear significantly in the odes, and "en" (the Latin equivalent of "lo") does not appear at all.[15] Only in the *Silviludia*, a set of beautifully active hunting eclogues wrongly attributed to Sarbiewski, do we find the word "en," and the context is instructive: "Lo the many-colored flower with the painted lips of its leaves *silently* proclaims the divine graces."[16] Epiphany—the recognition of the outside world—is silent revelation. There is no revelation in Sarbiewski because there is too much noise.

Once more we return to Coleridge. First, because he installs the epiphanic appearance of an outside event; his "hark" and "see" replace Sarbiewski's theatrical "effect of suddenness" with a better prepared and more deliberate influx from outside. And second, because he corrects the imbalance between voice and eye with a perfect correlation between the sound and sight of the storm, between the music and the "glitter" of the lyre.

But the recovery in Coleridge's poem is almost too complete. His simplicity masks the complexity both of the problem and of its solution. On the one hand, he attempts to recover a temporal continuum. On the other, he attempts to restore the possibility of description, that is, of expressing the Other, the discontinuity between the self and the world. Epiphany functions, in other words, as a *discontinuous continuity*. In order to clarify its structure, we need to see it gradually emerge in response to the challenge implicit in Sarbiewski's poetry. Coleridge's poem will then find its place as the culmination of a long series of efforts to translate and assimilate Sarbiewski's odes.

* * *

Given the prominence of military imagery in Sarbiewski, one could describe the failure of his poetry as the result of a lack of discipline. Correspondingly, the one universal characteristic of the English translations is an increased formal discipline. In the couplet versions both line and couplet tend to function as units of sense, and even the freest Pindaric imitations are divided on the page into numbered stanzas that force the translator to organize his material more clearly and distinctly than do Sarbiewski's continuous stanzas. Similarly, the frequent aphorisms in the Latin can be of any length; in the translations they usually fill out one or two lines.[17]

Among the many choices to be made by the conscientious translator is that between fidelity to sound and fidelity to sense. The rare telltale Latinisms or punning translations show that it was possible to prefer sound, but the English prefer overwhelmingly to preserve the sense and simplify the rhetoric; they neglect the intricate Latin harmonies and eliminate much of the exotic paganism and many merely decorative sensuous topoi.[18] In one sense such choices impoverish the original, but in return the translations are often more general and more widely applicable than the Latin poems. Henry Vaughan, for instance, omits most mythological and geographical references, titles, direct address, and other particularizing features so as to transform poems about specific historical conflicts into utterances concerning "all" peoples.[19]

Though none simplifies so radically as Coleridge, all who discipline the excessive flamboyance of the originals endeavor to compensate for what has been sacrificed, "to supply the lost Excellencies of another *language* with new ones of their own" (Cowley, *Poems* 156). Therefore the translators countless times replace pagan, classical, or foreign details with Christian, modern, or (most often) English ones.[20] But nationalizing forms only a part of the overall endeavor of the translators, which might better be described as naturalizing. Faced with poems as dislocated in time and place as are Sarbiewski's revivals of an obsolete form, the translator attempts to place the text with respect to himself and his culture.[21] An examination of the ways in which the earlier translators attempted to localize the poems in a real time and a real space will illustrate the intentions which are more fully realized in Coleridge's version.

I will begin with a few examples of temporal placement that aims to clarify the narrative structure or point of view of the odes. Both translators of the lines "Stat tacitus cinis, / Cui serus inscribat viator: / *Cum populo jacet hic et ipso / Cum rege Regnum*" (2.5.54–57) felt the need to make the role of the "late traveler" more precise. Hils turns him into a pilgrim and emphasizes his temporal relationship to the destruction: "The silent dust remains, to let / The weary Pilgrim this Inscription set / (In after times, as hee goes by)" (23). Hughes insists on the extent of the destruction, specifies where the inscription will be placed, and leaves no doubt that the traveler is a fictive personage: "nought remains / But dust above and desert plains, / Unless some stone this sad inscription wear, / Rais'd by some future traveller" (lines 83–86). Isaac Watts's versions are the most thoroughgoing in this regard; he strengthens or eliminates indirect constructions, simplifies complicated subordinations or turns them into independent clauses, changes rhetorical questions into exclamations, adds finite verbs, often in lieu of infinitives and participles, and supplies many vivid narrative details. The result is a complete transformation of the originals; as Coleridge says, "A few of the Odes have been translated in a very animated manner by Watts." Here is a sample:

> Vobis fugaces vidi ego Bistonum
> Errare lunas, signaque barbaris
>   Derepta vesillis, et actam
>   Retro equitum peditumque nubem.
>
>   (4.4.65–68)

I saw Thracian crescents fleeing you, and banners torn from barbarian standards, and a cloud of horse and infantry driven back.

>   Then the *Turkish* Moons
> Wander'd in Disarray. A dark Eclipse
> Hung on the Silver Crescent, boding Night,
> Long Night, to all her Sons; at length disrob'd
> The Standards fell; the barbarous Ensigns torn
> Fled in the Wind, the Sport of angry Heav'n:
> And a large Cloud of Infantry and Horse
> Scattering in wild Disorder, spread the Plain.[22]

Watts's strongly visualized, painterly landscape illustrates how narrative depends on a feeling for movement and therefore on a sense of space. Even in poems with less narrative interest the translations regularly define an absent spatial perspective or clarify an existing one. Thus, Vaughan converts Sarbiewski's baroque lament on the universal weary homelessness of mankind (*Odes* 4.15) into a Horatian satire directed against those who displace themselves by traveling abroad. The feeling of belonging to a place pervades Vaughan's version down to the smallest detail. Sarbiewski's traveler, for instance, departs from "patriis . . . arvis" (paternal fields); Vaughan expands this bare phrase in order to humanize and localize it: "those *hills* our *fathers* walkt on here" (line 12). When Sarbiewski's traveler becomes ill, he takes his disease with him even if he returns home—home or nature is associated with illness, as elsewhere with a wound: "Frustra fideles si dominum retro / Morbi sequuntur" (in vain if faithful diseases follow their lord home; lines 17–18). Vaughan's traveler, on the other hand, takes his illness as a sign to return to where he, like all men, belongs: "And then (too late with *home* Content,) / They leave this *willful banishment*" (lines 25–26). For Sarbiewski, in fact, there is no home or place of rest on earth: "Tandemque nobis exsulibus placent / Relicta" (and at length what exiles have left behind delights them; lines 21–22). The good place is not a real place but heaven. And nature is not a place but an absence, the place where I am not, the place where God is not, the place of the wound.

The emergence of a concept of real place can best be observed in the translations from the most popular of the odes, the fifth of book 2. The poem is one of many heavenly ascents in Sarbiewski; he leaves the natural world, sees the earth "vanish into a point" ("vanescit in punctum," line 83), and is submerged in a vast, ineffable sea of light. Though the poem is long, only one phrase has anything resembling a descriptive function: "hic mite coelum" (here the sky [is] mild). And this phrase belongs to an anaphoric series of clauses in which "hic" shifts confusingly in meaning between "here on earth" and "here in heaven"; Johann Nikolaus Götz, the most literal of the translators, can only make sense of the passage by rendering "hic . . . hic . . . hic" (lines 13–16) with "hier . . . doch anderwärts . . . dort" (here . . . but elsewhere . . . there; Götz, 2: 39). There is no real definition of place but only a polarity between absence and mysterious presence, the nothingness of earth and the indescribably transcendent heaven.

In the first of the translations, Cowley's "Exstasie," this is already changed. Cowley's heaven is not a mystical state of being, but a sublime version of the familiar sky of earth; far from overwhelming the speaker's consciousness, it adapts itself to his capacities.

> Without *affright* or *wonder*
> I meet *Clouds* charg'd with *Thunder*,
> And *Lightnings* in my way
> Like harmless *Lambent Fiers* about my Temples play.
>
> (stanza 3)

In subsequent translations the distant earth increasingly assumes its own descriptive characteristics. Two sentences out of many are particularly revealing: "Oh! Object well deserving tears!" in John Hughes's "Ecstasy" (line 17) and, in Aaron Hill's "The Transport,"

> Oh! thou dim speck!
> Thou dusky earth! farewel,
> From height, like this, I see thee, plainly now!
> Thou art, at best, a kind of hope-cool'd hell.
>
> (*Works* 3: 232)

The translations develop a new polarization, not between presence and absence but between the world of the perceiving subject and the distant world of objects, between the warm, animated world here and the world out there which is also real (otherwise it could not be addressed) but cold and inanimate. The individual's possibilities are divided not between the irreconcilable poles of life and death, but between the world in which he is now participating and the world beyond his horizon, in which he is not now a participant, though he might be at some other time.

From these observations we can begin to understand the epiphanies with which English odes abound—all those "lo"s and "see"s and "hark"s, and indeed most of the innumerable references to seeing which the translators add. They are the gesture which opens up the world to the poet. The world has always been there—objectively—but now he chooses to make it part of *his* world.[23] The term "epiphany" is unfortunate and misleading. There is no sudden change in the world, no startling self-revelation of a mystery which was formerly hidden. Rather, it is the poet who suddenly opens his eyes and looks out; he casts his light on the world and enters into a living bond with it. The English ode is not a poetry of the observing eye; it is a poetry of the illuminating eye, shedding its light on the universe.[24]

This explains the possibility of a discontinuous continuity. The objective world remains what it was. Suddenly something startling *seems* to happen: suddenly something *seems* to stream in at the poet. But nothing sudden has happened out there—*natura non facit saltus*—rather, he has suddenly blinked, turned his gaze, let the light of his countenance shine upon it.

The theological coloring which I have given this definition derives from an important fragment by the German Romantic Novalis.[25] To the sublime poets of the eighteenth century, epiphany is not yet a divine act but only the imitation of one. God remains the prime source of illumination, "one immense and ever-flowing light," as Norris's version of 2.5 has it ("The Elevation," st. 6). But the incessant epiphanizing of the eighteenth-century Pindarics is the very reverse of the continual illumination which it is designed to echo: it is bombast and completely unable to establish the desired temporal continuum bridging a spatial discontinuity. What began as a potentially expressive gesture rapidly declined into mere gesticulation. Cowley, for one, could commemorate the *middle* of his journey heavenward with, "And lo! I mount."[26] And of Aaron Hill it has been said that "perhaps no poet of his century penned a noisier page" (Aubin, *Topographical Poetry* 98).

Poetry should be continual illumination, but the poet's inspiration is both flickering and overbearing. The eye of the poet, in other words, is antithetical to the eye of poetry. The pathos of this dilemma is evoked in Hughes's "Ecstasy." "The Wond'ring Muse transported sees," in this poem, "groves of trees" on the moon. What she thought were spots were instead the result of the steady light which appears "no more in shadowy spots." Almost immediately the poet interrupts her with his "when lo!" In contrast to the Muse, the poet sees the earth, now *with* spots and with intermittent light: "And to her Sister-Moon by turns gives light" (lines 130–38). The Muse is pure imagination; at another point in the poem she looks into the future and conjures up a nostalgic world of uniform pastoral harmony. But the poet rudely interrupts with his intermittent epiphany ("and lo!") and sees, instead, present death and devastation.

> Around the space of earth I turn my eye;
> But where's the region free from woe?
> Where shall the Muse one little spot descry
> The seat of happiness below?
> Here peace wou'd all its joys dispense,
> The vines and olives unmolested grow;
> But, lo! a purple pestilence
> Unpeoples cities, sweeps the plains,
> Whilst vainly thro' deserted fields
> Her unreap'd harvest Ceres yields
> And at the noon of day a midnight silence reigns.
>
> (lines 42–52)

In the reversals of Hughes's poem we can detect the incipient stage of that troubled Wordsworthian dialectic where the light of the poetic imagination finally supersedes and disrupts the poet's "light of sense" ("the eye and progress of my Song").[27] The earlier translators imposed a discipline on Sarbiewski—in order to illuminate his fundamental message for them—but they failed to discipline themselves. The excessively emphatic eighteenth-century translations do not so much recover a foreign tradition as appropriate a foreign authority for their own poetic conventions. In translation and in its homologue, epiphanic discovery, in the confrontation both with tradition and with nature, the poet-observer illuminates the outside world, but the act of illumination is properly a passive act of participation in a common experience. The task of the Romantics in this connection is clear: epiphany must be purged of its hubris. We seem, indeed, to look beyond Coleridge toward Keats's Mnemosyne-Moneta, the goddess who links past and future and whose blank eyes "beam'd like the mild moon" (*The Fall of Hyperion*, line 269).

* * *

But for now I remain with the "eye of Day." As a response to the contradictions outlined here, Coleridge's poem shows its originality in its consistency and stylistic decorum. New-Critical immanent interpretation cannot take proper account of the poem's continuities, for immanent interpretation rests on distinctions that "open" the work, using what has been called a "hermeneutic wedge," such as a verbal or structural irony, as an initial foothold.[28] An immanent approach will not necessarily "falsify" the poem, but it will inevitably slight what is undoubtedly the poem's greatest asset, the smooth, simple flow of its verse.

What then are the continuities of the poem? Note, first, some possible ironies (that is, possible discontinuities) which are avoided. "Clouds rise thick with heavy louring." There is a possible irony of personification; the clouds seem to stare at the poet. I will return to this. There is a possible irony in the treatment of substance: the clouds are thick, filmy matter is seen as dense. And this irony, barely hinted, is virtually absorbed in a third possible irony of motion: the clouds rise heavy. In another context there would appear to be a conflict of directions, but in this poem there is a perfect merging of directions. The light emanates upward from the glittering lyre and is watched by the eye of day. The lyre hangs down but shines up. The wind seems simultaneously to rise and fall—to hover and die. A generalized diffusion of energy—energy simultaneously of sight, of sound, and of motion—replaces a limited directionality.[29] Only the lines devoted to the poet gently—and as will be seen, significantly—emphasize the downward direction: "lying," "waterfall," "reclin'd."

A related diffusion of semantic energy results in the avoidance of a number of possible puns. Puns depend on a concentration of meaning; they split one word into two meanings or else yoke two words into one. But Coleridge presents us with a paronomastic spectrum that overthrows the whole notion of a plurality of distinct meanings. The lyre glitters "to" the sun: does the word mean "toward" or "in response to"? Which is the source of light, which the recipient? The "air" is ended. This "pun" occurs repeatedly in early Coleridge. The air is the atmosphere, Sarbiewski's "aer." Can the atmosphere end? Or is this the tune? Surely Coleridge perceives the end of the musical air. But a tune does not breathe except figuratively; literally the air breathes: the wind, as the poem says, "sighs." Or is "sighs" a figurative expression, a metonymy applying to the wind what really belongs to the harp? Can the wind be "solemn" or does that word really apply to the music? It becomes impossible to speak of two meanings, literal and figurative, proper and metonymic; there is one air, not two, a generalized diffusion of music informing both the atmosphere and the lyre.[30] What about "lay"? There is another possible pun. The lyre—or the air—sings its "lay" and the poet lies down. Does the poet imitate the lyre? Does he imitate metaphorically (he wants to be like it) or metonymically (it charms him to sleep)? Dare one say that the lyre makes him a lie-er? Surely not; at least, the text shuns any such semantic outrage. There is a generalized participation by the poet in the music but no definable yoking together of distinct meanings, no pun. What about "louring"? Again there is a possible pun, suggested by the editions which print the word as "lowering" (Shedd) or "low'ring" (E. H. Coleridge). Could "louring" mean "sinking lower"?[31] That would perhaps rhyme better with "roaring" than the primary meaning does. It would also make nonsense of the line: "clouds rise sinking lower." Clearly, there is no pun here either. Still, the suppressed second meaning ("sinking") does have a function: it deflects attention away from the witty personification which yokes the cloud to a glaring human face and thus it further relaxes the tone. These are all examples of what William Empson would call emotive language: they are simple words, with a fluid range of meaning.[32] Coleridge's artfulness thus restores the native emotional force of language.

Astonishingly, the diffusion of power affects the event. Even an attentive reading must miss the significance of the third stanza unless the historical substructure has first been revealed: we must know that we are to look for an epiphany which is a streaming out, directed by mind, and not a streaming in directed by matter. While Sarbiewski first sees clouds then hears the actual sound of rain, Coleridge hears distant sounds then sees gathering clouds. We presume that in Coleridge's version a storm looms, breaks in on the poet's slumber, wets the instrument. This natural inference in fact is made explicit in Johann Gottfried Herder's version of the ode ("Die flüchtige Freude," *Werke* 3: 339). But Coleridge does not sleep; he only expresses an intention to sleep. We infer that Coleridge goes to sleep after stanza 2, as we infer that it rains after stanza 3, but the poem, like "A Slumber Did My Spirit Seal," does not report the external occurrences.[33] Even the epiphanic moments in stanza 3 do not designate external actions; they mark the instant when consciousness is directed to ongoing processes. Coleridge's poem concerns itself above all with states of mind. Indeed, it is not certain that anything forceful, abrupt, or discontinuous actually happens outside. For in a beautiful displacement, Coleridge has added a waterfall to the ode. Somewhere water is already falling, in a natural anticipation of the storm. Coleridge *may* leave, in melancholy, after the rain. But he may leave out of prudence, his attention called to the anticipated effect of the rain by the spray which has already collected on the lyre. Such is the diffusion in Coleridge's poem that ultimately we do not know what occurs when.

Is the poem just an elaborate pun, a deceitful action by nature (by the waterfall) imitating a true epiphanic interruption (the fall of rain) and warning Coleridge, with a kind of comic catharsis, not to mistake the real sources of natural power? Is there, behind the sublime exclamations of the third stanza, an implied theology, however vague? No, the concept of power and of action is too diffuse even for that. It cannot confidently be said that anything in nature makes the lyre wet. The rainstorm is never explicitly described. The waterfall is present but only out there in the distance ("*yon* waterfall"). And even before the waterfall is mentioned, the lyre appears, by a further anticipation, *already wet*. For what glitters in Coleridge is always water.[34] Thus, in "The Eolian Harp," "Through my half-clos'd eyelids I behold / The sunbeams dance, like diamonds, on the main" (lines 36–37); in "Religious Musings," "dewy glitter" (line 101); and in "Separation," "Wealth's glittering fairy-dome of ice" (line 11). *The Aeolian harp, for Coleridge, is that thing which is always already wet*, always ecstatically out there in the world, even when it is here. As a bright and glittering object, it is always the focus of attention, always monitory, always epiphanic. It is continual illumination. And it is poetry.[35]

What does this mean? It means that poetic, "Aeolian" simplicity mediates a radically new conception of events. An event is no longer merely an "occurrence," something that "runs into" one. Instead, an event is a diffusion of power. An event is an occurrence (for example, a rainstorm) that the observer takes into his or her world. Its effect is not highly localized—in a particular moment of time and a particular word of the poem—but it spreads out, coloring the future and also the past. An event is the interpretation of an occurrence; more specifically, it is the reevaluation of the observer's position, as it is, as it was, and as it will be. The cardinal event in Coleridge's poem, an event described in the text and not merely implied between the stanzas, is a change of mind, the replacement of one intention ("I will slumber") by another ("Let me seize thy wetted string").

An event colors the past and future as well as the present. No longer is time divided into two exclusive categories, the *now* and the *not-now*, the quick and the dead. Instead, the past, to the extent that it is capable of being thought at all, is still in some sense with us, affecting our behavior and capable of being affected by it. And the future, to the extent that it can be imagined at all, is already in some sense with us, influencing our intentions and influenced by them.

The poem's verb tenses flesh out this conception of experience. From the present perfect of the first line[36] through the imperative, the abundance of present participles, and the varieties of present indicative—the iterative "sighs," the momentary "hark," the incipient or durative "rise" and "blackens"—to the future-directed intentional present of "let me seize" and the gnomic, generalized present of the moral, there is a sense of continued presence, continually changing. (Herder's translation, by contrast, gives the reader a jolt with one past tense: "Dunkle Wolken umhülleten / Den heitern Himmel" [dark clouds have covered o'er the cheerful sky; *Werke* 3: 339].) The experience possesses an extraordinary ductility; there is not one single occurrence but a constellation of a dozen different ones, each with its own impetus, which combine to make the rainstorm. The sources of action are many and widely diffused.

Yet it would not be accurate to call this simply a subjectivization of the concepts of time and experience, for the observing subject is suppressed to the same extent as the rainstorm. The approach of the storm seems sudden primarily because Coleridge is slumbering; he, the subject, has decided to absent himself from the occurrence. The crucial lines in this connection are the pair which forms something of an exception to the general pattern of the poem: "I will slumber, careless lying, / By yon waterfall reclin'd." Here is the one verb not in the present tense, the one element of apparently unfettered choice, and the one passage in which a single direction of movement predominates. But the direction is downward, a movement of inertia, toward the object earth and away from the principle of life. Paradoxically, free choice—the act of subjectivity—has as its goal this gravitational movement, absence of will, slumber.

Experience is participation in the "life of things," "identifying the Percipient & the Perceived," as Coleridge comments on Wordsworth's phrase (*Notebooks* 921). More accurately, in view of the repeated anticipations and the crucial future tense in the poem, one could say that experience is an anticipatory self-projection into the world.[37] It is active—you bring things into your life. It is also passive—you enter into the life of things. Really, it is active and passive at once and indivisibly, for "self-experience . . . is not possible without an intermediate faculty"—the imagination, and above all the poetic imagination—"which is at once both active and passive" (*Biographia Literaria* 72).[38] It demands a will to enter in, somewhere: a partial submergence of things (you cannot attend to everything at once) and also a partial submergence of self. Full active presence of mind is unthinkable (though entry 2026 in the *Notebooks* does attribute to poetic geniuses the power of "*pure Action*, defecated of all that is material & passive"); it would mean that everything passed in review as an indifferent spectacle, without once casting the mind into a state of passive receptivity and affecting it. Coleridge's will to indolence in this poem, as a translation of Sarbiewski, is a form of discipline; it is the proper disciplining of egotism.[39]

*   *   *

Such is the nature of Coleridge's response to the problems of vision and temporality in Sarbiewski's baroque odes. Yet Coleridge's imitation, though a fine poem, is not a great one, and its shortcomings help to identify one of the fundamental ambitions of the Romantic poets.

It seems evident that the weakest lines are the somewhat top-heavy moral. Having established a continuous flow, Coleridge cannot close it off without breaking it. A similarly broken progression toward a moral is found throughout Coleridge, in "The Eolian Harp," in "The Rime of the Ancient Mariner," in "Christabel," in "Dejection," as indeed in Coleridge's life.[40] Yet it is difficult to pinpoint the nature of the break. In the version by Coleridge's friend Joseph Hucks a new, reflective speaking voice supervenes and draws the moral by rational analogy; the outcome is a false identification of the fleeing man with the figure of pleasure: "O my harp, my companion, my treasure, / Let us rise, let us *hasten away*: / 'Tis thus flies the phantom of pleasure, / With quick step ever *hasting away*" (182, my italics). But Coleridge grafts on his moral in a more subtle, seemingly less arbitrary fashion. He links it phonically ("swiftly flies"—"softly sighs") and rhetorically ("on the wing"—"on thy wires hov'ring") to the wind. Furthermore, he links it as a personification to the earlier personifications—to the personification of the wind, to the subdued but paradoxically threatening personification of the clouds, and especially, by rhyme and similarity of function, to the personification of the lyre ("parent of the *soothing* measure"—"the *flatterer*, Pleasure"). Coleridge thus aims at a generalized diffusion of relationships between the event and the moral. The moral appears to arise not out of a posterior reflection but rather as a musical echo, a sympathetic vibration in the mind.

Still, there is an evident break in tone, and it colors our sense not so much of the last two lines as of the first fourteen. In contrast to Sarbiewski's eroticism, Coleridge's poem is cool, almost inert, with its soothing parental figure, for instance, replacing what Coleridge's punning ear must have taken to be a "buxom" daughter. But abruptly "the flatterer, Pleasure," emerges as a new character for whom nothing in the earlier lines has prepared the reader. Instead of an interpenetration of human awareness and natural process, an external agency now seems to frustrate Coleridge's desires. In particular, we are reminded of another concealed flatterer, Sarbiewski's "whistling Eurus," hidden behind the sibilants of Coleridge's sixth line. In the light of the closing lines, we are led to see the wind as a seducer, playing on the harp in order to attract the poet; Coleridge's slumber in the distance then appears as a rejection of nature's advances and the scowling storm clouds as the lover's angry reaction. Thus, despite Coleridge's efforts to link the moral to what precedes, it is a new event that affects, as events often do, what seems already past. The language has seemed completely compact, with no distinction of levels, of literal and figurative, of sense and significance. But from the later perspective the event is seen merely as a literal level on which an allegorical interpretation can be imposed. The event seemed rich; it now seems less completely rich. It seemed eloquent, but now it seems to need a spokesman. The precarious continuity has been broken.

As a summary indication of the subsequent course of development I should like to juxtapose Coleridge's poem with the work of a major post-Romantic poet, Stéphane Mallarmé. Needless to say, there is even less occasion to speak of Coleridge's "influence" on Mallarmé than of Sarbiewski's on Coleridge. Nevertheless, in both cases the later poet's solution sheds light on the problems of the earlier poet: Mallarmé's poetry, that is, helps to show what was needed in order to complete the project begun in works such as "Ad Lyram."

Even in the absence of a direct line of historical influence, Coleridge and Mallarmé share important concerns. What Hugo Friedrich has identified as "the three fundamental forces of [Mallarmé's] poetry and of his thought" are named in a line of the poem "Salut" which introduces the collected poems: "solitude, récif, étoile" (*Struktur* 90). The two poles of experience are thus virtually identical for the two poets: on the one hand, the isolated consciousness, on the other, the distant star (the "eye of Day" in "Ad Lyram," "the star of eve" in "The Eolian Harp"). What is more striking is that the mediating objects also correspond, since both Coleridge's Aeolian harp and Mallarmé's reef are always already immersed in the spray of the world. This implies, as we have seen, that for both poets the unity of experience is provided by an existential projection.

But there remains a crucial difference. Coleridge's Aeolian harp is the pure poetic voice of the world, corresponding to the sound of waters in Wordsworth or (more precariously) in Joseph von Eichendorff; it is the goal of a profound, though sometimes ambivalent desire. Mallarmé's reef, by contrast, is a place of shipwreck and destruction; it is "time, the cape," whose sinking ship reflects "night, despair, and precious stones" ("Au seul souci de voyager"). The shipwreck, unlike the harp, is "silent," and its instrument—not a lyre, of course, but a (fog)horn—is "without virtue" and "enslaved even to echoes" ("A la nue accablante tu"). Throughout Mallarmé's poetry runs the yearning for an echoing song that is the reverse of the voice of the harp, not protected and edenic but destructive; he likens poetry to a swan that remains whole even when it dies and that causes more pain to the human poet than to itself ("Petit air II"). If Coleridge's harp is the pure voice of poetry, then Mallarmé's reef answers with an elusive siren voice that destroys the poetic voice.[41] Mallarmé's poetry calls for a destruction of the poetic image.

The obstacle in Coleridge's poetry is the dependence on a symbolic image, an object or occurrence which is not really literal, which does not mean itself but something else: "My heart plays an incessant music / for which I need an outward Interpreter" (*Notebooks* 2035).[42] This is the residual discontinuity in his work. Some 25 years later Shelley was still struggling to achieve a musical fusion with nature in a fully organic language, though he experienced the struggle with the greater anguish of a generation-long ambition still unfulfilled: "Make me thy lyre, even as the forest is . . . Be thou, Spirit fierce, / My spirit! Be thou me!" ("Ode to the West Wind"). In Mallarmé, subject, object, and language are all absorbed into pure, unbroken relationships—what Derrida has called an "irreducible excess of the syntactic over the semantic"[43]—into "an extraordinary appropriation of structure, limpid, from the primitive fires of logic" ("Le Mystère dans les lettres"). Two works name their primitive structure in the title—*Igitur* (therefore) and "Or" (now); in others it forms the obvious backbone of the text—"comme si" in "Petit air I" and in part of the *Coup de dés*, for instance—and always there is an attempt to abolish objects. The book itself is no longer an object; it effervesces into a "spiritual instrument."[44]

The Romantics continue to need an instrument, a symbol around which to organize their experience. For them, to return to the theme of

Coleridge's poem, an event is a re-placement of the self *by means of something*. In Mallarmé, an event is pure placement: "RIEN N'AURA EU LIEU QUE LE LIEU" (*Un Coup de dés*, *Oeuvres* 474–75).

The task the Romantics face in their great works is the submergence of the symbol. This task itself is symbolized in their abiding fascination with dangerous vessels[45] and (above all in Wordsworth and Goethe) with floods and drowning. In Coleridge himself the effort to repress or submerge the symbolizing activity of the mind is perhaps the strongest of all. It is for this reason, for example, that his odes never summon but rather dismiss the powers of the imagination: one thinks of the titles "Ode to the Departing Year" and "The Recantation: an Ode" (later retitled "France: an Ode"), of the apostrophe in "Dejection: an Ode," "Hence, viper thoughts, that coil around my mind," and of the inevitable refrain of "An Ode to the Rain," "Do go, dear Rain! do go away!" From this perspective the poem that should form the center of a future study is not a conversation poem or a poem of imagination (though the symbolic albatross sinks "like lead into the sea") but rather a poem that lies somewhere in between—a song whose title, incidentally, is a phonetic elaboration of the word "lute"—the strange love chant, "Lewti": "Nay, treacherous image! Leave my mind— / For Lewti never will be kind."

CHAPTER 8

Romanticism and Enlightenment

> The new age proclaims itself fleet-footed, sole-winged; the dawn
> has put on seven-league boots.—Long has lightning flashed on the
> horizon of poetry; all heaven's stormy force was compressed into
> a mighty cloud; now it thundered mightily, now it seemed to retreat
> and flashed only from afar, soon to return all the more fearsomely:
> soon there will be no more talk of a single storm, but all the heavens
> will burn with one flame, and then all your petty lightning rods will
> avail no longer. Then the nineteenth century begins in earnest. . . .
> Then there will be readers who can read.
> —Schlegel, "Über die Unverständlichkeit"

Romanticisms and Enlightenments

ARTHUR O. LOVEJOY'S famous essay "On the Discrimination of
Romanticisms" showed the problem decades ago: Romanticism cannot
be defined. To write an essay called "Romanticism and Enlightenment"
seems, then, to be an impossibility compounded. In any reasonably
comprehensive view, the eighteenth century was not dramatically more
uniform than the early nineteenth. Indeed, in one crucial respect it was
less so, for no fact so inescapably galvanized the Enlightenment mind as
that of revolution did the mind of Romanticism. There are many versions of Enlightenment—aristocratic and bourgeois, rationalist and empiricist, modernist and classicist, mercantilist and laissez-faire, urban
and pastoral, religious and secular. Properly speaking, this chapter
should be entitled "Enlightenments and Romanticisms," a multiplicity
that leaves no hook except the little word "and" to hang a hat on.

That is what I propose to do. Though we may not be able to define
either Enlightenment or Romanticism, we may succeed better at defining their relationship. The historical sensibility was more fully developed in the Romantic period than earlier, and this means that how the
present relates to the past can be more important than what that past
was. We may be able to understand the "and" that connects Enlighten-

ments with Romanticisms without needing to fix either period as an entity. It is clear that such an approach—focusing on the process rather than the materials or the product—will not give us objective determinations. The "and" of the title is a vector without a precise location. I shall not ask what Enlightenment and Romanticism were in their essence, for they are each too manifold. Moreover, I shall compound the turn away from a goal of "objectivity" by asking how the Romantics sensed their relationship to the preceding generations rather than by attempting to ascertain the external facts.

For the truth is that the facts are contradictory. It is a truism, on the one hand, that the Romantics rebelled against their predecessors. The typical Romantic—so conventional wisdom runs—went to extremes. He was a godless revolutionary in his youth and, if he lived long enough, an orthodox traditionalist in his age but in neither case an Enlightened progressive. Somewhere along the line, the humanist tolerance best typified by Voltaire, Lessing, and Johnson (see Barnouw, "Erziehung des Menschengeschlechts") lost its appeal, giving way on the one hand to the libertinism of a Shelley or a Byron, on the other to the bigoted Catholicism of several of the older German Romantics. A common intellectual enemy was Newtonian rationalism, whose desiccated narrowness was attacked by Blake, by Keats (in *Lamia*), and, with otherwise uncharacteristic savagery, by Goethe in his vast *Theory of Color*. Romanticism, on this view, attacked Enlightened, classicizing, conformist rationalism in recognition of unstated emotions and unconscious instincts.

The evidence for the Romantic attack on Enlightenment lies everywhere at hand. The antirationalism of a De Quincey comes late enough that one might hesitate to identify it as an original impulse of Romanticism. But already among the first generation of Romantics one finds the geologist and poet Novalis (Friedrich von Hardenberg, 1772–1801) who, before his early death, composed the *Hymns to the Night*, the dream-dominated medievalizing romance *Heinrich von Ofterdingen*, the mystical, orientalizing story "The Apprentices at Sais," and the aphorisms collected under the titles *Pollen* and *Belief and Love*, most famous among them being the utterance "The secret way goes inward." Novalis was the subject of influential early essays by Carlyle: he was widely admired in mid-nineteenth-century France (see Besset, *Novalis et la pensée mystique*); and he has been taken (by Hugo Friedrich) to be, like Poe, a fountainhead of symbolist and expressionist poetry. If there had been one Romanticism confronting one Enlightenment in all of Europe, dark against light, Novalis would have been it. Were that the case, our story would be quickly told.

That simple story, finally, is easily corroborated in the English context. Blake assaulted all the canons of eighteenth-century art along with all the preconceptions of Lockean empiricism; Wordsworth vilified the diction of eighteenth-century poetry; supernatural sensationalism, such as Fielding reduces to ridicule in *Tom Jones* (8.11; 16.5), became the norm in the Romantic novel in England, France, Germany, and America; and Enlightened cosmopolitanism gave way to nationalism and the revival of indigenous mythologies. The eighteenth century wrote satire in heroic couplets, moral odes, local poetry, and extended didactic poems in Miltonic blank verse; the Romantics wrote sonnets, blank verse meditative lyrics, ballads, mythological or metaphysical odes, and first-person epics. Eighteenth-century novels were picaresque or epistolary; Romantic novelists satirized the picaresque or else wrote social, historical, or Gothic fictions. Eighteenth-century philosophy was empiricist and materialist; Romantic philosophy, after passing through the inhuman rigors of neo-Spinozism, became transcendental and idealist (see McFarland, *Coleridge and the Pantheist Tradition*).

Much in that conventional account is true. But inevitably a closer look complicates the picture. Writers such as Morse Peckham (*The Triumph of Romanticism*) and Virgil Nemoianu (*The Taming of Romanticism* 34) have shown the degree to which Enlightenment values persist despite the changed atmosphere of the nineteenth century. Formal philosophy, which became transcendental in Germany, remained rationalist with a tinge of mysticism in the French ideologues, rationalist with a tinge of metaphysics both in the English tradition that leads from David Hartley to William Godwin and Jeremy Bentham and in the later Scottish school of Thomas Reid, Dugald Stewart, and William Hamilton. Wordsworth's aesthetics, through the influence of Archibald Alison, remained strongly in the associationist tradition. Voltaire's ideal of tolerance continued in the writings of Schlegel, Shelley, and French Revolutionary thinkers— contemporaries often more different from one another than from their common ancestor. The "and" hinging Romanticism to Enlightenment links as much as it separates.

Literary developments are similarly complex. Neoclassicism, which was a formative element in the Enlightenment, remained a powerful if variable current in Goethe (who translated two of Voltaire's tragedies), Schiller, the later Schlegels, the artists of the French Revolution, Shelley, Keats, and the later Wordsworth ("Laodamia"). The mythological works of Keats, Shelley, and Friedrich Hölderlin in many respects remained faithful to the syncretic and euhemerist traditions of the Enlightenment, partly because they drew on many now forgotten seventeenth- and eighteenth-century mythographic compendia (see Hungerford, *Shores of Darkness*). In verse, Popean satire was not only reborn in Byron but also strongly colored Blake's prophecies and left traces in some of Shelley's works and even a few of Keats's. The development of stage drama is at once too complicated and (in Britain at least) too uninteresting to examine in detail here, but broadly it may be said that both in England and in France the main forms of Romantic drama (melodramatic tragedy, domestic comedy, and opera) grew continuously out of the eighteenth-century traditions, while in Germany the marked shift in style beginning around 1760 was more a turn from French to English models than an advance from Enlightenment to Romanticism. Nor did the Romantic novel simply reject earlier forms: Austen modeled her moralism and her meticulous prose on Johnson, while the epistolary novel survived, largely through the mediation of Goethe's *Werther*, in Hölderlin's *Hyperion*, Ugo Foscolo's *Jacopo Ortis*, Scott's *Redgauntlet*, and numerous others. These manifestations added up to a great deal of important writing in the Romantic period that prolonged Enlightenment paradigms, even while the mainstream—Romantic lyric, mythological closet drama (*Manfred, Prometheus Unbound, Faust*), and the familiar essays of Lamb and Hazlitt—differed profoundly from Enlightenment norms. Hence, writers like Marilyn Butler (*Romantics, Rebels and Reactionaries* 1–10), Jerome J. McGann ("The Anachronism of George Crabbe," *Beauty of Inflections* 294–312), and Anne K. Mellor (*Romanticism and Gender* 209–12, where the term *post-Enlightenment* is even briefly proposed) have increasingly objected that the simple view of Romanticism as a rejection of Enlightenment delivers a woefully impoverished picture of what was actually written by major figures in the decades after 1800.

A converse objection, long familiar, is that many elements of Romanticism are present in writers of earlier generations. Romantic nature feeling—affectionate dwelling on particulars, along with dreaming or daydreaming in dark grottoes, amid vast wildernesses, or on high mountains—is widespread in the writing of the second half of the eighteenth century, and it can easily be traced further back, to James Thomson and Edward Young, to moments in Pope's *Windsor Forest* and *Eloïsa to Abelard*, or, on the Continent, to such works as the precise descriptive poems of Thomson's German translator, Barthold Heinrich Brockes (1680–1747). The ballad revival, the Spenserian revival, the Gothic novel, the cult of sentiment, all date from the middle of the eighteenth century. Blank verse lyric really begins not with Wordsworth and Coleridge but with Akenside and his circle. Wordsworth's attack on poetic diction is foreshadowed in Oliver Goldsmith's *Life of Parnell* and again in chapter 8 of *The Vicar of Wakefield*, with its criticism of the "false taste" of the period that admires "a string of epithets that improve the sound without carrying on the sense." Countercurrents of Enlightenment culture, on this view, become main currents of Romantic thought: Swedenborg and Young lead to Blake (who illustrated Young's *Night Thoughts*), with the nine parts of *The Four Zoas* and of Shelley's *Queen Mab* modeled on Young's nine (see Curran, *Shelley's Annus Mirabilis*, chap. 1); Berkeley funnels into Coleridge, Friedrich Klopstock's Biblical dramas into Byron's, and Rousseau and Diderot (virtually exact contemporaries of Johnson, Gray, and Hume) into everybody. These countercurrents, it often used to be said (best by Henri Monglond in *Le Préromantisme*), constituted a preromanticism that coexisted with the official Enlightenment.

To be sure, few scholars still use the term *preromanticism*. Dislodging individual themes and motifs from the contexts where they occur gives a distorted picture of their significance: however steadily Brockes and Thomson may look at their subjects, devotional descriptions of birds and flowers do not greatly resemble Wordsworth's personal memory poems. And isolated and imperfect anticipations, such as Mark Akenside's *Inscriptions* or Horace Walpole's *Castle of Otranto* (written in 1764 but, as K. K. Mehrotra's *Horace Walpole and the English Novel* showed, not really influential until about the time of Ann Radcliffe), or even the handful of nature sonnets written by William Lisle Bowles in the years around 1790, do not equate with the prolific and controlled achievements of the Romantics. "Preromanticism," though widely diffused, turns out to be an unwitting and accidental by-product of other impulses, and hence radically different from the consciously worked out aims of the various Romantic writers, richly elaborated in a coherent body of works.

Nevertheless, accounts of an eighteenth-century preromanticism and of a Romantic post-Enlightenment conjointly remain valuable. What they lack in a spurious coherence they make up in a genuine complexity. They have taught us that many and often clashing forces were at play in both periods. We have been taught to view our traditional period concepts, as McGann says, more "critically." From Arnold to Yeats and beyond, Wordsworth and Shelley alike (let alone Keats and Blake) had been treated as elite, essentially private poets. A scholarly counterwave in the 1950's and 1960's stressed the fashionable, popular or populist dimensions of their writing. Yet the most recent criticism—partially returning to and contextualizing some Arnoldian themes (such as that poetry is the criticism of life)—has recognized that fashions respond to countervailing fashions. (This has always been evident in the German case, where the "Romanticism" of Novalis and the Schlegels encountered the simultaneous "Classicism" of Goethe, Schiller, and Wilhelm von Humboldt in a sometimes loyal, sometimes embittered opposition.) Recognizing "post-Enlightenment" values has meant learning again to highlight the oppositional elements in Romantic poetry. Wordsworth praising peasants, Shelley free love, Blake intellectual warfare, Byron libertine heroism, or Austen the traditional virtues of agrarian society— these all mean something different in the abstract from what they mean in a world of growing industrialism and antirevolutionary turmoil and repression.

Whatever one's assessment of individual arguments, critical and ideological readings of Romantic works have greatly increased our perception of covert and implicit meanings embodied within them. But they have also greatly complicated the task of the literary historian. It was all too easy to take Romantic values as the new and Enlightenment values as the old—or, worse, as the waves of the future and the past respectively in a world perpetually lacking a present. But if writing is oppositional (designed, one might simply say, to persuade someone of something), then we are dealing with a clash of contemporaneous values whose historical dimension remains to be investigated. The same considerations apply to the now outmoded accounts of preromanticism. Preromantic traits are undoubtedly present throughout the eighteenth century, and we owe a debt of gratitude to the scholars who have pointed them out. But these traits are oppositional features of the Enlightenment itself, not glimmerings of a new dawn; they need to be referred to their contemporary context in order to be understood. The Enlightenment can no more be limited to the *Essay on Man* than Romanticism to the cuckoo-and-daffodil vein.

And that is just as well. The traditional historical picture suffered from the illusion that we could simplify our task by assigning some features of a period to some other period. But the procedure is obviously circular. We need to know which values are Romantic in order to disentangle Romantic writing from post-Enlightenment writing, or preromantic from Enlightenment. But we need first to have disentangled them in order to know which values are Romantic. And the separation, could it be performed, is inimical to historical understanding. It tells us, at most, the difference between Enlightenment and Romanticism, but it does not explain the relationship between the two. Suppose we say that Enlightenment, to use Abrams's terms, is the mirror of wit, Romanticism the lamp of genius; that Enlightenment is collective and social and Romanticism private and individual (or, in accounts by Theodor Adorno and some others, the reverse); that Enlightenment is universalizing, Romanticism historicizing—any such characterizations obscure the processes by which Romanticism emerges out of Enlightenment. A taxonomic approach to periodization denies the rights of history. For all these reasons, we need to develop a more dialectical account than has hitherto been customary. Using an antithetical idiom, we can say that Romanticism *grows out* of Enlightenment. The new turns against the old, but it does so from a historical logic already inscribed in the old and still preserved in the new. The historical thrust of Enlightenment and the historical memory of Romanticism must alike be recognized if their succession is to be comprehended. Romanticism and Enlightenment differ from one another in consequence of the ways in which each differs internally from itself—in which Enlightenment is driven toward its opposite and in which Romanticism incorporates its antithesis.

The Darkness of Enlightenment

From a certain perspective it appears natural to pit the optimism or elation of the post-Restoration decades against the satiric impulse that dominated in the early eighteenth century. While the party of faith reacted to the Restoration with the resignation of the blind Milton, typified by the gloomy classicism of *Samson Agonistes*, or else with the bitterness of Marvell's "Last Instructions to a Painter," the party of Enlightenment welcomed what we call the "Glorious Revolution" in a mood of exalted panegyric. Dryden served as its spokesman, for despite the ever-popular *MacFlecknoe* and *Absalom and Achitophel*, he was only occasionally a satirist. It can easily be made to seem, then, as if the radiant fabric of Enlightenment gradually unraveled, with didacticism steadily giving way, for better or worse, before satire. With *The Rape of the Lock* leading to *The Dunciad*, Pope to Johnson, and the bright Augustan Age to the gloom of sensibility, the pattern seems to continue. From this scheme derives the oversimplified account, discussed in the first section of my chapter, which treats Romanticism as the rejection of Enlightenment and as the embrace of darkness.

By recognizing that darkness lies at the heart of Enlightenment, we can rearrange and clarify the received historical picture. If Dryden is at all representative, the mood of elation preceded the facts that were to justify it, for he celebrated Cromwell as a bringer of peace in the "Heroic Stanzas" before celebrating Charles in the same role in "Astraea Redux." Enlightenment rationalism, in other words, existed as an anticipatory cast of mind, even before it had any genuine reason to celebrate. And the hopes proved to be excessive, as genuine hope must always be. In that excess already lay the seed of the self-division that characterizes Enlightenment and that eventually destroyed it.

Here, from Dryden's "Annus Mirabilis," his greatest poem of the 1660's, are some euphoric stanzas that portray the Royal Society:

> This I fore-tel, from your auspicious care,
>   Who great in search of God and Nature grow:
> Who best your wise Creator's praise declare,
>   Since best to praise his works is best to know.
>
> O truly Royal! who behold the Law,
>   And rule of beings in your Makers mind,
> And thence, like Limbecks, rich Idea's draw,
>   To fit the levell'd use of humane kind. (657–64)

The bravado of this mood lies in its ready linkages of the divine and the human. The explosive formula of Spinozistic pantheism, *deus sive natura* ("God, i.e., nature," as it might be rendered), lurks close at hand. Milton's Adam, a year later, was to seek what the Archangel Raphael calls "knowledge within bounds" (*Paradise Lost* 7.120). His aim closely resembles Dryden's; he desires revelation in order, as he says, "the more / To magnifie his works, the more we know" (7.96–97). Yet Adam's priorities are clear: knowledge exists to further praise. Dryden's *ands*, by contrast, obscure the priority of God and nature, praise and knowledge, the rationality of law and the authority of rule. Likewise, the "is" in line 660—an uncommon and pointedly vague usage in Dryden's early style—obscures the relationship between present accomplishment and future potential: reason prevails at the expense of any clear ordering of values. And the last two lines run further risks in their implicit correlation of science with commerce, speculation with profit. "Reasoning I oft admire," Adam was soon to say, "How Nature wise and frugal could commit / Such disproportions, with superfluous hand / So many nobler Bodies to create, / Greater so manifold, to this one use" (*Paradise Lost* 8.25–29). Raphael immediately corrects Adam's rationalism with the injunction to "be lowlie wise" (8.173); there are many mysteries, he says, and the lights of heaven do not exist solely to enlighten man's mind. Reason reduces all things to man's measure.

Dryden in 1666 was no Leveller. The specious humility of his word "levell'd" betrays reason's dangerous reductions. Immediately, the perils of conflict arise to haunt the smooth progress of mind: "But first the toils of war we must endure" (665). Reason's alchemy promises to put all things on an even keel, but its anticipated glorious dawn is irremediably shadowed by the unpredictable terrain of experience. (The mixed metaphors are implied by Dryden's text and combine with the willed simplicity of the diction to constitute the complex strength of his style and of his insight.) Enlightenment begets self-scrutiny: the greater the aspirations of reason, the more difficult it is for humans to realize them. Thus does the elation of the 1660's prepare the way for the "unpolish'd, rugged Verse" (*Religio Laici* 453) of Dryden's doctrinal poems and of his fables.

> Dim as the borrow'd beams of Moon and Stars
> To lonely, weary, wandring Travellers,
> Is Reason to the Soul: And as on high,
> Those rowling Fires discover but the Sky
> Not light us here; So Reason's glimmering Ray

> Was lent, not to assure our doubtfull way,
> But guide us upward to a better Day.
> And as those nightly Tapers disappear
> When Day's bright Lord ascends our Hemisphere;
> So pale grows Reason at Religions sight;
> So dyes, and so dissolves in Supernatural Light.
>
> (*Religio Laici* 1–11)

Whether in religion or in politics, the Enlightenment yearned for the splendor of the sun. But it never forgot that light is born out of darkness. Charles II, Dryden says, began subject to a "black Star," and the "thaw" in 1660—so Dryden wishfully writes—came as but a heightening of the palette of experience.

> Yet as wise Artists mix their colours so
> That by degrees they from each other go,
> Black steals unheeded from the neighb'ring white
> Without offending the well cous'ned sight:
> So on us stole our blessed change; while we
> Th' effect did feel but scarce the manner see.
>
> ("Astraea Redux" 113, 134, 125–30)

The Enlightenment never basked in light; it was a world groping its way out of the darkness or seeing feelingly.

> The Gods are just;
> But how can finite measure infinite?
> Reason! alas, it does not know itself! . . .
> Whatever is, is in its causes just,
> Since all things are by fate. But purblind man
> Sees but a part o'the chain; the nearest links;
> His eyes not carrying to that equal beam,
> That poises all above.—
>
> (Dryden, *Oedipus* 3.1, in *Works*,
> ed. Scott 6: 174)

These lines, anticipating *Religio Laici* by some three years, typify the "Romantic" Enlightenment; in introducing the play, Dryden's Romantic editor Walter Scott calls them "excellent poetry, [which] expresses more sound truth, than a whole shelf of philosophers" (6: 123). If only the play were not so gruesome, Scott thinks the "complete management of light and shade" on the modern stage would let it "be represented with striking effect" (6: 120). We are not used to thinking of the Enlightenment as too extreme in its passions for the Romantics, but it could be. (For Wordsworth's complex response to *Religio Laici* and to Pope see Sanford Budick's brilliant essay "Chiasmus and the Making of Literary Tradition.")

The great philosophical image of the age was that of Descartes, sitting in the wintry darkness of Germany and seeking out reason by the light of his stove, "like a man who walks alone and in the shadows" (*Discourse on Method*, part 2). Like Dryden some decades later, Descartes was writing out of an experience of religious warfare with one claimant to sovereignty pitted against another (opening sentences of *Discourse*, part 2), but he acknowledges the violence and the homelessness that Dryden conceals. He will not, he tells us, preach a revolution that would overthrow the foundations of the state, but he will thrown down the house of his own experience in order to build it afresh. Locke, to be sure, never talks this way, but he too is very unsure of his ground in the "vast Ocean of Being" (*Essay Concerning Human Understanding* 1.1.7), and his famed cautiousness, as Leo Strauss beautifully put it, "is a kind of noble fear" (*Natural Right and History* 206).

Part of the oversimplification that neglects the dark side of Enlightenment results from concentrating on one or at most two genres at a time. While Dryden was writing poems in praise of reason, the nation, art, and science, comic playwrights—Dryden prominent among them—were excoriating the dissoluteness of the age. After 1700, the comic stage grew more sentimental and polite, and the Addisonian manner made the harsh polemics of a Jeremy Collier or a John Dennis unfashionable in essays. But in the verse satire of Swift, Pope, and, later, Churchill (see Lockwood, *Post-Augustan Satire*), the Juvenalian mode increased in importance (even—as Howard Weinbrot has shown—in imitations of Horace), becoming ever more personal and even vulgar in its attacks on vice and on vulgarity. Yet, on a comprehensive view, overlap between satire and sentimentality remains great: Pope and Thomson are the leading masters of eighteenth-century poetic diction; Pope and his older contemporary Young were closely associated in the popular mind; and it is not even difficult to find cases of the same poem appearing in both couplet and Pindaric dress (John Dyer's *Grongar Hill*) or in ironic and sentimental styles (William Shenstone's Spenserian imitation, *The Schoolmistress*). As the end of the century approaches, the temptation to compartmentalize grows ever greater. Vulgar spoofing seems to have been claimed by Fielding for the novel (*Humphrey Clinker*, *Tristram Shandy*). The heritage of Richardson goes its own separate way to fuel the explosive emotionalism of writers like Frances Burney and Elizabeth Inchbald. Satire, in Johnson and Goldsmith, turns increasingly toward an exaltation of feeling in recognition of what *Rasselas* calls "the uncertain continuance of reason." Yet stage comedy enjoys a revival noted for its decorousness of language and situation and its traditional values.

A less insular perspective can show us that these disparate phenomena must all belong to a single complex of values. In Germany, for instance, Klopstock's emotional religion and nationalism combined with Lessing's liberalism to beget the violent antics of storm and stress drama; in France, Diderot was at once the century's most extravagant admirer of both Richardson and Sterne, the responsible editor of the *Encyclopédie*, which was the great summa of Enlightenment thought, and the founder of a theatrical tradition that led to the protorevolutionary farces of Beaumarchais (the French Sheridan, who was formally even more conservative than his British counterpart but politically far more dangerous). The various literary traditions of the later eighteenth century in Britain will continue to look like the frayed ends of the Enlightenment until we decide to regard them as various positions in a continuum of values that, without ever being fully articulated, regulated the thought processes of the entire period.

Historically, the bright sides of Enlightenment dominated at first, and the dark sides—satire and then sentiment—prevailed later, especially after 1740. But the ideological and emotional precedence goes the other way. Before Charles entered the limelight, he was under a "black Star." That star—as Dryden's text makes extraordinarily plain underneath its decorative obscurity—was as much his personal dissoluteness as his political destitution.

> Such is not Charles his too too active age,
> Which govern'd by the wild distemper'd rage
> Of some black Star infecting all the Skies,
> Made him at his own cost like Adam wise.
> ("Astraea Redux" 111–14)

The more fully elaborated sequence of "Alexander's Feast" (1697) leads music through rape, drunkenness, "joyless" military victory, the "pain" of erotic desire, nightmare, and madness, before Cecilia brings harmony to earth. The melancholy overview in Dryden's last poem, *A Secular Masque* (1700), images the completed century as a succession of bestial revelry, pointless war, and faithless love. Dryden begins his career by claiming or implying that a new age has dawned:

> Some lazy Ages lost in sleep and ease
> No action leave to busie Chronicles;
> Such whose supine felicity but makes
> In story chasmes, in Epoche's mistakes;
> O're whom Time gently shakes his wings of Down
> Till with his silent sickle they are mown:
> Such is not Charles his too too active age.
>
> ("Astraea Redux" 105–11)

He ends, literally on his deathbed, by wishing for that new age, in the gloomy recognition that "supine felicity" has been the best of man's experiences hitherto: " 'Tis well an old age is out, / And time to begin a new" (*Secular Masque* 90–91).

Given the consistent pattern and the regression of confidence, I think we can use the "black Star" passage of 1660 to interpret the stage comedies of the Restoration in relationship to the ideals of Enlightenment. Even though many of the leading playwrights were also elevated poets (Dryden, William Congreve, William Wycherley) or respected statesmen (George Etherege, Sir John Vanbrugh), our impulse is to take the comedies as an outlet that vented energies antithetical to Enlightened rationalism. Such readings underrate the integrity of the age and the comprehensiveness of its vision. The plays generate happy endings out of immoral, foolish, and chaotic actions. There is little logic in this progression, but I think that we can take it as literally as the equally illogical yet psychologically compelling progressions of Dryden's poems. "Apollo's . . . drunk ev'ry Night," sings Sir Wilfull Witwoud in Congreve's *The Way of the World* (1700), "and that makes him so bright." "The Sun's a good Pimple, an honest Soaker, he has a Cellar at your Antipodes" (4.10). That is Dryden's black star all over again, and as willful and wishful as *The Secular Masque* of the same year. Mirabell, a more thoughtful spokesman, especially in soliloquy, has this to say of the force of reason and of its habitation:

To think of a Whirlwind, tho' 'twere in a Whirlwind, were a Case of more steady Contemplation; a very Tranquility of Mind and Mansion. A Fellow that lives in a

Windmill, has not a more whimsical Dwelling than the Heart of a Man that is lodg'd in a Woman. There is no Point of the Compass to which they cannot turn, and by which they are not turn'd; and by one as well as another; for Motion not Method is their Occupation. To know this, and yet continue to be in Love, is to be made wise from the Dictates of Reason, and yet persevere to play the Fool by the force of Instinct. (2.6)

The lesson of stage comedy, which is also the lesson of the greatest poetry of the age, is that reason and instinct, wisdom and passion, must coexist and that their dwelling place is a frantic bosom or a turbulent windmill.

What we see in the exemplary cases of Dryden and the comic playwrights we can learn to recognize throughout the age. In his meager refuge from the Northern cold, Descartes has to tear down before he rebuilds; that is, he is a satirist before he is a rationalist. The contents of Hume's philosophy are different, but the founding gesture is the same: he must tear down the house of epistemology before he can build those of sociability and morality. What Norman O. Brown called Swift's "excremental vision" (*Life Against Death* 179–201) haunts even so complacent-seeming a work as Goldsmith's *She Stoops to Conquer*. The disorderly house with its unruly servants here may seem too tame to count as prefigurations of Beaumarchais's riotous *Marriage of Figaro*. But when Kate possesses herself of her hereditary jewels stolen from the locked casket of Aunt Hardcastle, in a sequence that leads to a wild night-time ride ending, for the Aunt, in the horse-pond at the bottom of the garden, the dark passions at the perimeter of human rationality are unmistakably acknowledged.

"Wherefore," Walter Shandy asks at the conclusion of Sterne's masterpiece, "when we go about to make and plant a man, do we put out the candle?" (9.33). *Tristram Shandy* is arguably the century's profoundest response to Locke. Historically, readers have argued whether it is an application, a commentary, or a critique of Locke. I do not think the question has as much importance as has sometimes been thought because Locke's *Essay*, like any great book, undertakes a self-critique of its own illuminations. We will not properly understand the relationship of Romanticism to Enlightenment if we see only the light of the eighteenth century and ignore the generative darkness in the background.

Tristram Shandy includes various pages that contain no text but are eloquent in their silence. The first is the black page that covers the dead

Yorick (1.12). Much later comes the white page belonging neither to perceptivity nor to reason, but to the imagination that is left free to represent its own desire as a picture of the Widow Wadman (6.38). Whiteness likewise represents vacancy in the omitted chapters 9.18–19. When these chapters are later incorporated at 9.25, they prove to contain Toby's abortive proposal to the Widow, with its confusion of discourse with "the Real Presence," in the belief, "That talking of love, is making it." A whole century, we realize, talked of reason too, without necessarily making it. Between the black and white pages comes the mottled page of 3.36: "Without much reading, by which your reverence knows, I mean much knowledge, you will no more be able to penetrate the moral of the next marbled page (motly emblem of my work!) than the world with all its sagacity has been able to unravel the many opinions, transactions and truths which still lie mystically hid under the dark veil of the black one." It was Wordsworth who wrote that, "mid all this mighty sum / Of things forever speaking," "The eye it cannot choose but see" and that one should not fear "That nothing of itself will come" ("Expostulation and Reply"). The Enlightenment was less confidently open and took the marbled page as its motley emblem. In modern reprints that page is black and white and looks like an image produced and reproduced. (The marbled page is reproduced in color in the Florida Edition of *Tristram Shandy*, but not successfully.) But in the first edition it is an actual piece of beautifully marbled paper, seamlessly inlaid. It is an emblem, but it is also the thing itself, a real presence that brings the self-image of the age bodily into our chamber. For once, in a way perhaps only possible in a book, the image is at one with the object, in ambiguous fulfillment of age-old yearnings for a self begetting clear and distinct idea.

The images that I have been tracing regulate the fundamental impulses of epistemology, psychology, and politics alike in the Age of Reason. Yet they are rarely acknowledged in their full extent—perhaps only in Hume and Sterne, which may be what makes those the two most disturbing authors of the age. The story I have told is one of the concealment of darkness under a utopian optimism and of the gradual and reluctant acknowledgment of the darkness—let me now call it the Romantic darkness—at the origin of life. It is the story of an age coming to know itself. The knowledge, at last, burst upon it in ways that were never entirely comfortable. That self-knowledge of Enlightenment is what we know as Romanticism.

The Great Awakening

My first section demonstrated how both the Enlightenment and Romanticism contain similar contradictions within them. The second section discusses the genealogy of reason in the Enlightenment. That genealogy is implicit in Enlightenment texts but recognized only in incomplete or fragmentary ways. Far from being a repudiation of Enlightenment, Romanticism was its summation. Of all Enlightenment authors, Hume comes closest to an overview of the dialectic of Enlightenment, and Kant says (in the introduction to the *Critique of Pure Reason*) it was Hume who awakened him from his dogmatic slumbers. Romanticism, I will suggest, is the fulfillment and awakening of Enlightenment.

To see what this formula entails, I begin with the early Wordsworth poem I have just quoted. We need first to reconstruct the situation. Matthew, the aged schoolmaster who is Wordsworth's interlocutor in the poem, represents the wisdom of an earlier generation. In the companion poem, "The Tables Turned," Wordsworth disparages his "meddling intellect," his "science," and his "art." Both poems are bantering in tone; these lines do not state settled doctrines or reflect a fundamental antipathy between the two friends, but they do associate Matthew—who appears throughout the poems devoted to him as a figure of light—with the Enlightenment. What, then, does Wordsworth mean by telling Matthew, "The eye it cannot choose but see"? The eye, after all, is the one sense organ that can be closed off. Indeed, Wordsworth's eyes in this poem must be either closed or at least vacant, for he is "dream[ing] my time away." His reverie is devoid of cause and effect or of what Keats was to call "consequitive reasoning" ("You look round on your mother earth, / As if she for no purpose bore you"), and it appears to be thoughtless ("When life was sweet I knew not why"). Yet he says it is full, not empty.

The debate between Wordsworth and Matthew—that is, I believe, between Romanticism and Enlightenment—is rooted not in alienation or incomprehension but in a common ground. For it is Enlightenment doctrine that Wordsworth turns against his teacher. Ever since Descartes, the principle that the soul always thinks had been espoused by Enlightenment rationalists and empiricists alike. As applied to the sense of sight, that principle was interpreted to mean that the eye is always on the watch, whether the lid is open or shut. Even when nothing registers, as Gottfried Wilhelm Leibniz had said in the preface to his *New Essays on Human Understanding*, we still have an unending stream of "little perceptions," though we may be unaware of them. "This mighty sum / Of things forever speaking" is the full, punctual world of empiricism, a world without empty space. "Methinks, it should have been impossible / Not to love all things in a world so fill'd," Coleridge wrote in 1817, in the lines added to "The Eolian Harp" as a reflective summing up. In "Expostulation and Reply" Wordsworth does not think (he only "deem[s]" and "dream[s]"), but he enjoins Matthew to "think" in order to accede to the totality of Enlightened experience. That is the message addressed by Romanticism to its forebears.

One mistake often made is to link Romanticism too closely with the world of dreams. *L'Ame romantique et le rêve*—Albert Béguin's title is virtually a cliché. Yet the French tradition in which he wrote traces Romanticism well back before the generation of '98. Reverie—empty dreaming or daydreaming—was at its most fashionable around the 1780's, with writers such as Rousseau and William Cowper. The writers whom we know as Romantics are distinguished from this earlier generation by virtue of the fact that they tell their dreams, and, indeed, the more haunted they are (as with De Quincey), the more they try to share and illuminate their hauntings. It is not dreaming that is the distinctive emblem of Romanticism—for even Dryden had his "black Star"—but the moment of awakening in which the dream is preserved.

Such moments are ubiquitous in Romantic poetry. There are the literal awakenings like the Arab Dream in book 5 of *The Prelude*, "Kubla Khan," Lambro's awakening of Haidée and Don Juan in canto 4 of Byron's poem, the apocalyptic moments that conclude Blake's major epics, or the image of Adam's dream in Keats's letter of November 22, 1827. Equally prevalent, especially in the younger poets, are failed or uncertain awakenings like those in "The Idiot Boy," "Christabel," the "Ode to Psyche," the "Ode to a Nightingale," Keats's *Hyperion*, and "The Triumph of Life." Moneta, the warner in *The Fall of Hyperion*, admonishes Keats that "The poet and the dreamer are distinct, / Diverse, sheer opposite, antipodes" (1.199–200); most of Keats's narratives involve struggles to awaken, and the earliest, "Sleep and Poetry," contrasts the good imaginative sleep that leads to the dawn with the self-deluding imaginative death of neoclassical "handicraftsmen" who work in "The name of one Boileau" (200, 206). Just in the weeks when he was avidly attending Hazlitt's lectures on the eighteenth-century poets, Keats penned a blank-verse sonnet ("O Thou Whose Face") that ends with the line, "And he's awake who thinks himself asleep." The full scope of mind necessarily encompasses an alertness to dreams. The Enlightenment's limitation came when it thought itself awake.

The schema of awakening or of failure or struggle to awaken is repeated even more often by analogy and metaphor. Before further considering the implications of this schema, I will present two familiar examples at somewhat greater length. The first is Wordsworth's "Tintern Abbey." The earliest experiences described in this poem are "The coarser pleasures of my boyish days / And their glad animal movements." The earliest stage of genuine humanity is Wordsworth's interpretation of empiricism: it is all elementary perceptions ("Their colours and their forms") and generically classified objects ("The sounding cataract," "the tall rock," and so forth). Pope—from whose poetry Wordsworth knew thousands of lines by heart—uses the phrase "the language of the heart," and Wordsworth, nostalgically, speaks of "the language of my former heart" as he attributes to Dorothy the "shooting lights" and the natural eyes associated with Enlightenment. (See also Griffin, "Wordsworth's Pope.") Beyond mere empiricism comes—and here Wordsworth quotes and acknowledges Young—"the mighty world / Of eye and ear, both what they half-create, / And what perceive." Half-creation is not pure imaginary guess-work, "as is a landscape to a blind man's eye," but rather a dream-world that recomposes the perceived world, when "we are laid asleep / In body, and become a living soul: / While with an eye made quiet by the power / Of harmony, and the deep power of joy, / We see into the life of things." The dark world is at once memory, dream, and imagination. Through it Wordsworth passes beyond the mechanistic and empiricist psychology of "An appetite: a feeling and a love, / That had no need of . . . any interest, / Unborrowed from the eye," toward the revived humanism of the active mind.

In the fourth paragraph of "Tintern Abbey," as Wordsworth recomposes the genesis of his current maturity, "thought" is introduced as the key term, and reasoning processes begin to govern the poem's rhetoric (paragraph 4 has "And so," "For," "Therefore," whereas the "If" in paragraph 3 lacks its consequent "then"). Yet the earlier stages of feeling, the "gleams / Of past existence," are preserved and honored, not rejected. "Day-light" is "joyless," and so Wordsworth wishes the light of the moon on his sister, yet the development leads to a renewal of vision (as the verbs of sensation in the first paragraph proceed from "hear" to "behold," "view," and finally "see") and a return to the now tamed "light of setting suns." Romanticism comes into its own by recapitulating its prehistory. "Tintern Abbey" means a great many things, and in pointing out these elements of structure I have not begun to interpret the poem. Even from the purely epistemological perspective an interpretation would need to account for the various elements in Wordsworth's assessment of empiricism: why, for instance, does he link elementary perception with such eagerly appetitive feelings? The coming-to-consciousness of Romanticism is not itself the content of Romantic belief; rather, it is the ground on which Romantics arrived at their often conflicting assessments of the world they experienced. It is the grammar rather than the text of their thinking.

Shelley's *Prometheus Unbound* depends on a more abstract version of the same grammar of consciousness. It alludes chiefly to political history (the French Revolution and the Ancien Régime) rather than to intellectual history, and its judgments of past eras differ from those of "Tintern Abbey." But it too portrays—indeed repeatedly—the dawning of a new age and the awakening of a new humanity. The necessitarian tyrant Jupiter is resisted darkly by Prometheus. Yet Prometheus is unable to free himself: mere denial is servitude, not liberation. It is, of course, a grave simplification of Shelley's multiple perspectives to identify Jupiter with light and Prometheus with night and consequently even a graver one to present the play as the triumph of the Romantic imagination (or of Revolutionary freedom) over Enlightenment reason (or aristocratic tyranny). For the victory of one power would merely perpetuate a cycle, whereas Shelley's concluding vision is of an everlasting day (4.14: "We bear Time to his tomb in eternity"), modeled on the dance of lights in Dante's *Paradiso*. It is not the evil past that is vanquished by present good, but rather the entire Miltonic conflict of evil and good that is transcended. Critics often treat the play as a lyrical effusion whose dramatic conflict ends in the very opening speech, when Prometheus says, "Disdain? Ah no! I pity thee" (1.53). Could the authority of the past be so easily put down, the force of history would be very weak indeed. But the pity is in fact both mutual (Mercury, Jupiter's messenger, twice says, "I pity thee," 1.356 and 428) and ineffective: Jupiter moans in his only appearance that Demogorgon, who eventually has the last word in the play, has "No pity" (3.1.64). Both Prometheus and Jupiter live in the post-Saturnian world where time appears as a shadow (2.4.33–34) that opposes past to present, necessity to desire. Asia's long narration in 2.4 (the center of the play, as Stuart Curran points out in *Shelley's Annus Mirabilis* 221) describes how Promethean invention mastered time and how Jovian law then mastered invention. But neither did away with the temporal cycle of negation and domination that is Shelley's real concern.

The psycho-historical dynamic issues in a characteristically Shellyan punning ambivalence. Immediately after expressing his pity, Prometheus says, "The Curse / Once breathed on thee I would recall" (1.58–59). Prometheus's recall, like his pity, is inferior because it remains oppositional. Though masked as a retraction, it is really a negation. As in Freud's account of negation, it serves as a pretext to recollect what he has forgotten. Prometheus wishes to deny power to Jupiter, but not to eliminate the whole idea of power (e.g., 1.272–73). In the process he shows his likeness to Jupiter in many ways, such as in the exultation that he condemns yet often seems to express, as well as in his victory over the Furies ("Methinks I grow like what I contemplate / And laugh and stare in loathsome sympathy / . . . . Yet am I king over myself, and rule / The torturing and conflicting throngs within / As Jove rules you"; 1.450–51, 492–94). Reminded of the curse at last, he repents (1.303: "It doth repent me"); falteringly, he asks to change his state. In all these ways he is wrong, even as he pities Jupiter. In the closing speech Demogorgon preaches a forgiving retraction or else an enduring resistance before which oppressive evil merely vanishes:

> To forgive wrongs darker than Death or Night;
>   To defy Power which seems Omnipotent;
> To love, and bear; to hope, till Hope creates
> From its own wreck the thing it contemplates.
>
> (4.571–74)

Far from terminating with Prometheus's expression of pity, the play's dramatic action only begins there; its dramatic action is a complex process of development leading to Demogorgon's corrective concluding injunction, "Neither to change nor falter nor repent" (4.575).

If that process is Prometheus's way of dealing with his past, it is also symptomatic of Romanticism's way of dealing with its past. Repudiation and triumph are its most visible gestures, which have led to conventional accounts of the war of Romanticism against Enlightenment reason. Pitying condescension is another gesture that is not infrequent in writings about Enlightenment figures by second-generation Romantics. But all these gestures are surface signs of a yet more complex process that was the Romantic working-through of its roots. What was to be overcome had to be thoroughly remembered. And if the chain of necessity is overthrown, the Promethean rebellion too must give way to the eternal day of rectified Reason.

In her narration Asia speaks as if all value derived from Prometheus: "He gave man speech, and speech created thought, / Which is the measure of the Universe" (2.4.72–73). But Earth speaks differently in the closing scene—more impersonally as well as with a reformed priority that puts thoughts before an ordering language rather than after a creative language. His is the play's considered judgment of the birth of consciousness. "Language is a perpetual Orphic song, / Which rules with Dædal harmony a throng / Of thoughts and forms, which else senseless and shapeless were" (4.415–17). The "Godlike," "divine" (2.4.79, 82), creative ambitions of a Promethean Romanticism give way in the play to the synthetic and syncretic dance of all forms, thoughts, and eras with one another in the coadunative imagination. Much in Asia's praise of music replays Dryden's various shadowed panegyrics on the celestial mission of the arts, whereas Earth reminds us of their grounding and paves the way for Demogorgon to "waken Oblivion" (4.543).

The deluded "all-prophetic song" (2.4.76) that Asia recounts is really a denial of the past. The destiny of Romanticism was to proceed beyond this immature or premature stage toward a reconciliatory recollection. English provides us with the fortunate puns re-collect and re-member. The Enlightenment, as we have seen, aimed at masking and forgetting the itinerary by which it arrived at reason. Its self-knowledge was therefore only partial. Romanticism, with the same goal, undertook a synthetic itinerary. Collecting the members of the path of reason, it aimed at knowing the light through knowing the dark and the present by means of the past. Locke and Kant, for instance, shared the desire to clarify the mechanisms of consciousness. But Locke begins with perception, that is, with the bright or visible part of the process, without studying the faculties that precede and empower perception. Kant's theory of knowledge, by contrast, focuses specifically on the preexisting, imperceptible structures that beget conscious perception. And philosophy beyond Kant concentrated increasingly on the paths leading from the predisposing structures toward fully developed cognition—on what Hegel called the history of consciousness—as well as on analogously idealized histories of society and of nature. The heroines of Austen, the heroes of Scott, and the great Romantic poets all know themselves by remembering what they have experienced. That distinguishes the novels even from picaresques like those of Defoe, whose narrators recount their errors in order to segregate the renegade past from the reformed present. And it distinguishes poems of return like "Tintern Abbey" or Eduard Mörike's "Besuch in Urach" even from Gray's "Ode on a Distant Prospect of Eton College," which masks childhood recollections in an allegorical vision of future woe, an "all-prophetic song."

Consider William Hazlitt's judgment on Jeremy Bentham, a transitional figure and the eldest of the notables portrayed in *The Spirit of the Age*:

Mr. Bentham's method of reasoning, though comprehensive and exact, labours under the defect of most systems—it is too topical. It includes every thing; but it includes everything alike. It is rather like an inventory, than a valuation of different arguments. Every possible suggestion finds a place, so that the mind is distracted as much as enlightened by this perplexing accuracy. The exceptions seem as important as the rule. By attending to the minute, we overlook the great; and in summing up an account, it will not do merely to insist on the number of items without considering their amount. (Hazlitt, *Works* 11.14)

Bentham forgets nothing and hides nothing, but he also synthesizes nothing. Such indiscriminate visibility, says the great Romantic portraitist, is not true Enlightenment. "By attending to the minute we overlook the great": that is the charge leveled by Romanticism at even the most inclusive minds of the eighteenth century. Hogarth was another such. Though a notorious hater, Hazlitt treasured Hogarth. Yet even Hogarth failed to satisfy the hunger for imagination of even the most empirically minded of the great Romantics:

He had an intense feeling and command over the impressions of sense, of habit, of character, and passion, the serious and the comic, in a word, of nature, as it fell within his own observation, or came within the sphere of his actual experience; but he had little power beyond that sphere . . . [to] make the dark abyss pregnant, . . . making all things like not what we know and feel in ourselves, in this "ignorant present" time, but like what they must be in themselves, or in our noblest idea of them, and stamping that idea with reality . . . : this is the ideal in art, in poetry, and in painting. (*Works* 6.146)

In the long passage from which these phrases are excerpted, Hazlitt challenges Hogarth to bring the dark abyss to light, to lift the world around us into "the empyrean," and to give ideas reality by raising them "above the ordinary world of reality." The best of the Enlightenment, as Hazlitt saw it, was striving toward a Romantic potential.

There is no way to reduce the diffuse prose and the incommensurate ambitions of Hazlitt's critique of Enlightenment to a formula or a common denominator. Its virtue, rather, lies in its comprehensiveness. Thus does Romanticism claim not to reject but to refine, subsume, and transcend its predecessors.

Revolution

Richard Brinsley Sheridan was the great Georgian playwright who then became a leading Romantic politician. His politics looked forward, whereas his dramaturgy looked backward to the comic playwrights of the Restoration. Yet when he became manager of Drury Lane Theater in 1776, his most important reform was to increase the number of new plays produced. So representative a figure looks backward and ahead at once.

Lamb, in his permanent nostalgia, seems to me less representative of his age. Still, his comments on the comedies he saw in his youth are telling. Utterly unreal because utterly amoral, they were (as he says in "On the Artificial Comedies of the Last Century") a dream-world to which audiences repaired "to escape from the pressure of reality." They were relaxing because they were aggregates without a synthesis:

For what is Ben [in Congreve's *Love for Love*] . . . but . . . a dreamy combination of all the accidents of a sailor's character. . . . But when an actor comes, and instead of the delightful phantom . . . displays before our eyes a downright concretion of a Wapping sailor— . . . when . . . he gives to it a downright daylight understanding, and a full consciousness of its actions . . . we feel the discord of the thing; the scene is disturbed; a real man has got in among the dramatis personae, and puts them out. ("On Some of the Old Actors," *Works* 2.140)

Let us call that real man Romanticism. It was an awakening from the comic dreams of Enlightenment. Yet that awakening entailed (to Lamb's regret) a "full consciousness" of what had been superseded. You cannot look ahead if you do not know which road lies behind you.

And let us call the process of awakening, revolution. Lamb's language for the artificial comedy of the last century bears a remarkable resemblance to Carlyle's language for the artificial society of old France: "Such visual spectra flit across this Earth, if the Thespian Stage be rudely interfered with: but much more, when, as it was said, Pit jumps on Stage, then is it verily, as in Herr Tieck's Drama, a *Verkehrte Welt*, or World topsy-turvied" (*The French Revolution* 2.1.10). In the first paragraph of this chapter, I said that all the Romantics shared a consciousness of revolution. By that I did not mean only of the French Revolution. For one thing, the Revolution itself—as Carlyle's masterpiece shows—was many different things at different times, in different places, to different people. And, for another, the course of political revolutions was and is often guided by revolutions in ideas, feelings, behavior, the Industrial Revolution, Kant's Copernican Revolution in philosophy, revolutions in life style, even in poetic style. For much of Wordsworth's life the revolution in Cumberland mores preoccupied him far more than did events abroad. Even Carlyle, in the midst of proclaiming the French Revolution "the crowning Phenomenon of our Modern Time," recognized that revolution is permanent and ubiquitous:

All things are in revolution; in change from moment to moment, which becomes sensible from epoch to epoch: in this Time-World of ours there is properly nothing else but revolution and mutation, and even nothing else conceivable. Revolution, you answer, means speedier change. Whereupon one still has to ask: How speedy? At what degree of speed; in what particular points of this variable course, which varies in velocity, but can never stop till time itself stops, does revolution begin and end; cease to be ordinary mutation, and again become such? It is a thing that will depend on definition more or less arbitrary. (1.6.1)

But if we say that Romanticism was the revolutionary reawakening of Enlightenment, we need to recognize that revolution meant something different in 1800 from now. The word meant a turning back before it meant a turning away. In the seventeenth century revolution was the opposite, not the consequence of rebellion, and it retained some of these connotations even into the nineteenth century. When Hazlitt wrote that Horne Tooke "had none of the grand whirling movements of the French Revolution, nor of the tumultuous glow of rebellion in his head or in his heart" (*Works* 9.53), he continued to reflect a sense that revolution is greater and more embracing than rebellion. Even Carlyle, for whom "Time is rich in wonders, in monstrosities most rich; and is observed never to repeat himself, or any of his Gospels" (2.5.1), projects an affinity of the whirling of the Revolution with the great cycles of nature. His monumental book of memory, perhaps the first historical essay to treat modern times as a receding experience that must be reconstructed archeologically, was prompted by a passion to return to what Wordsworth's Intimations Ode had called "the fountain light of all our day."

Understand it well, the Thing thou beholdest, that Thing is an Action, the product and expression of exerted Force: the All of Things is an infinite conjugation of the verb to do. Shoreless Fountain-Ocean of Force, of power to do; wherein Force rolls and circles, billowing, many-streamed, harmonious; wide as Immensity, deep as Eternity; beautiful and terrible, not to be comprehended: this is what man names Existence and Universe; this thousand-tinted Flame-image, at once veil and revelation, reflex such as he, in his poor brain and heart, can paint, of One Unnameable, dwelling in inaccessible light! From beyond the Star-galaxies, from before the Beginning of Days, it billows and rolls,—round thee, nay thyself art of it, in this point of Space where thou now standest, in this moment which thy clock measures. (2.3.1)

Such is the sense in which Romanticism was revolutionary. It had its moments of rebellion, yet it was not fundamentally a rebellion against its predecessors. Rather, it was revolutionary in that older and more encompassing sense (discussed by Reinhart Koselleck in " 'Neuzeit': Remarks on the Semantics of the Modern Concepts of Movement," *Futures Past* 231–66) in which a revolution gathers up and recollects, as it sweeps all with it toward the future.

CHAPTER 9

Origins of Modernism
Musical Structures and Narrative Forms

COMPARISON OF LITERATURE and the visual arts is much more common than comparison of literature and music. For, as Roland Barthes wrote in a late essay that in part exemplifies the problem, "It is . . . very difficult to speak about music. Many writers have spoken well about painting; none, I believe, has spoken well about music, not even Proust. The reason is that it is very difficult to link language, which is of the order of the general, and music, which is of the order of difference." Music, as Barthes says in another essay, is "inactual," or, as I should put it, abstract.[1] Nonspecialists often feel that they can look at a painting and discern what it represents; and even those who know nothing about painting techniques are liable to have imbibed a few useful elementary notions of pictorial form. Far fewer stare at a musical score with anything but discomfort. Music suffers doubly: first from being nonrepresentational, and second from being written in a script that is arduous to learn. Even the most avid listeners would no sooner write about a piece of music than about a poem in a language they cannot read.

Yet despite Barthes's engagement on behalf of a purely affective approach, the analysis of music holds great potential. For what music lacks in external referentiality, it gains in the distinctness of internal relationships. If it is the most abstract art, it is also the most highly formalized. Or, to put this in yet a third way, while the *meaning* or denotation of a piece of music is far less explicit than that of a work of verbal or pictorial art, the *structure* is far more explicit.

The contrast among the arts can be described in semiotic terms. Language has what is known as a double articulation: a limited system of discrete sounds out of which is composed an essentially unlimited and unsystematic lexicon of discrete words. While literature intermittently exploits the phonetic system, it primarily communicates through the much more fluid lexical register. Painting, of course, has at its disposal only the lexical or conceptual articulation. A painting may represent discrete objects or actions, but its material basis is an unarticulated continuum of colors, brushstrokes, and the like. No general system of "huemes" and "valuemes" corresponds to the phonemes of language. Music, finally, has in general only the lower or systematic articulation. The elements of a musical composition are pitches, rhythms, instruments, dynamic levels, and types of articulation: more elements, in other words, than there are phonemes in any natural language but a finite number nevertheless. That is why music can be notated. The extensive writing on musical semiotics rarely seems to acknowledge the basic fact that music does not, in general, have words.[2] More specifically, since music sporadically has symbolic motifs, one should say that music does not distinguish words from sentences. Music has its own identity because it is not like language, and the manipulations of its building blocks can be described far more concretely than the manipulations of words, whose meanings and formal properties are by nature complex and overlapping.[3]

Therefore, if we are interested in the formal sense of a period or a movement, we may well look to its music for the clearest, most easily describable examples. By formal sense I mean such characteristics as the types of closure that are permitted, the nature of segmentation and transition (relationship between adjacent parts), the relative importance of local and long-distance relationships, and the types of hierarchy or equivalence that are recognized. Geoffrey Tillotson's *Augustan Studies* contains a well-known essay on the "manner of proceeding" in eighteenth-century poetry, and his phrase conveniently sums up what I mean by style. In all the arts there are characteristic manners of proceeding or formal principles by which we recognize the style of a creator, a group, or a period. In literary works the principles take the form of norms, often only loosely defined and frequently unrecognized in analysis. In music, on the other hand, the formal outlines of a piece can generally be described with a high degree of precision (or a low degree of ambiguity), and the generalizations based on a group of such formal descriptions appear much more like laws than like the flexible norms of literary form.

A preliminary example of structuring principles can usefully precede the main exposition in this chapter. One norm of plot structure in the nineteenth century is surely that there must be a satisfactory resolution. Vladimir Propp has shown that this norm has the force of an invariable law in the case of fairy tales—or at least of those collected during that epoch. But the resolutions in novels and short stories do not always take the canonical forms of marriage or death; it is not easy to define the limited number of plot functions and thereby to specify acceptable outcomes. With music, on the other hand, we are on firm ground. A precise, inflexible law that everyone acknowledges governs most music of this period, even though few bother to state something so obvious: every piece must end with a cadence in the same key in which it began.

To be sure, even the firmest laws sometimes get tested. Schumann and Chopin experimented with what Charles Rosen has called "tonal unity" without a focused "central tonality" (*Sonata Forms* 295), but only under carefully controlled conditions: in "Romantic" forms, but not in sonatas, and with the prevailing keys a third apart, usually a major and its relative minor. More radical departures—in a couple of iconoclastic forays by Beethoven and in programmatic gestures by Schubert, in songs exclusively—remain even more isolated. Such departures, furthermore, acknowledge the law of resolution through their attempt either to amend it or to motivate a repeal. Even these few works, that is, have determinate not suspended or cyclical endings.[4] In the absence of obviously Shandean characteristics (as in "Variety Without Method," a late eighteenth-century setting in various keys and meters of the psalm, "O God thou hast been displeased," by the American hymnist William Billings), should one meet a nineteenth-century piece where the first movement ends in F major while the last movement ends in D major, one would have no recourse but to conclude that the composer was terminally syphilitic. Indeed, in this particular instance—the Second String Quartet of Bedřich Smetana—the contributors to the earlier editions of *Grove's Dictionary of Music and Musicians* were unable to face the music; J. A. Fuller Maitland, the general editor of the second edition, put the piece in C major (vol. 4, p. 486), while Rosa Newmarch in the third edition put it in C minor (vol. 4, p. 789).

Now it is not difficult to see how a closely related norm of closure likewise applies to the nineteenth-century novel. Flamboyant exceptions like Charlotte Brontë's *Villette* and Melville's *The Confidence-Man*, of course, confirm the norm by the self-conscious way they reject it. But we might risk losing our critical nerve with what seems like half-cadences or half-hearted conventionality in the works of Flaubert, Eliot, or Hardy—indeed an increasingly long list of major writers. Here the musical parallel should encourage us to view the endings as adequate resolutions of problems to be critically identified. It teaches us the principle of reading the novels in the light of their conclusions, just as we analyze a symphony from the perspective of its tonal resolution rather than, say, in the light of prevailing textures or of organizational symmetries.[5]

In the spirit of this example, then, I will take up a central paradigm in nineteenth-century music, its parallel in literary form, and its fate in the twentieth century. What follows is an experiment at compactly surveying the prehistory of modernism. The intention is to show how the patterns of music history can help to organize our understanding of the more fluid patterns of literary history.

The language of nineteenth-century music was based on a series of polar oppositions that had gradually crystallized from the musical practice of the preceding centuries: the contrast of consonance with dissonance, tonic with dominant (or other nontonic) harmonies, symmetrical with asymmetrical phrasing, melodic outline with rhythmic configuration, treble with bass, strong with weak beats, solo with accompaniment, string with wind sonorities. Each such polarity functions somewhat differently from the others, and their complex interplay defines the inner form of any given piece. But all have in common that one term is the normal, neutral, stable, or principal one, while the other is abnormal, expressive, unstable, or subordinate.

String sound, to expand on one of the oppositions, is neutral. Winds characteristically gain prominence in the more excited or colorful inner sections of a movement or a piece, and they are lavishly used in ballet and opera to accompany visual spectacles.[6] Yet wind-band music virtually disappears from mainstream composition, since it would have the effect of being all message and no code: it is a sign of unreality when Mendelssohn's Overture to *A Midsummer Night's Dream* opens with wind chords and an obvious archaism when the theme of Brahms's *Variations on a Theme of Haydn* is stated by winds alone over no more string stability than is offered by cello and bass pizzicato. The string quartet, on the other hand, is the most neutral or purest medium, used only for fully structured abstract pieces and never for short character pieces or for program music. A list of exceptions shows how rare they are: apart from two or three quartet movements by Beethoven, Hugo Wolf's *Intermezzo* and *Italian Serenade*, and Tchaikovsky's sextet, "Souvenirs de Florence," you have to descend to the level of Nikolai Afanasiev's quartet "The Volga" or return to the hapless Smetana's quartet "From My Life" to find programmatic or evocative string music. And it could be argued that Schoenberg's first decisive attack on nineteenth-century musical language came with his writing a full-scale symphonic poem for string sextet, *Verklärte Nacht*.

Taken as a whole, the various oppositions define a manner of proceeding that every listener recognizes as the nineteenth-century norm: most simply, pieces oscillate between stability or resolution and excitement or expressivity, and, in particular, pieces begin in normality (in the tonic key) and move through areas of greater or lesser tension in the middle until they arrive at a concluding resolution. These patterns of what linguists call markedness are obvious; just as obviously they do not structure much of the most characteristic music of our century, and they apply only in a partial and weaker way to music of the baroque era, which depends more heavily on symmetrical balance than on pointed contrast.

The formal structures of nineteenth-century fiction are likewise defined by oppositions between tension and relaxation, complication and resolution, colorful dissonance and restored harmony. The categories for analyzing these structures are, to be sure, more flexible and imprecise than the musical categories, but they were acknowledged at the time, they remain discernible now, and, however approximate they may be, I believe that they are nevertheless essential to an understanding of nineteenth-century fiction.

The structural oppositions in nineteenth-century fiction can only be illustrated here; a full description must be left for another occasion. The terms that we most often find in nineteenth-century discussions are the true or the real and the interesting or the romantic. The struggle of the nineteenth-century writer is to accommodate both the true and the interesting or—to borrow the musical terms—both consonance and dissonance, tonic and dominant. Trollope, for instance, objects to the designation of himself as realistic and Wilkie Collins as sensationalistic: "A good novel should be both, and both in the highest degree" (*Autobiography* 194). Hardy says, "The writer's problem is, how to strike the balance between the uncommon and the ordinary so as on the one hand to give interest, on the other to give reality" (*Life and Work* 154); *Bleak House* (according to Dickens's preface) was intended to portray "the romantic side of familiar things"; and Henry James is employing only a superficially different vocabulary when he writes, "Every good story is of course both a picture and an idea, and the more they are interfused the better the problem is solved" ("Guy de Maupassant," *Partial Portraits* 269).

Just as certain composers lay bare the skeleton of the period's formal sense by simplifying and rigidifying the polarizations in harmony and rhythm,[7] so certain authors and works likewise render the polarizations of literary form in a purified and thus unmistakable way. *Bleak House* experiments with juxtaposing a pitiless, objective, foggy narrator with a romantic and sunny one and moves toward reconciling the two at the end. Stevenson's best-known work pits the real scientist Dr. Jekyll against the nightmarish romantic villain Mr. Hyde. And detective stories in the mold of Arthur Conan Doyle regularly fall into two main parts: the recital of the actual situation in the present tense with all the scattered clues of the crime, and the recital in the past tense of the romantic and exciting history of the criminal and the crime.

At the end of the nineteenth century these polarized forms become formulaic. Their interest slips, and eventually they lose their coherence. The artist who preserves the traditional forms becomes an artisan, often a miniaturist, like many of the nationalist composers or the numerous superb short story writers native to almost every country except imperial England. The grand formal problems all but vanish and hitherto subordinate resources of nuance and tone color are featured, such as piquant chords and dialect words. Increasing formal ease and virtuosity mean that a whole piece may be generated out of a kernel phrase, as in the famous Maupassant story "The Necklace," about a string of diamonds ("rivière de diamants") that is lost near the river, making martyrs out of the poor bourgeois of the nearby Rue des Martyrs.

Finally, as the charisma of the dialectic is routinized, all that matter are color and atmosphere—tone-painting or word-painting. From the other side of the great stylistic divide Schoenberg made merry over the minimal character of a language based on color: "When songs from the southern portion of West-Farinoxia," he writes in an essay on "Symphonies from Folksongs," "show Lydian tendencies in a prevailing Phrygian, whereas dances from the neighboring northern part of Franquimonia show the opposite, namely traces of Phrygian in decidedly Lydian melodies, such differences may, to a specialist in the region, indicate signs of autochthonous originality."[8] But late in the nineteenth century such minimal originality was often a composer's or a short story writer's primary resource. The character piece is a distillate, the passion without the story of the passion, "not the tale, but the sketch of a tale," "only the point of departure and that of arrival," as Giovanni Verga says in the programmatic introduction to "Gramigna's Lover" (1880; *Tutte le novelle* 1: 167–68), or, in other words, a contrasting beginning and end that virtually dispenses with the mediating middle. This type of colorful sketch, popular in both literature and music toward the end of the century—and the inspiration for verismo opera—ultimately became in its turn a commonplace convention.

When normal coherence of the old sort is abandoned in favor of such fragmentary evocation, larger structures become problematic, as most obviously in the monstrously episodic works of Bruckner, Mahler, and Zola. In longer works one solution—particularly associated with Wagner and his followers and, in literature, with Flaubert—was to sustain interest by refusing to come to rest: perpetual unresolved dissonance, a middle with very little end. This is, of course, signally the mode of Henry James's *The Turn of the Screw*, which seeks to turn the screws of intensity higher in each of its twenty-four chapters so as to maintain a constant frenzy of excitement, so different from the carefully paced, intermittent horror of romantic gothic. Alternatively, by the end of the century, impressionists such as Debussy and Chekhov (exact contemporaries, though Chekhov wrote more quickly and died younger) preserve compositional depth by melancholy or ironic reminiscences of traditional motifs and forms, the sunken cathedrals of the past: think of all the unsent letters, untold stories, and unnoticed crimes and cruelties of Chekhov's early tales.

Creators like these can now construct larger forms only as a patchwork based on recognizable motifs but lacking a prevailing tonality. Chekhov's first longer story, "The Steppe," is a degenerate picaresque. The indifferent plain (the two words pun in Chekhov's text) through which Egorushka passes decomposes into contrasting story types, the idealized princess Dranitskaya and the mysterious Varlamov, but Egorushka remains equally untouched by the tonic stability of the one and the dominant excitement of the other: "Egorushka felt that, with these people disappeared for him, eternally, like smoke, all that had been lived through until now" (*Izbrannye Sochinenia* 1: 134).[9] Such halting, uncertain cadences mark endings that are not culminations but dissolutions. Debussy's composites are games ("Jeux"); for the gloomier Chekhov they constitute "A Dull Story," but for both the climactic, structuring elements of traditional forms remain but a hollow shell. The bang of excitement may resound, as it does, almost at the end of "A Dull Story"—"There are terrible nights with thunder, lightning, rain, and wind, that among the people are called sparrow's nights. One such sparrow's night occurred in my personal life . . ." (1: 420, Chekhov's suspension points)—but the end is at best a gloomy thud. The organization, though not the texture, of "A Dull Story" resembles that of Debussy's later Cello Sonata, where an excited climax of plucked dominant seventh chords on G, instead of resolving, is followed by a return of an earlier melancholy, wailing recitative and then by a series of D minor chords, loud, to be sure, but ending low and abruptly muffled, with the marking "dry." Point and line come unglued, leaving structures that are heaps of fragments, not well shored up against ruin.[10]

By the early years of this century, post-Wagnerian continual modulation combined with the dissonant expressive leaps of Mahler's melodies and the rhythmic freedom of what Schoenberg called "the progressive Brahms" to undermine totally the stability of the tonic, of the octave, and of the beat. If tension never relaxes, then tension also never builds and the internal dramatic shape of the work is lost. There is no longer a progress from tonic to dominant, consonance to dissonance, the true to the interesting, and back again. Hence, a work like Schoenberg's *Erwartung* becomes an extended, slow rhapsody of unfulfilled expectation, its texture pervaded by the disembodied sonority of the celesta, its epiphanic moment utterly subdued (see measure 390, text "Liebster, der Morgen kommt" [Beloved, the morning comes], marked

"Ruhig, fast freundlich! ohne Leidenschaft!" [Calm, almost friendly! without passion!]).

In the absence of an audible internal structure, music for a short period predominantly seeks its coherence from some external principle of reference. Ballet, program music, and song become the norm. (The omission of ballet is an uncharacteristic blind spot in Carl Dahlhaus's magisterial *Nineteenth-Century Music*.) Out of the heart of darkness there must emerge a voice, without which pure form retains only the briefest sustaining power: it is not by chance that Kurtz ("short") is the name of the mysterious central figure in the story that climaxes with the anguished cry, "A voice! a voice!" Or else music seeks a symbolic meaning, a fugitive vision that lies beyond words, the song of the nightingale perhaps. In some posthumously published program notes to his *Orchesterlieder*, opus 22 (1915), Schoenberg speaks of this striving. Conventional program music, he says, had attempted to bring the represented object directly into the music; in semiotic terms, it had assimilated the musical sign to the verbal signified. But Schoenberg envisioned a new music that could function like enactments, not like designations, and that would ultimately circumvent or surpass language in its meaningfulness. "If an actor will speak in a different cadence of a rough sea and of a calm one, my music will be no different: . . . the music will not become agitated like the sea, but *differently*, like the actor. . . . A word describes the object and its condition; . . . music . . . *carries* the thing and its essence *up before the eye of the mind*" (*Gesammelte Schriften* 290).[11] A new semiosis is born that overcomes the disjunction between signifier and signified; the nature of meaning changes.

To illustrate the transition from the literary side, I quote from the well-known "Letter to Lord Chandos" of 1902 by Hugo von Hofmannsthal: "Everything fell apart into pieces around me; they coagulated into eyes which stared at me and into which I had to stare back: they are whirlpools into which I gaze in giddiness, which revolve incessantly and through which one reaches the void. . . . Since then I have led a life which you, I fear, can hardly grasp, so spiritlessly, so thoughtlessly does it flow by. . . . A watering-can, a harrow left in the field, a dog in the sun, a poor churchyard, a cripple, a small farmhouse, any of these can become the vessel of my revelation. . . . It is all a kind of feverish thought, but a thought in a material which is more immediate, more fluid, more glowing than words" ("Ein Brief," *Ausgewählte Werke* 2: 342–43, 347–48). Literature was striving toward the condition of music, just as music was striving toward the condition of language, and these apparently opposite strivings arose out of a single impulse, to substitute embodiment for denotation in order to restore expressivity where formal control had been lost.[12]

The limit case of the polarized forms of the nineteenth century is thus a fragmentation of form. A curious passage in *Dr. Jekyll and Mr. Hyde* seems to predict this development from polarized form to fragmented form. It comes early in the concluding section of the story, which contains Dr. Jekyll's coherent explanation of the mystery, just before he loses all control over his identity:

> I thus drew steadily nearer to that truth, by whose partial discovery I have been doomed to such a dreadful shipwreck: that man is not truly one, but truly two. I say two, because the state of my own knowledge does not pass beyond that point. Others will follow, others will outstrip me on the same lines; and I hazard a guess that man will be ultimately known for a mere polity of multifarious, incongruous, and independent denizens. (*Complete Short Stories* 520)

Those who outstrip nineteenth-century form arrive at the incoherence of what might well be called atonal literature. A reference to Stéphane Mallarmé's "Un Coup de dés" would seem to be called for at this point, and that randomized flotsam of interwoven motifs is surely one type of literary atonality, following a shipwreck like Dr. Jekyll's. But even more revealing, because less flamboyant, examples of what Schoenberg was to call the emancipation of dissonance, may be found in the meandering inarticulacy of Hardy's *Jude the Obscure* and the coolly dissonant, "uglified" Romanticism of his later poetry. "So Various" is the programmatic title of a poem from the volume *Winter Words* that concerns the fragmentation of identity. Here is its discordant conclusion:

> Now ... All these specimens of man,
> So various in their pith and plan
> Curious to say
> Were *one* man. Yea
> I was all they.

Through the preceding twelve stanzas of contradictory self-portraits and all the way to the final harshly fragmenting plural pronoun, the poem shows Hardy as precisely what Dr. Jekyll had predicted, "a mere polity of multifarious, incongruous, and independent denizens."[13]

Before the turn of the century, of course, large-scale dramatic structure was already often tending to yield to motivic consistency as a shaping force, as in Tchaikovsky's *Symphonie Pathétique*, an episodic work that is almost entirely generated by the four-note motif heard at the very start. And many works of the period seem to enact the struggle between opposing forms of organization. Thus in the last song of Mahler's *Das Lied von der Erde* the dissonant final chord, C-E-G-A, synopsizes one of the two leading motifs of the movement while refusing to come to rest harmonically and while the text likewise refuses closure through its repetitions of the word, "ewig" (eternal). James's *Turn of the Screw* is a work similarly in transition; a few years ago we were treated to the spectacle of an elegant, intricately knit essay concerning the fragmentation of identity in the story, published simultaneously with an equally brilliant if disheveled structuralist reading that demonstrated how it is permeated by a systematic symmetry of motivic relationships.[14]

Ultimately Schoenberg developed the twelve-tone system as a means for integrating larger works. He systematically subordinated dramatic modulations of intensity to the continuous fabric of intervallic relationships dispersed throughout the work. The local intelligibility of a melodic curve is replaced by long-range relationships that confer a meaning on each interval only in terms of its place in the tone-row and its employment elsewhere in the piece. The ecstatic semiosis of atonality thus eventually leads to a style where meaning is felt to arise from outside the local phrase.[15] Musical expression no longer seems natural and immediate. Stravinsky, Bartók, and even to a considerable extent the greatest of the traditionalists, such as Ravel and Prokofiev, are less schematic in their procedures, but fundamentally they share the same formal sensibility. The manner of proceeding common to all these composers derives from the breakdown of the polarizations that had structured music for the preceding 150 years.

Whereas each subsystem of nineteenth-century musical language (harmony, rhythm, and so forth) is divided into an unmarked and one or more marked components, in twentieth-century musical style these internal subdivisions no longer exist or—in more traditional composers who partially preserve them—their force is reduced. As Schoenberg says in the essay "Composition with Twelve Tones," "In this space . . . there is no absolute down, no right or left, no forward or backward" (*Style and Idea* 223). Thus, for instance, dissonance is no longer expressively marked with respect to consonance. The dominant, similarly, is no longer marked with respect to the tonic, so that even when polytonal music continues to use triads, movement away from a given triad loses its significance. And melody loses its primacy through being fragmented in early twelve-tone music, demonized by pulsing ostinatos in Bartók, skeletonized by rhythmic displacement and pointillist instrumentation in Stravinsky.

As a result of such changes, formal unity and totality can no longer be generated "organically" through tension (internal division) and relaxation (reconciliation). The work is no longer an organism, self-defining and self-limiting. Instead, most often composers adopted historical forms to impose an arbitrary recognizable shape on their works. The forms of music in this period were therefore not a product of the musical langauge, as they had been earlier; the language generates only fragments, and the larger forms actually employed are alien to the language.[16] And this contradiction between form and language leads in turn to the second main result of the stylistic transformation, namely that a division between internal and external components replaces a series of internal divisions as the semiotic foundation of musical expression. The style has no internal limits—anything goes, so to speak—and only the bounded forms of the past that lie outside the modern style carry any special charge. Where dissonance is the norm, for instance, consonance becomes an expressive device, but always, in music of this type, as an untimely sonority, forbidden by some composers, archaic for the others.[17] Consequently, expressivity is always attached to devices that break the stylistic conventions of the form. And these devices— semiotically marked, expressive, and disruptive—are precisely those features of melody, harmony, form, and so forth that are the familiar elements of the older style.

Thus, we arrive at the law for music of this period, which is that the familiar is always destabilizing, while the stable elements are always estranged. Coherence and shape are at odds: the former, the unity of the piece, comes from the modern style, most often from the dense texture of microscopic motifs that permeate the whole, while the latter, the expressive totality, comes from the larger units such as melody and structure that are borrowed wholesale from the past. From this permanent division arises the unstably ironic or elegiac character that seems inescapable in the period: the music always seems to be saying one thing and meaning another or to be pointing toward a position it does not occupy. Yet the irony rarely seems to arise from the kind of firm ground that supports the puns of Haydn or the parody so frequent in late Beethoven. Indeed, the very key migrations that signal abnormality in Schubert or Chopin and madness in Smetana become unremarkable after 1900, and can be found in works like Zoltan Kodály's Cello Sonata, opus 4, Ravel's Sonata for Violin and Cello, and the first of Richard Strauss's *Four Last Songs*. The great music of the twenties seems not to take a position; it rarely has the pronounced and unmistakable ideological character found in the music of powerful revolutionary composers such as Mozart, Beethoven, and Wagner or of powerful consolidators such as Haydn and Brahms. It has no home base: even composers who preserve the notion of tonality use devices such as a confusion of major and minor modes or oblique tonal relations in order to undermine the stability of the tonal system.

Music is not a referential art, and the homelessness of musical style in this period is a structural necessity, not a biographical or sociological one. This realization may offer us one way of understanding what Hardy once called "the ache of modernism" (*Tess of the D'Urbervilles* 105)—the condition of homelessness or exile that besets the literature of the period. The happy ending and the tragic but redemptive one have become equally obsolete; the inability of the citizens of Joyce's Dublin to get along with one another is an aesthetic precondition for the energy and movement required of a narrative. Thus, Joyce's *Exiles* ends with Richard's confession of a wound "which can never be healed," consisting of the "restless living wounding doubt" that makes love possible (112).

What is a law of musical form is merely a norm of literary expression. When Joyce spoke, for instance, of the "scrupulous meanness" of his writing,[18] he did not mean that every sentence must be discordant, but he still wanted to emancipate dissonance; in consequence, catachresis or category error becomes one of his most frequent and characteristic stylistic devices: "A bell clanged upon her heart" ("Eveline," *Dubliners* 41); and "A light began to tremble on the horizon of his mind" ("A Little Cloud," *Dubliners* 73). The old organic forms are reduced to a fragmentary residue; where there is a conflict and resolution, as in "The Boarding House," the climactic scene is omitted; where there is a plot, like the friends' scheme in "Grace" to get Kernan on the wagon, it seems to turn into a raucous imposition, parodied for instance by a millinery redemption in lieu of a genuine millenary one: "His hat, which had been rehabilitated by his wife, rested upon his knees" (*Dubliners* 173). Consistency comes from the web of motivic connections. There is no law, such as in the dodecaphonic system, requiring every note to be derived from the tone-row, but there is a principle of economy; literally, "scrupulous meanness" proclaims concentration on a narrow repertoire of motifs. Totality or closure, on the other hand, comes from the archetypal patterns of aging, of the progression of the seasons, of the growth of social organization, that pervade the collection as a whole and that are entirely disjunct from the shape of the individual stories. And whereas tonal music is selective—some notes are in the scale, others are out—twelve-tone music substitutes what Rosen calls the saturation of the musical space: all notes must be represented equally (*Schoenberg* 69–70). Likewise, Joyce's encyclopedic impulse saturates the narrative space: all walks of life are represented, as are all ages of man, and the absence of spring from the cycle of seasons is the one significant structural irony in the collection: there is no pastoral and no regeneration.

At the very least, such parallels can confirm one's sense of what is truly general in the artistic culture of a period. No influence is in question here, no common heritage, no particular shared problematic, not even necessarily the same public—only a common sensibility. And I think, as well, that these parallels can aid those of us on the literary side with some of our interpretive problems and judgments. For the "laws" of musical structure offer firmer guidelines to interpretation than the more approximate principles of verbal expression. They can help guide our interpretive tact by clarifying for us what constitutes a message and what belongs to a cultural code and thus by indicating which features of the work we should decide to rely on or to stress.

In Joyce's case the musical parallels can help us with the peculiar tonelessness of *Dubliners*, that deadpan succession of declarative sentences, poor in connectives, that characterizes his prose. There is a temptation to regard this feature as a savage irony, an Irishman's pitiless exposé of Dublin, as if Joyce might have written differently of London, Paris, or Trieste. But, of course, the great artists of this period hardly wrote differently of these other cities: "scrupulous meanness" could well describe the tone of Italo Svevo's Trieste, Proust's Paris, or to a considerable degree even Woolf's London. Svevo even makes one of the apparent villains in *The Confessions of Zeno* a musician, the sort of violinist who plays Bach's Chaconne smoothly and sweetly. According to the title character, by contrast, "mistuning is the path to unison" (*La Coscienza di Zeno* 101). Yet Zeno's paradox reminds us that unison—the point of rest or the perspective point—can never be reached but only approached through the increasing acuteness of permanent mistuning. Thus does the modernist sense of structure differ radically from the nineteenth-century principle that dissonance is the road to consonance—or in the Hegelian language of dialectical musical aesthetics, "in the suspension [*Aufhebung*] of equilibrium lies the tendency to return to a condition of equilibrium."[19] There is no implied superior position, ideological or utopian, from which the creator looks down on his creations; the disjunctions in the works are not a judgment but the very form of modernism.

*   *   *

What are the consequences of the formalist history that the preceding pages sketch out? On one reading, they entail a fatalism or a Foucauldian power play. I have invoked Debussy, Schoenberg, Stevenson, Hardy, Chekhov, and Hofmannsthal to suggest how the European spirit was Balkanized alongside the European polity. The fate of *Realpolitik*, this account would claim, was merely one expression of the fate of *Realismus*. A terrible beauty was born, with all the violence that we have come to associate with the term revolution. It happened to Hofmannsthal in 1902, to Schoenberg in 1911, and eventually to Europe in 1914.

There is a second reading of my argument that is closer to what I would like to believe. The second reading, like the first, claims a linkage between matters of the spirit and matters of history, for I hope that any reader of this chapter feels that music matters to life. But the second reading would equate what I have called form not with fate but with what others would call ideology. A Marxist such as Fredric Jameson has drawn powerful inspiration from the formalists Northrop Frye and Algirdas Greimas as well as from Adorno's musical writings. Students of music almost invariably regard form (as literary critics also normally do) as an abstraction from meaningful substance. Yet those who oppose an empty formalism often do so, mostly without acknowledgment, in the service of an enriched one. Edward T. Cone's concluding words in *The Composer's Voice* sound the watchword: "The formalist is justified in demanding a purely musical context for music only if he recognizes that . . . the musical context and the human context are inseparably intertwined" (175). To the extent that form subconsciously regulates the possibilities of articulate thought, then I would like to think that formal analysis is the vehicle of self-reflexive ideology critique. A case in point would be Ruth Solie's essay on Schumann's *Frauenliebe und Leben*; contesting formalism ("or what," she says, "we might more pointedly call autonomism," 240), she in fact brings the resources of formal analysis to bear in an ideologically aware defense of the seemingly indefensible. Or one could invoke that other Marxist *malgré lui*, Charles Rosen, for his commitment—implicit throughout *The Classical Style*—to the view that music is the essential or inescapable carrier of our cultural determinants, precisely because it is free of the corrupting—or deconstructive—entanglements of words. On this second reading of my argument, we could say that formal analysis unveils the birth of ideology out of the spirit of music.

PART IV

Finale

Unheard Melodies

The Force of Form

for MHP

If you have any music that may not be heard, to't again.
—Shakespeare, *Othello*

PRELIMINARY POSTSCRIPT. Readers may wonder how an essay on silence finds its way (as this one originally did) into a collection on performance. The match was made at the last minute, not by author or coordinator of the issue where it appeared but at the suggestion of the editor and the editorial board. Perhaps they wanted to frame a debate? No incidental comments on orchestral seating will disguise the Shelleyanism of an argument for which, as Joel Fineman intimates of *Othello*, sound appears to stain the white radiance of sense. "Rome's azure sky, / Flowers, ruins, states, music, words, are weak / The glory they transfuse with fitting truth to speak" (Shelley, *Adonais* 464–66). To the committed idealist, the best artist lacks hands.

Still, if the ideal is to convey a truth without corrupting it in the utterance, perhaps music may come closer to adequacy than more denotative expressions. Free from specific markers, it might tap the empyrean. In this spirit Shelley writes in one of his lyrics "To Jane":

> Though the sound overpowers
> Sing again, with your dear voice revealing
> A tone
> Of some world far from ours,
> Where music and moonlight and feeling
> Are one.

A tone is better than a word and all the more so in the nocturnal somnolence of Shelley's dream world. If it enters into activity, it suffers corruption: in *Adonais* music is discredited by its association with the daytime azure sky and with the productions of nature and of man. But released from consciousness, music becomes redemptive. So it is in the minimalist world of "To Jane"; where the guitar is "tinkling," the moon "soft," the light "faint," and the voice "most tender," the aim clearly is to evoke the lower threshold of awareness. When Shelley wrote that "the sound overpowers," he was not thinking of Guns 'n Roses; he intended, certainly, a lullaby that hypnotizes or anesthetizes. Music transfigures to the degree that it escapes perceptual fixation. Gabriel Conroy in Joyce's "The Dead," "strain[ing] his ear to listen" in the "stillness" after a song, captures the symbolic perfection that Joyce called an epiphany: "*Distant Music* he would call the picture if he were a painter" (*Dubliners* 209–10). Joyce and Shelley join Shakespeare's clown in adhering to the credo that the perfection of music is silence.

Yet Shelley's idealism was committed to paper. And *Othello* ends not with Gratiano's despondent last line—"All that's spoke is marr'd" (5.2.358)—but with the active emissary Lodovico, promising a performance allied in spirit to what the audience has just seen: "Myself will straight aboard, and to the state / This heavy act with heavy heart relate" (5.2.371–72). Even as we teeter at the edge of the intense inane, the mission to communicate—to inform and to reform—warps us home again. There will be no show without a tell.

In what sense this counts as performance remains to be seen. For the senses of performance are multiple. For every thinker who pits form against matter or against body, there is one who ranks it against soul or spirit. Form is the visible and the invisible, the measured and the felt, the analytic and the radiant. And whether it casts forms or casts scripts into form, performance, caught between ideals of fidelity and release, lists to every wind. By implication even if not by original intent, this chapter can, I hope, contribute to a reconciliation of the energetics of performance with the contemplative repose of the creative imagination—or else of the impulsive imagination with the disciplined body of the interpreter. "For of the soule the bodie forme doth take: / For soule is forme, and doth the bodie make" (Spenser, *An Hymne in Honour of Beautie* 132–33).

* * *

Early formalism, we know, was embarrassed enough of the historical subject or Spirit . . . to transform poems into artifacts as seemingly emptied of historical subject as a Grecian Urn. (Liu, "The Power of Formalism" 740)

What does a work of art contain? The question stumps all reflection theories, however complex their mediations. For them the contents lie outside the work or on its surface. A mirror traveling down a road has no inside; on its uncertain glass lie only shadows, a Platonic cavern turned inside out. Its transcendent Ideas repose in the looking-glass world beyond the mirror, within the warp that it pretends not to have. So much do the revelations of literature or painting conceal. What then of an art that, deep down, does not reflect or denote? Even for Plato—for Aristotle even—mimesis belonged preeminently to music and to the passions of the soul. What does the musician of the *Politics* convey? What do the Sirens sing? Utterance and its cognate gestures—externalization, outreach—are at best the outer limits of expression. Art's secrets lurk within.

Within the urn. Keats's passionate music leaves his surfaces troubled and confused. Questions proliferate in "a kind of 'wild ecstasy' of syntax" (Wolfson, "The Language of Interpretation" 40). What are these, gods or men? What men, or what gods? The speaker's mind wanders, beyond and outward, to a world unknown, unfindable. Abruptly, passions fall silent, to no end. A catharsis both overwrought and cold stills life. Does it slake desire? What kind of doom, or what kind of consolation, is proclaimed to those "on earth"? It's hard to know what an ode says.

What the ode doesn't say is easier to discern. In the first stanza Keats tries to overhear the "tale" or "legend" haunting "about thy shape," but by the last stanza his meditations have redirected him to the "shape" itself, the "attitude," the "silent form." For a "silent" urn speaks ("thou say'st") through ellipsis. Its beauty and truth stem from an ancient triad. Notable for its absence is the triad's third member: between the truth of pure reason and the beauty of aesthetic judgment, the poem voids the goodness of practical reason. Its action supplants Action.[1] Whatever the tonality of Keats's coda, "on earth" means in the forest or the wilds ("trodden weed"), not in the "little town, . . . little town," to which the fourth stanza bids its lingering adieu. From Auburn to urn: desert the village and let the earth figure the ground of being.[2] Beneath the hot pipes, themselves unheard, the urn's cold bass will not be seduced by the passions on its surface. What would its quietism deny? What reject? And what enable?

"Shape," "attitude," "form." The well-wrought urn, beloved of formalists, sings an allied song. Donne's "hymns" ("The Canonization" 34) link mimesis to contradiction and death. But here, too, the emptying out of sense and the ironic reduction of three dimensions to two ("the glasses of your eyes") prove a mysterious and sacred askesis. The contradiction that is at once a lessening, an infecting, and a betrothing looks ahead to resurrection and divine reward. Could Donne's "pattern" too be a mystic equation—the truth of beauty and the beauty of truth—secured by the privitude of his music?

The path I have chosen for investigating these questions lies through some dry, even abstruse empirics. It has the virtue of taking my topic as literally as possible, over a restricted domain. In real music—real, nonexistent music—I will look for the key to the urns. But first I want to dwell with beauty a few paragraphs longer, fleshing out this particular Keatsian swoon.

*   *   *

> Heard melodies are sweet, but those unheard
>   Are sweeter; therefore, ye soft pipes, play on;
> Not to the sensual ear, but, more endear'd,
>   Pipe to the spirit ditties of no tone.

For a poem so well studied as the "Ode on a Grecian Urn," these lines have elicited remarkably little commentary. What could they mean? The "unheard melodies" above or within the urn are the secrets of art. First, Keats suggests that art is like life, only more so. What we hear is sweet; what's on the urn is even sweeter. It is endeared to more than just our earthly ears. To be sure, "endear'd" is an odd word, a bastard cross between endearing and endowed, and a bad pun to boot. Keats strains here, trying to make a comparison between art and life that won't stand scrutiny. For there is a second layer in the lines that contrasts art to life. Unheard melodies are the opposite of heard melodies. The urn pipes *not* to the ear *but* to the spirit. Life is "sensual"—rich and full—whereas art is toneless. By the end of the sentence Keats seems to have reversed himself; he began by saying that art is more than life—precisely, that it is "sweeter," that is, more sensual—whereas by the end he says that it's less than life, with "ditties of no tone." The sounds of the word "note" lurk in this richly musical phrase, shadowing its denial with an unheard antiphon. (See Garrett Stewart, *Reading Voices* 156–60, a section entitled

"Unheard Melodies," for other such "graphonics" in Keats.) But the status of sound remains undetermined. On the one hand, we have comparison between art and life, on the other hand, contrast. Art is life intensified, or it is life denied.

The awkward combination of comparison and contrast reappears in the word "soft": "Therefore, ye soft pipes, play on." Obviously, Keats doesn't mean "soft" here. The pipes are not just soft but silent, that is, ultra-soft, softer than soft; an unstated superlative or absolute comparative is implied. Yet really those pipes aren't soft at all; they are solidest marble. If we take soft materially, it is the opposite of the truth. It's another litotes—an understatement, message unspecified. The comparative reading points to the spiritual story the pipes should be ever so softly telling, the contrastive reading to the physical art object. Comparison, contrast; story, picture. The one thing absent is the tune. Music gets lost in the shuffle.

The strangely casual-sounding word "ditties" heightens the paradox. A ditty is a ballad, and etymologically it comes from the old French word for speaking or dictating. "Ditties of no tone" are, precisely, the words without the music, appropriately piped to the spirit and not to the ear, sentiment rather than sensation. Curiously, the other well-known place where Keats uses the word "ditty" also has an aura of silence: "He play'd an ancient ditty, long since mute, / In Provence call'd, 'La belle dame sans mercy'" ("The Eve of St. Agnes" 291–92). Revived in romance, as here, the ditty proves a dangerous charm. Better the toneless ditty than the opiates of Provençal song, with their life-denying, hypnotic incantation. Music is bad for the soul. In the ode Keats first mentions the pipes in connection with danger, "What pipes and timbrels? What wild ecstasy?" He says nice things to the pipes to flatter them—"Therefore ye soft pipes, play on"—knowing full well that they aren't playing at all and that he wouldn't want them to. "Therefore" is the most devious word of all. Logically, Keats should have said, "Heard melodies are sweet, but those unheard / Are sweeter; therefore, ye soft pipes, shut up." Indeed, what he does say amounts to much the same thing, more tactfully worded.[3]

A crisis, then, haunts these lines. The unheard melodies really aren't there because they have always already turned into something else. Words or pictures, more or less, comparable or contrasting: the poem gives us everything but the thing we are looking for, the music—or the muse—itself. No wonder that Keats says near the end, playfully but sadly, "Thou silent form dost tease us out of thought."

* * *

Dans cette métaphysique héliocentrique, la force cédant la place à l'eidos (c'est-à-dire à la forme visible pour l'oeil métaphorique), a déjà été séparée de *son sens* de force, comme la qualité de la musique est séparée de soi dans l'acoustique.

In this heliocentric metaphysic, force, yielding its place to eidos (i.e., to form that is visible to the metaphoric eye), has already been separated from *its sense* of force, as the quality of music is separated from itself in hearing. (Derrida, "Force et signification" 45)

Composers didn't need Keats to imagine unheard melodies. The idea is as old as the famous and widespread mystical notion of the music of the spheres and as new as John Cage's 4 minutes and 33 seconds of silence. When the bustle of daily existence falls silent, you hear the universe or else, as Cage says (13), the nervous system and the circulation of the blood—the world or else the self. Keats wasn't inventing in his ode but rethinking a long-familiar conception, as we might see from his word "spirit," which means both something transcendental and something internal, world or self. He is in tune with tradition here, and hence it makes sense to juxtapose his ode with musical passages that may have something related in view.

There is no more outspoken example of an unheard melody than that in Schumann's *Humoresque*, opus 20, so blatant a case of secrecy that it's almost funny and certainly more outrageously teasing than Keats's urn (see Example 5). The middle line in the score is a melody published with the explicit direction not to play it. Quite soberly, we can say that the "inner voice" line orients the performer's thoughts. The melody is also outlined and, indeed, discreetly highlighted in the treble part. The "inner voice" reminds the performer to think about it and to emphasize those notes in performance. Yet the inner voice also differs from the treble notes: it's written an octave down, with a rest in one bar where the right hand plays, and with dynamic indications—unplayed dynamics!—that in some cases vary from those in either the treble or bass parts. We can retain from this curiosity the simple yet vital notion that the piece is composed of two levels, outer and inner voice, sounds and thoughts. The sounds are directed at what Keats calls "the sensual ear." But the

*)Diese innere Stimme soll nicht mitgespielt werden. Der Spieler soll hier gleichsam „zwischen den Zeilen" lesen.
This inner part is not to be played. The player is to "read between the lines" here, as it were.
Cette partie intermédiaire ne doit pas être jouée. Ici, l'exécutant doit savoir „lire entre les lignes".

Example 5. *Humoresque*, by Robert Schumann. Reproduced from *Complete Works for Piano Solo in Six Volumes*, vol. 4, Melville: Belwin Mills, n.d., a reprint of a nineteenth-century edition of Schumann's works.

performer must think about the sounds in order to shape the performance: that shaping thought is the inner voice, a ditty of no tone that is
piped to the spirit. There's nothing very startling about this, yet it remains quietly perplexing to feel that the thought is somehow different
from the music or that the sense or quality of the notes is not exactly in
what you hear. Schumann, too, wants music to be "eerie"—for the spirit
and not, or not just, for the ear.[4]

Now this Schumann passage is obviously eccentric. We need to ask
whether he is doing here something that has never been done, or, on the
contrary, something that we always do and therefore rarely bother to
think about. I will rest my case that it is the latter on a series of other
examples that range gradually from the odd to the normal.

Tchaikovsky, one of the most underrated of the great masters, is distinctly odd. His unheard melody is the theme of the last movement of
the *Symphonie Pathétique*. Example 6 shows its guise on first appearance,
Example 7 a reprise later in the movement. In the reprise the first violins
play the tune. But initially it is broken between the first and second
violins. The lines they play are never heard individually, and no one
plays the melody that audiences have always heard and analysts always analyzed. Why Tchaikovsky did that is a mystery. But clearly he
had a reason. The mystery, then, is a controlling design. Something is
heard, and something, whatever it may be, is thought, beneath what is
heard. To be sure, in Tchaikovsky's day the second violins sat opposite
the firsts rather than behind them, and attentive listeners might have
caught a delicate stereophonic effect (Porter, *Music of Three Seasons* 451).
But for my purposes it doesn't even matter, finally, whether the unheard

Example 6. Symphony no. 6 (*Pathétique*), by Pyotr Ilich Tchaikovsky. Finale,
opening.

Example 7. *Pathétique* Symphony. Finale.

melody is really unheard or almost unheard. What matters is that the scoring conveys an attitude toward the melody or a thought about it. There is an undersense of strain, later relieved, that the performers must feel and that should be communicated through the intangibles of interpretation.

By interpretation musicians (and actors) normally mean expressive performance, whereas critics normally mean the elucidation of thought, design, or ideology. Unheard melodies bring the two meanings together. The undersense of strain belongs to an overall structure of feeling, expression, and import that pervades the whole symphony. From the murky vastness of its low bassoon and bass opening onward, the symphony is an epic work, the tale of a world at risk. It breaks precedent by ending with a slow movement—Mahler followed suit a few years later—and the fragmented theme is but one sign among many of an impending doom. The whole story would be too long to tell here, but some such undersense must be what led Tchaikovsky's brother to give the name *Pathétique* to the symphony. As the unheard melody in the bars that I have reproduced lies in the way the voices are fitted together, so the larger unheard melody lies in the adjustment of voices and parts in the whole symphony. Donne's "legend," epitome, and "pattern," Keats's "attitude" and "silent form"—those are what a fuller analysis could unfold and what Modeste Tchaikovsky named for us in his title.

Musical Romanticism's last gasp came some 50 years later, with the *Four Last Songs* of Richard Strauss. The last song, in the usual ordering, is called *Der Abschied* (The Farewell). The unheard melody that I single out here is found in the horn parts in the last bars, the end of the end of the end (see Example 8). From amid the whole orchestra, playing its

Example 8. "Der Abschied," from *Four Last Songs*, by Richard Strauss. Conclusion.

softest, the horns fall silent. Those horns were Strauss's father's instrument, his own favorite and that of the Romantic poets, particularly Eichendorff, who wrote the poem that Strauss set here. Strauss keeps his own counsel as to why he allows the horns to die out before everyone else. Perhaps the reasons are partly acoustical, but the silence is unmistakably an expressive gesture as well. It can be read, I think, as Strauss's secret farewell to Romanticism. More to the purpose here, however, is simply the assertion that the silence ought to be read somehow, as a commentary on the piece.[5]

In short, there is more to a piece of music than meets the ear. We can call that something more an attitude, a conception, or a thought. In the odd examples given so far the something leaves an unheard trace in the score, and they do offer glimmerings at least of what is at stake, of what really matters to the composer. More typically, of course, what really matters is also audible. But in any piece some things are more audible than others. You don't notice all the melodies that are hearable but the subliminal effect remains. The difference between a good and a bad listener is that the good listener knows how things fit together, hears the inner voices, and makes the connections. And often the composer helps things along.

In the song from *Pierrot Lunaire* called *The Pale Washerwoman*, Schoenberg silently guides the listener by printing a piano reduction in the score even though the piano doesn't perform in this piece. Amid all the "ugly" music reflecting an ugly world, the conventional minor chords of bar 4 sound pale and washed out. It's another adieu to Romanticism, shaded differently from Strauss's. But the piano reduction doesn't tell all, nor is even a careful listener of these quick moments likely to realize why the pale chords sound so very odd and out of place. What matters is less the harmonies that show up in the piano reduction than the distribution of the voices that, perhaps, only the performers can really hear (see Example 9). Three instruments play three notes each. But a different voice is on top each time, and each sounds the notes of a different chord. The violin plays an A-major arpeggio, the clarinet a dominant seventh on E, the flute a C-sharp-major arpeggio. While the chords are innocuous, the lines are polytonal. Only preternaturally swift ears could hear the counterpoint consciously, yet the sequence sounds alien. Heard melodies, in this case, are sweet, but unheard ones are acid.

Example 9. "Eine blasse Wäscherin," from *Pierrot lunaire*, by Arnold Schoenberg. Opening. Used by permission of Belmont Music Publishers, Pacific Palisades, CA 90272.

You can hear sounds, but you can't hear patterns or attitudes; those you have to think or hear with the mind. For to know what constitutes a pattern you have to know what belongs together, what feels right or wrong, tense or relaxed, complete or incomplete. The feelings and emotions come through the patterns that project the attitudes. Satisfaction means making full, filling up the pattern, rounding off; emotion means moving, changing, altering or breaking the form, making it expressive by pressing something out of it. In an important sense, melodies are never heard. Only notes are heard. What E. H. Gombrich has ceaselessly argued about art applies with a vengeance to music: the meaning lies in the mind's apprehension of conventions that are being manipulated.

I will therefore conclude my music section with a mainstream example that is free of the idiosyncracies of the other examples yet still features an unheard melody. All music does—all art does—so long as you stretch the meaning of the word melody to include any type of pattern. But this example has an unheard melody that's really a melody, and because it isn't there, any good listener will have to listen for the pattern instead (see Example 10). This, following eleven tumultuous introduc-

Example 10. Symphony no. 3 (*Eroica*), by Ludwig van Beethoven. Finale, bars 12–52 and 76–83.

tory bars, is the opening of the last movement of Beethoven's *Eroica* Symphony, much the most ambitious symphony yet composed by anyone. What must Beethoven's first listeners have thought, coming so far—musically speaking—in order to arrive at the puny excuse for a theme that is plunked out in the bass? Something is missing. There's not much to listen to here. Where is the tune?

A really sophisticated listener would know where the tune is, because Beethoven had already written it, in the finale of his ballet, *The Creatures of Prometheus*. If you know enough you can hear the unheard melody. But if you aren't one of the favored few, about the best you can do is think. You could think about the weather while waiting for something pretty to happen, but more likely Beethoven wanted you to think back over the symphony.

Starting on the tonic—or key—note of E-flat, the tune stretches an octave between high and low B-flat (the fifth, or dominant, note of the scale), stretching an extra note to low A at one point. It might call to mind the opening theme of the first movement, which is also a bass line covering an octave between B-flats (see Example 11). The first theme of the slow movement covers an octave between the dominant tones, G in this case, stretching an extra note to high A-flat at one point (see Exam-

Example 11. *Eroica* Symphony. First movement, opening.

Example 12. *Eroica* Symphony. Second movement, opening.

Example 13. *Eroica* Symphony. Third movement, opening.

Example 14. *Eroica* Symphony. Trio section of the third movement, opening.

ple 12). The first theme of the third movement covers an octave between B-flats, stretching an extra note to high C at one point (see Example 13). Even the theme of the trio section of this movement begins by covering an octave between B-flats (see Example 14). Altogether, the absence of a melody at the opening of the finale leaves room for reflection and helps call attention to the unity of the symphony. The skin is stripped away leaving the bones; or the decoration, leaving the framework. The unheard melody is the structural coherence of the whole.

In the *Eroica* Symphony the summing up is simultaneously a redemption of the earlier movements. The first movement theme begins with the notes of an E-flat-major triad, sinks to D, and then sinks further to a note that doesn't belong, C-sharp. Musical training is not requisite to hear the effect because the music changes character at this point, with the agitated entry of the syncopated violins (Example 11, bar 7). In the last movement, the bass line also sinks to D, but then returns to E-flat (Example 10, bars 16–17). The last movement begins, in other words, by correcting a disruption in the first movement. It also echoes in a brighter vein the tragic second movement, with rising pairs of notes (E–F, D–E-flat, A–B-flat; Example 10, bars 17–19) replacing the heavy descents of the earlier theme.

There are no such problems with the third movement. But that movement does raise another problem perhaps overlooked earlier on. The most distinctive characteristic of the third movement theme is the repeated notes. The trio is also built up of repeated notes. Repeated notes also form the introductory flourish in the slow movement theme. Even earlier they constitute the accompaniment to the first movement theme (Example 11, third staff). In other words, repetition is present from the start, adjacent to the themes, and the symphony gradually makes repetition a part of its thematic material. Now, in the last movement we also find repeated notes, and again they don't seem to be really part of the theme. They are, first, the echo effect as the winds repeat the string notes (Example 10, bars 20–25), and then, second, the loud flourish on B-flat where the motion pauses (bars 28–31). That sort of pause on the dominant was a common feature of variation themes at the time, but Beethoven seems in desperate straits when he does it so baldly. This isn't part of the tune but a crude structural device. How is he going to pull it all together? What is going to happen next?

What happens next is truly extraordinary. Beethoven does not simply fashion a unifying motif but instead stages the gesture of producing that unity. For, before the unheard Prometheus melody is at last sounded, Beethoven writes variations on the bass line. By holding off the melody, Beethoven lets us hear the motivation for it. Repetition occurs first as the interrupting element, then as echo, next as an accompaniment figure (bars 44 and 46), and at last, when the Prometheus theme appears, as part of the melody itself (bars 80–81). All the parts contribute to the whole that has grown organically. Consequently—to mention just one other effect among a large number that a full analysis might disclose— the very opening of the symphony may now be heard differently. For it

opens with another flourish. Before the agitated first-violin syncopations, even before the ostinato eighth-note accompaniment in second
violins and violas, come two—repeated—opening chords. Listeners may
treat them as an empty gesture, and I suspect that analysts never attach
them to the first theme. But in hindsight they should be reckoned with.
At first sounding like a vestigial introduction, these too subsequently
prove to be an integral building block of the structural whole.[6]

So let me repeat my equation. Unheard melodies are structure, skeleton, attitude, feeling: they are the inside of the piece, or of the urn.
Though my examples have been a little out of the ordinary, it's really an
ordinary point, worth taking a little less for granted than is often done.
It's a commonplace, for instance, that themes for variation often aren't
very pretty; you don't listen to them for their own sake. You listen in
anticipation of the unheard elaborations to come later. And during the
variations you listen back to the theme that is no longer being played.
Even for a relatively naive listener the pleasure of the form lies in comparison and contrast: the invariant substructure and the potential that
unfolds from it. Keats was right after all to tell the soft pipes to play on
rather than to shut up. The unheard melodies aren't unplayed; they are
the undertone that make their presence felt through their persistence.

The point is equally applicable to the other arts. Keats's urn, after all,
features a painting, not a tone poem. His interest is excited by what can't
be known about the urn or by what can't be seen on it. "What men or
gods are these?" he wants to know, "What maidens loth?" "To what
green altar, O mysterious priest, / Lead'st thou that heifer lowing at the
skies?" The first questions ask for information that isn't forthcoming,
the last for a scene that isn't painted. We hardly ever look at a painting
without wanting information: who or what is portrayed, what is the
story, what is the conventional or personal significance of the details?
Not everything that we need to know to look at a work of art is contained within it. The iconographic quest may not concern unseen pictures in the strict sense, but it certainly concerns things unseen within
the picture that are essential for a proper understanding of it.

Even more to my point, however, is the formalist quest. Looking at a
painting is not the same as looking at an object, just as listening to a
musical composition is not the same as listening to the tunes. Poussin's
self-portrait (Figure 1) is full of unseen pictures, canvases viewed from
the back or in part. The man stands behind his works, and you haven't

Figure 1. *Self-Portrait*, by Nicolas Poussin, 1650. Oil on canvas, 38½ × 29 in. (98 × 74 cm). Musée du Louvre, Paris. © Photo R.M.N.

seen everything if you have just looked at them. Yet more famous is Velázquez's *Las Meninas* (Figure 2), whose giant concealed canvas captured the imagination of painters throughout the ages (Kronik, "The Web, the Hive, and the Looking Glass"), as it has captured the imagination of critics of all stripes. But it doesn't take much to remind us of the unseen picture behind the canvas (Figure 3). A little spot of white at the center, something as chancy as a playing card facing the other way can be the signal that the world in the painting isn't our world but a self-contained, imaginary, fictive world. The boy in Chardin's *Card Castle* doesn't care about us or relate to us in any way; he is absorbed in his

Figure 2. *Las Meninas*, by Diego Velázquez, c. 1656. Oil on canvas, 125 × 108⅔ in. (318 × 276 cm). Museo del Prado, Madrid. Photo: Alinari/Art Resource, New York.

own thoughts (Fried, *Absorption* 46–51). Chardin loved to paint a world of thoughts, a world beyond pure visibility, or beyond the eye, so typically down-turned in this magical portrait.

Thought—reflection. Isn't that what every serious painting is—not a copy of reality but a thoughtful reflection that composes the usual surface into something more deeply meaningful? Painters love mirrors (Cook, "The Wilderness of Mirrors"). They love them for painterly reasons, because of the fascinating softening of contours in the painted mirror image that seems to idealize the scene. Remember the royal cou-

Figure 3. *The Card Castle*, by Jean-Baptiste-Siméon Chardin, c. 1735. Oil on canvas, 32⅜ × 26 in. (82 × 66 cm). National Gallery of Art, Washington; Andrew W. Mellon Collection.

ple in Velázquez's mirror, miniaturized but still conceptually dominant, at the visual center of the picture. Manet's *Bar at the Folies-Bergères* (Figure 4) is another famous and fascinating mirror, which doesn't reflect the scene in front of it but some other skewed version in the painter's imagination. Enacting Manet's "attitude toward the Folies-Bergère," as a Marxist critic has written, the mirror turns the scene into something "almost real" in order to communicate "a form of explana-

Figure 4. *The Bar at the Folies-Bergère*, by Edouard Manet, 1882. Oil on canvas, 37¾ × 51¼ in. (96 × 130 cm). Courtauld Institute of Art, London.

tion" for the "social circumstances" it depicts (Clark, *The Painting of Modern Life* 253–54). Reflection isn't copying but thinking; that's what painters do and what Monet paints in this remarkable canvas that might be called a visualization of an unseen picture.

It wouldn't be hard to come up with more paintings of hidden pictures, or of mirrors reflecting scenes that aren't there, let alone of the unpainted areas of canvas that from Cézanne to Jackson Pollock and beyond have increasingly been part of the painter's repertory. (Kenneth Noland, for instance—according to Fried, *Three American Painters* 27—"make[s] the raw canvas itself work as optical space with unprecedented intensity.") But let me move on to at least one "ordinary" painting that seems to be a painting of the world rather than of the painter's activity in transforming the world. But has any of us ever seen what the world "really" looks like? Don't we always think as we see, connecting the dots on our retina, in order to turn pure visual sensations into visual pictures? We see green and black splotches but we perceive grass and

Figure 5. Detail from *Regatta at Argenteuil.*

shadows: the splotches are unperceived by us, the forms perceived, but in a literal sense unseen. Music is composed of sounds and sound shapes, and there is only noise if we don't hear the forms within the sounds—as sometimes happens to us with music from an alien culture. The same is true of visual things; unless the unseen shadows the seen, the world is no better than a hallucination.

That was the lesson of the Impressionists. Figure 5 is a detail from Monet's *Regatta at Argenteuil.* Is it possible to see the picture in the splotches? In context, however (Figure 6), their identity as a tree and a

Figure 6. *Regatta at Argenteuil*, by Claude Monet, 1871. Oil on canvas, 19 ×
28¾ in. (48 × 73 cm). Musée d'Orsay, Paris. © Photo R.M.N.

house is beyond question. Yet there is more to the painting than mere
linear decipherment.

The semantic relation between top and bottom, evidently works in both directions. First, the top names the bottom: this aggregate of spots that means nothing to you, presto! it's a tree, it's a house, it's a boat. Second, the bottom reveals
the top: this boat, this house that you find drab in fact secretly contain these
color harmonies, those elementary figures, such expressive possibilities.

In a painting like this one, what is above corresponds to what we recognize, to
the reality we are accustomed to; the lower part, which conveys these houses or
these boats toward us, corresponds to the painter's activity. Thus the water
becomes a metaphor for painting. The broad strokes that make up these reflections vigorously affirm the material and the tools used by the artist. The liquid
surface gives us an example in nature of this activity. (Butor, "Claude Monet,"
285)

By separating form from visual content, the reflective surface within
Monet's paintings becomes the figure of the unseen limit where mind
and matter, the known and the felt, meet. Some of my examples are

especially dramatic, self-conscious expressions of the reflective character of art, but my message is that all art is reflective. To a thoughtful
audience art reveals the buried inside of things: the moving patterns
that make sense of the world's surface, of sounds, of sights, of words.

*   *   *

Of words? I have talked about music and about pictures but not yet
about my own field. Where are the unread poems?

That's an easy one. One example is the passage I quoted early on from
Keats's *Eve of St. Agnes*: "He play'd an ancient ditty, long since mute, /
In Provence call'd, 'La belle dame sans mercy.' " Keats wrote a ballad
called *La Belle Dame sans Merci*, but later. It would be an easy parlor
game to accumulate poetic references to unquoted or unwritten poems,
novelistic allusions to other works of literature, real and imaginary,
stage directions that call for wordless communication by the actors or
that contain voluminous background information that can never be
communicated in the theater. Harold Bloom has built his career on the
premise that the meaning of a poem is always another poem: behind the
words that you read lie others—usually from *Paradise Lost*—that motivate them and give them their significance. The notions of a poem
behind the poem or of a story behind the novel are too common for
words.

Such things, however, are not quite unheard melodies. They are iconographic backgrounds, explanations of the surface content of the works.
But in music and painting we have been looking at structural patterns
that reflect the shape and tone of the work. Aren't the unheard melodies
of poems less innocuous and more like the inner movement of the Grecian urn? Their type is the complex interplay of comparisons and negations in Keats's lines. Isn't such a shuttling among similarities, inten-
sities, and contrasts the very essence of the mind's structuring activity,
teasing us into thought? Don't we have in those lines a portrait of precisely the kind of thought that I have called the unheard melodies of our
existence?[7]

A portrait of thought. A reflection on reflection. You can say what
Keats means, but in saying it you have only the surface meaning, the
heard melody, the visual transcription. But if you show his meaning,
if you perform it, you have created something "more endear'd," of

greater value, deeper. That performance is what makes a poem poetic. What makes a poem is not what it says but what it does in saying it. What makes a mind is not what it thinks but that it thinks, not the content but the activity. The reflecting surface is fluid; it breaks up appearances in order to perceive substrates. The meaning of a work is never identical to what it says, or depicts, or sings. Even if it utters truths—and works often do—even then the enacted meaning, the unseen picture, the unheard melody is never the same as the statement. The meaning of a poem can be described in words—that is what we literary critics do for a living—but it cannot be reduced to words. "Ditties of no tone" is a great phrase, for what works of art contain is not a meaning that is uttered but one that is carried by force of example from mind to mind, spirit to spirit, soul to soul.

*   *   *

I will conclude by mentioning a few poems and citing some utterances by a later and simpler poet than Keats: Stéphane Mallarmé. (For a fine discussion of formalism and expressivism in Mallarmé see McDonald, *Dispositions* 37–69.) Mallarmé is not simpler, of course, in his verbal surface, but he is in what matters more—the directness with which he calls our attention to the organizing thoughts underneath. The very name of Mallarmé, to be sure, popularly evokes an impressionism in which all definite realities dissolve into the shimmering expressive immediacy of pure voice: "Je dis: une fleur! et hors de l'oubli où ma voix relègue aucun contour, en tant que quelque chose d'autre que les calices sus, musicalement se lève, idée même et suave, l'absente de tous bouquets" (I say: a flower! and, beyond the oblivion to which my voice consigns any outline, as something other than known calyxes, musically arises—the suave idea itself—the One absent from all bouquets; *Oeuvres* 368). But you shouldn't read those well-known lines from the end of the essay "Crise de vers" out of context, as is normally done. If you have the whole essay before you, you will have read this, three sentences earlier: "Un désir indéniable à mon temps est de séparer comme en vue d'attributions différentes le double état de la parole, brut ou immédiat ici, là essentiel" (An undeniable desire of my time is to separate as if with an eye to different predications the dual status of the word, raw or immediate here, there essential; 368). The musical flower, the suave idea, is a word after all, not a pure, wordless impression, though indeed it is a deeper, essential, inapparent word, a ditty of no tone. How do we discern that essential word? The immediately preceding paragraph describes as unmistakably as anyone could desire how Mallarmé discerns it, at concerts:

Certainement, je ne m'assieds jamais aux gradins des concerts, sans percevoir parmi l'obscure sublimité telle ébauche de quelqu'un des poëmes immanents à l'humanité ou leur originel état, d'autant plus compréhensible que tu et que pour en déterminer la vaste ligne le compositeur éprouva cette facilité de suspendre jusqu'à la tentation de s'expliquer. . . . Car, ce n'est pas de sonorités élémentaires par les cuivres, les cordes, les bois, indéniablement mais de l'intellectuelle parole à son apogée que doit avec plénitude et évidence, résulter, en tant que l'ensemble des rapports existant dans tout, la Musique.

Certainly, I never take my seat in the tiers of the concert hall, without perceiving amid the dark sublimity some sketch of one of the immanent poems of humanity, or their original state, all the more comprehensible because silenced and because the composer, so as to determine their vast line, felt a readiness to suspend even the temptation to explain himself. . . . For, it is not from elementary sonorities by the brass, the strings, the woodwinds, undeniably but from the intellectual word at its apogee that there should result, in full and demonstrably, as the entirety of the relations existent in everything, Music. (367–68)

Music is, undeniably, relationships and not sounds, the perfection of utterance and not visceral feeling, not the channeling or taming of noise but the intellectual word that manifests the silent pulse of being. The unheard melody resides in shape and pattern, as Mallarmé says two paragraphs earlier: "Tout devient suspens, disposition fragmentaire avec alternance et vis-à-vis, concourant au rythme total, lequel serait le poëme tu, aux blancs" (All becomes suspense, fragmentary arrangement with alteration and juxtapositon, concurring in the total rhythm, which would be the silent poem, in the blanks; 367). Go back to the previous page, and Mallarmé has said it all, in a one-line paragraph setting the topic that these concluding pages have merely been explicating: "Cette visée, je la dis Transposition—Structure, une autre" (This [preceding] aim I call Transposition—Structure [is] something else; 366).[8] Structure, as the something else within expression, is the silent poem, the essential word, the flower absent from all bouquets, the musical idea.

Such is the context for the impressionistic musical disappearance of the contour of the flower. One could hardly dream of a more explicit declaration of the themes concealed within the urn. And so, when Mallarmé, in his poetry, praises the pale reflection of a portrait of Saint Cecilia ("Sainte"), I think there can be no question but that his "Musicienne du silence" (Musician of silence) evokes the perfect organization without which all would be blank to the mind. Or, that the denials of another sonnet ("Une dentelle s'abolit")—the self-canceling lace of the title, the "absence éternelle de lit" (eternal absence of bed) the "unanime blanc conflit / D'une guirlande" (unanimous white conflict of a garland) with its mirror image, and the "musical hollow void" within the mandolin—are likewise all enabling virtualities underneath the world of appearances, making it possible to end the poem not, as one might predict, with nonbeing (*n'être*), but instead with birth (*naître*). (Like so much in Mallarmé, the lines "Tristement dort une mandore / Au creux néant musicien" [Sadly sleeps a mandolin / In the hollow musical void] seem to echo Coleridge, specifically the silent music of "The Eolian Harp": "and the mute still air / Is Music slumbering on her instrument.") Another poem opens with the utter silence of dark, formless matter:

> A la nue accablante tu
> Basse de basalte et de laves
> A même les échos esclaves
> Par une trompe sans vertu. . . .
>
> Silent in the overwhelming cloud
> Basalt and lava shoal
> Enslaved even to echoes
> By a horn without force. . . .

But even this beginning opens out into the bright afterglow ("le si blanc cheveu" [the so white hair]) of a submerged musician ("Le flanc enfant d'une sirène" [The childlike side of a siren]). In resisting the chaos of "enslaved echoes" into which our lives are forever falling, art transmits to us the shaping power of the unseen, the unheard, and the unspoken that enables expression to take place.

*   *   *

Decant, descant, discount. Have I done nothing more in these pages than pour old wine into a new bottle? Aired it, refreshed it, embellished it, yet left it fundamentally untouched, taken it for granted even? Yes, to be sure. And no, by no means. Yes, in that the spirit of Cassirer and Langer rightly lives. Formalist is an epithet to be honored, not blushed at. Without form there is no power of resistance to the immediate, nought but the "enslaved echoes" of an abject consciousness. But no, if it be supposed that the new bottle is as rigid a container as the old one. The glass exists to be broken, the wine of form to be drunk, as in that drunken, distorting mirror of Manet.

> Le vierge, le vivace et le bel aujourd'hui,
> Va-t'il nous déchirer avec un coup d'aile ivre
> Ce lac dur oublié que hante sous le givre
> Le transparent glacier des vols qui n'ont pas fui!

> The virgin, lively and fair today,
> Will it with a drunken blow of its wing
> Tear our hard, forgotten lake haunted beneath the frost
> By the transparent glacier of flights that have not fled!

The icy surface that transmits without reflecting is the form of the dead present, forgotten because closed to its own possible unfolding. Mallarmé resolves to reawaken form, but not by remembering the forgotten surface or capturing the unflown and (in French) thievish flights. The divine parousia is not to be chained in bonds of ice or marble, freeze or frieze. Rather, form becomes the personifying force that liberates today into its unknown possibilities of action and of expression, of remembering and projecting, transcending the inert ideality of the moment and the inert materialism of the thing itself.[9]

By taking my cue from music, I have stacked the cards in favor of a thesis that form is energy, expression, and movement. But in truth that thesis is inscribed in the restiveness to be felt in the most inert or the most mimetic of paintings (see Bryson, "Chardin"),[10] as well as in poetry's recurrent envy of what it is not—of the pictorial balance that a sequential art can never attain, or of the musical pulse beyond the waywardness of natural life (see Paz, "El Ritmo," El Arco y la lira 49–67). Apollo is Dionysus.[11] The noble, intact today is the drunken pugilist of tomorrow and yesterday. I do not know why the critics of Keats, who tend to divide between the Apollonians and the Dionysians, should so seldom have seen this mutuality in the Ode on a Grecian Urn, where it seems so inescapable, let alone in the unseen landscapes of the Ode to a Nightingale or the dreaming wakefulness of the Ode to Psyche. All you need to know, on earth, is that beauty is . . . as truth, and truth . . . as beauty. The one *becomes* the other—how delightfully colloquial are our philosophical puns in English—in the vital round dance that lets form give life and meaning to content, and content give substance and expression to form. Base materialisms and empty formalisms alike may pretend to ignore the unheard call, but they cannot escape their destinies.

Reference Matter

Notes

Overture

1. Need it be observed that a worm in a garden path is an emblem of evil? The circles in *Bleak House* are discussed by J. Hillis Miller (*Charles Dickens* 185–90) and more fully by Robert Newsom (*Dickens* 18–39).

2. In two excellent feminist essays, Mary Jacobus and Margaret Homans describe Eliot's dialectic in analogous terms ("The Question of Language," "Eliot, Wordsworth, and the Scenes of Critical Instruction"). These essays take the sexual problem to be primary; I take it to instance a dialectical position. The feminine, an indispensable concept and quality, is not necessarily coextensive with the female.

3. Stuart M. Tave encloses the first chapter of *Some Words of Jane Austen* with fine discussions of dance as order (1–2, 34–35). "Every savage can dance," however (Darcy, quoted by Tave, 34), and Anne Elliot, the Austen heroine with the greatest mastery over her confused feelings (275), is also the one who "never dances" (262). C. J. Rawson surveys dancing in the eighteenth century and after (*Henry Fielding* 3–44); see esp. p. 29 on the "mincing, ambiguous figure" of the dancing master. See also Derrida and McDonald, "Choreographies" 68.

4. Or does Zola surreptitiously activate the mental sense of "balancer"? What, precisely, does the verb mean when he says of the "toy soldier" lover Zéphyrin, "il ne répondait ni oui ni non, se balançait comme si on l'eût chatouillé, puis s'élargissait d'aise" (he answered neither yes nor no, rocked [hesitated?] as if he had been tickled, then stretched out comfortably; part 5, chap. 1, p. 1168)?

5. The word ἀνατρέπω is not used by Plato to mean "refute," but Aristophanes uses it prominently in his satire of Socratic philosophy, *The Clouds*, which is centrally concerned with exploring turns (the character Strepsiades, the "vortex," etc.). The other locus for ἀνατρέπω in this sense is a late commentator who refers to some of Plato's dialogues as διάλογοι ἀνατρεπτικοί.

6. I have been unable to locate any extended discussion of *aporia* in Plato. The

major commentaries on the *Meno*, for instance, ignore the relevant passages, as if *aporia* belonged only to the interlocutors and not to the Socratic method. The absence of a word for *aporia* in modern languages may have contributed to the impression one gets that *aporia* is neither regarded as a concept nor acknowledged to have a function. Hans-Georg Gadamer at least recognizes the problem: on the one hand, he says that the *aporia* of presentation "fills us with confusion and uncertainty" (*Dialogue and Dialectic* 113) and that "because of the apeiron, human life can never be absolutely successful" (154–55), but on the other hand, he does allow that "this source of all aporia is also the source of the *euporia* which we achieve in discourse" (11). Gadamer's translator, typically, omits *aporia* from the index.

7. A transitional state of the word "revolution" may be found at the end of letter 83 of Goldsmith's *Letters to a Citizen of the World*: "The world is like a vast sea, mankind like a vessel sailing on its temptestuous bosom. Our . . . judgment is the rudder, without this last the vessel is tossed by every billow, and will find shipwreck in every breeze. In a word, obscurity and indigence are the parents of vigilance and œconomy; vigilance and œconomy of riches and honour; riches and honour of pride and luxury; pride and luxury of impurity and idleness, and impurity and idleness again produce indigence and obscurity. Such are the revolutions of life" (*Works* 2: 341). I believe that Blake's line, "And the Male gives a Time & Revolution to her Space" (*Jerusalem*, pl. 69, line 23), offers another transitional example; "revolution" here seems to imply (1) circling, (2) orgasm, and (3) the Fall. Leslie Brisman discusses "revolution" as circling and as violence in Wordsworth (*Romantic Origins* 328–29). Koselleck's *Kritik und Krise* is a brilliant account of the birth in the eighteenth century of a prolific crisis mentality (especially "in the philosophers professing a cyclical view of history," 134) and its degeneration into the hostile dualisms of politicized critique.

8. *Vom Schwindel* is cited from the enlarged 1791 edition, whose preface indicates that the principal changes are in the later, technical parts of the book.

9. For the view that dance teaches order see John C. Meagher, "The Dance." He concedes some of the difficulties of his position on p. 276.

10. Thomas M. Greene's masterful study affirms stability, but I believe that Jonson's works can be reread from the standpoint of his "centrifugal spirit" and of the present essay.

11. Antinous does not render the notion of twins any more stable when he later alludes to Castor and Pollux as "the victorious *twinns* of Laeda' and *Jove*" (71), hardly a tactful periphrasis to address to Penelope in the midst of her entanglement with the actions of Leda's other twins.

12. "*Brawles*: the *branle*, a dance distinguished by movement from side to side" (Davies, 369n). Love, that is, teaches a tottering dance.

13. The association of Penelope with mind is fairly consistent. True, st. 11 refers to *Antinous*'s mind. But the context is the power that Penelope's eyes exert

(and that Antinous merely receives) over "the noblesse and the splendour of his mind." In st. 46 Antinous calls music "the soft minds Paradice, the sick minds Leach"; clearly he is siding here with emotion, not with thought.

14. Rousset derives his notion of classicism from the customary misreading of Heinrich Wölfflin, who is discussed later in this volume.

15. Jacques Derrida discusses the turn against turn on 252–63 of the Hegel column of *Glas*: "Essayer de *penser* (mais ce mot déjà retient dans le cercle) un reste de *temps* (mais le temps déjà engage dans le cercle) qui ne serait pas, qui ne relèverait pas d'un présent, d'un mode d'être ou de présence et qui par consé-quent tomberait hors du cercle du *Sa*, n'en tomberait pas comme *son* négatif, tout prêt à reprendre la tangente pour rester collé au cercle et se laisser par lui réentraîner" (252a). Puns make Derrida's prose untranslatable, so that I can only give an approximate rendition: "To try to *think* (but this word already retains in the circle) a remainder of *time* (but time already engages in the circle) that would not be, that would not participate in a present, in a mode of being or of presence and that consequently would fall out of the circle of *absolute knowledge*, would not fall out as *its* negative [as a negative *sound*], quite ready to resume the tangent so as to remain stuck to the circle and to let itself again be swept along with it." While the processes described in *Glas* are most intriguingly bizarre (*anthérection, coupture*, etc.), I believe that my concluding turn toward process is compatible in a general way with Derrida's contention (as in the paragraph on "gl," p. 262b) that we remain indissolubly glued to the ring of difference.

16. Nature, in Harry Berger's beautiful expression, is "*too* perfect" ("The *Mutabilitie Cantos*" 171 n). Patricia A. Parker's entire book is an important treat-ment of my subject; see esp. pp. 54–64 on the *Mutability Cantos* and pp. 16–31 and 64–77 on error in Ariosto and Spenser. Typical of the difficulty in disentan-gling these cantos is William Nelson, *The Poetry of Edmund Spenser* 309, where Boethius is pressed into service in an awkward attempt to distinguish Muta-bility's "perdurability" from genuine "eternity."

17. St. 2 of canto 6 says, "As I have found it registered of old / In Faery Land mongst records permanent." St. 2 of canto 7 says, "for who, but thou alone / That art yborne of heaven and heavenly Sire, / Can tell things doen in heaven so long ygone, / So farre past memory of man that may be knowne?"

18. Angus Fletcher advocates a more hopeful view of Mutability in *The Pro-phetic Moment* 217–28. Arguing that the cantos subsume rebellion under revolu-tion (in the old sense of cycle), he concludes that error is redeemed, or at least "continually reborn" (227), in the anagogical Sabbath vision. How to translate theological truth (Fletcher quotes Tillich to confirm his reading) into sublunary experience remains, of course, the question. I think Fletcher answers it as I do; at least, he returns to the Mutability Cantos at the end of the same chapter ("Error and Experience," 215–57) in a section called "The Fall into History" (253–57).

19. "Poets' verses cannot really be endless; poems end, and, like every other

thing we make, they die." So says Isabel G. MacCaffrey (*Spenser's Allegory* 431), in the course of linking Spenser to Stevens in a more resigned fashion than I am about to do. Indeed, poems stop, even *The Faerie Queene*. But the issue is qualitative potency, not quantitative bulk. See also Altieri, "The Qualities of Action," and Kümmel, *Platon und Hegel*.

20. Commenting on the double meaning of Yeats's question, Paul de Man attributes its ambiguity to the split between the grammatical and the rhetorical functions of language, without remarking on the simpler semantic ambiguity of the expression, "to know from" (*Allegories of Reading* 11–12).

21. Frank Kermode, in a seminal, proto-feminist essay, "The Dancer," discusses the negativity, the faceless, sphinxlike quality of the dancer. I would like to suggest here what is achieved through this negation.

22. Jonathan Goldberg's *Endlesse Worke* puts a historian's question, "Where does *The Faerie Queene* move from its vantage point?" then immediately re-phrases it in a categorically deconstructive mode: "Where *can* the text go . . . ?" 166, my emphasis). The answer, in the book's final phrase, must then be this: "into the reality of loss" (174).

23. Donald G. Marshall, "Ideas and History," attacks the still extant notion that an idea has a "true meaning." "On such a model," he writes, "we would have a history of errors and of glimpses of truth with a clear terminus." In view of this dilemma, he expresses "scepticism that 'imagination' in fact has a history" (358). My belief, on the contrary, is that in fact ideas like "imagination" have *only* a history. A valuable history of crisis-consciousness itself has now appeared: Eugene Hollahan, *Crisis-Consciousness and the Novel*.

Chapter 1

1. Weinstein, *Hippolyte Taine* 51. Despite its dated attitudes, however, this is a serious, careful book that remains well worth reading.

2. My quick sketch identifies books by their definitive titles; in several cases the first book publications, whose dates are given, have somewhat different titles. There is some uncertainty in the dates since bibliographies and reference works sometimes differ; in any case, many essays and chapters were published earlier in periodicals (or, in the case of the Mill chapter of the *History of English Literature*, as a separate book).

3. Taine seldom wrote at length about women: a brief essay of 1857 about Mme. de la Fayette; an even briefer late essay (1876) about George Sand; and a somewhat fuller discussion (1866) of Spanish culture and domesticity with reference to Mme. d'Aulnoy. (Giraud's *Essai sur Taine* also excerpts four uncollected reviews of books—including one on contemporary women—by Camille Selden, the pseudonym for Heinrich Heine's *Mouche*, Elise von Krienitz.) The *History of English Literature* mentions a substantial number of women writers but

features none. Given the obsession with the dead father and with surrogate fathers portrayed in *Etienne Mayran*, together with Taine's personal reticence and late marriage, there is evident occasion for a revealing essay concerning sexuality in his writing. While I do not examine the topic further, I use masculine pronouns throughout this essay in order to signal the problem.

4. The only full-scale analysis of Taine in many decades, Jean-Thomas Nordmann's *Taine et la critique scientifique*, presents Taine as my initial paragraphs have sketched him. It is a philosopher's account that puts *De l'intelligence* at the center while intentionally downplaying the more personal travel writings and the French history and that emphasizes structural unity over temporal division and literary character over style. (There are some pages on Taine's own writing, but no mention of his views on style.) Few of the passages I quote even appear in the book, and those that do are evaluated quite differently. Thus, Nordmann regards Taine's striking remark about the history of pants cited in note 32 below as deviant (304–5) and notices the "difficulties of transitional periods" (357) in preference to the achievements that Taine also celebrates. It is an admirably full and clear portrait from an entirely different angle.

5. Michelet's history, Taine complains in the essay devoted to him, is a work of inspired art, but not of thoughtful reflection and science (*Essais* 95). Typically, Taine was more charitable about Michelet when he was focused on assessing the strengths and weaknesses of another writer; see the glowing comparison of Michelet with Victor Cousin in *Les Philosophes classiques* 117–19.

6. Some examples of Taine's reportage of the Revolution: A chapter opening, "Through their carmagnoles there pierces a calculation which they will later acknowledge" (*La Révolution* 2: 137), is the only allusion to these popular orgies. Here is the only mention of regicide, the first clause of a many-headed sentence: "Consequently we have dethroned the king and cut off his head" (3: 90). The Terror gets most of a paragraph, of which the following is the most explicit part: "Indeed, before guillotining Robespierre and consorts for their orthodoxy, [the Convention] guillotined the Girondins, Danton and Hébert, as heretics" (3: 553). Nothing could be further from the magniloquent Greek tragedy constructed for Robespierre by Carlyle (*French Revolution* 6.7).

7. See the materials assembled by Victor Giraud in "Taine et le pessimisme," *Hippolyte Taine* 83–102. Colin Evans's "Conflict and Dualism in Taine" scrutinizes Taine's divided legacy, relying heavily on early manuscripts, some excerpts from which he prints for the first time.

8. Zola, "La Formule critique appliquée au roman," *Le Roman expérimental* 225–30. Taine's hostility to method is one of many British characteristics or tendencies in his writing; see the general account of this (racial?) tendency by David Simpson, *Romanticism, Nationalism, and the Revolt Against Theory*.

9. The preface to *Les Philosophes classiques* is frank and explicit about Taine's calculation as a writer. "I know that these manners are irreverent, and that one

should never call a thing by its name. My excuse is that this book was not made for established persons. I wished to persuade my reader, and my reader should not be more than thirty years old" (iv). The relation of creator to audience is a regular, important, and, indeed, markedly original focus of Taine's criticism as well as a feature of his own writing.

10. Drawing on Claude Bernard's notion of the *milieu intérieur*, on the double meaning of the French *expérience* as (subjective) experience and (objective) experiment, and on the general tendency of his imagination to polarize exterior and interior spaces, Zola's criticism silently converts Taine's three factors into six: nationality and blood line (exterior and interior race), environment and psychology (exterior and interior milieu), public and personal history (exterior and interior moment). He aims not to explain particular convergences so much as to correlate inner and outer truths, as in the oft-repeated naturalist slogan, "a corner of creation seen through a temperament," or in his advocacy of "the ascertainment of the states of external world corresponding to interior states of the personages" ("De la description," *Le Roman expérimental* 232). The resulting system might arguably be clearer and more coherent than Taine's, but it is certainly, at any rate, different.

11. Patrizia Lombardo's "Taine scrittore" finely evokes Taine's dual nature, stressing his vitalism, colorism, and passion for style. It is a corrective to the same author's "Hippolyte Taine Between Art and Science," which casts a harsh light on the Spinozism of the *Essai sur Tite Live*.

12. Bergson was born in 1859 and was a student at the height of Taine's influence. The only significant discussion of connections I have located is Günther Pflug's *Henri Bergson*, where Taine's *De l'intelligence* becomes the constant reference point: "Thus the debate with Taine's thesis is fundamental to 'Matière et mémoire,' even if Taine's name is nowhere mentioned" (139). Pflug stresses the differences—and certainly Bergson rejects the Hegelian and historicist components of Taine's vitalism—but then I will be stressing the internal differences between Taine's own vitalism and the systematics of *De l'intelligence.*

13. Edmund Wilson gives a harsh but just appraisal of Taine's failure of imagination in *Origines*—together with a strongly mixed appraisal of the *History of English Literature*—in *To the Finland Station* 53–64, which should be compared with Remy de Gourmont's almost unqualified praise in his chapter, "La Question Taine: Les Idées et les images," *Le Problème du style* 67–82.

14. Fritz Schalk gives a balanced account of Taine's empiricized Hegelianism in "Zu Taines Theorie und Praxis."

15. On Guizot see the useful pages (240–44) in Lucien Febvre's essay, *"Civilisation*: Evolution of a Word and a Group of Ideas," in *"A New Kind of History"* 219–57. Febvre, however, does not clearly distinguish the concepts of progress *of* (evolving) civilization and of progress *toward* (an ideal of) civilization, a tension that Jean Starobinski ("The Word *Civilization*," *Blessings in Disguise* 1–

35) considers fundamental to the development of the concept. Also relevant is the critique of Febvre by Fernand Braudel in "The History of Civilizations: The Past Explains the Present," *On History* 177–218.

16. Taine here footnotes Darwin, whose *Origin of Species* was published in 1859 and appeared in French in 1862.

17. Thus, in an uncollected 1865 review of a history of Greek literature, Taine writes that "literary style . . . brings to light the sentiments of men whose portrait or history we are making. A great historian said to me: I accumulate, I check and I arrange my materials, as I should do in a Memorial for the Academy of Inscriptions; then, I write my book like a novel" (Giraud, *Essai sur Taine* 236).

18. Yet the *annalistes* often seem rooted in Taine despite themselves. What, after all, are Braudel's triad of *longue durée*, conjuncture, and event—or, as Febvre puts it, "permanent forces" like "the Mediterranean," "stable forces" associated with "the space of time occupied by the reign of Philip II of Spain," and the "chance" of "events"—what are these other than race, milieu, and moment? (See Braudel, "History and the Social Sciences: The *Longue Durée*," *On History* 25–54, esp. 44, and Febvre, "A New Kind of History," "*A New Kind of History*" 37.) To be sure, there is a crucial difference in Taine's resistance to the illusions of scientific permanence. Still, Febvre's repeated denunciations of Taine and his followers in *La Terre* must, in this instance, be acknowledged as a sign of influence and kinship.

19. See also Albert S. Cook's fine analysis (*History/Writing* 119–35) of Michelet's jerky narrative rhythms and "nervous lapses of time" (124), which project the movement of time as a deep or "subterranean" (126) progress only fitfully and unevenly manifest in experience.

20. Taine is careful to specify that Milton's poetic output virtually ceased during the decades of the Puritan Revolution.

21. "Beside the permanent impulse and the given surroundings, there is the acquired momentum" (1: 16/1: xxix). A passage in the *Voyage en Italie* dismisses "vitesse acquise" as mere "inertia" and "dead forces," preferring "active forces . . . continuously renewed by new impulses" (1: 384–85). Despite the shift in vocabulary and in emphasis, the core of vitalism is recognizably the same in both books. Though Wellek correctly reports that after the introduction "Taine never again speaks of acquired speed" (31), the conception is pervasive; see, for instance, the passage quoted in note 33, where the translator has introduced the phrase for a slightly different French phrase.

22. Here are bits of some typical, extended paeans to realism. While quality is routinely praised (as with Donatello's formulaic originality and energy, just below), it is vastly outweighed by the realists' quantitative achievements. "What power! What foreground and background the endless enumeration gives the figure! how well he is known in all his actions and all his parts! how real he becomes! . . . For such is nature: the details are infinite and unravel infinitely"

("Balzac" 20). "By [Titian's] intelligence of real things, the field of art increases tenfold. . . . The infinite diversity of nature . . . opens to him" (*Italie* 2: 353).

23. In *George Sand and Idealism* (35–42) Naomi Schor usefully contrasts the rigidly masculinist Proudhon with Taine (one of whose two essays on women novelists concerns Sand), concentrating on the two books from 1865.

24. There are numerous passages praising realism in the *Voyage en Italie*, and one notable one in the *History of English Literature*, concerning Defoe: "Never was such a sense of the real before or since. Our realists of to-day, painters, anatomists, partisan men of business, are a hundred leagues from this naturalness; art and calculation crop out amidst their too minute descriptions" (2: 192 / 4: 88–89). Also relevant is the following, in *Notes sur l'Angleterre*: "No painter, nor artist is a pure copyist; he invents, even when he confines himself to translating; for, what nature executes by one system of means and values, he is obliged to render by a different system of values and means.—Such is the error of contemporary English painters; they are faithful, but literally" (354).

25. "Whether you come from the deep sky or rise from the abyss, / O Beauty! your look, infernal and divine, / Pours charity and crime all confused" (*Les Fleurs du mal* 28). On Baudelaire's infatuation with Proudhon around 1848, see T. J. Clark, *The Absolute Bourgeois* 164–69.

26. For a helpful new perspective on the instability of mid-century aesthetics see Pierre Bourdieu, *The Field of Cultural Production*, esp. "Field of Power, Literary Field and Habitus," trans. Claude DuVerlie, 161–75.

27. "A beautiful falsehood is always shocking; better an ugly truth" ("Du style," from Giraud, *Hippolyte Taine* 236). Giraud, a great authority on Taine, prints "Du style" as a companion to a "Lettre sur l'idéal," for which, on stylistic grounds, he rejects a date of 1851 and conjecturally suggests the period of *De l'idéal dans l'art* (i.e., around 1865, or just after the *History of English Literature*). The dating seems untenable. The "Lettre sur l'idéal" lambastes the French classical authors, for whom a series of essays from the late 1850's tries to develop a more sympathetic understanding. "Du style" extols Shakespeare for his realism, the *History of English Literature* for his soaring imagination that did not "confine [it]self to the imitation of nature" but instead "br[oke] loose from the laws of the real world" (1: 412 / 2: 259). The early book analyzing Livy as an "oratorical historian" already seems to be working free of the hostility to artistry of "Du style."

28. The only essay I have found on Taine's conception of style is Ulrich Schulz-Buschhaus, "Taine und die Historizität des Stils," with well-contextualized praise for Taine's style analyses, a deficient notion of "historicity," and, surprisingly, no discussion of the *History of English Literature*. Jean-François Revel's sensitive introduction to his selection of Taine's art criticism also points to the centrality of style in Taine's thought. And Fredric Jameson at least mentions style in joining Taine to Oswald Spengler as historians who focus on "the total *style* of a

culture" (*Marxism and Form* 324). Yet style is nowhere in evidence in such formative writings as Sainte-Beuve's sympathetic reviews (which fault Taine at length for failing in sympathy, particularly toward Pope, and in passing for his unforgivable sympathy toward Stendhal), Emile Faguet's scowling assault, Giraud's intellectual biography, Louis Juglar's ponderous *Le Style dans les arts* (whose extended and carping critiques of other aspects of Taine's thought perhaps constitute a backhanded acknowledgment that Taine *also* discussed style), or—most surprisingly of all—the *History of French Literature* by Taine's English translator, Henri van Laun.

29. Shakespeare is perhaps another example of absolute pastness: "His style and our style—two languages not to be reconciled" (1: 374/2: 192). In Shakespeare's unique case, however, historicity is problematized by absolute genius.

30. Wellek mentions style only in the second half of a paragraph about form, unity, and Taine's "purely emotionalistic point of view" toward modern poetry. He praises Taine's "nontechnical but often acutely observant" comments on style (49). To put Taine in perspective, here is the paltry best I could find in his translator, about Molière's types: "The language which they employ is always natural to them, and is neither too gross nor over-refined. His verse has none of the stiffness of the ordinary French rhyme, and becomes in his hands, as well as his prose, a delightful medium for sparkling sallies, bitter sarcasms, and well-sustained and sprightly conversations" (van Laun, *History of French Literature* 2: 224).

31. Hans Aarsleff's "Taine and Saussure" (*From Locke to Saussure* 356–71) is a learned and persuasive account of Taine's influence. Aarsleff rests with too simple a structural dualism, however, when he calls race and milieu synchronic concepts in contrast to the diachronic moment. Also informative, though less sympathetic to Taine, is Antoine Compagnon, *Troisième république* 174–97.

32. The passage about Burns (which ends book 3 of the history) concludes by shifting from verbal style to dress. "When Roland, being made a minister, presented himself before Louis XVI. in a simple dress-coat and shoes without buckles, the master of the ceremonies raised his hands to heaven, thinking that all was lost. In fact all was changed" (2: 282/4: 232). There are parallels in other periods, such as the Elizabethan, when the rapier replaced the shield and two-handed sword, "a little, almost imperceptible fact, yet vast, for it is like the change which, sixty years ago, made us give up the sword at court, to leave us with our arms swinging about in our black coats" (1: 172/1: 243). More startling is a moment in the *Voyage en Italie* where Taine says, "since I dare to speak without mincing words and to speak things as I feel them, my decided opinion is that the great change in history is the arrival of pants: all the Northern barbarians already wear them in the statues; they mark the passage from Greek and Roman to modern civilization.—This is not a quip or a paradox; nothing is more difficult than changing a universal and daily habit" (138). Taine protests too

much, of course; the spirit of the age is a habit of mind more than it is a habit of dress. But then, style is precisely the dress of thought.

33. Under the Puritans, to be sure, England did fall into the morass of a revolution that was fashioned "without style" and lived without joy by men whose "style [was] borrowed from the prophets" and who made their "fears of conscience . . . into laws of the state" (1: 484, 561 / 2: 381; 3: 7). But the soil was too fertile, even in Scotland, for "the indistinct forms of gloomy despots, of bilious sectarians, of silent victims" to prevail; and "deliverance, . . . like a checked and flooded stream, . . . with all its natural force and all its acquired momentum [*poids naturel et . . . masse acquise*] carried away the dams" (1: 562 / 3: 9–10).

34. Cf. Bourdieu, the contemporary thinker who seems to me closest to Taine's spirit: "An aesthetic revolution could only occur aesthetically. . . . The revolution of the gaze, and the rupture of the bond between ethics and aesthetics implied by that revolution, effected a total conversion of lifestyle" ("Flaubert's Point of View," *The Field of Cultural Production* 208–9). Or, again: "Struggles over words . . . will consist in . . . putting into action a symbolic revolution which may be at the root of political revolutions" ("Reading, Readers, the Literate, Literature," *In Other Words* 97). Bourdieu's sense of the working of time within consciousness likewise bears comparison with Taine.

35. The chapter on the Romantics expresses unreserved admiration only for *The Excursion*, a taste that I at least can share, provided it remains subject to the precisely evocative image Taine uses, comparing the poem to "the grand and monotonous music of the organ, which in the eventide, at the close of the service, rolls slowly in the twilight of arches and pillars" (2: 337 / 4: 322). The place of music in Taine's thought is discussed below.

36. Van Laun translates "agreement" rather than "accord"; it will be seen how much is lost in that translation.

37. Using the English word, since "there is no French word," Taine says he was "roused" by hearing Beethoven on the piano (*Notes sur Paris* 323).

38. For a more technical statement concerning formalism, expression, and historicity in music, see my review of John Daverio.

39. My formulations concerning style as ethos in the Renaissance are derived from, though not directly found in, the classic studies of Croll, Williamson, and especially Wallerstein (who speaks on p. 91, for instance, of "a half symbolic or allegorical view of style which transforms the idea of decorum").

40. The *Oxford English Dictionary* does not distinguish normative from non-normative uses of "style." In other words, it does not distinguish usages according to whether the implied alternative is a different style, a poor style, or a lack of style. Citations consequently were not selected to illustrate these distinctions; however, they seem to support a date of around 1800 for the semantic development. It was surely part of a general cultural development; for instance, Stephen Orgel's "Shakespeare and the Kinds of Drama" locates a shift from a descriptive

to a normative sense of dramatic genre in roughly the same period. Klaus Dirscherl's "Stillosigkeit als Stil" turns on Marivaux and Rousseau, without recognizing that stylelessness was, seemingly, not conceivable previously. Nor does Hans Ulrich Gumbrecht's richly informative history of the concept of style go beyond shifting categorizations (individual, collective; conventional, invented; etc.) to acknowledge the paradigm shift in the very construction of the categories, when style becomes an optional rather than an obligatory element of expression.

41. See Thomas Pfau, "Immediacy and the Text," for a good account of Schleiermacher's insights into the conflicted nature of style. For general worries about the identity of style see Charles Rosen, *The Classical Style* 19–23. The desultory closing discussion in Thomas Sebeok's symposium, *Style in Language* (420–34), is an object lesson in the frustrations attendant upon single-valued definitions of style; if there is a focus, it is on the tension between descriptive and normative definitions.

42. Barthes: "Whatever its refinement, style always has something ugly about it. . . . Its references are at the level of a biology or a past, not of a History" (*Degré zéro* 14). "Enough will never be said about the ravages of 'style' on our bourgeois stages. Style excuses everything, dispenses with everything, and notably with historical reflection" ("Deux mythes du jeune théâtre," *Mythologies* 110, and cf. in "La Critique ni-ni," p. 146, the critique of the bourgeois "euphoric reference to the writer's 'style' as an eternal value of Literature"). Among nineteenth-century enthusiasts for bad style are Kant (see Jean-Luc Nancy, *Discours de la syncope*) and Hazlitt (see Mary Jacobus, "The Art of Managing Books" 225–31); related in effect is Herbert Spencer's praise for economy, which is tantamount to a disparagement of style for its own sake: "to have a specific style is to be poor in speech" (*Philosophy of Style* 47).

43. Berel Lang's essays on style as uncategorizable expression and intention analyze the force of style (though not its historicity) in ways related to Taine's. Also illuminating is John Guillory, "Canonical and Non-canonical" 517–19, discussing style as "both a mode of apprehension irreducible to reason, and the sign of a cultural capital always unequally distributed" (518–19, not in the rewritten version of this essay in Guillory's book *Cultural Capital*).

44. Even at that, many of Taine's analyses and assessments hold up remarkably well or return to fashion; though Wellek, for instance, scorns Taine's admiration for *Aurora Leigh*, many current readers would share his devotion to Barrett Browning and George Sand.

45. Readers will surely wonder about comparing Taine with the greatest twentieth-century historian of style, Erich Auerbach. Auerbach, indeed, greatly admired Taine's essays on French writers and even cites the social analysis of *L'Ancien régime* with approval (*Scenes* 244). Yet Auerbach was, or at least became, a pessimist who recognized only a limited possibility, or none, for indi-

viduals to shape culture. About Balzac, for instance, he writes, "Balzac's atmospheric realism is a product of his period, is itself a part and a result of an atmosphere" (*Mimesis* 417). In the long section of his Balzac essay concerning Balzac's style, Taine writes more circumspectly that Balzac's "stylistic habits fit our habits of life, and that the author is authorized by the public" (*Nouveaux essais* 41), and the essay moves on toward Balzac's greatest imaginative inventions. While Auerbach's sensitivity to stylistic innovation has never been equaled, it remains for him either "a well-nigh incomprehensible miracle" (*Mimesis* 159, on Dante) or at best a self-confirming accomplishment with no definable agency, as when he writes about a unique and beautiful narration by Antoine de la Sale: "It is apparent that the late-feudal epideictic style is able to produce a visual representation of such a genuinely tragic and genuinely real scene" (*Mimesis* 215, continuing for pages with impersonal and even passive constructions).

Even where Auerbach comes closest to Taine's vision and imagery for cultural emergence, the language of representation supplants the language of agency. Thus, on Baudelaire: "The visionary power of such combinations exerted a crucial influence on later poetry; they seemed the most authentic expression both of the inner anarchy of the age and of a still hidden order that was just beginning to dawn. In an entirely new and consummate style, this poet . . . expressed the naked, concrete existence of an epoch. For his style was not based on his personal situation and his personal needs; it became apparent that his extreme personality embodied a far more universal situation and a far more universal need" (*Scenes* 225; Taine is mentioned with resounding approval in a note to the essay on p. 249). Even though "dawn" sounds Taine-like, the affect for Auerbach lies with light and not with flow. Though Auerbach's early Dante book praises the poet for "preserving the *Evidenz* [clarity, visibility] of appearances" (*Dante* 76), a decisive turning point comes in the 1944 explication of *figura* as a shadow (*umbra*) awaiting revelation (*Scenes* 34, 63, 66). Thus, the last chapter of *Mimesis* ends with a visionary play of lights, in a kind of terrified celebration of the impending end of history. History remains deeply problematic for the later Auerbach (as it was to become for the later Taine), and he contrives to write a discontinuous account of innovations with no concept of emergence. In Taine's terms, to put it bluntly, Auerbach is not a historian at all.

46. As the author of a book entitled *Preromanticism* that has sometimes been reviled for its teleology, I welcome the teleological leanings implied by "early modern," but not the telescoping of history that "emphasiz[es] larger historical divisions at the expense of smaller ones," as Heather Dubrow says in one part of her fine critique of the current fashion (Letter to the Forum 1026, and see also Marcus, "Renaissance / Early Modern Studies" 41–44).

47. On p. 1 of *Learning to Curse*, Greenblatt speaks of his early fascination with "radical uncertainty (what would now be called *aporia*)." For Greenblatt's

use of "dialectic," the conclusion to the Sir Thomas Wyatt chapter of *Renaissance Self-Fashioning* is telling. "His achievement is dialectical," Greenblatt says. But it isn't. "We sense, in short, a continual conflict between diplomatic self-representation . . . and inwardness. . . . Neither triumphs: hence the *suspension* of Wyatt's court lyrics" (156). On p. 1, Greenblatt says that "the early modern . . . structures that govern [!] the generation of identities" arrived in "complex but resolutely dialectical" ways. Yet it remains hard to discern either the resolutions or the resoluteness in Greenblatt's perpetually subtle and (to use one of his favorite words) anamorphic analyses. The essay on *The Tempest* that concludes *Shakespearian Negotiations* illustrates the uses of "circulation" as unproductive circling. An awkward preposition can mark it, indeed, as shuttling: "This complex circulation *between* the social dimension of an aesthetic strategy and the aesthetic dimension of a social strategy" (147, my emphasis). And when "Prospero's magical power and princely authority . . . pass, in a startling display of the circulation of social energy, from the performer onstage to the crowd of spectators," the play turns into "a model of unresolved and unresolvable doubleness" (157–58). "Introduction," "Towards a Poetics of Culture," and "Resonance and Wonder" (*Learning to Curse* 1–15, 146–60, 161–83) argue that the profit from the "negotiation" or "exchange" involved in art is found in a pleasure that cannot readily be analyzed or historicized.

A related evaporation of history tied to a concept of circulation surfaces in Patricia Fumerton's *Cultural Aesthetics*. Fumerton proposes the anthropological cycle of gift exchange as a "more positive" alternative to deconstructive deferral (58), whose "most striking example is Jonathan Goldberg's *Endlesse Worke*" (224). Circulation accomplishes something: it produces "trivia," and more specifically aesthetic articles of consumption. Still, when we find "the self . . . chasing its self-image *endlessly* along an empty corridor of vision between facing mirrors" (129, my emphasis), with a "status" that remains "undecidable" on the last page of the text (206), we may wonder what effect the redescription or "uncanny double" (24) of deconstruction has. Fumerton's polarities are no more mediated than Greenblatt's; in privileging the oblique, the fragmentary, or the trivial over the central, the total, or the "wholly representative" (11, with misleading reference to Taine), her "highly idealizing" view of gifts (William Flesch's critique, *Generosity* 99) functions as a kind of send-up of Theodor Adorno—negative dialectics without the dialectic.

48. *Shakespearean Negotiations* begins with an emotional—and surely in some sense Oedipal—attack on William Wimsatt, the most exact student of style in his generation. I have noted "style" once in *Renaissance Self-Fashioning* as a background term (16–17, offering the alternatives either of referring More's *contemptus mundi* to "the style of late medieval culture" or else of taking stock of its "actual effect in his life and writings"), and once in *Shakespearian Negotiations*, italicized even, but only in a quote from Bourdieu in a note (178–79). While I

have not searched the writings systematically, I suspect these instances are symptomatic.

49. Frank Lentricchia tars Taine with Greenblatt's feather in his acute critique of the latter, "Foucault's Legacy." For another comparison of Taine and Greenblatt see Edmundson, *Literature Against Philosophy* 186–87.

50. Apparently coining a phrase, Catherine Gallagher scrutinizes the "emphasis, . . . in 'oppositional' American criticism, on indeterminate negation" ("Marxism and the New Historicism" 41). In substance Brook Thomas's *The New Historicism* makes the same critique. It shows how both Renaissance and Americanist New Historicists totalize chiasmic polarities. Lacking a concept of limited negation, they relegate art to the unsatisfactory alternatives of reproductive complicity in the real or utopian evasion. Thomas proposes instead a "description of literature as a rhetorical means to question present constructions of rhetoric" (217), which he further concretizes in an essay devoted to what formal logic calls subaltern negation. While it seems natural here to move from rhetoric to style and from Aristotelian limitation to Hegelian determination, Thomas instead falls back on Wolfgang Iser. To my mind, the issues are deflected, not resolved, by Iser's notion of negation as textual blanks and by his focus on the phenomenology of reading. (Iser's fullest discussion of negation and negativity, which Thomas does not cite, is *The Act of Reading* 212–31.)

51. Impersonation: Stephen Greenblatt, "Psychoanalysis and Renaissance Culture" (*Learning to Curse* 131–45). Thomas Greene's "The Flexibility of the Self" is the first scholarly study cited in *Renaissance Self-Fashioning*. Greenblatt misleadingly implies that the essay concerns undirected, fictive selfhoods: "Greene's starting point is the assertion in Pico that man may choose to fashion (*effingere*) himself in whatever shape he prefers" (258). True, but starting from there the essay in fact surveys the specific and differential kinds of self-positioning found in many diverse authors.

52. McGann more characteristically deprecates Hegel (for instance in comparison to Kierkegaard) as a totalizer. And he avoids the term style (except in the technical, typographical sense), preferring less fraught words such as procedure. For the reasons why I nonetheless invoke him here, see "What's in a Text?"

Chapter 2

1. The fullest survey of Wölfflin's milieu is given in Walther Rehm's monograph *Heinrich Wölfflin als Literarhistoriker*.

2. See also the nominalistic critiques of Wölfflin in Walter Bockelmann, *Grundbegriffe*, and Arnold Hauser, *The Philosophy of Art History* 139–66.

3. The early essay on ancient triumphal arches gives no hint of a notion of rebirth; instead, it says that "a playful beginning . . . , a period of classicism . . . ;

finally a period of dissolution . . . where the forms lose sense and meaning . . . , will be observable in every style in art history" (KS 70). Evidently, the notion of continuous historical change, not the notion of cycle, was Wölfflin's starting point.

4. The slogan "Kunstgeschichte ohne Namen" is often quoted but rarely attributed. It comes from the suppressed preface to the first edition of *Kunstgeschichtliche Grundbegriffe*, which has not been translated into English.

5. "The concepts of multiple unity and unified unity require special treatment here too. It is just in architecture that the concepts attain an unusual lucidity" (PAH 186).

6. See Talcott Parsons, "Value-freedom and Objectivity" (and the discussion following) 27–82. Weber comes closest to Wölfflin in passages concerning the scholar's role in resisting the chaotic movement of history, such as the astonishing conclusion of the essay "Die 'Objektivität' sozialwissenschaftlicher und sozialpolitischer Erkenntnis," 206–14. Hauser compares Wölfflin and Weber in *Philosophy of Art History* 212–15, and the question of Wölfflin's "objectivity" is well discussed at the end of "Sense and Sensibility" 35–50. A recent, interesting, ideological reading is Martin Warnke, "On Heinrich Wölfflin."

7. The published translation uses the passive "posed" rather than "posing," a slight but revealing instance of the repression of Wölfflin's dynamism.

8. Since I wrote this, Jacques Derrida has expressed himself decisively on this point: "The gesture that has been called deconstructive . . . is accompanied, can be accompanied (in any case, that is how I would always prefer to accompany it) by an affirmation; it is not negative, it is not destructive" ("Table ronde sur l'autobiographie: Réponse de Jacques Derrida," in Lévesque and McDonald, eds., *L'Oreille de l'autre* 117).

9. The "contrasted handling of . . . right and left" could also describe the great innovation of Wölfflin's classicizing, coolly objective lecture technique: using tandem slide projectors to enable constant comparison of different pictorial modes.

10. Notable polarizing theoreticians—apart from Wölfflin's followers and from Alois Riegl and his disciple Wilhelm Worringer—include the philosopher Johannes Volkelt, *Ästhetische Zeitfragen*, chap. 4, and *System der Ästhetik* 3: 300–37; the psychologist Herman Nohl, *Stil* esp. 7–11; the art historian August Schmarsow, *Unser Verhältnis*; and the literary historian Ernst Elster, *Prinzipien*, vol. 2. Elster clearly reveals the Schillerian affiliation through his habit of realigning and subdividing categories; Wölfflin's teacher Volkelt (who was a notoriously indecisive thinker) waffles on the question of a possible synthesis of opposing categories and thus highlights the incisiveness of Wölfflin's logic.

11. See Wind, "Zur Systematik der künstlerischen Probleme" 480–86, and Venturi, *History of Art Criticism* 288–89. Wölfflin himself concedes that "in every chapter the baroque standpoint has meant a kind of obscuring" (PAH 224).

12. Italian critics have been particularly guilty of assimilating Wölfflin's position to that of Fiedler and Hildebrand: see Benedetto Croce's attack in *Nuovi saggi* 251–57, and the even less discriminating treatments in Lionello Venturi's *History of Art Criticism* 288–89 and in Carlo Ragghianti's essays collected under the title *L'arte e la critica*.

13. Lipps, *Grundzüge der Logik* viii. Lipps's preexistentialist idealism seems to me closer in spirit to Wölfflin than are Wölfflin's actual predecessors, Robert Vischer, Herman Lotze, and Gustav Fechner, who are more empiricist in temperament; see esp. Fechner's *Vorschule* 1: 108–11.

14. "Tiepolo composed a *Last Supper* which, while it cannot be compared with Leonardo as a work of art, stylistically presents the absolute opposite. The figures do not unite in the plane, and that decides" (*PAH* 88).

15. See the conclusion of Jacob Burckhardt, *Force and Freedom* 369–70. Wölfflin's numerous essays on Burckhardt harp on the classicizing, static quality of his presentation and a notation of 1891 is preserved to the effect that "development receives too little emphasis" in Burckhardt's book on Renaissance architecture (*Jacob Burckhardt und Heinrich Wölfflin* 70). Given the intimate personal relations between the two men, it is not surprising that Wölfflin's critique never became more explicit.

16. A letter of January 14, 1889, demonstrating Wölfflin's early and approving familiarity with the school of Taine is printed in Rehm, *Wölfflin als Literarhistoriker* 116.

17. Cf. Burckhardt's judgment, "Baroque architecture speaks the same language as the renaissance, but a barbarian dialect of it" (*Gesammelte Werke* 9: 305). On Goethe, see Wölfflin, "Goethes italienische Reise," *Gedanken* 49–56. On Schiller, see Peter Szondi, "Das Naive ist das Sentimentalische." On Humboldt, see my "Humboldt and the Mediation Between Self and World." In art history, this line is continued by Erwin Panofsky, for instance *Renaissance* 112–13.

18. The whole enterprise of Heidegger's "grant of Being" can be understood as a commentary on the impossible tautology, The classic is the classic. Derrida has warned against the temptations of this introduction to metaphysics that never quite succeeds in being a reintroduction of metaphysics, but even Heidegger himself readily acknowledged the antithetical logic of being toward which this study of Wölfflin has been pointing: "*existasthai*, 'existence,' 'to exist,' meant for the Greeks precisely nonbeing" (Heidegger, *An Introduction to Metaphysics* 64). See also Derrida, "The Supplement of Copula."

19. The spirit of Hegel's logic of existence could have been transmitted to Wölfflin through the epistemological discussions in Conrad Fiedler's 1887 essay, "Über den Ursprung der künstlerischen Thätigkeit," *Schriften* esp. 200–201: "The origin of language does not resemble a process of crystallization in which matter accretes toward a definite form in which it continues to exist; rather the

work is like the bloom, the fruit of a plant; in the bloom, in the fruit the plant develops something from itself which is no longer itself, a metamorphosis begins, but the plant is not destroyed thereby."

20. The example of the Romanesque is based on Paul Frankl, "Der Beginn der Gotik"; the example of the primitives is based on Wölfflin's *Dürer*: "The heads are expressive in the manner of the sixteenth century, to whom the art of earlier times seemed to be a mute art" (158). Apropos of heads that are stylized (formalistic) in background detail and naturalistic (expressive) in principal features, Wölfflin writes: "The essence of greatness is the same at all stages [of history]: it means that an artist recognizes the one feature in the large variety of visible objects which is of essential significance. He need not abandon the other features but only make them subordinate so that the leading voice can be heard distinctly. The subject does not matter; it may be simply a head or a history-piece: this relation of predominant to subordinate parts must be maintained and the eye must be capable of recognizing the essential feature immediately and without difficulty" (*Dürer* 247; modified translation).

21. Henri Meschonnic, *Pour la poétique* 2: 62. Meschonnic's direct critique of Macherey is on 124–29.

22. See Michel Foucault, *The Order of Things*, chap. 1, and John Searle, "*Las Meninas*." Searle's exposition has been decisively refuted by Joel Snyder and Ted Cohen, "Reflexions on *Las Meninas*"; the refutation confirms one point of my essay, that we are dealing with an ideal of classicism, not with an "objective" view of actually existing classic works. The authoritative Velázquez scholar of Wölfflin's day, Carl Justi, and Wölfflin himself both offer illuminating comments on the visual uncertainties of *Las Meninas*: Justi, *Diego Velázquez* 418, and Wölfflin, *Gedanken* 78.

Chapter 3

1. Crucial to the "postmodern," dialogic forms in McGann's criticism is the closing section (161–75) of "The Poetry of Truth: A Dialogue (on Dialogue)," *BR* 151–75.

2. See, for instance, *SV* 91, where the issue is distilled: "Poetry is obliged, as it were, to present all sides of a question. This includes bringing forth, *within a sympathetic structure*, those details and points of view which are by ordinary measures incommensurate with themselves and with each other. . . . The consequence is a certain kind of nonnormative discourse: not a discourse *without* norms, but one in which we observe the collision of many different and even contradictory norms." I find the generally dialectical tenor hard to reconcile with the sovereign embrace of the phrase that McGann italicizes. On Goethe and Marx, see Marc Shell, "Money and the Mind."

3. "How one decides which parts of the strategic programme need to be emphasized in particular case studies is always a difficult question. I am not even sure that one can theorize these sorts of problem at all" (*BI* 9).

4. *SV* 128–29, my italics. (McGann italicizes "natural" and "Eros.") Since the categorical is, in fact, the determinative (*die Bestimmung*, in post-Kantian usage), the passage ends by rejecting the very emphasis that it began by declaring "fundamental."

5. For an excellent case study, see Peter J. Manning, "The Hone-ing of Byron's Corsair."

6. See the forceful critique of would-be divisions of intrinsic from extrinsic factors in Lee Patterson's essay, "The Logic of Textual Criticism." McGann's basically intelligent reading of Kant's aesthetics as a cardinal instance of the individualist and idealizing "romantic ideology" is a case in point. When he criticizes de Man for "bracket[ing] our attention to the way 'Kant' performs. . . . in his sociohistorical field" (*SV* 104), McGann overlooks both extrinsic and intrinsic factors that would *conjointly* condition his account. Externally, Kant's political and theological reputation was generally radical, at the opposite pole from the later Coleridge. And, textually, McGann's proof passages from early in the "Critique of Aesthetic Judgment" should be registered as a transitional moment of idealism on the way back to the natural science of the "Critique of Teleological Judgment."

7. *Black Riders* analyzes schools of postmodern writing in which verbal meanings are undecipherable and messages are carried chiefly by the physical appearance of the work. Even in these cases, however, there does not appear to be a contradiction between material and verbal meaning. In the still-troubling case of Pound ("The *Cantos* of Ezra Pound, the Truth in Contradiction," *BR* 96–128), McGann does seem to defend Pound by splitting off aura and effect from sense, meaning from saying: "while the face of these texts says one thing, their converse says something very different" (*BR* 107). However, the road to a more adequate and sympathetic understanding comes through closer attention to the text: "Lauber has not *read* the passage" (120); "when readers dismiss writing of this kind they are often merely exposing . . . their failure to read, and to think through their reading" (120); "The *Cantos* is remarkable because when we read it—the whole of it and not simply selected parts," we come to appreciate its "disturbing mode of truth" (125, 128). While many critics these days want to embed texts in contexts outside of them, McGann stands out as one for whom the primary context is what the word primarily means—*the rest of the text*.

8. McGann, "Some Forms of Critical Discourse." The four forms are listed on p. 399, the first two examples are given in the footnote on p. 416, the others are developed in the text.

9. See, for instance, the following: on scientific essays, Charles Bazerman, *Shaping Written Knowledge*; on Euclid, Gilles-Gaston Granger, *Essai d'une philoso-*

phie du style 24–42; on cookbooks, Susan J. Leonardi, "Recipes for Reading" 340–47. With respect to the array form, Hayden White's essay needs to be consulted ("The Value of Narrativity"). McGann says that White narrates what is really a pseudo-progress from nonnarrative to narrative forms. He does not say that White demonstrates how we can actually read annals narratively, thus effectively effacing the distinction that McGann wants to make.

10. *Critical Inquiry* version, 414 (my emphasis). Symptomatically, the dialectic is attenuated in *SV* 149: "Although these three types of critical discourse (array, narrative, dialectic) exhibit the *form* of criticism, that form is no guarantee that the discourse will in fact be critical."

11. See the change from the original uncompromising formulation: "the array and the dialectic offer especially clear contrasts with narrative forms of discourse, both critical and noncritical" (*Critical Inquiry* 400), to the later version: "In this respect the forms of array and dialectic are particularly important, not merely as alternative critical modes, but as forms which cast an important critical light on the structure of narrativized discourse" (*SV* 133).

12. The treasured modernist text is not so pure a conception as McGann's phrasing might seem to imply. For the material complexities—i.e., the social dimension—involved in producing the first edition, see Hugh Kenner, " 'The Most Beautiful Book.' "

13. Verdi repeatedly added, subtracted, and recomposed material (musical and verbal) in response both to his own second thoughts and to aesthetic and political promptings from outside—a fairly normal situation for nineteenth-century opera composers, and not unparalleled in symphonic music (e.g., orchestration in Mahler or Schumann). Some literary authors also have been tinkerers producing uncontrolled textual forms—McGann's immediately preceding essay on *Urizen*, "The Idea of an Indeterminate Text: Blake and Dr. Alexander Geddes," presents a great instance, Philip Gaskell's "*Night and Day*: Development of a Play Text" (*TCLI* 162–79) a minor one, not very interestingly analyzed. Other authors, such as William Dean Howells and Thomas Wolfe, have written in complex collaboration with editors. And manuscript transmission, of course, is prone to unresolvable indeterminacies, such as Dickinson's or Hölderlin's punctuation. (Heidegger's exegesis of Hölderlin depends crucially on an attributed line-end comma ["Des gemeinsamen Geistes Gedanken sind, / Still endend in der Seele des Dichters"] in a poet who characteristically neglected line-end punctuation.)

14. There is a less dismissive reading of "A slumber did my spirit seal" in chapter 6 (*RI* 68–69).

15. For a challenging, unnecessarily difficult, but often profound extension of McGann's impulse into (among other things) the psychological dimension, see Marjorie Levinson, *Keats's Life of Allegory*.

16. More in McGann's spirit is Gerald MacLean's "What Is a Restoration

Poem? Editing a Discourse, Not an Author," which argues that "authors are never entirely in control of their texts" (339) and which brilliantly demonstrates how an unnormalized text can reveal significances hidden by emendation according to principles of authorial meaning.

Chapter 4

1. For a less Byronic view of aporia see the Overture to this book, "Errours Endlesse Traine." In "Displacing Post-Structuralism" 451–74, Tilottama Rajan argues congenially that "displacement" should edge out "aporia," because the latter is misunderstood too often in a romantically demonized way (see esp. notes 4 and 5).

2. "No Apocalypse" 20–31. And see *Memoires: For Paul de Man*, whose topics are "deconstruction in America" (implying that deconstruction, as America knows it, is not in France) and Derrida's Parnell-like concern for finding a path out of the graveyard (132: "it seems to me [not to 'deconstruction in America'] that the experience of the aporia, such as de Man deciphers it, gives or promises [the experience gives to Derrida, but perhaps not to de Man who merely deciphered the experience] the thinking of the path"). Derrida's itinerary in the lectures is from Hegel to Heidegger, allowing him to predicate "non-dialectizable opposition" (134) of de Man; de Man's itinerary, biographically, was from Heidegger to Hegel. Only in the early, Sartrean de Man, I believe, is the path beyond death a concern, as in "Hölderlin et Heidegger" (816): "For us, however the pain of mediation is always that of finitude and we can only conceive it in the form of death. . . . The task of the poet then becomes to internalize this death, to think of the death of God." Or even more clearly in "Mallarmé, Yeats, and the Post-Romantic Predicament" 60: "To be conscious of death is to be conscious of the self as *becoming*, to know that it moves us toward an unknown." The later de Man puts death aside through what seems to me a dialectical renaming: "Death is a displaced name for a linguistic predicament" ("Autobiography as De-Facement," *Rhetoric of Romanticism* 81), which does not enlighten death, but makes light of it. The American bravado is moving; equally so, but contrasting, is the European's troubled, meditative response (see *Memoires* 87–88 n. 4).

3. J. Hillis Miller ("The Critic as Host" 230) says cozily that " 'Deconstruction' is . . . simply interpretation as such." True, but beware of his "simply," which has the same rhetorical status as Parnell's "surely."

Chapter 5

1. For a fuller discussion of the philosophical and literary revolutions of the 1780's, see my *Preromanticism* 75–81.

2. Hoffmann, *Betrachtungen über Musik* 78. More recent scholarship has invalidated the traditional attribution of this review to E. T. A. Hoffmann; see Hoffmann, *Schriften zur Musik* 402.

3. For an account of the Bagatelles themselves that typifies the negative view of Romantic reverie, see Riccardo Bacchelli, *Rossini* 444–48.

4. Julie Anne Vertrees reviews the Fétis debate in "Mozart's String Quartet K. 465." Mozart's principal defender in the controversy, A. G. Leduc, stressed the intentional harmonic obscurity of the introduction: see "Ueber den Aufsatz des Herrn Fetis" 124.

5. Commentators generally have concentrated on the harmonic chaos of the introduction and have ignored the metrical chaos. Fétis, however, was primarily troubled by the lawlessness of the rhythm in the contrapuntal imitation and would have normalized the piece by means of an alteration in the rhythm alone, delaying the entry of the first violin by a beat.

6. In less technical (and less precise) language, it could be said that C-sharp, which is the second in the normal cycle of sharps, neutralizes the E-flat, which is the second in the normal cycle of flats. The repeated accented sharps of these final bars introduce an unclassical note of dynamism as the reverie works toward clarification; hence, they are ignored in Antoine-Elisée Cherbouliez's otherwise exhaustive analysis, which attempts to assimilate the introduction to canonical classical patterns.

7. It was common practice in the classical period to reinforce a pulsing cello C in this register with an occasional open C string, combining the resonance of the lower octave with the clearer articulation of the higher octave. Examples may be found in Mozart's C-Major Quartet (first movement, bar 72; second movement, beginning), at the opening of Beethoven's C-Minor Quartet, opus 18, no. 4, and elsewhere.

8. See Joseph Kerman's analyses of the introduction to opus 59, no. 3, and of the "La Malinconia" introduction to the last movement of opus 18, no. 6, in *The Beethoven Quartets* 135–37 and 77–80. Slow introductions, while still the exception, are far less rare in other chamber combinations (duo sonatas, trios, quintets) than in string quartets and solo piano sonatas.

9. There is some good analysis of the Fantasia's harmonic ambiguities and descending tendencies in Wilhelm Keller, "Modulationen." At times overly literal, Keller concludes that the movement ends not in C but in F-quintuple-flat (is that also the key of the associated C-Minor Sonata?); he might consider the final three-octave ascending scale as a compensation for the downward harmonic cycling (marked by three enharmonic modulations) and as a movement out of the depths of harmonic confusion and back up to conventional form. The rising gesture is repeated in the arpeggio that opens the sonata.

10. For a differing view, see Lieselotte Theiner, "Das Phänomen der atonikalen Werköffnung," where Mozart appears among the most conventional of

composers. This article stands as an example of the dangers of a purely mechanical study, arbitrarily limited not by genre but by instrument and with no
regard to the structural function, weight, or (except in a very limited sense)
complexity of the material. So narrow is the definition that the C-Minor Piano
Fantasia is not even mentioned! Potentially interesting formal issues are raised
by example 45 (p. 157), a third movement introduction used as a transition in a
sonata by Johann Ladislaus Dussek.

11. On the significance of the key of C, see Douglas Porter Johnson, *Beethoven's
Sketches* 932–39. How far did the C-major phenomenon spread? To Johnson's
examples may be added the Symphony no. 33 (1780), subtitled *Il Maniatico*, by
the Madrid composer Gaetano Brunetti. This symphony has two introductions:
the standard fanfare and then a programmatic introduction, where the waver-
ing pitch of slow trills in the solo cello is used to symbolize mental alienation.
Reason (and C major) triumphs over unreason at the end of the piece. For an
even earlier example, see Wilhelm Heinse's extraordinary rhapsody (in a letter
to J. W. L. Gleim of August 1776) about the great C bell in Erfurt, whose resonant
harmonics he compares to the pure Row of time: "*Becoming, being, and decaying,
and renewed becoming,* eternally creating and eternally decaying harmony. . . . *The
first breath of beauty out of the bosom of night, of the invisible,*" *Werke* 9: 292–94. On
the other hand, none of the models for the Piano Fantasia cited by Oskar Sigmund is in C.

12. A typical Mozart-Raphael comparison is Emil Naumann, "Wolfgang Mo-
zart"; a typical Mozart-Goethe (vs. Beethoven-Schiller) comparison is Ludwig
Nohl, *Mozart.* The best studies of Mozart's reputation that I have found are Leo
Schrade, "Mozart und die Romantiker" and "Vom Nachleben Mozarts." Of
course, the revolutionary character of Mozart's libretti is widely recognized: see
Jean Starobinski, *1789* 25–30; Rosen, *Classical Style* 321–35; and Angus Fletcher,
"On Two Words."

13. This Mozart-as-child tradition is most accessible in Stendhal's brief *Vie de
Mozart.* The justly famous literary embodiment is Eduard Mörike's story "Mozart auf der Reise nach Prag," which perfectly fuses all three strains of Mozart's
reputation: the naive, the demonic, and the classically pure. It should be added
that Ingmar Bergman's *Magic Flute* and *Amadeus* have resuscitated the demonic
Mozart since my essay was first published.

Chapter 6

1. I have left the Heidegger translation unmodified because its highly evaluative rhetoric so well illustrates the risks to which historians of philosophy are
exposed. As I read Heidegger (2: 167–68 in the German edition), his concern is
with a universal philosophical situation, not with improvements made by Descartes. In particular, for "superficially" the German has "von außen her"—from

an outside perspective, not a foolish or ignorant one. For "inappropriately," which also sounds like a condemnation, the German has the more neutral "unangemessen" (not tailored to the occasion); rather than a "contingency" that "threatens" thought it speaks of a "Vorgang" (procedure) to which thought is "exposed" (ausgesetzt). In that context, "Descartes was forced to discourse at the already prevailing level" is more accurately translated, "Descartes was forced to speak from a prior level" (aus der Ebene des Bisherigen zu sprechen)—not particularly a lower level. My essay is intended to make the case that the history of philosophy (like the history of poetry and the arts) is not a progress from lower to higher levels but rather a continuing mutation of language and point of view.

2. Edmund Husserl argues that Descartes mistakes his own transcendental reduction as a merely psychological insight. But while *Die Krisis der europäischen Wissenschaften* persuasively demonstrates what is termed Descartes's "self-misinterpretation" (sect. 18), Husserl does not even ask why Descartes should have made so fundamental a mistake; that is to say, he does not view the problem on Descartes's level. The deficiency lies in Husserl's philology. Though at one point he appeals to "the grammatical sense of the statement *ego cogito*" (*Cartesianische Meditationen* 24), he constantly presumes the "world" and material things as the contents (and grammatical objects) of thought. As I shall show below, *cogito* is a mental construction (judge or imagine), not a mere mental response (mediate or ponder); consequently, the analysis offered by Husserl remained beyond Descartes's horizon. Even if the "self-misrepresentation" belies the logical implications of Descartes's thought, it remains the only interpretation that his language permits.

3. Contending that philosophy concerns the search for eternal verities not dependent on language, Alquié undertakes to demonstrate that "Kant rediscovered the true essence of Cartesianism" (152). This is my argument turned inside out. What it does not explain is why Descartes failed to discover the true essence of his own philosophy and why Kant was so misled by Leibniz that he failed to notice how that essence lay implicit in the earlier philosopher. Jean Ferrari (*Sources françaises* 22–78) decisively refutes Alquié's essay (though he does not cite it) by demonstrating Kant's lifelong disregard for Descartes; he finds Kant's critique of the *cogito* "in flagrant contradiction with the Cartesian text" and concludes, "it is clear that the properly Cartesian meaning of the cogito ergo sum has been completely forgotten" (65, 69).

4. In this chapter, Kant is quoted in Norman Kemp Smith's translation, with modifications. In particular, as with Heidegger's *Nietzsche*, I have again altered the translation of *Satz* to "sentence," replacing Smith's "proposition."

5. Berel Lang's clever account of the genre of the *Meditations* clarifies the priority of the movement of truth over its fixity in this text.

6. Kemp Smith translates "ich bin einfach" adjectivally, as a determinate judgment: "I am simple"—a grammatical possibility that, however, falsifies the con-

tentlessness Kant always attributes to the *cogito*. Likewise, in the preceding sentence, by emending the gender of a relative pronoun, Kemp Smith makes "simplicity . . . involved in every thought," whereas the unemended text says that "the sentence 'I think' " is "involved in every thought."

7. In the *Discourse*, the translation reads, "attente examinans quis essem" and "mens per quam solam sum is qui sum" (6: 558), where Descartes writes, "examinant avec attention ce que i'estois" and "l'Ame par laquelle ie suis ce que ie suis" (6: 32–33); in the *Meditations*, Descartes writes, "Nondum verò satis intelligo, quisnam sim ego ille" (9: 19), where the translation reads "Mais je ne connais pas encore assez clairement ce que je suis" (7: 25) and where the long ensuing discussion similarly drives insistently at "what" (quid) and even "what kind of thing" (qualis res) I am (7: 25–29). Curiously, Gilson's commentary on the *Discourse* does not discuss this discrepancy.

8. *Meditations* 3 (*Oeuvres* 7: 44 Latin = 9: 35 French). The fulfilled type of this image is common in Kant's era, notably in Wordsworth: see my *Preromanticism*, chap. 12.

9. A noteworthy contradiction concerns another famous passage in the *Discourse on Method*: "like a man who walks alone and in the shadows, I resolved to go so slowly, and to use so much circumspection in all things, that, if I advanced but very little, I should keep myself, at least, from falling" (*Oeuvres* 6: 16–17). By translating "circonspection" with "caution," F. E. Sutcliffe's version makes this sound like the reverie of a solitary wanderer who holds back from an encounter with the world. The Latin translator finds a different tonality of genuine attentiveness here: "so diligently looking about at all things" (tam diligenter ad omnia circumspicere; *Oeuvres* 6: 549). By emphasizing alertness, he edges the passage toward Descartes's discussion of method in the *Rules for the Direction of the Spirit*, which warns against shadows: "all those who thus accustom themselves to walk in the shadows so weaken their eyesight in consequence that they can no longer support the light of day" (*Oeuvres* 10: 371).

10. While the notion of Descartes as *bon vivant* certainly does not reflect all of his moods, the parallel with Hume's view of the world theater shows that this translation of the motto is not a philosophical absurdity. It could serve to characterize a Humean great man: Hume writes in the chapter "Of Greatness of Mind" "that a genuine and hearty pride, or self-esteem, if well concealed and well founded, is essential to the character of a man of honour, and that there is no quality of the mind which is more indispensably requisite to procure the esteem and admiration of mankind" (*Treatise* 532). On the personality of the philosopher as reflected in the philosophy, see Henri Gouhier's beautiful book.

11. "M. Descartes . . . arose at once, changed countenance, drew his sword with unforeseen pride, spoke to them in their language with a tone that seized them, and threatened to pierce them through on the spot, if they dared offer him any insult. It was in this encounter that he perceived the impression the bold-

ness of a man can make on a low soul; I mean a boldness rising far above one's forces and power of execution: a boldness which, on other occasions, could pass for pure bravado." Descartes, *Oeuvres philosophiques* 51.

12. Nancy concludes his analysis with the image of a camera; he compares Descartes's convulsive self-assertions to the "brutal shutting of the diaphragm" (*Ego Sum* 152). Abandoning his usual philological caution, he presents his principal piece of evidence in this fashion: "*ego sum* is true 'every time that *I* utter it or that *I* conceive it in my mind' (it is *I* [*moi*] who underline *I* [*je*])" (150). The French text (with which Nancy has taken some slight freedoms) is, however, not Cartesian, and the Latin ("quoties a me profertur, vel mente concipitur"; *Meditations* 2; 7: 25) contains no *I* to be snapshotted, or to misfire. Anachronism is misused here; it can properly illuminate historical difference and direction, but it does not properly support assertions of systematic deficiency.

13. Jaakko Hintikka calls the *cogito* a performative. His plausible account is controversial but, I think, less for the reasons given by his critics than because the notion of a performative suggests the creation of something enduring beyond the performance. The misjudgment concerns Cartesian temporality rather than Cartesian linguistics. From a different perspective, see Nancy's punning discussions of Descartes's *for* (Latin "speech," French "conscience, internal tribunal").

14. There are good overviews of the problem of consciousness in Descartes and after in Francisque Bouillier, chap. 3; Kurt Joachim Grau; Theodor Kehr, chap. 7; and Heinrich Scholz. Vendler gives the most careful account of the *cogito* in the Cartesian system. Etienne Gilson's edition of the *Discours de la Méthode* has been indispensable, although I have risked proposing differing interpretations of the phrases "ego cogito" and "sum, sive existo."

15. On Descartes's confidence see Bouillier, 1: 74. On clarity see the important pages in Gilson, *Etudes* 264–65, contrasting Descartes with the Pantheist Tommaso Campanella. Georges Poulet's brilliant reading of the famous dreams reported by his biographer recuperates even their passages of bizarre terror as experiences of hyperbolic doubt within a framework that anticipates the mature system of the *Meditations*.

16. On Descartes's voyage to construct a worldly self, see the subtle interpretation of the *Discourse* in Gerald L. Bruns, *Inventions* 63–87. Nathan Edelman's more conscientious survey takes similar imagery to reflect a yearning for a solid foundation; though he speaks of insecurity, his findings are not inconsistent with the self-assertiveness claimed by other scholars. William Kerrigan and Gordon Braden (*Idea of the Renaissance* 135–53) suggestively, though not always convincingly, relate Descartes's enterprise to the will to power within Renaissance individualism.

17. In his often subtle study of Descartes's style, Pierre Alain Cahné (*Un Autre Descartes* 49–52) misleadingly limits the formula "is or exists" to God—which is

true of the French text of the *Discourse*, but not of the Latin text, nor of other occurrences of the doublet—and regards *exists* as an "intensifier" of *is*: "The coordination with 'or' signifies perhaps that the second term corrects the first, or *rather* erases it" (52). But the Latin *sive* that renders *ou* means "in other words" not "or rather"; in the *Meditations*, *sive* is regularly rendered *c'est-à-dire*.

18. Semantically, *cogito* approximates "deliberate," as opposed to "contemplate." Hence in the Vulgate it often renders λογίζομαι. Only one citation in the entire *Thesaurus Linguae Latinae* resembles the Kantian misreading of Descartes's *cogito* as an intransitive verb, and it is the exception that proves the rule. It is the very first example, s.v. *cogito*: "sed cum cogito, equidem certo idem sum qui semper fui." This comes from Plautus's *Amphitryon*, line 447. Comparing himself with his double (Mercury in disguise), Sosias is baffled in the attempt to construct a self-intuition. This apparent approximation of "cogito, ergo sum" is thus a mark of delusion, or even madness. In all other recorded examples of *cogito* used absolutely, the sentence is clearly elliptical, with a judgment as the implied object. Vendler appears to be alone in recognizing that *cogito*, in Descartes, "is a propositional verb" ("Descartes' 'Res Cogitans'" 198), yet demonstrably wrong in declaring "that the verb *cogitare*, unlike its kin *putare*, is not a propositional verb in Latin" (199).

19. Gerhart Schmidt, *Aufklärung und Metaphysik* 169. To refer to thought stripped of all its objects, Schmidt uses the Kantian word "bloß," which literally means "nakedly." The equivalent French and Latin phrases mean "thought alone" and would not connote empty thought. Similar claims are widespread. The most extreme formulation is that of G. E. Barié: "thought alone is concrete without the aid of anything else, for it has, by its very nature as thinking activity, its first object in itself: *ego cogito me*" (225). Related misconstructions of Descartes's *cogito* include Dalia Judovitz, *Subjectivity and Representation* 116 ("The *cogito* is presented here as a primitive act of knowledge, one based on a *simple act of mental vision*—in other words, *intuition*"—her emphases), Roger Lefèvre, *Pensée existentielle* 31 ("The Cogito [takes place] in a limpid intuition where the subject and the object form a single certainty. The essence [*propre*] of the thinking being is for it to think its very self [*de se penser soi-même*], I can never think without being"), and, in a more general context, A. Carlini "Grundeigenschaften des Geistesaktes" 356 ("Thinking here means: *thinking oneself* [*Sich-Denken*]," his emphasis). Hintikka, " 'Cogito, Ergo Sum'" 117–18, recognizes correctly that the *cogito* is "a conceptual operation" but accuses Descartes in consequence of "shortcomings" and "ambiguity."

20. Andreas Kemmerling has argued, with considerable finesse, that the *cogito* must logically be reflexive. Its proper formulation, he deduces, is, "The thinker of this thought-occurrence exists" ("Reflexive Deutung" 165), a formulation in which "the 'cogito' inheres in the subject, the 'sum' in the predicate, and the 'ergo' in the origin" (166). But an "Entstehungsgeschichte"—a notably difficult

word to translate—presupposes a temporal continuity and a substratum enduring through time; in other words, it gives an ongoing life to "thought-occur-
rences." The point, as I shall be arguing more fully, is that Descartes has no
language for such subsistence and consequently no way to conceive it. Kemmerling's conclusion adroitly recognizes that his reconstruction, however necessary,
may be impossible. "Cogito Ergo Sum [is] a thought revolving in itself. [But it
isn't a "thought"; it's a statement, in a language.] The I that it concerns is
possibly very ephemeral. . . . Whether all that speaks against the above interpretation or against its object is one of the many difficult questions that I here
leave aside" (166). If only philosophy were a matter of logic!

21. See *Principia* 1.66–71, where it becomes evident that it is indeed difficult to
arrive at clear and distinct ideas of our sensations—and hence to take sensation
as a first principle—yet, apparently, it is not logically impossible.

22. See my *Preromanticism*, chap. 4.

23. Intuition, for Descartes, is yet another form of judgment, as he describes at
length in the third of the *Rules for the Direction of Spirit* (*Oeuvres* 10: 368). So too, I
think, is perception. In the *Meditations*, at any rate, *percipio* and *perceptio* are
regularly rendered with *connaître* and *connaissance* (last paragraph of *Meditations* 2; 7: 34 = 9: 26; *Meditations* 3; 7: 35 = 9: 27; *Meditations* 5; 7: 65 = 9: 52;
Meditations 5; 7: 71 = 9: 55 [*reconnaître*]). Particularly interesting is a phrase in the
preface: "ex eo quod mens humana in se conversa non *percipiat* aliud se esse
quam rem cogitantem" (de ce que l'esprit humain, faisant réflexion sur soi-
même, ne se *connaît* être autre chose qu'une chose qui pense; *Oeuvres* 7: 7–8 =
Meditations, ed. Rodis-Lewis, 6–7, my emphases in both quotes). The passage
does not appear in the original translation and was not reviewed by Descartes.
Still, the seventeenth-century translator seems to be in conformity with the rest
of the work when he takes *percipiat* as a stylistic variant for *cognoscat*. Even the
mind turned in upon itself is reflecting, not intuiting in the modern sense. In a
letter written in French concerning the Fifth Objections to the *Meditations* (9:
208), Descartes equates (true) perception with both knowledge and thought, but
not with judgments, which come after. By "judgments" here he appears to mean
inferences or conclusions; he is not denying propositional form to the "perception or thought" (his phrase) preceding the judgment.

24. Cahné (*Un Autre Descartes* 43–44) quotes the following decisive passage
from Augustine's *Confessions* 10.18, though he uses it for other purposes: "Cogenda rursus, ut sciri possint, id est uelut ex quadam dispersione colligenda,
unde dictum est cogitare. Nam cogo et cogito sic est, ut ago et agito, facio et
factito" (They are to be brought together [*cogenda*] so as to be known; that is,
collected as if from a state of dispersion, whence this is called *cogitare*. For *cogo* is
to *cogito* as *ago* to *agito*, *facio* to *factito*). The issue here is one of linguistic resonance, not of doctrine. Consequently, Augustine's testimony is powerful even
though Descartes had little interest in or knowledge of his writings.

25. Scholz discusses fully the iterative adverbs that regularly accompany Descartes's reasoning, though without signaling the iterative character of thought itself. See also Hintikka, " 'Cogito, Ergo Sum' " 113: "Descartes's insight emerges from his own descriptions as a curiously *momentary* affair. It is a consequence of the performatoriness of his insight. Since the certainty of my existence results from my thinking of it in a sense not unlike that in which light results from the presence of a source of light, it is natural to assume (rightly or wrongly) that I can be really sure of my existence only as long as I actively contemplate it." "Momentary" is right, but from Descartes's perspective the momentariness is inevitable not curious. And the example is wrong: it is durative where Cartesian thought is iterative. To be sure, Descartes sometimes uses the durative conjunction *quamdiu* in *Meditations* 2: "for he will never cause me to be nothing so long as I think myself something"; "I am, I exist; that is certain. But for how long? For so long as I think" (7: 25, 27). But these durations remain composed of particles: "every time I utter it," "every time I consider myself to be something" (7: 25, 26).

26. "Semper" gives the translator difficulties. In French it becomes "actuelle et éternelle" (9: 52). The doublet recaptures (in reverse order) the two faces of "est ou existe": action and subsistence. Descartes emphatically calls this conception of God clear and distinct, suggesting that he had less difficulty than his translator with the notion of a worldly, iterative eternity.

27. On error in Descartes, see the speculative essay by Ralph Flores. More generally, see the chapter "Substance at Risk" in Grene, *Descartes* 88–109, which concludes as follows: "It is the real distinction and the concomitant double reduction of mind to thought and nature to machinery that have plagued our thinking. . . . The bare unstable Cartesian world does indeed demand a foundation and must indeed fail to find it" (108). The central argument of the book is that Descartes neglected "the category of life" (21). That is, in substance, exactly my conclusion, which I have formulated as the absence from Descartes's texts of a certain (vitalist) temporality. However, I do not regard the absence as a failure, but rather as a linguistic-conceptual gap that only Descartes's conceptual and stylistic rigor could render visible, and then only to or through subsequent writers such as Kant.

28. Jean Wahl's booklet *Du rôle de l'idée de l'instant* celebrates Descartes's "actualism." Yet the features that he singles out are largely negations (the infinitesimal and history that "becomes the negation of the importance of history," 43) or insubstantial images (fire and light). Such achievements are prone to melt away, like wax.

29. "Pars itaque temporis quaelibet est tempus, et, quae sunt in tempore, simplicia, nempe *momenta*, non sunt partes illius, sed *termini*, quos interiacet tempus." In a note to *Le Monde* (*Oeuvres philosophiques* 347), Alquié says, "space is the a priori condition of all external representation. The Cartesian affirmation is quite close to that of Kant's *Transcendental Aesthetic*." But Descartes at this point is talking about matter and not, as Kant would, about space.

30. Cahné (*Un Autre Descartes* 142–43) attributes to Descartes imagery of dark labyrinths, but his only textual citation (from *Regulae* 5; 10: 379–80) concerns finding one's way through a labyrinth. Asserted parallels from Bacon and Leibniz do not consolidate the case. Nor do Cahné's examples make the phonetic linkage of *Icarus* and *cera* plausible. Edelman's essay is a helpful account of some of the relevant imagery. Gouhier, *Essais sur Descartes*, chap. 2 (esp. pp. 78–79 and 98–102) explains Descartes's apparent prudence in withholding *Le Monde*.

Chapter 7

1. *Watchman* 2: 68–70.

2. Derrida relates the problematics of "natural" language to the image of the sun in "White Mythology." See esp. 53: "With every metaphor, there is no doubt somewhere a sun; but each time that there is the sun, metaphor has begun. If the sun is already and always metaphorical, it is not completely natural. It is already and always a lustre: one might call it an *artificial* construction if this could have meaning in the absence of nature." Notice that Coleridge adds the metaphorical sun ("the eye of Day"), which is not mentioned in the Latin.

3. The first edition of the odes, in three books, was published in 1625; the first complete edition of the odes and epodes appeared in 1634, and there were some two dozen before 1800. Volume 1 of *The Happy Man* by Maren-Sofie Røstvig discusses Sarbiewski's influence in England at length, generally without considering the differences between Latin and English versions, though there is a useful contrast of Vaughan and Sarbiewski on 272. To my knowledge, the only good introduction to Sarbiewski in the neo-Latin context is Gerald Fitzgerald's "*Cenodoxus* and Baroque Latin": see esp. 10–12 and 130–31 (on "momentalism") and 44–46 and 69 (on strange sonorities and linguistic excesses). Leonard Forster's inaugural lecture, *The Temper of Seventeenth-Century German Literature*, surveys problems of baroque temporality with emphasis on northern Europe. On baroque opulence and its relation to sonority and the rhetorical voice, see Angus Fletcher, *The Transcendental Masque*, chap. 1.

4. Compare, for example, Horace's very supple use of the rare Ionic *a minore* (˘˘‒‒) in his *Odes* 3.12 with Sarbiewski's leaden succession of two- and four-syllable words in his *Od.* 2.28.

5. *Od.* 2.4.13–14: "Multi magna loqui possumus: ardua / Raros ausa vocant." Cf. also *Od.* 4.3.33–36: "Ad prima si quis vulnera non gemit, / Solo peregit bella silentio; / Celare qui novit sinistros, / Ille potest bene ferre casus," and *Od.* 4.11.13–16: "Vera laus sciri fugit. Ipse pulcher / Se suâ Titan prohibet videri / Luce: qui totus potuit latere, / Major habetur."

6. *Od.* 1.6.29–34: "Frustra Novembres dicimus ad focos / Pugnata Rhaetis bella sub Alpibus: / Frustra renarramus Gelonum / Versa retro retulisse signa: / Si non & ipsi stringere Noricos / Audemus enses." Observe the characteristic accumulation of "re-" prefixes.

7. The ode just cited continues (lines 45–46): "To him Tempe, bought with much blood, will afford recreation" (Hunc empta multo sanguine recreent / Tempe). The opposition of martial iron and degenerate gold appears in lines 14–15: "Ferro, Quirites, si lubet, abditum / Mercemur aurum."

8. When Sarbiewski attempts the description of nature in movement, the result is liable to be as absurd as the following, from the very first ode: "The hills moo, and breathless the wood from the tired calves. In peace the ridges spring up, in peace the foul rocks smile" (lines 31–34: "Mugiunt colles, & anhela fessis / Silva juvencis. / Pace subsultant juga, pace rident / Tetricae rupes").

9. *Od.* 4.8.29–30: "Humana quidquid composuit manus, / Humana rursus disjiciet." *Od.* 2.6.33–36: "Et qui conspicuus tot populis heri / Spectabar tacito non sine gaudio; / Ridens e mediâ plebe vicariam / Cras spectabo Trag-oediam." Cf. the phrase "taciti . . . Dies" in *Od.* 1.7.36, an otherwise more conventional poem about natural mutability. Contrast the well-known sonnet 3.8 of Andreas Gryphius ("Du siehst, wohin du siehst, nur eitelkeit auf erden"), which describes nature's noisy destruction of human vanity. The contrast is apposite because Sarbiewski translated Gryphius's sonnet 3.7. On Gryphius's translations from Biedermann and Sarbiewski, see Fitzgerald 96–100 and 116–18.

10. *Od.* 3.23.5–7: "Mitte sectari, quis amoena praeter / Prata non parco fluit amnis auro. / Sit satis Virtus." *Od.* 1.23.21–28: "Numquam . . . / Auri deciduis vestierat jubis / Graium pellis Iasona; / Si non difficiles imperii boves / Egisset dominâ vertere dexterâ / Ferratis Chalybum saucia dentibus / Colchi litora Phasidis." Cf. also *Od.* 44.26.18–20: "In arma ferrum / Sit satis. Rapto malè pugnat olim / Miles in auro."

11. *Od.* 4.19.9–12: "At te quae tacitis distinet otiis, / o JESU, regio? quis mihi te locus / Caecis invidet umbris, / Aut spissâ nemorum comâ?"

12. *Od.* 2.12.33–41. I call the sound effects false because (1) they are unclassical, (2) they ignore etymology ("ite . . . iterate . . . te"), and (3) they apparently ignore vowel quanity ("culmis . . . orbis").

13. Observe that the problems of time and space are fundamentally inseparable. On the relation of vision as sight to vision as prophetic foresight see Bishop Berkeley's *New Theory of Vision*, § 148, and Meyer H. Abrams, *Natural Supernaturalism* 373–84.

14. *Od.* 1.7.41–44: "Et sunt quae, *Lyce*, cernimus? / An peccant fatuis lumina palpebris, / Et mendax oculi vitrum? / An longi trahitur fabula somnii?"

15. There are no epiphanic formulae in Horace either; their origins in English poetry need to be investigated. On the use of "ecce," see Erich Auerbach, *Mimesis* 157.

16. *Silviludia* 4.6: "En pictis foliorum / Multicolor labellis / Flos *tacitus* divinos / Eloquitur honores" (my italics). "En" in *Epodes* 3.37 is also not original with Sarbiewski but derives from the same source as *Silv.* 4. On the attribution

of the *Silviludia*, which were regularly printed with the *Odes* and translated as Sarbiewski's by R. C. Core in 1848 under the title *Wood-Notes*, see John Sparrow, "Sarbiewski's *Silviludia*."

17. Thus the epitaph in *Od.* 2.5.56–57 ("Cum populo jacet hic et ipso / Cum rege regnum") is one-and-a-half lines in the Latin spanning a stanza break, one line in G. Hils, two full lines (though of differing lengths) in John Hughes's "The Ecstasy." There is similarly a strong tendency to force anaphoric repetition into a uniform position at the beginning of the line; examples can readily be found in the Oxford *Miscellany* translations and on almost any page of Hils's bilingual edition. It should be noted that there is no alternative principle of formal balance in Sarbiewski, such as could be achieved, for example, by a careful management of clause lengths. Even where isocolon is found, the effect in context is not so much balance as urgency (as in the lines, "Integram nobis sine labe vitam, / Prosperam nobis sine clade mortem," found in *Od.* 4.24.13–14 and again in *Ep.* 9.33–34).

18. Examples of punning translations based on sound rather than sense are "regent" for "regina," "sublimes and takes me" for "me eripit sublimem," and "oh what a *longing*, Jesu, thus / With thy delay thou mak'st in us?" for "*Longam ducis*, JESU, / In desideriis moram" (Hils 91, 63, 79; my italics). The last pun, not noticed in the *Oxford English Dictionary*, is also found in Donne, e.g., *Metempsychosis*, lines 63–64, and *The Litanie*, line 83.

19. Sarbiewski, *Od.* 4.28 ("Cum novi e Germania, Gallia, Italiaque motus bellici nuntiarentur"): "Punctum est, sors avidis quod secat ensibus / Inter tot populos." Vaughan, lines 17–20: "It [the world] is a *ball* / Which *Fate* and *force* divide 'twixt all / The *sons* of *Men*."

20. We can see the process of compensation at work in the translations of *Od.* 2.5. First, Cowley in "The Exstasie" replaced figures from the Trojan War with Galileo and with St. Paul, who, in turn, being insufficiently modern, gives way to Columbus ("Not *Paul*, who first did thither pass, / And this great *Worlds Columbus* was," st. 6). Then Hughes, in his version of "The Ecstasy," substitutes Newton for Paul and directly compares the modern figures to their outmoded classical prototypes: " 'Tis he—as I approach more near / The great Columbus of the skies I know, / 'Tis Newton's soul! that daily travels here / In search of knowledge for mankind below. / O stay, thou happy Spirit! stay, / And lead me on thro' all th'unbeaten wilds of day; / As when the Sybil did Rome's father guide" (lines 175–81).

21. Hans-Georg Gadamer's *Wahrheit und Methode* generalizes the principle by arguing that any creative inheritance of a tradition is in fact a translation, involving such a re-placement and redefinition of style. For an elegant literary demonstration of the principle, see Emil Staiger, "Entstellte Zitate."

22. "The Celebrated Victory . . . ," Watts, *Horae Lyricae*, No. 204. Watts's monosyllabic strong verbs (hung, fell, fled, spread) sound like participles or adjectives

and thus manage to combine the monumentality of the Latin with the vivid animation of true narrative.

23. Cf. Paul de Man, "Intentional Structure of the Romantic Image," *Rhetoric of Romanticism* 5: "Strictly speaking, an epiphany cannot be a beginning, since it reveals and unveils what, by definition, could never have ceased to be there." The sentence which follows seems less appropriate to the optimistic early English romantics than to de Man's immediate subject, Hölderlin: "Rather, it is the rediscovery of a permanent presence which has chosen to hide itself from us— unless it is we who have the power to hide from it."

24. G. Wilson Knight's *The Starlit Dome* contains a fine study of illumination in Coleridge. The key sentence is on 119: "We have disentangled a progress from normal sexuality . . . towards the specifically artistic consciousness, which is, however, generally entwined with some literary or musical feminine figure; while the whole progress is, as it were, *lighted* by a nostalgic memory of youthful love, felt as a still existing, but somehow mislaid, experience" (Knight's italics).

25. "Everything seems to stream in on us because we do not stream out. We are negative because we want to be—the more positive we become, the more negative the world around us becomes—until at last there will be no more negation, but we are all in all. *God wants gods*" (Novalis's italics), *Schriften* 2: 584.

26. "The Exstasie," stanza 2. Willis, too, springs an epiphany in mid-ascent: "Go, go, my Muse, the winged horse prepare; / I purpose now to take the Air / Take solid Judgement for the Bit, / And put on the rich Ornaments of Wit; / Where sense does shine like Dawn of Morn, / (Not dazzled by the thick, / And gaudy Flowers of Rhet'rick;) / Thro' Interspaces which the work adorn; / Lo! now I mount and (lo!) I take my flight," and so on (*Miscellany Poems* 27).

27. Wordsworth, *Prelude* (1805) 6:534, 525. As here, so too in Hughes and Coleridge (see the discussion below), "past and future overtake the present," as Hartman says (*Wordsworth's Poetry* 46).

28. "Hermeneutic wedge" is Hartman's phrase in "The Voice of the Shuttle," *Beyond Formalism* 351. Cleanth Brooks's search for ironies is a privileged mode, but not the only mode of hermeneutic inquiry.

29. Two roughly contemporary translations of 4.23 attempt this effect, but achieve only a sense of reciprocal directionality, rather than Coleridge's diffusion of directionality. For "Et te voce, *Cicada*, / Et mutum recreas nemus" (lines 3–4), Joseph Hucks has "lull the listening grove" (83) and Götz has "den horchenden Hain" (2: 16).

30. On the ambiguities of the light and the air cf. the following sequence in *Notebooks* 2936: "—like a lake beneath the Sun seemed to possess in its own right & prodigally give the fiery Light, which by not receiving it flashed forth"; 2937: "Aeolian Harp motive for opening the Sash; & at once lets in music & sweet air," and so on. On the harp and the light see also 2435.

31. This is apparently a common and spontaneous ambiguity; see *Oxford English Dictionary*, "lour."

32. Empson, *Structure*, chap. 1. See chap. 4 ("'All' in Milton") for Empson's analysis of a purely emotive word. For an argument that words are inherently simple though not "natural," see Emile Benveniste, "Nature du signe linguistique." Martin Price has some interesting comments on Blake's avoidance of irony in the *Songs of Innocence*; see *To the Palace of Wisdom* 390–97.

33. Among the many relevant commentaries on Wordsworth's poem, see in particular that by Paul de Man in "The Rhetoric of Temporality" 204–6.

34. The association of glitter (also glimmer and gleam) with water is peculiar to the early Coleridge (before about 1805). Wordsworth's glitter, by contrast, is dry, as in "A Farewell," lines 53–54: "The steep rock's breast / Glittered at evening like a starry sky." Wordsworth's usage eventually impinged on Coleridge, as in the second paragraph of *Biographia Literaria*. See also Josephine Miles, "Wordsworth and Glitter."

35. It would take another essay to trace the implications of the imagery linking water-eyes-illumination-expansion-animation (one life)-Aeolian harp. Some key passages are "Dejection," lines 73–75; "Hymn before Sunrise in the Vale of Chamouni," lines 23–25 and 70–85; and "The Night-Scene," lines 42–45. Ecstasy, not epiphany, is the proper term for the poetical "lo!"—it is more descriptive and more accurate historically. See, for instance, the odes entitled "The Ecstasy," cited above, and also the analysis in Heidegger, *Sein und Zeit*, § 65.

36. Gustave Guillaume's discussion of perfects compounded with "to be" (*être*) could be applied *in toto* to Coleridge's poem. The so-called "Passé composé intégrant," according to Guillaume, is characterized by a passive agent, by the absence of a strong distinction between subject and object, and by a conception of event as a participatory, continuous totality. See "Existe-t-il un déponent en français?"

37. I choose the term "self-projection" not because Heidegger later adopted it to describe the "transcendent" unity of subject and object but rather because it is used by the Romantic philosophers. See, for instance, the page on "Entwerfen" beginning, "Wer bin Ich? Subjekt und Objekt in Einem," in Johann Gottlieb Fichte's *Bestimmung des Menschen* (*Sämmtliche Werke* 250). Heidegger, however, is more lucid; see *Sein und Zeit*, § 31 (definition of "der Entwurf"), and §§ 63, 64, and 69 (on transcendent unity). It is worth remembering the characteristic seventeenth-century rejection of anticipation in George Herbert. Prudence (pro-videntia) belongs to divine providence, not to men, who should live in the present and whose only future is death. "Men and the present fit: if he provide / He breaks the square. / This houre is mine: if for the next I care, / I grow too wide, / And do encroach upon deaths side" ("The Discharge," lines 31–35).

38. Cf. also *Notebooks* 2439: "patiendo agam . . . et agendo patiar." Hegel's *Science of Logic* contains the most searching philosophical analysis of the fusion of action and passion into what is called "determinate simplicity"; see the concluding sections of vol. 1: "Action and Reaction" and "Reciprocity."

39. Before Coleridge, Hume had already seen the "indolent belief in the general maxims of the world" (and later "indolence and pleasure") as the remedy for "philosophical melancholy and delirium" (*A Treatise of Human Nature* 1.4.7). In the preceding section of the *Treatise* Hume describes the spectacle of perception in a way that is relevant to—and indeed answered by—Coleridge's "simple" style: "The mind is a kind of theatre, where several perceptions successively make their appearance; pass, repass, glide away, and mingle in an infinite variety of postures and situations. There is properly no *simplicity* in it at one time, nor *identity* in different, whatever natural propension we may have to imagine that simplicity and identity" (Hume's italics). The topic is well surveyed in Spiegelman, *Majestic Indolence.*

40. Coleridge's comment to Mrs. Barbauld concerning the moral of the "Ancient Mariner" is well known. Richard Haven traces the problem of Coleridge's moralizing conclusions in chap. 2 of *Patterns of Consciousness.*

41. See Maurice Blanchot, *Le Livre à venir* 9–19 (part of the essay, "Le Chant des sirènes"). Mallarmé's closest approach to the Aeolian harp—a relatively recent invention first described by Athanasius Kircher in his *Musurgia universalis* of 1650—is an obsolete instrument hanging in an enclosed showcase, "musicienne du silence" ("A la fenêtre recelant").

42. Contemporary with Coleridge and closely allied to him in spirit is the French aphorist Joubert (1754–1824); see Blanchot's eloquent essay "Joubert et l'espace," *Le Livre à venir* 75–98, where (in the section entitled "Une première version de Mallarmé") the following is quoted: "I am an Aeolian harp. No wind has blown over me" (94).

43. "The Double Session," *Dissemination* 220–22, apropos of the word *entre.* Cf. also 262–64 and Philippe Sollers, "Littérature et totalité," esp. 78–82. After Mallarmé the self-sufficiency or "littéralité" (Sollers, 81) again perhaps declines; see, for instance, J. Hillis Miller's analysis of Wallace Stevens's revision of the Arab dream passage in the *Prelude*: *Linguistic Moment* 390–422.

44. "Le Livre, instrument spirituel." The fundamental study of the effervescence of Mallarmé's imagery is Jean-Pierre Richard, *L'Univers imaginaire de Mallarmé*, esp. 377–409.

45. Northrop Frye, "The Drunken Boat" 200–217, and also *Fearful Symmetry* 138–39.

Chapter 9

1. Roland Barthes, "La Musique, la voix, la langue" and "Le Chant romantique" in *L'Obvie et l'obtus* 247 and 253. See further the useful survey by Françoise Escal, "Roland Barthes: Fragments d'un discours."

2. An exception to the word-envy of musical semiotics is Theodor Adorno's essay, "Fragment über Musik und Sprache." Most prominent among the exam-

ples of the yearning to assimilate music to language is perhaps Jean-Jacques Nattiez, *Fondements*, esp. 76–82. More extreme is B. M. Gasparov, "Nekotorye deskriptivnye problemy muzykalnoi semantiki." More attuned to the specificity of music is Vladimir Karbusicky; see, for instance, his "Zeichen und Musik," though even here we read: "Since musical symbols are more nearly [iconic] characterizations than arbitrary encodings [eher Charakteristika als willkürliche Chiffren] they point toward early stages in the development of language" (240). In "Das Verstehen der verbalen Sprache und das 'Verstehen der Musik,'" Adam Schaff says that music has phonemes but not words. In consequence, he argues, whereas language communicates meaning, music communicates only feelings. The reduction is like that of Barthes or, before him, of Suzanne Langer. Schaff's essay is part of a collection containing numerous valuable essays of a general nature that are relevant to the present discussion.

3. My semiotic account applies to musical texts, not to performance. Indeed, it has been argued that no formal semiotic analysis is possible of music as actually realized: see François Delalande, "L'Analyse." The objection is true, but not relevant, since the same objection would apply to plays as performed or to poems—or even novels—as read aloud.

4. Harold Krebs discusses examples of wandering tonality in Schubert songs and in Chopin in "Alternatives to Monotonality." In some cases, he argues, Schenkerian analysis reveals the initial sonority to be a false tonic; in the others the harmonic movement is genuine and is textually motivated. The key relation between beginning and end in the latter cases is always a third. Even rarer are the works (always songs or programmatic character pieces) that end on a suspension; see the list in Vladimir Jankélévitch, *Fauré* 26. One domain where the law of tonal consistency does not regularly apply is opera, particularly in the *bel canto* tradition and in Wagner.

5. Drawing on Peter Brooks's book *Reading for the Plot*, Anthony Newcomb's "Narrative Archetypes" illustrates the origin of a modernist sense of closure in Mahler's Ninth Symphony. For another interesting modernist account that regards closure as a repression, see D. A. Miller, *Narrative and Its Discontents*. I have criticized this approach on other grounds in "Plan vs. Plot."

6. Cf. Jérôme J. de Momigny, *Cours complet d'harmonie et de composition*, cited in Leonard Ratner, *Classic Music* 146: "the general plan is established by these instruments [the strings] and the wind instruments, when they are not assigned a leading part, only serve to reinforce the plan with a clearer or more decisive color."

7. So, in connection with the "antinomy that everything should be at once understandable and striking [verständlich und apart]," Adorno writes even of so complex a work as *Tristan* that "the socially conformist demand of comprehensibility and the artistic one of plasticity split asunder," "Versuch über Wagner" 51.

8. Arnold Schoenberg, "Symphonien aus Volkslierdern," *Gesammelte Schriften* 134. I have retranslated this from Schoenberg's German version, which is a little more colorful than the original English, found in "Folkloristic Symphonies," *Style and Idea* 161.

9. The remainder of Chekhov's conclusion reads: "He descended in exhaustion into the shop and, with hot tears, greeted the new, unknown life which was now beginning for him. . . . How was this life to be?" (Chekhov's suspension points). The pun on "ravnodushno" (indifferently) and "ravnina" (plain) appears on 261, in the first chapter. For a more extended analysis, see the brilliant essay by Michael Finke, "Chekhov's 'Steppe': A Metapoetic Journey," 79–120, where the "irreconcilable, disharmonious directions" of the anticlimactic plot (91) are shown to be resolved in a "drama of motifs" and a musicality of structure (107–12) in which "words more than characters are the story's actors" (102).

10. The emergence of modernist features in Debussy's style is well traced in Arthur B. Wenk, *Claude Debussy*. There is a nice comparison of temporality in Debussy's *Canope* and in Proust in Claudia Zenck-Maurer, *Versuch über die wahre Art, Debussy zu interpretieren*.

11. Jankélévitch, *La Vie et la mort dans la musique de Debussy* 93: "The voice of things is captured as closely as possible, and by so immediate an intuition that the human voice, that human presence, that the human person are finally effaced." This book also contains a sensitive appreciation of Debussy's temporality.

12. Gérard Genette, *Mimologiques* 257–314, gives a fine account of the turn toward embodiment in both linguistics and poetics (Mallarmé, Valéry, Sartre, and Jakobson). See esp. pp. 286–88 on the musicalization of language and pp. 298–99 on "signification that has 'fallen into immanence,' [and] 'become a thing.' "

13. A similar programmatic fragmentation is enacted in Luigi Pirandello's novel *Uno, nessuno e centomila*; see the analysis in Gregory Lucente, *Beautiful Fables* 116–55.

14. Shoshana Felman, "Turning the Screws of Interpretation"; Christine Brooke-Rose, "The Squirm of the True." Christopher Lewis speaks of "a general trend in the arts away from a linear perception toward the idea of a multidimensional network of implications and cross-relations in all directions" ("Mirrors and Metaphor"). The term "trend," however, does not adequately capture the conflict between opposing modes reenacted so often in works of the period and well illustrated by the article's own examples of interference between Schenkerian monotonality and post-Wagnerian dual tonality.

15. In Schoenberg's atonality, as Carl Dahlhaus well expresses in the essay "Emanzipation der Dissonanz," "consequentiality is taken away from the chord, but not comprehensibility"; see Dahlhaus, *Schönberg und andere* 148.

16. There is an excellent, nuanced description of the disjunction between style and form in Charles Rosen, *Schoenberg* 79–116. He characterizes the aims as "a

move to resurrect an old classicism" (82) and "as much a defiant proclamation of freedom as an exercise in nostalgia" (103), but the attribution of a mood is risky at best. Along similar lines, see the precise and eloquent analysis of musical structures in Thomas Mann's *Doktor Faustus* in Harry Redner, *In the Beginning Was the Deed* 216–41, though Redner appears to understand Schoenberg differently (236–37).

17. In Schoenberg's *Pierrot Lunaire*, for instance, consonances (never comfortably scored and in root position) always allude to the lost past. They appear at the opening of No. 4, "Eine blasse Wäscherin" (A Pale Washerwoman), in the nostalgic postlude of No. 5, "Valse de Chopin," and on occasion in the last song (No. 21) in connection with the text "O alter Duft aus Märchenzeit" (Old aroma from fairy tales of yore).

18. Letter to Grant Richards, March 13, 1906, *Letters of James Joyce* 2: 134. By "meanness" Joyce presumably understands parsimoniousness but with an unpleasant affect, as in "A Little Cloud," *Dubliners* 83 ("He found something mean in the pretty furniture which he had bought for his house on the hire system"), and "A Painful Case" 107 ("He found all the other suburbs of Dublin mean, modern and pretentious").

19. Theodor Lipps, "Das Wesen der musikalischen Konsonanz und Dissonanz" 195. The key word is equilibrium, in contrast to the modernist sense of an ending that is illustrated in D. A. Miller's *Narrative and Its Discontents*. Or, similarly, contrast the "resting place" in "The C Major of this life" at the end of Robert Browning's *Abt Vogler* with the conclusion of Thomas Pynchon's story, "Entropy": "[Aubade] turned to . . . wait with him until . . . the hovering, curious dominant of their separate lives should resolve into a tonic of darkness and the final absence of all motion" (*Slow Learner* 98).

Finale

1. My invocation of "action" and the pun on "void" allude to Kenneth Burke's excremental reading of Keats's ode, "Symbolic Action." What that essay refused to say, "Body is turd, turd body," finally came out elsewhere, still not verbally, but with sufficiently explicit hints: *Rhetoric* 204.

2. The Platonic and the Heideggerian Keats have come under attack lately. Yet they revive, for this poem at least, if we recognize "The Deserted Village" as an intertext. (Keats gave his sister a collection of Goldsmith's works in February 1819, about three months before the ode was composed.) Keats's "sylvan historian" replaces the figure in Goldsmith's frontispiece, "The sad historian of the pensive plain" (136). His "flowery tale" replaces the village garden: "Near yonder copse, where once the garden smiled, / And still where many a garden flower grows wild" (137–38). His reiterated "sweet" is even more emphatic in Goldsmith; his lovers' chase, his empty town, his wasted generation, all

likewise sublimate more realistic motifs in Goldsmith; and the urn's valedictory replaces that of Goldsmith's "loveliest maid" (407), Poetry, whose voice can "Aid slighted truth" (423). Readers who willingly suspend disbelief will enjoy seeing in the "broken teacups" on display in Auburn (235) a type of the Grecian Urn.

3. See further Geraldine Friedman's "Erotics of Interpretation" for penetrating observations on the gender trouble wrought by (among other things) the poem's acoustics: "bride of quietness," lowing heifer, silent town, and so forth.

4. Charles Rosen has recently discussed the "inner voice" in Schumann's *Humoresque* in nearly identical terms; see *The Romantic Generation* 7–9.

5. I feel that a sketch of the interpretive support is more necessary here than with my other musical examples. Characteristic of Strauss's scores following the Ovidian death-music of the wartime *Metamorphoses* is a revival of the Romantic past: the unending triads of the Second Horn Concerto, or the melodic lyricism of the Oboe Concerto (redeeming for Romanticism an instrument that had not had a distinguished solo piece since the era of the baroque concerto grosso—a form recently renewed by the likes of Stravinsky and Manuel de Falla). Characteristic of the *Four Last Songs* are (1) prosopopoeia (such as flute trills where the text mentions birds, low tessitura at the word "tief" [low] in *Beim Schlafengehen*, and a quotation from Strauss's own *Death and Transfiguration* at the word "Tod" [death] in *Im Abendrot*); (2) controlled, calm lushness, over a firm, steady bass line; (3) a preference for pure instrumental colors (little wind doubling or foreground mixing of wind timbres); (4) a sparing use of the horn, which is, however, featured as the sonority of peaceful repose at the end of the second and third songs, *September* and *Beim Schlafengehen*, to modern poems by Hesse. It is in this context that I take the final fade-out of the horns in the only song with a Romantic text to signify a loosening of all the links so lovingly forged by the songs—of text with music, sound with meaning, and present with past. A closely related effect is the absence of the English horn from the final chord of Wagner's *Tristan und Isolde*.

6. David Epstein, *Beyond Orpheus* 128–29, discusses the unusual spacing of Beethoven's opening chords, which, he observes, if one stray clarinet note is discounted, "spells out" the opening theme. Unlike the clearly audible effects I have discussed in this symphony, or the guidance to expression given by those in the other works I have discussed, Epstein's effect is an inaudible abstraction. This mapping of the axis of succession onto the axis of simultaneity is persuasive, if at all, as an indicator of the will to spatial form that motivates the effects I have discussed. On pp. 133–34, there are some excellent comments about the structural function of repeated notes in the symphony, including a number of passages that my limited remarks omit and of a more technical nature than is appropriate for a literary audience.

7. Frank Kermode's brief reflections on the poem (*The Art of Telling* 134–35

and 154) are particularly suggestive on its imitation of mental action. In the phrase I have echoed, Kermode says, "I've been teasing Keats's poem into thought," but three sentences later he reverses the direction of flow: "Of course the poem encourages us to do these things" (135). Different in rhetoric yet allied in spirit is Barthes's discussion of "The Pensive Text" at the end of *S/Z* (216–17), in conjunction with his notions of "structuration without structure" (5) and with what might be called the supplement of deficiency (24, 143, 175).

8. Leo Bersani sees Mallarmé's essay as floating among disparate positions, and he drives a wedge between the two poles that my chapter seeks to reconcile: the structural, where "*the author is omitted by his structure*," and the musical, "conveying the opposite message," which embraces "not only . . . a view of poetry as the music of individual souls, but also . . . other (non-structural *and* non-psychological) notions of art" (*Death* 39, Bersani's italics). In the following later summary, I emphasize the terms at issue: "In . . . the speculative turbulence of the essay 'Crise de vers,' Mallarmé seems to be proposing a view of literature as an unlocatable—perhaps even *unheard* and unseen—*performance* devoid of any semiotic or epistemological authority. And yet it is in the erasing of his own capacity for making authoritative statements—indeed, in his apparent unlearning of the very technique by which what we call statements are *formed*—that Mallarmé sought to define the historical, even the political interest of his career" (Bersani, *The Freudian Body* 25; the words from "unlocatable" to "authority" also appear in *Death* 45, except that "performance" is there "activity"). The gaps in this reading that my chapter addresses are, first, the unspecified location where "interest" inheres (the "in" of "in the erasing") and, second, the undefined dialectic that generates definition out of the negations "erasing" and "unlearning."

9. Marjorie Levinson explores and deconstructs the pun on frieze-freeze-frees in order to bring Keats's depths to the surface and to remake his "Ideas" into "a conceptual physics" (*Keats's Life of Allegory* 105–6, and see also 130, 133, 140, and 175 on ideas and Ideas). Ultimately, I suggest, her materialism cannot be distinguished from a properly dynamic formalism, such as her title word "allegory" designates.

10. Bryson's book, *Looking at the Overlooked*, considers at length the implications of a kind of painting that suppresses narrative (see especially 60–95) and also contains a section (145–55) on some still life paintings with hazy scriptural scenes in the background, where "transcendental truth does not belong to the realm of the visible" (150).

11. "Le différend, la *différance* entre Dionysos et Apollon, entre l'élan et la structure, ne s'efface pas dans l'histoire car elle n'est pas *dans* l'histoire. Elle est aussi, en un sens insolite, une structure originaire: l'ouverture de l'histoire, l'historicité elle-même" (The dispute, the *differance* between Dionysus and Apollo, between thrust and structure, is not erased in history because it isn't *in* history. It too is, in

an unaccustomed sense, an originary structure: the opening of history, historicity itself; Derrida, "Force et signification" 47). Missing from Hegel's accounts of form and force—particularly the relatively accessible, but highly segmented presentation in the *Enzyklopädie*, sections 131–38—is the history-begetting thrust that inspires Keats and Derrida.

Works Cited

Aarsleff, Hans. *From Locke to Saussure: Essays on the Study of Language and Intellectual History.* Minneapolis: University of Minneapolis Press, 1982.

Abert, Hermann. *W. A. Mozart.* 3 vols. Leipzig: Breitkopf und Härtel, 1956.

Abrams, Meyer H. *The Mirror and the Lamp: Romantic Theory and the Critical Tradition.* New York: Oxford University Press, 1953.

———. *Natural Supernaturalism.* New York: Norton, 1971.

Adorno, Theodor. "Fragment über Musik und Sprache." In *Gesammelte Schriften.* Ed. Gretel Adorno and Rolf Tiedemann. Vol. 16. Frankfurt am Main: Suhrkamp, 1978. 251–56.

———. "Versuch über Wagner." In *Die musikalischen Monographien. Gesammelte Schriften.* Ed. Gretel Adorno and Rolf Tiedemann. Vol. 13. Frankfurt am Main: Suhrkamp, 1971. 7–148.

Adorno, Theodor, and Max Horkheimer. *Dialectic of Enlightenment.* Trans. John Cumming. New York: Seabury, 1972.

Alquié, Ferdinand. "Une Lecture cartésienne de la Critique de la raison pure est-elle possible?" *Revue de métaphysique et de morale* 80 (1975): 145–55.

Altieri, Charles. "The Qualities of Action: A Theory of Middles in Literature." *Boundary 2* 5 (1976–77): 323–50, 899–917.

Anderson, Benedict. *Imagined Communities.* London: Verso, 1991.

Antal, Frederick. "Remarks on the Method of Art History." *Burlington Magazine* 91 (1949): 49–52, 73–75.

Arendt, Hannah. *On Revolution.* New York: Viking, 1963.

Aubin, Robert A. *Topographical Poetry in XVIII-Century England.* New York: Modern Language Association of America, 1936.

Auerbach, Erich. *Dante als Dichter der irdischen Welt.* Berlin: de Gruyter, 1929.

———. *Mimesis: The Representation of Reality in Western Literature.* Trans. Willard Trask. Garden City, N.Y.: Doubleday, 1957.

———. *Scenes from the Drama of European Literature.* Trans. Ralph Manheim and Catherine Garvin. New York: Meridian, 1959.

Austen, Jane. *Pride and Prejudice*. Vol. 2 of *The Novels of Jane Austen*. Ed. R. W. Chapman. London: Oxford University Press, 1933.

Bacchelli, Riccardo. *Rossini e saggi musicali*. Milan: Mondadori, 1968.

Banfield, Ann. *Unspeakable Sentences: Narration and Representation in the Language of Fiction*. Boston: Routledge and Kegan Paul, 1982.

Barié, G. E. "Du 'cogito' cartésien au moi transcendental." *Revue philosophique de la France et de l'étranger* 141 (1951): 211–27.

Barnouw, Jeffrey. "Erziehung des Menschengeschlechts: Die Formierung bürgerlichen Bewußtseins (Voltaire, Johnson, Lessing)." In *Propyläen Geschichte der Literatur*. Ed. Erika Wischer. 6 vols. Berlin: Propyläen, 1981–84. 4: 11–39.

Barthes, Roland. *Le Degré zéro de l'écriture, suivi de: Elements de sémiologie*. Paris: Gonthier, 1969.

———. *Mythologies*. Paris: Seuil, 1970.

———. *L'Obvie et l'obtus*. Paris: Seuil, 1982.

———. *S/Z: An Essay*. Trans. Richard Miller. New York: Hill and Wang, 1974.

Bass, Bernard, and Armand Zaloszyc. *Descartes et les fondements de la psychanalyse*. [Paris]: Navarin-Osiris, 1988.

Baudelaire, Charles. *Les Fleurs du mal*. Ed. Antoine Adam. Paris: Garnier, 1961.

Bazerman, Charles. *Shaping Written Knowledge: Essays in the Growth, Form, Function, and Implications of the Scientific Article*. Madison: University of Wisconsin Press, 1988.

Béguin, Albert. *L'Ame romantique et le rêve*. 2 vols. Marseilles: Cahiers du sud, 1937.

Behler, Ernst. "Die Auffassung der Revolution in der deutschen Romantik." In *Studien zur Romantik und zur idealistischen Philosophie*. Paderborn: Schöningh, 1988. 66–85.

Benveniste, Emile. "Nature du signe linguistique." In *Problèmes de linguistique générale*. Paris: Gallimard, 1966. 49–55.

Berger, Harry, Jr. "The *Mutabilitie Cantos*: Archaism and Evolution in Retrospect." In *Revisionary Play: Studies in the Spenserian Dynamics*. Berkeley: University of California Press, 1988. 243–73.

Bersani, Leo. *The Death of Stéphane Mallarmé*. Cambridge: Cambridge University Press, 1982.

———. *The Freudian Body*. New York: Columbia University Press, 1986.

Besset, Maurice. *Novalis et la pensée mystique*. Paris: Aubier, 1947.

Blanchot, Maurice. *Le Livre à venir*. Paris: Gallimard, 1971.

———. "The Main Impropriety." Trans. June Guicharnaud. In *Literature and Revolution*. Ed. Jacques Ehrmann. Boston: Beacon, 1970. 50–63.

Bloomfield, Robert. *Remains*. Ed. J. Weston. 2 vols. London: Baldwin, Cradock, and Joy, 1824.

Bockelmann, Walter. *Die Grundbegriffe der Kunstbetrachtung bei Wölfflin und Dvorák*. Dresden: Baensch Stiftung, 1938.

Bouillier, Francisque. *Histoire de la philosophie cartésienne.* 2 vols. Paris: Delgrave, 1868.

Bourdieu, Pierre. *The Field of Cultural Production: Essays on Art and Literature.* Ed. Randal Johnson. New York: Columbia University Press, 1993.

———. *In Other Words: Essays Towards a Reflexive Sociology.* Trans. Matthew Adamson. Stanford: Stanford University Press, 1990.

Brands, Hartmut. *"Cogito ergo sum": Interpretation von Kant bis Nietzsche.* Freiburg: Alber, 1982.

Braudel, Fernand. *On History.* Trans. Sarah Matthews. Chicago: University of Chicago Press, 1980.

Brisman, Leslie. *Milton's Poetry of Choice and Its Romantic Heirs.* Ithaca: Cornell University Press, 1973.

———. *Romantic Origins.* Ithaca: Cornell University Press, 1978.

Brooke-Rose, Christine. "The Squirm of the True: An Essay in Non-Methodology," "The Squirm of the True: A Structural Analysis of Henry James's *The Turn of the Screw*," and "Surface Structure in Narrative: The Squirm of the True, Part III." *PTL: A Journal for Descriptive Poetics and Theory* 1 (1976): 265–94, 513–46, and 2 (1977): 517–62.

Brown, Marshall. "Humboldt and the Mediation Between Self and World." *Genre* 6 (1973): 121–41.

———. "Plan vs. Plot: Chapter Symmetries and the Mission of Form." *Stanford Literature Review* 4 (1987): 103–36.

———. *Preromanticism.* Stanford: Stanford University Press, 1991.

———. Review of John Daverio, *Nineteenth-Century Music and the German Romantic Ideology.* In *Nineteenth-Century Music* 18 (1995): 290–303.

Brown, Norman O. *Life Against Death.* Middletown, Conn.: Wesleyan University Press, 1959.

Bruns, Gerald L. *Inventions: Writing, Textuality, and Understanding in Literary History.* New Haven: Yale University Press, 1982.

Bryson, Norman. "Chardin and the Text of Still Life." *Critical Inquiry* 15 (1989): 227–52.

———. *Looking at the Overlooked: Four Essays on Still Life Painting.* Cambridge, Mass.: Harvard University Press, 1990.

Buffon [Georges-Louis le Clerc]. *Oeuvres philosophiques.* Ed. Jean Piveteau. Paris: Presses universitaires de France, 1954.

Burckhardt, Jacob. *Force and Freedom: Reflections on History.* Trans. James Hastings Nicols. New York: Pantheon, 1943.

———. *Gesammelte Werke.* 10 vols. Basel: B. Schwabe, 1955–59.

———. *Jacob Burckhardt und Heinrich Wölfflin: Briefwechsel und andere Dokumente ihrer Begegnung.* Ed. Joseph Gantner. Basel: B. Schwabe, 1948.

Burger, André. "Phonématique et diachronie: A propos de la palatalisation des consonnes romanes." In *A Geneva School Reader in Linguistics*. Ed. Robert Godel. Bloomington: Indiana University Press, 1969. 218–31.

Burke, Kenneth. *A Rhetoric of Motives*. Berkeley: University of California Press, 1969.

——. "Symbolic Action in a Poem by Keats." In *A Grammar of Motives*. New York: George Braziller, 1955. 447–64.

Butler, Marilyn. *Romantics, Rebels and Reactionaries: English Literature and Its Background, 1760–1830*. Oxford: Oxford University Press, 1981.

Butor, Michel. "Claude Monet ou le monde renversé." *Art de France* 3 (1963): 277–301.

Cage, John. *Silence*. Middletown: Wesleyan University Press, 1961.

Cahné, Pierre Alain. *Un Autre Descartes: Le Philosophe et son langage*. Paris: Vrin, 1980.

Carlini, A. "Grundeigenschaften des Geistesaktes als Selbstbewußtseins überhaupt." *Logos* 20 (1931): 352–62.

Carlyle, Thomas. *The French Revolution: A History*. New York: Modern Library, 1934.

Cavell, Stanley. "Naughty Orators: Negation of Voice in *Gaslight*." In *Languages of the Unsayable*. Ed. Sanford Budick and Wolfgang Iser. New York: Columbia University Press, 1989. 340–77.

Champigny, Robert. "The Theatrical Aspect of the Cogito." *Review of Metaphysics* 12 (1959): 370–79.

Chekhov, A. P. *Izbrannye sochinenia*. 2 vols. Moscow: Khudozhestvennaya Literatura, 1979.

Cherbouliez, Antoine-Elisée. "Zur harmonischen Analyse der Einleitung von Mozarts C-Dur Streichquartett (K.V. 465)." In *Bericht über die musikwissenschaftliche Tagung der Internationalen Stiftung Mozarteum in Salzburg*. Ed. Erich Schenk. Leipzig: Breitkopf und Härtel, 1932. 102–11.

Christensen, Jerome. " 'Like a Guilty Thing Surprised': Deconstruction, Coleridge, and the Apostasy of Criticism." *Critical Inquiry* 12 (1986): 769–87.

Clark, T. J. *The Absolute Bourgeois: Artists and Politics in France, 1848–51*. Princeton: Princeton University Press, 1982.

——. *The Painting of Modern Life: Paris in the Art of Manet and His Followers*. New York: Knopf, 1985.

Coleridge, Samuel Taylor. *Biographia Literaria*. Ed. George Watson. New York: Dutton, 1956.

——. *Complete Works*. Ed. William Greenough Thayer Shedd. 7 vols. New York: Harper and Brothers, 1854–56.

——. *Notebooks*. Vols. 1–2. Ed. Kathleen Coburn. New York: Pantheon, 1957.

——. *Poems*. Ed. E. H. Coleridge. London: Oxford University Press, 1935.

——. *The Statesman's Manual*. In *Lay Sermons*. Ed. R. J. White. Princeton: Princeton University Press, 1972.

——. *The Watchman*. Ed. Lewis Patton. Princeton: Princeton University Press, 1970.

Collingwood, R. G. *The Idea of History*. Ed. T. M. Knox. London: Oxford University Press, 1956.

Compagnon, Antoine. *La Troisième république des lettres, de Flaubert à Proust*. Paris: Seuil, 1983.

Cone, Edward T. *The Composer's Voice*. Berkeley: University of California Press, 1974.

——. "Three Ways of Reading a Detective Story—or a Brahms Intermezzo." *Georgia Review* 31 (1977): 554–75.

Congreve, William. *Comedies*. Ed. Bonamy Dobrée. London: Oxford University Press, 1969.

Conrad, Joseph. *The Secret Sharer*. In *'Twixt Land and Sea*. Vol. 19 of his *Complete Works*. New York: Doubleday, 1924. 91–145.

Cook, Albert S. *History/Writing: The Theory and Practice of History in Antiquity and in Modern Times*. Cambridge: Cambridge University Press, 1988.

——. "The Wilderness of Mirrors." In *Dimensions of the Sign in Art*. Hanover, N.H.: Brown University Press / University Press of New England, 1989. 62–83.

Cowley, Abraham. *Poems*. Ed. Alfred Rayney Waller. Cambridge: Cambridge University Press, 1905.

Croce, Benedetto. *Nuovi saggi di estetica*. Bari: Laterza, 1948.

Croll, Morris W. *"Attic" and "Baroque" Prose Style*. Ed. J. Max Patrick and Robert O. Evans. Princeton: Princeton University Press, 1966.

Culler, Jonathan. "The Uses of *Madame Bovary*." *Diacritics* 11.3 (1981): 74–81.

Curran, Stuart. *Shelley's Annus Mirabilis: The Maturing of an Epic Vision*. San Marino, Cal.: Huntington Library, 1975.

Dalhaus, Carl. "Emanzipation der Dissonanz." In *Schönberg und andere*. Mainz: Schott, 1978. 146–53.

——. *Nineteenth-Century Music*. Trans. J. Bradford Robinson. Berkeley: University of California Press, 1989.

Davies, Sir John. *The Poems of Sir John Davies*. Ed. Robert Krueger. Oxford: Clarendon Press, 1975. 87–126.

Delalande, François. "L'Analyse des conduites musicales: Une Étape de programme sémiologique." *Semiotica* 66 (1987): 99–107.

de Man, Paul. *Allegories of Reading*. New Haven: Yale University Press, 1979.

——. "Hölderlin et Heidegger." *Critique* no. 100–101 (Sept.–Oct. 1955): 800–19.

——. "Mallarmé, Yeats, and the Post-Romantic Predicament." Harvard diss., 1960.

——. *The Rhetoric of Romanticism*. New York: Columbia University Press, 1984.

——. "The Rhetoric of Temporality." In *Interpretation: Theory and Practice*. Ed.

Charles S. Singleton. Baltimore: Johns Hopkins University Press, 1969. 173–209.

Derrida, Jacques. "Cogito et histoire de la folie." In *L'Ecriture et la différence*. Paris: Seuil, 1967. 51–97.

———. *Dissemination*. Trans. Barbara Johnson. Chicago: University of Chicago Press, 1981.

———. "Le Facteur de la vérité." *Poétique* 21 (1975): 96–147.

———. "Force et signification." In *L'Ecriture et la différence*. Paris: Seuil, 1979. 9–49.

———. *Glas*. Paris: Galilée, 1974.

———. "Living On: Border Lines." In *Deconstruction and Criticism*. Ed. Harold Bloom, et al. New York: Continuum, 1984. 75–176.

———. *Memoires: For Paul de Man*. Trans. Cecile Lindsay, Jonathan Culler, and Eduardo Cadava. New York: Columbia University Press, 1986.

———. "No Apocalypse, Not Now (full speed ahead, seven missiles, seven missives)." Trans. Catherine Porter and Philip Lewis. *Diacritics* 14.2 (Summer, 1984): 20–31.

———. "The Supplement of Copula: Philosophy *Before* Linguistics." Trans. James Creech and Josué Harari. *Georgia Review* 30 (1976): 527–64.

———. "Tympan." In *Marges de la philosophie*. Paris: Minuit, 1972. i–xxv.

———. *La Voix et le phénomène*. Paris: Presses Universitaires de France, 1972.

———. "White Mythology." Trans. F. C. T. Moore. *New Literary History* 6 (1974): 3–74.

Derrida, Jacques, and Christie V. McDonald. "Choreographies." *Diacritics* 12.2 (Summer, 1982): 66–76.

Descartes, René. *Correspondance*. Ed. C. Adam and B. Milhaud. 8 vols. Paris: Alcan, 1936–63.

———. *Discours de la Méthode: Texte et commentaire*. Ed. Etienne Gilson. Paris: J. Vrin, 1947.

———. *Discourse on Method and Other Writings*. Trans. F. E. Sutcliffe. Baltimore: Penguin, 1968.

———. *Meditationes de prima philosophia. Méditations métaphysiques*. Ed. Geneviève Rodis-Lewis. Paris: Vrin, 1978.

———. *Oeuvres*. Ed. Charles Adam and Paul Tannery. 13 vols. Paris: Cerf, 1897–1913.

———. *Oeuvres philosophiques*. Ed. Ferdinand Alquié. 3 vols. Paris: Garnier, 1963–73.

Dickens, Charles. *Bleak House*. Ed. George Ford and Sylvère Monod. New York: Norton, 1977.

Dirscherl, Klaus. "Stillosigkeit als Stil: Du Bos, Marivaux und Rousseau auf dem Weg zu einer empfindsamen Poetik." In *Stil: Geschichten und Funktionen eines kulturwissenschaftlichen Diskurselements*. Ed. Hans Ulrich Gumbrecht. Frankfurt am Main: Suhrkamp, 1986. 144–54.

Donington, Robert. *Wagner's "Ring" and Its Symbols*. London: Faber and Faber, 1963.

Dryden, John. *Oedipus*. In *The Works of John Dryden*. Ed. Walter Scott. London: William Miller, 1808. 6: 117–225.

———. *The Works of John Dryden*. Ed. Edward Niles Hooker and H. T. Swedenberg, Jr. 18 vols. to date. Berkeley: University of California Press, 1956–.

Dubrow, Heather. Letter to the Forum. *PMLA* 109 (1994): 1025–26.

Edelman, Nathan. "The Mixed Metaphor in Descartes." *Romanic Review* 41 (1950): 167–78.

Edmundson, Mark. *Literature Against Philosophy: A Defence of Poetry*. Cambridge, Eng.: Cambridge University Press, 1995.

Eliot, George. *The Mill on the Floss*. Boston: Estes and Lauriat, n.d.

Elster, Ernst. *Prinzipien der Litteraturwissenschaft*. 2 vols. Halle an der Saale: Niemeyer, 1897–1911.

Empson, William. *The Structure of Complex Words*. Ann Arbor: University of Michigan Press, 1967.

Epstein, David. *Beyond Orpheus: Studies in Musical Structure*. Cambridge, Mass.: MIT Press, 1979.

Escal, Françoise. "Roland Barthes: Fragments d'un discours sur la musique." *Semiotica* 66 (1987): 57–68.

Evans, Colin H. "Conflict and Dualism in Taine and Taine Criticism." In *Gallica: Essays Presented to J. Heywood Thomas*. Cardiff: University of Wales Press, 1969. 165–81.

Faguet, Emile. "Taine." In *Politiques et moralistes du dix-neuvième siècle*. Vol. 3. Paris: Société française d'imprimerie et de librairie, n.d. 237–314.

Febvre, Lucien. *"A New Kind of History" and Other Essays*. Ed. Peter Burke. Trans. K. Folca. New York: Harper and Row, 1973.

———. *La Terre et l'évolution humaine: Introduction géographique à l'histoire*. 1922; Paris: Albin Michel, 1970.

Fechner, Gustav. *Vorschule der Ästhetik*. 2 vols. Leipzig: Breitkopf und Härtel, 1876.

Felman, Shoshana. "Turning the Screws of Interpretation." *Yale French Studies*, no. 55 / 56 (1977): 94–207.

Ferrari, Jean. *Les Sources françaises de la philosophie de Kant*. Paris: Klincksieck, 1979.

Fichte, Johann Gottlieb. *Die Bestimmung des Menschen*. In *Sämmtliche Werke*. 8 vols. Ed. Immanuel Hermann Fichte. Berlin: Veit, 1845–46. 2: 167–319.

Fiedler, Conrad. *Schriften über Kunst*. Ed. Hans Marbach. Leipzig: S. Hirzel, 1896.

Finke, Michael. "Chekhov's 'Steppe': A Metapoetic Journey." *Russian Language Journal* 39 (1985): 79–120.

Fish, Stanley. "Consequences." *Critical Inquiry* 11 (1985): 433–58.

Fitzgerald, Gerald. "*Cenodoxus* and Baroque Latin." Harvard diss., 1963.

Flesch, William. *Generosity and the Limits of Authority: Shakespeare, Herbert, Milton*. Ithaca: Cornell University Press, 1992.

Fletcher, Angus. "On Two Words in the Libretto of *The Magic Flute*." *Georgia Review* 29 (1975): 128–53.

———. *The Prophetic Moment: An Essay on Spenser*. Chicago: University of Chicago Press, 1971.

———. *The Transcendental Masque*. Ithaca: Cornell University Press, 1971.

Flores, Ralph. "Cartesian Strip-Tease." In *The Rhetoric of Doubtful Authority: Deconstructive Readings of Self-Questioning Narratives, St. Augustine to Faulkner*. Ithaca: Cornell University Press, 1984. 66–87.

Forster, Leonard. *The Temper of Seventeenth-Century German Literature*. London: H. K. Lewis, 1952.

Foucault, Michel. *The Archaeology of Knowledge*. Trans. A. M. Sheridan Smith. New York: Random House, 1972.

———. *The Order of Things*. New York: Pantheon, 1973.

Frankl, Paul. "Der Beginn der Gotik und das allgemeine Problem des Stilbeginnes." In *Festschrift Heinrich Wölfflin*. Munich: H. Schmidt, 1924. 107–25.

Fried, Michael. *Absorption and Theatricality: Painting and Beholder in the Age of Diderot*. Berkeley: University of California Press, 1980.

———. *Three American Painters*. Cambridge, Mass.: Fogg Art Museum, Harvard University, 1965.

Friedman, Geraldine. "The Erotics of Interpretation in Keats's 'Ode on a Grecian Urn': Pursuing the Feminine." *Studies in Romanticism* 32 (1993): 225–43.

Friedrich, Hugo. *Die Struktur der modernen Lyrik: Von Baudelaire bis zur Gegenwart*. Hamburg: Rowohlt, 1956.

Fry, Paul. "History, Existence, and 'To Autumn.' " *Studies in Romanticism* 25 (1986): 211–19.

Frye, Northrop. "The Drunken Boat." In *The Stubborn Structure*. Ithaca: Cornell University Press, 1970. 200–17.

———. *Fearful Symmetry*. Princeton: Princeton University Press, 1969.

Fumerton, Patricia. *Cultural Aesthetics: Renaissance Literature and the Practice of Social Ornament*. Chicago: University of Chicago Press, 1991.

Gadamer, Hans-Georg. *Dialogue and Dialectic*. Trans. P. Christopher Smith. New Haven: Yale University Press, 1980.

———. *Wahrheit und Methode: Grundzüge einer philosophischen Hermeneutik*. Tübingen: Mohr, 1960.

Gallagher, Catherine. "Marxism and the New Historicism." In *The New Historicism*. Ed. H. Aram Veeser. New York: Routledge, 1989. 37–48.

Gaskell, Philip. "*Night and Day*: Development of a Play Text." In *Textual Criticism and Literary Interpretation*. Ed. Jerome J. McGann. 162–79.

Gasparov, B. M. "Nekotorye deskriptivnye problemy muzykalnoi semantiki." *Trudy po znakovym sistemam* 8 (1977): 120–37.

Genette, Gérard. *Mimologiques*. Paris: Seuil, 1976.

Gilson, Etienne. *Etudes sur le rôle de la pensée médiévale dans la formation du système cartésien*. Paris: Vrin, 1951.

Giraud, Victor. *Essai sur Taine: Son oeuvre et son influence*. Paris: Hachette, 1932.

———. *Hippolyte Taine: Etudes et documents*. Paris: Vrin, 1928.

Goethe, Johann Wolfgang. *Faust*. Trans. Walter Arndt. New York: Norton, 1976.

———. *Neue Gesamtausgabe der Werke und Schriften*. 22 vols. Stuttgart: Cotta, 1950–68.

Goldberg, Jonathan. *Endlesse Worke: Spenser and the Structures of Discourse*. Baltimore: Johns Hopkins University Press, 1981.

———. *James I and the Politics of Literature: Jonson, Shakespeare, Donne, and Their Contemporaries*. Stanford: Stanford University Press, 1989.

Goldsmith, Oliver. *The Collected Works of Oliver Goldsmith*. 5 vols. Ed. Arthur Friedman. Oxford: Clarendon Press. 1966.

Gombrich, E. H. *Norm and Form: Studies in the Art of the Renaissance*. London: Phaidon, 1966.

Götz, Johann Nikolaus. *Vermischte Gedichte*. Ed. Karl Wilhelm Ramler. 3 vols. Mannheim: Schwan, 1785.

Gouhier, Henri. *Essais sur Descartes*. Paris: Vrin, 1949.

Gourmont, Remy de. *Le Problème du style*. Paris: Mercure de France, n.d.

Granger, Gilles-Gaston. *Essai d'une philosophie du style*. Paris: Odile Jacob, 1988.

Grau, Kurt Joachim. *Die Entwicklung des Bewusstseinsbegriffes im XVII. und XVIII. Jahrhundert*. Halle: Niemeyer, 1916.

Greenblatt, Stephen. *Learning to Curse: Essays in Early Modern Culture*. New York: Routledge, 1990.

———. "Loudun and London." *Critical Inquiry* 12 (1986): 326–46.

———. *Renaissance Self-Fashioning: From More to Shakespeare*. Chicago: University of Chicago Press, 1980.

———. *Shakespearian Negotiations: The Circulation of Social Energy in Renaissance England*. Berkeley: University of California Press, 1988.

Greene, Thomas. "Ben Jonson and the Centered Self." *Studies in English Literature* 10 (1970): 325–48.

———. "The Flexibility of the Self in Renaissance Literature." In *The Disciplines of Criticism*. Ed. Peter Demetz, Thomas Greene, and Lowry Nelson. New Haven: Yale University Press, 1968. 241–64.

Grene, Marjorie. *Descartes*. Brighton: Harvester, 1985.

Griffin, Robert J. "Wordsworth's Pope: The Language of His Former Heart." *ELH* 54 (1987): 695–715.

Gryphius, Andreas. *Werke*. 3 vols. Ed. Hermann Palm. Darmstadt: Wissenschaftliche Buchgesellschaft, 1961.

Guillaume, Gustave. "Existe-t-il un déponent en français?" In *Langage et science du langage*. Paris: Nizet, 1964. 127–42.

Guillory, John. "Canonical and Non-Canonical: A Critique of the Current Debate." *ELH* 54 (1987): 483–517.

Guizot, [François]. *Cours d'histoire moderne.* No publication information.

Gumbrecht, Hans Ulrich. "Schwindende Stabilität der Wirklichkeit: Eine Geschichte des Stilbegriffs." In *Stil: Geschichten und Funktionen eines kulturwissenschaftlichen Diskurselements.* Ed. H. U. Gumbrecht. Frankfurt am Main: Suhrkamp, 1986. 726–88.

Gusdorf, Georges. *Les Principes de la pensée au siècle des lumières.* Paris: Payot, 1971.

Halpern, Richard. *The Poetics of Primitive Accumulation: English Renaissance Culture and the Genealogy of Capital.* Ithaca: Cornell University Press, 1991.

Hardy, Thomas. *An Autobiography.* Ed. Michael Sadleir. London: Oxford University Press, 1953.

———. *The Life and Work of Thomas Hardy.* Ed. Michael Millgate. Athens: University of Georgia Press, 1985.

———. *Tess of the D'Urbervilles.* Ed. Scott Elledge. New York: Norton, 1965.

Hartman, Geoffrey H. "The Voice of the Shuttle: Language from the Point of View of Literature." In *Beyond Formalism.* New Haven: Yale University Press, 1970. 337–55.

———. *Wordsworth's Poetry.* New Haven: Yale University Press, 1964.

Hauser, Arnold. *The Philosophy of Art History.* New York: Knopf, 1959.

Haven, Richard. *Patterns of Consciousness.* Amherst: University of Massachusetts Press, 1969.

Hegel, Georg Wilhelm Friedrich. *Enzyklopädie der philosophischen Wissenschaften, 1830.* Ed. Friedhelm Nicolin and Otto Pöggeler. Hamburg: Meiner, 1959.

———. *Phänomenologie des Geistes.* Ed. Johannes Hoffmeister. Hamburg: Meiner, 1952.

———. *Science of Logic.* Trans. A. V. Miller. London: Allen and Unwin, 1969.

———. *Werke.* Ed. Eva Moldenhauer and Karl Markus Michel. 20 vols. Frankfurt am Main: Suhrkamp, 1969–79.

Heidegger, Martin. *An Introduction to Metaphysics.* Trans. Ralph Manheim. New Haven: Yale University Press, 1959.

———. *Nietzsche.* 2 vols. Pfullingen: Neske, 1981.

———. *Nietzsche.* Trans. Frank A. Capuzzi, David Farrell Krell, and Joan Stambaugh. 4 vols. San Francisco: Harper and Row, 1979–87.

Heinse, Wilhelm. *Sämmtliche Werke.* Ed. Carl Schüddekopf. 15 vols. Leipzig: Insel, 1904.

Helgerson, Richard. *Forms of Nationhood: The Elizabethan Writing of England.* Chicago: University of Chicago Press, 1992.

Herder, Johann Gottfried. *Werke.* Ed. Heinrich Düntzer. 24 vols. Berlin: Gustav Hempel, n.d.

Herz, Marcus. *Versuch über den Schwindel.* Berlin: Vossische Buchhandlung, 1791.

Hildebrand, Adolf von. "Über das Vorstellen und das Körpergefühl in der Kunst." In *Gesammelte Schriften zur Kunst*. Ed. Henning Bock. Cologne: Westdeutscher Verlag, 1969. 358–61.

Hill, Aaron. *Works*. 4 vols. London, 1754.

Hils, G. *The Odes of Casimire*. 1646; Rpt. without Hils's introduction. Ed. Maren-Sofie Røstvig. Los Angeles: Augustan Reprint Society, 1953.

Hintikka, Jaakko. " 'Cogito, Ergo Sum': Inference or Performance?" In *Knowledge and the Known: Historical Perspectives in Epistemology*. Dordrecht: Reidel, 1974. 98–125.

Hoffmann, E. T. A. *Betrachtungen über Musik*. Ed. Walter Florian. Stuttgart: P. O. Rohm, 1947.

——. *Schriften zur Musik*. Ed. Friedrich Schnapp. Munich: Winkler, 1963.

Hofmannsthal, Hugo von. *Ausgewählte Werke*. 2 vols. Ed. Rudolf Hirsch. Frankfurt am Main: Fischer, 1957.

Hollahan, Eugene. *Crisis-Consciousness and the Novel*. Newark: University of Delaware Press, 1992.

Holly, Michael Ann. "Wölfflin and the Imagining of the Baroque." In *Visual Culture: Images and Interpretations*. Ed. Norman Bryson, Michael Ann Holly, and Keith Moxey. Hanover, N.H.: Wesleyan University Press, 1994. 347–64.

Homans, Margaret. "Eliot, Wordsworth, and the Scenes of Critical Instruction." *Critical Inquiry* 8 (1981): 223–41.

Howarth, Herbert. *The Tiger's Heart*. New York: Oxford University Press, 1970.

Hucks, Joseph. *Poems*. Cambridge: Deighton, 1798.

Hughes, John. *Poetical Works*. 2 vols. Edinburgh: Apollo, 1779.

Hume, David. *A Treatise of Human Nature*. Garden City, N.Y.: Doubleday, 1961.

Hungerford, E. B. *Shores of Darkness*. New York: Columbia University Press, 1941.

Husserl, Edmund. *Cartesianische Meditationen*. Ed. Elisabeth Ströker. Hamburg: Meiner, 1987.

——. *Die Krisis der europäischen Wissenschaften und die transzendentale Phänomenologie*. Ed. Elisabeth Ströker. Hamburg: Meiner, 1982.

Iser, Wolfgang. *The Act of Reading: A Theory of Aesthetic Response*. Trans. David Henry Wilson. Baltimore: Johns Hopkins University Press, 1978.

Jacobus, Mary. "The Art of Managing Books: Romantic Prose and the Writing of the Past." In *Romanticism and Language*. Ed. Arden Reed. Ithaca: Cornell University Press, 1984. 205–46.

——. "The Question of Language: Men of Maxims and *The Mill on the Floss*." *Critical Inquiry* 8 (1981): 207–22.

James, Henry. *Partial Portraits*. Westport, Conn.: Greenwood, 1970.

——. *The Turn of the Screw*. In *The Complete Tales of Henry James*. Ed. Leon Edel.

Philadelphia: Lippincott, 1961–64. 10: 15–138.

Jameson, Fredric. *Fables of Aggression: Wyndham Lewis, the Modernist as Fascist.* Berkeley: University of California Press, 1979.

———. *Marxism and Form: Twentieth-Century Dialectical Theories of Literature.* Princeton: Princeton University Press, 1971.

———. *The Political Unconscious.* Ithaca: Cornell University Press, 1981.

———. *Sartre: The Origins of a Style.* New Haven: Yale University Press, 1961.

Jankélévitch, Vladimir. *Fauré et l'inexprimable.* Paris: Plon, 1974.

———. *La Vie et la mort dans la musique de Debussy.* Neuchâtel: La Baconnière, 1968.

Johnson, Douglas Porter. *Beethoven's Sketches in the "Fischhof Miscellany," Berlin Autograph 28.* 2 vols. Ann Arbor, Mich.: UMI Research Press, 1980.

Jonson, Ben. *The Complete Masques.* Ed. Stephen Orgel. Vol. 4 of *The Yale Ben Jonson.* New Haven: Yale University Press, 1969.

Joyce, James. *Dubliners.* Ed. Robert Scholes and A. Walton Litz. New York: Viking, 1969.

———. *Exiles.* New York: Viking, 1961.

———. *Letters of James Joyce.* Ed. Richard Ellmann. Vol. 2. London: Faber and Faber, 1966.

Judovitz, Dalia. *Subjectivity and Representation in Descartes: The Origins of Modernity.* Cambridge: Cambridge University Press, 1988.

Juglar, Louis. *Le Style dans les arts et sa signification historique.* Paris: Hachette, 1901.

Justi, Carl. *Diego Velázquez and His Times.* Trans. A. H. Keane. London: Grevel, 1889.

Kant, Immanuel. *Briefwechsel.* Vol. 10 of *Kants gesammelte Schriften.* Berlin: Walter de Gruyter, 1922.

———. *Critique of Pure Reason.* Trans. Norman Kemp Smith. London: Macmillan, 1929.

———. *Gesammelte Schriften.* 29 vols. Berlin: G. Reimer, 1910–70.

———. *Werke.* 6 vols. Ed. Wilhelm Weischedel. Wiesbaden: Insel, 1956–64.

Karbusicky, Vladimir. "Zeichen und Musik." *Zeitschrift für Musik* 9 (1987): 227–49.

Kayser, Wolfgang. "Der Stilbegriff der Literaturwissenschaft." In *Die Vortragsreise.* Berne: Francke, 1958. 71–81.

Keats, John. *The Poems of John Keats.* Ed. Jack Stillinger. Cambridge, Mass.: Harvard University Press, 1978.

Kehr, Theodor. *Das Bewusstseinsproblem.* Tübingen: Mohr, 1916.

Keller, Wilhelm. "Die Modulationen in Mozarts Fantasie KV 475." In *Festschrift Erich Valentin.* Ed. Gunther Weiss. Regensburg: G. Bosse, 1976. 79–88.

Kemmerling, Andreas. "Eine reflexive Deutung des Cogito." In *Theorie der Subjektivität.* Ed. Konrad Cramer, et al. Frankfurt am Main: Suhrkamp, 1987.

Kenner, Hugh. "The Most Beautiful Book." *ELH* 48 (1981): 594–605.

Kerman, Joseph. *The Beethoven Quartets.* New York: Knopf, 1967.

Kermode, Frank. *The Art of Telling: Essays on Fiction*. Cambridge, Mass.: Harvard University Press, 1983.

——. "The Dancer." In *The Romantic Image*. London: Collins, 1971. 62–106.

Kerrigan, William, and Gordon Braden. *The Idea of the Renaissance*. Baltimore: Johns Hopkins University Press, 1989.

Kleinbauer, W. Eugene. *Modern Perspectives in Art History*. New York: Holt, Rinehart and Winston, 1971.

Kleist, Heinrich von. *Sämtliche Werke und Briefe*. Ed. Helmut Sembdner. 2 vols. Munich: Hanser, 1984.

Knight, G. Wilson. *The Starlit Dome: Studies in the Poetry of Vision*. London: Oxford University Press, 1971.

Koselleck, Reinhart. *Futures Past*. Trans. Keith Tribe. Cambridge, Mass.: MIT Press, 1985.

——. *Kritik und Krise: Eine Studie zur Pathogenese der bürgerlichen Welt*. Frankfurt am Main: Suhrkamp, 1973.

Krebs, Harold. "Alternatives to Monotonality in Early Nineteenth-Century Music." *Journal of Music Theory* 25 (1981): 1–15.

Kronik, John. "The Web, the Hive, and the Looking Glass: Self-Consciousness in Hispanic Literature." Mid-America Conference on Hispanic Literature. University of Colorado, Boulder, October 3, 1986.

Kümmel, Friedrich. *Platon und Hegel: Zur ontologischen Begründung des Zirkels in der Erkenntnis*. Tübingen: Niemeyer, 1968.

Lamb, Charles. *The Works of Charles and Mary Lamb*. Ed. E. V. Lucas. 1903; New York: AMS Press, 1968.

Lang, Berel. "Descartes and the Art of Meditation." *Philosophy and Rhetoric* 21 (1988): 19–37.

——. "Looking for the Styleme." *Critical Inquiry* 9 (1982): 405–13.

——. "Style as Instrument, Style as Person." *Critical Inquiry* 4 (1978): 715–39.

Lasky, Melvin J. *Utopia and Revolution*. Chicago: University of Chicago Press, 1976.

Leduc, A. G. "Ueber den Aufsatz des Herrn Fetis." *Allegemeine musikalische Zeitung* 32 (1830): 117–32.

Lefèvre, Roger. *La Pensée existentielle de Descartes*. N.p.: Bordas, 1965.

Lentricchia, Frank. "Foucault's Legacy: A New Historicism?" In *The New Historicism*. Ed. H. Aram Veeser. New York: Routledge, 1989. 231–42.

Leonardi, Susan J. "Recipes for Reading: Summer Pasta, Lobster à la Riseholme, and Key Lime Pie." *PMLA* 104 (1989): 340–47.

Lévesque, Claude, and Christie V. McDonald, eds. *L'Oreille de l'autre: Textes et débats avec Jacques Derrida*. Montreal: VLB, 1982.

Levinson, Marjorie. *Keats's Life of Allegory: The Origins of a Style*. Oxford: Blackwell, 1988.

——. *Wordsworth's Great Period Poems*. Cambridge: Cambridge University Press, 1986.

Lévi-Strauss, Claude. "Introduction: History and Anthropology." In *Structural Anthropology*. Trans. Claire Jacobson and Brooke Grundfest Schoepf. Garden City, N.Y.: Anchor, 1967. 1–28.

———. *The Savage Mind*. Chicago: University of Chicago Press, 1966.

Lewis, Christopher. "Mirrors and Metaphor: Reflections on Schoenberg and Nineteenth-Century Tonality." *Nineteenth-Century Music* 10 (1987): 229–42.

Lipps, Theodor. *Grundzüge der Logik*. Hamburg: Voss, 1893.

———. "Das Wesen der musikalischen Konsonanz und Dissonanz." In *Psychologische Studien*. Leipzig: Dürr, 1905. 115–230.

Liu, Alan. "The Power of Formalism: The New Historicism." *ELH* 56 (1989): 721–71.

Locke, John. *An Essay Concerning Human Understanding*. Ed. Alexander Campbell Fraser. 2 vols. New York: Dover, 1959.

Lockwood, Thomas. *Post-Augustan Satire: Charles Churchill and Satirical Poetry, 1750–1800*. Seattle: University of Washington Press, 1979.

Lombardo, Patrizia. "Hippolyte Taine Between Art and Science." *Yale French Studies* no. 77 (1990): 117–33.

———. "Taine scrittore." In Hippolyte Taine, *Etienne Mayran*. Ed. Patrizia Lombardo. Milan: Adelphi, 1988. 143–78.

Lovejoy, Arthur O. "On the Discrimination of Romanticisms." In *Essays in the History of Ideas*. New York: Putnam, 1960. 228–53.

Lucente, Gregory. *Beautiful Fables: Self-Consciousness in Italian Narrative from Manzoni to Calvino*. Baltimore: Johns Hopkins University Press, 1986.

Macaulay, Thomas Babington. *Critical and Historical Essays*. 5 vols. Leipzig: Bernhard Tauchnitz, 1850.

MacCaffrey, Isabel G. *Spenser's Allegory: The Anatomy of Imagination*. Princeton: Princeton University Press, 1976.

Macherey, Pierre. *Pour une théorie de la production littéraire*. Paris: Maspero, 1966.

MacLean, Gerald. "What Is a Restoration Poem? Editing a Discourse, Not an Author." *Text* 3 (1986): 319–46.

Major, John M. "The Moralization of the Dance in Elyot's *Governour*." *Studies in the Renaissance* 5 (1958): 27–36.

Mallarmé, Stéphane. *Oeuvres complètes*. Ed. Henri Mondor and G. Jean-Aubry. Paris: Gallimard, 1961.

Manning, Peter J. "The Hone-ing of Byron's Corsair." In *Textual Criticism and Literary Interpretation*. Ed. Jerome J. McGann. 107–26.

Marcus, Leah S. "Renaissance / Early Modern Studies." In *Redrawing the Boundaries: The Transformation of English and American Literary Studies*. New York: The Modern Language Association of America, 1992. 41–63.

Marshall, Donald G. "Ideas and History: The Case of 'Imagination.'" *Boundary 2* 10 (1982): 343–59.

McCorkel, Christine. "Sense and Sensibility: An Epistemological Approach to the Philosophy of Art History." *Journal of Aesthetics and Art Criticism* 34 (1975): 35–50.

McDonald, Christie V. *Dispositions: Quatre essais sur les écrits de Jean-Jacques Rousseau, Stéphane Mallarmé, Marcel Proust et Jacques Derrida.* Québec: Hurtubise, 1986.

McFarland, Thomas. *Coleridge and the Pantheist Tradition.* Oxford: Clarendon Press, 1969.

McGann, Jerome J. *The Beauty of Inflections: Literary Investigations in Historical Method and Theory.* Oxford: Clarendon Press, 1985.

———. *Black Riders: The Visible Language of Modernism.* Princeton: Princeton University Press, 1993.

———. *A Critique of Modern Textual Criticism.* Chicago: University of Chicago Press, 1983.

———. *Fiery Dust: A Study of Byron's Poetic Development.* Chicago: University of Chicago Press, 1968.

———. [Anne Mack, J. J. Rome, and George Mannejc, pseud.] "Literary History, Romanticism, and Felicia Hemans." *Modern Language Quarterly* 54 (1993): 215–35.

———. *The Romantic Ideology: A Critical Investigation.* Chicago: University of Chicago Press, 1983.

———. *Social Values and Poetic Acts: The Historical Judgment of Literary Work.* Cambridge, Mass.: Harvard University Press, 1988.

———. "Some Forms of Critical Discourse." *Critical Inquiry* 11 (1985): 399–417.

———. *Towards a Literature of Knowledge.* Chicago: University of Chicago Press, 1989.

———, ed. *Textual Criticism and Literary Interpretation.* Chicago: University of Chicago Press, 1985.

Meagher, John C. "The Dance and the Masques of Ben Jonson." *Journal of the Warburg and Courtauld Institutes* 25 (1962): 258–77.

Mehrotra, K. K. *Horace Walpole and the English Novel: A Study of the Influence of "The Castle of Otranto," 1764–1820.* Oxford: Basil Blackwell, 1934.

Meinecke, Friedrich. *Historism: The Rise of a New Historical Outlook.* Trans. J. E. Anderson. New York: Herder and Herder, 1972.

Mellor, Anne K. *Romanticism and Gender.* New York: Routledge, 1993.

Meschonnic, Henri. *Pour la poétique.* 5 vols. Paris: Gallimard, 1970–78.

Miles, Josephine. "Wordsworth and Glitter." *Studies in Philology* 40 (1943): 552–59.

Miller, D. A. *Narrative and Its Discontents: Problems of Closure in the Traditional Novel.* Princeton: Princeton University Press, 1981.

Miller, J. Hillis. *Charles Dickens: The World of His Novels.* Bloomington: Indiana University Press, 1969.

——. "The Critic as Host." In *Deconstruction and Criticism*. Ed. Harold Bloom, et al. New York: Continuum, 1979. 217–53.

——. *The Linguistic Moment: From Wordsworth to Stevens*. Princeton: Princeton University Press, 1985.

Miscellany Poems and Translations by Oxford Hands. London: Anthony Stephens, 1685.

Monglond, Henri. *Le Préromantisme français*. 2 vols. Grenoble: Arthaud, 1930.

Murry, J. Middleton. *The Problem of Style*. London: Humphry Milford / Oxford University Press, 1925.

Nancy, Jean-Luc. *Discours de la Syncope*. Vol. 1: *Logodaedalus*. Paris: Flammarion, 1976.

——. *Ego Sum*. Paris: Flammarion, 1979.

Nattiez, Jean-Jacques. *Fondements d'une sémiologie de la musique*. Paris: Union générale d'éditions, 1975.

Naumann, Emil. "Wolfgang Mozart." In *Sammlung Musikalischer Vorträge*. Ed. Paul Graf Waldersee. 6 vols. in 5. Leipzig: Breitkopf und Härtel, 1879–98. 1: 193–211.

Nelson, William. *The Poetry of Edmund Spenser: A Study*. New York: Columbia University Press, 1963.

Nemoianu, Virgil. *The Taming of Romanticism: European Literature and the Age of Biedermeier*. Cambridge, Mass.: Harvard University Press, 1984.

Newcomb, Anthony. "Narrative Archetypes and Mahler's Ninth Symphony." In *Music and Text: Critical Inquiries*. Ed. Steven Paul Scher. Cambridge: Cambridge University Press, 1992. 118–36.

Newsom, Robert. *Dickens on the Romantic Side of Familiar Things*. New York: Columbia University Press, 1977.

Nietzsche, Friedrich Wilhelm. *Also Sprach Zarathustra*. In his *Werke in drei Bänden*. 3 vols. Ed. Karl Schlechta. Munich: Hanser, 1969. 2: 275–561.

Nohl, Herman. *Stil und Weltanschauung*. Jena: Diederichs, 1920.

Nohl, Ludwig. *Mozart: Ein Beitrag zur Aesthetik der Tonkunst*. Heidelberg: Bangel und Schmidt, 1860.

Nordmann, Jean-Thomas. *Taine et la critique scientifique*. Paris: Presses Universitaires de France, 1992.

Norris, John. *A Collection of Miscellanies*. London: E. Parker, 1730.

Novalis [Friedrich von Hardenberg]. *Schriften*. 5 vols. Ed. Paul Kluckhohn, Richard Samuel, and Hans-Joachim Mähl. Stuttgart: Kohlhammer, 1960–75.

Orgel, Stephen. "Shakespeare and the Kinds of Drama." *Critical Inquiry* 6 (1979): 107–23.

Panofsky, Erwin. *Renaissance and Renascences in Western Art*. 2 vols. Stockholm: Almkvist and Wiksell, 1960.

Parker, Patricia A. *Inescapable Romance: Studies in the Poetics of a Mode*. Princeton: Princeton University Press, 1979.

Parnell, Thomas. *Collected Poems*. Ed. Claude Rawson and F. P. Lock. Newark: University of Delaware Press, 1989.

Parsons, Talcott. "Value-Freedom and Objectivity." In *Max Weber and Sociology Today*. Ed. Otto Stammer. Trans. Kathleen Morris. New York: Harper and Row, 1971. 27–82.

Pater, Walter. *Appreciations, with an Essay on Style*. New York: Macmillan, 1905.

Patten, Steven C. "Kant's Cogito." *Kant-Studien* 66 (1975): 331–41.

Patterson, Lee. "The Logic of Textual Criticism and the Way of Genius." In *Textual Criticism and Literary Interpretation*. Ed. Jerome J. McGann. 55–91.

Paz, Octavio. *El Arco y la lira*. Mexico City: Fondo de Cultura Económica, 1967.

Peckham, Morse. *The Triumph of Romanticism*. Columbia: University of South Carolina Press, 1970.

Pfau, Thomas. "Immediacy and the Text: Friedrich Schleiermacher's Theory of Style and Interpretation." *Journal of the History of Ideas* (1990): 51–73.

Pflug, Günther. *Henri Bergson: Quellen und Konsequenzen einer induktiven Metaphysik*. Berlin: de Gruyter, 1959.

Piaget, Jean. *Structuralism*. Ed. and trans. Chaninah Maschler. London: Routledge and Kegan Paul, 1971.

Plato. *Platonis Opera*. Ed. Ioannes Burnet. 5 vols. Oxford: Clarendon Press, 1900–07.

Pope, Alexander. *Poems*. Ed. John Butt. New Haven: Yale University Press, 1963.

Porter, Andrew. *Music of Three Seasons: 1974–77*. New York: Farrar, 1978.

Poulet, Georges. "The Dream of Descartes." In *Studies in Human Time*. Trans. Elliott Coleman. New York: Harper, 1956. 50–73.

——. *Mesure de l'instant*. Paris: Plon, 1968.

Price, Martin. *To the Palace of Wisdom*. Garden City, N.Y.: Doubleday, 1965.

Propp, Vladimir. *Morphology of the Folktale*. Trans. Laurence Scott. Austin: University of Texas Press, 1968.

Proudhon, Pierre-Joseph. *Les Carnets de P.-J. Proudhon*. Ed. Suzanne Henneguy and Jeanne Faure-Fremelet. Vol. 2. Paris: M. Rivière, 1961.

——. *Correspondance de P.-J. Proudhon*. 14 vols. Paris: A. Lacroix, 1875.

——. *De la justice dans la Révolution et dans l'Eglise*. Ed. C. Bouglé and J.-L. Puech. 4 vols. Paris: M. Rivière, 1935.

——. *Du principe de l'art et de sa destination sociale*. Paris: Garnier, 1865.

——. *Les Majorats littéraires*. Paris: E. Dantu, 1863.

——. *Philosophie du progrès*. Brussels: A. Lebègue, 1853.

Proust, Marcel. *A la recherche du temps perdu*. Ed. Pierre Clarac and André Ferré. 3 vols. Paris: Gallimard, 1954.

Pynchon, Thomas. *Slow Learner: Early Stories*. London: Little, Brown, 1985.

Quintero, Vicente. "El 'Cogito' cartesiano en la 'Crítica de la razón pura' de Kant." In *Homenaje a Descartes en el tercer centenario del "Discurso del Método."*

Ed. Luís Juan Guerrero. Buenos Aires: Imprenta de la Universidad, 1937. 2: 335–39.

Ragghianti, Carlo. *L'arte e la critica*. In *Critica d'arte* 45 (Jan.–June 1980).

Rajan, Tilottama. "Displacing Post-Structuralism: Romantic Studies After Paul de Man." *Studies in Romanticism* 24 (1985): 451–74.

Ratner, Leonard. *Classic Music: Expression, Form, and Style*. New York: Schirmer, 1980.

Rawson, C. J. *Henry Fielding and the Augustan Ideal Under Stress*. London: Routledge, 1972.

Redner, Harry. *In the Beginning Was the Deed: Reflections on the Passage of Faust*. Berkeley: University of California Press, 1982.

Rehm, Walther. *Heinrich Wölfflin als Literarhistoriker*. Munich: Bayerische Akademie der Wissenschaften, 1960.

Revel, Jean-François. "Introduction." In Hippolyte Taine, *Philosophie de l'art*. Ed. Jean-François Revel. Paris: Hermann, 1964. 9–19.

Richard, Jean-Pierre. *L'Univers imaginaire de Mallarmé*. Paris: Seuil, 1961.

Romanowski, Sylvie. *L'Illusion chez Descartes*. Paris: Klincksieck, 1974.

Rosen, Charles. *The Classical Style: Haydn, Mozart, Beethoven*. New York: Norton, 1972.

——. *The Romantic Generation*. Cambridge, Mass.: Harvard University Press, 1995.

——. *Schoenberg*. London: Fontana, 1976.

——. *Sonata Forms*. New York: Norton, 1980.

Røstvig, Maren-Sofie. *The Happy Man*. 2 vols. Oslo: Akademisk Vorlag, 1954.

Rouges, Alberto. "La Refutación kantiana del Idealismo problemático: El realismo empírico." In *Homenaje a Descartes en el tercer centenario del "Discurso del Método."* Ed. Luís Juan Guerrero. Buenos Aires: Imprenta de la Universidad, 1937. 3: 161–70.

Rousseau, Jean-Jacques. *Oeuvres complètes*. Ed. Bernard Gagnebin, Robert Osmont, and Marcel Raymond. Vol. 1. Paris: Gallimard, 1959.

Rousset, Jean. *La Littérature de l'âge baroque en France: Circé et le paon*. Paris: José Corti, 1954.

Sainte-Beuve, Charles-Augustin. "Divers écrits de M. Taine." In *Causeries du lundi*. Paris: Garnier, 1926. 13: 249–84.

——. "Histoire de la littérature anglaise, par M. Taine." In *Nouveaux lundis*. Paris: Calmann-Lévy, n.d. 66–137.

Sarbiewski, Matthias Casimirus [Maciej Kazimierz]. *Matthiae Casimiri Sarbievii Carmina*. Argentoratum [=Strasbourg]: Societas Bipontina, Anno XI [=1803].

Saussure, Ferdinand de. *Course in General Linguistics*. Ed. Charles Bally and Albert Sechehaye. Trans. Wade Baskin. New York: McGraw-Hill, 1959.

Schaff, Adam. "Das Verstehen der verbalen Sprache und das 'Verstehen der Musik.'" In *Musik und Verstehen: Aufsätze zur semiotischen Theorie, Ästhetik und*

Soziologie der musikalischen Rezeption. Ed. Peter Faltin and Hans-Peter Reinecke. Cologne: Volk, 1973. 276–88.

Schalk, Fritz. "Zu Taines Theorie und Praxis." In *Beiträge zur Theorie der Künste im 19. Jahrhundert.* Ed. Helmut Koopmann and J. Adolf Schmoll gen. Eisenwerth. 2 vols. Frankfurt am Main: Klostermann, 1971. 1: 352–59.

Schmarsow, August. *Unser Verhältnis zu den bildenden Künsten: Sechs Vorträge über Kunst und Erziehung.* Leipzig: Teubner, 1903.

Schmidt, Gerhart. *Aufklärung und Metaphysik: Die Neubegründung des Wissens durch Descartes.* Tübingen: Niemeyer, 1965.

Schoenberg, Arnold. *Gesammelte Schriften.* Ed. Ivan Vojtech. Frankfurt am Main: Fischer, 1976.

———. *Style and Idea.* Ed. Leonard Stein. New York: St. Martins, 1975.

Scholz, Heinrich. "Über das Cogito, ero sum." *Kant-Studien* 36 (1931): 126–47.

Schor, Naomi. *George Sand and Idealism.* New York: Columbia University Press, 1993.

Schrade, Leo. "Mozart und die Romantiker." In *De Scientia Musicae Studia atque Orationes.* Ed. Ernst Lichtenhahn. Berne: Haupt, 1967. 519–36.

Schulz-Buschhaus, Ulrich. "Taine und die Historizität des Stils." In *Stil: Geschichten und Funktionen eines kulturwissenschaftlichen Diskurselements.* Ed. Hans Ulrich Gumbrecht. Frankfurt am Main: Suhrkamp, 1986. 189–99.

Searle, John. "*Las Meninas* and the Paradoxes of Pictorial Representation." *Critical Inquiry* 6 (1980): 477–88.

Sebeok, Thomas, ed. *Style in Language.* New York: John Wiley and Sons, 1960.

Shell, Marc. "Money and the Mind: The Economics of Translation in Goethe's *Faust.*" *Modern Language Notes* 94 (1980): 516–62.

Shelley, Percy Bysshe. *Shelley's Poetry and Prose.* Ed. Donald H. Reiman and Sharon Powers. New York: Norton, 1977.

Sigmund, Oskar. "Mozarts Phantasie in c-Moll, KV 475." In *Gustav Becking zum Gedächtnis: Eine Auswahl seiner Schriften und Beiträge seiner Schüler.* Ed. Walter Kramolisch. Tutzing: Schneider, 1975. 483–94.

Simpson, David. *Romanticism, Nationalism, and the Revolt Against Theory.* Chicago: University of Chicago Press, 1993.

Snyder, Joel, and Ted Cohen. "Reflexions on *Las Meninas*: Paradox Lost." *Critical Inquiry* 7 (1980): 429–47.

Solie, Ruth. "Whose Life? The Gendered Self in Schumann's *Frauenliebe* Songs." In *Music and Text: Critical Inquiries.* Ed. Steven Paul Scher. Cambridge: Cambridge University Press, 1992. 219–40.

Sollers, Philippe. "Littérature et totalité." In *L'Ecriture et l'expérience des limites.* Paris: Seuil, 1971. 67–87.

Sparrow, John. "Sarbiewski's *Silviludia* and Their Italian Source." *Oxford Slavonic Papers* 8 (1958): 1–48.

Spencer, Herbert. *Philosophy of Style: An Essay.* New York: D. Appleton, 1897.

Spenser, Edmund. *The Faerie Queene*. Ed. J. C. Smith. Oxford: Clarendon, 1909.

Spiegelman, Willard. *Majestic Indolence: English Romantic Poetry and the Work of Art*. New York: Oxford University Press, 1995.

Spinoza, Benedict de. *Chief Works*. Trans. R. H. M. Elwes. 2 vols. London: George Bell and Sons, 1901.

Staiger, Emil. "Entstellte Zitate." In *Die Kunst der Interpretation*. Munich: Deutscher Taschenbuch-Verlag, 1971. 138–54.

Starobinski, Jean. *Blessings in Disguise: Or, the Morality of Evil*. Trans. Arthur Goldhammer. Cambridge, Mass.: Harvard University Press, 1993.

———. *1789: Les Emblèmes de la raison*. Paris: Flammarion, 1973.

Sternberg, Meir. *Temporal Modes and Expositional Ordering in Fiction*. Baltimore: Johns Hopkins University Press, 1978.

Sterne, Laurence. *Tristram Shandy*. Ed. James A. Work. New York: Odyssey, 1940.

Stevens, Wallace. "Adagia." In *Opus Posthumous*. Ed. Samuel French Morse. New York: Random House, 1982. 157–80.

———. *Collected Poems*. New York: Knopf, 1959.

Stevenson, Robert Louis. *The Complete Short Stories*. Ed. Charles Neider. Garden City, N.Y.: Doubleday, 1969.

Stewart, Garrett. *Reading Voices: Literature and the Phonotext*. Berkeley: University of California Press, 1990.

Strauss, Leo. *Natural Right and History*. Chicago: University of Chicago Press, 1953.

Strich, Fritz. *Zu Heinrich Wölfflin's Gedächtnis*. Berne: Francke, 1956.

Svevo, Italo. *La Coscienza di Zeno*. Milan: Dall' Oglio, 1969.

Szondi, Peter. "Das Naive ist das Sentimentalische: Zur Begriffsdialektik in Schillers Abhandlung." In *Schriften*. Ed. Jean Bollack. 2 vols. Frankfurt: Suhrkamp, 1978. 2: 59–105.

Taine, Hippolyte. *L'Ancien régime* (part 1 of *Les Origines de la France contemporaine*). 2 vols. Paris: Hachette, 1899.

———. *De l'intelligence*. 2 vols. Paris: Hachette, 1923.

———. *Derniers essais de critique et d'histoire*. Paris: Hachette, 1923.

———. *Essai sur Tite Live*. Paris: Hachette, 1923.

———. *Esssais de critique et d'histoire*. Paris: Hachette, 1923.

———. *Etienne Mayran: Fragments*. Ed. Paul Bourget. Paris: Hachette, 1910.

———. *Histoire de la littérature anglaise*. 5 vols. Paris: Hachette, 1877 (vols. 1–4), 1873 (vol. 5).

———. *History of English Literature*. Trans. Henri van Laun. 2 vols. New York: A. L. Burt, n.d.

———. *La Fontaine et ses fables*. Paris: Hachette, 1907.

———. *Notes sur l'Angleterre*. Paris: Hachette, 1923.

———. *Notes sur Paris: Vie et opinions de M. Frédéric-Thomas Graindorge*. Paris: Hachette, 1921.

————. *Nouveaux essais de critique et d'histoire*. Paris: Hachette, 1923.

————. *Les Philosophes classiques du XIXᵉ siècle en France*. Paris: Hachette, 1895.

————. *Philosophie de l'art*. Ed. Stéphane Douailler. N.p.: Fayard, 1985.

————. *La Révolution* (part 2 of *Les Origines de la France contemporaine*). 3 vols. Paris: Hachette, 1881–85.

————. *Voyage aux Pyrénées*. Paris: Hachette, 1920.

————. *Voyage en Italie*. 2 vols. Paris: Hachette, 1907.

Tave, Stuart M. *Some Words of Jane Austen*. Chicago: University of Chicago Press, 1973.

Theiner, Lieselotte. "Das Phänomen der atonikalen Werköffnung in der Klaviermusik von Ph. E. Bach bis R. Schumann." *Studien zur Musikwissenschaft* 28 (1977): 115–69.

Thesiger, Sarah. "The *Orchestra* of Sir John Davies and the Image of the Dance." *Journal of the Warburg and Courtauld Institutes* 36 (1973): 277–304.

Thomas, Brook. *The New Historicism and Other Old-Fashioned Topics*. Princeton: Princeton University Press, 1991.

————. "Parts Related to Wholes and the Nature of Subaltern Opposition." *Modern Language Quarterly* 55 (1994): 79–106.

Tillotson, Geoffrey. "The Manner of Proceeding in Certain Eighteenth- and Early Nineteenth-Century Poems." In *Augustan Studies*. London: Athlone Press, 1961. 111–46.

Tillyard, E. M. *Five Poems*. London: Chatto and Windus, 1948.

Trollope, Anthony. *An Autobiography*. Ed. Michael Sadleir. London: Oxford University Press, 1953.

————. *Can You Forgive Her?* Ed. Michael Sadleir and Frederick Page. London: Oxford University Press, 1948.

Valéry, Paul. *Oeuvres*. 2 vols. Ed. Jean Hytier. Paris: Gallimard, 1957–60.

van Laun, Henri. *History of French Literature*. 3 vols. London: Chatto and Windus, 1883.

Vaughan, Henry. *Complete Poetry*. Ed. French Fogle. New York: Norton, 1969.

Vendler, Zeno. "Descartes' Res Cogitans." In *Res Cogitans: An Essay in Rational Psychology*. Ithaca: Cornell University Press, 1972. 144–205.

Venturi, Lionello. *History of Art Criticism*. Trans. Charles Marriott. New York: Dutton, 1964.

Verga, Giovanni. *Tutte le novelle*. 2 vols. Milan: Mondadori, 1961.

Vertrees, Julie Anne. "Mozart's String Quartet K. 465: The History of a Controversy." *Current Musicology* 17 (1974): 96–114.

Volkelt, Johannes. *Ästhetische Zeitfragen*. Munich: Beck, 1895.

————. *System der Ästhetik*. 3 vols. Munich: Beck, 1905–14.

Wagner, Richard. *Sämtliche Schriften und Dichtungen*. 16 vols. Leipzig: Breitkopf und Härtel, 1911.

Wahl, Jean. *Du rôle de l'idée de l'instant dans la philosophie de Descartes.* Paris: Vrin, 1953.

Wallerstein, Ruth. *Studies in Seventeenth-Century Poetic.* Madison: University of Wisconsin Press, 1965.

Ward, Aileen. "The Forging of Orc: Blake and the Idea of Revolution." *Tri-Quarterly* no. 23–24 (1972): 204–27.

Warnke, Martin. "On Heinrich Wölfflin." *Representations* no. 27 (Summer 1989): 172–87.

Watts, Isaac. *Horae Lyricae.* London: J. Clark and R. Hett, 1727.

Weber, Max. "Die 'Objektivität' sozialwissenschaftlicher und sozialpolitischer Erkenntnis." In *Gesammelte Aufsätze zur Wissenschaftslehre.* Ed. Johannes Winckelmann. Tübingen: Mohr, 1951. 206–14.

Weinbrot, Howard. *The Formal Strain: Studies in Augustan Imitation and Satire.* Chicago: University of Chicago Press, 1969.

Weinstein, Leo. *Hippolyte Taine.* New York: Twayne, 1972.

Wellek, René. "Hippolyte Taine." In *A History of Modern Criticism: 1750–1950.* Vol. 4: *The Later Nineteenth Century.* New Haven: Yale University Press, 1965. 27–52.

Wenk, Arthur B. *Claude Debussy and Twentieth-Century Music.* Boston: Twayne, 1983.

White, Hayden. "The Value of Narrativity in the Representaton of Reality." *Critical Inquiry* 7 (1980): 5–27.

Wilkes, G. A. "The Poetry of Sir John Davies." *Huntington Library Quarterly* 25 (1962): 283–98.

Williams, Bernard. *Descartes: The Project of Pure Enquiry.* Atlantic Highlands, N.J.: Humanities Press, 1978.

Williamson, George. *The Senecan Amble: A Study in Prose Form from Bacon to Collier.* Chicago: University of Chicago Press, 1951.

Wilson, Edmund. *To the Finland Station: A Study in the Writing and Acting of History.* New York: Farrar, Straus and Giroux, 1972.

Wimsatt, William. *The Prose Style of Samuel Johnson.* New Haven: Yale University Press, 1941.

Wind, Edgar. "Zur Systematik der künstlerischen Probleme." *Zeitschrift für Ästhetik und allgemeine Kunstwissenschaft* 18 (1925): 480–86.

Wölfflin, Heinrich. *The Art of Albrecht Dürer.* Trans. Alastair Grieve and Heide Grieve. 1905; New York: Phaidon, 1971.

———. *Classic Art: An Introduction to the Italian Renaissance.* Trans. Peter Murray and Linda Murray. 1898; London: Phaidon, 1952.

———. *Gedanken zur Kuntsgeschichte.* Basel: Benno Schwabe, 1941.

———. *Kleine Schriften.* Ed. Joseph Gantner. Basel: Benno Schwabe, 1946.

———. *Principles of Art History: The Problem of the Development of Style in Later Art.* Trans. M. C. Hottinger. 1915; New York: Dover, 1950.

——. *Renaissance and Baroque*. Trans. Kathrin Simon. 1888; Ithaca: Cornell University Press, 1966.

——. Review of Alois Riegl, *Die Enstehung der Barockkunst in Rom*. In *Repertorium für Kunstwissenschaft* 31 (1908): 356–57.

——. *The Sense of Form in Art*: *A Comparative Psychological Study*. Trans. Alice Muehsam and Norma A. Shatan. New York: Chelsea, 1958.

Wolfson, Susan. "The Language of Interpretation in Romantic Poetry: 'A Strong Working of the Mind.' " In *Romanticism and Language*. Ed. Arden Reed. Ithaca: Cornell University Press, 1984. 22–49.

Wood, Allen W. *Kant's Rational Theology*. Ithaca: Cornell University Press, 1978.

Wordsworth, William. *Poetical Works*. 5 vols. Ed. E. de Selincourt and Helen Darbishire. Oxford: Clarendon Press, 1940–49.

Yeats, William Butler. *Collected Poems*. New York: Macmillan, 1956.

Young, Edward. *Works in Prose*. London: P. Brown, H. Hill, and S. Payne, 1765.

Zenck-Maurer, Claudia. *Versuch über die wahre Art, Debussy zu analysieren*. Munich: Emil Katzbichler, 1974.

Zola, Emile. *Une Page d'amour*. In his *Oeuvres complètes*. 15 vols. Ed. Henri Mitterand. Paris: Cercle du livre français, 1966–69. 3: 959–1209.

——. *Le Roman expérimental*. Ed. Aimé Guedj. Paris: Garnier-Flammarion, 1971.

Index

In this index an "f" after a number indicates a separate reference on the next page, and an "ff" indicates separate references on the next two pages. A continuous discussion over two or more pages is indicated by a span of page numbers, e.g., "57–59." *Passim* is used for a cluster of references in close but not consecutive sequence.

Library of Congress Cataloging-in-Publication Data

Brown, Marshall
   Turning points : Essays in the history of cultural expressions /
Marshall Brown.
      p.   cm.
   Collection of previously published material.
   Includes bibliographical references and index.
   Contents: Why style matters : The lessons of Taine's History of
English literature — The classic is the baroque : On the principle
of Wölfflin's art history — What's in a text — Deconstruction and
Enlightenment — Mozart and after : The revolution in musical
consciousness — Kant's misreading of Descartes — Toward an
archaeology of English Romanticism : Coleridge and Sarbiewski —
Romanticism and Enlightenment — Origins of modernism : Musical
structures and narrative forms — Unheard melodies : The force of
form.
   ISBN 0-8047-2708-2 (cloth)
   1. Criticism.   2. Criticism, Textual.   3. Literature—History and
criticism.   I. Title.
PN81.B695   1997
001.3—dc20   96-21910
                                                              CIP

⊛ This book is printed on acid-free, recycled paper.

Original printing 1997
Last figure below indicates year of this printing:
06   05   04   03   02   01   00   99   98   97

D0915191

What Others Say

"This fascinating, insightful book is more than technique; it has very practical suggestions on 100+ common issues most parents and educators face. It breathes a sound philosophy and way of thinking that empowers us, instead of our constantly looking to others for solutions."

Stephen R. Covey, Ph.D.
Author of *The 7 Habits of Highly Effective People*

"Marvin Marshall's insights, innovative ideas, and ingenuity provide a clear plan for raising responsible children. The benefits to schools and families are enormous."

Gene Bedley, National Educator of the Year
Author of *Character Lessons for Life*

"The strategies that Dr. Marshall describes for developing humane, responsive, and responsible classrooms are grounded in research AND good practice. They link classroom management concerns to the more fundamental issues of how teachers can create powerful curriculum, teaching, learning, and lasting motivation. I recommend this book to anyone who wants to create a 'right to learn' in all classrooms."

Linda Darling-Hammond, Ed.D., Professor of Education
Stanford University
Author of *The Right to Learn*
Director, National Commission on Teaching and America's Future

"Discipline is not easy in our culture. Our Puritanical past has led to many wrong assumptions about how to channel behavior. In this book, Marvin Marshall shows us how to overcome these counterproductive patterns while promoting responsibility and growth in young people. It is an important work, and I highly recommend it."

Jim Cathcart
Author of *The Acorn Principle: Know Yourself—Grow Yourself*

"This book has great payoffs. It shows how to raise responsibility—a basic desire and need of our society. The quality of family life and school life will improve as the principles of this book are put into practice. School and workplace leaders will make many applications to management practices as well."

Steve Barkley, Executive Vice President
Performance Learning Systems

"Several years ago, I had the opportunity to do a lengthy interview with B.F. Skinner. I concluded that I do not subscribe to much of what he taught—for example, his rejection of all inferred states such as attitudes and motivation . . . . Dr. Marvin Marshall's book addresses a fundamental problem that every society must solve: how to produce individuals who will take responsibility for doing the important tasks that need to get done. He focuses on what is the essence of good citizenship in the home, school, and nation. Using some of the latest findings of social science, Dr. Marshall has developed an approach that enables parents and teachers to help young people grow into responsible citizens and live satisfying and rewarding inner-directed lives."

Gene Griessman, Ph.D.
Author of *The Words Lincoln Lived By*

"Marv Marshall makes a compelling argument that stress, punishment, and rewards are counterproductive in raising or teaching children. At best they merely create temporary compliance. More likely, they corrode relationships, deter risk-taking, overlook the underlying causes of behavior, and subvert the learning process. Marshall points the way to successful strategies such as reframing perceptions and initiating specific intervention techniques. Parents, teachers, and principals should read this book—and rush to do so."

Elaine Haglund, Ph.D., Professor
Education, Administration, & Counseling
California State University, Long Beach, CA

"This book is a potent contribution to the field of child service. Not only has Dr. Marshall shown us a philosophy that works, he makes it easy to understand and implement. Everyone wins—especially our young people."

James Sutton, Ed.D., Child Psychologist
Author of *If My Kid's So Nice...Why's He Driving ME Crazy?*

"Self-directed people are resourceful. They engage in cause-effect thinking, spend energy on tasks, set challenging goals, persevere, are optimistic, feel good about themselves, and control anxiety. To achieve this human potential, the focus of education needs to shift. Both teachers and students must become internally-driven learners: self-analyzing and self-modifying. Marvin Marshall's book provides the science, structures, and strategies that further this cause."

Arthur Costa, Ed.D., Professor Emeritus
California State University, Sacramento
Co-Founder, Institute for Intelligent Behavior

"I have been struggling with my 5-year-old who knows his own mind. Coercion was not working. I was at a complete loss until I read your book. My son is responding very well, and the approach has improved our relationship. Thank you for giving me a practical method for teaching responsibility."
Karen McCormick, Norco, California

"When I'm stuck, I like to review *Discipline without Stress.* They say that a classic is something you can refer to over and over and still get something new out of it each time. Well, that definition fits here. The more I look back through it, the more it helps me to see things in a different light."
Anna Nyman Daley, Bluffdale, Utah

"Marshall's system has major strengths beyond those found in other systems of discipline. It makes sense and rings true for teachers. It focuses on developing responsibility, an enduring quality that remains useful throughout life. It removes the stress that students and teachers normally experience in discipline. It is easy to teach, apply, and live by. It is long lasting because it leads to changes in personality. Educators find these strengths especially compelling; hence, the surge of interest in Marshall's model."
C. M. Charles, *Building Classroom Discipline -8th Ed* (Boston: Pearson, 2005) pages 106-107

"Knowing that one of the principles of the system is to be positive, I knew that I had to start using the hierarchy in positive situations. Now, I not only try to use the hierarchy a lot to acknowledge higher-level behaviour, but also to be *proactive.* In other words, I use it *before* a lesson, *before* an activity, *before* an event, etc. In that way the students are set up for success. They know EXACTLY what higher-level behaviour looks like, and I find that when you have helped them create that vision in their minds, they are motivated to reach for it. That's when teaching becomes joyous. You start spending a larger percentage of your time acknowledging good choices, instead of dealing with problems. That's what makes this system so extraordinary! It's an exciting way to teach!"
Kerry Weisner
Duncan, British Columbia
Canada

Discipline
without Stress®
Punishments
or Rewards

Second Edition

Discipline

without Stress®

Punishments

or Rewards

How Teachers and Parents Promote
Responsibility & Learning

Marvin Marshall, Ed.D.

Second Edition

Piper Press ◆ Los Alamitos, California
Division of Marvin Marshall & Associates, Inc.

Published by Piper Press
Division of Marvin Marshall & Associates, Inc.
P.O. Box 2227
Los Alamitos, CA 90720 U.S.A.
www.MarvinMarshall.com

Copyright © 2001, 2002, 2004, 2005 by Marvin L. Marshall
Second Edition Copyright © 2007 by Marvin L. Marshall

Discipline without Stress® is a registered trademark belonging to
Marvin L. Marshall
DISCIPLINE WITHOUT STRESS®

Structural Breathing™ is a trademark of William Hanrahan

All rights, including that of translation, reserved under International and
Pan-American Copyright Conventions. No part of this book may be
reproduced or transmitted in any form or by any means, electronic or
mechanical, including photocopying, recording, or by any information
storage and retrieval system, without the prior written permission of the
publisher, except by a reviewer who may quote brief passages in a review.

ATTENTION: SCHOOLS AND ASSOCIATIONS
Substantial discounts on bulk quantities are available to corpora-
tions, professional associations, and educational or other organizations. For details and discount information, contact the special sales
department at Piper Press: 800.606.6105

Publisher's Cataloging-in-Publication
Marshall, Marvin L.
   Discipline without stress, punishments, or
rewards : How teachers and parents promote
responsibility & learning / Marvin Marshall. --
2nd ed.
   p.cm.
   Includes bibliographical references and index.
         ISBN-13: 978-0-9700606-2-4
   ISBN-10: 0-9700606-2-9
   1. Discipline of chidren. 2. Responsibility.
3. Learning. 4. Parenting. 5. Stress management.
I. Title.

LB3025.M37 2001   371.5
                  QBI00-500158

Printed in the United States of America

Cover Designer: Robert Howard
Interior Designer: Pamela Terry

10 9 8 7 6 5 4 3 2 1
Second Edition, First Printing

To my elementary, middle, and high school students who taught me that no one wants to fail or get into trouble and that young people want to be responsible—but too many adults are using counterproductive approaches to help them.

TABLE OF CONTENTS

DETAILED TABLE OF CONTENTS

FOREWORD

"What should I do to this kid?" is the most common question I receive from the readers of my book, my monthly column on *teachers.net,* and my in-service presentations.

I answer by saying that you do not "do" things to people. Rather, you need to teach people to do things for themselves. Classroom management teaches procedures for accomplishing this.

Discipline is a distinctly different subject. Discipline deals with how people behave, whereas procedures deal with how things are done.

Marvin Marshall has created a program that challenges many current assumptions and practices used with today's young people. He clearly and concisely demonstrates how the external approaches of relying on rules, imposing consequences, rewarding students for appropriate behavior, and punishing students to make them obey are all counterproductive.

This landmark book is a must-read whether you are a starting or experienced teacher, parent, youth worker, counselor, administrator, professor of teacher education, or anyone with an interest in promoting responsibility and growth in young people. You will find each chapter full of insights and strategies that will improve your influence and effectiveness with others.

Harry K. Wong, Ed.D.
Author of *How to Be An Effective Teacher –The First Days of School*
www.HarryWong.com

ABOUT THIS BOOK

Who is this book for?

If you experience stress, this book can help you diminish it. If you are a teacher or parent, this book will be especially useful.

What areas does this book include?

This book is a crossover of three areas: education, parenting, and personal growth. It offers practical solutions to real problems in each area. The following is a typical comment: A teacher approached me at a character education conference in St. Louis and said, "*I learned things from you today that I am going to use with my own teenage daughter.*"

Where can the ideas be used?

The strategies in this book can be used in any classroom, type of school, subject area, grade level, or with any youth or youth group. Most also can be used by anyone in a relationship with another person—parent with child, husband with wife, supervisor with supervised.

When can the strategies be implemented?

Every suggestion can be implemented immediately.

Why this book?

When I returned to the classroom after twenty-four years in counseling and guidance and supervision and administration, I met with an awakening. Society and youth had changed, but adults were using approaches no longer successful with so many of today's young people.

Here are three examples of what I learned: (1) If you focus on obedience you may engender resistance and even defiance—whereas focusing on responsibility brings obedience as a natural by-product. (2) Using rules places you in the position of a cop, rather than a coach. (3) Although you can *control* a person, you cannot *change* another person. People change themselves, and coercion is the least effective approach for influencing another person to change.

Many young people today do not demonstrate the level of responsibility necessary to continue our civil democracy. The program that I developed and used in my classrooms eliminated discipline problems—the bane of today's teaching.

I began sharing my approach and strategies in seminars. "Do you have a book?" became a common question. This publication is the result.

How should I read the book?

Each chapter is self-contained. The book need not be read in any particular order. For example, if your highest priority is to learn and implement the stress-reducing, noncoercive discipline program, go right to Chapter 3 and read about *The Raise Responsibility System.*

Chapter 1 shows how to reduce stress.

Three principles to practice are demonstrated: the power of positivity, the empowerment of choice, and the importance of reflection and self-evaluation. The chapter concludes with an exercise demonstrating that life is more successful and satisfying when these principles are used.

Chapter 2 is about motivating others.

People attempt to influence others based upon a theory. After an explanation of theories, the difference between external and internal motivation is explored. Then comes a discussion of rewards, punishments, and how these are two sides of the same motivational coin. The effectiveness of *telling* follows. The chapter concludes with a discussion of mindsets—those perceptions that drive motivation.

Chapter 3 focuses on fostering responsibility.

The Raise Responsibility System describes a discipline program that is noncoercive, is based on internal motivation so youth *want* to be responsible, and is easy to implement. The program has three parts: (1) Four critical concepts are presented. (2) When a student acts irresponsibly, checking for understanding is applied. (3) When a youngster continues to disrupt, authority is used without being punitive.

Chapter 4 is devoted to promoting learning.

The chapter begins with a discussion of the learning climate.

Suggestions are given for improving relationships between the teacher and the class, among students themselves, and between the teacher and individual students. Strategies are described for classroom meetings, collaboration—rather than competition—for quality learning, and reducing perfectionism. The chapter concludes with specific strategies for handling impulse and anger management, resolving conflicts, and dealing with difficult students.

Chapter 5 describes fundamentals for classroom teaching.
Topics include brain hemisphericity (including mindmapping), multiple intelligences, modalities of learning, emotions, styles, lesson planning, levels of intellect, instructional questions, group questioning strategy, choosing key words to frame questions and statements, imaging, stories, metacognition, the senses, additional suggestions for aiding recall and memory, laser learning, seminal shifts, classroom management, and home assignments.

Chapter 6 offers essential practices for parenting.
Topics include practicing positivity, offering choices, encouraging reflection, using effective questions, listening to learn, limiting lecturing and telling, checking assumptions, focusing on the important, asking for assistance, recognizing implicit messages, fostering responsibility, exhibiting personal responsibility, maintaining standards, using authority without being punitive, letting the youngster lead, teaching procedures to deal with impulses, intervening in sibling squabbles, being aware of gender differences, using acknowledgments more than praise, honoring home assignments, working smarter rather than harder, nurturing your child's nature, and reaping the joy of parenthood.

Epilogue – Argues that business is a poor model for learning.
Government, business, and even education leaders often compare schooling to business. Schools are referred to as workplaces, students as customers, and performance is measured in terms of accountability. Equating young people's learning processes with what adults do to make money is a false equation. Using a business model for learning is a practice that has been described by the comic strip character Dagwood Bumpstead, who said, "You know, that makes a lot of sense if you don't think about it."

ABOUT THE AUTHOR

Marvin Marshall is an international speaker and staff developer who shows how to promote responsibility and learning using noncoercive—but not permissive—approaches.

His writings on discipline, social development, human behavior, motivation, and promoting learning have been published internationally.

His professional education experiences include:

Classroom teaching at the primary and upper elementary grades, every grade 7–12, and as a full-time instructor in the Division of Education at California State University, Los Angeles.

Counseling and guidance experiences as a middle school counselor, high school counselor, guidance department chair, and certification in *Reality Therapy* and *Choice Theory* by the William Glasser Institute.

Curriculum and instruction as a demonstration teacher, department chair, instructional coordinator, and high school assistant principal of curriculum and instruction.

Supervision and administration as an elementary school principal, middle school assistant principal, high school athletic director, high school assistant principal of supervision and control, high school principal, and district director of education.

Masters thesis in business and economics at California State University, Los Angeles, on leadership and participatory management.

Doctoral Dissertation at the University of Southern California in the combined areas of curriculum, instruction, and guidance.

After 24 years of service in the above areas, Dr. Marshall returned to the classroom where he developed *The Raise Responsibility System.*

The program is now used across the entire teaching spectrum—in small childcare centers to large high schools and in rural, suburban, and urban schools. The strategy can be used in any home or youth setting. The system is an intergral part of *The Marvin Marshall Teaching Model* outlined on page 112.

On a personal note, he enjoys theatre and music, and occupies his spare time playing the great highland bagpipes, for which he has served as a pipe major and is certified by the College of Piping in Glasgow, Scotland.

His professional mission is influencing educators, parents, and leaders away from using "external" manipulative and coercive approaches to using more powerful "internal" approaches to promote responsibility and learning, increase effectiveness, improve relationships, and reduce stress for both the young and mature. He offers a free monthly electronic newsletter on these topics by subscription only at *www.MarvinMarshall.com.*

Contacting the Author

The author can be reached in the United States of America at
Marvin Marshall & Associates, Inc.
P.O. Box 2227, Los Alamitos, CA 90720
800.255.3192 ♦ 001.714.220.0678 International
Marv@MarvinMarshall.com
www.MarvinMarshall.com

PREFACE TO THE SECOND EDITION

The Marvin Marshall Teaching Model was developed after the original publication of the book. The model categorizes the key concepts for easy reference.

A few articles illustrating the key concepts have been included. They were written after the original publication.

The first article entitled, *A Principal's Experience*, describes how implementing the three principals described in Chapter I made a significant difference in the quality of people's professional and personal lives.

The second article entitled, *A Primer,* shares a teacher's journey from using the external manipulators of rewards for appropriate behavior to that of using the internal approach described in *The Raise Responsibility System* of Chapter III.

The third article is entitled, *Curriculum, Instruction, Classroom Management, and Discipline.* Clarity is essential for solving problems. For example, classroom management and discipline are often used interchangeably—as if they are synonymous. A clear understanding of the four areas enhances teaching and is so important that I have included a short description of each.

A small sampling of communications is included in the section entitled, *Letters Worth Reading.* These experiences could only have been written *after* implementing ideas in the original publication. Reading them will enhance your interest and encourage you to implement the ideas presented in the book.

The hierarchy of *The Raise Responsibility System* has been extended to promote effort in learning and improve academic proficiency. This is now Part IV of the teaching model.

Reference to differentiated instruction and a sample lesson are included in this edition.

Since motivation is a prime subject of the book, additional ideas for prompting students to learn are included. The article entitled, *Suggestions for Motivation,* is the first section in the Appendix.

Teaching procedures is the basis of effective classroom management. Much instructional time is often lost in obtaining students' attention. The reason is that a procedure for obtaining attention immediately has not been taught, practiced, and reinforced. The Appendix now includes an example of *Attention*

Management that I use in my staff development presentations and that so many teachers have asked me to share.

The Appendix also includes a wonderful analogy for teaching the four levels of social development, the foundation of the *Raise Responsibility System*. Of the three parts of the system described in Chapter III, students need to understand only these four concepts. The article is on pages 278-279.

This edition emphasizes *eliciting a procedure before* using the essay and self-diagnostic referral forms in the Appendix.

Society has changed and so have societal influences on youth. Many adults are often not so successful as they could be with younger people because these adults continue to use practices that worked in a society that had a factory-type ethos promoting obedience rather than promoting responsibility. Traditional authoritarian approaches are difficult to implement successfully in today's society that emphasizes individuality and personal responsibility.

The practical suggestions in the book are so simple that you may wonder why you have not been using them already. Be aware, however, that implementing the practices may feel awkward at first. Unlike youth, who find little risk in attempting new activities, adults have established patterns and often feel anxious and uncomfortable when attempting something different from what they have been doing. Realizing this at the outset will make it easier for you to attempt them. Doing something different requires making new habits, new neural connections. Practice makes permanent, and you will soon find that practicing the simple suggestions will soon become easier.

Finally, six months after the original publication in February of 2001, I started a free, monthly electronic newsletter. Each issue has short sections on promoting responsibility, increasing effectiveness, improving relationships, promoting learning, and disciplining without stress. You are invited to subscribe at *www.Marvin Marhsall.com*. This site also contains many interesting readings in the *Articles & Publications* link.

Marv Marshall
February 2007

ARTICLES

A Principal's Experience

Last April, I started a new life journey that has dramatically changed who I am as a principal as well as who I am as a person. I was completing my fifth year as an elementary public school principal. One of my colleagues recommended I attend the National Association of Elementary School Principals (NAESP) Convention in Anaheim, California. He had attended the conferences in the past and found them highly worthwhile.

Excitedly, I registered and began to think of my main goals during the conference. In reflecting on my abilities as an educational leader, I felt that I could improve my interaction skills with students encountering behavioral issues. In one third-grade class for example, the teacher and I had been meeting on a weekly basis to help a child who seemed to be continually making poor choices and becoming exceedingly more angry each day. We met with the parents who worked together with us on several behavior plans. Nothing seemed to change the child's behavior. I kept thinking there must be something else in the land of educational ideas that could provide my staff and me with additional strategies or suggestions to help children with behavioral difficulties.

Armed with a mission, I attended every workshop in the program concerning "at-risk," "disruptive," or "difficult" children. It was at one of these sessions that I first heard Dr. Marvin Marshall speak. As he talked about the system and the power of positivity, choice, and reflection, I knew in my heart that I had hit upon something that might work for my school and me.

Immediately following the conclusion of Dr. Marshall's presentation, I turned to a gentleman sitting next to me. He seemed to know about Dr. Marshall's system so I asked him if he used the system in his school. When he said, "Yes," I asked his opinion and he responded by stating, "The teachers who incorporate Dr. Marshall's principles are sad at the end of the school year because they don't want their students to leave. The ones who do not use the system can't wait for the school year to end!" That was all the vindication I needed. I hurried to the conference bookstore and purchased Dr. Marshall's *Discipline without Stress, Punishments or Rewards.*

Before the plane landed back in New Jersey, I had finished the book—complete with highlighting, tabs, and notations in the margins. Since April, I have read Dr. Marshall's book at least twice and some chapters three or four times! I carried the book everywhere I went: school, home, to lunch with friends, and at family gatherings. What is remarkable about it is not that there are profound statements or earth-shattering revelations. Instead, it is a primer for a way of life—a new way of thinking, a new way of helping children act responsibly.

Back at school, I began to make attempts to implement Dr. Marshall's philosophy in some small way each day. The first three chapters of the book stress positivity, giving students choices, and using reflective questions to help students assess their behavior and accept responsibility for their actions. I decided to start by waking up each morning telling myself to think and act in positive ways.

Each morning, I greeted staff and students with a smile, wished them a happy day, and tried to think of ways to state comments to students in a positive manner. I practiced saying things like, "We walk from the bus to the classroom," instead of, "No running! " In the lunchroom, I called clean up time, "quiet clean-up," instead of, "no talking." In the past, we clapped out a rhythm for getting students' attention in the lunchroom or during an assembly. At Dr. Marshall's suggestion, I started raising my hand and timing how many seconds it took the students to become quiet. If it took more than a few seconds, I would say, "That took 10 seconds. I bet we can do it even faster." Then we would try again and of course they improved the time.

As the idea of positivity began to become a habit with me, I started to notice how good it felt. People responded to me in the same way I interacted with them. I also noticed when other staff made statements in negative terms. It began to bother me. I hadn't noticed before how often educators speak to students and others in negative terms.

I wanted to share the knowledge I had gained from *Discipline without Stress, Punishments or Rewards*, but I did not want my staff to feel this was a top-down directive. I decided that after I had practiced a bit, I would begin to have conversations with my staff about student behavior and their style of interacting with children.

In the meantime, I began to experiment with giving students choices. This was an easier change for me because I had used this strategy to some degree in the past. I have always felt that children should be active participants in solving problems and resolving conflicts. When speaking to students about their behavior at recess, in the lunchroom, or on the bus, I would try to solicit from them what choices they had and how they could make the correct choice. If a consequence were needed, we would talk together about some of the choices. If I was satisfied, I would say, "I can live with that." This came straight from Dr. Marshall. Every time it worked, I would wonder at the simplicity of the process.

Finally, I began the hardest part of Dr. Marshall's system: reflective questions. This is especially challenging for educators because we feel we are not doing our job unless we are constantly teaching or telling children what they should do, when, how and why. Actually, we are doing children a great injustice when we do this. Who is doing all the thinking and reflecting? Certainly not the children! When reflective questions are used, the student is prompted to respond. These reflective questions do not come naturally. They take practice. At first, I fumbled a little. I felt like my brain was on overload deciding what questions I needed to ask. Many times I would go back to the book and reread examples of reflective questions so I could get a better feel for them.

In May, teachers began to notice I was carrying *Discipline without Stress, Punishments or Rewards* everywhere I went in school. At team planning meetings, I asked them if they were satisfied with the behavior of their students. We talked about the different procedures in their classroom and how they handled behavior concerns. They agreed that sometimes behavior modification plans did not work. Sometimes they ran out of ideas and were frustrated and stressed out. I started telling them about Dr. Marshall's ideas. Teachers expressed an interest in reading Dr. Marshall's book and trying his approach.

I purchased *Discipline without Stress, Punishments or Rewards* through my administrator's account for each staff member who expressed an interest. At our last faculty meeting in June, I distributed the books and invited the teachers to read them over the summer. In September, the entire faculty was ready to go. We watched Dr.

Marshall's instructional video prior to the first day of school. That served as a good reminder for teachers who read the book over the summer and important information for those who had not. Teachers made bulletin boards with the four levels of behavior: Anarchy (A), Bullying/Bossing (B), Cooperation /Conformity (C), and Democracy (D). We printed and laminated the posters from Dr. Marshall's website for each classroom.

By the end of September, we were all speaking the same language. I could walk up to any student in the building and ask him/her: "What level of behavior is that?" and they could identify it correctly. The goal of course was for students to be at levels C or D. Some students got it right away and made efforts to make the right choices. One second grade student was concerned because a classmate was ill on Halloween. He was worried that his friend would not be well enough to go Trick or Treating. He asked his parents if he could take half of his "goodies" to his friend and so the parents drove him to his friend's house. What a great example of Level D behavior! I would not have even known about it except that the sick child's mother called me the next day to praise the child.

Other students needed to be reminded more often. Special education students with behavior problems have had the greatest difficulty behaving at the appropriate levels. At team planning meetings each week we shared experiences, asked questions, and helped each other implement the program. We also held several after-school gatherings. We called it a "Book Club." Teachers volunteered to come and talk about Dr. Marshall's book and their experiences with the system. I especially enjoyed sitting back and listening to others share their stories.

It is almost a year since I heard Dr. Marshall speak. My life has not been the same since that momentous day. I continue to work each day at being positive. Reflective questions now come more naturally to me. Most of my interactions with students are calm events that challenge students to think about what they did and come up with plans for how they can be at Level C or D more frequently. One first grade student was worried that her classmate would not be able to bring in a treat for his birthday, so she asked her mother if they could make cookies for him. They did and the child was so excited when she brought them in on his birthday to share with the class. This is another example of a child doing the right thing because it was the right thing to do!

In conclusion, I would like to make the comparison of a Sonicare Toothbrush with what we now call "The Marshall Plan." All my life I had used a manual toothbrush: Reach, Oral B, or whatever the dentist gave me after a checkup. I never thought there could be something better to clean my teeth until the Sonicare Toothbrush entered my life. Was it easy to use? Not at first.

My husband and I read the instruction book. Then we practiced. The toothbrush felt tingly during our first few times using it, as the book indicated. Did we give up? No, we felt it was worth the effort to continue trying. There were many things to remember when using the Sonicare Toothbrush. You must keep your mouth shut, or the toothpaste will dribble down your chin. If you take the toothbrush out of your mouth without turning it off first, the toothpaste splatters all over the mirror, sink, and your clothes! The toothbrush has an internal clock; it runs for two minutes. With a manual toothbrush, you can just stop or start whenever you want.

Despite all these adjustments and changes to my tooth brushing habits, the end result is so effective and my teeth are so much cleaner that I will never go back to my old toothbrush again! This is exactly how I feel about my post Dr. Marshall life. I will never go back to who I was before. Was it easy? No. Was it worth the effort? Yes! The new me is a happier, more positive person and administrator—and it has made all the difference in my life.

Mary Lou Cebula, Ed.D.
Principal, Central School
Warren, New Jersey

A PRIMER

NEARLY 25 years ago, as a beginning teacher struggling somewhat with classroom discipline, I eagerly scanned teacher magazines in search of tips. One technique came well recommended: I should divide my class into teams; offer points for good behaviour, kind deeds, and diligent work habits; and then each week present the winning team with something special—perhaps a chocolate bar, a comic book, or a fancy pen. The magazine promised that this system would build self-esteem and motivate students to behave, do their best work, learn well, and be kindhearted. Armed with enticing treats for incentives, I had great expectations for improved behaviour from those few students who occasionally challenged me and for an increased level of motivation from the rest of the class. This was so easy. Why hadn't I thought of it myself?

Easy? Well, not for me! I didn't seem to have the necessary skills to get this straightforward little plan to work. It turned out that I wasn't a very accurate judge of who should be awarded points. I could never pay enough attention to determine which team was truly the quietest at dismissal time, and I found it almost impossible to accurately assess which group had the tidiest handwriting. Since I was not alert enough to notice *every* act of kindness in the room, the children themselves began to interrupt lessons to point them out to me.

As it happened, my students, grade five that year, were quick to pick up on my obvious lack of skill, and the more vocal ones were not about to let any errors go by unnoticed. Often squabbles broke out, and eventually even the "good kids" started to complain if I awarded points in a way with which they didn't agree. Somehow, this wasn't what I had envisioned! Instead of becoming more cooperative, self-disciplined, and focused on lessons, these children were becoming greedy and resentful, interested in only one thing— getting points, *more* points than their neighbors.

Where were those thoughtful, well-behaved, motivated students who wanted to learn simply for the joy of learning? What happened to that respectful and purposeful classroom atmosphere that I was trying to create? Why were the children more interested on Monday mornings in the nature of the Friday prize than in the wonderful lessons that I had spent long hours preparing? I was sadly disappointed in myself as a teacher.

A QUEST

Fed up with conflict and never one to really enjoy competitive activities anyway, I knew I couldn't follow through with the magazine's suggestion. After three weeks, I accepted what seemed obvious: I wasn't cut out to be the truly effective teacher the magazine described. When it came to classroom discipline, I simply didn't have the talent. Somehow I would have to find another way.

Discouraged with my inability to successfully follow popular educational advice as outlined by that upbeat teaching article, I turned instead to personal experience for direction. I started to reflect on the teachers who had taught *me* over the course of my schooling. Certain ones clearly stood out in my memory as powerful and inspiring. What characteristics did they share?

They had cultivated personal bonds with students by
- treating us with respect and kindness,
- using an honest, direct teaching approach.
- showing interest in us as individuals.
- sharing stories from their own lives.
- maintaining an approachable manner so that we felt safe, and displaying a willingness to give extra help and encouragement.

They had held high expectations by
- requiring us to work hard,
- insisting that we try,
- challenging us to think, and
- expecting us to behave appropriately.

They had employed best teaching practices by
- capturing interest through an engaging classroom environment,
- providing a reason to want to attend class,
- making learning fun,

- using a variety of carefully planned teaching strategies, and
- giving varied and meaningful assignments.

For the next 20 years, I tried to emulate these memorable educators. Although I gradually developed an increasingly clearer sense of direction, I still struggled on a day-to-day basis with students who misbehaved, were insensitive, or avoided responsibility. I felt as if I had a pretty good idea of *where* I wanted to go, but only the vaguest notion of *how* to get there. Eventually I began to investigate motivation research and was greatly affected by what I found.

With great conviction, I set out to find an approach to classroom teaching and discipline based on *internal motivation*. Forget the gimmicks, the quick-fix approaches, the prizes, the stickers, the pizzas for reading, and those merit points for good behaviour. The studies clearly showed that none of these things would bring about long-term, lasting results. I was determined to find a program that would encourage the children in my charge to work consciously toward becoming compassionate, self-disciplined, responsible individuals; nothing less would do. Yet the challenge remained: How on earth could *anyone* do that with 6-year-olds?

Although this idealistic vision certainly captured my imagination, I knew that in a practical teaching sense I didn't have much to go on. What I needed were concrete teaching strategies that would allow me to assist students who daydreamed class time away, ridiculed classmates, or deliberately hurt others in the schoolyard. Once again, feeling discouraged, I felt destined to spend the rest of my career searching for something that didn't exist.

And then one day, all of that changed with just a quick click of my computer mouse. Prompted by mail-ring conversations regarding discipline plans based on behaviour modification and other imposed approaches, I entered the phrase "rewards and punishments" into a search engine. Up came a site titled "Dr. Marvin Marshall – Discipline Without Stress, Punishments, or Rewards" *(www.MarvinMarshall.com)*.

Eureka! Here was the information for which I had been endlessly searching. The website described a simple system based on internal motivation that focused on promoting responsibility rather than on promoting obedience. It was *exactly* what I needed to inspire children to lead responsible lives.

THREE PRINCIPLES TO PRACTICE

Excited, I decided to start by implementing three recommended practices:

1. I was *positive* in everything I said. Students do better when they feel good about themselves.

2. I taught students that they always have the freedom to *choose their responses*—regardless of the situation. Realizing that they had choices, the students became more self-controlled and responsible. They felt empowered.

3. I learned to ask questions that would effectively guide students to *reflect* and *self-evaluate.*

Practicing these three principles of adopting *positivity,* empowering through *choice,* and encouraging *reflection* greatly reduced my stress as a teacher and allowed me to view misbehaviour as I would any academic difficulty—as *an opportunity to teach and learn* instead of as a problem. My goal became to influence students, rather than trying to coerce them into making constructive changes in their behaviour.

THE THREE PHASES OF THE RAISE RESPONSIBILITY SYSTEM

In Part 1 of this article, Marvin Marshall detailed the theories behind his *Raise Responsibility System.* As applied in the classroom, the system has three phases: 1) *teaching,* 2) *asking,* and 3) *eliciting.*

Phase 1: Teaching the hierarchy. The foundation of the *Raise Responsibility System* is the hierarchy of social development. Classroom behaviours can be assigned to different levels of the hierarchy. I chose behaviours appropriate to my grade and displayed them on a chart:

Level D: Democracy Develops self-discipline. Shows kindness to others. Develops self-reliance. Does good because it is the right thing to do. *The motivation is internal.*

Level C: Cooperation/Conformity Listens Cooperates. Does what is expected. *The motivation is external.*

Level B: Bossing/Bullying Bosses others. Bothers others. Bullies others. Breaks classroom standards. *Needs to be bossed to behave.*

Level A: Anarchy Noisy. Out of control. Unsafe.

Using the familiar situation of a piece of trash lying on the classroom floor, I introduced the concepts underlying the hierarchy. I described the type of behaviour with regard to the trash that would be indicative of each successive level of social development.

At the lowest level of behaviour, Level A, a student might pick up the trash but then throw it at someone. Moving up the ladder, a student operating on Level B also would not feel compelled to pick up the trash but instead might kick it around the room. At an acceptable Level C, a student would pick up the trash at the request of the teacher. At Level D, a student would take the initiative to pick up the trash and deposit it in the trash can without being asked—whether or not anyone was watching—simply because this was the *right* thing to do.

The important points for students to understand are:

1. Levels A and B behaviours are always *unacceptable.* The use of authority by the teacher is required at both of these levels.

2. Level C behaviour is acceptable, but the motivation is *external* —to gain approval or avoid punishment.

3. Levels C and D differ in *motivation,* not necessarily in their behaviours.

4. Level D is the goal, where the motivation is *internal*—taking the initiative to do the right, appropriate, or responsible thing.

I was astonished at how quickly my young students grasped these concepts and were able to generate novel examples of their own. With understanding in place, I was ready to implement the second phase of the program: reflective questioning.

Phase 2: Asking students to reflect on their behaviour. The point of this phase is to guide a misbehaving student to self-evaluate. The first question I always asked was, "On what level was that behaviour?" It was clear that the effectiveness of this phase was the result of *asking* the child to identify the level of behaviour, rather than using the traditional approach of *telling* the child that the behaviour was unacceptable. Also, by referring to a level—rather than to the student's specific behaviour—the deed was separated from the doer. Students did not feel a need to defend themselves.

Having learned the hierarchy, the students found it easy to accurately assess their levels of behaviour, and when they identified an action as being on an unacceptable level, they felt a strong sense of responsibility for correcting it or at least not repeating it.

I was taken completely by surprise as I immediately began to see positive changes and significant improvements in the students' behaviours. They began to analyze their actions and take responsibility for their choices. The little girl who nearly drove me crazy by constantly making noises suddenly started to display excellent self-control. The impulsive youngster who often bullied others on the playground started having peaceful noon-hour experiences. The disorganized little boy who could never keep track of his belongings made a commitment to return a special book that he wanted to borrow. Proudly and responsibly, he followed through with his plan! Having experienced the powerful feelings of satisfaction that emerge from being capable and responsible, my students began acting with more empathy and caring toward others.

Although I believed strongly in the power of internal motivation, I had always assumed that any success based on such a teaching model would be measured in years, rather than in days and weeks. I had mistakenly equated *lasting results* with a lengthy and delayed process.

Phase 3: Eliciting changes in behaviour. On rare occasions, a student continued to misbehave even after having identified a behaviour as being on an unacceptable level. Then I used the process of "guided choices." I gave the student an activity to prompt self-reflection—with the goal of eliciting (rather than imposing) a plan of action. In this way the student could develop a procedure that would redirect impulses and assist in preventing a similar inappropriate behaviour in the future. This approach demonstrates that one can use authority when necessary—but without being punitive.

A GIFT FOR LIFE

Moment by moment, choice by choice, we each create a life, the quality of which depends largely upon the choices we make. With awareness, we can consciously choose to make decisions that will lead to positive results. *The Raise Responsibility System* gives young people, even young children, the awareness they need in order to look at their choices and plan future behaviour.

Although initially it appeared that the children who often misbehaved were the ones who were benefiting from the Raise Responsibility System, it wasn't long before I realized that *every* student had been given an incredible gift. The very nature of the hierarchy inspires young people to set their sights at the highest level. They found that they could better themselves by consciously choosing to aim for Level D, the level at which they could be autonomous—making appropriate choices without relying on the teacher to direct them.

I noticed that by adding to the list of descriptors for Level D, I could easily influence the children to operate more consistently at this level. For instance, when I added the phrase *shows initiative*, those who had always shown initiative got reinforcement and a boost to their self-esteem because they recognized this quality in their own actions, and those who tended to operate at lower levels had yet another trait to which they could aspire.

EXTENDING THE HIERARCHY TO LEARNING

Gradually, as I experienced continued success with the Raise Responsibility System, I realized that the way in which I understood the system was evolving. I no longer viewed it in a limited way—as only a tool for handling classroom discipline. I began to see that there was enormous potential and value in using the hierarchy to inspire young people in all areas of their lives.

One day I decided to have a discussion with my students about how they could use their understanding of the four levels of development to help themselves become better readers. We talked about the 30-minute "Whole School Read" session in which we participate each morning. I asked the youngsters to describe hypothetical behaviours of students operating at each of the four levels during this daily reading time.

They were able to clearly describe conduct at each level:

At level A, students wouldn't be practicing reading at all. They would be deliberately misbehaving and causing a disturbance. At level B, students wouldn't be doing much reading either. They would be annoying or distracting others, perhaps by poking them or making jokes. They would probably flip through the pages of a book but wouldn't put in the effort to actually read. We reviewed that when students are behaving at Levels A and B, a teacher must step in and use authority because neither Level A nor Level B conduct is ever acceptable.

Then we discussed the higher and acceptable levels of development, C and D. Students operating at Level C would be reading—but more or less only when an adult (the teacher or a parent) was directly watching or working with them. When an adult was not supervising in their area, they probably wouldn't disturb anyone but wouldn't put in much effort, either. Their motivation for reading would be external—they would willingly cooperate and do what was necessary in order to avoid the disapproval of the adults in the room.

At this point in the discussion, I felt it was important for students to fully understand another aspect of Level C. I stressed the idea that people operating at this level sometimes comply with expectations simply in an effort to impress someone else with their conduct. In other words, their reason for reading is again *external.* They feel the need to be noticed while reading so as to "look good" in the teacher's eyes. I wanted the students to understand that a lot of energy can be wasted worrying about what others think—energy that in this particular situation could more profitably be devoted to actual reading.

When we moved on to Level D, the class imagined students who would be using reading time each morning to truly practice reading. It wouldn't be necessary to have an adult directly with them at all times; they would stay on task simply because they knew what was expected of them. They would read and re-read sections of their books because they knew that by doing so they would become better readers. Their motivation would be *internal.* They wouldn't be wasting any time watching the teacher in the hope of being specially noticed as "someone who was reading."

Having run through examples of all the levels of development in this particular situation, I asked, "Which of these students from our discussion will learn to read?" The class understood that it seemed unlikely that students operating at levels A and B could ever learn to read very well. Their choices and actions were leading them in the opposite direction.

We then went on to the benefits of operating at the two higher levels of the hierarchy. We discussed that students operating at Level C probably *would* learn to read but would be unlikely to get much pleasure from reading or to become proficient readers because they were reading *only* when directly supervised. They complied with the classroom expectation of reading, but their hearts weren't in it. With only a so-so effort at practicing, they would get only so-so results.

Then we discussed Level D—which is always the goal in the Raise Responsibility System. This is the level at which people take the initiative to do what is right or appropriate. People at this level *motivate themselves* to put forth effort and achieve. The results are long-lasting and powerful. These people strive to become good readers and therefore can get a lot of enjoyment from reading. Because they experience enjoyment, they keep reading and therefore become even better readers. People at this level feel good about themselves because they experience improvement and are aware that it comes as a result of choices that they have consciously made.

After these discussions, I wanted to prompt some reflection, and so I simply asked the students to analyze their own developmental level in the reading session that had just passed. After giving them a moment to think "in their heads," I asked them to honestly evaluate their own choices. I wanted them to think about whether or not their choices were leading them in a positive direction. Nothing more was said aloud, either by me or by the students, and they were left to reflect for a minute before we moved on to another lesson.

THE RESULTS

That night, without any suggestion or prompting on my part, the poorest reader in the class went home and read his reader over and over again. Prior to this, the kindly parents of this child had been sincerely concerned about his lack of reading progress and fairly supportive of the school, but they hadn't understood the value or importance of conducting nightly reading sessions with their struggling youngster, as the school had requested.

That evening they watched as their little boy independently read and re-read his reader. Both the parents and the child could see a dramatic improvement in his reading skills. They experienced the powerful impact that internal desire, coupled with just one night of true effort, could have on someone's ability to read. The boy came back to school the next day bursting with pride and determination to practice more and more so that he could move on to a new, more difficult reader. It only took one more night of practice, and he was able to do just that.

The Raise Responsibility System prompted this youngster to learn a powerful lesson that is bound to influence his behaviour in the future. He could clearly see the connection between his own choices and the results from them. *I could never have bribed him into such a learning experience by offering a sticker or a prize for having read a certain number of pages.*

As a result of *promoting responsibility*, I discovered that obedience followed as a natural by-product. As a result of *teaching a hierarchy*, which inspired students to aim for the highest level, I observed children choosing to be more responsible and becoming willing to put forth the effort needed to learn. As a result of *encouraging self-reflection in a noncoercive manner*, I witnessed students doing what they knew to be appropriate and aiming to fulfill the highest expectations.

I am elated to have finally found an effective approach to discipline that creates a classroom in which young people feel safe, care for one another, and enjoy learning. Teaching becomes a joy when students demonstrate more responsible behaviour and become motivated to put more effort into their own learning.

Kerry Weisner
Duncan, British Columbia
Canada

CURRICULUM, INSTRUCTION, CLASSROOM MANAGEMENT, AND DISCIPLINE

An understanding of each distinctive concept is essential for effective teaching.

"The Brilliant Inventiveness of Student Misbehavior: Test Your Classroom Management Skills" was the title of an article in a well-respected educational journal. The article had some good suggestions. However, there was a glaring misnaming in that the article had nothing to do with classroom management. The article was entirely about discipline.

Confused?

So are many educators—even college professors. When speaking at an international conference on character education, a college professor said to me, "I don't like the word 'discipline'; it's too harsh, so I use the term 'classroom management' instead." This teacher of teachers had not a clue to the differences.

I was honored as the Distinguished Lecturer at a conference of the Association of Teacher Educators (ATE). The membership of this association is primarily composed of university professors who teach methods and other educational courses. At my behest, the name of the Special Interest Group (SIG) was changed from "Classroom Management" to "Classroom Management *and Discipline.*"

Although related, these are *distinctly different topics* and should not be lumped together as if they were synonymous.

CLASSROOM MANAGEMENT deals with *how things are done.* *DISCIPLINE* deals with *how people behave.*

CLASSROOM MANAGEMENT has to do with *procedures, routines,* and *structure—sometimes to the point of becoming rituals. DISCIPLINE* is about *impulse management* and *self-control.*

CLASSROOM MANAGEMENT is the teacher's responsibility. *DISCIPLINE* is the *student's* responsibility.

CLASSROOM MANAGEMENT is enhanced when procedures are:

1. explained to students

2. practiced by students, and periodically (when necessary)

3. reinforced by practicing again.

When procedures are learned, routines are established. Routines give order and structure to instruction.

Good classroom management is essential for efficient teaching and learning. Chances are that when you walk into a room, you do not pay much attention to the floor. But if it were missing, you would. The analogy works for classroom management. You don't notice it when it is good. But without it, the lack of it is readily apparent.

The differences between "classroom management" and "discipline" are two of the four distinctive concepts necessary for an understanding of effective teaching. The other two concepts are "curriculum" and "instruction."

CURRICULUM refers to the subject matter and skills to be taught. The curriculum is determined by state departments of education, boards of education, the "federal agenda," professional associations, the community—and, more recently, corporate performance accountability models for learning.

It is the teacher's responsibility to make the curriculum relevant, interesting, meaningful, and/or enjoyable.

INSTRUCTION has two components: (1) teaching and (2) learning. The former refers to what the teacher does, the latter to what students do.

Good *teaching* of a lesson has at least three parts: (1) grabbing interest, (2) the actual presentation of the material, and (3) reflection on the experiences for enhanced understanding, reinforcement, and retention. (See pages 183–184.)

Learning pertains to the activities in which students are engaged to learn.

Here is the essential point: If you have an unsuccessful lesson, ask yourself, (1) Was it the *curriculum?* (I just didn't make it appealing, interesting, relevant, or meaningful.)

or?

(2) Was it *instruction?* (I had a wonderful lesson planned, but I did all the work; the students were not involved enough in learning activities,)?

or?

(3) Was it poor *classroom management*? (I had a wonderful lesson, but it took 10 minutes to get everything organized.)

or?

(4) Was it a *discipline* problem? (I prompted the students' curiosity, taught a good lesson with meaningful student activities, had everything implemented efficiently, but I a few students still behaved inappropriatcly?)

Reflecting on these questions enhances a clear understanding of the differences bctween curriculum, instruction, classroom management, and discipline. It is a fundamental first step of an effective teacher.

LETTERS WORTH READING

A Parent's Experience

When my elementary school first implemented the *Raise Responsibility System*, I was somewhat apprehensive about how such a program would work in my classroom. I have always felt that I created a positive learning environment in my class and, frankly, this system seemed like just one more passing fad to add to our classroom management file.

However, after reading Dr. Marshall's book, "*Discipline Without Stress, Punishments or Rewards*," I realized that if I was going to use this in my classroom, I should try it at home first. As a mother of two teenagers, creating an environment that was stress-free really appealed to me. I talked to my children about how stressful things had been at home and shared with them a little bit about the program that I was "trying out" on them.

Later that day, I heard my daughter slamming doors and screaming at the top of her lungs at her brother. Before, I would have stormed in to intervene and quickly reacted to the situation without even thinking. Instead, I calmly began using such questions as: "Is what you are doing something that is beneficial?" My daughter stopped and looked at me and said, "Oh, this is that discipline thing you are using at school, right? Okay, so, no! No, it's not." I asked, "Is what you are doing something that falls in line with the standards of our family?" She sighed, "No." I said, "Would you tell me what our family rule is regarding yelling?" She relayed to me that yelling was not allowed and that if we had anything to say we could say it in a calm manner. Finally, I said, "Well, what do you think we should do about this?"

I told her to go to her room and reflect on what we should do about what had happened between her and her brother. A little while later, she came back in and asked to talk to her brother. She apologized for yelling at him and proceeded to give us a list of consequences that she had decided on. "I guess I should not use the computer for three weeks, or talk on the phone, or go to the movies with my friends," she began to list. We were stunned!

Honestly, this was the first time that she had really accepted responsibility for something so calmly. The next three weeks were very interesting. She answered the phone and we could hear her explain, "I can't talk on the phone right now because my parents...I mean, I have restricted myself."

Since using this in our home, life seems so much more enjoyable. The truth is that our children do know what is expected of them. Holding them to a higher level of responsibility has made all of our lives more peaceful.

Thank you.
Wendi Hall
Vestavia Hills, Alabama

A Primary Teacher's Experience

On the second day of the new system, a miracle happened. The student who had driven me crazy all year chose to take time out for reflection at his desk (instead of outside in the hall) after he belched five times in less than ten minutes during story time on the rug.

I explained that if he chose to sit at his desk, he would still have to allow the rest of us to concentrate. He agreed. When after two minutes he began belching loudly again, I said he must have changed his mind and decided now to sit outside. When he started to fuss, I asked him whose decision it was to bother the class. He sheepishly said, "Mine" and walked quietly out of the room. Nothing that simple had ever happened with that child before.

But even more miraculous, when he returned to the classroom he said, with no prompting, "Mrs. Clark, I'm really sorry about how I behaved on the rug." I was stunned and so was the rest of the class. So I asked, "Do you know what level of behavior that is?" He didn't, so I told everyone that this is an example of level D, Democracy, taking responsibility for your own actions and caring about others at the same time.

Thanks for helping me regain a bit of sanity. This will be my fourth year of teaching, and before your approach I had begun to think that starting this new career at 56 might have been more than I could bear, but I guess I should be good for another ten years. Thank you.

Sincerely,
Rachel Clark
Berkeley, California

A First Grade Teacher's Experience

I have taught for 29 years, mostly in first grade. This year I learned of the *Raise Responsibility System.* I have taught the levels of behavior, and we role-played how the levels would look and sound in various school settings.

We are in our 5th week of school. On Tuesday morning, we were to be given one-on-one testing for beginning reading skills in the media center. When we got there, testing was running behind, so I had to turn the class around and return to our room. Needless to say, it was a situation that quickly slid into anarchy when they got back to our room and headed to the front to finish our morning meeting. They began to fuss over someone sitting in their spot, not having enough room, etc. One of my more challenging students looked at me and said in a loud voice to be heard over the others, "This is level A, isn't it?"

I merely nodded but he had been heard by many of the children and what happened next was simply amazing. ALL the children found a seat on the circle without any further upset, sat "criss-crossed" with their hands in their laps, lips together and eyes on the teacher. I was blown away. This system is certainly a stress reducer for me! Thank you, Dr. Marshall!

Melissa Mathews
Lake George Elementary
Orlando, Florida

An Algebra Teacher's Experience.

About a week before school started I went online looking for a way to provide a suitable reward system to make sure that my classes were positive and motivated. I knew that rewards were more effective than punishments, or so I thought.

I did a search for "Discipline Rewards" and your site popped up. I started reading your website and I was immediately on-board. After spending about an hour on your site, I decided to try your system this year.

I spent the second day of school talking to my classes about the hierarchy. Their homework was for them to go online and research the *Raise Responsibility System.* We discussed their viewpoints the 3rd day of school and the changes started immediately.

I realized for the first time in over 25 years of teaching that I was not having enough faith in my students. As High Priestess of the Control Freaks, I had to learn to step back and give them the chance to analyze their own behavior and come up with their own responsible responses.

The entire atmosphere in my algebra class is changed to one of maturity, self-discipline, helpfulness, and respect. I am not exhausted by the end of the day from trying to control all my students. No more adversarial confrontations!

I am now frequently impressed by the maturity that my students are showing. I have gone from bossing to trusting.

Thank you for your website, your book, and for your sound principles. I am a much calmer and happier teacher now.

Sharon Miles
Crownsville, Maryland

A Story About Grades and Rewards

My name is George H. Orfe, and I am the guy from South Dakota who told you the story of the boy and the $5 his father gave him for each "A" grade. You asked that I relate the story to you. Here it is.

I had a father of a fifth grader who gave his son $5 for each A on his report card. The first marking period the child received eight A's, and $40 from his father.

The second marking period ended in January, and report cards went home at the beginning of February. The father was quite upset, since his son had dropped to only one A, 2 B's and the rest C's.

In the conference with the father, I suggested we call his son in and see what the problem was. The boy came into my office, sat down, and we began to talk. My first question was, "How come your grades have slipped so much this marking period," and the boy quickly responded, "I didn't need the money!"

The father slumped in the chair.

ACKNOWLEDGMENTS

I am indebted to Kerry Weisner and Darlene Collinson of British Columbia, Canada, who have added a new dimension to using the hierarchy of social development—the teaching part of the *Raise Responsibility System* described in Chapter Three. By continually referring to the higher, acceptable levels—rather than emphasizing the lower, unacceptable levels—Kerry and Darlene have used the principles described in Chapter One to make the system even more effective.

In addition, they have demonstrated how to use the hierarchy more effectively to reduce student apathy and have students want to put forth effort to improve their learning—as well as increase their desire to behave responsibly.

Kerry is also the prime contributor to Internet support found at *www.MarvinMarshll.com.*

INTRODUCTION:
THE CALF PATH

One day, through the primeval wood,
A calf walked home, as good calves should;
But made a trail all bent askew,
A crooked trail as all calves do.

Since then two hundred years have fled,
And, I infer, the calf is dead.
But still he left behind his trail,
And thereby hangs my moral tale.

The trail was taken up next day
By a lone dog that passed that way;
And then a wise bellwether sheep
Pursued the trail o'er vale and steep,
And drew the flock behind him, too,
As good bellwethers always do.

And from that day, o'er hill and glade,
Through those old woods a path was made;
And many men wound in and out,
And dodged, and turned, and bent about
And uttered words of righteous wrath
Because 'twas such a crooked path.

But still they followed—do not laugh—
The first migrations of that calf,
And through this winding wood-way stalked,
Because he wobbled when he walked.

This forest path became a lane,
That bent, and turned, and turned again.
This crooked lane became a road,
Where many a poor horse with his load
Toiled on beneath the burning sun,
And traveled some three miles in one.
And thus a century and a half
They trod the footsteps of that calf.

The years passed on in swiftness fleet.
The road became a village street;
And thus, before men were aware,
A city's crowded thoroughfare;
And soon the central street was this
Of a renowned metropolis;
And men two centuries and a half
Trod in the footsteps of that calf.

Each day a hundred thousand rout
Followed the zigzag calf about;
And o'er his crooked journey went
The traffic of a continent.
A hundred thousand men were led
By one calf, near three centuries dead.

They followed still his crooked way,
And lost one hundred years a day;
For thus such reverence is lent
To well-established precedent.

A moral lesson this might teach,
Were I ordained and called to preach;
For men are prone to go it blind
Along the calf-paths of the mind,
And work away from sun to sun
To do what other men have done.

They follow in the beaten track,
And out and in, and forth and back,
And still their devious course pursue,
To keep the path that others do.

But how the wise old woods-gods laugh,
Who saw the first primeval calf!
Ah! Many things this tale might teach,
But I am not ordained to preach.

Sam Walter Foss

1
REDUCING STRESS

PRINCIPLES TO PRACTICE

You cannot coerce people into changing their minds.
–Benjamin Franklin, protesting the
Stamp Act to King George III

L ife is a conversation. Interestingly, the most influential person we talk with all day is ourself, and what we tell ourself has a direct bearing on our behavior, our performance, and our influence on others. In fact, a good case can be made that our self-talk creates our reality. Many psychologists have argued that, by thinking negatively, we cause ourselves mental and physical stress. Stress is related to perceiving the world as manageable or unmanageable. By practicing the three principles below, we can reduce stress because these principles enhance the management of our world. Practice of the principles also improves relationships and increases our effectiveness in influencing others to change their behaviors.

POSITIVITY, CHOICE, AND REFLECTION

The first principle to practice is *positivity*. We know that we learn and do better when we feel good, not bad. Unfortunately, rather than communicating in positive terms, we often communicate in negative terms, such as by using consequences. Although consequences can be positive or negative, when we refer to them we usually mean punishment, which is negative and coercive. A more effective approach than consequences is the use of contingencies. Rather than reactive and negative, contingencies are proactive and positive. In addition, when using contingencies responsibility remains with the person with whom we want to foster responsibility. Communicating positively reduces stress, improves relationships, and is more effective than negativity in influencing change in others.

The second principle to practice is the use of *choice*. Choice empowers. Many practitioners who have written about behavior maintain that choice is the *prime* principle of empowerment. These include Covey, Deci and Flaste, Deming, Ellis, Frankl, Glasser, Kohn, McGregor, Oakley and Krug, and Senge, among others. Young people learn that regardless of the situation, external stimulus, or internal impulse or urge, they still have the freedom to choose their responses.

The third principle to practice is *reflection*. Reflection is essential for effective learning and retention. In addition, reflection engenders self-evaluation—the critical component for change and an essential ingredient for happiness. The authors listed above all strongly advocate self-evaluation. Perhaps Covey put it most succinctly when he stated, "In all my experiences I have never seen lasting solutions to problems, lasting happiness and success, that came from the outside in." (Covey, p. 43)

KEY POINTS

◆ Stress is directly related to perceiving the world as being manageable or unmanageable.

◆ Practicing the three principles of positivity, choice, and reflection can reduce stress because they enhance the management of our world.

◆ Practicing positivity, choice, and reflection with ourself and with others improves quality of life.

THE POWER OF POSITIVITY

People do better when they feel better, not when they feel worse.

Positivity is a more constructive teacher than negativity. Positive messages elevate, encourage, and foster growth.

ACCENTUATE THE POSITIVE

When thoughts are guided to focus on the positive and constructive, then the self is nourished and enriched. Self-worth is intangible, and much of its cause, as well as its effect, is a matter of choosing thoughts that expand and strengthen the human psyche— rather than constrict or weaken it. A monkey is smart enough to eat only the nourishing banana and throw away the bitter peel. Yet, humans often "chew on the peel" of criticism, ridicule, embarrassment, failure, or other negatives. *It is important that teachers and parents help young people learn to throw away the peel by teaching them to focus on the positive.*

One salesgirl in a candy store always had customers lined up waiting while other salesgirls stood around. The owner of the store noted her popularity and asked for her secret. "It's easy," she said. "The other girls scoop up more than a pound of candy and then start subtracting some. I always scoop up less than a pound and then add to it." People are like magnets. They are drawn to the positive and are repelled by the negative. This is an important principle to understand when working with others. People who are effective in influencing other people phrase their communications in positive terms.

CONSEQUENCES VS. CONTINGENCIES

Consequences are associated with everything we do and can be positive or negative. An imposed consequence, however, only works when a person finds value in the relationship or when the person sees value in what he is being asked to do. Otherwise, an imposed consequence is perceived in negative terms.

When a consequence is imposed, it is often associated with a threat. Such is the case when the adult says, "If you continue to do that, here is what will happen to you." Telling a youngster, "You chose to do that and must now realize the consequence," is a pseudo choice and plays a mind game. It causes the young person to feel as if he punished himself. "If your work is not finished, you're not going," is also perceived in a negative sense. In this case, the adult also has added to his own workload because now the *adult* has the task of checking on the condition that has been established, namely, to check when the work is finished before giving permission. This approach transfers the responsibility away from the young person— where it belongs—to the adult.

In contrast to imposed and reactive consequences, proactive *contingencies* rely on internal motivation and are perceived in a positive way. "You can *do that as soon as you do this.*" *"If/then"* and *"as soon as"* assist in sending both a positive message and placing the responsibility on the young person—where it belongs. Notice these in the following examples: *"If your work is finished, then you can go to one of the activity centers." "Sure, you can go as soon as your work is finished."*

Although the result of a contingency is the same as that of a consequence, the *message and emotional effect are markedly different.* As already mentioned, when using a consequence the responsibility for checking is placed on the enforcer—the *adult.* When using a contingency, the responsibility is on the *youngster.* In addition, whereas a consequence implies a lack of trust, a contingency conveys a message of confidence and trust. The crucial difference can be best understood in personal terms. Which would you prefer to hear your supervisor say to you: "If you leave and are not back on time, we will have a real problem," or "Sure, you can leave as long as you are back in time"?

An example of the difference between a consequence and a contingency was illustrated on a television sitcom featuring Bill Cosby playing the role of Dr. Cliff Huxtable. He was sitting at the dinner table with Rudy, his youngest daughter. The father would not let the daughter leave the table until she had eaten all of her dinner. Rudy refused to finish her dinner. The father gave her a choice of finishing her dinner and leaving the table or remaining at the dinner table until she did finish. Still, she refused to eat, whereupon the father went on and on about this other 5-year-old who would not finish her dinner, and all her friends went to middle school, graduated from high school, and went to college, but the young girl remained at her dinner table. Rudy, apparently, was not impressed; she still would not finish her meal.

Denise, Rudy's older sister, came into the house, and Rudy could hear Denise and her friends move the living room couch, roll up the carpet, start to play music, and begin to dance. Just then, Denise came into the kitchen, and Rudy asked her older sister, "Can I dance with you and your friends?" Denise said, "Sure, as soon as you finish your dinner." Dr. Cliff Huxtable, the father, gave his daughter what amounted to a consequence: finish your dinner, or stay at the table. Denise, on the other hand, offered a contingency—whereupon Rudy ate her three Brussels sprouts, placed the plate in the sink, and went out to dance. Too often, we say to young people, "Eat your Brussels sprouts or else," and we don't understand why they are not motivated.

WHEN CONSEQUENCES ARE NECESSARY

My experiences with discipline as an elementary school principal, middle school assistant principal, high school assistant principal, and high school principal have all had a common thread: Young people need structure; they want to know where they stand. Consequences provide that security. Ironically, knowing the consequences beforehand provides many young people an invitation for mischief.

Some students will push as far as they can, in part, because they already know the amount of risk involved. Having knowledge ahead of time as to what will happen gives them security and reduces their risk. For example, the youngster is referred to the office for misconduct. The administrator inquires into the cause of the referral. The student pleads ignorance. He is told to stand against the wall for five minutes until he remembers. The student will stand against the wall for five minutes. The same scenario is repeated, except this time the administrator tells the student to stand until he remembers. The student inquires, "How long do I have to stand here?" The administrator responds, "I don't know." The youngster inquires again, "How long do I have to remain here?" The administrator says, "I don't know; I guess until you remember." The student will remember in fewer than five minutes because of the uncertainty of how long he will need to remain standing. The same principle is at work in the high school where the student is stopped in the hallway after the bell has rung. The administrator queries the student, who replies, "This is only my second tardy. I have one more to go before I get detention."

Announcing consequences ahead of time is counterproductive when dealing with young people. Uncertainty is much more effective. Knowing the consequence focuses on the consequence. It is better to have students focus and think about what is appropriate.

If a consequence is deemed necessary, rather than *impose* it, a more effective approach is to *elicit* the consequence from the young person. For example, whenever I was absent from my class, my substitute folder contained a form that requested the substitute leave the names of those students who acted inappropriately. Upon my return, I would speak to those students who had not been good hosts to the visitor in our classroom. The students understood that their behaviors were unacceptable, and I inquired of them what should be done. Having dealt with so many behavior problems at all grade levels, in urban as well as suburban schools, I learned that in the majority of cases the student chose something more effective for changing his or her behavior than I would have imposed. If what the student chose was not acceptable to me, the student would be given other opportunities until we could both agree on the consequence that would help the student to become more responsible. The key response I had ready was, "What else? What else?"

Here is another example of how *eliciting a consequence*—rather than *imposing one*—was used. The school year was almost over, and a student had done something that could not be overlooked. The eighth-grade party, the big event of the year, was fast approaching. The student understood that what he had done could not be ignored. The question was put to him, "What shall we do?" He said, "I guess I shouldn't go to the eighth-grade party." I responded that I could live with that decision. By my *eliciting* the consequence, ownership and responsibility remained with the student. The teacher was not the villian, and the student was not the victim.

To be effective for long-lasting results, the person must feel ownership. Lack of ownership is a prime reason why student discipline contracts do not work. A contract agreed to under duress engages little ownership from a young signer.

PROJECT POSITIVE EXPECTATIONS

Attitude is the mind's paintbrush; it can color any situation. The teacher who says, "This is a very important test. Be careful," paints a negative picture that shakes confidence. Saying, "This is a very important test and I know you can handle it and do well," paints a positive picture.

Which would you rather hear when you walk into a restaurant: "I can't seat you for thirty minutes" or "In thirty minutes I will have a wonderful table for you"? The result is the same, but the perception is different. The child who wets his bed conjures up one image when the parent says, "Don't wet your bed tonight" and a completely different picture when the youngster hears, "Let's see if you can keep the bed dry tonight." The message we convey can have a dramatic effect on young people's behavior.

The first step is awareness. To assist in becoming aware of negative statements, listen to yourself. When catching yourself saying something that paints a negative picture, take the extra step of thinking how it could be rephrased to paint a positive picture. "I'm afraid that I will forget my keys," becomes, "I'm going to remember that I placed my keys in the top drawer." Adults do not purposely set out to deprecate young people; awareness of positive language can ensure they do not. For example, rather than saying, "Did you forget again?" say, "What can you do to help yourself remember?" Rather than, "When will you grow up?" say, "As we grow older, we learn how to solve these problems from such experiences."

Positive attitudes affect teaching. Many years ago, the first day of school began on a bright note for the new teacher, who was glancing over the class roll. After each student's name was a number 118, 116, 121, and so on. "Look at these IQs," the teacher thought. "They have given me a terrific class!" As a result, the elated teacher challenged his students, raised their expectations, and communicated his confidence in them. The teacher tried innovative techniques and involved students so they became active learners. The class did much better than expected. Only later did the teacher find out that the numbers placed by students' names on new class roll sheets were locker numbers.

Here is a simple way to start off each year, especially at the elementary level. At the end of the previous year, each teacher writes one positive comment about every student that will be passed on to the student's new teacher. The comment can relate to an interest, a talent, a personal skill, an attitude, or anything else worth sharing.

The result is that the student's new teacher is equipped at the very outset with a positive viewpoint toward each student.

Students at risk often think about what they are *not* good at doing. These students are often right-hemisphere dominant, so their strengths do not lie in the left-hemisphere (logical, linguistic) areas in which schools focus after the primary grades. These students may have some hidden talent in art, psychomotor skills, leadership, or personal relations. Find one interest, talent, or skill these students possess and, in private, say something positive to them. "I see you draw well. I can tell because of the detail in your drawing." The message with students who have low self-worth needs to be repeated a number of times in different ways. Sometimes young people have to believe in someone else's belief in them until their own belief in themselves kicks in. Building on the positive gives a positive mindset. *The pictures that young people have of themselves drive their behaviors.*

We always want to refer to the behavior, never the person. If you say, "You are late all the time; you are just one of those late people," the person will work to that expectation. On the other hand, saying, "You have such great work habits in many areas, and punctuality is something that you can improve on. I know you are capable of being here on time each day," then the young person has something for which to strive. A positive picture has been created.

Also, consider the fact that mood follows action. Grandmother knew this, which is why she said to mother, "If you don't feel good, clean the stove." Similarly, doing something productive engenders positive feelings, in contrast to doing something negative or doing nothing at all. The advice is sound: *Change what you do and you change your view.*

Research has shown that optimism, whether "natural" or "learned," results in better health. People who are optimistic have a better handle on dealing with their emotions, which has an impact on the immune system, heart, and other body functions.

Positivity brings hope, which is a cousin of optimism. A series of tests on hope was given at the University of Kansas, and results were compared to the Scholastic Aptitude Test (SAT) scores, which are supposed to determine success as a college freshman. It was found that the test scores on hope were better predictors than the SAT scores. Hope and optimism are learned. They are teachable. A starting point is always to ask yourself, *"How can I say that in a positive way?"*

KEY POINTS

◆ People do better when they feel good, rather than when they feel bad.

◆ Consequences are usually imposed, which is the prime reason why they are perceived negatively and why they do not change the way a person wants to behave.

◆ Advertising consequences ahead of time is counterproductive because it focuses on consequences, rather than on expected behaviors.

◆ If a consequence is deemed necessary, rather than assign it, a more effective approach is to *elicit* the consequence, thus placing ownership and responsibility on the young person.

◆ Contingencies promise with the positive and place the responsibility on the young person, where it belongs, rather than on the adult.

◆ Negative comments engender negative attitudes. Positive comments engender positive attitudes.

◆ People who are most effective in influencing other people phrase their communications in positive terms.

◆ Positivity brings hope.

◆ The pictures that people have of themselves drive their behaviors.

◆ Positivity prompts feelings of being valued, enthusiastic, supported, respected, motivated, challenged, capable, and proud.

THE EMPOWERMENT OF CHOICE

They offer sufficient proof
that everything can be taken from a man but one thing
...to choose one's attitude in any given set of circumstances.
–Viktor Frankl

Teaching young people about choice-response thinking—*that they need not be victims*—may be one of the most valuable thinking patterns we can give them. Students become more responsible when they learn that in almost any *situation*, or with any *stimulus*, or with any *impulse* or *urge*, they still have freedom to choose a response.

CHOICE-RESPONSE THINKING

Situation

I was comfortably seated in an airplane ready for take-off on a flight to California. I had just started reading a book when the pilot announced there would be a two-hour delay; Los Angeles International Airport was fogged in. After a few minutes of additional reading, I gazed up from my book and discovered that I was one of the few passengers who had not deplaned. Even with a good read, adding two-hours to the three-hour flight seemed a little long to remain seated. I left my materials, already in the overhead storage compartment, and returned to the airport terminal. After a half-hour of strolling and shopping, the thought occurred to me that, if the fog in Los Angeles lifts, the plane might take off sooner than the two-hour announced time. I quickly returned to the loading area and watched my plane depart with my coat, seminar materials, and luggage.

This was a situation I could have avoided if I had not gone strolling and had stayed in the loading area. Although at that moment I could not change that situation, *I could still choose my response.* Getting angry would have been useless. I checked the departure schedule, arranged for a later flight to Los Angeles, and told an official my belongings were on the plane. Upon arrival in Los Angeles, I found my coat, materials, and luggage waiting for me. I felt pleased that I had taken a rational approach to the situation.

We all experience situations that are beyond our control, either momentarily or permanently. We are confronted with weather and other natural forces, with inconveniences, unpleasant assignments, unrewarding family or work relationships, and numerous situations that we cannot change. However, *we can choose our responses to these situations.*

Victor Frankl, the psychiatrist who survived Nazi death camps, experienced situations beyond his control. Yet, he taught that a person has the power to choose his thinking, his independence of mind, even in the most terrible conditions of psychic and physical stress. Although conditions such as lack of sleep, insufficient food, and various mental stresses suggest that the camp captives were bound to react in certain ways, in the final analysis it became clear that the sort of person the captive became was the result of an inner decision—not the result of camp influences alone. Even under such extreme circumstances, a person still has one freedom: "the last of the human freedoms—to choose one's attitude in any given set of circumstances, to choose one's own way." (Frankl, p. 104)

Stimulus

We also have the freedom to make a choice after something *stimulates* us. When a parent smiles at the infant, the infant smiles back. Such stimuli become less "automatic" with growth, as when the parent smiles at the teenager, but the teenager does not reciprocate with a like facial expression.

Assume for a moment that you are looking forward to watching a special broadcast on television. You have had your dinner, are comfortably reclining, and are engrossed in the program. The telephone rings. You can choose to answer it, or choose to let it ring, or choose to let the telephone-answering device respond to the call.

When you are driving and approach a red light in a busy inter-section, you choose to stop. Your initial response to answer a phone that is ringing or to stop at a red light are learned responses to stimuli. Neither of these stimuli *makes* a person do anything. Consciously or nonconsciously, we choose our responses to stimuli. These examples of reactions are everyday occurrences in daily living. In practical application, it doesn't make a particle of difference if these reactions are conscious or nonconscious. There is a problem, however, when we think our responses are automatically controlled by external stimuli. The harm comes when, by implication, we think that the ringing of the phone or the red light *causes* us to react—as if an outside force or person causes our behavior.

This same choice-response situation is operating when we are stuck in traffic and start to get angry. The traffic does not care; it is simply a situation that stimulates us. We allow ourselves to become angry. We could play a tape, a compact disc, or listen to the radio. We could think about past pleasant thoughts or future plans. *We can choose our responses to situations—no matter how unpleasant the situation may be.*

This was the situation during surgery when a very competent nurse was asked for a particular instrument and handed it to the surgeon a moment later than the surgeon expected it. The brilliant surgeon, who lacked people skills, turned to the nurse and berated her. Needless to say, the nurse's day was not very bright. She constantly thought throughout the day how the surgeon made her angry. She also reflected on the situation while driving home, and she then related the story to her husband at the dinner table. Her husband inquired what time the incident occurred. The wife responded that it took place around nine o'clock that morning. Her husband then inquired, "What time is it now?" She responded, "Seven o'clock." The husband then said, "You are telling me this incident took place ten hours ago and the surgeon is still making you angry." (I am indebted to Sam Horn for sharing this incident.) The nurse decided never again to give that surgeon the power to ruin her day, ride in her car, or be invited to her dinner table.

The nurse's original thinking was that the surgeon *made* her angry. This type of faulty thinking leads to an inference that one person can change another. Anyone who has lived with another person for any length of time discovers that no one can really *make* or *cause* another person to change. *People change themselves.* The environment can certainly be established where the person *wants* to change. This is the reason why very young people do things adults would like them to do. Youngsters value adults and *want* to please them. This is also true in the classroom. Young students like their teachers. Unfortunately, many teachers and parents use rewards and punishments thinking that these external manipulators *cause* young people to change.

Even after receiving a stimulus, an instant passes wherein a person can decide upon a response. Assume that Leo bullied Eddie. Young Eddie may choose to retaliate, he may choose to run away, he may choose to tell an adult, or perhaps he simply chooses to cry. We know that Eddie chooses what he does because he runs home, and only when he is in front of a parent, only then, does he begin to cry.

On the other hand, there are reflex actions that are automatic responses to nerve stimulation, like a sneeze. When the door slams, or someone shouts, or the dog barks, and you jump in response to the sudden noise, that is a reflex. All human beings inherit a certain level of reactivity to external stimuli. Some of us are highly reactive, while others can shut out certain amounts of incoming stimuli. As the brain matures, even highly reactive individuals tend to become less so. Reflexes are very important, and without them we would not function normally. The most basic reflex, the one that saves our lives—the so-called "fight or flight" reflex—is readily recognized. Think of what it was like when a friend who was watering the garden suddenly turned the hose on you. When we lived in a less protected environment, this startle reflex was caused not by the threat of a drenching, but by the possibility of a very real danger in the form of a tiger, a snake, or a spear. In order to survive against predators, we had to make an instant decision whether to stay and fight or run away. The situation engendered reflex thinking but even then involved some choice.

When confronted by a stimulus, a person needs to realize that a choice of responses exists. Imagine that in a classroom the teacher sees a student hitting another student. The teacher did not see the first student do the instigating; the teacher only saw the retaliation of the second student and calls him on it. The youngster tells the teacher, "He made me do it." Even though this student was stimulated to act, he still made the choice to hit back. No one else made the choice for him. The student had the freedom to choose a response, and he chose hitting. Students need to learn that regardless of the stimulus, each person still has some choice of responses.

Impulse

We also have the freedom to choose our response to an *impulse* or *urge*. Infants are given diapers to wear because they are not able to control their natural urges. As they grow, diapers are no longer needed. We learn to respond to our physiological urges. The same holds true for emotional impulses. When we become angry, there is a moment of awareness before the emotion takes over—before we may become "emotionally hijacked." (Goleman) As normal, healthy individuals—at that moment—we can exercise some choice of response. A response will occur, but the how, when, or where is often our choice.

Freedom to choose one's response is fundamental in a civil society. It is incumbent upon the adults of our society to teach young people that they have a choice in controlling their behaviors and that it is in young people's own best interests to choose appropriate responses.

Regardless of the situation, the stimulus, or the impulse, people choose their responses. To do otherwise means we would operate from compulsion. Jeffry Schmitt, a UCLA psychiatrist, refers to the beauty of being human, and not a rat or monkey. The difference is that we humans need not succumb to our emotions every single time. The less we succumb, the less we are bothered by tyrannical obsessions.

The following illustration summarizes choice-response thinking.

| Think: | CHOICE | > | RESPONSE |

SITUATION > (Information)	CHOICE	>	RESPONSE
STIMULUS > (from outside)	CHOICE	>	RESPONSE
IMPULSE > (from within)	CHOICE	>	RESPONSE

Because we have the freedom to choose our responses, we are responsible for our own choices (behaviors). By teaching young people that they choose their own behaviors, they begin to become conscious of the fact that no one else chooses their behaviors for them. Choice-response thinking encourages self-control and responsibility. In addition, having young people become aware of choice-response thinking can have a liberating effect, especially with those who feel they are helpless or victims.

As a young student explains his report card to his parents, he says, "No use debating environment versus genetic causes. Either way, it's your fault." As stated in the beginning of this section, teaching young people about choice-response thinking—*that they need not be victims*—may be one of the most valuable thinking patterns we can give them.

Victim-type thinking is counterproductive to engendering responsibility. Examples of such thinking can be heard in comments such as, "He made me do it," "I couldn't control myself," "I couldn't help it," and "I had no choice." *Merely being aware that such thinking relinquishes control has an empowering effect.*

A student has a test returned. The student did not do well and concludes, "I'm not good in this subject." The student sees a flaw in himself that he believes is beyond his control and becomes pessimistic. He gives up; he stops trying. Another student, an optimist, who receives the same grade concludes, "I guess that means I should have studied more." This student sees a setback as something *over which he has control.* The critical difference between optimistic thinking and pessimistic thinking has to do with the perception of control, which, in turn, depends upon perception of choice. We feel psychologically healthy when we believe we have choices.

Research on the value of choice is solid. Our brain generates different chemicals when we feel optimistic and in control than when we feel pessimistic and without control or power.

Choice, control, and *responsibility* are so woven together that one significantly affects the others. Make a choice, and control is enhanced. Fail to choose, and control is diminished. The more responsibility that is chosen, the more control follows. Deny responsibility, and control is given up.

People who regard themselves as victims do not see themselves as in control and often see the world as unfair to them in particular. Whatever happens in their lives only happens *to* them—as if they have no choice as to their responses. Victimhood people are often angry people. People who have chosen to regard themselves as victims cannot allow themselves to be happy because being happy would challenge their perceptions as victims. Such was the case on October 1, 1997, when a 16-year-old in Pearl, Mississippi, came to his high school campus and shot two students. When chased and caught by the school's assistant principal, the teenager was asked "Why?" The shooter replied, "The world has wronged me." Lack of a feeling of control is a prime factor in young people's anti-social behavior.

Too often, socially disruptive behavior is viewed as a "condition," resulting in students' being excused for socially irresponsible behavior. Thus, viewed through the prism of special handicaps, these students are too often not held accountable for irresponsible behavior.

When these students leave school and behave in socially unacceptable ways, giving excuses such as, "I'm compulsive," and "I couldn't help it," does not impress law enforcement or society, generally. A disservice will have been done to these students because the school world in which they have grown up is unlike the greater society. All young people need to learn that they have the freedom to choose their responses and that they will be held accountable for their choices.

Language shapes our thinking, particularly when it comes to self-talk. Taking conscious control of inner chat can act like a magic wand to shift to more empowering mental states. Victimhood is the result of thinking of outside forces rather than internal responses. Common thinking patterns are: "Someone else is at fault," "Something else caused my behavior; I am not responsible for it," and "I'm a victim."

Young people can be taught to self-talk in enabling and self-empowering ways. Phrases such as "prompts me" and "stimulates me" can be substituted for the powerless "made me" and "caused me." Additional words that reduce "victimhood" thinking are references to "influence," "persuade," "arouse," "irritate," "annoy," "pique," and "provoke." These words do not give away power; they merely describe the effect on oneself.

Another strategy to reduce powerlessness is to change adjectives into verbal forms. Notice the difference between, "I am *angering*," and "I am angry." As soon as we phrase it as an action, we become immediately aware of a choice.

Also, instead of thinking, "The task is too difficult," young people can be taught to take charge by eliminating the "too" and by changing the word "difficult" to "challenging"; thus, "The task is challenging." Another, more subtle language pattern is the ill use of "try." "Try" merely conveys an attempt. Self-talk should convey commitment. A person does not get out of bed by *trying* to get out of bed or make a phone call by *trying* to call. You get out of bed and you make a call. This type of self-talk is the hallmark of success. As Henry Ford so aptly put it, "If you think you can, you can; if you think you can't, you can't. Either way you are right."

Another approach that can be used is to teach young people to ask themselves proactive questions. "What would be the best way to act in this situation?" "How can I best respond to that?" "How can I prevent that urge from directing my behavior?" These types of questions empower people and assist in fostering individual as well as social responsibility.

It is no kindness to treat people as helpless, inadequate, or victims—regardless of what has happened to them. Kindness is having faith in people and treating them in a way that encourages and empowers them to handle their situations, stimulations, and urges.

KEY POINTS

◆ People can choose their attitudes and responses to any situation, stimulus, or impulse.

◆ Teaching young people about choice-response thinking—that they need not be victims—may be one of the most valuable thinking patterns we can give them.

◆ The critical difference between optimistic thinking and pessimistic thinking has to do with the perception of control, which, in turn, depends upon perception of choice.

◆ Choice, control, and responsibility are so woven together that each significantly affects the others.

◆ Students can be taught to self-talk in enabling and self-empowering ways.

Parts of this section first appeared in EDUCATION WEEK, May 27, 1998, as *"Rethinking Our Thinking on Discipline: Empower—Rather than Overpower"* by the author.

THE IMPORTANCE OF REFLECTION
AND SELF-EVALUATION

Learning is not compulsory, but neither is survival.
–W. Edwards Deming

Reflection is a powerful teaching and learning strategy that is too often overlooked. The key to reflection is the skill of asking self-evaluative questions. It is the most effective, yet neglected, strategy both in learning and in dealing with people. Using this skill also reinforces the other two practices of positivity and choice.

REFLECTION AND LEARNING

Reflection is necessary for long-term memory reinforcement. Its absence in the learning process can be likened to chewing—but not swallowing. The food is tasted, but unless it is digested, there is no nutritional value. Before elementary students leave a subject or middle and high school students leave a classroom, teachers should lead students to reflect upon the lesson. John Dewey phrased this concept in a formula: "Experience + Reflection = Growth."

In order to create meaning from a new informational experience, we need "internalizing time." The human brain is a meaning-seeking organ. Much of what we are exposed to in learning happens so fast that we need time to process it. The brain continues to process information before and long after we are aware of it. This is the reason why many of our ideas seem to "pop out of the blue." For this reason, a teacher can either call for learners' attention to new information or have them develop meaning—but not both at the same time. This "down time" (which is not really down) is a significant step for enhancing long-term memory.

Cramming more content per minute or moving from one piece of learning to the next without reflection virtually guarantees that little will be retained. Planning time for reflection also encourages students to let the teacher know when they did not understand or did not get a point the teacher made.

A quick-check technique is for the teacher to stop every so often and say, "In case you did not understand something, you and your partner write it down and turn it into me, and I'll read it over." Often, students will ask a question about something that the teacher thought was made clear but for some students was unclear.

A good way to promote reflection at the end of a class period is for students to keep a daily learning log. Students jot down at least one thought they had as a result of the lesson and explain the significance of the thought. Helpful prompt questions are, "What did I learn today?" "What do I need to work on tomorrow?" "In what did I do well?" and "What could I have done differently?" The questions asked are often more valuable than the answers.

A "keeper journal" is another reflective approach and has the advantage of feeling more personal. Students write down one comment, thought, or learning that they would like to *keep* (remember). If such a journal were started at the beginning of a typical American school year (although the activity can be started any time), each student would accumulate 170-200 specific remembrances from a teacher.

REFLECTION AND EVALUATIVE QUESTIONS

As important as reflection is in learning new information, the practice is equally as important for self-growth. *When applied to oneself, reflection is referred to as self-evaluation.* This practice engenders self-correction—the most effective route to improvement and growth.

Asking evaluative questions such as, "What can you do to accomplish that?" and "What would you do if you knew you could not fail?" are designed to provoke deep and reflective thinking. When you use these kinds of questions, you are directing the other person's thinking in a positive way. The answers can be a gift to the person asking questions because it is a quick way to obtain and understand the other person's perception and viewpoint, crucial in a student-teacher relationship and so many other settings.

In addition, asking these kinds of *evaluative questions* empowers the other person because the ideas that people support most are ones they come up with themselves; the answers that are most important to people are their own. *Ownership is a critical component for self-evaluation and change.*

The following four questions are extremely successful *for changing behavior*:
- What do you *want?*
- What are you *choosing to do?*

- If what you are choosing is not getting you what you want, then what is your *plan?*
- What are your *procedures* to implement the plan?

Here are additional questions for specific purposes:

For Getting On Task
- Does what you are doing help you get your work done?
- If you would like to get your work done, what would be your first step?
- What do you like to do that you can apply to this task?

For Commitment
- In the realm of *all things possible,* could you have kept your commitment?
- What are you going to do to make it happen?
- On a scale of 1 to 10, how would you rank your commitment to it?

For Improving Quality
- How does that look to you?
- What would you like to have improved even more?
- If there were no limitations on what you did, what would allow you to do it even better?

For Reducing Complaining
- How long are you going to continue this?
- Is what you are doing helping you get what you want?
- What do you notice about the experience you are having?

For Starting Conversations
- What was most pleasing for you today?
- What bothered you the most today?
- What was your biggest challenge today? How did you deal with it?
- If the situation came up again, what would you do?

The quality of the answers depends on the quality of the questions. Here are some ineffective questions that increase stress because of the responses they engender. Notice how reactive and counterproductive they are to changing behavior.
- What's the problem?

- What's your problem?
- Why are you doing this?
- Who did that?
- Why did you do that?
- Don't you know better than that?

GUIDELINES

Effective questions require a thinking response. Such questions:
- are usually open-ended. They require more than a "yes" or "no" answer.
- focus on the present or future (as opposed to the past).
- help people learn through the process of thinking.
- help people ask questions of themselves.
- are framed to fit the situation and clarify.
- often start with "What?" or "How?"

Questions that can be answered "yes" or "no" often close conversations. However, they can be used if they lead to *self-inquiry* or *self-evaluation*. In some instances, just asking a question is sufficient. In other situations, "yes" or "no" questions can be effective if followed up with another question that calls for a solution. Here are some examples of effective closed-ended questions:
- Is what you are doing working?
- Is what you are doing helping to get your work done? How?
- Is what you are choosing to do helping you get what you want? How?
- Are you willing to do something different from what you have been doing?
- Are you taking the responsible course? How?
- If you could do better, should you?
- Are you satisfied with the results?

Questions do not need to end with a question mark. For example, "Please describe to me . . . ." is an effective clarification question.

POTHOLES

Avoid asking a "Why?" question. Many times a young person does not know the reason for a behavior. Besides, such a question gives the student an excuse not to take responsibility. This is especially the case where youngsters are labeled. Even though the classification is meant to help, the label becomes a justification. "I can't help it. I have poor attention," is an example. Moreover, even if the "why" were to be known, articulating the explanation is very difficult. Most important, however, *asking a "Why?" question has little effect on changing behavior.*

"Why?" questions have an accusatory overtone. If you are really curious, ask a nonjudgmental question: "Out of curiosity, why did you choose this rather than that?" Change the structure of the question to eliminate any negative inference. A negative implication can be implied in other than "why" questions, such as, "When are you going to stop doing that?" Notice the unspoken demand and negative undertone. In contrast, asking, "How long will you be continuing that?" is inquisitive when asked in a non-accusatory tone. Of course, the tone of the voice is crucial. The adage, "What you are doing speaks so loudly that I can't hear what you are saying" rings true here.

QUESTIONS AS STRESS REDUCERS

Stress is reduced when we ask reflective, self-evaluative questions. The reduction of stress comes about because of the position in which we place ourselves. When influencing someone, only a *noncoercive* approach is effective. With this awareness, the first act is mental positioning. When practicing any skill, putting yourself in position always precedes the action. This is as true when asking evaluative-type questions as it is when holding a golf club before the swing, holding a baseball bat before the pitch arrives, shooting a basketball, holding a tennis racquet, or playing any musical instrument. The first step is placing yourself in a mental stance to employ noncoercion. You do not shout a question. The tone of voice communicates at least as much as the words. Even a horse understands this, as was reported by the trainer of Seattle Slew, the 1977 Triple Crown Winner. "Slew's a show horse. Thousands of people visit him each year. He's tough but kind, and he will do anything you ask him to do as long as you pose it as a question. If you give him an order, you are going to have a fight on your hands. And you're going to lose." (*Time*, April 28, 1997, p. 27)

THE SKILL

Asking evaluative questions is a skill. As with any skill, you will feel awkward at first, but the more you practice asking self-evaluative questions, the more comfortable you become, the more confidence you develop, and the more effective you are. In addition, regardless of how often the strategy is used with a person, it is still effective because the strategy is noncoercive and empowering.

Practice is the mother of skill. Thinking about a skill is not practicing it. Thinking is necessary for focus, but only the *actual asking of self-evaluative questions* will give you the skill. With this in mind, the question is asked, "How do you develop the skill?" Answered the sage, "With experience." "But," asked the disciple, "How do you get the experience?" Came the answer, "By asking poor questions." Remember: *you cannot learn a skill and be perfect at the same time.* Each question asked is a learning experience, and if the desired result is not obtained, it should be thought of as feedback, not as failure.

A final note: Some people have a talent and can naturally use a velvet-covered hammer. But most people need a technique. When you use a technique and understand the mechanism, your skill improves and you will have more success than relying on a talent.

KEY POINTS

◆ Reflection is a powerful teaching and learning strategy.

◆ When applied to oneself, reflection is self-evaluation—the most effective route to change and growth.

◆ The key to fostering reflection is the skill of asking evaluative questions—the most effective, yet neglected, strategy.

◆ Asking evaluative questions is a skill and is developed and becomes easy only through practice.

◆ Asking self-evaluative questions reduces stress.

◆ The best answer a teacher or parent can give is often a good question.

◆ If I were a student, would I want me as a teacher?

SUMMARY

We are just about as happy in life as we decide to be.
–Abraham Lincoln

Practicing the principles of positivity, choice, and reflection reduces stress. These three principles also improve relationships and increase effectiveness in influencing others to change their behaviors.

Negative comments engender negative attitudes. Consequences are usually perceived negatively, and they do not change the way a person *wants* to behave. Announcing consequences ahead of time is often counterproductive with young people because it focuses on the consequences, rather than on the desired behaviors. In addition, such information encourages certain types of students to push until the limit is reached. If a consequence is necessary, a more effective approach is to *elicit* the consequence—which should be reasonable, respectable, and related.

Positive comments engender positive attitudes. People who are effective in influencing others to positive actions phrase their communications in positive terms. Contingencies promise with the positive and place the responsibility on the young person, where it belongs. Positivity brings hope, which is a cousin of optimism. Positivity results in fostering others to feel valued, enthusiastic, supported, respected, motivated, challenged, capable, and proud.

Either consciously or nonconsciously, people choose their attitudes and responses to any situation, stimulus, or impulse. Teaching young people about choice-response thinking—*that they need not be victims*—may be one of the most valuable thinking patterns we can give them. This type of thinking teaches the difference between optimistic thinking and pessimistic thinking. Control depends upon one's perception of choice. Choice, control, and responsibility are so woven together that each significantly affects the others.

Reflection is a powerful teaching and learning strategy. It is also the most effective approach for bringing about change because reflection engenders self-evaluation, which is both noncoercive and empowering. The key to fostering reflection is the skill of asking evaluative questions, and, as this is a skill, it is only developed and improved through practice.

POSITIVITY, CHOICE, AND REFLECTION EXERCISE FOR STUDENTS

***Gratitude is not only the greatest of all the virtues,
but the parent of all the others.***
–Cicero

We think about what we lack more often than we think about what we have. The following exercise combines *positivity*, *choice*, and *reflection*. Hal Urban has conducted this exercise with his classes for twenty years with amazing results.

Inform your students to conduct themselves for the next twenty-four hours *without complaining*.

- Tell them not to stop the experiment even if they do complain. Just have them see how few complaints they can make in one day.

- Give each student a blank card. This makes it convenient to note each time a complaint comes forth and each time they catch themselves *about* to complain.

The next day, ask:

- What was the purpose of the assignment?

- What did you learn from doing it?

Students will have discovered the frequency and smallness of their complaints.

Then, have students label a paper, *"I am thankful for,"* and make three columns:

Column 1   <u>Things</u>   (They list all the material things they are glad they have.)

Column 2   <u>People</u>   (They list all the people they appreciate.)

Column 3   <u>Other</u>   (What will emerge will be things such as freedom, opportunity, friendship, love, intelligence, abilities, health, talents, peace, faith, God, security, learning, experiences, beauty, kindness, and the list continues.)

Instruct students to review the list four times within the next twenty-four hours:

- In the afternoon

- After dinner

- Before going to sleep

- Before school the next morning

When attention is given to the *positive*, when the option of *choice* is recognized, and when *reflection* is used, life is conducted more successfully and with greater pleasure.

2
MOTIVATING

THEORIES WE USE

We can control other people,
but we cannot change them.
People change themselves.

The beliefs and theories we hold direct our thoughts. Our thoughts mold our perceptions and direct our actions.

THEORY X AND THEORY Y

In 1960, Douglas McGregor, the late Sloan Professor of Management at the Massachusetts Institute of Technology, published *The Human Side of Enterprise*. His book was a major influence in promoting the application of behavioral science to improve productivity in organizations.

McGregor examined the reasons underlying ways people attempt to influence human activity. He studied various approaches to managing people, not only in industrial organizations but also in schools, services, and public agencies. He concluded that managerial approaches could be understood from the assumptions managers make about people. McGregor concluded that the thinking and activity of people in authority is based on two very different sets of assumptions. He referred to these assumptions as Theory X and Theory Y.

Theory X

McGregor labeled the assumptions upon which the top-down, authoritarian style is based as "Theory X." He concluded that this style is inadequate for full development of human potential. Theory X is based on the following beliefs:

1. The average person has an inherent dislike for work and will avoid it if possible.

2. Because of this human characteristic of dislike for work, most people must be coerced, controlled, directed, or threatened with punishment to get them to put forth adequate effort toward the achievement of goals and objectives.

3. The average person prefers to be directed, wishes to avoid responsibility, has relatively little ambition, and wants security above all.

These assumptions are not necessarily stated in any record, but one can see them in an organization's structure, policies, procedures, work rules, management methods, and actions. Responsibilities are delineated, goals are imposed, and decisions are made without involving individuals or requesting their consent. Rewards are contingent upon conforming to the system, and punishments are the consequence of deviation from the established rules.

Theory X styles vary from "hard" to "soft." A drill instructor uses a "hard" approach. A "soft" approach is used in less coercive strategies, such as coaxing and rewarding.

Theory Y

Theory Y assumptions are more consistent with current research and knowledge, and they lead to higher motivation and greater realization of goals for both the individual and the organization. The central principle of Theory Y is that of integration: the creation of conditions whereby members of the organization can achieve their own goals best by directing their efforts toward the organization's success. This integration is most effectively achieved using *collaboration* rather than *coercion*.

The assumptions of Theory Y are:

1. The expenditure of physical and mental effort is as natural in work as it is in play. The average person does not inherently dislike work. Depending upon controllable conditions, work may be a source of satisfaction and will be voluntarily performed, or it can be a source of punishment and will be avoided.

2. People will exercise self-direction and self-control toward objectives to which they are committed.

3. Commitment to objectives depends on the rewards associated with achieving them. *The most significant of such rewards is the internal reward of self-satisfaction.*

4. The average person learns, under proper conditions, not only to accept responsibility but also to seek it. Avoidance of responsibility is a general consequence of experiences. It is not an inherent human characteristic.

5. The capacity to exercise a relatively high degree of imagination, ingenuity, and creativity in the solution of problems is widely, not narrowly, distributed in the population.

6. Under the conditions of modern life, the intellectual potentialities of the average person are only partially utilized.

Theory Y encourages growth and development. It stresses the necessity for selective adaptation rather than for a single, absolute form of control. Above all, Theory Y points up the fact that the limits of human collaboration are not limits of human nature but of the authority figures' ingenuity and skill in discovering how to realize the potential of the people with whom they work.

Theory Y is not a soft approach to managing. It can be a very demanding style. It sets up realistic expectations and expects people to achieve them. It is more challenging to the participants—the teacher, the student, and the administrator.

Although McGregor's book is primarily about business management, he was an educator. He fully understood that these theories applied to education. While a growing number of people in education and family relations use Theory Y, many schools and households tend toward Theory X. People use external approaches in attempts to change behavior, especially when disciplining someone. They believe their own goals will be achieved by using coercion rather than by collaboration, or they are simply not familiar with Theory Y approaches. *A prime purpose of this book is to share strategies to implement Theory Y.*

Theory Y can be threatening to teachers, parents, administrators, and others in authority who are accustomed to using the power of their position. People who use Theory X rely on external motivators to influence, manipulate, and change others. The Theory Y person uses collaboration and realizes that improvement comes through desire, rather than control. In using Theory Y, for example, errors are viewed as feedback because it is the key characteristic for promoting growth and continual improvement. This is what Jerome Bruner meant when he said that the goal should be to help students experience success and failure—not as rewards and punishments—but as information. (Bruner, 1973)

The traditional model for attempting to change people has been authoritarian and aligned with Theory X. People have always submitted to a higher authority. The 1960s altered the effectiveness of the "submission" model. In the last number of years, society's model has been that nobody needs to be submissive to anyone else. Everyone has rights. Authority and expected submissiveness are out. *Everyone is equal.* Notice how often you are called by your surname preceded by a title. Not very! Using given names is much more equalizing.

The information revolution is a major reason why Theory X is not effective today. Information has always been a prime source of power and control. Only those in positions of authority possessed it, and they used it to their advantage. Not so today! Information is open to everyone, so individuals are on a more equal footing with their superiors. Restricting young people's information and access to it in today's electronically connected world is most difficult, if not impossible.

An old story dramatizes the effects of continuing to use Theory X. An expedition of scientists went on a mission to capture a Tonkin snub-nosed monkey. Only an estimated 100-200 of this particular species exists, and they reside only in the jungles of Vietnam. The objective was to capture one of the monkeys alive and unharmed.

Using their knowledge of monkeys, the scientists devised a trap consisting of a small bottle with a long narrow neck. A handful of nuts was placed in it, and the bottle was staked out and secured by a thin wire attached to a tree. Sure enough, one of the desired monkeys scented the nuts in the bottle, thrust an arm into the long neck, and grabbed a fistful. But when the monkey tried to withdraw the prize, his fist, now made larger by its contents, would not pass through the narrow neck of the bottle. He was trapped, anchored in the bottle, unable to escape with his booty, and yet unwilling to let go. The monkey was easily captured.

We may smile at such foolishness, but in some respects we operate in the same manner. We cling to the very things that hold us back, remaining captive through sheer unwillingness to let go. Peter Drucker, said that people fail because of what they will not give up. They cling to what has always worked, clearly after it has stopped working.

The person who holds on to coercion, in all its various forms, will remain captive like the monkey. In a sense, the person loses freedom. A person becomes liberated when willing to let go of the coercion and manipulation of Theory X with its stress, resistance, and poor relationships. The use of the collaboration and empowerment of Theory Y reduces stress, improves relationships, and is much more powerful in effecting change in others.

KEY POINTS

◆ How a person attempts to motivate others depends upon how the person views others.

◆ Theory X relies on control through direction and manipulation. This traditional top-down authoritarian style is inadequate in its approach in today's society.

◆ Theory Y encourages people to experience a sense of accomplishment and relies on collaboration, rather than coercion, to engender higher motivation.

◆ The use of collaboration and empowerment reduces stress, improves relationships, and is much more powerful in effecting change in others.

◆ If an adult views irresponsible behavior to be deliberatively disruptive, then coercive approaches of Theory X will be employed. Poor relationships and stress are natural outcomes of this approach. In contrast, if the adult perceives that the behavior is the youngster's best attempt to solve a frustration or problem, then the adult views the situation as an opportunity to help and uses approaches of Theory Y. In the process, resistance and resentment are reduced, and effectiveness is increased.

EXTERNAL AND INTERNAL MOTIVATION

Motivation is the art of getting people
to do what you want them to do
because they want to do it.
                    –Dwight David Eisenhower

The previous discussion of Theory X and Theory Y explained approaches people use to *influence others.* This section deals with two ways that people *become influenced* that have an effect on their motivation. The case can be made that no one really motivates another; people motivate themselves. Although this is technically true, motivation can occur in more than one way. When the legendary football coach, Vince Lombardi, started his half-time charge to the Green Bay Packers with, "Girls, let's have a talk," one would have a bit of a challenge convincing the players that they motivated themselves. Lombardi was a great motivator.*

EXPLANATION OF TERMS

The usual terms employed when discussing motivation are "extrinsic" and "intrinsic." Extrinsic motivation applies when the aim of the performance is to gain approval, to receive a reward, or to avoid punishment. The motivating force comes from outside the person. Intrinsic motivation applies when people perform for inner satisfaction or connotes something that emanates from within.

When referring to motivation, this book intentionally employs the terms *external* and *internal,* rather than "extrinsic" and "intrinsic." The reason is that this book is devoted to raising responsibility in young people, and responsibility is not a characteristic that we associate with "intrinsic" motivation. Acting responsibly may not be satisfying in the same sense as intrinsic motivation. The motivation to be responsible is more cognitive and rooted in ethics and values, in contrast to the emotion or feeling that is associated with the word "intrinsic."

The term *external* is used to connote something that comes from outside the youngster. Since motivation of the young is significantly influenced from outside, the term *external* makes the concept and

---

* Lombardi *stimulated* his players, but we do not refer to humans as stimulators.

power of peer pressure more effectively understood. The powerful pressure of peers significantly affects young people's behavior, and an awareness of this external motivation is the first step in analyzing it and determining when to accept the pressure and when to resist it.

Although humans operate from both external and internal motivation, the motivation itself often cannot be discerned by a person's actions. For example, if a youngster makes up her own bed because asked to by a parent (external motivation) or does so because she wants to (internal motivation), the action is the same; the bed has been made up.

EXTERNAL MOTIVATION

There is no discounting the significance that external motivation has in the "shaping" of the young. The modeling that parents and other role models display for youth is an essential part of their upbringing. This is evidenced by the first language babies learn, youngsters' experiences in forming and maintaining relationships, and their first lessons in appropriate—or inappropriate—behavior. Yankee wisdom referred to external influence on the young this way: "A young twig is easier twisted than an old tree."

Early in the 20th century, the concept of adolescence was developed and has had a profound change on young people's upbringing. In recent years, the emphasis on youth as a culture of its own is especially exemplified by the entertainment and fashion industries. The violence and lightning-speed actions of many videos, films, and television programs are aimed at the adolescent market. A look at almost any fashion advertisement on billboards, in newspapers, and in magazines attests to the focus on the young. A parent's purchase of the "wrong brand" of clothing is ample evidence of the strong desire of youth to "fit in" with what is popular with their peer group.

James Coleman's classic study, *The Adolescent Society: The Social Life of the Teenager and Its Impact on Education*, clearly showed that the age of adolescence could be thought of as its own ethnic group. Adolescents have their own language, their own uniforms, and they have a strong tendency to conform to their peers. Judith Rich Harris has since made the cogent point that when the age of adolescence is reached the traditional beliefs and discussions of *nature vs. nurture* are replaced by the reality of *peer pressure*.

External motivation plays an important part in people's lives. The behaviorist school of psychology is based on the principle that external motivation is pre-eminent in influencing a person's behavior. This approach can be seen in the strategy of rewarding young people when they do something good and punishing them when they do something bad. Notice that the responsibility here is on the person in authority initiating the action. The fundamental characteristic of this approach is that another person is necessary to change someone else's behavior. The responsibility rests with the other person, rather than with the one to be influenced.

It is also important to note that when teachers and parents employ external approaches, the aim is usually to have the young person do what the elder wants. This is basically teaching toward obedience. A major dilemma here is that obedience too often begets resistance. Even on the "positive" side, when an external motivator such as a reward is used, the motivation becomes not the desired prize of appropriate behavior but obtaining the reward. This is because the reward, not the desired behavior, drives the motivation.

Punishments are obviously external in nature. Their fundamental source of energy is fear. The power of fear underlies negative visions and can produce extraordinary changes—but only for short periods. William Glasser noted that attempts to apply external pressure upon students to try to motivate them generally fail. Direct motivation can be produced only with a "gun" or some other forceful method.

> But guns, force, threats, shame, or punishment are historically poor motivators and work (if we continue the gun example) only as long as they are pointed and as long as the person is afraid. If he loses fear, or if the gun is put down, the motivation ceases. (Glasser, 1969, p. 18)

INTERNAL MOTIVATION

Abraham Maslow stated the concept of internal motivation clearly:

> Human life will never be understood unless its highest aspirations are taken into account. Growth, self-actualization, the striving toward health, the quest for identity and autonomy, the yearning for

excellence (and other ways of phrasing the striving "upward") must now be accepted beyond question as a widespread and perhaps universal tendency. (Maslow, p. *xx*)

W. Edwards Deming believed that internal motivation (desire), performance, productivity, and quality work cannot be legislated or manipulated. He believed that all human beings are born with internal motivation—an inner drive to learn, to take pride in their work, to experiment, and to improve.

Thomas Armstrong writes that even when working with students labeled with Attention Deficit Disorder (ADD) and Attention Deficit Hyperactivity Disorder (ADHD), it may be far better to use behavioral strategies that *internally empower* them rather than those that externally control them. (Armstrong, 1999, p. 97)

In their explanatory book, *Why We Do What We Do: Understanding Self-Motivation*, Edward Deci and Richard Flaste show that internal, rather than external, motivation is at the heart of creativity, responsibility, healthy behavior, and lasting change. Internal motivation is the key to learning and educational success. The point was stated well in the perceptive Calvin and Hobbs cartoon where Calvin said to his teacher, "You can give me the information, but you can't make me learn." Calvin is correct; no one can make another person learn. However, a student can certainly be influenced to learn. With today's youngsters, the most effective approach for learning and changing behavior is to influence without coercion—in short, using Theory Y.

Imagine, for a moment, that you are Calvin in a classroom and are presented with the questions below. The italicized concept following each question describes the principles used in this book—most of which are rooted in internal motivation.

- You walk into your math classroom. The initial activity is to do 10 problems. Which assignment would you prefer to hear?

  A. Do the 10 problems on the board.

  B. Your choice: Do the 10 problems on the board or the 10 problems on Page 12.

Choice empowers.

- You disrupt the class. Which would have greater, more lasting impact?

  A. The teacher tells you that what you did was wrong.

  B. You realize that what you did was wrong—without the teacher's saying anything.

  Self-evaluation is essential for lasting improvement.

- You throw a wad of paper across the room. The teacher *sees it leave your hand.*

  Which would be more successful for controlling yourself in the future?

  A. The teacher tells you to pick it up.

  B. The teacher doesn't say anything—and you pick it up.

  Self-correction is the most successful approach for changing behavior.

- You walk into a classroom and notice the wastepaper basket on its side.

  Which would give you more satisfaction?

  A. Having the teacher suggest you turn it upright.

  B. Turning it upright without the teacher's saying anything.

  Acting responsibly is more satisfying through internal motivation.

- You enjoy one of the learning centers in the classroom and would like to go to it.

  Which would you rather hear?

  A. No, you cannot go to the center until your assignment is completed.

  B. Of course you can go to the center—as soon as your assignment is completed.

  Positivity is a more constructive teacher than negativity.

- You have disrupted the classroom again.

  Which would have the greater effect in changing your future behavior?

A. The teacher says, "You will serve detention tomorrow afternoon."

B. The teacher says, "With the assistance of your learning buddy, describe your behavior on this form."

Growth is greater when authority is used without punishment.

- The student sitting next to you hits you. You hit back.

Who caused your behavior?

A. The other student.

B. You.

People choose their own behaviors.

Most people choose answer "B" to these questions because this choice uses two dynamic motivators, both of which are internal. The first is integrity and a sense of fair play. The second is an appeal to pride. Neither of these indicates a sense of the external approach, which often carries with it a sense of control. Enthusiasm quickly evaporates in the face of being controlled. In this sense, internal motivation is closely related to choice. Deprive people of choice and you have likely deprived them of motivation. As one student said, "Being able to make choices leads to learning rather than just remembering."

People who are successful in relationships understand the differences between external and internal motivation. We can try to motivate others by advising, cajoling, exhorting, rewarding, demanding, and sometimes by punishing. However, these external approaches are far less powerful than those that tap into internal motivation. When a young person is given the choice of either being punished or of disappointing a parent, the answer universally forthcoming in my seminars is that people would rather be punished. People do not want to live with the feeling of disappointing a parent—or a teacher—whom they hold in esteem.

Aristotle concluded that an emotional outcome, like happiness, is the appropriate end of all behaviors because it is internally satisfying. (Scorseby, p. 37) Internal desire and satisfaction are far more effective in relations and in changing behaviors than are external or imposed approaches.

KEY POINTS

◆ External motivators are rooted in adult modeling and peer culture. They often influence through rewards and punishments.

◆ The term "external" motivation is used in this book, rather than "extrinsic" motivation, because the power of peer pressure is more easily conveyed.

◆ A fundamental characteristic of external motivators is that they rely on another person to stimulate a change, thereby placing responsibility on that person.

◆ The term "internal" motivation is used in this book because responsibility is more cognitive and rooted in ethics and values, in contrast to the emotion or feeling that is associated with the usual motivation term "intrinsic."

◆ Internal motivation is closely related to choice. Deprive people of choice and they lose motivation.

◆ Internal desire and satisfaction are far more effective in changing behaviors than are external or imposed approaches.

Preliminary Note:
The Epilogue of this book explains how business differs from learning. Although both require effort, the term *work* is usually associated with business and employment. Since I want to make a clear distinction between business and learning, in this book home*work* is referred to as *home assignment.*

REWARDS

Young people do not need bribes to act responsibly.

Rewards and acknowledgments can serve as great incentives. However, when used for expected standards of behavior, they can be counterproductive. Giving rewards for behaving appropriately encourages dependency, a process that is diametrically opposed to raising responsibility.

REWARDS AS INCENTIVES

Rewards serve as incentives. For example, grades are incentives and may motivate students to pay attention in class, study after class, complete home assignments, and do whatever else is necessary to receive the reward of a good grade. However, schools have great numbers of students who believe that a good grade is not an important enough reward to act as an incentive. *Rewards are effective only if the person is interested enough to work toward receiving them.*

Knowing this helps teachers and parents understand why some young people do not expend energy to improve their school grades. Rather than grades, learning should be the incentive. Jerome Bruner made the point in his classic, *The Process of Education*, in which he stated, "Ideally, interest in the material to be learned is the best stimulus to learning, rather than such external goals as grades or later competitive advantage." (Bruner, 1961, p. 14)

ACKNOWLEDGMENTS AS INCENTIVES

Acknowledgments encourage and motivate. They serve to give recognition without the disadvantages of praise. Praise has a price. It implies a lack of acceptance and worth when the youth does not behave as the adult wishes. Using a phrase that starts with, "I like...." encourages a young person to behave in order to please the adult. By contrast, acknowledgment simply *affirms* and *fosters self-satisfaction*.

Notice the difference in the following examples, first of praise followed by acknowledgment. "I am so pleased with the way you treated your brother," versus "You treated your brother with real consideration." "I like the way you are working," versus "Your working shows good effort." "I'm so proud of you for your grades," versus "Your grades show you are doing well."

Two characteristics usually determine whether the comment is one of praise or one of acknowledgment. The first is that praise often starts with a reference to oneself: *"I am so proud of you for...."* or *"I like the way...."* The second is that praise is patronizing. If you would not make the comment to an adult, then think twice before making it to a youth.

REWARDS FOR EXPECTED STANDARDS OF BEHAVIOR

When we give students rewards for expected behavior, we are sending a false message. In the world outside of school or the home, no one receives a reward for doing what is appropriate and expected. Rewards are not given for stopping at red lights or for not jaywalking.

Rewards for good behavior teach children that if they are good they will receive something in return. Young people soon learn that being good can be bargained for, can be bartered, and, in a very broad sense, has commercial worth. This can be understood in remarks like, "If I'm good, what will I get?" and "What's in it for me?"

Giving such rewards does not foster moral development. Good or bad, right or wrong, just or unjust, moral or immoral—these values are not considered. Winning the prize becomes the incentive, mitigating against questions such as, "Is this good?" "Is this a responsible thing to do?"

The message that a behavior is good because it is rewarded gives a false value: "What I am doing must be good because I am being rewarded for it." Rewarding appropriate behavior implies that such behavior is not *inherently* worthwhile. In addition, giving rewards for expected standards of behavior deprives students of the satisfaction that comes with doing what is socially responsible and right.

The effect of giving rewards also has an effect on character development. Studies at the University of Toronto, Arizona State University, and elsewhere show that external rewards or recognition for socially responsible behaviors are associated with *less* commitment for helping, caring, and sharing over the long haul. (Kohn, May 1997, p. 732)

In summary, giving *rewards for expected behavior is counterproductive* to fostering social responsibility, an expectation society has for schools. Young people do not need bribes to be cooperative or to be good. They actually want to be and do good. This is evidenced by the simple strategy of asking a young person for assistance. If the request is presented in a way that shows you genuinely need the person's assistance, rarely will the person refuse.

WHY WE USE REWARDS

Rewards are used because they create obedience. A primary teacher approaches a group of students working on task and says, "I just love boys and girls who do their work." Of course they will do their work. Boys and girls love their teachers. However, notice that another message has also been sent. "Unless you do your work, I'll abandon you; I won't like you; I won't be your friend unless you do what I want." Notice how, *inadvertently*, the comment has changed the students' motivation from the joy of the task to pleasing the teacher.

Rewards are quick and easy to use. Games, movies, free time, and M&Ms manipulate young people toward good behavior. But how long do the rewards last? The answer: Until the games have been played, the movies ended, the free time used up, and the M&Ms swallowed. Attitudes and commitments remain largely untouched.

Another reason we use rewards is that *we rely too much on stimulus-response psychology to change human behavior.* This "external" psychological approach is based on the theory that human beings can be motivated by the same approaches used with animals and, like animals, humans can be trained. This concept of training is reminiscent of the man who wanted to train his young dog. The owner figured that if the dog had an accident on the rug, the owner would take the dog and shove his nose in it, then pound him on the butt with a newspaper, and then push the dog out the little kitchen door into the backyard, where the dog was supposed to do his job. Sure enough, you can guess what happened. After three days, the dog would poop on the floor, and then run out the little kitchen door into the backyard. The dog did not learn what the master intended, but the little animal knew to clear out of the area.

We also use rewards because *we have come to believe they are necessary.* Carolyn Early, a teacher near Houston, Texas, told me about a parent whose seventh-grader was in her class. The father insisted that his son needed a positive note when he didn't make disruptive noises such as singing in class. A belief that a stimulus-response approach is necessary to change behavior is not unique to this parent. It is prevalent among many parents—and teachers.

Another reason rewards are used is *the desire to increase student self-esteem.* Yet, the self-esteem movement, as it is often practiced, has had disappointing returns on its investment. The fatal flaw in the self-esteem movement lies in the very belief that one person can change another's self-esteem through *external* motivators.

Praise is a prime strategy used to increase the self-esteem of young people, as can be witnessed when children sit in circles and compliment one another. Flattery may prompt us to feel good, but these feelings are transitory; they do not significantly change our self-perceptions. Our self-perceptions relate to our own thoughts of our capabilities. If a sense of worth is not *forthcoming from within the student,* even a positive external message may be interpreted as superficial.

Young people are very sensitive to our motives, even when we may not be clear about them ourselves. Even very young children can detect insincerity and manipulation, as when the kindergarten student crumpled up a paper the teacher had just gushed over. The teacher winced when she heard a neighbor say to the complimented youngster, "She just says that to get you to be good." The teacher's good intentions become counterproductive.

When rewards are given on a regular basis, as is often the practice in attempts to raise self-esteem, they become competitive. Young students compare and count stickers and compliments. This competition is counterproductive to raising self-esteem because of the measuring aspect. Measuring always connotes a purpose or goal—whether it is physical, emotional, or mental, and whether or not the goal is good for the person. Striving for self-esteem through measuring almost always leads to self-downing and self-deprecation because there is always a chance that the goal will not be achieved. This is the case when the person has not met with success or believes that someone else is superior. Even if self-esteem is raised, and the person feels good momentarily, the feeling is conditional because in order to maintain it, the individual must keep attaining the goals, which requires constant effort.

In addition, measuring oneself is disadvantageous because it tends to lead to anxiety. Measuring may result in the person's feeling less successful than desired and may produce a pessimistic belief of the inability to change or to improve. This, in turn, causes the person to try even less, resulting in even lower achievement. Here is a prime reason why self-esteeming is utterly deadly for those who are weak, slow, inadequate, or untalented. Unfortunately, these are some of the very people at whom the self-esteem movement is aimed.

An unspoken purpose of measuring is to be superior. Yet, self-esteeming and self-measuring may inadvertently lead to alienation from others and ruin relationships because they lead to self-absorption. The need for achievement increases while relationships with other humans diminish. When self-esteeming leads to bad feelings because the goal has not been accomplished, or when good feelings don't result, others may begin to disrespect the person because of the resulting self-downing. This, in turn, leads to the loss of respect, friendship, or love.

Unconditional self-acceptance, rather than self-esteem, should be the aim. "Non self-acceptance" really means that the person chooses to condemn herself, to feel undeserving. Unconditional self-acceptance is far more successfully accomplished when the *action*, rather than the person, is acknowledged. *It is the achievement itself that brings self-acceptance and self-satisfaction.* Unconditional self-acceptance laps over to others by accepting them, which, in turn, leads to better relations.

As Oseola McCarty, the Mississippi washerwoman who gained fame by donating $150,000 to the University of Southern Mississippi, said, "If you want to be proud of yourself, you have got to do things you can be proud of." Self-esteem is always the result of thoughts and actions emanating from within.

ADDITIONAL CONSIDERATIONS ABOUT REWARDS

Rewards punish. When a teacher rewards student "A" with praise while student "B" is not praised for the same behavior, this oral reward is counterproductive. "I really like the way Wallace is sitting in his seat," is not doing Wallace a service. In fact, the exact opposite occurs. Not only can children see the attempt to manipulate behavior, but also Wallace is not endeared to his fellow classmates. He feels punished by the teacher's comments, especially if he is the type of student who is embarrassed by the public recognition. In this regard, it is not uncommon for a teacher to compliment a student whose behavior has improved, only to have the student immediately misbehave again. Some students simply do not like to be pointed out, or the comment contradicts the self-image of the child, who then attempts to reinforce his own self-perception by acting out his usual behavior pattern.

Rewards change motivation. This is the prime principle to remember about the use of rewards. Teachers of upper elementary grades through high school know this by the most common questions students ask: "Will the material be on the test?" and "Will this count on the grade?" Rather than being motivated by curiosity, the challenge, or the enjoyment of learning, the students' motivation turns toward the external reward—the grade. The motivation is to do well for the teacher's evaluation, rather than for the learning itself. In addition, and this is rather obvious, the more emphasis placed upon the external reward of the grade, the more students look for the easiest way to obtain it.

Here is a paradox. Many studies have shown that the more we reward people for doing something for which they are not internally motivated, the more likely they are to lose interest in whatever they had to do to get the reward. (Kohn, February 1997, p. 430) In other words, the more emphasis we place upon the external motivator, the more students lose interest in what they are doing. Deci phrased it, "Stop the pay, and stop the play." (Ruenzel, p. 26) Rewarding students for reading is a typical example. When students read for pay or for some prize, their long-term interest in reading declines. They will be motivated to read in order to obtain the prize, but they read less after receiving the booty.

Creativity declines when more emphasis is placed upon grades. You can prove this to yourself with any group of students. Give them an assignment and let them know that you are very interested in seeing what they can do with it. Be clear that you will not assign a grade. Then give a similar assignment and inform the students that the activity will be graded. See for yourself the decline in creativity.

Another characteristic is that rewards *foster competition.* This concept is examined further in Chapter 4 in the section *Collaboration—Rather than Competition—for Quality Learning.* The important point to note here is that a person wins a reward at the expense of others. Everyone cannot be the winner. But even more important is the realization that cooperation is essential for the establishment and maintenance of a learning community. In "*Musings in the Wake of Columbine: What Can Schools Do?"* the authors conclude, "Until we make schools engaging learning communities whose members value those communities and feel welcome within them, we are right to think that the next Columbine could happen anywhere." (Raywid and Oshiyama, p. 449) Giving external rewards inevitably leads to competition, rather than cooperation and collaboration—two critical factors in establishing a learning community.

Giving external rewards for expected standards of behavior promotes the values of children, rather than the values necessary to promote autonomous behavior.

Adults who use external rewards focus on changing behavior—not on developing values. At best, values become of secondary importance—if they are considered at all.

When adults reward children with candy or other items for doing things—such as completing an expected task, being kind to others, or behaving appropriately—the values of children are being reinforced rather than the values that adults are hoping to instill.

While most young people will do what adults want them to do to get the reward, the adults have not moved one step closer to fostering values such as responsibility, integrity, and trustworthiness.

KEY POINTS

◆ A reward can serve as an effective incentive only if the person is interested in the reward.

◆ Acknowledgment is more effective as an incentive than is praise.

◆ The prime principle to remember about the use of rewards is that they change motivation. Winning the prize becomes the incentive.

◆ Rewards for good behavior teach children that if they are good they will receive something in return. This is a false message. Society does not give rewards for expected standards of behavior.

◆ Giving rewards for appropriate behavior is counterproductive to fostering internal motivation for raising responsibility and for promoting positive values.

PUNISHMENTS

People pressured against their will remain of the same opinion still.

Punishments in the form of penalties, retribution, isolation, and incarceration are traditional ways society attempts to achieve fairness and justice. *No argument is presented here against such societal practices for adults who have been convicted of socially harmful behavior.* If you believe that a youngster is an adult, then it may seem natural to treat a young person with the same approaches used to break socially harmful adult behavior patterns. However, if you believe that *young people are not adults,* then the use of *imposed* punishments to raise responsibility must be examined.

THEORY AND PROBLEMS WITH PUNISHMENTS

Punishment and threats of punishment have been our chief tools for dealing with irresponsible behavior. This is especially the case when it comes to disruptive classroom behavior. The rationale is that something must be done *to* the student. What is done usually involves some type of pain or threat of pain (not physical pain, of course). *Punishment operates on the theory that young people must experience pain in order to grow into responsibility.*

One reason we keep thinking punishment works is that sometimes the behavior stops. This may be the case with very young children if the behavior is caught early so that it has not become an established habit and if the punishment itself is a novel experience. However, we must also consider whether or not the subject understands which action is being punished.

Punishment may also be effective with the person who feels *connected* to the punisher. This is especially the case with young people who want to learn and do well. *They experience punishment as a reminder, not as an attempt to hurt them.* (Glasser, 2000, p. 154)

Punishment *is ineffective with far too many young people.* A testament to punishment's ineffectiveness is its escalation. When punishment fails to work, inevitably more punishment is prescribed, and the cycle perpetuates itself. By the time some students reach the secondary level, they have been talked to, lectured at, sent out of class, kept after school, referred to the office, referred to Saturday school, and suspended from school—and they simply no longer care.

Punishment is temporary and transitory. Fear and force only produce changes in the short run. Once the punishment is over, the student has "served his time" and is "free and clear" from further responsibility. A coercive approach that works in the short run does not mean it is effective in the long run. Threatening a youngster with punishment may force compliance—but only so long as the threat is present. Needless to say, it does not change behavior when the coercion is gone.

Punishment is teacher-dependent, rather than student self-dependent. The threat of punishment may coerce a student to act appropriately in one class but have no effect on the way she interacts with others outside of that class. In addition, because punishment is teacher-dependent, its use is inconsistently applied. What is a punishable offense by one teacher is not by another.

Punishment has little effect on fostering desired long-term changes because it deprives young people of taking responsibility for their own actions. It moves ownership of a problem from the student to the teacher, at the expense of engendering self-evaluation. The oft-punished child obtains few experiences in self-evaluation and in making sound judgments, a pattern of deficit that carries through to adulthood. In addition, when a youngster is punished, from his vantage-point the failure is no longer his fault. He becomes the victim and blames the adult for his predicament.

Punishment is based on avoidance, a negative response. Punishment stirs primal feelings of fear, fleeing, or fighting. Such emotions are counterproductive to the learning process. In addition, its use automatically puts the student and teacher in adversarial roles, which usually has predictable results: (1) the student tests the teacher to see what he can get away with and/or (2) it diminishes the person's motivation to learn. Punishment kills the very thing we are attempting to do—motivate the student to learn what the teacher desires. In addition, very sensitive young people retreat into feelings of low self-esteem where they begin thinking they are truly bad.

Punishment or the threat of it does not help the young person learn how to modify the behavior involved. What the young person learns—if the behavior is so strongly motivated that he or she continues it—is not to get caught the next time. Making excuses and covering one's tracks become the focus. Evasiveness increases rapidly under punishment, a sad situation in any class or family setting. Also, repeated or severe punishment has some very nasty side effects: fears, anger, resentment, resistance, revenge, even hate in the punished one—and sometimes in the punisher, too.

None of these mental states is conducive to learning. As educators, our goal should be to build self-reliant, responsible citizens. We want to foster the kinds of characteristics that emanate from a personality with an ethical self-image and a healthy sense of self-worth. Shaming, humiliating, and hurting students are counterproductive to both good teaching and to the ultimate objective, which is to encourage students to become responsible, cooperative, and motivated in socially healthy directions.

Not too many of us remember that the horse that pulled the buggy was urged on by a flick of the whip, and information was pounded into students by the cane, the strap, or fear of them. But since then, we have found better ways to teach; yet we are still using the horse and buggy approach to foster social responsibility in an era when both society and the nature of youth have dramatically changed.

An interviewer once related the following to me after a discussion of how society and youth have changed in recent generations:

> The other day, my teenage daughter, who is really a lovely child, was eating in a rather slovenly manner, and I *lightly* tapped her on the wrist and said, "Darling, please don't eat that way."
>
> My daughter replied, "Mother, don't abuse me."

The mother had grown up in the 1960s and volunteered the point that her generation tested authority but really was afraid to step out of bounds. She reiterated that her daughter was a good child and added, "*But the kids today not only disrespect authority, they have no fear of it.*"

When students are not afraid, punishment loses its efficacy. Yet, we often resort to punishment as a strategy for motivation. For example, students who are assigned detention and who fail to serve it are punished with more detention. Yet, in the hundreds of seminars I have conducted around the world, teachers who use detention rarely suggest that it is effective in changing behavior. If detention were effective, the same students would not be consistently assigned to it. The reason detention is ineffective is that it is punishment-based—a negative, coercive approach. The fact of the matter is that *people learn and act better when they feel better, not when they feel worse.*

The negative and stressful effects of using coercion take their toll on the coercer, as well. Education has been referred to as the "*profession that eats its young.*" "Thirty percent of teachers leave in the first five years and the exodus is even greater in some school districts." (Halford) In my home state of California, the rate has reached fifty percent. (Fuetsch) The Phi Delta Kappa/Gallup Polls of both teachers and the public consistently list disciplinary problems as a major cause of concern. *A prime reason—both for teachers' leaving the profession and the concern for discipline—is the clinging to coercive approaches as a strategy for motivating students to behave appropriately.*

If coercion were effective in reducing inappropriate behavior, discipline problems in schools would be a footnote in history. The irony of coercion is that the more you use it in an attempt to control others' behaviors, the less real influence is exerted over them. The reason is that coercion breeds resentment. In addition, if students behave because they are forced to behave, the teacher has not really succeeded. Little of the teacher as a positive influence will remain. Students should behave responsibly because they *want* to—not because they *have* to.

PUNISHMENT SATISFIES THE PUNISHER

In practice, coercive approaches such as punishment serve to benefit the punisher more than the punished. A cartoon demonstrates the point. It shows a father running after his son, strap in hand. The mother calls to her husband, "Give him another chance." The father retorts, "But what if he doesn't do it again?" *If the child does not do it again, then who is the punishment for?*

Punishment is reinforcing for the *punisher* because it demonstrates and helps to maintain dominance. Until the day when a child is big enough to retaliate, the adult is the dominant one. This, unknowingly, may be the main motivation behind our tendency to punish. The punisher may be primarily interested, not in behavior, but rather in proving higher status. In essence, the parties are engaged in a power struggle. The paradox of this situation is that the youngster knows which "button" to push to stimulate anger in the more powerful. When anger is demonstrated, the power desires of the vanquished become satisfied.

In all my school experiences, I observed more situations than I care to recall where the intent of the person referring a student to the office was focused on receiving satisfaction, basically revenge. I would like to think that the desire was to have the student become more responsible. It was not. Satisfaction for the punisher was the goal.

We are expecting students whom we "intentionally hurt" to act constructively. But can you recall the last time you felt bad and did something good? *You cannot think positively with negative feelings.* We do "good" when we feel good. *Coercion can force compliance but never commitment.* Have you ever seen anyone punished into commitment? Punishment kills the very thing we are attempting to do, viz., to change behavior into something that is positive and socially appropriate.

When a punishment does effectively halt a behavior, then the sequence of events becomes reinforcing for the punisher. The punisher tends to confidently punish again. This may be the prime reason why so many continue to use it, thinking that it is effective, even though other approaches can achieve better results without using punishment at all.

THE POWER OF NOT USING IMPOSED PUNISHMENTS

Self-punishment is the worst type and the most severe. Punishment is too often used for those who don't need it. These students will respond without punitive action. Kahlil Gibran makes the point when he asks, "And how shall you punish those whose remorse is already greater than their misdeeds?" (Gibran, p. 43)

All too often, the assumption is made that punishment is the only successful course of action to immediately halt inappropriate behavior. The paradox is that noncoercion can be far more effective than coercion. This point is brought home when we expect punishment but do not receive it. In such cases, we often remember the experience more than if we had been punished.

A friend of mine related a childhood incident. He and his brother expected some dire consequence when their father found out they had turned off the lights in the local restaurant as they ran out the door. Rather than meting out punishment, their father—knowing that his sons knew that he knew what they had done—did not resort to punishment. To this day, my friend remembers his own inappropriate behavior and the impact of his father's knowing of it and not punishing him. The fact that the father was disappointed by my friend's action was much more powerful than a transitory punishment would have been.

A fellow passenger on a flight told me an incident about this very point. Here is the story as Eric McDermott later wrote it to me.

> Though I haven't seen her in almost 20 years, my second-grade teacher has left a positive impression on me that has since, and will always, shape the way I treat people. It is with great affection for her creative direction that I share with you just one seemingly modest example of how a teacher's creativity can transform a young child's vision.
>
> I have always had a lot of energy, and second grade was no exception. In quiet period one morning, I was drawing a picture on a piece of paper. I was so excited about my drawing, I wanted to share it with my friend on the other side of the room. Knowing that I dare not get up to walk over to him, I transformed my piece of paper into a paper airplane. Waiting for just the right moment, I threw it to him.
>
> Having seen my launching from her desk, my teacher broke the quiet and said in a stern voice, "Eric, come over here right now, and bring that piece of paper with you."
>
> I walked over to her giant desk, terrified.
>
> "Hand me that piece of paper," she said gazing into my eyes.
>
> She inspected the paper airplane for several seconds as I awaited my sentence.
>
> "Hmm...," she said, never breaking her stern facade, "This is a very good paper airplane. I want you to go to the front of class and teach us all how to fold this kind of paper airplane. Afterwards, we'll all go outside and see whose flies the farthest."
>
> She handed paper out to everyone, and being the big ham that I was, I took great delight in teaching the class how to make it.
>
> At the time, I was in awe. Until that point, I had

always been punished by my teachers for what they viewed as undisciplined disturbances. Instead of scolding me, she had transformed my misbehavior into a learning opportunity. I loved her for what she had done.

While the class learned how to make paper airplanes, an essential skill in second grade, I learned the importance of using one's creativity to bring out the creativity in others.

I share this anecdote with all of my friends who have gone on to be teachers, and remember it even when I teach at my local Sunday school.

We moved away from Knoxville, Tennessee, in my third grade year and I now live in California. I went back to Knoxville just recently for the first time in 16 years. With great excitement I visited my Cedar Bluff Elementary School, but my teacher had retired just four years earlier and I never got to see her.

I don't know how she's doing, but according to the staff I spoke with when I visited, she is still residing in Knoxville. My second grade teacher, though she may not know it, and I may never get to see her and tell her so, will forever be in my thoughts and serve as an inspiration to make a difference in the lives of others.

Eric told me that if he were punished, he didn't think he would ever remember the incident. However, to this day he remembers how his second-grade teacher used the incident to teach him a lesson in a positive way by building on an incident that could very well have resulted in punishment.

These stories are but a sampling of those where the perpetrators still remember how a skillful adult used the opportunity to teach, rather than to punish.

KEY POINTS

◆ Punishment operates on the theory that young people must be "harmed" when they behave inappropriately in order to grow into responsibility.

◆ Punishment is temporary and transitory.

◆ Punishment has little effect on fostering desired long-term changes because it deprives young people of taking responsibility for their own actions.

◆ Punishment kills the very thing we are attempting to do—motivate students in positive ways.

◆ A prime reason for teachers' leaving the profession is the use of coercive approaches as a strategy for motivating students to behave appropriately.

◆ Coercive approaches such as punishment serve to benefit the punisher more than the punished.

◆ Coercion can force compliance—but never commitment.

◆ Self-punishment is the worst type and the most severe.

———————————————

REWARDS AND PUNISHMENTS:
TWO SIDES OF THE SAME COIN

Punishments ask, "What do you want me to do, and what happens to me if I don't do it?" Rewards ask, "What do you want me to do, and what do I get if I do it?" –Alfie Kohn

Bribing youngsters with rewards to behave appropriately and punishing them when they do not are two sides of the same motivational coin. Both are external approaches used to influence behavior.

WHERE WE STAND

Rewards and punishments can be likened to the use of the carrot in front of the mule and the stick behind it. The carrot only works with a hungry mule. If the mule is fed first, he has no interest in the carrot. When the mule becomes so hungry that it is worth the effort to get the carrot, then he will move. So, if the mule has been fed and a carrot is placed in front of him and he moves, we think the carrot motivates him. However, what really motivates the mule is the beating. The reason is that once you beat him hard enough, it is less uncomfortable for the mule to walk than to be hit. The response is to ease the pain of the discomfort, rather than to eat the carrot.

The Swiss psychologist, Jean Piaget, believed that adults undermine the development of autonomy in children when they rely on the use of rewards and punishments to influence their behavior. Punishment, according to Piaget, is an externally controlled behavior-management technique that often leads to blind conformity, deceit, or revolt in those being controlled. Children who choose to become conformists need not make decisions; all they need to do is obey. Other children practice deceit to avoid punishment. When parents or teachers say, "Don't let me catch you doing that again!" children respond by exerting every effort not to get caught—rather than focusing on appropriate behavior.

Kurt Lewin, the first to write in the area of social psychology, intentionally used the word "manipulation" when referring to these external approaches. Rewards and punishments amount to just that. The adult plays a game of power and control in which only the adult wins. The reason is that they are unilaterally imposed. The long-term use of this manipulative tactic requires raising the stakes. The teacher must keep these incentives ever present because children learn to depend upon these types of motivators. More and more treats must be offered or more threats or sanctions must be used to induce people to continue acting in the way the manipulator desires. They become self-perpetuating and need to be intensified to remain effective.

Not only does this reward-punishment approach become progressively more objectionable the older the person becomes, but it works only up to a certain point, up to a certain age. Anyone who works with adolescents and teens knows it gets tougher and tougher—because teenagers have shifted their reference group. Their desire for approval no longer comes from their parents and teachers. It now comes from their peers.

By using rewards and punishments, we give children the easy way out—at the expense of their development and maturation. Rather than empowering them with responsibility, they quickly learn that temporary compliance will get them off the hook, either in the form of accepting a loss of privileges or writing apology notes that will right all wrongs. Many children would rather take the pain of punishment than take the time to make difficult decisions and exert self-control.

When we use rewards and punishments as motivational strategies, we are teaching kids to make their decisions based on someone else's reaction. We reinforce the practice of people making their decisions based on how the other person is going to respond. The message tells people, "It's not what is best for you but how the *other person* is going to react." Teachers and parents are not around when peer pressure encourages young people to take up tobacco, get high on drugs, or do something that is destructive to themselves or society. The *ultimate* goal is not to obey and keep adults happy. The ultimate goal is for young people to act in a responsible way because it *pays off for them—because responsible behavior is in their own best interests.* If you have this vision—of what is good for *them*—it is going to reduce your stress in your relationships with them because it doesn't box you into manipulative and punitive modes.

The case bears repeating. In order for a person to take responsibility, the person must *want* to. *Obedience does not create desire.* Desire only comes through internal motivation, through *commit-*

ment—not compliance. Responsible behavior is a chosen behavior. It cannot be given; it can only be taken.

Rewards and punishments, then, are counterproductive to fostering self-discipline. The paradox here is interesting. Our goal is to assist students to become responsible, self-disciplined, self-reliant, independent problem solvers. Yet, giving rewards and using punishments for expected behavior set up students to be dependent upon an external agent. They set the person up to receive, rather than to give, *but it is in the giving that responsibility is developed.*

An inquiry into how external motivators affect behavior when no one is around reinforces the point. Here is the critical question: *How effective are rewards and punishments when no one is looking?*

WHERE ARE WE GOING?

There is an old Greek myth about a gentleman who was looking for Mt. Olympus. On his journey, he passed an elderly man and asked him for directions. The elderly man turned out to be Socrates. When the traveler asked him how to get to Mt. Olympus, the old sage responded in his reflective tradition: "Be sure every step you take is in that direction."

Rewards and punishments do not take us in the direction that fosters responsibility. Rather than doing things *to* young people, the most effective way to raise responsibility is to use noncoercive approaches by working and collaborating *with* young people.

KEY POINTS

◆ Rewards and punishments create obedience, but the problem is that they do not encourage responsible thinking.

◆ Rewards and punishments set the person up to receive, rather than to give, but it is in the giving that responsibility is developed.

◆ Rewards and punishments stimulate, but they do not encourage reflective thought such as, "Is this good for me?"

◆ Doing things *to* young people is not nearly so effective in changing long-term behavior as doing things *with* them.

TELLING

When I was a boy of fourteen, my father was so ignorant
I could hardly stand to have him around.
But when I got to be twenty-one, I was astonished
at how much he had learned in seven years.
–Mark Twain

Telling and mini-lecturing are generally ineffective with young adolescents, who are trying to assert their own independence.

TELLING OTHERS

The parent wants to save the adolescent from the consequence of what the parent sees as a negative experience, so the parent begins to lecture. After a few minutes, the glaze comes over the young person's eyes. The parent has been tuned out. The adolescent is thinking, "I'm being lectured again," or "Just because you tell me what to do, doesn't mean I'm going to do it." The intentions of giving guidance and counsel are good, but the young person who is attempting to assert independence perceives the advice as an attempt to control. People don't mind controlling, but they usually dislike *being* controlled.

Whenever we tell people to do something differently, we convey a message that the way they have been performing is wrong or not good enough. Telling implies that something has to be changed, but people tend to resist change that is thrust upon them. This often creates defensiveness and a tendency to resist.

I recall a friend sharing with me how he hated having his mother tell him to do something. Even though it was something he wanted to do, such as playing outside, because she *told* him to do it, he found an excuse not to do it. Just for a moment, think of a situation where someone told you that you *had to do something.* When someone tells us what we should do, most of us think, "Don't tell *me!*"

When a teacher tells a student what to do, the student perceives this as coercion, and it is often resented. Some teachers even keep a record of how many times a student is told—and often on the board for the entire class to see. The ineffectiveness of this approach can be verified simply by looking at names on a board in a classroom at the beginning of the year, and then revisiting the classroom again at the end of the year. The same—and additional—names appear with checkmarks.

By bringing to mind the all too familiar expression, "If I have told you once, I have told you a…." we see how ineffective telling is in changing behavior. If telling were successful, we would not have to repeat ourselves.

The ineffectiveness of telling, in contrast to the more effective approach of asking self-evaluative questions, is well illustrated by the classic story of people who started selling life insurance. These people went through the company's training program, and they were very successful for about a year and a half. After this period, sales dropped off.

The company made quite an intensive investigation as to the reasons, and they found that the people followed the prescribed sales approach for about eighteen months. The training approach taught by the company showed how to ask specific kinds of questions, which fostered a bonding with clients because the sales people not only learned about the clients' financial situations and future plans, but also something about the people as individuals.

However, after about eighteen months, the salespeople had learned so much that they thought to save time. They began asking fewer questions and talking more. Sales dropped because the salespeople did not bond with the prospective customers. When sales plummeted, the salespeople began talking even more. They soon began focusing on the fear of losing sales, became discouraged, and the downward spiral of performance went into full gear. The time that telling saved came at the expense of success.

TELLING OURSELVES

Telling a person what to do is not nearly so effective as a person's deciding for oneself. Asking reflective and self-evaluative questions engenders this. If we stop and reflect, we realize that when we are successful in obtaining something we really want from someone, *we don't tell*; we ask. If you are now or ever have been married, ask yourself whether the proposal was *asked* or *told* you. Chances are that the proposal was asked.

Simply stated, telling does not engender the *desire* in people to do what you would like them to do.

KEY POINTS

◆ Even though the intent of telling a youngster is worthwhile, the actual telling is perceived as an attempt to control, and people do not want to be controlled.

◆ Telling creates defensiveness and a tendency to resist.

◆ Telling does not engender desire.

MINDSETS

"How do I make Johnny learn?" is a question
that has plagued all teachers since the beginning of time.
The answer is simple. It can't be done!
No one can make a child or anyone else learn.
                                        –Madeline Hunter

Mindsets are attitudes, dispositions, intentions, and inclinations. If Johnny's mindset is one of little or no interest in learning (and this includes learning appropriate behavior), Johnny will not learn much. Therefore, *a major task of adults working with young people is to promote mindsets that promote learning and appropriate behavior.*

James Sutton is a psychologist in Pleasanton, Texas, who trains child service professionals. Jim emphasizes how perceptions are as important as reality. If a child is afraid, behaviors will reflect that fear, regardless of whether there is anything to be afraid of or not. Jim's experiences have led him to conclude that there are youngsters who are damaged more by their perceptions of their lives than by the realities of their lives.

Roger was a perfect example. He had undergone the successful removal of a brain tumor (benign, fortunately). Following the surgery, Roger began to fall apart in academics and in social relationships. Dr. Sutton was consulted. As best as he could determine from hospital and surgical records, there was no medical reason why this boy should have trouble after the surgery. In fact, it was expected that he would improve. While working with the young boy, Dr. Sutton asked a question that was not on his usual interview list.

> "Roger, do you think that when the surgeon removed the tumor he also took out part of your brain?"
>
> "No, sir," the boy replied softly. "I thought he took all of it."
>
> Good grief! No wonder this boy was having trouble. He thought he had to function with no brain at all. Jim explained the surgery to Roger and assured him that he still had all of his brain and the ability to use it.
>
> "Really?" he asked with an obvious sense of relief

in his voice. His young face broke into the first smile
Jim had seen from him.

"Absolutely!"

Over the next few days and weeks Roger improved, and he kept on improving in both his academic and social relationships.

All people visualize, and these *visualizations play a large role in determining mindsets.* A noted example of this is the saga of James Nesmeth, an average golfer who shot in the 90's. For seven years, he completely left the game; he did not touch a golf club nor set foot on a fairway. Major Nesmeth spent those seven years imprisoned in a small cell as a prisoner of war in North Vietnam. During almost the entire time he was imprisoned, he was isolated. He believed that he could keep himself sane in his tiny cell under hideous conditions by occupying his mind. He decided to practice his golf game. He was in no hurry. He had no place to go. He imagined that he was at his favorite golf course playing a full round of golf. Every day he experienced each detail. He saw himself dressed in his golf clothes. He smelled the fragrance of the trees and the freshly trimmed grass. In his mind's eye, he experienced different weather conditions—windy spring days, overcast winter days, and sunny summer mornings. He visualized every single step, from how he positioned himself before each swing to the follow-through afterwards. Starting at the first tee, he looked down and saw the little ball. He visualized addressing it, the feel of the grip of the club, and the position of his stance. He instructed himself as he practiced smoothing out his downswing and the follow-through on his shot. Then he watched the ball arc down the exact center of the fairway, bounce a couple of times and roll to the precise spot he had selected. Not once did he ever miss a shot, never took a hook or a slice, never missed a putt. Day after day he played a full 18 holes of golf. When he was liberated, one of the first things he did was to go to the golf course and play a round of golf. The first time out, without touching a golf club in seven years, he shot a 74, knocking 20 strokes off his game. That is the power of visualization!

Because mindsets are partly at an unconscious level, they often need assistance to be changed. Teachers and parents can assist by the pictures they help young people create in their minds. This motivational approach is the foundation of the program to raise responsibility and is described in the following chapter.

KEY POINTS

◆ Mindsets drive our behavior.

◆ Perceptions of self-efficacy, or the lack thereof, are critical to motivation.

◆ Adults can assist young people by the pictures they help create for them.

◆ If an adult views irresponsible behavior to be deliberatively disruptive, then coercive approaches of Theory X will be employed. Poor relationships and stress are natural outcomes of this approach. In contrast, if the adult perceives that the behavior is the youngster's best attempt to solve a frustration or problem, then the adult views the situation as an opportunity to help and uses approaches of Theory Y. In the process, resistance and resentment are reduced, and effectiveness is increased. (p. 31 duplicate)

———————————————

Suggestions for prompting student motivation towards learning are found in the first Appendix.

SUMMARY AND CONCLUSION

I skate where the puck is going to be,
not where it has been.

–Wayne Gretsky

External motivators are used in attempts to change behavior. Significant and long-lasting behavior is changed through desire, rather than through manipulation and coercion.

SUMMARY

How a person attempts to motivate others depends upon how the person views others. Generally, these views can be categorized by Theory X and Theory Y. The former relies on control through direction and manipulation. Theory Y, in contrast, encourages people to experience a sense of accomplishment and personal growth and relies on collaboration and empowerment to engender motivation. Theory X relies on external motivation. Theory Y is based on internal motivation. Theory Y's use of collaboration and empowerment reduces stress, improves relationships, and is much more powerful in effecting change in others.

Internal motivation is closely related to choice. Deprive people of choice and they lose motivation.

A reward can serve as an effective incentive only if the person is interested in the reward. The principle to remember about the use of rewards is that they change motivation. Winning the prize becomes the incentive. Rewards for good behavior teach children they will receive something in return. This is a false message. Society does not give rewards for expected standards of behavior. Giving rewards for appropriate behavior is counterproductive to fostering internal motivation for raising responsibility.

Coercive approaches such as punishment serve to benefit the punisher more than the punished. The punisher receives satisfaction, but the punished has relinquished responsibility and often feels victimized. Punishment is temporary and transitory. It has little effect on fostering desired long-term changes because it deprives young people of taking responsibility for their own actions. In addition, punishment kills the very thing we are attempting to do—motivate students in positive ways.

A prime reason for teachers' leaving the profession is the use of coercive approaches as a strategy for motivating students. Coercion can force compliance but never commitment, and coercion disheartens teachers.

Even though the intent of telling a youngster is worthwhile, the actual telling is perceived as an attempt to control. Telling creates defensiveness and a tendency to resist and does not engender desire.

Mindsets drive our behaviors. These perceptions of efficacy, or the lack thereof, are critical to motivation. Adults can help young people by the pictures they help create.

CONCLUSION

Language shapes our thoughts. George Orwell pointed out that without having a word such as "freedom," the concept of freedom would be difficult to conceive. Also, the use of language shapes the meanings of both words and concepts. For example, when we say, "He is making me so angry," we perpetuate the concept that the other person is shaping our anger. Actually, how much we allow others to stimulate us depends on *our* choices—consciously or nonconsciously. Although people are easily stimulated, we technically motivate ourselves.

The only way that you can "motivate" another person—whether spouse or partner, child, friend, or employee—is to provide an environment by which that person *wants* to change. This is especially the case when it comes to a *lasting* change in behavior. Reflect on the story that originated during World War II. A young lieutenant explained the new GI insurance program to thousands of troops who were to be sent overseas. After a lengthy presentation, the young lieutenant asked for a showing of hands of those who were interested. No hands were raised. The lieutenant was rejected until an old sergeant raised his hand and asked permission to say a few words to the troops. The lieutenant nodded affirmatively.

The sergeant took the microphone and announced that within the week, they all would be sent overseas. Some of them would be sent to the front lines, and, unfortunately, some of them would not be coming back.

He went on to say, "As the lieutenant has already explained, for those of you who enroll in this new GI insurance plan and who are killed, the U. S. Government will be obligated to send your families a check for $10,000. But for those who do not enroll in this new GI insurance and are killed, the U.S. Government will not be obligated to send your families one single dime."

The old sergeant paused and then inquired, "Do you believe the U.S. Government will be sending to the front lines those of you who are enrolled in the new GI insurance and the U.S. Government will be obligated to send your families a check for $10,000, or those who are not enrolled and the U.S. Government will not be obligated to send your families one single dime?"

Outside situations and stimulations have powerful effects on us, but they do not motivate us. Technically, motivation comes from within.

Rewards, punishments, and telling are external in their approaches. As such, their usefulness in effecting long-term behavioral change and raising responsibility is limited. A more effective approach is to use an internal approach, which is the basis of *The Raise Responsibility System.*

3
RAISING RESPONSIBILITY

DISCIPLINE

The best discipline is the kind nobody notices—
not even the one being disciplined.

W hen teachers and parents discipline with stress, they are
deprived of joy in relationships. Discipline, however, can be
an opportunity, rather than a problem. As the French sociologist
Emile Durkheim observed, discipline provides the moral code that
makes it possible for the small society of the classroom to function.

DISCIPLINE AS OPPORTUNITY

Discipline is a tool for teaching responsibility. The ultimate goal
of discipline is self-discipline—the kind of self-control that underlies
voluntary compliance with expected standards. This is the discipline
that is a mark of mature character and that a civilized society expects
of its citizens. John Goodlad, one of my former professors, said that
the first public purpose of schooling is to develop civility in the
young. Civility can only be achieved with self-discipline.

Discipline is derived from the Latin word *disciplina*, which means
instruction. The original meaning of the word connotes the self-
discipline necessary to master a task. This is the self-discipline of
the competitive athlete, of the professional musician, of the master
craftsman, of the expert in any field.

Another meaning of discipline refers to our nature. We may have
little control over the thoughts that spring into our minds and little
control over our initial emotions. But consciously or nonconsciously
(habitually), we *choose our responses* to both our thoughts and our
emotions. This is the discipline to which Durkheim referred that is
so necessary for a civil community.

In order for a society or classroom to be civil, discipline needs to
be fostered. Yet, according to Richard E. Clark, Chair of the Division

of Educational Psychology at the University of Southern California:

> Discipline is understood in a very limited way by most educators—"How do we get these children to behave?"—rather than, "How do we support the people in our charge as they learn to channel and direct their positive energy in ways that accomplish their goals and those of their community?" (Clark)

This limited understanding of discipline to which Dr. Clark refers is reminiscent of the teacher standing in front of the class who states, "I expect you all to be independent, innovative, critical thinkers who will do exactly as I say." As humorous as this statement is, many teachers operate with a focus on obedience rather than on self-discipline. If a child does not obey, punishment seems in order.

Lee Salk, the famous child psychologist, emphatically states, "What discipline is *not* is punishment." (Salk, p. 47) The National Congress of Parents and Teachers agrees:

> To many people, discipline means punishment. But, actually, *to discipline means to teach.* Rather than punishment, discipline should be a positive way of helping and guiding children to achieve self-control. (National P.T.A.)

In her book *The Caring Teacher's Guide to Discipline: Helping Young Students Learn Self-Control, Responsibility, and Respect,* Marilyn Gootman writes that discipline is teaching self-control, not controlling or managing students. (Gootman, p. 17)

As Richard Sagor notes, an effective discipline program requires three particular, vital educational functions:

- The maintenance of order
- The development of internal locus of control
- The promotion of prosocial behavior (Sagor, p. 150)

All three are accomplished in an approach where the *student* acknowledges ownership of behavior, where the *student* self-evaluates, and where the *student* develops a plan. In the process, the student grows by becoming more self-regulated. As Sagor notes, the locus of control is *internal.*

This is in contrast to an *external* control approach where the *teacher* takes possession of the problem, where the *teacher* presents the student with a plan, and where there is overpowerment of some kind—usually in the form of punishment—which often results in enmity against the adult.

Teachers who largely rely on external methods of control may succeed in getting students to toe the line under their supervision, but what happens when the teacher is not around? As one teacher who uses external controls said, "My children are very good for *me*, but they can be holy terrors when I'm not around." Research points to the same conclusion: Children subjected extensively to discipline based on external controls develop low internal commitment to good behavior. *The real power, the real influence of teachers, is not what students do when the teacher is with them; it's what students do when the teacher is not.*

Self-development is most effective if the person is committed, rather than just complying to someone else's desires. Commitment comes through *internal* motivation. Internal motivation is fostered in a *positive learning environment* where people feel they will not be harmed, where they are given *choices* that encourage ownership and empowerment, *where self-evaluation and self-correction* are the dominant avenues to growth, and where people learn that appropriate, responsible behavior is in *their own* best interests. *The Raise Responsibility System* makes full use of these approaches.

KEY POINTS

◆ Discipline means both to teach and to learn.

◆ Discipline is a tool for teaching responsibility.

◆ A good discipline program requires the maintenance of order, the development of an internal locus of control, and the promotion of social behaviors.

◆ The real influence of teachers is reflected by what students do when the teacher is not with them.

NOTE:
Read pages 278-279 for a preview and additional suggestion on how to teach the four concepts.

THE RAISE RESPONSIBILITY SYSTEM

Young people want to be responsible,
but we are using wrong approaches to help them.

The Raise Responsibility System handles disruptive behavior simply and easily. The three phases of the system are: *Teaching the Concepts, Checking for Understanding,* and *Guided Choices.*

TEACHING THE CONCEPTS

IMAGING THE CONCEPTS

Since learning is retained best from experiential activities, you will gain greater insight if you participate in a simple recursive activity—one that will teach you how to teach it by actually doing the activity yourself. It will take only a few minutes and is a worthwhile investment because the instructions are given in the manner in which you can teach the concepts.

You will need a blank sheet of paper. Standard computer printer or loose-leaf-size paper is preferable because that size is large enough to complete the exercise. (Young children may use larger paper and would not do the short writing phase.)

Fold the paper horizontally as in a hamburger shape (rather than vertically as in the shape of a hot dog).

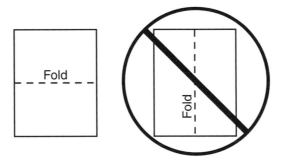

NOTE: For youngsters in kindergarten and preschool, the terms may seem too advanced. It is helpful to remember that young children are constantly learning new words and abstract concepts and readily absorb them. They have no context for deciding whether a word is more advanced or difficult than any other. For them, it is just a new word.

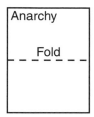

On the upper half of one side of the paper, print the word "Anarchy."

Explain that "anarchy" is behavior in which there is no law or order, and anyone can do anything he or she wants to do without consideration for anyone else.

Now *draw* any scene that comes to mind representing *anarchy*— any situation anywhere that shows a lack of law or order. Stick figures will do. The drawing is to cover only the top half of the page. After making the drawing, describe what you drew on the same upper half of the paper.

When finished, you are ready to make another drawing on the bottom half of the same side of the page.

Below the fold, separating the top half of the page from the bottom half,

print the word "Bullying."

Now *draw* a picture that shows someone bullying someone else.

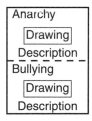

After making the drawing, describe what you drew.

When finished, turn your paper over. *Label* the top half of this second side "Conformity." On the top half of this side, *draw* something that conjures up people *behaving in an expected manner*—any scene where people are conforming or doing what is expected of them. After making the drawing, describe what you drew.

One more drawing needs to be made. *Label* the bottom half of this side "Democracy." *Draw* a picture of whatever you think connotes the idea of someone taking responsibility without being told to do so. After making the drawing, describe what you drew.

If this activity were to be used to introduce the four concepts in a classroom, each student would take turns describing the drawings or explaining their concepts to a partner.

ANALYSIS OF THE ACTIVITY

Processing the Concepts

Five learning activities were used. First, a scene was *visualized* for each of the four concepts. Second, a scene was *drawn* for each concept. Third, a description was *written* for each concept. Fourth, the scene for each concept was *orally* described to someone else. Fifth, each student *listened* to someone else's descriptions of the concepts.

Ownership

You were actively engaged in making the four concepts meaningful because *you* created them. What we do ourselves is remembered longer than what is presented to us. The principle of ownership is a prerequisite for growth and is a fundamental characteristic of *The Raise Responsibility System.*

Meaningfulness

Learning the four concepts through the foregoing exercise is brain-compatible. The brain is hard-wired to remember images more so than words or text. This explains why it is easier to remember faces more than names. It is for this same reason that we remember stories. We make mental images as we read stories or as they are told to us. Similarly, when students create examples for each of the four concepts, the images conjured up in the mind assist in both meaning and memory. It is for this reason that the four vocabulary words were introduced as concepts and examples rather than as definitions. *Because examples bring real understanding, the concepts can be taught to any person, at any grade level, in any subject area, and to any class.* With this in mind, we can proceed to explain and refine an understanding of the concepts.

EXPLANATION OF THE LEVELS

Level A – Anarchy

Anarchy is the lowest level of behavior. The word comes from Greek and literally means "without rule." This level refers to absence of government, aimlessness, and chaos. Alan Bennett summarized the concept well:

> We started off trying to set up a small anarchist community, but people wouldn't obey the rules.

Shortly after my presenting *The Raise Responsibility System* to an elementary school, the counselor called me and shared what she experienced. She had walked into a primary classroom and heard the teacher give the assignment to the first-grade students. The teacher announced that when the assignment was completed the students could go to one of the learning centers. A few minutes later, the noise level began to grow substantially louder. One of the first graders stood up and called out, "Anarchy! This is anarchy!" The noise level immediately subsided. The teacher had not said a word. The students controlled their own learning environment. An *awareness* of the concept of anarchy facilitated self-management.

Level B – Boss*ing*/Bully*ing*

Bully<u>ing</u> is the level of behavior above anarchy. (Young people have no problem with the term "bullying," but some teachers do. "Bothering" is an alternate choice for these teachers.) A student behaving at this level violates the courtesies of class operations and accepted standards. The bully attempts to become the ruler by making the rules and standards. Bullies boss others by violating others' rights.

Accommodating a bully only encourages bullying behavior. We make our biggest mistake in not understanding the nature of a bully. If a bully prevails, irresponsible and provocative behavior will be repeated. The sooner a person stands up to bullying, the easier it will be to handle and the sooner the bullying behavior will stop.

Though it can be scary for a very young child to confront a bully, most people are surprised at how quickly bullies back off when someone stands up to them.

Leonard Eron, professor of psychiatry at the Institute of Social Research at the University of Michigan, conducted a 26-year study that tracked eight-year-old aggressive boys. He reported:

> If a child is the tormentor not the tormented, don't dismiss his bullying as a phase. The earlier you intervene, the better. Studies show that aggressive kids tend to grow into, not out of, their behavior. (Jameson, p. 3E)

Classroom bullying is more prevalent than many educators think, and experts say it should no longer be tolerated as part of growing up.

> Because bullying is so often an underlying cause of school violence, the National School Safety Center now calls it "the most enduring and underrated problem in American Schools." (Mulrine, p. 24)

The research suggests that teachers and principals underestimate the amount of bullying that takes place under their noses—on playgrounds, in hallways, even in classrooms—and that too many educators are reluctant to get involved. Charol Shakeshaft, a professor at Hofstra University in Hempstead, New York, reported, "When we talked to teachers, they said they didn't think it was acceptable and they didn't like the adolescent climate at all. But they didn't know how to stop it." (Viadero, p. 21) What was surprising in the studies was that students were picked on quite often in classrooms. While boys are more often the perpetrators and victims of direct bullying, girls tend to bully in more indirect ways. They manipulate friendships, ostracize classmates from a group, or spread malicious rumors. Researchers who have studied the issue say that bullying starts in elementary school and peaks in middle school. It is too pervasive and too damaging to ignore, according to John Hoover, an associate professor of teaching and learning at the University of North Dakota. He asserts that ten to twelve percent of kids are miserable in school because of bullying. (Ibid., p. 20) Assuming the lower figure of ten percent, that means in a school of 600, sixty students are coming to school fearful for their well being.

Not much learning takes place when students are in constant fear because of being bullied.

Only this level uses the gerund or verb form, "bullying," instead of the noun form of "bully." This reduces any tendency to refer directly to a youngster as a "bully." Reference is always made to the *level of behavior*, never to the person. Also, the verbal form emphasizes that a student chooses his own level of behavior.

In a classroom, when a student disrupts the class, he is making his own standards. He is bullying the teacher by interrupting instruction and bullying the students by interrupting their learning. When this concept of bullying is first introduced to students, they register surprise because they had not thought of irresponsible behavior as bullying others—especially the teacher.

> **Some key points to remember: First, the teacher *never* labels or calls a student a "bully." Second, the *level* of behavior is identified, not the behavior itself. Third, as we shall see later, the responsibility for acknowledgment is the *student's*— not the teacher's.**

Level C – Cooperation/Conformity

Conformity is the next level of behavior and is as essential for classroom decorum as it is for a civil society. No society can exist without some measure of conformity. The term means to comply and cooperate with expected standards. *The term does not mean or connote regimentation.* Rather, it means to be connected and involved with others. It refers to the accommodations people make when they are naturally inclined to accept the values and mores of their immediate group and society.

The need for conformity on the part of young people brings to mind the newspaper cartoon showing a group of girls dressed in school uniforms. All of their blouses, skirts, socks, and shoes are identical. The girls are talking with a group of boys who attend a different school that does not require school uniforms. However, the boys are wearing identical caps, shirts, pants, and shoes. One boy says to the girls, "At our school, we don't have to wear uniforms." However, the boys are wearing uniforms—of their group. Their dress is motivated by peer pressure to conform.

So compelling is the pressure to fit in that many young people lack the strength of character to resist. This pressure affects student achievement. It is largely because of peer pressure that some students do not want to show they can do well in school. Being smart does not fit into some student subcultures. The *Washington Post* profiled a girl who allowed her grades to drop from A's and B's to C's and D's in order to win back her friends. (Chase, 1999, p. 37) The president of the National Education Association even reported that he personally knows a teacher who resorts to a ruse in order to protect her high-achieving students from peer retribution. The teacher writes an F on the students' test papers with the note, "See me after class"—at which time she confidentially reveals their real grades of A's or B's. (Ibid.)

Gardner Reynolds, of Laredo, Texas, shared some thoughts on peer pressure at the middle and high school levels.

> Peer pressure: now here is a force most pernicious and most powerful in the lives of teenagers. It can make a youngster who is friendly and cooperative in a "one-on-one" with a teacher turn into a complete hellion when he has a group of his classmates to impress with his "cool." A student who does try to accomplish something worthwhile in class is immediately labeled a "teacher's pet" or a "nerd" by the "cool" students.
>
> This is a rather "topsy-turvy" view of things: good is bad and bad is good. Try to work within the system and achieve something and you are an outsider from the "in-crowd"—a nerd or a dork or whatever the current colloquialism is. Rebel against authority, exhibit disrespect and insolence to teachers and administrators and you are a "cool dude" worthy of respect and emulation by your peers. Fail your classes, get sent to the office on a repeated basis and you are "with it." (Reynolds)

As pointed out by James Coleman in the section on *External Motivation* in Chapter 2, adolescents have a strong tendency to conform. In *The Nurture Assumption: Why Children Turn Out the Way They Do,* Judith Rich Harris concluded that the peer group in today's society often displaces the family's influence when youngsters reach middle-school age.

It is important to keep in mind the power that peer pressure has on this age group. It does not matter that the adult is asking for legitimate behavior. If the youth believes that his or her peers will perceive the request as disrespectful, the youth will react negatively, even if he likes the adult. If dignity is at stake, consideration of how peers will react takes precedence over the consideration for the adult.

The key concept of level C is that the *motivation is external.* Once young people become aware that external forces are manipulating them, they begin to feel liberated. Such awareness and subsequent articulation assists adolescents to resist group temptations of an "anti-learning subculture." Understanding peer pressure helps young people to become more autonomous and to decide against engaging in socially irresponsible acts, both inside and outside of school.

Level D – Democracy

Level D is the highest level of behavior. At this level, the motivation to be responsible is *internal.* The person has integrated the regulation of important behaviors. Dr. Edward Deci, professor of psychology at the University of Rochester, who has studied motivation extensively, refers to behavior undertaken or carried out without outside pressure as "autonomous."

> Autonomous functioning requires that an internalized regulation be accepted as your own; the regulation must become a part of who you are. It must be integrated with your self. Through integration, people become willing to accept responsibility for activities that are important but not (necessarily) interesting—activities that are not intrinsically motivating. (Deci, p. 94)

Behavior at this level is manifested by qualities of character that individuals habitually recognize as the right thing. The four classical virtues of *prudence, temperance, justice,* and *fortitude*—as old as Aristotle—are just as compelling today. *Prudence* is practical wisdom—recognizing and making the right choices. *Temperance* involves much more than moderation in all things. It is the control of human passions and emotions, especially anger and frustration. *Fortitude* is courage in pursuit of the right path, despite the risks. It is the strength of mind and courage to persevere in the face of adversity. *Justice*, in the classical sense, includes fairness, honesty, and keeping promises.

My own state of California has joined the growing character education movement and refers to these attributes as follows:

- *Caring*: To be compassionate, considerate, helpful, and understanding of others

- *Civic Virtue & Citizenship*: To hold to the values and principles basic to American constitutional democracy; to accept the rights and duties of citizenship; to act for the common good

- *Justice & Fairness*: To be considerate, unbiased, and equitable

- *Respect*: To show regard for self, others, property, and the environment

- *Responsibility*: To be answerable; to be accountable for one's actions

- *Trustworthiness*: To be worthy of trust and confidence; to be reliable and honest (California State Department of Education, 1999)

Whether classical or current, the characteristics depend upon self-discipline—level D behavior. Clearly, this, the democratic level, is the level to which we hope our youth will aspire. *Responsibility and democracy are inseparable.* In teaching this level, a critical point is communicated, namely, that young people are not only capable of behavior at this level, but this is the level of *expected* behavior. John F. Kennedy, 35th President of the United States, articulated the point in his Pulitzer Prize winning book, *Profiles in Courage*:

> For, in a democracy, every citizen, regardless of his interest in politics, "holds office"; every one of us is in a position of responsibility; and, in the final analysis, the kind of government we get depends upon how we fulfill those responsibilities.
>
> (Kennedy, p. 255)

The teacher communicates that "every citizen" includes young people. The hierarchy not only offers an inherent motivation for students to act on level D, but the teacher communicates that this is the level of expected behavior. As "location, location, and location" are the three prime factors for success in real estate, so "expectation, expectation, and expectation" are the prime factors to be communicated to young people.

The difference between levels C and D is fundamentally in the motivation, rather than the action. The motivation on level C is *external,* but the motivation on level D is *internal.* Observing the difference between these two levels is often very difficult, if not impossible. For example, assume a student spotted a piece of trash on the classroom floor. If the student picked up the trash at the teacher's direction, the student was acting on level C. The student complied by implementing the teacher's request to assist in keeping the classroom clean. This is good behavior. Conforming is necessary for community. However, if the student picked up the trash without anyone's asking or telling him, the action then is at level D. The piece of trash was picked up because it was the right thing to do. The *behavior* was the same at both levels, but the *motivation* was external in the first case and internal in the second. Similarly, if a parent asks a youngster to help carry in the groceries, and the youngster complies, level C behavior is demonstrated. However, if the youngster knows that the expectation is to assist the mother and does so without being asked, level D behavior is demonstrated. These are simple explanations that young people of any age can understand. *A critical component for growth and development is for students to understand the difference between level C (external motivation) and level D (internal motivation).*

During the initial learning phase, reference is made to the name of each level: anarchy, bully*ing*, conformity, and democracy. However, after becoming familiar with the ABCD's of social development, reference is only made to their letters. Also, little time is spent in differentiating between the levels. Neither A nor B are acceptable behavior levels, while levels C and D both meet expected standards.

REVIEW OF CONCEPTS

D   Democracy
    ◇ **Highest level of behavior**
- Develops self-discipline
- Demonstrates initiative

- Does good because it is the right thing to do
- Demonstrates responsibility because it is essential for democracy

The motivation is in̲ternal.

C   Cooperation/Conformity
◇ **Appropriate and acceptable level of behavior**
- Considerate
- Complies
- Conforms to peer pressure

NOTE: Conformity does not mean regimentation.
The motivation is ex̲ternal.

B   Boss*ing*/Bully*ing*
◇ **Neither appropriate nor acceptable level of behavior**
- Bothers others
- Bosses others
- Breaks laws and makes own rules and standards

Must be bossed to behave.

A   Anarchy
◇ **Lowest level of behavior**
- Absence of order
- Aimless and chaotic
- Absence of government

Anarchy is the fundamental enemy of civilization.

PRIMARY POINTS

The primary points to emphasize *when teaching* the levels are:

(1) The lower levels of A and B will result in the use of authority.

(2) The higher levels of C and D are both acceptable.

(3) The motivation at level C is *ex*ternal.

(4) The motivation at level D is *in*ternal.

CONCEPT VARIATION

The concepts can be varied to meet the needs of any class. Dianne Capell has a bulletin board entitled "**Behavior Plan**." Under this title, she has the following four posters:

D   Democracy
- Develops self-discipline
- Shows kindness to others
- Does good because it is the right thing to do

C   Conformity
- Listens
- Practices
- Cooperates

The motivation is external.

B   Bully*ing*/bother*ing*
- Bosses others
- Bothers others
- Breaks classroom standards

A   Anarchy
- Noisy
- Out of control
- Unsafe

In her letter from Japan, Dianne wrote me:

> Several other teachers have begun using the same language to reinforce the children's understanding, and some have actually started using the same plan. Of course, this has added a great deal to its effectiveness. All of my students can now recognize their own level of behavior and label it appropriately. They know almost instantly when they need to make better choices. This takes much less time away from instruction and keeps the classroom climate stress-free and positive. (Capell)

APPLYING AND TEACHING THE CONCEPTS

As mentioned at the outset, images are more effective in understanding the concepts than are definitions. The images are examples that people create themselves. The key to understanding the concepts is to make the examples relevant to the learner. The examples need not be limited to classroom situations only. Young people can also create examples of situations found in their neighborhood or in the larger societies that will exemplify each of the four levels. The point is emphasized that for optimum understanding, young people need to be actively engaged in constructing examples specific to their classroom, playground, social, or community setting. Questions are posed such as, "What would anarchy look like here? Give an example." The same questions are asked regarding levels B, C, and D. In a classroom, students share their examples in pairs, small groups, and then with the entire class.

The concepts can be taught and used with any grade level, in any class, with any subject matter, or in any situation because the examples created are what make the concepts personal, meaningful, interesting, and relevant. For example, "bullying" in the first grade will be different from "bullying" in the fourth grade, where name calling and similar activities are often more subtle.

The manner in which the concepts are taught depends upon the age of the youngsters, their maturity level, and the subject area. In the case of very young people, one concept can be introduced each day. Stories and literature are excellent ways to introduce the concepts. For example, *Miss Nelson Is Missing* illustrates level A. This story is about a primary classroom that is out of control until an authoritarian substitute takes over. After decorum is established, the regular teacher reappears. The story illustrates that when things are chaotic, authority is the most expeditious approach to establishing order. *The Three Little Pigs* can be used for level B to show how the wolf bullied the little pigs. *Snow-White and the Seven Dwarfs* can be used to illustrate level C in that the dwarfs, although all different, complied with their responsibilities by going to the ore mine to work each day. *The Hole in the Dike* can be used for level D by illustrating how the little Dutch boy put his finger in the dike and saved the town. Peter exercised self-reliance and a concern for the community. As students become more familiar with the levels, further discussions about external and internal motivation will aid the maturation process. *Ira Sleeps Over* is a good primary story that contrasts external pressure with internal desire in the decision-making process.

At the upper elementary and middle school levels, the four concepts can be introduced by the activity used at the beginning of this chapter. Students create examples to show how each level of development would look in their particular class. The Appendix contains a butterfly analogy to explain the hierarchy as well as a sample implementation procedure used in grades five to eight. At the high school level, the program can be taught in one short lesson by creating examples for the particular class. *The point is emphasized: examples, rather than definitions, bring understanding and applicability.* The critical exercise is to relate examples of specific behaviors to each concept.

At the middle and high school levels, the program even can be adopted school-wide without having the concepts taught in every classroom. For example, if all students have a social studies requirement, the concepts can be taught in these classes because the concepts particularly lend themselves to analyzing current, historical, and sociological events. Teachers in other subjects only need make the concepts pertinent to their own classes.

COGNITION AND MORAL DEVELOPMENT

Awareness of the hierarchy is the foundation of this approach to raising responsible behavior. When a young person can say that a behavior is on a level that is unacceptable, that young person has taken the first step toward moving to more responsible behavior. The reason is that *awareness comes before acknowledgment.* Teaching the concepts fosters the necessary awareness. Awareness and acknowledgment are both cognitive activities. Both are necessary to change one's own behavior. Both Piaget and Kohlberg—the Swiss and Harvard University psychologists, respectively—believed that moral and, therefore, civic responsibility depended on cog-nitive growth.

William Glasser, the psychiatrist and originator of Reality Therapy and Choice Theory, goes a step further. He believes that morality should be discussed in schools. The discussion should be part of a nonthreatening, nonpunitive environment so children can learn to commit themselves to living a moral life, not just paying lip service to it. "In schools without such an environment, morality and responsibility will be only words for most children." (Glasser, 1969, p. 192) An introduction of the four concepts serves as the first phase for establishing and maintaining a noncoercive, nonthreatening environment as well as an introduction to moral and ethical development.

Awareness as it relates to moral development has an emotional component. When young people perform an inappropriate action, often their only emotion is the negative feeling of getting caught. Instead, the negative feeling should be related to the inappropriate action itself. Young people need to be helped to see that the negative emotion should be the result of *what they do*, rather than the result of being found out.

ADVANTAGES TO TEACHING THE HIERARCHY

Oliver Wendell Holmes said, "The human mind, once stretched by a new idea, never regains its original dimensions." When young people become aware of levels of social development, they become conscious of social responsibility in their own behaviors and in relationships with others.

The hierarchy *serves as a means of communication.* It offers young people and adults the same conceptual vocabulary. The vocabulary brings clarity of understanding and assists communications both between teacher and student and among students themselves.

The hierarchy encourages *students themselves to maintain an environment conducive to learning,* rather than always relying on the teacher. Members of the class take on leadership roles to retain decorum. When students help each other to maintain an atmosphere conducive to learning, they are taking a major step in creating a learning community. A community is most successful when members look to themselves to solve problems.

The hierarchy *raises awareness for responsible citizenship.* Our society is based on great autonomy for its citizens. However, citizenship assumes values such as responsibility, respect, caring, fairness, and trustworthiness—the values that transcend divisions of race, creed, politics, gender, and wealth. These values are fostered in the hierarchy and are reinforced in the examples students create for level D—democracy.

The hierarchy *raises awareness for individual responsibility.* Teaching for democratic living requires more than just choosing when to conform and when not to conform. When peer pressure is so compelling as to prompt people to do something that is personally or socially irresponsible, just knowing the levels of social development can have a liberating and responsibility-producing effect. For example, a problem in many middle and high schools relates to studying and doing home assignments. Many students do not study or complete learning assignments because such effort is discouraged in the peer culture. The hierarchy can be a motivator in this regard. Students begin to realize that not turning in home assignments or not studying because of peer pressure is level C behavior. After exposure to the concepts, students begin to evaluate the level of their choices. Internalizing the levels can do much to foster desired behavior and individual responsibility.

Using the hierarchy *calls attention to the fact that people are constantly making choices* and that students choose their own level of behavior, consciously or nonconsciously. Students learn that their behaviors are self-chosen, a product of their decisions. They learn that they have a choice in how they respond in a situation, to a stimulus, and even to an urge.

The hierarchy *empowers young people.* It sets the groundwork for students to analyze and correct their own behaviors. It shows students they can be in control of their lives, be agents of their own empowerment, and can resist a *victimhood* mentality.

The hierarchy *encourages students to achieve the highest level of behavior.* The very nature of a hierarchy serves as an inspiration. Young people have an internal desire to be as competent and successful as they can be. We deprive them of opportunities if we do not expose them to possibilities. Using the hierarchy fosters internal motivation so students *want* to act responsibly.

The hierarchy *encourages mature decision making.* Adolescents are looking for roles, more than goals. Exposing young people to the levels has a natural effect of encouraging them to think about long-term decisions. This is a significant consideration since so much advertising, peer pressure, and behavior of young people is aimed at instant gratification rather than at fostering character development and growth.

The hierarchy *fosters character education,* as described under the explanation of level D, without ever mentioning what some communities would consider red flags of teaching values, ethics, or morals.

The *hierarchy serves to distinguish between the inappropriate behavior and the person who acts inappropriately.* It separates the *act* from the *actor* (Kohn, 1996, p. 123), the *deed* from the *doer,* a *good person* from *bad behavior.* A fundamental advantage of the hierarchy is that it naturally accomplishes what adults talk about but have a most difficult time in accomplishing, namely, separating a person's behavior from the person himself. For example, reflect on the last time you were evaluated. Did you separate what the evaluator was telling you about your *performance* from you as a *person?* While the evaluation session was taking place, were you aware that the supervisor was not really talking about you personally, just about your on-the-job actions? My surveys with hundreds of teachers and administrators have indicated that only an extremely small number of people consciously separate themselves from their behavior during an evaluation. If the separation is difficult for adults, imagine how much more difficult it is for young people. Even though we try desperately to make it clear to a young person that we are not criticizing the student as a person—that we are just not approving of inappropriate behavior—it is extremely difficult for a young person to perceive the difference. Teaching the hierarchy makes this challenging task quite easy. We never talk about the student's behavior; we only talk about the *level* of behavior.

The hierarchy focuses on *labeling behavior, not people.* Labeling people often has negative overtones and is not conducive to building relationships. In contrast, labeling a description is far less antagonizing. One summer day on a long drive, my wife was describing a story she was writing. She was, in effect, thinking aloud. After what I thought was a somewhat lengthy pause, I turned on an audio tape cassette that was already in position to be played. After listening to it for a minute, I ejected the tape, turned to my wife, and asked, "Is everything O.K.?" She answered, "Sure, you're from Mars!" (alluding to John Gray's book *Men Are from Mars, Women Are from Venus*). We had often discussed natural differences between males and females and were familiar with John Gray's metaphors of men being from Mars (action-oriented) and women being from Venus (relations-oriented). By labeling my action as Martian, she dispersed in a matter of seconds what otherwise might have created great tension. She knew where I was coming from, and I realized my behavior was inappropriate. It was the understanding communicated by labeling the behavior that allowed us to continue on a pleasant ride. The important learning from this episode is that we had a common vocabulary; we were both familiar with the Mars and Venus metaphors. We understood that reference was made to a type of behavior, not a personal attack on the person. My wife did not tell me I was a rude person; she merely referred to my actions as being Martian. I did not feel personally attacked. Labeling the behavior was non-confrontational, aided communication, assisted understanding, and encouraged readjustment.

The hierarchy fosters understanding about *internal and external incentives.* Understanding the difference between an external incentive and an internal incentive can have a significant impact on motivation. It is common for elementary and middle school teachers to offer incentives for students to behave. When these students move on to a different teacher, they often ask what will be given to them if they behave properly. The incentive has become getting the reward, rather than commitment to appropriate behavior. In this process, students have fallen under the control of the external reward at the expense of autonomy. The paradox is that we want to assist students to become self-disciplined, independent problem solvers; yet, external incentives set up students to be dependent. Students quickly understand that external incentives are really bribes to manipulate their behavior. Although they are influenced by incentives, they learn that they can choose to be or not to be motivated by them.

The hierarchy leads to *improved self-esteem.* After students have discussed the differences between external rewards and internal satisfaction, the stage is set for understanding self-esteem. Teachers give external rewards such as certificates and praise in attempts to build self-esteem. However, according to *Toward A State of Esteem: The Final Report of the California Task Force to Promote Self-esteem and Personal and Social Responsibility:*

> The building blocks of self-esteem are skills. The more skillful a person, the more likely he or she will be able to cope in life and situations. By fostering skills of personal and social responsibility, schools can help students increase their behavioral options. (California State Department of Education, 1990, p. 64)

Self-esteem is closely related to self-satisfaction. A person who is satisfied with an accomplishment has a tendency to repeat it. The more often one completes a task successfully, the more proficient in it the person becomes. This reinforcement builds feelings of competency and self-worth, critical elements of self-esteem. Rather than being the result of external rewards, these feelings are the result of internal thoughts—often resulting from an internal feeling of satisfaction.

Students learn that their *behavior plays a role in determining how they want their teachers to relate to them.* Neither A (anarchy) nor B (bossing/bullying) is an appropriate or acceptable behavioral classroom level. Behavior at either of these levels encourages a *controlling* reaction from the teacher. When students operate on these levels, they are telling the teacher, "Use authority on us." When students understand the levels, a teacher can stop an unpleasant situation with a simple question, "Do you want me to become a level B teacher today?" Given the choice, students invariably say, "No, we will be on level C." What a simple way to resolve the situation! In addition and most important, students soon learn that when the class operates on level C or D, the atmosphere encourages autonomy and supportive behavior on the part of the teacher.

Teaching the hierarchy *fosters self-management.* While learning the concepts, young people are also learning the underlying value system. For example, level B, which implies selfishness, is at a lower level of social development than level C. Cooperation/conformity, which implies order and fairness, must prevail before democracy can exist. Democracy calls for responsibility and doing the right thing—*whether or not someone else is watching.*

The concepts are the foundation of *The Raise Responsibility System.* The second part of the system, is simply checking for understanding.

KEY POINTS

◆ *The Raise Responsibility System* is *proactive.* The plan is to set the stage for dealing with disruptive behaviors *before* they occur. This is in contrast to a reactive strategy of dealing with disruptive behaviors after they occur.

◆ A *deductive* approach is used. Four concepts are taught first. This is in contrast to the more common inductive approach of first teaching specifics in order to arrive at general concepts.

◆ The *person* identifies a *level* of development—separating the *behavior* from the *person*—eliminating the natural tendency to self-defend.

◆ The more often that reference is made to the higher, acceptable levels—rather than the lower, unacceptable levels—the more often students want to increase their desire to behave responsibly.

◆ The program uses *internal* motivation so the young person develops a *desire* to be responsible—both individually and socially.

Using the Concepts to Promote Learning

Before students engage in a lesson (or any activity), create examples pertaining to the levels. *After* the lesson, ask students to take just a moment to reflect on their chosen levels. Creating examples and then reflecting promotes motivation to perform at the highest level.

The more the hierarchy is used, the more it becomes a tool for self-evaluation.

Example 1: THE HIERARCHY RELATING TO MATH

Level D (*INTERNAL* motivation to learn)
- Displays a desire to learn
- Stays focused during math lessons
- Willingly practices to improve math skills
- Practices *without* the necessity of adult supervision
- Completes assignments because it is in one's self-interest

Level C (Relies on E*XTERNAL* motivation to prompt effort)
- Practices when an adult is nearby
- Applies effort mainly to impress or satisfy others
- Fulfills the assignment primarily to get a good grade

Levels B/A
- Spends little if any effort to learn
- Distracts others by taking them off task

Example 2: Use an alarm clock analogy to teach the importance of establishing a procedure to get to school on time.
- Level D - You set your alarm clock, wake up, and get to school on time.
- Level C - You depend on your parents to wake you up to get to school on time.
- Levels A/B - You harm yourself by ignoring your alarm clock and come to school late.

CHECKING FOR UNDERSTANDING

People need to know you mean them no harm.

This section explains how to have a young person acknowledge and take ownership of inappropriate behavior. The strategy is referred to as *Checking for Understanding.* In order to foster ownership, the youngster, not the adult, must do the talking. This approach is more than a paradigm shift. It is a *metanoia*—the Greek word meaning a profound conversion. It is a fundamental change in thinking from an external control mentality to internal control thinking. Although the strategy can be used in any school or non-school setting, it is explained here in a classroom setting.

MENTAL FRAMING

The strategy for *Checking for Understanding* starts with the teacher's own mental framing. The mental framing is essential in order to remain in control. Otherwise, when the classroom is disrupted, the disrupting student is controlling the situation. This is evidenced by the stress the teacher feels. Therefore, the teacher first establishes or reclaims a positive outlook, viewing the situation as one for guiding rather than punishing, as an opportunity to help the student readjust behavior. The positive mental reframing reduces the teacher's stress and has a significant effect on communications and relationships. The student perceives the teacher as attempting to *help*, rather than punish.

After teaching the hierarchy but before using the *Checking for Understanding* strategy, many unobtrusive techniques may first be considered. The following suggestions allow the teacher to stop a disruption by using a minimum of effort to refocus a student's behavior.

UNOBTRUSIVE TECHNIQUES

These include body language, mannerisms, posture, inflections and nuances in tone of voice, the pacing of speech, and the feelings that language evokes.

Visual

- Your face is a powerful tool of communication. Use a friendly smile.

- Change your facial expressions, such as widening your eyes or moving your eyebrow(s).

- Use a "beat beyond" eye contact by looking at the person for a second or two beyond the normal time—and then smile. This is in contrast to a stare that is often accompanied by a stern expression. Staring is aggressive and works against a noncoercive relationship.

- Lower your head or nod as you look at the student.

- Employ a group signal for attention, such as all raising hands or lowering the lights.

Verbal

- Use a pause—perhaps the least used and most effective technique.

- Change your voice inflection or reduce the volume of your voice.

- Use a release of tension, such as breathing out and then taking a deep breath.

- Make a variety of sssshhhh sounds, such as, "You sssssshhhhhould be listening now."

- Give a subtle hint, such as, "Thank you, Sheldon," or "Please, Sandy."

- Use a friendly request, such as, "Thanks for considering others," or "Thank you for your attention."

- Ask an evaluative question, such as, "Please ask yourself if that meets the standards of our class," or "If you could do something about changing that, what would you choose?"

- Combine a need with a request, such as, "The noise you are making is disturbing us. Is there a way you can work so that we won't be distracted?"

- State your needs, such as, "I need your help in this."

Kinetic

- Move to a different location. You may even establish a special place in your classroom to where you will move when students' behaviors need changing.

- Use proximity by standing next to the student and perhaps including a gentle touch on his or her desk.

- In cases of a tapping pencil or some other tapping sound of which the student may not be aware, redirect the object to the student's thigh, or slip a tissue underneath the area on the desk so the sound will not be heard.

- Use the principle of entrainment. Entrainment is a form of communication that occurs when we "get on the same wavelength." In the case of a rhythmic sound, such as a tapping pencil, the teacher can tap a foot or stretch a rubber band at the same tempo as the student is tapping the pencil. When the teacher slows the tempo of the foot tapping or rubber band stretching, the tapping of the pencil will also slow down. Entrainment can also be used by the teacher's stretching or deeply inhaling. Students will follow the same action.

- Use a positive—rather than a negative—rapport position. Standing side-by-side or at an angle with the student is non-confrontational. This is in contrast to a head-to-head, face-to-face confrontational pose. Also, lowering your body below that of the student by stooping places the student in an empowering position. This easily diffuses unwanted situations.

- Entrainment and positive rapport can be combined. When you are speaking to a student, mirror his body posture. For example, if a student is slumped over, then the teacher slumps. When the teacher straightens up, the student will follow the new posture.

- Use your hands in an inviting posture. A palms up, open hand is an invitational position. A hand-down, finger-point position is a repelling position.

- When near a student, you can safely assume that the student is listening to you. It is often counterproductive to demand a

student look you directly in the eyes. The student may be embarrassed or is showing respect by not looking directly at you.

QUESTIONS AS INQUIRY

The Raise Responsibility System uses the simple cognitive learning
theory of teaching and then testing. The first phase is teaching the
levels. The second phase simply tests the disrupting student to
acknowledge the level of chosen behavior. The testing—*Checking
for Understanding*—is simple inquiry.

Asking questions encourages the respondent to clarify thoughts,
which in turn leads to acknowledgment of actions. This inquiring
approach also assists the inquirer in setting a positive mental frame.
One does not normally become stressed while asking questions.

When administrators and counselors use guidance techniques with
students who have acted inappropriately, the conversation takes
place on a one-on-one basis. How can a teacher establish such a
relationship in a classroom full of students? The answer lies in having
taught the hierarchy. By having this instructional base, the teacher
moves into a guidance mode when a disruption occurs. The teacher
uses a non-accusatory, noncoercive questioning approach because
the purpose is solely to inquire whether or not the student
understands the level on which the action belongs. The teacher
simply *asks* the student to identify the *level* of the behavior. Note
that the student is *not asked to describe the behavior itself*—just the
behavioral *level*.

Although it is always preferable to speak to students about
misbehavior problems on a one-to-one basis, an advantage of the
strategy is that the questioning can be done in front of the class
without alienating the disruptive student. An additional advantage
to the strategy is that instructional time is not wasted during the
short teacher-student interchange because the levels of social
development are being reinforced to the class.

A STARTER FOR EFFECTIVE QUESTIONING

The purpose of the questioning is simply to check for
understanding, to see whether the student can identify the level of
unacceptable behavior. If the student appears not to know, then the
teacher guides or coaches the student to acknowledge level B because

this is the level of making one's own standards, rather than following the standards of the class. Once the hierarchy has been learned, the questioning process is extremely short. The student knows that level B is the level of irresponsible and unacceptable behavior.

Following are some sample dialogues between a **Teacher (T)** and a *Student (S).*

T: On what level is that behavior?
S: I don't know.

T: Tell me a civility or standard in our class.
S: Not to be talking when the teacher is.

T: Then you are making your own standards. What level is that?
S: B.

T: Thank you.

*   *   *

T: On what level is that behavior?
S: He was doing it, too.

**T: That was not the question. Let's try it again.
On what level is that behavior?**
S: I don't know.

T: What level is it when someone bothers others?
S: I don't know.

**T: The letter comes right after A in the alphabet.
What letter comes after A?**
S: B.

T: Thank you.

*   *   *

T: Would it be right for everyone to operate on that level?
S: No.

**T: What level do we call it when someone makes his own rules
and bothers others?**
S: I don't know.

**T: As capable as you are, I don't believe that.
CLASS, can anyone help?**

ASKING IS THE KEY

Notice that in the second illustration, the student was evasive. The teacher, however, persevered. This point is critical: *The person who asks the question controls the situation.* The question directs the conversation. If this type of situation occurs, continue to question. Remain in control by continuing *to ask* until an answer is satisfactory.

When first starting, a student may "test" by pleading ignorance, as in the examples. Waste no time. Just ask the class, *"What level do we call it when a person makes his own rules?"* After the level is acknowledged, the teacher immediately returns to the lesson. Nothing more is said because the objective has been met; *level B behavior has been acknowledged.*

The power of the strategy is that when a student acknowledges an inappropriate level of behavior, the misconduct not only stops but younger students often apologize. The reason is that an apology is a natural by-product of accepting responsibility. Note: An apology is *never* requested; that would be coercive.

CAUTIONS

The effectiveness of the answers depends on the effectiveness of the questions. For example, asking a disruptive student, *"What are you doing?"* will lead to a potential confrontation and frustration because the student will most likely respond, *"Nothing."* The teacher would have been better off not asking that question. The strategy is made simple, however, by always starting the questioning process with, *"On what level is that behavior?"*

Be careful when it comes to using closed-ended questions. In the above examples, open-ended questions were asked. Close-ended questions ("yes" or "no") should be used only if the question calls for self-inquiry or self-examination. Here is an example of using a well-placed closed-ended question where (**T**) **is the Teacher** and *(S) is the Student:*

> **T: On what level is that behavior?**
> *S: I don't know.*
>
> **T: Tell me what the other students are doing.**
> *S: They're working together.*

T: Were you doing your best to work together with them?
(Closed-ended question calling for a "yes" or "no" answer but involving reflection)
S: No.

T: What is the level when someone makes his own rules?
S: Level B

T: Thank you

SIMPLE BUT NOT EASY

Asking effective questions is a skill, not a talent. In order to be successful, the questioning needs to become a conscious, practiced strategy. Otherwise, we remain prisoners of what seems natural.

Alan Schneider grew up in New York City and drove a taxicab to put himself through Columbia University. He knew how to drive quite well. He now lives in upstate New York where one day he encountered "black ice," which cannot be seen but is felt when the car goes into a skid.

Alan was driving to work one day when he drove over some black ice, and his car started to skid to the right. The more the car skidded to the right—straight towards the trees—the more he turned the wheel desperately to the left. The car kept skidding. He related to me that it felt like experiencing slow motion. The car finally hit a tree. Fortunately, Alan was not injured, but the car had to be towed. When the tow truck came and the driver looked at the ice on the pavement, he said, "You know, you should have turned with the skid in order for the car's tires to regain traction with the road." Alan thought to himself, "I knew that." Why didn't he do what he knew? He told me, "I did what came naturally."

Alan lives by a lake, and that winter the lake was over two feet thick with ice. In order to practice, he put his car on the ice, revved his car up to 15 mph, and slammed on the brakes. Naturally, the car went into a skid and Alan turned the steering wheel in the same way he did when he had his accident. He made a second attempt and again turned the steering wheel the wrong way. Alan told me it took him three tries before he actually turned the steering wheel in the direction he knew he should—with the skid, not against it. When he turned the steering wheel in the same direction as the skid, the tires gained traction and Alan regained control of his car.

One thing is certain. When you start asking self-evaluative questions, you are going to feel slightly strange. You will be doing something that does not feel natural or comfortable. You need to be aware of this. A skill becomes comfortable and feels natural *only after practicing it.*

The most effective way to become habituated is to consciously put yourself in the proper mental position—as before hitting a golf ball or baseball, or before playing a musical instrument. Your proper mental position is that of a counselor. Using this mental framing, stress is immediately reduced and the short dialogue will be very pleasant.

TONE

Tone is an essential ingredient of communication. It doesn't matter what the verbal communication is if the tone is one of anger. The tone negates the message. It takes time and practice to speak in a nonconfrontational tone when your impulse is to display verbal anger.

TONE OF VOICE

It's not only what you say
But the manner in which you say it;
It's not only the language you use
But the tone in which you convey it.

"Come here!" I sharply said,
And the child cowered and wept.
"Come here," I said. He looked and smiled
And straight to my lap he crept.

Words may be mild and fair
But the tone can pierce like a dart;
Words may be soft as the summer air
But the tone can break my heart.

Words come from the mind
And grow by study and art—
But tone leaps from the inner self,
Revealing the state of the heart.

For if you want behavior to change,
Of this you must remain aware—
As much as the words you use, *it is the tone of your voice*
Which communicates how much you care.
(Author Unknown)

KINESICS

In addition to how the question is asked and the tone in a person's voice, kinesics also communicates. Kinesics is non-verbal body language. Gestures, facial expressions, movements, and posture all communicate. If a teacher is *checking for understanding* with a frowning face, arms folded, body stiff, and eyes glaring while asking, "What level is that?" a very clear coercive message is sent. However, when the same question is asked with a slight smile, arm extended with the palm up, body slightly forward, and eyes wide open, the resulting message is completely different.

PRACTICE IS THE MOTHER OF SKILL

When we first learned how to walk, we wobbled, were unsteady, and fell down. When learning to ride a bicycle or drive a car, most of us went through an awkward stage. Remember how awkward you felt the first time you stood before a class? The awkwardness leaves when we get the "hang of it." *We cannot learn a skill and be perfect at the same time.* We don't expect it of our students, and we should not expect it of ourselves. Using the strategy and expecting perfection the first time or even the first few times is unrealistic. *Give yourself permission to be a learner.*

The skill improves with use. Each question is a learning experience. After starting to ask self-evaluative questions, you will begin to ask more and more of them. You learn which ones bring desired outcomes and which do not. It helps to think of developing a skill as a direction, rather than as a destination. The story is told of two camels with riders in the desert. The rider on the first camel looked back over his shoulder to a woman and two children on the second camel, and said, "Stop asking when we are going to get there; we're nomads for crying out loud!"

With practice, the teacher develops an "ear" for effective and ineffective questions. Following are two questions attempting to get the same result, but notice the subtle differences in sound and message: "When are you going to stop doing that?" is demanding and has an "attack" overtone. "Have you planned your time for getting on track?" is inquisitive—not accusatory. The significant difference is in the direction of the questions. The first aims at stopping a negative. The second aims at the power of positive direction. Certainly, the tone of voice is crucial, but notice how the questions themselves can influence the tone.

Learning the skill is simple but not easy—until the skill is regularly practiced. As Ralph Waldo Emerson said,

> That which we persist in doing becomes easier—
> not that the nature of the task has changed,
> but our ability to do it has increased.

The simple tasks of teaching the concepts and learning the skill of effective questioning handle the great majority of socially irresponsible classroom behaviors. However, when a student has *already acknowledged level B behavior* and *again* disrupts the class, authority is used—but without being punitive. This is the third phase of the program, *Guided Choices.*

KEY POINTS

◆ The strategy starts by setting the mental frame: irresponsible behavior is viewed as a teaching opportunity for fostering responsibility.

◆ First use unobtrusive visual, verbal, or kinetic techniques to stop distractions.

◆ When handling disruptive behaviors, a *stress-reducing mode* is used. A noncoercive guidance approach is employed, rather than an authoritarian coercive approach.

◆ An *asking*—rather than a telling—approach is employed because asking is a more effective strategy for encouraging self-evaluation.

◆ A disrupting student is asked to identify the *level* of chosen behavior, not the behavior itself.

◆ If the questioning is done in front of the entire class, classroom time is not wasted. During the short interchange, the class is reinforcing the levels of development.

◆ The classroom maintains a positive learning environment at all times, even when a student demonstrates irresponsible behavior.

_____

NOTE:

The first step in using Guided Choices in the next section should be to *elicit* a procedure to help the youngster help himself and, thereby, avoid being a victim of impulses. The conversation sounds something like, "Every time you stick your foot out when your friend walks by your desk, you are a victim of your impulses. Do you really want to be a victim? If you want to me a victor, instead of a victim, then let's develop some procedure so that when you get that impulse, you will be able to redirect or refocus. Without some procedure to use and practice, the temptation will continue to be so great that you will continue to be a victim of your impulses." (See page 155 for an example of a procedure.)

Also, review page 6, for the example of *eliciting a consequence—* rather than *imposing one.*

GUIDED CHOICES

You can be tough without being punitive.

OVERVIEW

If a student has acknowledged unacceptable behavior and continues to disrupt learning, the third phase, *Guided Choices,* is employed. *This third phase is used only with those who are constantly disruptive.*

Simply stated, *Guided Choices* refers to using authority without being punitive. Employment of authority is essential with youth who go beyond acceptable behavioral standards. However, the authority is used without being authoritarian because authoritarianism is coercive and shuts down any *desire* for change and growth. The disrupting student is given a choice, thereby maintaining self-respect and avoiding an adversarial relationship.

The strategy is to offer choices in the form of questions. Authority is used because *the person who asks the questions controls the situation.* However, as long as the student can make a decision, regardless of how minor it may be, dignity is preserved and confrontation is avoided. Madeline Hunter stated, "A student who loses dignity usually becomes rebellious and resistant in the situation and retaliatory to the person who caused the loss of dignity." (Hunter, 1967, p. 61) The overriding principle always to keep in mind is, *"Not losing is more important than winning."* No one really wins in a confrontational relationship. Solving a problem is much more difficult when people are in conflict because their egos interfere.

Guided Choices is a "win/win" strategy. In "I win/you lose" situations, the teacher only wins a form of satisfaction but the student is left with dejected feelings. In "lose/lose" situations, neither wins; the teacher gets aggravated and the student again takes the brunt. In "you lose/I win" situations, the student has outsmarted the teacher. By using *Guided Choices,* the teacher wins by using a non-confrontational guidance approach that avoids stress. The student wins because dignity has been left intact. In addition, the relationship wins because it is not fractured.

Guided Choices fulfills four purposes: (1) stops the disruption, (2) isolates the student from the class activity, (3) gives the disrupting student a responsibility-producing activity to encourage reflection, and (4) allows the teacher to return to the lesson promptly.

GUIDED CHOICES ACTIVITIES

In *primary grades*, activities will depend upon the teacher's style and creativity. Primary teachers are continually developing ways to isolate a disrupting student from the rest of the class. *Rather than just a time out, the activity should encourage self-evaluation.* Some examples are: having the student draw what the student did, describe the incident while talking into a tape recorder, or create a story that illustrates the type of behavior the student demonstrated. A simple approach is for the youngster to just relate the incident to another student; it is in the telling that reflection and self-evaluation start.

Primary teachers are cognizant that learning a behavior is similar to learning content or a skill in that children are not punished when they have not learned some information or mastered a skill. Similarly, developing responsibility and successful group interactions are skills. When disruptive behavior is thought of as a *learning opportunity* rather than as a punishment opportunity, everyone wins.

ESSAY

The strategies described in the rest of this chapter are for *upper elementary, middle, and high school classes.* The first activity consists of the student's completing a form referred to as an *Essay.* (See Appendix.) It is simply a self-evaluation activity that has three questions:

- What *did* I do? (Acknowledgment)
- What *can* I do to prevent it from happening again? (Choice)
- What *will* I do? (Commitment)

The form is handed to the student while asking, in a noncoercive tone, *one* of the following questions: (a) "Would you rather complete the activity in your seat *or* in the rear of the room?" (b) "Would you rather complete the activity by yourself *or* have someone help you?" (c) "Would you rather complete the activity in the classroom *or* in the office?" The specific question asked depends upon the teacher's appraisal of the student and the situation. As long as the student has a choice, then that student's power, respect, and dignity are retained. It is when a student feels powerless, feels a loss of respect and dignity, or feels cornered that confrontation usually takes place. Offering a choice avoids confrontations. An axiom to remember is to use the *A*, *B*, *C* approach: *A*lways *B*e *C*ourteous.

I had one student who, upon receiving the *Essay*, informed me that he would not complete it. I told the student that I understood. I also told him that he needed to understand that I am employed by the board of education and that they would not tolerate any student defying their authority. I then said, "If your pencil is not to the paper within a minute, you are telling me that you are defying the board of education, in which case you are not eligible to remain in the classroom. I would like you to stay, but the board of education would not approve." *I then immediately moved away.* The student picked up his pencil and completed the form—the only one that was ever needed with that student.

Any form used should meet two criteria: (1) it should foster student reflection, and (2) it should involve future planning.

The vast majority of students are capable of completing the form by themselves. However, if the disrupting student works with another person, that is perfectly acceptable. Having to relate and admit to something has a great emotional impact by itself.

Before a student leaves the classroom, a short discussion takes place. The student is first asked if he knows *why the activity was assigned*. The student is not asked to agree, but it is important for the student to understand why the activity was given. The short discussion reinforces the point that when a person makes his own standards, the use of authority is the most expedient approach to stop the behavior and enable the teacher to continue teaching. The point is also made that the teacher is solely interested in the student's impulse control, not in punishment. Second, the student is asked *whether or not the activity was assigned for personal reasons*. This second question is asked in order to reduce any ill feelings.

Using the essay form or other similar activity followed by the short discussion with students handles the vast majority of disruptive problems.

The completed form need not be kept on file. One way to show the student that the teacher is only interested in the student's growth, and not in punishing the student, is for the teacher to ask the student what should be done with the form. At this point, the form has served its purpose, namely, halting disruptive behavior by isolating the student and fostering student reflection. My approach was to tear up the form in front of the student and drop it in the nearby wastepaper basket. I wanted the student to leave my classroom (1) feeling good and (2) knowing I had no ill will.

Every day is a new day for student growth. If a student disrupts the class on a subsequent day, the teacher begins again with *Checking for Understanding.* That is, the student is always given an opportunity to acknowledge the level of behavior before *Guided Choices* are used.

SELF-DIAGNOSTIC REFERRALS

In those cases where a student continues to disrupt the lesson, a *Self-Diagnostic Referral* is used. This is different from the *Essay,* which is often discarded. Keep these completed referrals for the entire school year, not just for each quarter.

When presenting the student with this form, the student is again given a choice as to how he would like to complete it: by himself or with assistance from another student, in the student's own seat or in another seat, in the classroom or in the office. As with the essay, the *student* completes the form, remembering that it is the *student* with whom we want to foster responsible behavior. The following are examples of items on the form. (Items tailored to specific grade levels are included in the Appendix.)

- Describe the problem created that resulted in getting this assignment.

- Tell the level of behavior.

- Explain this level.

- Explain how the behavior is on this level.

- When acting on this level, on what level must the teacher act?

- Is this how you want to be treated?

- Why or why not?

- On what level should you have acted to be socially responsible?

- If you had acted on this level, how would the situation have been different?

- On the back of this *Self-Diagnostic Referral,* list three solutions to the problem you could use to act more responsibly.

Because the referral may find its way to the office or to a parent, all questions are answered completely. As with the essay, the form needs to be completed before the student rejoins the class activity. If the form is not completed to the teacher's satisfaction, a new form is given to the student.

ADDITIONAL SELF-DIAGNOSTIC REFERRALS

If a second *Self-Diagnostic Referral* form were to be used, a copy of the first as well as the second are mailed home along with a very short note explaining the recurring problem. (See *Parent Note* in the Appendix.) If a third referral were to be necessary, "Three strikes and you are out" is employed. Copies of all three self-diagnostic referrals would be mailed to the parent along with a second parent note indicating that the teacher exhausted every means to foster social responsibility and that any future disruption will be referred to an administrator.

Although the process may sound cumbersome, it rarely reaches the stage of a third referral. In addition, since the student's growth is the concern, the student is the person who expends the effort in completing any form or activity. The teacher's involvement in record keeping is minimal. The only form completed by the teacher is the brief parent note.

WHEN ALL ELSE FAILS

Some people see the light only when they feel the heat. Two seventh-grade students come to mind who already had three referrals sent home. Jason and Robert were students who will "push" as far as they can, the kind who cause a teacher to wake up in the morning with a first thought of, "I hope Jason and Robert are absent today."

I had gone as far as I could to help the boys become more socially responsible. The students understood "After three strikes, you are out." This was still the first quarter and I had expected to send the boys to the office, as all their other teachers had done. To my surprise, I never had to send either boy to the office the entire year.

Here is what I did. With the attitude that every day is a new day, the boys had one opportunity to self-correct. When they disrupted the lesson, the first step was to have them identify their behavioral level. This became their warning. Since I had already completed the standard office referral, ready to go except for the date, I placed the office referral on the student's desk right after the disruption and said, "My preference would be to have you stay in the classroom. However, if you act on level B again, you are telling me that you want to continue to make your own standards for the class. That is not acceptable. You may stay in the classroom only if your behavior is at level C or D." (Notice the use of the contingency.)

The boys could see and touch the referral. They knew they had pushed as far as would be allowed and that their staying in class was contingent upon their choosing an acceptable level of behavior.

Unfortunately, schools have students who will push to the brink. Once they are standing on the edge, however, they rarely jump. Students can control themselves and do, although authority needs to be used.

Guided Choices, then, uses a "no one loses" strategy. The class does not lose because the disrupting student is isolated from the class activity so that instruction can continue. The dignity of the student is not diminished because the approach uses authority but is not authoritarian, and the disrupting student also benefits because he is given an activity that assists reflection and leads to a plan for improvement. By using a non-stressful, non-confrontational guidance approach, the teacher resists becoming stressed—or distressed, as is so often the case.

KEY POINTS

◆ *Guided Choices* refers to using authority without being punitive. The strategy is based on offering choices.

◆ Any such activity fulfills four purposes: (1) stops a disruption, (2) isolates the student from the class activity, (3) gives the disrupting student a responsibility-producing activity to encourage reflection, and (4) allows the teacher to return to the lesson promptly.

◆ Primary students are given an activity that is similar to a time out but includes the young person's becoming engaged in a self-evaluating activity.

◆ With older students, the first activity consists of the student's completing a form referred to as an *Essay*. In cases where a student continues to disrupt the lesson, *Self-Diagnostic Referrals* are used.

◆ Authority is combined with guidance, and sending a student to an administrator becomes unnecessary.

◆ The first step in using Guided Choices should be to ***elicit*** a procedure to help the youngster help himself and, thereby, avoid being a victim of impulses.

SUMMARY, REVIEW, AND CONCLUSION

The real power, the real influence of parents and teachers,
is not what young people do when they are with adults;
it is what young people do when they are not.

The Raise Responsibility System activates internal motivation. The system handles classroom disruptions simply and easily, creates a noncoercive classroom, raises individual and social responsibility, promotes interest in learning, increases the joy of teaching, reduces office referrals, reduces suspensions, and reduces everyone's stress.

SUMMARY

Raising responsibility starts with teaching a hierarchy of developmental levels. Exposure to the levels encourages responsible behavior. Students want to reach the highest level of the hierarchy because it uses the motivating principle of challenge.

(1) Teaching the Concepts

The concepts comprise four levels of development that are made meaningful by the examples students create for their own classroom. The levels are:

(D) Democracy (<u>In</u>ternal motivation—because democracy is inseparable from responsibility)

(C) Cooperation/Conformity (<u>Ex</u>ternal motivation—as with peer pressure)

(B) Boss*ing*/Bully*ing* (Rather than following accepted standards, makes own rules and standards)

(A) Anarchy (Absence of order)

Levels A and B are not acceptable levels of classroom behavior. Although levels C and D are both appropriate classroom levels, behavior at level D is the goal.

(2) Checking for Understanding

Disruptions are handled by *Checking for Understanding*. The purpose is for the disrupting student to acknowledge the level of inappropriate behavior (level B). Acknowledgment is the first step towards accepting responsibility. *The vast majority of situations are handled by using this basic learning theory of teaching (the concepts) and then testing (Checking for Understanding)*. Surveys across the country indicate that teachers use the second phase, *Checking for Understanding*, with fifteen to twenty percent of students. The self-evaluative questioning strategy encourages students to reflect on their level of self-chosen behavior. The effect of this procedure is, to quote one teacher, "They (students) know almost instantly when they need to make a better choice. This takes less time away from instruction and keeps the classroom climate stress-free and positive." (Capell)

(3) Guided Choices

Continued or repeated disruptions are handled by guided choices. The purpose is to stop the disruption and give the student a responsibility-producing activity. In these situations, authority is used but is not punitive. Surveys indicate that teachers need to use *Guided Choices* with only two to five percent of students.

In both *Checking for Understanding* and *Guided Choices*, the teacher is asking—not telling. By asking, the teacher controls the situation. However, as long as the student can make a decision, dignity is preserved and confrontation is avoided.

A major reason for the effectiveness of the system is that students know and feel that they will not be harmed. Students understand that the teacher's intention is for student *growth*, not punishment. In the process, students learn that taking responsibility, which comes from internal motivation, is more satisfying than being externally motivated.

REVIEW

1. When a disruptive student is sent to the office, the counselor or administrator invariably starts the conversation by asking a question. That conversation is on a one-to-one basis. But how does a teacher employ such an approach while teaching with so many other students in the classroom? The answer is a strategy that is proactive. *Teaching* the concepts is done at the outset.

2. When a student acts inappropriately, the teacher starts by asking a self-evaluative question. The question is aimed at having the student reflect by identifying the level of chosen behavior. Since a *level* is referred to, *rather than the student's*

behavior, the student feels no need to be defensive. The noncoercive approach prevents confrontations and reduces stress for both teacher and student. In addition, the disruption is viewed as a teaching opportunity to raise social responsibility.

3. The approach uses simple cognitive learning theory. First we teach; then we test. The testing is referred to as *Checking for Understanding*. Effective questions are asked to ensure that the student reflects, self-evaluates, and understands that he or she chose to act on level B.

4. After the student acknowledges the level of behavior, the teacher continues with the lesson. The questioning process takes no more than a few moments and can be done either individually or in front of the entire class.

5. Acknowledgment and ownership are the first steps in changing behavior. Students need to feel that the teacher's desire is for them to accept responsibility, rather than to be coerced or punished.

6. During the short checking for understanding interchange, responsibility is being reinforced to the class. Instructional time is not wasted.

7. The power of the strategy is that when the student acknowledges the level of behavior, the misconduct not only stops, but also the student oftentimes apologizes—a result of accepting responsibility.

8. Asking self-evaluative and reflective questions is a skill and, therefore, is developed only with practice. You will probably feel uncomfortable when first using it because adults are more habituated to telling young people, rather than asking them reflective questions. During the questioning, be aware of your tone of voice and non-verbal body language (facial expression, body stance, gestures). Be inquisitive, not coercive.

CONCLUSION: OBEDIENCE VS. RESPONSIBILITY

External motivators are used extensively in schools. This includes *telling* young people what to do, *punishing* them if they do not, and *rewarding* them if they do. These approaches teach young people obedience. The shortcomings of obedience appear when teachers and parents are not around to use these external motivators.

The Raise Responsibility System focuses on internal motivation, which builds the vision to act with responsible, autonomous behavior— whether or not anyone else is around.

If America is to continue the civil democracy that has been our heritage, we must do more than just talk about civil democracy and responsibility; we must actively foster it. We can do this in a classroom by providing opportunities for students to take responsibility and by showing them that virtuous behavior is in their own best interest.

By teaching a developmental hierarchy, by using a guidance approach when irresponsibility occurs in the classroom, and—when necessary—by using authority without being punitive, we empower students to manage themselves to be responsible. When we foster responsibility, which in the final analysis requires internal motivation, we foster the type of citizenship that will perpetuate a civil society.

KEY POINTS

◆ The foundation of the system lies in being proactive by teaching four concepts that can be understood at any age—although the depth of the meanings will vary depending upon age and maturity.

◆ The lower two levels are unacceptable while the two higher levels are acceptable. By having *two acceptable* levels, people generally want to aim at the highest one—simply because of having an option and the nature of a hierarchy.

◆ A reward should never be given for Level D. If it were, one would never know if the behavior was to get the reward or because it was the right thing to do. In addition, the difference between Level C and Level D is in the *motivation*—not necessarily the behavior.

◆ The adult's goal is to have youth operate on Level C—the level of following procedures, conformity to laws and regulations, and pro-social behavior. Level D is for people who choose to make it a goal.

◆ No one operates consistently on the same level. Although a person has acted on one level, the person may act on a different level with the next decision. When choosing a higher level, youth reap the benefits of improved self-esteem and increased self-satisfaction.

The Marvin Marshall Teaching Model

(I) CLASSROOM MANAGEMENT vs. DISCIPLINE

The key to effective classroom management is teaching and practicing procedures. This is the teacher's responsibility. Discipline, on the other hand, has to do with behavior and is the student's responsibility.

(II) THREE PRINCIPLES TO PRACTICE

POSITIVITY	CHOICE	REFLECTION
Teachers practice changing negatives into positives. "No running" becomes "We walk in the hallways." "Stop talking" becomes "This is quiet time."	Choice-response thinking is taught—as well as impulse control—so students are not victims of their own impulses.	Since a person can only control another person temporarily and because no one can actually change another person, asking REFLECTIVE questions is the most effective approach to actuate change in others.

(III) THE RAISE RESPONSIBILITY SYSTEM (RRSystem)

TEACHING THE HIERARCHY (Teaching)	CHECKING FOR UNDERSTANDING (Asking)	GUIDED CHOICES (Eliciting)
The hierarchy engenders a desire to behave responsibly and a desire to put forth effort to learn. Students differentiate between internal and external motivation— and learn to rise above inappropriate peer influence.	Students reflect on the LEVEL of chosen behavior. This approach SEPARATES THE PERSON FROM THE BEHAVIOR, thereby negating the usual tendency to defend one's actions. It is this natural tendency toward self-defense that leads to confrontations between student and teacher.	If disruptions continue, a consequence or procedure is ELICITED to redirect the inappropriate behavior. This approach is in contrast to the usual coercive approach of having a consequence IMPOSED.

(IV) USING THE SYSTEM TO INCREASE ACADEMIC PERFORMANCE

Using the hierarchy BEFORE a lesson and reflecting AFTER a lesson increases effort and raises academic achievement. www.MarvinMarshall.com/hierarchy.htm
www.MarvinMarshall.com/aletterworthreading.html

4
PROMOTING LEARNING

LEARNING CLIMATE

If learning is what we value,
then we ought to value the process of learning as much as the
result of learning.

Learning is promoted in a climate where people feel safe and cared for. The adage, *"People don't care what you know until they know you care,"* is applicable. When working with one middle school, William Glasser stated,

> The teachers stopped almost all coercion—an approach that was radically different from the way most of these students had been treated since kindergarten. When we asked the students why they were no longer disruptive and why they were beginning to work in school, over and over they said, "You care about us." (Glasser, April 1997, p. 601)

The result of a caring interest in those with whom we work was documented in a classic study on human relations and became known as the "Hawthorne Effect." It came from a study that took place in 1927 at Western Electric's Hawthorne plant in Cicero, Illinois. Researchers went into the factory to see if, by increasing room lighting for a group of employees, productivity would increase. Improvements did indeed seem to boost worker output. But much to their surprise, when the researchers analyzed a comparable group with no change in the lighting, their productivity also improved. Further study and analysis of this puzzling result showed that productivity increased because the workers were delighted that management was showing some interest in them. *The workers felt that management cared about them and that they were valued.*

People have difficulty understanding that someone cares for them when coercion is used. W. Edwards Deming, the American who showed Japan in the post–World War II years how to improve quality, understood this. (His approach is further discussed in the section *Collaboration—Rather than Competition—for Quality Learning*.) One of his core principles was to *"Drive out fear."* Deming understood that motivation, performance, productivity, and quality are optimum when coercion is at a minimum and when a trusting, caring climate is at the maximum.

In a classroom where the teacher and class have a forced relationship, the student who disrupts the class becomes a hero. The reason is that a coercive climate is an adversarial one. In a climate of positive relationships, the disrupting student does not receive support from the other students.

V*oluntary* relationships are chosen as, for example, between friends. However, classroom relationships are *involuntary*. Students are mostly assigned to their classes; relationships between teachers and students and between students and students are not chosen. The approaches promoted in this chapter help turn involuntary relationships into voluntary ones.

Where learning is promoted, certain activities are unacceptable. These include ridiculing, threatening, forcing, compelling, punishing, bribing, manipulating, blaming, complaining, putting down, nagging, and badgering. We rarely use these coercive tactics with our friends. Coercion is simply not effective in influencing others while trying to keep good relationships.

The first section of this chapter deals with *relationships*, the second with *strategies*, and the third with *challenges*. Although addressed to classroom teachers, the discussions are appropriate in parenting and in other social settings.

KEY POINTS

◆ Learning is optimal when coercion is at a minimum and a trusting, caring climate is at the maximum.

◆ Involuntary relationships become voluntary when people are where they *want* to be. Learning is promoted in this climate.

RELATIONSHIPS

Meaningful relationships establish
a genial place conducive to growth.

Three categories of relationships that promote learning are discussed. The first is between the teacher and the class, where the negative orientation of *rules* is contrasted to the positive orientation of *expectations*. The second concerns reducing *anonymity*, both between the teacher and students and among students themselves. The third is the intimacy between the teacher and each individual student that occurs during *tutoring*.

RULES VS. EXPECTATIONS

I do not dress like a cop; nor did I become a teacher to be one.

The relationship between the teacher and the class improves as rules are reduced.

REDUCING RULES

A common practice in this country is to establish classroom rules, either by the teacher alone or by the teacher and students cooperatively. *Rules are necessary in games, but in relationships they are counterproductive.* Although the establishment of rules has good intentions, their implementation often produces deleterious effects.

When Johns Hopkins University researchers analyzed data from more than 600 schools, they found six characteristics associated with discipline problems. Notice that the first three concerned rules.

1. Rules were unclear or perceived as unfairly or inconsistently enforced.

2. Students didn't believe in the rules.

3. Teachers and administrators didn't know what the rules were or disagreed on the proper responses to student misconduct.

4. Teacher-administrator cooperation was poor or the administration was inactive.

5. Misconduct was ignored.

6. Teachers tended to have punitive attitudes. (Gaustaud, p. 18)

When a student does not follow a class rule, the tendency is to think in negative terms: "You broke the rule." The reason is simple. Rules in a classroom imply "or else." A rule that is not followed often leads to an accusatory encounter and results in some type of psychological pain, anger, or resentment for both teacher and student. The rationale is that there must be a consequence for breaking the rule—a punishment that, by its very nature, is coercive. It encourages feelings of enmity, which are not very conducive for positive relationships.

Rulemaking breeds enforcement, which promotes punitive attitudes and results in a teacher's moving from *the role of a coach to the role of a cop,* as was verified in the Number Six finding of the Johns Hopkins study.

Glasser affirms that "traditional education often produces problems that stem from poorly conceived and poorly administrated rules." (Glasser, 1969, p. 195)

> At present, in both elementary and secondary schools, we usually establish rigid rules that lead to punishment when they are broken. The rigid rules of the average central-city school cause even those who have more to gain, the intelligent, to rebel and to refuse to accept the education available. (Ibid., p. 194)

Glasser concludes that an inflexible, punitive approach works poorly especially with central-city children, "most of whom have difficulty obeying rules." (Ibid.) Classroom rules often work against the very reason for their existence: to have students self-discipline and maintain decorum. Quality schools and quality workplaces do not rely on rules. (Glasser, 1992, p. 123) Neither does citizenship education rely on rules. Citizenship education has to do with appropriate and inappropriate classroom conduct, and rules are kept to a minimum—such as "respect for one another and safety." (Farivar, p. 61) Citizenship is really little more than the conscious practice of civic etiquette—the public manners that make the places where we live workable when we practice them, and unbearable when we don't.

Neither are rules effective in teaching moral development.

> Many parents, teachers, and religious leaders find out too late that a concentrated or exclusive focus

on rules is problematic. Using rules and attempting to enforce them as the principal method of producing compliance has not been successful. In fact, it often creates defiance. Many schools, for instance, have established school-wide citizenship programs because large numbers of students are tardy, absent, or otherwise fail to comply with school policies and procedures. This program consisted of an enforcement system that required noncompliant students to participate in hours of community service or other educational programs for each failure to comply. 'Teeth' were added by announcing that failure to comply or complete the service hours would prevent students from graduating. It was not long until schools were forced to create large-scale service and educational programs that required extra record keeping because large and increasing numbers of students failed to comply. The rule system designed to decrease noncompliance actually appeared to promote it. (Scoresby, p. 28)

The mere fact that one knows a rule does not mean it will be followed, in much the same way that information that has been taught does not mean it was learned. When we discover that a teaching has not been learned, we try to assist the student. Similarly, *behavior* is learned and the student should be helped, not hurt or caused to suffer.

Rules are "left-hemisphered." They are sensible, orderly, and structured. However, students who "break the rules" often operate spontaneously and process randomly—typical "right-hemisphere" behavior. In addition, rules often engender a search for loopholes. Rather than using rules, teachers would be better served by using *expectations.*

EXPECTATIONS

The term "expectations" connotes a positive orientation. When an expectation is not met, a helping mentality is engendered, rather than an enforcement mentality. Expectations repair a major finding of the Johns Hopkins study, namely, that many students believe "rules" are mandates that adults put on students, but do not apply to adults.

Expectations engender student empowerment and are responsibility lifting. They tap into internal motivation and foster commitment, rather than compliance.

The following were the expectations posted in my classroom:

- Do my tasks
- Have materials
- Be where I belong
- Control myself
- Follow directions
- Speak considerately

MANNERS

Edmund Burke, the 18th century British statesman, said that manners are more important than laws. According to George Bernard Shaw, the Irish playwright, "Without good manners human society becomes intolerable and impossible." Manners are what make civilization civil. Hal Urban is a teacher, speaker, and author of *Life's Greatest Lessons: 20 Things I Want My Kids to Know*. He suggests holding discussions on manners.

Following are some questions that Urban suggests:

- Would a society be better if people treated each other with respect?

- How are classrooms and schools societies?

- How can good manners be one of the most important keys to success in life?

- What is the Golden Rule? How is it civilizing?

- Which impresses people more: being cool or being courteous?

The following questions promote additional reflection on the topic:

- What do you think about getting up, walking across the room, throwing something in the wastebasket, and then walking back across the room while the teacher is talking?

- What do you think about speaking to others and especially adults in a defiant manner?

- What are disadvantages of swearing in classrooms and in conversations between classes?

- What difference does it make when approaching someone with, "May I please have. . . ." in a pleasant tone versus saying, "I need. . . ." in a demanding tone?

- What are the advantages of using, "Please" and "Thank you"?

- What do you think about listening when the teacher is talking versus feeling the right to ignore the teacher and have a private conversation?

- What do you think about listening when a fellow class member asks a question?

- What do you think about demonstrating an interest in other people versus being solely concerned with yourself?

PROCEDURES

Very often, what a teacher refers to as a rule is really a *procedure*. We need look no further than to one of the first rules primary students are given. They are taught the classroom rule of raising one's hand to be recognized by the teacher before speaking out. The same rule is taught year after year. I have even seen this rule posted in eighth-grade classrooms! Simply reminding students that this is a procedure, rather than a rule, places the teacher in the position of a coach and eliminates an enforcement mentality.

We too often assume that students know what we know and what we would like them to do. This assumption is faulty. Teach procedures—such as how to enter the classroom, how to use an activity center, how to distribute supplies, or anything else that requires a mode of operation. A successful classroom has routines and procedures, which give organization and structure to learning. (See *Classroom Management* in Chapter 5 for more on this topic.)

KEY POINTS

◆ Rules are necessary in games but are counterproductive in relationships.

◆ Relationships improve as rules are reduced.

◆ Rules foster obedience rather than responsibility.

◆ Discussing manners is more effective than posting rules.

◆ The use of *expectations* accomplishes what rules purport to do, but without their disadvantages.

◆ Examine your rules. You will find that they are either expectations or procedures. When you see any that are procedures, *teach* them.

REDUCING ANONYMITY

Anonymity must be banished.
–National Association of Secondary
School Principals

Many students feel isolated at school and are alienated from the learning process. Such feelings were captured in the school film *Cipher in the Snow.* The main character was a young student who felt as if he were a person of no importance or value; he felt like a non-entity, a cipher. Even though the student was in the midst of others, he felt alone. He felt anonymous and simply disappeared.

TEACHER AND STUDENT

The National Association of Secondary School Principals (NASSP) emphasizes the need to reduce student anonymity (Tamara). In *Breaking Ranks: Changing an American Institution,* their seminal publication for changing the American high school, NASSP lists six themes that schools must incorporate to break ranks with the status quo. On the top of their list is that better education depends on personalizing the school experience for students. (NASSP, p. 5) The report goes so far as proclaiming that anonymity must be banished. (NASSP, p. 46)

Dale Carnegie, in his best-selling book on winning friends and influencing people, states that a person's name is—to that person—the sweetest and most important sound in any language. Calling a student by the name the student *prefers* to be called not only reduces anonymity but also sends a powerful communication of interest and caring on the part of the teacher.

Chuck Glover of Richmond, Virginia, illustrates the power of showing interest in a student's name.

> During my tenure as an itinerant elementary physical education teacher, while walking down the empty school hall during a short break between classes, Sam, a second-grade student from Southeast Asia, emerged from his classroom to go to the water fountain. After getting his drink and turning back towards his classroom, he waved, and I reciprocated. I interrupted his return by squatting down as he

came by and asked him if his name really was Sam. He quickly replied that his name was Sambohem but that his parents told him to say his name was Sam because Americans have difficulty pronouncing his real name.

I reflected momentarily on what Sam had just told me, and then I asked if he minded if I called him by his real name. He smiled from ear to ear and reassured me that it would be all right. He and I practiced for a couple of minutes right there on the spot. After he felt comfortable with my pronunciation of his name, he continued on his way. But after only a step or two, he turned back towards me, tears in his eyes, gave me a hug, and said, "Thank you," then disappeared through the door of his classroom.

For the rest of that school year, whenever I would see Sambohem, he seemed to have an especial affinity for my class.

Asking a student how the student prefers a teacher address him or her sends a powerful communication.

A simple way to learn the name of every child, is to play identification. A student states his or her name. The next student repeats the first person's name and then states his or her own name. The third child does the same. This is repeated until every student is identified. A variation is to identify a hobby or something that the student enjoys doing. Including an item with the name elongates the time between repeating each name. Also, including an item with the name enhances retention. Knowing something about someone else further reduces anonymity between students.

Another simple approach to reducing students' anonymity is to request parents to write a letter of introduction about their child. These letters give quick parental insight as well as other information that the teacher might not otherwise obtain. In addition, the letters encourage parental support. Here is a sample letter of request from an elementary teacher to parents:

Dear Parents:

It will be my pleasure to be your child's teacher this school year. I look forward to having your child in my class.

Please assist me by writing a letter of introduction about my new student. The letter will help me to learn your child's interests, what you want me to pay particular attention to or lend particular assistance in, and perhaps something personal or something about your child's personality.

I encourage you to compose the letter with your child.

Thank you,

(Signed by the teacher)

A prime reason that anonymity should be reduced is that it can have a socially deleterious effect. With some people, anonymity breeds irresponsibility. Imagine yourself driving on a freeway on a Saturday morning when traffic is light and the road looks more like a ribbon of pavement rather than a slow moving parking lot. Your eyes have time to meander as you notice the azure sky, the various architectural styles, and the landscape of the area. You gaze in your rear view mirror and you notice a car so close to the rear of yours that you can almost feel its bumper against yours. At your earliest opportunity, you move to the right lane and, as the car starts to pass you, the driver begins to give you an unwarranted familiar gesture. At that moment, his eyes meet yours, and you recognize each other. Suddenly, his gesture changes into a familiar wave of his hand. Why did he change his intended gesture? He is no longer anonymous. Anonymity does interesting things to attitudes and behavior.

STUDENT AND STUDENT

One reason young students try to learn is that they love their parents and caregivers and want to please them. Similarly, young children like their teachers and try to please them. But as young people move into middle school and then high school, where teachers necessarily become less personal and less available, students lose some of the school caring that was more available in elementary grades. As young people move up the grade ladder, they turn more and more to their friends for belonging, and as they grow older, they depend still less upon teachers and even parents.

As much as we wish learning were the major attraction for students in attending school, during the adolescent years we find that relationships are often the major motivational factor. Kids want to be with other kids. According to Theodore Sizer, "Personalization is the single most important factor that keeps kids in school." (Shore, p. 1) When a student lacks a sense of belonging, when the student feels anonymous or isolated, motivation for school attendance is diminished. One reason why students drop out of school is lack of friendship.

Teachers can address this issue by planning activities where students spend some time interacting, where they can relate and get to know each other. This can be accomplished in any classroom in just a few minutes. Students share their interests, hobbies, experiences, and things they are proud of with a partner. Some students will not willingly tell a large group about themselves, but they do not mind sharing with one other person, and they don't mind if that person shares the information with a larger group. After a little sharing of personal information, one student introduces the other and states the partner's name and something of interest about the partner. Another activity is for students working in groups to tell three things about themselves that are true and one that is false. In the process of guessing for the false item, students learn three bits of information about each member of the group. Such activities need only to be done periodically for class members to feel a sense of belonging. Involving students in *occasional* activities such as these demonstrates that the teacher is aware of the importance emotions play in learning. (This topic is addressed in Chapter 5 in the section *Emotions.*)

Using activities where students get to know other students—not just as members of the class but as real people—can prevent mean-spirited behavior among students. A bully situation outside of class is stopped with the simple statement, "Leave him alone. I know him."

Trained professionals working with suicidal youngsters attempt to reduce anonymity as soon as possible. A high school named Columbine brings an immediate sense of urgency to this challenge.

KEY POINTS

◆ Reducing feelings of not belonging and anonymity plays a key part in promoting positive feelings for learning.

◆ Learning something personal about each student reduces teacher-student anonymity.

◆ Learning something personal about each other reduces student-to-student anonymity.

TUTORING

If you treat someone as he is, he will stay as he is.
But if you treat him as if he were what he could and ought to be,
he will become what he could and ought to be.
                                    –Johann Wolfgang von Goethe

Tutoring is the easiest, quickest, and most effective way to establish relationships with students. Daily tutoring, more than any other activity, can reduce anonymity, foster a student's sense of belonging in a caring environment, and bring satisfaction and joy to the teacher.

Aside from what is learned cognitively, the impact on the affective level is significant. A few moments at eye level with the teacher gives the student a feeling that the teacher cares about him or her as an individual.

Encouragement is often a spark that ignites motivation. Tutoring affords the perfect opportunity for this type of communication. Time and again one hears that the most powerful factor in student effort is, "The teacher believed in me." Marlon Brando wrote that one of his middle school teachers, Burton Rowley, paid special attention to him. Brando reported that the attention of his teacher so dramatically boosted his self-image that he gained the courage to pursue acting. "His words of encouragement affect me to this day," Brando wrote in his autobiography. (Hicks)

Although every student cannot be tutored every day, *a few minutes can be planned for some daily tutoring*. This applies at any grade level. Especially at the middle and high school levels, too many teachers deprive themselves of working with individual students and establishing a personal relationship with them. Every teacher can afford to invest a few minutes with individual students on a daily basis. Spending time at the student's desk offers an excellent opportunity to see the student's organization and work pattern, and to observe specific skills.

In the old days in England in the city of Broadway near Bath and Nottingham, people would bring their horse and carriage to the inn and leave them with the carriage boy. Because people wanted to encourage the carriage boy to do well—because people thought the carriage boy *could* do well—the owner would give a tip *before* the carriage boy helped with the horse. When the carriage boy was given that tip—the value of his services up front—he wanted to prove his worth. Using this same approach, teachers can tip their students about their potential, give encouragement, share ideas, and foster enthusiasm.

A personal connection is the best gift that a teacher can give to those students who traditionally have not done well in school. We know that the brain is a seeker of connections. When new information is given to students, chaos in the brain may take place until a connection or hook is made. For some students, cognitive connections are not made easily. The human connection can serve as the part of what provides a hook for persistence that is so necessary for success with these students.

A teacher is an encourager. Jim Bellanca stated it succinctly: "Teaching is a strategic act of encouragement." (Bellanca, p. 659) Letting students know we care is the most important thing we can communicate, and seeing a student on a one-to-one basis offers the perfect opportunity.

Much of the success of tutoring is due to personal association and personal attention. One reason why cross-age tutoring is so successful is that the student who does poorly, when asked to help another student, begins to identify himself not as a failure, but as a success.

Ralph Waldo Emerson's idea can well be applied to the teacher and tutoring:

> It is one of the most beautiful compensations of life
> that no man can sincerely try to help another without
> helping himself.

KEY POINTS

◆ Tutoring is the easiest, quickest, and most effective way to establish relationships with students.

◆ Encouragement is often a spark that ignites motivation. Tutoring affords the perfect opportunity for this type of communication.

◆ A few minutes can be planned to do some tutoring daily.

STRATEGIES

Tell me the strategies you use to promote learning,
and I will tell you if you do.

Three strategies for promoting learning are described. The first, *classroom meetings,* establishes an environment conducive to learning, resolving conflicts, fostering empathy, and promoting community. The second strategy, *collaboration,* offers suggestions for enhancing and improving the quality of learning and is far more effective than having students compete against each other. The third strategy, *reducing perfectionism,* is included because the concern for perfection hinders and harms too many young people.

CLASSROOM MEETINGS

He drew a circle that shut me out
Heretic, rebel—a thing to flout.
But love and I had the wit to win:
We drew a circle that took him in.
–Edwin Markham

Classroom meetings provide excellent opportunities for students to practice communication and socialization skills. They facilitate solving classroom problems and engender both improved instruction and student learning. Classroom meetings differ from usual class discussions in that, to some extent, *the process is the point.* These meetings not only give ownership of the class to the students, they also provide a venue to gain understanding of how other people think and feel—both aspects of getting along with others.

POSITIVE RELATIONSHIPS

Classroom meetings facilitate positive relationships because they provide opportunities for building trust and respect—which in turn leads to a caring environment. Such an environment of mutual respect is necessary in order for each class member to develop the confidence to make a statement or voice an opinion and feel safe doing so.

Self-empowerment is increased when opinions are listened to with respect and when it is seen that an individual's particular contribution has led to a worthwhile solution to a problem or has been of interest to other people.

Teachers who use class meetings develop a closer relationship with their students. The relaxed conversation often reveals things about students, their families, and their circumstances that teachers might never have found out otherwise. An "unmanageable class" can become a learning and caring community because meetings provide a support that calls forth students' best behaviors.

DEVELOPMENT OF SKILLS

The ability to listen attentively and with real understanding is a vital skill for students to acquire. Students soon realize that if they let their attention wander, they miss some key interesting points, lose track of the conversation, and even miss some of the fun arising from humorous contributions.

Students learn the skill of *reflective* listening. Teachers model the skills of paraphrasing and asking clarifying questions, e.g., "Harold, before you give your idea, would you please tell us what you heard Sharon's idea to be." This type of reflective dialogue also helps listening with understanding.

Students gain needed experiences in skills of reading nonverbal clues such as tone of voice, facial expressions, and gestures. Clear and concise speech is another important skill that is developed. It does not take long for students to learn that if their speech is unclear or disjointed, they will be unable to make their point of view known.

Empathy is fostered by asking questions such as, "Would you want to be treated like that?" and "Would you want all persons to act that way in a similar situation?" In fostering empathy, students learn to set aside their own desires, views, and values as they *hear* another person's. Sensitivity to others' feelings makes it less likely that students will hurt, taunt, or isolate others. As Robert Fulghum so aptly stated,

> Sticks and stones may break our bones,
> but words will break our hearts. (Fulghum, p. 20)

In addition to empathy, values basic to our democratic system such as fairness, tolerance, respect, and helpfulness are nurtured. Students learn civil and peaceful ways to deal with different points of view, that there is more than one way to deal with challenges, and that *being different is not synonymous with being wrong*.

Outside the world of school, academic information is not nearly as important as being able to succeed in human relations. Almost all of us interact with others—continually initiating, responding, and negotiating. Much work gets done by informal and formal teams of workers. Employers want employees who are team players, who can understand the culture within a group, and who can work successfully with others. The U.S. Secretary of Labor published a widely quoted report referred to as the SCANS competencies. (Secretary's Commission on Achieving Necessary Skills - Teaching the SCANS Competencies) The report lists skills and personal qualities that are identified as necessary in the workplace. High on the list were interpersonal skills: working on teams, teaching others, serving customers, leading, negotiating, and working well with people from culturally diverse backgrounds. Classroom meetings provide excellent opportunities to practice these necessary skills and gain required understandings.

Several years ago, I was in a one-person store standing in line to pay for my purchase. Six people were in front of me. Gary was the only employee in the store. He answered the phone and helped customers with their questions while at the same time operating the cash register. When I finally became first in line, he greeted me, and I complimented him on his skill in handling the stress of his job so well. Gary said, "I realized no one else was going to be hired; I'm it. We're all in this boat together." Classroom meetings convey this same message: "We are all in this classroom together."

MODELING CIVILITY

A prime reason why class meetings assist in the development of social skills is that they use procedures of civility. Put-downs, snide remarks, or untimely giggles are not appropriate or acceptable. Primary students can use cardboard slips with sad faces on them to keep students aware when a civility has not been followed. Courtesies that are used include respecting the opinions of others whether or not you agree with them, acknowledging others' positions, listening attentively, making constructive rather than destructive contributions, taking turns, and not interrupting others when they are speaking. Once these procedures have become internalized and are regularly observed, it is only necessary to mention them periodically or when there is an infringement.

PURPOSES AND OBJECTIVES

Some meetings have specific purposes such as instructional reflection, discussing pertinent items, articulating and applying the values that schools engender toward civility, character development, and solving problems.

Specific objectives for classroom meetings include the following:

- Improving communication skills of listening and speaking

- Providing opportunities for insightful, creative, and critical thinking

- Learning the process of respectful interaction and promoting teamwork

- Increasing social intelligence, such as empathy

- Fostering social skills, such as reducing shyness

- Enhancing aspects of character education, such as being trustworthy and fair

- Reducing anonymity and promoting feelings of acceptance and worthiness

- Building a trusting and caring relationship between teacher and student and among students themselves

- Creating and maintaining an open, trusting atmosphere for risk-taking in learning

- Creating a sense of community by increasing class cohesiveness

- Providing a channel for relevancy, where students talk about subjects that interest, affect, or concern them

THREE PARTS

Most meetings should have three parts in addition to rehearsing the procedures at the beginning and, on some occasions, summarizing at the end. The first part, *defining the topic*, ensures that everyone understands the issue or topic so that everyone talks about the same thing. The second part, *personalizing*, gives participants the opportunity to relate the topic to their own knowledge and experiences. The third part, *challenging*, provides an opportunity for the teacher to stretch the students' minds by applying the ideas to hypothetical questions or situations. In problem-solving meetings, this third part should be designed to lead to possible solutions to the problem.

CHALLENGING SITUATIONS

With students who tend to monopolize a discussion, after a reasonable period of time, gently intervene and/or talk to them individually outside the class meeting. Suggest that they limit themselves to three contributions per meeting. For students who create disturbances, sit next to them or directly across from them where you are easily visible. Arrange a special signal so the prearranged cue can help them refocus. Over time, changes will begin to appear in these students.

To reduce teacher intervention and obtain maximum student participation, some primary teachers use an index card or some object to pass around or across the circle to the next person who wants to speak. Another technique for very young students is to use a yarn ball, which can be tossed (underhanded) to the next speaker. For students who do not participate when a discussion is free flowing, emphasize the importance of their contribution. Encourage them to talk by saying, "For the next five minutes I'd like to hear from people who haven't had a chance to contribute yet." Invite reluctant members to contribute by saying, "Linda, what are your thoughts about this?" or "Since you have been listening attentively, you may want to share some of your ideas." Making a special effort to acknowledge, outside of the meetings, some positive things reluctant participants do will assist in their willingness to participate during the meetings.

If particular students are the cause of constant irritation either in or out of class, are friendless because of their behavior or poor social skills, or repeatedly violate expected standards, the situation can be a topic of discussion. In these situations, the student under discussion must be present to hear what is being said. When peers, in the safety of a class meeting, sensitively explain to a fellow student their specific feelings and how particular behaviors affect them, the student is more likely to internalize the message and grow in empathy than when an adult tries to say the same thing. Peers can often explain in ways that are more meaningful to their age group than can adults. It is most important that, at all times, *the discussion focuses on the action rather than on the person.* Blame is not attached because the emphasis is always on what the student can do to help improve the situation.

To discourage putting inappropriate or unnecessary problems on the agenda, some teachers use the following "Ground Rule": You can make a complaint about a problem, but you must also have a recommendation for solving it.

A cautionary note needs to be made about problem-solving meetings because their overuse may adversely affect students' attitude toward class meetings in general. This is especially the case if such meetings are used to address "people problems." It is predominantly the open-ended and evaluative types of meetings that stimulate students, are challenging and enjoyable, and are largely responsible for the development of the range of skills referred to earlier.

LENGTH, TIME, AND FREQUENCY

Plan on meetings of ten minutes for young children. The meetings can be expanded to twenty minutes with older students—depending on their age, the nature of the group, their interest level during the meeting, the complexity of the topic, and their experience with class meetings. The meetings should be planned at the same time in the schedule. Many teachers hold meetings before a mandatory dismissal time, such as before lunch, the end of the period, or the end of the day. Many middle and high school teachers begin once each week with a classroom meeting where students talk for a few minutes about how the class is going and how individual and group projects are progressing. Students discuss topics such as whether they think it makes more sense to review home assignments in teams or as a whole class. Because learning is more effective when students are part of the planning process, learning increases even though fewer minutes are devoted to formal instruction. Also, if a class is a particularly difficult one, a class meeting can set the tone for learning.

CREATING THE PHYSICAL ENVIRONMENT

A tight circle is by far the most satisfactory arrangement. Teachers who try the circle format for the first time are often surprised at the difference this face-to-face arrangement makes in the amount and quality of discussion. A circle format ensures that everyone can read the body language as well as hear the spoken word. It is easier to hear all speakers when they are facing the center. Rows can be used, but they are less effective. Rows of people usually result in some comment from the back being misheard or not heard at all. When a funny, witty, or particularly interesting remark is made during the discussion, many of the people sitting in rows will squirm around to see who was responsible for the contribution. In this situation it may be difficult to maintain concentration for the full time of the discussion.

FURNITURE

If furniture needs to be moved, practice in moving the furniture should precede any meeting. It will take students a few practices to move quickly and quietly into a circle formation. As with any procedure, explanation and practice are essential for smooth and successful implementation. Also, if chairs are used, they should all be the same height, thus making it less likely that the teacher is seen as being too overbearing. For younger grades, sitting on the floor often means less movement of furniture and less loss of time both before and after the meeting.

THE TEACHER AS FACILITATOR

The role of the teacher is to facilitate the discussion. This includes reviewing the procedures, posing some questions, monitoring participation, avoiding judgment, and concluding the session. When starting, there is often a tendency for the teacher to over contribute. A helpful strategy to avoid falling into this trap is to audiotape a few sessions. Listening to the ebb and flow of discussions leads to improved skills.

Another tendency is to insert judgment. By making a simple statement about one student's comment—regardless of how affirmative it may be—judgment is implied. This is especially the case if a comment is made about one student's comment and not another's. A judgmental statement may be very subtle and unintended but can have a detrimental effect on the reluctant participant who does not receive this affirmation. That student makes his own interpretation that his contribution may not have been worthwhile. Examples of judgmental statements are, "I like that," "What a good idea," or "I agree." Comments such as, "Do you think so?" or "Really?" have a negative effect and can be equally damaging. Class meetings should provide a supportive, encouraging environment that develops students' confidence to speak and make comments. Passing judgment destroys this environment. Most teachers find refraining from judgment very challenging, but it is extremely important that continuing effort be made to create a non-judgmental environment.

A mental strategy for helping in this regard is to fully concentrate on what each student is saying, rather than thinking about what to do or say next. One technique for accomplishing this is to wait a few seconds after a student is finished talking before doing or saying anything. The procedure sends the message that you care about what the student is saying—merely by the fact that your full attention is with that student. It also models good listening for the students and emphasizes the importance of reflection.

AGENDA

The agenda for meetings can be kept in a folder with easy access for both the teacher and students, since both can submit agenda items. On the primary level, the teacher can take dictation from very young students who wish to submit an item.

Primary teachers find classroom meetings not only helpful in resolving conflicts but in handling minor nuisances. Comments such as, "Someone is touching me," or "He is making fun of me," can be handled by the teacher's saying, "Put it in the classroom meeting folder." Similarly, when students raise issues for discussion about some aspect of the classroom operation, the teacher does not feel personally threatened. Merely raising the issue is a confirmation that students have developed the confidence to share because the teacher has demonstrated a willingness to listen. Similarly, the teacher can use a meeting for instructional reflection by stating, "Folks, how can we make this lesson better for the next time I teach it?"

FORMULATING QUESTIONS

The goal of the meeting needs to be clearly established in the teacher's mind in order to formulate questions that will achieve the goal. Questions should be open-ended to elicit more than one-word answers. Closed-ended questions—those which require only a one-word answer—usually bring a conversation or discussion to an abrupt halt. Unless it is a reflective-type question, closed-ended questions rarely show that any thinking has been employed in arriving at an answer. If a question requires a one-word answer, it should incorporate a second part, which starts with "Why?" or "How?"

When a discussion relates to a problem-solving situation, the best procedure is to pose it as a question. For example, "Several people have said there has been a lot of name-calling on the playground lately. Is name-calling acceptable?" "Why?" Then follow up with, "What should we do if it starts again?" This could then be followed up with a commitment question, such as, "Now that we know what *should* be done, who is willing to say he or she will do it?"

Here are some suggestions for question development and facilitation of discussions:

- Start with personalizing the question and relate it to the students' world.

- Ask questions that start with: Why? What if? Could we? Should we?

- Request clarification.

- Look for relationships.

- Encourage examination of assumptions.

- Guide discussions to encourage extension, application, and evaluation of ideas.

- Assist with the formulation of generalizations and recognition of underlying principles.

- Push questions to depth rather than skimming across the surface.

- Play the role of "devil's advocate" on occasion.

- Defer judgment, and encourage both conventional and creative answers.

- Search for unusual ways of doing or looking at something.

- Encourage students to question opinions.

- Use interesting ideas students present and follow these ideas with a new *define-personalize-challenge* sequence discussed earlier in the section *Three Parts.*

CLOSING THE MEETING

A final aspect of the teacher's role is to use reflection to bring the discussion to a positive close. Sometimes it will be necessary to summarize the discussion, draw out the consensus, or clearly state the final agreed-upon solution in a problem-solving discussion. Examples are, "The main ideas expressed today are...." "It seems that most people think...." "Have we agreed that...?" "I think we will have to disagree because there are so many different ideas."

Following are additional reflective techniques:
- Keepers - "Name one thing you want to *keep* from the meeting," or "Restate something that was said that you thought was a good point—even if you didn't agree with it." Have students share with a partner or share in the circle.

- Complete a sentence - Invite all to complete a sentence, e.g., "At the end of this meeting, I hope...."

- Silence - "Take a minute to think about an aspect of today's meeting, such as a new idea or something you will do differently as a result of our discussion. If you would like, take a moment to write it down."

- Post Mortem - Share a few comments asking, "What did you like about today's meeting?" "What made it a good discussion?" "What could or should we do differently next time?"

EVALUATION

After each class meeting, the teacher should evaluate or reflect on the meeting in order for skills (both of students and teacher) to be continually improved. Some considerations are:

- Am I becoming more comfortable and skillful at questioning and leading/facilitating discussions?

- Are the students expressing and supporting their own opinions?

- Are the students willing to challenge others' opinions?

- Is there evidence of insightful thinking?

- Are students talking with each other rather than speaking to the leader?

- Am I using class meetings for one purpose only, or am I using them for a variety of purposes, such as discussing pertinent items and for instructional reflection?

After experiencing many class meetings, further items of evaluation can be considered:

- Achievement towards the goal of each meeting

- Assessment of the level of participation, such as (a) whether everyone had an opportunity to express an opinion, (b) whether anyone dominated the meeting, and, if so, to plan for intervention approaches, and (c) whether anyone consistently avoided participation

- Whether changes from one aspect of a topic to another (the segues) were at appropriate points

SUGGESTED TOPICS AND SOURCES

Thirty topics are listed below that foster communication and socialization skills. Additional topics come from students, the teacher, or are raised from current affairs, television, radio, newspapers, and magazines. Community and social issues are also natural sources for topics.

1. Why do people come to school?

2. Why do schools have report cards?

3. What would you do if you found out at lunch time that you lost your lunch?

4. How can you tell if a person is healthy?

5. What is peer pressure?

6. What would happen if people have rights without responsibilities?

7. What would you do if you found a $5.00 bill on the playground, and why?

8. Would you rather be little again or just like you are now, and why?

9. Why do we call each other names?

10. If you could change our classroom, how would you make it different?

11. Why are people your age given chores to do at home or at school?

12. Does having a reason for doing something make it o.k. to do?

13. What is prejudice?

14. What is discrimination?

15. How do you deal with anger?

16. How do you deal with frustration?

17. What does thinking like a victim mean?

18. What does being bored mean?

19. What does honesty mean?

20. What does having fun mean? How is it different from being happy?

21. What does being grateful mean?

22. How do you deal with jealousy?

23. If you could watch only one TV program, what would it be? Why?

24. What is learning?

25. What are things that trouble people of your age?

26. Is it worth undergoing short-term *pain* for long-term *gain*? If no, why not? If yes, what are some examples?

27. What is the difference between being influenced and being made to do something?

28. How do you control your reaction to impulses and urges?

29. What is the difference between something that is appropriate and something that is acceptable?

30. What are some things that you learn at school that will be helpful to you later in life?

KEY POINTS

◆ Classroom meetings foster communication, social, and other curriculum skills.

◆ In classroom meetings, the process is as important as the content.

◆ Meetings have specific purposes: instructional stimulation and reflection, discussing pertinent school items, articulating and applying the values that schools engender toward civility and character development, and solving problems.

◆ Most meetings have three parts: defining the topic, personalizing, and challenging.

◆ Classroom meetings augment learning even though fewer minutes are devoted to more formal instruction.

◆ Elementary classrooms should hold class meetings daily. Middle and high school classes deprive themselves of the many advantages of class meetings if they do not hold them regularly.

COLLABORATION
—RATHER THAN COMPETITION—
FOR QUALITY LEARNING

*Competition increases performance, but
collaboration increases learning.*

One needs to look no further than the business or sports sections of any newspaper to see how pervasive competition is in our culture. Athletic teams, bands, and other performing groups practice for hours spurred on by the competitive spirit. Fair competition is valuable and can be lots of fun. Competition in classrooms, however, is fun for the winner but is often dispiriting for the others because the same children usually win. If a student rarely finds himself in the winner's circle, competitive approaches kill his drive for learning.

COMPETITION

Teachers of early grades work with children who come to school eager to learn, but competition dulls their spirit. For example, when the kindergarten teacher says, "Boys and girls, let's see who can make the best drawing," the competitive spirit is fostered. The assumption, of course, is that this charge will spur the youngsters to do their best. Unfortunately, however, the teacher has unwittingly set up only one of the students to be the winner. Competition, by its very nature, engenders winners and losers. In band and athletic competitions, losing can build character. However, when a student is first learning a skill, *successes* build character and self-esteem.

A common example of competition is the use of ratings, where students are ranked according to their grades, accomplishments, or some other criteria. *But ratings are an incentive only for those students interested in the reward*—in this case, ranking high. And even though the incentive of ranking high may influence some students in a positive way, it does not necessarily enhance the quality of their learning. The reason is that the focus becomes whatever is necessary to achieve the ranking, which is not necessarily the same as quality learning. Competitive approaches influence students to work against each other, rather than for each other and with each other. "Serve yourself" is the theme. In addition, some people who get good ratings—especially those caught up with perfectionism—often register a paradox; they feel that they don't deserve to be ranked above some of their classmates. On the other hand, those who received low ratings often feel they have been misjudged. To put it simply, class rankings destroy team spirit and community.

It is imperative to understand that grades serve as an incentive in much the same way that rankings do. Many students are interested in achieving high grades. However, today there are thousands of young people in classrooms across America who show little interest in grades. When grades are an incentive, the focus is on this external reward, often at the expense of the internal satisfaction of quality work. In addition, there are many areas across the country where earning good grades is frowned upon by youngsters. The attitude even of some parents is illustrated by the bumper sticker, "My kid beat up your honor-roll student."

Joseph Duran taught that whenever there is a problem, 85% of the time it is with the system. Only 15% of the time will it be the fault of the people. W. Edwards Deming went further and suggested that the ratio is closer to 95-5. This is certainly the situation with cheating in schools, the product of competition. If the emphasis is on grades—rather than learning—students will do whatever it takes to get grades. The answer is not to crack down harder on cheaters and somehow enforce honesty; the answer is to change the system, or at least in a classroom to change the emphasis.

Grades change motivation. Teachers know this from the questions students ask. "Will it be on the test?" or "Will it be counted in the grade?" The focus is not on quality or learning but, rather, on the external reward of the grade. This is not the case in areas like performing arts and vocational classes. It is the excitement of the process that generates quality work. Can you imagine a surgeon or an airline pilot pleased with anything other than best effort? The same holds true with students. A student working in an auto shop is interested in having the car start all of the time, not 75 percent of the time. A person baking a cake is interested in the entire cake, not just part of it, tasting good. This same drive for quality work can be fostered in academic classes.

Grades will not disappear from the education scene, but they need not drive teaching since they do not drive quality work. Grades should be thought of as goals, which are mutually established by the class and the teacher. Rubrics, for instance, can show students how every-one willing to learn and work can earn an A or B.

JOY IN LEARNING

A reason people enter the teaching profession is that they have experienced the joy of learning, and they want to pass it on to others. Focusing on quality is a natural approach to achieving this objective. A quality experience hooks a student on learning. Mastery, of course, requires effort. However, when there is joy in learning, it does not *seem* like great effort because it feels good—as when a student spends hours on the basketball court, working up a sweat while practicing a particular shot. When a person *wants* to do something, the labor seems incidental. Quality work involves exertion, but it may even seem like fun.

When people are engaged in quality work, a few indicators can be observed. They choose to be engaged in the activity; it is meaningful to them. The effort involves some creativity and skill and involves more than a simple task; it is usually complex. The activity results in some success. Personal control is present. Self-assessment is involved. The activity may not be perceived as stressful; it may even feel relaxing.

STARTING ON THE PROCESS

Quality in learning is influenced by the quality of the process. A sense of *purpose* needs to be established. A discussion of the following questions assists in this regard:

Why are we here?

What are we trying to do?

What does it mean to do something well?

How will we know if we are doing it well together?

When students move from the child development emphasis in primary grades to that of greater accountability in upper grades, they need to evaluate their own work. Therefore, the first few sessions of the class should be devoted to a discussion of each of the following topics:

What does it mean to do quality work?

How will each student know that a quality level has been attained?

How will the teacher know that a quality level has been attained?

What does the student need to do in order to attain the level?

What can the teacher do to help students attain the level?

How will a third party be assured that the level has been attained?

The result of such discussions is that during the remainder of the semester, student enthusiasm and drive increase so that the students learn much more. Time "lost" by having these discussions is more than regained over a period of weeks.

Once students believe that the task is worth their time and effort, discussion then focuses on how the learning is to take place. This discussion revolves around such subjects as the following:

Testing: How often? What kind? How to evaluate? What is the purpose?

Home Assignments: Why? How often? When?

Evaluation: How will we know how we are doing? Against what shall we make comparisons (benchmarks)?

Class Management: How do we make ourselves most efficient?

Documentation: How shall we persuade others that we have really done a good job?

Once students have tasted the joy of learning and responsibility for quality work, they may not want to return to something inferior. Some students respond more quickly than others, but all students need to be engaged continually in discussions about quality.

TEACHING VS. LEARNING

The following story illustrates the difference between learning and teaching. The dog owner says, "Last Wednesday I taught my dog to whistle. I really did. I taught him to whistle. It was hard work. I really went at it very hard, and I taught him to whistle. Of course, he didn't learn, but I taught him."

Learning depends upon how enthusiastically the students tackle their assignments. To get students to do home assignments, teachers have employed "carrot and stick" approaches. By a combination of rewards and threats, we have tried to force students to do home assignments, often tying them to a grade. The students, in return, have done their best to outwit the teacher. To change the situation requires harnessing the internal motivation of students. Collaboration is one very powerful method for doing this.

COLLABORATION AND QUALITY

W. Edwards Deming (1986) clearly showed the advantages of collaboration over competition for improved quality of work. Using collaboration to improve quality, Dr. Deming brought Japan from producing cheap and shoddy products to being the world's leader in quality production. Deming's approach that quality can *reduce* cost went against common sense. The thinking at that time was that improved quality would cost more. Deming showed—by using collaboration—how quality of work would increase while costs simultaneously would be reduced. The underlying principle of the Deming approach is continuous worker self-inspection so that quality is built into each step of the process, rather than inspection by someone else at the end of the process. Deming understood that no one can legislate or dictate internal motivation (desire), performance, productivity, or quality. His approach was to use the power of ownership to empower the worker by encouraging self-evaluation. Deming diminished the use of exhortations, threats, prizes, and special rewards for doing what people are supposed to do. In a nutshell, Deming demonstrated that for improved quality of work, *working together is better than working competitively.*

The key to quality learning is to structure student interaction for maximum participation. For example, today's common approach is to *ask* students a question. Students compete for the teacher's attention by raising their hands. The only "winner" is the person the teacher calls upon. Instead of *asking* a question and then calling on a single person, *pose* the question. *Posing* implies open-endedness, invites students to engage in thought, and engenders dialogue. Have students collaborate in pairs or small groups for responses. When collaboration is used, *all* the students participate. Also, notice that students first grapple with the idea or concept. This approach of challenging students at the outset is the approach used so effectively in Japanese schools. Curiosity, interest, and motivation are fostered. Then the teacher facilitates solutions. When activities are structured to be primarily collaborative, learning becomes noncompetitive— an essential principle for increasing quality.

Here is another example of how collaboration improves the quality of learning. A high school student accustomed to above-average test scores was disappointed in her last two test results. The student had grasped the prime concepts but did not do well on reporting details. The teacher told the students that in order to place concepts in long-term memory details need to be remembered. The student's father suggested that as his daughter reads she should mindmap. The father explained that when the brain attempts to remember *words* alone, *semantic* pathways to memory are being used. Semantic pathways require much repetition in order to be retained. On the other hand, he explained, when the brain attempts to remember *images* or *icons*, it uses *episodic* pathways, which require fewer repetitions. Episodic pathways are contextual or spatial and always involve location. To make his point, the father asked his daughter what she had eaten for dinner the previous Saturday and requested that as she answers she relate her thinking process out loud. The daughter responded by saying, "Where was I last Saturday?" "Exactly the point! You looked for a location because we are always somewhere, and we remember through context and images," said the father. "This is the reason that episodic memory is more efficient than semantic memory. It is easier to remember illustrations and pictures than it is to remember information from textbooks and lectures, which usually involves only words."

After this explanation, the daughter suggested to two of her friends that they also mindmap their next reading assignment and share it. All three met and discussed their notes. During the discussion, each became aware of a few additional details that the others had included. Subsequently, all three students' test scores dramatically increased. The strategy of mindmapping assisted, but collaboration made the activity enjoyable and even more effective.

CONTINUOUS IMPROVEMENT

Schools generally use an old approach to evaluation, as when students submit work solely to the teacher. Before Deming showed the superiority of self-evaluation for improved quality of work, American managers hired inspectors to check the work of employees. Quality did not really improve; rather, the poor-quality work just did not get out. Costs went up because items that did not pass inspection were discarded.

> Dr. Deming told me that when he went to Western Electric in the 1920's there were 30,000 people making telephone sets and 10,000 people inspecting their work. The job of the workers was to get their product past the inspectors, and the job of the inspectors was to catch them if they did something wrong. This is no way to reduce cost. It is no way to achieve improved telephones. It is no way to work. (Tribus)

Rather than use this outdated factory model of the teacher as inspector at the end of the process, improved quality of work results if *continuous* improvement and *continuous* feedback are built into the learning process. It is learner-generated feedback that increases motivation and that is so critical to improved quality of work. When we are pleased with our efforts, especially when we see improvement, we invest more effort. Improvement comes through self-evaluation, practice, and more evaluation. The better the quality of our work, the more we are pleased and the more we engage in the activity.

COLLABORATIVE EVALUATION

> Stephen Covey refers to the concept of collaboration as "synergy." Simply defined, it means that the whole is greater than the sum of its parts. It means that the relationship that the parts have to each other is a part in and of itself. It is not only a part, but the most catalytic, the most empowering, the most unifying, and the most exciting part. (Covey, pp. 262-263)

The brain is innately social and collaborative. Although the processing takes place in our individual brains, learning is enhanced when the environment provides opportunities to discuss our thinking and to bounce ideas off peers. The act of shared thinking, of having to put one's own views clearly to others, of finding defensible compromises and conclusions, is evaluative and, therefore, educative.

Teachers' workloads can be reduced, while simultaneously increasing the quality of student work, by applying approaches of collaborative evaluation through feedback. For example, after an essay assignment is given, but before it is started, students pair with each other and share their understanding of the assignment. Then the procedure of "*three before me*" is explained, which is that before the teacher corrects any paper, it will have been seen by one other student three times. (A variation is to have the work seen by three different people, which may include someone other than a classmate. A parent qualifies.) After the original sharing of ideas, each student writes a first draft, which is exchanged with another student. Each student gives feedback to the other. A second draft is then written, again with each giving the other feedback. The third copy undergoes the same, and then the final draft is completed and submitted to the teacher.

As a general principle for quality work, a first draft should never be considered a final draft. The story is told about Henry Kissinger, who submitted a report when he first started working for the government. His supervisor inquired whether the report was his best work. Kissinger worked on the report for an additional two days, fine-tuning it and giving the report greater clarity before resubmitting it. Again, a similar inquiry was forthcoming, "Is this the best you can do?" The report was worked on for an additional day. After further revisions, Kissinger submitted his work with some anger and confidence asserting that the report was the best he could do. His supervisor said, "Good! Then I will read it."

KEY POINTS

◆ Competition serves as an incentive to improve *performance* but often has a negative effect on *learning* when first learning a skill. If a student rarely finds himself in the winner's circle, competitive approaches kill his drive for learning.

◆ Working for quality is what hooks a student on learning.

◆ Collaboration results in improved quality of work because of continual self-assessment and feedback.

◆ Discussions about what constitutes quality improve student work.

◆ The key to quality learning is to structure student interaction for maximum participation, as in *posing* questions rather than asking them.

◆ When activities are structured to be primarily collaborative, learning becomes noncompetitive—an essential principle for increased quality.

◆ Collaborative learning strategies reduce teachers' workloads.

REDUCING PERFECTIONISM

You cannot learn and be perfect at the same time.

When young people perform *academic-type* tasks and are corrected before obtaining feelings of empowerment or success, they become candidates for discouragement.

A friend of mine related an incident that occurred at the birthday party of his young daughter. After his daughter opened a present he had just given her, my friend asked, cajoled, and finally coerced his daughter into sharing her new toy with the other children. It is hard for a child to share or open to others that which the child does not yet "own." The same principle holds true in learning. Young people need to feel some degree of ownership or success in performing a task—or have a feeling that they are capable of it—before correction becomes beneficial. Otherwise, the good intentions of correction are perceived as criticism, which leads to a dampened desire to perform the task.

Unless a student is very motivated, he normally does not like doing something for which he will be criticized. However, once possession is felt—once he feels competent—he can open himself to others.

Misguided attempts to correct before possession is taken can have unfortunate results.

> In the first grade, when I finished my picture with the sun in the sky, I brought it to my teacher. He looked at it and said that there is no such thing as a green sun. The sun is yellow. Everyone knows that. He said that my picture wasn't realistic, that I should start over. Nightfall came to me in the middle of the afternoon.
>
> The next year my second-grade teacher said to the class, "Draw something—anything you want." I stared at my paper and when the teacher came around to my desk, I could only hear the beating of my heart as he looked at my blank page. He touched my shoulder with his hand, and whispered, "How big and thick and nice is your cloud." (author unknown)

The awareness of the negative effects of criticism and the positive effects of empowerment may be one of the most distinguishing marks of superior teachers—and parents. When our daughter was first learning to speak, she made the sound of "s" in a nonstandard way. We called attention to it—only once. For the next several weeks, every time our daughter spoke any word that contained the sound of an "s," she hesitated and tried to make the sound perfect. We witnessed the first stage of stuttering. Attention was never called to her speech again, and my wife and I were greatly relieved when her natural speech pattern returned. You can prove this phenomenon by concentrating on the process of walking down a flight of stairs the next time you attempt it.

When an infant first attempts to walk, we offer encouragement because we know that learning comes by degrees. We do not expect the child to stand up and walk in one day. Similarly, we encourage an infant to speak even though the sounds are only approximately right. "Exactly right" is made up of a whole series of "approximately rights." Suppose you want an infant to say, "I want a glass of water." If you wait until the child articulates that request with a flawless, complete sentence, you will have a dehydrated, dead child.

Young children are cute, and it is easy to empower them through encouragement. But, when young children become adolescents, we treat learning differently. Should we? Whatever the age, having an orientation for participation should hold a higher priority than perfection. *Participation is the way to success. Perfection is too often a burden.*

The tendency adults have to correct should be modified by a consideration of where the child is in his stage of learning. For example, when the child is desperately struggling to express an idea or use his brain to solve a problem and is put down by constant correction, he may simply not want to continue attempting that or similar activities.

One way to look at the orientation of a classroom is to watch for both the teacher's and students' reactions to mistakes. When mistakes are welcome, learning is enhanced. The reason is that mistakes are invaluable clues to how students are thinking and that to welcome mistakes is to create a climate of safety that ultimately promotes more successful learning. A simple way to foster learning is to constantly remind students that mistakes are opportunities to learn.

A focus on perfection has opened pathways for many students to live with the idea that they have to be perfect for people to love them. The perception that if a person makes a mistake rejection will follow—the sense that she has to be perfect for people to find her acceptable—is an idea that plagues young people all too often.

Striving for perfection, *rather than for continual improvement,* leaves students reluctant to admit mistakes or apologize when in the wrong.

Another manifestation of perfectionism is that students stop learning; they simply give up. Perfectionism becomes so tyrannical that students develop anxiety attacks. This leads to the thinking pattern that they cannot perform or engage in the activity because they will not be good enough. The next stage is total paralysis.

Adults should foster *failure as feedback.* Failing is a natural outcome of trying, and it is a great teacher. That is, it *can* be if the choice is to learn from it rather than be crushed by it. The teacher's message to students, therefore, is to emphasize that experiences—including learning—should be *viewed as processes* and *as information,* not as weapons for self-punishment. This positive mindset breeds a willingness to experiment, to try, to risk. This is extremely important since improvement only comes with practice. Especially at the early stages of learning, *"Implement now; perfect later!"* should be our teaching principle.

KEY POINTS

◆ When young people perform tasks and are corrected before obtaining feelings of success, they become candidates for discouragement rather than for empowerment.

◆ The tendency of adults to correct should be modified by a consideration of where the child is in his stage of learning.

◆ Participation and practice lead to success; perfectionism is a burden.

◆ Accuracy and precision come later with a focus on continual improvement.

◆ Failure is feedback, not an end state.

◆ "Implement now; perfect later!" should be the principle when learning something new.

CHALLENGES

Decent behavior is non-negotiable.

Three challenges that can make the difference between success or frustration are discussed. The first describes a technique for making better decisions when reacting to situations, stimuli, or impulses. The second describes a simple approach to resolving conflicts. The third offers suggestions for dealing with difficult students.

IMPULSE AND ANGER MANAGEMENT

When annoyed, count to 10 before you speak;
if very annoyed, count to 100.
                    –Thomas Jefferson

Impulses and emotions surge within us, even though something outside of us may have prompted the stimulation. These impulses and emotions can reinforce themselves and become more frequent and even more intense. However, impulses can be diminished, both in intensity and in frequency, when we employ a conscious strategy for responding to them.

First, we must recognize that regardless of the emotion or impulse, a person still has a choice of responses. As earlier discussed in Chapter 1, we can choose our responses when stuck in traffic. We can allow ourselves to become angry or we can choose to play a tape, listen to the radio, or think of a pleasant experience. Similarly, when someone cuts in front of our car or does something that stimulates us to a state of road rage, we either can allow that emotion to direct our behavior, or we can choose to redirect our response to that surge of emotion.

Even very young people in an aggravated emotional state can change their responses. One of my favorites in this area occurred when a kindergarten teacher summoned me for assistance with a youngster having a crying fit. I reached into my bag of tricks and pulled out a stethoscope given to me by my physician and placed it around my neck. When I entered the kindergarten room, I knelt down to the child and applied the stethoscope to a few places on the child's chest. The crying immediately stopped. I then proclaimed the child healthy. The strategy of redirecting a child's attention worked every time.

This same diversionary phenomenon is often seen with teenagers. The adolescent is having an emotional argument with a parent. The phone rings; it is one of the teenager's friends. The tone of voice immediately changes; it is suddenly friendly, even sweet. Upon termination of the conversation, the previous surge of emotion reappears, proving that by redirecting their attention even teenagers can control their tempers.

Here is a strategy that anyone of any age can use to prevent becoming hijacked by his or her impulses or emotions. The strategy can be used when sitting or standing, but to realize its fullest effect, I suggest standing this time to learn (and teach) the strategy.

First, slowly and silently breathe as though you were *gasping* for a breath.

Do this a second time, and notice that your jaw drops open and your tongue goes to the bottom of your mouth.

Take a third long, slow, deep *gasp*. As you breathe in through your open mouth, notice your back expanding. This is Structural Breathing™ and is more effective in filling the lungs and oxygenating the system than the so-called diaphragmatic or abdominal breathing, which constricts the rib cage and allows only part of the lungs to expand to their fullest.

This simple procedure of taking a *gasp* of air releases the jaw and the emotional tension of the nearby nerves that otherwise would send the tension throughout the body.

In the moment that it takes to slowly *gasp* and release the tension, the mind has the opportunity to redirect thinking by considering options.

When working with young people, a traffic signal can be used to visualize and reinforce the three steps.

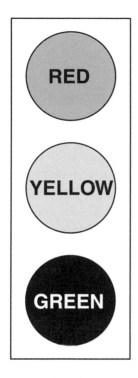

Stop
and *gasp* a long,
deep breath.

Think
of options.

Go
with your best
choice.

We should be teaching that we can recognize an impulse or emotion such as anger, that we have a choice of how to react to it, and that we can choose a constructive response.

We should also teach young people to differentiate between anger at a person and anger at a situation. When people are upset, they often misdirect their anger. Ask, "Are you angry at me or the situation?" This reflective question leads to redirection of behavior.

KEY POINTS

◆ A conscious strategy can be used to respond to impulses such as anger.

◆ Using a slow, silent, deep gasp releases the tension in the body and allows us to redirect our thoughts and behaviors.

◆ Asking, "Are you angry at me or the situation?" redirects behavior.

The author is indebted to William Hanrahan of Vocal Integration Concepts, Marina del Rey, California, for demonstrating the effectiveness of Structural Breathing™.

CONFLICT RESOLUTION:
SOLVING CIRCLES

Changing ourselves is the most effective way
to change others.

Solving circles is a very effective strategy for resolving conflicts between two people.

In order to understand this strategy, a simple question needs to be answered. Think of any one person with whom you have had a personal association—it may be a spouse, child, parent, fellow worker, friend, or acquaintance. Now, ask yourself whether *you* ever changed that person, and if the person did change, consider whether *you* did the changing or if the person *changed him/herself.*

The realization that no one really changes another person, but that people change themselves, is the theory behind using solving circles.

Of course, a person can control others in the sense of exercising authority over them, or directing or commanding them, as, for example, when a parent "grounds" a son or daughter or when a teacher sends a student to "time out." Temporary compliance, however, does not change how a person *wants* to behave. People are not *changed* by other people.

With this in mind, here is how solving circles works. Two interlocking circles are drawn. The first circle represents person A; the second circle represents person B. The overlapping area between the circles represents the common goal, such as solving a problem or getting along better.

In a disagreement, the usual approach is for each person to tell the other person what the other person needs to do or stop doing—basically, how the *other* person needs to change. With the realization that one does not change another person, that a person can only change him/herself, person A describes what *he* himself or *she* herself will do to reach the common goal. Person B is naturally drawn to do the same. By discussing one's *own* behavior, instead of the other person's behavior, each individual takes responsibility for his or her own actions. No additional assistance or third party is needed.

With young students, the strategy can be taught on the playground by drawing two large overlapping circles in chalk or by using two hula hoops. The teacher then asks two students to describe some problems they encounter on the playground. After a situation is chosen, role-playing is conducted by having one of the students stand in one circle and the other stand in the other circle. The conflict resolution is played out.

As long as people psychologically stay in the circle and realize that *they can change only their own behavior*, they can negotiate almost anything. Each is sending the message, "I want to improve the situation. Here is what I am willing to do."

When the parties are angry, first have a cooling-off period. With young children, have them sit down with the direction that neither can get up without the other's permission. Once they realize the situation they are in, anger dissipates, and the situation often turns humorous. With older students and adults, call a short time-out period. Leave the situation. The parties need to cool down because, when angry, the focus is rarely on a solution. When tempers have cooled, resume solving circles.

Do not recycle the past. When the focus is on the past, the misery is revisited because the past does not change. The discussion must be future-oriented since we can only plan for the future. Realizing that people can change only themselves and that the conversation is future-oriented are the reasons that solving circles resolves conflicts in a simple and effective way.

KEY POINTS

◆ We cannot change other people. We can influence them to change by what we do.

◆ Rather than talking about how the other person needs to change, each person volunteers what he or she will do to resolve the conflict.

◆ Discussion is focused on the future, rather than on the past or on the cause of the conflict.

◆ Two people can resolve their own dispute; a third person or mediator is unnecessary.

The author is indebted to William Glasser, M.D., for this strategy.

DEALING WITH DIFFICULT STUDENTS

Kids would rather be bad than stupid.
A reason they misbehave is they don't want to be failures.

The Raise Responsibility System is the foundation for handling irresponsible behavior. However, some students require special attention in order to help them become more responsible. Review the unobtrusive techniques at the beginning of the discussion on *Checking for Understanding* in Chapter 3. Additional suggestions follow.

USE POSITIVITY

When a youngster is off task or exhibiting behavior you do not like, be positive by informing him what you *want*—not what you do not want. Simply tell the student what you would like to see happen. This helps the student understand your desires and stops the student from engaging in one undesirable behavior only to engage in another non-productive one.

EMPOWER WITH CHOICES

Offering more than one activity affords choice and ownership. For a math assignment, students may be given the choice of doing assigned problems on a certain page, doing the odd-numbered problems, or doing the even-numbered problems. For an essay assignment, students can choose from among several topics. Asking students how they believe they can best learn the material is always a possibility.

ASK REFLECTIVE QUESTIONS

Work on the skill of asking reflective questions, such as, "Since you are having a challenge staying on task, what would you suggest to help?" Use an inquiring tone and a smile. Before starting an activity, ask, "What are the benefits of what we are going to do?" The discussion will take a few minutes but is worth the time to encourage "buy-in" for self-control.

COACH

Think of young people as lacking skills, rather than as being non-compliant. Few students are maliciously non-compliant. We teach young people how to swing a baseball bat, how to play a musical instrument, and how to drive a car. We do not give up on them, nor do we resort to punishment. We coach them.

GIVE START DIRECTIONS

Students with short attention spans have a difficult time getting started on a task. Give clear, concise start directions, such as, "Feet on the floor, back straight, pencil and paper in proper position." Have students complete the following to themselves, *"The first thing I see myself doing is...."* Helping a youngster set his own mental frame assists him in taking responsibility for his actions.

USE CREATIVE APPROACHES

When there are distractions, teach students to label them. One teacher used this strategy when construction was going on outside her classroom. She taught her students to label the noise "*distraction*" and that doing so would help them refocus on their task. She told me that this strategy saved her semester.

Have students count the number of times they return to their tasks. Tracking them increases the likelihood that students will stop and think about what they are doing.

ACKNOWLEDGE ON-TASK BEHAVIOR

Acknowledge *in private* when the student is on task. Do not be concerned about interrupting the student at work; the student will let you know if it is bothersome.

ENCOURAGE

Encourage students. It raises their aspirations. Robert Danzig rose from office boy to president of his company because Margaret Mahoney, his office manager, said to him, "You are full of promise." That comment prompted him to begin seeing possibilities and generated his rise from sweeping floors to becoming the president of the Hearst Newspaper Corporation. (Danzig)

Equally important is that a word of encouragement during a failure is worth more than a whole book of praise after a success. When a student has not been successful, ask, "What can we learn from this experience?"

CHANGE A SEAT

Arrange for a student who has poor self-control to be seated near the teacher's desk or at the front of a row so that the student's back will be to other students. Position the student away from distracting stimuli such as doors, high-traffic areas, and pencil sharpeners.

ASSIGN A BUDDY

Select a responsible student as a "buddy helper" to assist the student by answering questions, explaining directions, and making transitions to new activities. Periodically, rotate "buddies" to avoid burnout and to give other students the "tutor" experience.

DEVELOP SIGNALS

Develop a secret verbal or nonverbal signal or cue for redirecting a student's energy or attention to refocus. An "ahhuum" throat-clearing sound works well.

PROGRESS IS POWER

Progress is measured by improvement in oneself, not in comparison to others. Periodically, find some improvement that the youngster has made and acknowledge it. Success breeds further success.

KEY POINTS

◆ Be positive by informing students what you *want*, rather than telling them to stop doing something.

◆ Ask reflective questions, such as, "What are the benefits?" before starting an activity. This encourages "buy-in" and self-control.

◆ Think of youngsters as lacking skills, rather than as being non-compliant. This will engage you as a coach to help them.

◆ Give clear, concise start directions.

◆ Teach youngsters to label a *"distraction"* as such. It helps them refocus on their task.

◆ Encourage progress and acknowledge it.

◆ Develop a verbal or nonverbal signal to redirect students when necessary.

_____

SUMMARY AND CONCLUSION

*The ultimate use of power should be to empower others.
That's what our Constitution is about.*
                                    –William Glasser

The most effective way to promote learning is to establish a noncoercive environment where students *want* to learn and *want* to behave appropriately.

SUMMARY

Relationships - Three types of relationships foster this type of learning climate: relationships between the teacher and the students as a class, relationships among students, and relationships between the teacher and individual students.

Relationships between the teacher and the students as a class improve as rules are reduced. Rules are necessary in games but are counterproductive in relationships because the teacher is placed in a position of being a cop, rather than a coach. This often produces adversarial relations between the teacher and class members. In addition, rules foster obedience rather than responsibility. A more effective approach is to teach procedures and to use expectations.

Student relationships improve as anonymity among students decreases. Students should not feel alone in a crowd. Having students interact and share information about themselves builds community.

Tutoring is the easiest, quickest, and most effective way for the teacher to establish relationships with individual students. It offers an excellent opportunity for learning more about each student and for giving encouragement. Encouragement is often a spark that ignites motivation. A few minutes daily can be planned to do some tutoring.

Strategies - The first strategy discusses classroom meetings—their purpose, importance, and implementation. The second is collaboration in promoting quality learning. The third focuses on reducing perfectionism.

Classroom meetings turn a classroom into a learning community. Meetings have specific purposes: instructional stimulation and reflection, discussing pertinent items, articulating and applying the values that schools engender toward civility and character development, and solving problems. Classroom meetings augment learning even though fewer minutes are devoted to more formal instruction. Elementary classes should hold class meetings daily. Middle and high school teachers should include meetings as part of their lesson plan.

Collaboration results in quality work because of continual self-assessment and feedback. Working for quality is what hooks a student on learning. The key is to structure student interactions for maximum participation, as in posing questions rather than asking them. When activities are structured to be primarily collaborative, then learning becomes noncompetitive. Collaborative learning strategies also reduce teachers' workloads.

Perfectionism interferes with learning. When young people perform academic tasks and are corrected before obtaining feelings of success, they become candidates for discouragement. The tendency of adults to correct should be modified by a consideration of where the child is in his stage of learning. Accuracy and precision come later with a focus on continual improvement. "Implement now; perfect later!" should be the principle when learning something new.

Challenges - Three challenges that teachers encounter are students' lack of impulse control, conflicts between students, and dealing with difficult students.

A conscious strategy can be taught for responding to impulses, even anger. A diversion can redirect behavior. Using a slow, silent, deep *gasp* releases the tension in the body and allows us to redirect our thoughts and behaviors.

Conflicts between two people can be resolved by the use of solving circles. Since people change themselves, rather than talking about how another person needs to change, in solving circles each person volunteers what he or she will do to resolve the conflict. Discussion is focused on the future, rather than on the past or on the cause of the conflict. Using this approach, two people can resolve their own dispute without the involvement of a third person or mediator.

When dealing with difficult students, be positive by informing them of what is wanted, rather than telling them to stop doing something. Ask reflective questions, such as, "What are the benefits?" before starting an activity. This encourages "buy-in" and promotes self-control. Think of youngsters as lacking skills, rather than as being non-compliant. Give clear, concise start directions. Teach youngsters to label a "distraction" as such. This helps them refocus on the task.

CONCLUSION

Niccolo Paganini (1782-1840) is still considered one of the greatest violinists of all time. One day, as he was about to perform before a sold-out house, he walked out on stage to a huge ovation but felt that something was terribly wrong.

Suddenly he realized that he had someone else's violin in his hand. Horrified, but knowing that his only prudent choice was to begin, he started playing.

That day, he gave the performance of his life.

After the concert, Paganini was in his dressing room speaking to a fellow musician and he reflected, "Today I learned the most important lesson of my entire career. Before today, I thought that *the music was in the violin.* Today, I learned that *the music is in me.*"

Establishing a noncoercive learning environment and implementing the suggestions of this chapter promote this kind of thinking in our students.

Subscribe to the free monthly newsletter
PROMOTING RESPONSIBILITY and LEARNING
at <u>www.MarvinMarshall.com.</u>

Articles include how to promote responsibility and learning, increase effectiveness, and improve relationships.

Discipline *without* Stress®
Punishments
or Rewards

How Teachers and Parents Promote
Responsibility & Learning

"What you are doing is one of the most
important tasks in education in our lifetime."
—Richard E. Clark, Director of the seminar
Psychology, University of Southern California

Dr. Marvin Marshall
Author of FOSTERING SOCIAL RESPONSIBILITY

5
TEACHING

CURRICULUM AND INSTRUCTION

If telling were the same as teaching,
we would be such good teachers we could hardly stand it.

Although classroom disruptions may stem from problems that students bring to school, they may also arise from curriculum, instruction, or classroom management. Curriculum and instruction are discussed in this section. The following sections offer suggestions for classroom management and home assignments.

CURRICULUM

Curriculum has to do with content or *what* is taught. Every level of government, local boards of education, professional subject matter and professional associations, individual schools, and local communities all impact on what is taught.

Skills such as reading, writing, arithmetic, and problem solving are part of the curriculum. The curriculum also includes basic information about our history, health, and a whole range of other subject matter that is important to our lives and perpetuates the priorities of society.

INSTRUCTION

Instruction is about *how* content, skills, and problem solving are taught and learned.

What many teachers refer to as discipline problems actually stem from instruction. *Behavior problems are at a minimum when instruction is effective.* A lesson is most effective when (1) is made interesting (by engendering curiosity), meaningful (by informing students the "why" of the lesson), relevant, or useful; (2) the lesson involves thinking; and (3) students are actively involved. This means planning instruction in ways that students *want to learn.* Glasser makes the point: "It does no good to push a student who does not want to learn any more than it does to get tough with a worker who is looking for another job." (Glasser, *Choice Theory in the Classroom,* p. 74)

This chapter gives an overview of basic instructional considerations using the components of the acronym "LIMES," which refers to *L*eft-right brain hemisphericity, *I*ntelligences, *M*odalities of learning, *E*motions, and *S*tyles. This is followed by a discussion of lesson planning, levels of intellect, instructional questions, a group questioning strategy, and choosing key words to frame questions. A short discussion of imaging, stories, metacognition, and the senses follows. The chapter concludes with additional principles for aiding recall, laser learning, and three seminal shifts regarding instruction. The overriding theme of the chapter is to offer multiple connections to the brain so students have multiple ways of knowing in order to increase the odds of understanding, application, and transference.

Left-Right Brain Hemisphericity (The "L" in LIMES)

We start with the concept of *left*-right brain hemisphericity. (The terms "left brain" and "right brain" are meant as generic locations for easy reference. More specifically, the terms refer to the hemisphericity of the cerebral cortex. This area of the brain is the core location for cognitive learning.) Understanding how the brain functions is important to the design of effective teaching and learning experiences.

Brain hemisphericity originated when medical practitioners were trying to stop epilepsy so that seizures in one side of the brain would not travel to the other side. This was accomplished by severing the corpus callosum, the thick cable of nerve fibers that connects the two cerebral hemispheres. A pioneer in this movement was Roger Sperry, who won the 1981 Nobel Prize in medicine for his work. Much has been learned in the intervening years, but the concept of hemisphericity remains useful and valid. The concept can help us in teaching and learning *as long as we use the two sides as a construct for understanding.* We should not pigeonhole behavior into either a left-brain or right-brain blueprint or fall into inaccurate assumptions and conclusions, such as making a relationship to handedness (lateral dominance) or intelligence. No relationship exists in either.

When we talk of brain hemisphericity, we are always talking about integrating both sides of the brain because the hemispheres of the brain are continually interacting. In fact, since the two hemispheres do not function independently, it is impossible to educate only one hemisphere in a normal brain. The reason is that the brain reduces information into parts while perceiving wholistically at the same time. For example, when we look at something that is in motion, numerous locations in the brain are activated to combine its form, dimension, perspective, color, and movement in order to see the object as a whole. Neuroscientists refer to this as operating in a "modular" fashion with autonomous systems devoted to different mental acts.

The left and right hemispheres of the brain have some distinctly different functions, but both sides are involved in nearly every human activity. For example, both sides work together to integrate words for proper speech intonation. The left side produces the correct speech, and the right side mediates the feelings attached to it. Words produced only with the left side will be intelligible but will sound flat or indifferent. Conversely, if only the right side is involved, then the language will sound like gibberish although the feelings accompanying them might be recognizable.

Another example of both hemispheres of the brain working together pertains to memory. The formation of memories involving words is concentrated in the left hemisphere of the brain, but visual memories stimulate greater activity in the right hemisphere. Specialization in a part of the brain does not mean exclusivity. In fact, hemispheric dominance runs the gamut from neutral (no preference) to strongly left or right. However, most people do have a dominant hemisphere that affects personality, abilities, and learning modalities.

In most people, the left cerebral hemisphere is the hemisphere of logic. It controls analytical and verbal intelligence. It is methodical, sensible, and processes sequentially. The right cerebral hemisphere controls spatial and artistic skills. It is intuitive, processes randomly, and involves feelings, expressiveness, and creativity.

The functioning of brain hemispheres can be categorized as follows:

Left Hemisphere of the Brain	Right Hemisphere of the Brain
• Analytical and methodical	Creative and expressive
• Deals with the sensible	Deals with fantasy and the imaginative
• Logical	Intuitive
• Processes information linearly	Processes randomly and wholistically
• Stimulated by function	Stimulated by appearance
• Detailed, orderly, likes instructions	Spontaneous, goes with the flow
• Sequence is important	Context is important
• Deals with time	Deals with space
• Interprets through words, symbols	Interprets through pictures, letters, graphs, charts
• Responsible for verbal expression	Responsible for gestures and facial movements
• Spoken, written language	Tone of voice
• Reading	Seeing or experiencing
• Recognizes letters, words, numbers	Recognizes faces, places, objects, music
• Deals with inputs one at a time	Integrates many inputs at once
• Parts first, then whole	Whole first, then parts
• Structure, predictability	Open-ended, surprises
• Main center for language	Main center for nonverbal ideation

Mindmapping

Challenge, complexity, and *novelty* stimulate the brain, light up both hemispheres, grab attention, and lead to greater learning and memory. The key point to remember is to plan for experiences so *the brain learns.* For example, the activity of plotting words *and* graphics integrates both sides of the brain and increases learning.

This type of activity is referred to as mindmapping, concept mapping, graphic organizing, "webbing," or clustering.

Here is a mindmap of this book up to this point.

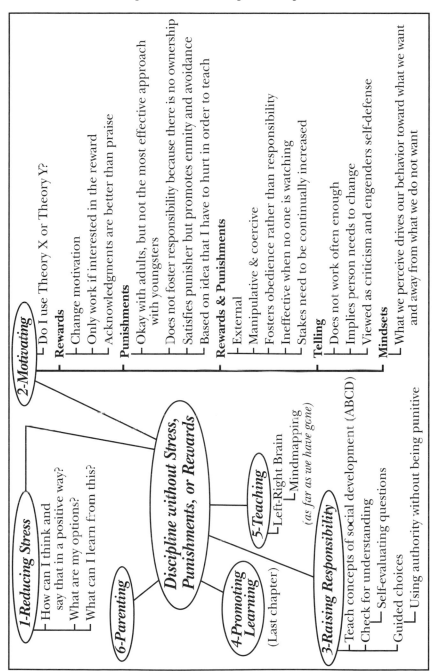

Variations include drawings or icons (in place of words) and use of colors.

In addition to traditional outlining, which is linear, use this type of visual organizing to string relationships in a less sequential, more visual manner. Information organized into wholistic conceptual frameworks is more easily remembered and understood than bits of discrete information.

At about grade three or four, teaching often moves from using activities, many of which appeal to the right hemisphere of the brain, to almost exclusively using methods and activities that appeal to the left hemisphere of the brain. The result is that many right-brained students, who need more creative and visual work (not to be confused with reading, which is a special skill), are nurtured less by schooling processes and move toward becoming at-risk students.

(The "I" in LIMES)

Students are smart in ways other than those measured by intelligence quotient (IQ) tests. These tests measure essentially the same characteristics that Alfred Binet devised at the turn of the 20th century to predict which French children would succeed or fail in school: memory, vocabulary, spatial thinking, and the ability to draw analogies and solve puzzles.

In 1983, Howard Gardner's *Frames of Mind: The Theory of Multiple Intelligences* was published. Gardner listed seven intelligences, has since added an eighth, and indicated that there may be even more. (Gardner, 1993, 1997) Two fundamental propositions are central to Gardner's theory: (1) Intelligence is not fixed. Every time something is learned, the brain changes, and we have the ability to develop the intellectual capacity of our students. (2) Intelligence is not unitary. There are many ways to be smart, which Gardner refers to as *kinds of minds.*

The concept of multiple intelligences (MI) has had a profound influence on how we think about teaching. Emphasis shifts from "how smart students are" to "ways that students can be smart." This means teaching in many ways to provide varied learning experiences beyond the typical linguistic and logical ones predominantly used in American classrooms beyond the primary grades.

According to Gardner, intelligence must relate to those competencies that are valued in the world. School matters, but only insofar as it yields something that can be used once students leave school. (Gardner, 1997, p. 12) "An intelligence is the ability to solve problems, or to create products, that are valued within one or more cultural settings." (Gardner, 1993, p. *x*)

The eight (8) intellegences are categorized as follows:

Verbal-linguistic	*word smart*
Logical-mathematical	*logic/number smart*
Visual-spatial	*picture smart*
Musical-rhythmic	*music smart*
Body-kinesthetic	*body smart*
Interpersonal	*people smart*
Intrapersonal	*self smart*
Naturalist	*nature smart*

Here are the eight intelligences at a glance:

- *Verbal-linguistic* - This is the most commonly shared and crucial competence of the human species. It allows us to comprehend the meaning of words in verbal and written form. It also allows us to follow the rules of grammar and syntax and appreciate the sounds, rhythms, and inflection of words. Students show they are *word smart* when they are good at reading, writing, spelling, speaking, telling stories, and playing with words. They learn best through verbal presentations, reading, writing, and discussing.

- *Logical-mathematical* - This is the area of math-science. This intelligence allows us to work with objects, assess their qualities, and assign numbered symbols. It allows us to order, align, and sequence in the world around us. Students show they are *logic/number smart* when they are good with numbers, sequencing, synthesizing, evaluating, and solving math problems easily. They often learn best through logic.

- *Visual-spatial* - The prime function of this intelligence is to form images and perceive the world accurately. It is linked to verbal intelligence in that the mind stores and recalls its information in pictures, which may then be verbalized. Imaging is a valuable asset in recall and in problem solving. Students show they are *picture smart* when they have good artistic capabilities, an eye for detail and color, spatial awareness, can manipulate perceptions mentally, and enjoy painting, drawing, and sculpturing. They visualize easily and are good with spatial relations. They learn best through imagery, films, videos, and visual aids.

- *Musical-rhythmic* - One of the earliest intelligences to appear, its core functions deal with rhythm, music, tone, pitch, and patterns. Of all the intelligences, the consciousness or mood altering effect of music and rhythm on the brain is the greatest. When words are combined with melody and rhythm, as in song, they are easier to recall. Music has the ability to inspire, to excite, to express joy and sorrow; it also has the ability to calm and soothe. Students show they are *music smart* when they have the ability to communicate or gain meaning from music; listen to music frequently; play an instrument or sing; and are sensitive to pitch, timbre, timing, tone, and rhythm. Students using their music smarts often think in rhythms, melodies, or lyrics. They like to sing, hum, chant, rap, read, or create music. They learn best through music or lyrics and when music is part of the lesson.

- *Body-kinesthetic* - The main characteristic of this intelligence is to use the body for expressive purposes. Involving the body in any learning event increases the neural activity of the brain and increases the chances for information to be stored in the muscles of the body. Students show they are *body smart* when they unite body and mind for physical performance, have good motor skills, use their bodies to communicate, are good at dancing or athletics, and use the body in skilled ways. They are coordinated; use gestures and body language; and enjoy acting, role-playing, dancing, or athletics. Students using their body smarts think in movements, gestures, and body language. They often learn best when there is movement or when the content is presented in a "hands-on" form.

- *Interpersonal* - This intelligence gives us the ability to communicate verbally and nonverbally with other people. It is the capacity to perceive emotions, moods, motivation, and intentions. It also allows us to empathize with another person.

Students show they are *people smart* when they make and maintain friends easily; are sensitive to the feelings, moods, and motives of others; are good mediators, leaders, and organizers; put themselves in the role of the other; and see things from the other's perspective. They often learn best when they interact with other people over subject content or skills.

- *Intrapersonal* - This intelligence involves knowledge of the internal aspects of oneself, such as feelings and emotional responses. Self-image and personal identity are part of intrapersonal intelligence. It also gives us our capacity to see wholeness and unity, to discern patterns as they relate to self, and see connection with large orders of things or higher states of consciousness. Students show they are *self smart* when they have access to their own feelings, strengths, ideas, values, and beliefs; set and meet goals; and enjoy private time to think and reflect. They know themselves well and have the ability to use that information when making decisions. They often learn best when they are given time to formulate their ideas and reflect on their learning.

- *Naturalist* - This intelligence describes the ability to recognize flora and fauna and classify like objects. Students show they are *nature smart* when they have keen observation skills, an ability to make distinctions, and to form classes among natural objects. They have an awareness of the natural world and phe-nomena, and discriminate among animals, insects, birds, rocks, plants, trees, flowers, stars, planets, or even some non-natural items like cars, airplanes, shoes, or hairstyles. They enjoy gar-dening or caring for animals. They often learn best when the content is sorted and classified and is related to the real world.

Using the theory of multiple intelligences can have a very positive effect on learning. Learners forget a great deal of what is taught, but the problem may be a reliance on only one intelligence. By appealing to several intelligences, we can enhance long-term memory. Attending to students' intelligences accommodates more learners and gives students a greater repertoire of problem-solving tools. Another reason to include several intelligences when planning activities is to aid students in building self-esteem. This occurs when students identify an area in which they have a natural competence. Knowledge about one's own intelligences helps in this regard.

Thomas Armstrong suggests that one way to ascertain students' most highly developed intelligence is to observe how they *misbehave* in class. The strongly linguistic student will be talking out of turn, the highly spatial student will be doodling and daydreaming, the interpersonally inclined student will be socializing, and the body-kinesthetic student will be fidgeting. These intelligence-specific behaviors can be thought of as a cry for help—a diagnostic indicator of how students need to be taught. (Armstrong, 1994)

Another good indicator of proclivities is to observe how students spend their free time. Highly linguistic students might gravitate toward books, social students toward group games and gossip, spatial students toward drawing, and body-kinesthetic students toward hands-on activities.

Two caveats regarding multiple intelligences need to be made clear: (1) Do not design lessons for each intelligence. Planning such lessons misinterprets the brilliance of the concept. The approach should be to *plan activities that incorporate as many intelligences as are purposeful*—rather than preparing lessons for each intelligence. (2) It is nonsensical and far too demanding to plan on teaching something seven or eight ways. The point of multiple intelligence theory is to realize that any important topic can be taught in more than one way. The maxim to remember about multiple intelligences is *the more ways we teach, the more students we reach.*

Modalities of Learning (The "M" in LIMES)

The *modalities* refer to visual and print, auditory, kinesthetic and tactile, olfactory, and gustatory learning. Whereas the intelligences tell us how people are smart, learning modalities explain how people learn.

Information comes to us through our senses of sight-*visual*, hearing-*auditory*, touching-*tactual or tactile*, taste-*gustatory*, and smell-*olfactory*. Home economics, science, and some fine arts activities employ the senses of taste and smell. But the visual, auditory, and tactual senses are used in the preponderance of lessons. In practice, the tactual sense is expanded to imply any body movement (kinesthetic). Although print is usually considered visual (for the blind it is tactile), *interpreting print requires other skills.*

The brain learns in many ways at once. As we grow and engage in various activities, some senses develop more than others, but none grows in isolation. The concept can be likened to use of the right and left hand. Although we use both, we prefer one to the other. Similarly, we do not have a single, dominant lifelong learning mode. We learn our first language through sound, but many adults find it easier to learn vocabulary of a second language by seeing words visually as objects or in print.

Visually-oriented people prefer seeing instructions. They form mental pictures, scenes, and even words by projecting them with the mind's eye. Auditory people prefer an oral briefing. They recall things that have been said, music, and other sounds. Kinesthetically-oriented people like to get physically involved and get their hands on the activity and often are the first to try things.

During teacher presentations, visual and verbal cues can help tap into various learning modalities. The following lists offer some suggestions:

Visual learners

> like to see things in writing
>
> picture in their minds
>
> organize by pictures
>
> like colors
>
> like to take notes
>
> like flash cards
>
> enjoy mindmapping and graphic organizers
>
> want to be shown how to do something rather than be told how to do it
>
> match clothes and colors
>
> enjoy looking at a drawing or diagram rather than hearing an explanation.

The following examples of *verbal connectors* both indicate and cue into a visual style:

> "You can see the situation."
>
> "See what I mean?"
>
> "It appears that...."

"In your mind's eye…."

"Show me what you mean."

"Do you get the picture?"

"Is it becoming clear?"

"This looks good."

"Here is a bird's eye view."

Auditory learners

need to hear themselves talk

learn by repeating

read out loud

study out loud

often request to have directions repeated

like oral directions

sub-vocalize when reading

like the sound of their own voice

remember directions better if they repeat them to a neighbor

The following examples of *aural connectors* both indicate and cue into an auditory style:

"I hear what you are saying."

"Does that sound reasonable?"

"That rings true."

"I hear you loud and clear."

"Does it sound right?"

"We're on the same wavelength."

"I remember it word for word."

"That rings a bell with me."

"I'm trying to hear you but you're going too fast."

We often assume auditory learners can learn just by listening. It is important to note that auditory learners need to *hear themselves*. They learn by verbal repeating. An aural learner who is not cued beforehand may listen and then turn to a neighbor and say, "What did he say?" This is particularly true regarding home assignments. Before giving students an assignment, cue them ahead of time by simply saying, "In a moment I'm going to give the home assignment." Also, after giving the assignment, have students turn to a learning buddy and repeat what was said.

Kinesthetic/tactile learners

like manipulates

enjoy flash cards—as long as they can hold them

need movement

use lots of hand gestures

tend to have shorter attention spans

tend to be leg and arm movers

create energy to stay focused even though their movement itself does not teach anything

The following examples of *kinesthetic/tactile connectors* both indicate and cue into a kinesthetic/tactile style:

"I've got a handle on that."

"I can really get a hold of that information."

"This helps me grasp the issue."

"Raise your hand if you get a feeling for her point."

"Get a grip on this point."

"Hold on a second."

"Can you put your finger on it?"

"Does it touch you?"

Whereas colors and visuals can be used for visual learners and lyrics and rhythm can be used for auditory learners, finding movement for kinesthetic learners in the classroom can be far more challenging. Spelling words, for example, can be put on posters around the room. Students go to the various locations where the posters are, say a word out loud, and even draw the word with their hands through the air. The same procedure can apply to vocabulary, multiplication tables, geography, or other subject areas.

A fine line often exists between kinesthetic students and those labeled with Attention Deficit Hyperactivity Disorder (ADHD). The latter student will wiggle no matter what. A kinesthetic learner will only wiggle while he is concentrating. Kinesthetic learners will ask more often than others to go to the bathroom, sharpen pencils, and get out of their seats. Just allowing them to stand helps. Also, they will wait longer to ask questions or to ask for help.

A student's modality of learning can often be ascertained by observation. Visual learners usually follow the teacher with their eyes. Aural learners repeat out loud and want things repeated. Kinesthetic learners like to move while learning. Providing choices allows students to choose the modes that best suit them.

We need to recognize our own learning styles because we have a tendency to teach the way we learn. A teacher whose learning modality is highly visual will have a natural tendency to use visual activities, often to the exclusion of activities directed toward other modalities.

Emotions (The "E" in LIMES)

Achieving change is emotional as well as intellectual. Emotions can enhance the learning process or interfere with it.

Our emotional system drives our attention, which drives learning and memory. (Sylwester) Specifically, how a person "feels" about a situation determines the amount of attention he or she devotes to it. Students need to feel an emotional connection to their tasks, their peers, their teachers, and their school. For an increasing number of students, school is a place where making emotional connections is more important than anything else. This is especially true for so many adolescents, where a feeling of belonging almost overshadows all other needs. As indicated in Chapter 4 in the section *Reducing Anonymity,* this need is often the most important factor that keeps kids in school.

We generally focus on cognition when we teach, and we tend to avoid the emotions. Yet, students must feel physically and emotionally secure before they can process information. Threats are counterproductive because they stimulate emotions that interfere with higher-order thinking skills. Armstrong calls negative emotions such as humiliation, shame, guilt, fear, and anger "paralyzing experiences." (Armstrong, 1994) When students are anxious, the emotions interfere with thinking and disrupt the learning process. In short, negative emotions are counterproductive to learning.

Some knowledge of how emotions and thinking are intertwined is important because in every encounter there is an emotional subtext.

Within a few moments of seeing or hearing something, we react. There is a very subtle, and sometimes not so subtle, liking or disliking. The brain evolved this way for survival. In case of a dire threat, we needed an immediate response. Not much time was allowed for a rational decision. "I'll get it or it may get me." The emotional mind still reacts before the thinking mind. Sensory signals from the eye or ear travel to the thalamus. The thalamus acts as a relay station for information and branches to both the neocortex, the thinking or cognitive part of the brain, and to the amygdala. The amygdala is an almond-shaped ganglion (mass of nerve tissues) perched above the brain stem adjoining the temporal lobe. The amygdala stores our emotions, especially fear and aggression. It is our emotional memory since the time we were infants. But there is one long neuron connection from the amygdala to the gastrointestines. That is why you may have a feeling that seems like it emanates from the pit of your stomach. It does. The branching allows the amygdala (emotions) to respond before the neocortex (thinking) because the circuit to the amygdala is smaller and shorter. This explains why we get angry before we think. This threat-response is great for escaping from predators, but not for learning. The short-term impact of this brain response includes impaired spatial episodic memory, weakened ability to prioritize, and greater likelihood of repeated behaviors that impinge on learning.

The brain biologically is going to pay attention and remember longer those things that have strong emotion, either negative or positive. Since emotional climate is critical for learning, we need to invest the first few minutes of every class in activities that allow students to get into a positive learning state and make the lesson "enjoyable" to the learner.

The implication for the classroom is to add emotional hooks to what we are teaching. The art of this craft is to create experiences, rather than just present information. For example, a high school history class is reading about immigration to the country in the early part of the 20th century. The textbook contains a graph showing great numbers coming from Eastern Europe. A simulation could give students some idea of what the experience was like for these people, who were mostly very poor, and who traveled across the Atlantic Ocean on ships as steerage. A group of students huddles sitting on the floor in one corner of the classroom. Crowded together, they move their upper bodies back and forth to simulate not only the movement of the ship but also how people were seasick for much of the voyage. No wonder they were elated to see the Statue of Liberty in the calmer waters of New York Harbor! When we add emotion to learning experiences to make them more meaningful and exciting, the brain deems the information more important, and retention is increased. (Wolfe and Brandt)

The human brain has a built-in attention preference for certain stimuli, such as novelty and pleasure. We can take advantage of the brain's preference for *novelty* by eliciting states of *curiosity, oddity, intrigue, suspense, anticipation, awe, confusion, surprise,* and *challenge.* We can increase *pleasure* by creating states of *anticipation, hope, security, fun, acceptance, success,* and *satisfaction.*

Knowing that we respond emotionally when fear and anxiety are involved should always be a classroom consideration. If a student feels helpless or incompetent, anxiety sets in and impedes learning. Conversely, when students are encouraged and challenged without coercion or fear of failure, they feel the likelihood of becoming more competent.

To move towards competence, students need to learn to accept feedback, *whether positive or negative,* without any emotional connotation or judgment. They need to learn to treat failure as an opportunity, not a disaster. Failure gives information one would not otherwise have. The approach is to see failure as a guide and not allow an emotional rush to swamp them. But we have done a funny thing with failure. Instead of keeping it as a lookout, we have too often given it the helm. Failure is a natural part of any learning. *You cannot learn and be perfect at the same time,* as indicated in Chapter 4 in the section *Reducing Perfectionism.* This phenomenon can be observed by watching very young children before they put on their belief systems. They take one shaky step and fall down; they take another step and plop. Without emotional freight, babies know instinctively that failure is a signal to try another way. If failure is feared, learning will never be optimal. If failure is used as a guide, not an accuser, success will be swifter.

Styles (The "S" in LIMES)

Styles refer to modes of behavior and communication. They have little to do with intelligences, abilities, or aptitudes.

No style is good or bad, right or wrong. Neither is one style better or worse than another; they are just different. For example, perhaps you have sometimes wondered why it seems so difficult to communicate with some people and why at other times you instantaneously hit it off with someone you have just met. The answer can be found in our styles.

Carl Jung, the Swiss psychiatrist who founded analytic psychology, was the first to develop the concept of behaviorial styles. Jung articulated a theory of personality behavior types, which he believed are genetically determined. They can be discerned by watching young children and discovering how they process experiences in different ways. Jung postulated that every individual develops a primacy in one of four major behavioral functions: intuiting, thinking, feeling, and sensing.

Over the years a number of inventories have been developed using Jung's "forced-choice" approach. If you have ever taken such an inventory, you might have had difficulty making choices between two opposites because the answers are not mutually exclusive. That is, one choice may be more representative but not to the complete exclusion of the other. Therefore, any inventory that uses a forced-choice approach is an artificial attempt to categorize and describe. If we keep this in mind and do not pigeonhole people by the results of such an inventory, the general concept can be useful.

From the many instruments now available using this forced-choice approach, four behavioral styles seem to emerge. To help understand this approach to styles, visualize a directional scale with a *thinker* in the north, a *feeler* in the south, a *doer* in the west, and a *relater* in the east.

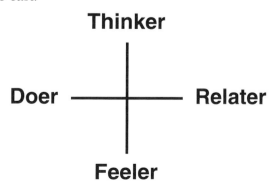

A *thinker* (north) analyzes and can be described as logical and structured, and as someone who *processes cognitively*. Jung describes a person in this category as processing analytically and inferentially. A *feeler* (south) can be described as personalized, spontaneous, emotional, and animated. Jung describes a person in this category as one who *processes subjectively*. A *doer* (west) is *orientated toward results* and can be described as assertive and directed, while a *relater* (east) is *into relationships*. Since directions are not limited to the ordinates of north, south, east, or west, thinking north *and* west, south *and* east, etc., is more useful. For example, my styles are predominantly in the thinker and doer quadrants. I am cognitive and project-oriented. My wife's are in the thinker and relater quadrants. She is a writer and desires interactions with others. Our daughter is predominantly in the feeler and relater quadrants. She is guided by her feelings and has a great desire to be with people. Knowing our daughter's styles allows my wife and me to be much more understanding of her. A parent who is aware of styles has a decided advantage in relating to the child. The same holds true for a husband and wife. Just knowing that my wife needs time to relate allows me to respond more successfully to my impulse of "getting on with the task." Being aware of styles enhances communications. Alessandra and O'Connor refer to this awareness as the *Platinum Rule:* "Do unto others as they would like done unto them." Relate to other people according to *their* styles.

In a classroom, a teacher whose own style is predominantly that of a thinker will have a propensity to plan fewer activities that tap into feelings, sentiment, or excitement. Similarly, a teacher who is predominantly a doer may have a tendency to plan too few activities where students interrelate. Knowing about behavioral and communication styles allows the teacher to plan activities that afford opportunities to appeal to all styles. This is especially important for at-risk students. Many students who drop out of school are "feelers," those who process subjectively. *If they feel school is not successful for them, why continue?*

To summarize, the "LIMES" acronym assists in remembering that some students are sequential learners and others need to see the whole picture (*l*eft-right brain). Every student can be smart in some way (*i*ntelligences). Some need to hear themselves while others need to move or touch (*m*odalities of learning). Anxiety should be reduced and feelings of enjoyment increased (*emotions*). Finally, learning can be enhanced by considering behavior and communication patterns (*styles*).

It is critical to remember that lessons are not planned around each entity. The purpose is to be *aware of them* so that when lessons are planned and implemented, learning will be enhanced and understanding of student differences will be increased.

Lesson Planning

Madeline Hunter's lesson-planning model is very useful in considering teaching and learning. Unfortunately, over the years her model has come under some criticism mainly because of faulty interpretation. The model has been incorrectly perceived as an inflexible recipe or cookbook approach. That is, if all the ingredients are not included and used in sequence, then the model is not being followed.

This is *not* how the model was supposed to work. Madeline Hunter saw the model as flexible and open-ended. The steps should be *considered* when planning a lesson. Having considered them, teachers should select, abandon, or judiciously include any or all of the steps.

Anticipate

1 **Mental Set** - Break Preoccupation/Get Attention.

- Link past experiences or future plans and interests to the lesson.
- Engage curiosity.

2 **Objective** - Give the intended objective of the lesson.

- Explain the purpose, meaning, and/or use of the lesson.

Participate

3 **Teach the lesson** - Facilitate the learning.

- Bear in mind (LIMES) left-right brain considerations, intelligences, modalities of learning, emotional considerations, and styles of behavior and communication to involve students.

4 **Check for understanding** - Obtain feedback.

- Check that students have learned what you have taught.

5 Practice - Apply.

- Give students an opportunity to practice the lesson, first independently and then with learning partners.

Reflect

6 Closure - Reflect/Reinforce.

- Have students articulate and share what they have learned.

- Think, pair, and share.

7 What next - Plan for long-term memory.

- Through inquiry and example, relate how the learning is meaningful, useful, relevant, or interesting. Have students use a learning log to record, "What did I learn?" and "What do I need to work on?"

Organizing the steps into the three categories of **anticipation, participation**, and **reflection** assists in both planning and implementation. This categorizing serves to remind us of the importance of reducing anxiety and increasing novelty when a lesson is introduced (anticipation). It also helps to focus on what the *students* will be doing to learn (participation). Likewise, reflection at the conclusion of a lesson aids long-term memory. Traditionally, not much time of a lesson has been devoted to reflection because the assumption has been that the teacher must be active in teaching. But it is in the processing time that learning becomes solidified. (Jensen, 1998, p. 47)

Levels of Intellect

A look at levels of intellect is useful, especially since the advent of media technology, where students are exposed to so much information, perhaps at the expense of higher levels of thinking.

Benjamin Bloom's taxonomy of educational objectives in the cognitive domain helps teachers and learners understand levels of thinking. (Bloom) The taxonomy categorizes higher-order thinking in ascending order, from the simplest to the most complex:

1. *Knowledge* - Remembering previously learned material (recall).

2. *Comprehension* - Grasping the meaning of material.

3. *Application* - Using learned material in new and concrete situations.

4. *Analysis* - Breaking down material into its component parts so that its organizational structure can be understood.

5. *Synthesis* - Putting parts together to form a new whole (creativity).

6. *Evaluation* - Judging the value of material for a given purpose.

At the lowest rung on the ladder, students can be asked to *recall* information. Second, if students can recount information in their own words, they probably *comprehend* it. If students can *apply* the information, they are at the third level. When students can *analyze* or examine components of the information, they have reached the fourth level. If students can combine or assemble information to draw a solid conclusion, they are at the *synthesis* level. Finally, when students make a judgment about the information expressing their opinion, they are at the *evaluation* level.

Levels from *application* upward require recall and comprehension. If students cannot recall and comprehend the information, they will not be able to apply it, analyze it, synthesize it, or make a considered evaluative judgment.

Following are two subject area examples.

Government

1. *Knowledge* - What students *remember*.
   What is the electoral college?

2. *Comprehension* - What students *restate* in their own words.
   How does the electoral college work?

3. *Application* - What information is to be *used* to solve the problem.
   Predict what would happen if the electoral college were to be eliminated.

4. *Analysis* - What is *broken down* into what parts.
   Differentiate between what the electoral college did before the 12th Amendment to the Constitution and its present role.

5. *Synthesis* - What two pieces of information are to be *combined*.
   How can the electoral college and the popular vote produce different results?

6. *Evaluation* - What students are to express an *opinion* about.

In your opinion, should the electoral college be retained or abolished? Defend your choice.

Literature

1. *Knowledge* - Describe one of the main characters in the story.

2. *Comprehension* - Compare characteristics between two main characters.

3. *Application* - Write a conversation between you and one of the characters.

4. *Analysis* - Explain how one of the main characters moves the plot forward.

5. *Synthesis* - Rewrite your own ending of the story for the main character.

6. *Evaluation* - Describe the author's message and how the main character fits into it.

Here are some key words to assist in planning and evaluation:

1. *Knowledge* (recall)	list	fill in
	describe	identify
	locate	recall
	define	what
	label	when
	repeat	who
	name	
2. *Comprehension*	paraphrase	translate
	explain	interpret
	discuss	summarize
	compare	convert
	review	how
	match	why
	give an example	
3. *Application*	apply	employ
	construct	restructure
	draw	predict
	simulate	calculate
	sketch	practice
	demonstrate	how

4. *Analysis*	analyze	contrast
	classify	deduce
	dissect	categorize
	distinguish	separate
	differentiate	break down
	compare	subdivide
	infer	
5. *Synthesis*	compose	create
	combine	integrate
	design	formulate
	relate	assemble
	produce	rearrange
	put together	collect
6. *Evaluation*	judge	rate
	argue	debate
	assess	evaluate
	appraise	choose
	decide	defend
	criticize	support

Notice that the lower three levels—knowledge, comprehension, and application—describe a *convergent* thinking process whereby the learner recalls what is known and comprehended to solve a problem through application. In contrast, the upper three levels—analysis, synthesis, and evaluation—describe a *divergent* thinking process. These levels of processing result in new insights and discoveries that were not part of the original information.

Use of the taxonomy is especially pertinent today where so much information gathering becomes an end unto itself, as is the case with the expanding use of computers. For students to gain wisdom, higher-order thinking skills must be incorporated into instruction. Even students with learning difficulties can handle this successfully.

David Sousa offers some questions to stimulate higher-order thinking:

> What would you have done?
> What are some of the things you wondered about
>   while this was happening?
> What might happen next?

Why do you think this was the best choice?
What do you think might happen if...?
What do you think might have caused this?
Predict what will happen in the future.
How is it like...?
How is it different from...?
Give an example.
Where could we go for help on this?
Have we left out anything important?
In what other ways could this be done?
How many ways can you use this?
Do you agree? Why or why not?
What was the most important idea to you?
How would you change it?
What details can you add to give a clearer picture?
How can you test the theory?
How can you tell the difference between...and...?
(Sousa, 1995, p. 127)

A note of caution is necessary here. The brilliance of the taxonomy is that it helps to ensure that lessons are not exclusively aimed at only lower-level thinking. The government and literature examples were given to explain the concept—*not to expect each lesson to include all six levels of the taxonomy.*

Instructional Questions

Effective teachers ask effective questions because questions direct the thinking process.

The following will assist in more active thinking and increased student participation.

1. Ask "what" questions. Continually and repeatedly ask, "What if?" and "What else?" When students start thinking about answers to these questions, their mental images take on far more detail and their language takes on far more differentiation. In addition, they begin to "own" the information.

2. Use wait time to encourage thinking. Learn to be comfortable with silence. When you call on a student for a response, wait 10 seconds (not the usual 1-2 seconds) after your question. Responses will be longer, responses will be at higher intellectual levels, and students will demonstrate more confidence in their

answers. Also, this wait time will encourage students to offer a response instead of assuming another student will be called on.

3. Wait after an answer is given. Immediately following an answer, wait 5-10 seconds (not 1-2 seconds) before giving feedback or making another instructional move. This will both encourage other students to volunteer and model reflection on an answer.

4. Use levels of intellect. Instead of requesting only recall or information, ask questions that require higher-order thinking skills of analysis, synthesis, and evaluation. Students automatically will include lower intellectual levels in their answers.

5. Call the student's name *after* asking the question. When a student is called on before the question, other students do not pay as much attention or prepare a response. The exception may be for the student who is shy or has a disability and is not comfortable with "taking risks."

6. Do not repeat responses. When teachers do not repeat answers, students pay greater attention and show increased respect for their classmates' responses.

7. Pose, rather than ask, questions. Asking often implies a correct answer. Posing implies open-endedness, engenders dialogue, and invites students to think. Posing increases student involvement.

Group Questioning Strategy

Spencer Kagan of Kagan Cooperative Learning in San Clemente, California, believes that teachers often disempower themselves with the traditional approach to answering questions. All a student has to do is hold up a hand, and the lesson can be derailed with an off-the-wall question. This is a three-way lose situation. The teacher is disempowered because the question needs to be answered, the student may get a cursory or irritated response, and the class loses because it is time away from the class activity while the teacher deals with the question—which may be of no interest to the other students.

Another approach is to tell students to hold questions until interaction time. When students work together as pairs and if one does not know the answer, then two students have the question. When students work in teams, the questioner asks the other team members.

Chances are one of the team members will know. If no one in the team knows, that means there is a team question since now a few people have the same question and the team has exhausted its resources. When all team members raise their hands, this signals to the teacher that the team needs help.

When using group questions, the teacher randomly chooses one member of the group to ask the question. This guards against a student's saying to the other members of the team, "I've got a question; so all of you put up your hands." In responding to the group's inquiry, the teacher has a few options. The question may be answered, thinking may be redirected, resources may be pointed out so the team can do their own research, or the question may be shared with the class. *The key is that the teacher is the filter for what goes on in the classroom.* Group questions are a three-way win because the students get a quality response, the teacher retains the agenda, and time is not wasted for the rest of the class.

Choosing Key Words to Frame Questions and Statements

Robert Greenleaf of Greenleaf Learning in Providence, Rhode Island, suggests paying particular attention to key words when asking questions. Specific words determine the levels for both thinking and group interaction. For example, key words in the three following questions evoke (even dictate) a predetermined, specific type of response.

The question, *"When was gold first discovered in California?"* evokes *"1848"* and may even conjure up James Marshall's discovering the gold nugget at Sutter's sawmill. Notice, however, that *"when"* and *"first"* in the question send a message that *only one correct answer is sought.* Once the answer is provided, there is no purpose in further deliberation. Also, a risk is involved. If the question were asked of the entire class, a student volunteering an incorrect answer would have been better off not participating.

A second question such as, *"What kinds of things do you think the pioneers heading for the promise of California gold would have brought with them?"* evokes a *multiplicity of responses.* A list of items would be engendered, such as water, food, clothes, shovels, pickaxes, and gunpowder. All responses are viable. The plurals, *"kinds"* and *"things,"* indicate that more than one response is necessary; thus learners continue to search for probable items. Students make use of their understanding (prior knowledge) of the time period and its technology and posit likely things the pioneers would have brought with them. In this case, students are encouraged to continue to search for additional responses, as the list is potentially extensive. Notice that little, if any, risk is involved in this processing to attempt additional answers.

A third question, *"How do you think the U.S. might have developed differently if gold had been discovered on the Gulf Coast instead of the West Coast?"* evokes a different type of response. *"Might"* and *"if"* indicate full license for the learner to explore possibilities, that developing ideas and relationships in one's thinking are sought. Minds stay engaged and connections are made. Also, the responses will be offered in more complete thoughts and full sentences, such as, "Fewer people would have gone west," "The people who discovered the gold would have become rich and bought most of the Caribbean," "It would have taken a lot longer for pioneers to move westward because there would have been less incentive," and "New Orleans would have been the economic center of the country instead of New York."

As key words in questions trigger very specific responses, key words in statements can also stimulate thinking. "Put your paper on your desk" requires only that the student process a simple direction. "The bell is about to ring. Think about what you need to do before you are ready to be excused," engenders much more complex, intellectual processing. Instead of simply following directions, students must determine what to do and then direct themselves to do it. Therefore, *choose words that mentally engage students.*

Imaging

Visualization of objects and events is a powerful way of storing information. (In contrast to *imagining*, which has no limits, *imaging* is specific and focused.)

We can even improve reading comprehension by encouraging students to make mental pictures as they read and use their own experiences. For example, students can mentally image the entrance to their residence—the first room they enter, then the kitchen, and then other rooms. This imaging encourages focusing and generates additional richness of detail. In this example, one can mentally stop in any room and visualize the furniture and decor. Using this technique, students can visualize or "peg" information in any location.

Any image can be created to enhance recall. For example, to learn Stephen Covey's seven habits of highly effective people (Covey) correctly and in proper order, I conjured up the following image.

Habit	Mental placement on my body
1. Be Proactive	head
2. Begin with the End in Mind	shoulders
3. Put First Things First	chest
4. Think Win/Win	belly
5. First Seek to Understand, ...Then to be Understood	hips
6. Synergize	back
7. Sharpen the Saw	thighs

By creating this visualization, I have immediate recall. In addition, it took less time to create the image than if I had attempted to memorize the list through repetition—and reinforcement takes but a matter of moments.

Conjuring up vivid images (right brain) while reading a book (left brain) encourages hemispheric integration and leads to improved memory and more efficient learning. If you think of engaging both sides of the brain, no matter what you are teaching, the learner builds up more hooks and cues to ensure long-term memory. The brain can keep on making connections and, therefore, grow throughout life. *Learning builds learning* because, as we continue to learn, the neural networks of the brain augment, creating ever-abundant connections.

In *How the Brain Learns,* David Sousa says:

> Imagery should become a regular part of classroom strategies as early as kindergarten. In the primary grades, the teacher should supply the images to ensure accuracy. Later, teachers should encourage students to form their own images. Research studies continue to attest to how the power of imagery aids in recalling word associations, visual arrays, prose learning, complex procedures, and motor learning. (1995, p. 96)

Here is a simple experiment you can do with your students. Find two similar reading selections. Have students read the first selection and then ask questions about the reading. Then take your students through a visualizing exercise. Use their bedroom as an example. Say, "As you read something that is important or that you wish to remember, make an image of it or describe it in two or three words and then place it on the bed. Place the next item in a different location and continue the procedure until the end of the reading selection." Have the students answer similar questions as they did before the imaging exercise. Explain to your students the reason for their improvement: the brain remembers experiences and images better than words.

Let your students also know that their memory can be improved when they think in images. Often the more unusual the image, the better the retention. A simple exercise proves the point. Envision a cow. The cow's name is Georgette. It's a Jersey cow. The cow is on the Empire State Building and is singing a couple of Christmas carols. Under the cow's chin is a ham. It's a Virginia ham. The cow is wearing yellow underwear. In the cow's hoof is a pencil. And the cow is making a connect-the-dots drawing of Marilyn Monroe who is walking down a road going to Mass.

You just named all original thirteen colonies: Georgia, New Jersey, New York (Empire State), the two Carolinas, Virginia, New Hampshire (ham), Delaware (underwear), "Pencilvania," Connecticut (connect the dots), Maryland, Rhode Island, and Massachusetts.

If you want to increase involvement and enhance recall even more, use oral repetition. The exercise would go as follows:

Envision a cow. The cow's name is Georgette.
What's the cow's name?

It's a Jersey cow.
What kind of a cow?

The cow is on the Empire State Building.
Where is the cow?

It's singing a couple of Christmas carols.
What is it singing?

Under its chin is a ham.
What's under its chin?

It's a Virginia ham.
  What kind of ham?

The cow is wearing yellow underwear.
  What's the cow wearing?

In its hoof is a pencil.
  What's in its hoof?

And the cow is making a connect-the-dots drawing.
  What kind of a drawing?

Of Marilyn Monroe.
  Of whom?

Walking down a road.
  Down a what?

Going to Mass.
  Going where?

This visualization could be reinforced with a quick oral review. Ask the following questions, and have students repeat the word and the state the word represents.

What is the cow's name?

What kind of a cow is it?

Where is the cow?

Singing a couple of _____.

Under its chin is a _____.

What kind of a ham?

The cow is wearing _____.

In its hoof is a _____.

It is making what kind of a drawing?

Of?

Walking down a _____.

Going to _____.

An additional reinforcement would be to have students sketch a picture (on paper or by moving their hands in the air) and identify the parts of the picture using the names of the states.

"SAVER" is a simple acronym to remember when using imagery. "S" refers to *seeing* the image in the mind's eye. "A" refers to *associating* the image to some *action*. "V" refers to *vivid*. The more colorful and clearly defined the image, the easier recall will be. "E" refers to *exaggerate*. The more extraordinary the better. "R" refers to *reviewing* the image periodically. Reviewing assists long-term retention.

Visualization should be encouraged regularly. It is a simple technique to improve performance in reading comprehension, vocabulary development, and other areas. Most important, because imaging increases comprehension and recall—two of the most tested skills in schooling—it gives students considerable confidence and faith in themselves.

Stories

Take every opportunity to simplify the written word so that information can be created in a picture or experience. One way to do this is to convey information in story form. When we use this approach to communication, we help create meaning and improve retention for the listener. Stories are retained longer than facts because they create visual images. Images touch emotions because they arouse sensations, which are remembered longer than facts.

When the history teacher was asked the secret for making the subject so interesting and students so enthused, the response was, "I can tell you in two words: Tell stories." An old storyteller's tale makes the point.

TRUTH walked around naked, and everyone shunned him.

STORY walked around in colored clothes, and everyone liked him.

TRUTH inquired of STORY, "What is it that you do that people like you?"

STORY lent TRUTH some colorful garb and interesting clothing.

Everyone began liking TRUTH.

Metacognition

Metacognition is awareness of one's own thinking. Arthur Costa, co-founder of the Institute for Intelligent Behavior in El Dorado Hills, California, Professor Emeritus at California State University, Sacramento, and former president of the Association for Supervision and Curriculum Development (ASCD), speaks and writes on the importance of this area.

Metacognition is essential for developing critical thinking skills. The objective of metacognition is to have the *learner* become aware of his own cognitive processes and to become involved in understanding what he is thinking as he proceeds. The student is reflecting to see whether or not what he is doing is working.

Reflect on whether or not you hear yourself talking to yourself while solving this problem: *How much is half of two plus two?*

When we hear ourselves thinking, we are metacogitating. But do not assume that every student does it. For example, a student works on and solves a problem, and the teacher says, "Tell us how you solved that problem." And the student says, "I don't know; I just did it." This shows a lack of metacognitive awareness.

Students often attempt to solve a problem or analyze a situation without thinking. The answer may be so obvious that they just say it. There are many situations that can be dealt with successfully in this way. However, a problem arises when this approach does not work because the task has become too complex. For students who are habituated to thinking at the perceptual level, and who have not developed cognitive tools, such problems appear to be "too much" for them to deal with, and they just give up. *The inability to take charge of one's own cognitive processes is a very large part of the at-risk/dropout problem—as well as of discipline problems.*

Although mastering subject matter is important, strategies to increase thinking power are equally important. Schooling today too often emphasizes "correct" answers and single solutions. But in so many situations, it is not how many answers one knows, but rather how one proceeds when one does not know, as when confronted with problems, dilemmas, enigmas, and situations to be addressed, the answers to which are not immediately known or readily available. This is becoming truer every day in the rapidly-changing information age.

When faced with a task, most of us just start doing what seems to be the proper thing, giving thought to what we do *only if it becomes necessary.* For example, when driving an automobile, we stop at a red light "automatically" because we have habituated the process. If we encounter a flashing red light, a situation that is not quite so common, we then start thinking. In school, the difference between those who succeed in doing the more complex tasks of cognition and those who do not is that successful students have learned to be conscious of what they are doing. They do not act impulsively or intuitively when it is inappropriate to do so.

When a routine has been developed, thinking is reduced. This is the time to introduce a more difficult or complex task. Conscious thinking is forced back into play. This oscillation between a routine way of dealing with a task and the development of new approaches to deal with more complex tasks increases thinking power.

A good way to build awareness and improve thinking skills is to *have students talk about what is going on inside their heads when they are approaching a task,* instead of focusing on their getting the right answer. Practice with the intent of keeping the thinking process going—to sustain "openture" rather than coming to closure. Ask questions such as, "What was going on inside your head to come up with that answer?" "What was your strategy?" "How else could you have done that?" *Talking about thinking begets more thinking.* Teachers can model their own metacognition process to help students.

Still another approach is to ask questions such as, "Give me three reasons why this is the wrong choice." In answering such a question, students learn to make comparisons—one of the essential cognitive functions. In the process, students not only learn to develop criteria for making comparisons, they *become aware* that they are doing so.

Notice that asking questions, which encourages thinking and reinforces understanding, is more effective than the common approach of giving praise. Specific feedback is most useful. For example, rather than saying to a student, "That is a good job," the teacher would say, "You seem to be getting the hang of it, don't you think? Would you like to show me another example?" The student learns that he is gaining competence.

Rather than focusing on judging and ranking, the teacher becomes a mediator who helps students draw useful lessons from their own experiences. This includes understanding *why* success was attained or *why* there was a failure and what to do about it. The objective of metacognition is to gain insight into the student's reasoning—not for testing of information.

The Senses

A discussion of instruction would not be complete without mentioning the senses—the way humans receive all information. A snatch of a sensory memory and suddenly you are taken back to forgotten places, other faces. When golden oldies play, scores of long-forgotten words drift back into consciousness.

The more senses evoked while learning, the more anchors the student will have to hold that learning in memory. For example, adding colors could enhance the memory of the visioning exercise of Georgette, the Jersey cow on the Empire State Building. To realize the powerful effect of color, reflect on the one item the cow was using and see if you remember what it was as well as the color. Additional enhancement would occur if olfactory senses were used. Unlike other senses, smell speeds directly to the brain. Can you smell a banana? Can you smell coffee brewing in the morning? Using the same example, try smelling the tar of the freshly paved road Marilyn was using on her way to Mass.

Hearing, particularly music, hooks memory. Think of the tune "Twinkle, Twinkle Little Star," and the alphabet pops into mind. (Did you find yourself remembering a melody used in learning the alphabet? "ABCDEFG, HIJKLMNOP....") Music stimulates learning and retention. Studies in brain research suggest that the cells of the brain resonate to music. Some of the most beneficial effects are achieved by using music at a tempo of 60 beats per minute during quiet or study time. This tempo correlates with a relaxed heartbeat, causing the heart rate to slow and the body to relax, leaving the mind alert. Listening to the music of Mozart or 60-beat-per-minute baroque music (the largo or andante sections) in the background creates a refreshing and stimulating learning environment. Playing this type of music during reflection time enhances both the activity and recall. However, the rationale should be explained because some students prefer to study in quiet.

When kinesthetics are added, memory is enhanced even more. Here is an example combining arithmetic and rope jumping.

> Smart rope, smart rope, what's the trick
> to help me learn arithmetic?
> Denominator down—touch the ground
> Numerator top—give a hop.

The feet may trip, but weeks later the memory still does not.

It is worth noting that an attractive learning environment can heighten the senses. Secondary teachers can use the talents of their students to create as stimulating environments as are found in elementary classrooms.

Additional Suggestions for Aiding Recall and Memory

We tend to remember first impressions, that which is *repeated*, what strikes us as *outstanding*, what is *personal*, that which is *associated* with something we already know, and what was most *recent*. The acronym "PROPAR" assists in keeping the points in mind.

Primacy refers to the primary or first interaction. We remember our first impressions of people and experiences. This is the reason why the beginning of each classroom period is so important.

Repetition enhances recall. Anything that is repeated has a better chance of going to and remaining in long-term memory. Repetition during the lesson, and again in later lessons, aids recall. Distributive practice is more effective than elongated practice: practicing three times of short duration versus one time of a longer duration. Memory is especially enhanced when the repetition is done by the students—rather than only by the teacher—and when accompanied with some body movement.

We tend to remember anything that is *outstanding*, novel, different, or that catches our attention. We recall lasting impressions because they were out of the ordinary—be it a field trip, a special event, or a special manner in which the teacher is dressed or presents a lesson.

Similarly, we remember those things that are *personal* because they touch our emotions. We still remember a comment some teacher made because it encouraged us—or was disheartening.

Memory is enhanced when the brain *associates* something new with something already known or experienced. The introduction of a new skill or concept is a natural time to associate what will be learned with what students already know. Mnemonics, or memory associations, is an effective strategy to use. For instance, when teaching the planets in the order of moving out from the sun, use the sentence, "My Very Educated Mother Just Served Us Nine Pizzas." It helps remember Mercury, Venus, Earth, Mars, Jupiter, Saturn, Uranus, Neptune, and Pluto.

Recency refers to those things that were most recent (last). Recency is the reason why reflection time aids recall. In fact, often the best learning occurs during reflection time and is especially important for at-risk students. Reflection is best when it is both individual and shared. "Think, pair, share" is a useful strategy for reflection. For example, using this strategy, students first reflect individually by thinking of three things learned during the lesson. They then choose one of the three to describe to a learning partner (pair). Sharing takes place with the other in the pair, then in small groups or with the entire class.

Since recall is used so much for measuring success of schooling, here are a few additional points regarding the subject. Gestures serve to help people retrieve elusive words from their memory. (Begley, November 1998) People who are searching their "lexical memory" for a word often gesture in some way. The next time you are "fishing" for a particular word, notice how your hands or facial muscles become activated. Encourage gesturing when students have a memory blank. Another point has to do with eye movements. In a classroom when students are doing work or taking a test, the usual instructions are to look down at their own paper. Yet, recall is achieved best when it is accessed in the same way that it was stored. When visual learners take a test and look down, they may not be accessing information in the most efficient manner. After a test, when students are looking up, the visual memory comes flooding back. To improve examination performance, allow students to look up to access information in their memory.

Laser Learning

Laser learning refers to thinking and talking in short segments to increase retention.

Since the brain recalls in images and experiences, the learner first transforms key points into a few words to form a mental image. This is laser thinking. In order to get information to stick, the learner then "laser" talks by relating his image to another student—*in no more than thirty or forty-five seconds.* The short thinking and talking times generate just the right amount of stress to make learning most effective. This is a brain-chemical experience, not a social one. The process has nothing to do with the other person's listening or giving the learner feedback. It has to do with forcing the learner to think and say what he or she thinks he or she has just learned. For optimum benefit, this has to be done intermittently in short periods of time. It is only in the *saying* that the learner figures out what he gets or doesn't get. The strategy engenders the opportunity to self-correct.

The process needs to be explained to students. They need to understand that they will feel a little uncomfortable when they relate their learning to another person. They need to be told that when they think just miniscule things and put them into mental images, memory is increased because episodic pathways to memory are formed. (Sprenger). Students need to understand that they have to say it and hear themselves. It is in the saying that the brain's neurotransmitters get released. When the learner *states* what he has "learned," he realizes he has or does not "have it." You can see how this works by reviewing *The Raise Responsibility System*. Read the summary at the end of Chapter 3, then explain the program in one minute. You will see that only when the learner *says it* that he determines what needs to be reviewed more. Saying out loud what one has just learned is an excellent reflective strategy to improve learning. Again, the teacher's explanation of this process is necessary and assists students in becoming comfortable with the process.

Seminal Shifts

Four seminal shifts are important regarding instruction: (1) from changing others to self-change, (2) from a focus on teaching to one of learning, (3) from calling on individual students to 100 percent student participation, and (4) turn one-size fits all to differentiated instruction..

1. Shifting from a focus on changing students to a focus on self-change

Most people behave on the assumption that if something is not as they would like it to be, the change that is necessary is incumbent upon others. This specifically relates to instruction. If students are not performing as you would like, rather than expecting them to change, the question should be asked, "How can I, as the teacher, influence them to do what I would like them to do?"

2. Shifting from an instructional focus to a learning focus

Traditional teaching approaches have centered on getting and keeping student attention for most of the class time. According to Eric Jensen, the notion of continuously keeping the learner's attention is biologically and psychologically outdated. This is a model for control, rather than for learning. For optimal learning, the teacher need only have the attention of the student for a small amount of total time. Quality learning may begin by attracting the learner's attention with novelty, emotions, relevance, or curiosity. Then, once learners have had time to learn purposeful material in the way they do it best, it's time for integration, meaning, and memory. (Jensen, 1996, p. 37)

Cognitive research strongly affirms that we learn best when we are actively involved in interesting and challenging situations and when we talk about learning. (Sousa, 1998) Talking activates the brain's frontal lobe, which is necessary for understanding, meaning, and memory. Therefore, in most lessons, students should be actively engaged in activities other than sitting quietly and passively for long stretches of time. The brain simply learns best when it "does," rather than when it "absorbs." The old adage applies: *Students who do the talking and doing do the learning.* This is a way to close the learning gap, *the difference between what was taught and what was learned,* e.g., what was taught on Monday and what students remember on Tuesday. *Breaking Ranks* (with the status quo), the 1996 report of the National Association of Secondary School Principals, echoes this approach that students should take an active role in their learning rather than as passive recipients of information passed on by textbooks and lectures.

Two phrases always to keep in mind are *avoid boredom* and *avoid tedium.* Providing a variety of learning methods is the most effective approach to move from focusing on teaching to focusing on learning—to move from what is taught to what is caught. The more ways we teach, the more students we reach.

Consider the following statistics on learning. We retain 10% of what we read, 20% of what we hear, 30% of what we see, 50% of what we see and hear, 70% of what we say, and 90% of what we say and do. (Pike) An old Chinese proverb states the idea succinctly:

I hear and I forget. I see and I remember. I do and I understand.

Telling is not teaching, and listening is not learning. The best way to learn is to become a teacher—in part because staying active makes learning attractive. Learning occurs when the learner does work. This is one basis for cross-age tutoring. If you have large classes, teaching students to teach others should be considered, not only to reduce the teaching-learning ratio but also to increase personalization. Cooperative learning and think-pair-share activities can play an important role here. Pairing and sharing is especially effective because working with one other person poses little threat, prevents anonymity, and obtains high participation.

3. Shifting from calling on individual students (at the expense of not calling on others) to 100 percent student participation

Rather than asking the class a question and then having students raise their hands for attention, *pose* a question. Learning partners or groups then grapple with a response. Students quickly learn that the teacher is interested in everyone's involvement. Students who are correct still gain the internal satis-faction that comes from "being right."

A concluding comment: A significant thought to keep in mind is, "Asking is the key to the target." Asking questions starts the thinking process. Smart questions activate the brain. A good question can be the most effective hook for engagement. Asking effective questions is so important that much of this book relies on honing this skill.

4. Shifting from one-size fits all to differentiated instruction

Differentiated instruction is an attempt to create different pathways for optimal learning since students vary in academic abilities, learning styles, personalities, interests, knowledge, experiences, and motivation. The following is an example of differentiation for students in a middle or high school science class designed for learning the workings of a cell.

The teacher first reflects:

What should students KNOW? *The cell parts and their functions.*

What should students UNDERSTAND? *The cell has interrelated parts where everything affects everything else.*

What should students be able TO DO? *Analyze these interrelationships in a way that makes clear to their peers how the cell actually works.*

After a class lecture on cells, students choose from the following:

- Design a graph and label the parts with directional markers to be sure someone who is clueless about cells understands them.
- Relate cells to human interactions such as a family, an orchestra, basketball team where each has a different part to play. Emphasize the individual parts and the relationships.
- Use materials in the classroom room to make little cells.
- Compose a story as though the cell is the story: Who is the protagonist? Who is the antagonist? Who is trying to damage the cell?
- If you don't like any of these and have a different or better idea for your learning, talk to the teacher.

Students are then grouped in threes for two times:
  1st time: Share with others who used the same approach.
  2nd time: Share with people who used a different approach.

KEY POINTS

◆ When planning lessons, the acronym "LIMES" assists in keeping some key ideas in mind. The "L" refers to left-right brain hemisphericity to incorporate sequential as well as random organizing. The "I" refers to employing different types of intelligences. The "M" refers to varying activities by tapping into visual, aural, and kinesthetic modalities. The "E" refers to emotions that can either interfere with or enhance learning. The "S" indicates that people have different learning styles and that a variety of activities needs to be incorporated in lessons.

◆ In addition to planning activities to hook students to the lesson, time should also be planned at the end of the lesson for reflection.

◆ Using levels of intellect ensures that students learn thinking and evaluating skills in addition to simply gaining information.

◆ Asking "what" questions, using wait time, calling on students after a question, not repeating responses, and posing questions all enhance participation and learning.

◆ Using group questioning strategies allows the teacher to have more control over the direction of a lesson.

◆ Choosing key words to frame questions enhances thinking.

◆ Imaging and visualization techniques promote retention.

◆ Stories clothe facts, thereby aiding retention.

◆ Metacognition—being aware of one's own thinking process— improves thinking skills.

◆ Using music, bright colors, and other approaches that appeal to the senses enhances learning.

◆ Laser learning—having students frequently think and share in short segments—increases retention and lets students discover what needs to be reviewed.

CLASSROOM MANAGEMENT

*Effective classroom management relies on
the use of procedures—not rules.*

Classroom management is about strategies to make instruction and learning efficient. *Good classroom management reduces behavior problems.*

ESTABLISHING PROCEDURES

Just as teachers, administrators, and other staff members know what to do when entering school, so should students know what to do when they enter a classroom. (Wong)

Students need to be inducted into the organization of the classroom. The way to do this is to teach procedures. For example, before having a classroom meeting, the first procedure is to quickly and quietly arrange the chairs in a circle. No meeting starts until this procedure is implemented successfully. Procedures should be taught before content. The aphorism *process precedes product* should be noted.

Procedure gives structure, which is especially important for at-risk students. The label "at-risk" has nothing to do with intelligence. It simply means these students are in danger of failing or dropping out of school. Often, the lives of at-risk students are chaotic, and the only part of their lives that is stable is school. The reason they are in danger is simply because they don't do their work. A prime reason why they don't do their work is that they lack structure, and procedures can establish that needed stability.

Too often, we assume that children know what we know and what we want them to do. This is especially true with procedures. Assume nothing—other than the fact that students may not be sure what is wanted.

TEACHING ROUTINES

Structure activities or arrange the environment to reduce or eliminate conflict.

In the elementary grades, this pertains to both indoor and outdoor activities. Establishing a "getting drinks" routine after vigorous playground activities is an example of an outdoor procedure. Children whose last names are in the first half of the alphabet will use the fountain by the restrooms. Those in the last half will walk to another designated drinking fountain. The person behind the drinker will slowly count to ten and then tap the drinker softly on the shoulder. Before initiating the procedure, have students experience it. Line up everyone for a dry run.

Reinforce the routine for lining up before entering the room at the start of the day. One teacher reminds her students that when they enter to put their backpacks away, sharpen pencils, place home assignments and lunch money on the desk, and begin their proofreading. Another does not allow students to bend her ear as they enter the classroom at the beginning of the school day, or after recess, or after lunch. Rather, she carefully watches how students enter and watches to see them start immediately on the assignment on the board or overhead projector. Then, once all are on task, she gives her attention to those who need it.

Professional judgment is required at all times to bring about optimal behavior. In the morning, it may be preferable to have students enter the room and start working immediately. After lunch or a morning break, allowing the students time to settle down may be more practical.

It is good to remember that with any new activity, such as a special game or a chance to touch a visiting pet, conflicts will occur—unless some management procedures have been established first.

ATTENTION MANAGEMENT

Too much time is often wasted regaining students' attention during or when ending an activity. Even the procedure of raising hands needs to be taught and practiced because it has three parts: prompt, focus, and signal. The *prompt* is when the teacher's hand is raised. Students who see the raised hand of the teacher *focus* on the teacher by raising their hands and stopping their activity. The *signal* means these students, whose attention is back with the teacher, signal other students still involved in the activity to give their attention to the teacher. Note that the responsibility for bringing back the attention of the entire class belongs to the students, not the teacher.

Telling students the routine will not suffice. Students need to practice seeing the teacher's hand raised, focusing by raising their hands, and then signaling others whose hands are not raised. The routine should be practiced until the teacher is satisfied with obtaining the attention of the entire class within a very few moments. Periodically, the routine may need to be practiced again.

Fun can also be incorporated for elementary grades, such as in getting students' attention by saying "FREEZE," where students instantaneously hold their positions whatever they may be doing at the moment. The position is released with "UNFREEZE." Another technique is to say, "Clap once if you can hear my voice." "Clap twice if you can hear my voice." The second round of putting hands together will gain everyone's attention.

Students in any grade level or class can always be asked for their suggestions. The key here is to establish at least one attention management routine so the attention of all students can be gained within a matter of moments.

SPONGE ACTIVITIES

When students enter the classroom, they should immediately become engaged in a learning experience. They may write in a journal, analyze a cartoon projected by an overhead projector, complete some assignment on the board, identify significant learning from yesterday's lesson, or some other useful activity that soaks up time while the teacher takes attendance or engages in some other routine. Nonactivity at the beginning of a period is a waste of time because the beginning of the period is an important learning time. (Sousa, 1995, p. 58)

REDUCING TARDIES

If tardiness is a problem in middle or high school, use something positive.

Give students an occasional one-question quiz at the start of the period. The question can cover home assignments, recently presented information, or anything that the teacher wants to reinforce. The quiz is for extra credit only; it can help a grade, but not hurt one. When the tardy bell rings, the responses are collected, or, if the school does not use bells, collect the quizzes two minutes into the period.

Starting class with an interesting or novel activity can also reduce tardies. All students, even high school seniors, enjoy listening to good stories. Start reading the story right at the official starting time of the class. Do not expect students to automatically appear on time the next day. However, you will have more success with many chronic latecomers if you do not bring attention to their late entering. Do not fret that your lack of attention to these students will encourage others to enter late. After a few days, most of your latecomers will arrive on time and in an orderly manner. If students are boisterous when entering the class, reading an interesting story will have more success in their entering in a quiet manner than any means of coercion. Stop and wait until they settle down; then continue. After a few days, their manners will change.

If a student continues to come late, personalize your relationship. Ask the student if coming to class late is really what the student *wants*. Then ask what the student is *doing* that prevents him from arriving on time. Contrasting what the student *wants* with what the student is *doing* leads to self-evaluation and the opening to develop a *plan*. The plan must originate with the student, although the teacher can certainly make suggestions. If the student continues to come late, have the student develop specific *procedures* to implement the plan. The key to success with this type of student is for the *student* to develop the plan, for the *student* to itemize specific procedures, and for the *student* to visualize specific activities—even to the point where the student visualizes walking into the class before the class starts.

A final point with chronic latecomers: Many of these students do not enjoy being late. They mentally punish themselves when they are late. Adding external punishment does little to help them solve their time-management problem. A contract with a consequence may alter behavior temporarily but will not be nearly so effective as personalizing your relationship with the student.

TAKING ATTENDANCE

Taking attendance should not subtract from learning time. While students are engaged in the sponge learning activity, take roll. In middle and high schools, have a student assist. In the class where the master absence list is developed, the helper takes out the cards (if the system uses them) that need to be sent to the office. During other periods, the helper checks the absence list and assists by completing any necessary forms while the teacher enters appropriate marks in the rollbook. Attendance is taken in less than one minute.

PASSING AND COLLECTING MATERIALS

Establishing routines for supplies and materials should be one of the first management decisions.

Use student assistants. For example, if the sponge activity is to write in journals, have two students volunteer to pass out the journals before the class starts. These students will arrive at class early because they have that responsibility. Students know where other students sit and can place the journals on the appropriate desks before most of the students enter.

When books or supplies are distributed and returned, establish a traffic pattern for collectors and distributors to ensure a smooth operation. For example, establishing a clockwise walking pattern in a crowded classroom prevents unnecessary physical contact.

HOME ASSIGNMENTS FOR ABSENTEES

At middle and high schools, when a student returns from an absence, one of the first orders of the day is to obtain any assignments that were missed. A simple procedure is to label a standard composition book for each period. When an assignment is given to the class, a student records it in the "assignment book." Then, when a student returns after an absence, the returning student obtains the missed assignment from that book. If any additional explanation is necessary, it can be given at an appropriate time during the period.

If students collaborate by using learning buddies, then the buddy can be responsible for informing the absent student. The assignment can be shared upon the absentee's return or, even better, by the buddy who informs the absentee by telephone or e-mail.

LENDING PENCILS

Beyond primary grades, where materials should be readily available, lending pencils is a constant activity. Getting pencils back can be challenging.

Teach the term "collateral." When borrowing a pencil, the student leaves a personal item, such as a quarter or a house key. Students do not forget to retrieve personal items of value. Certain students who are constantly borrowing from others are met with the response, "What's your collateral?"

SHARPENING PENCILS

Sharpening a pencil while the teacher is talking can be avoided with a simple procedure. When a student wants to sharpen a pencil, the student holds the pencil up as a communication signal. At a convenient time, nod—granting permission to go to the pencil sharpener.

Some elementary teachers restrict pencil sharpening to the beginning of the school day and after lunch. At any other time, they trade for a pencil in one of the pencil boxes around the room. Boxes are marked "sharp" or "dull." Students put their dull pencils in a "dull" box in order to take a pencil from a "sharp" box.

USE OF SUPPLIES

Let students know that they need to make their supplies last. Unless students are taught and practice some procedures, the supplies will be depleted well before expected. Coloring pens are a case in point. Students need to practice listening for the cap to snap on the pen. Otherwise, pens will dry out sooner than expected.

TEACHER ASSISTANCE TO A GROUP

When students are working in groups, the teacher needs some indication of which teams need assistance.

When students are working collaboratively, the use of colored cups allows the teacher to prioritize attention according to student need. Each group has three cups (available at any party store). The cups are placed upside down, each inside the other. When the green cup is showing, no assistance is needed. When the yellow cup is showing, the group has a question. When the red cup is showing, the group needs help.

INDIVIDUAL TEACHER ASSISTANCE

The best way to learn is to teach. Make it a policy that a student who has a question asks two other students for assistance before requesting help from the teacher. The first question the teacher asks the student who needs help is, "Whom did you ask for assistance?" Aside from reinforcing the procedure, this also helps the teacher know if others have the same or a similar question.

INSTRUCTIONAL FEEDBACK

During a lesson, feedback from students lets the teacher know how successfully the lesson is going.

A simple technique is to have students point their thumbs up if they understand and thumbs down if they don't. For elementary students, another strategy is to use small cards of different colors. For example, when the teacher says, "Show me if you agree or disagree," students who do not agree raise a red card and students who do agree raise a blue card. Active participation makes students accountable and is more effective than calling on one student at a time to answer a question.

Another technique is to follow up a student's answer by asking the class, "Who agrees?" "Who disagrees?" Then follow up with, "Why do you disagree?"

Students who are not successful during guided practice time can be placed in a small group(s) for tutorial work with the teacher, while the other students can continue with independent work or another assignment.

CRUMPLING PAPERS—A PET PEEVE

When a student crumples papers while others are concentrating, the sound has a tendency to break preoccupation. The crinkling may be even more upsetting when it occurs as the teacher is talking. Showing students how to fold hot dogs and hamburgers can halt these unwelcome sounds. A paper folded vertically (left to right) is a hot dog. A paper folded horizontally (top to bottom) is a hamburger. Students have a choice of folding patterns when they want to discard a paper. Folding papers into hot dogs and hamburgers takes up no desk space because something else can be placed on top of it.

DISMISSAL PROCEDURES FOR MIDDLE AND HIGH SCHOOLS

The *teacher,* rather than an automated sound system, should dismiss students.

Depending upon the grade level and class, the dismissal may be by rows, sections, or in unison. Before dismissal, however, the teacher has the responsibility to ensure that the students leave behind them a classroom ready for the next class. Incoming students have a right to enter a clean and well-organized classroom.

This can be accomplished by assigning students various projects to be done toward the end of the period. Even though a teacher may be absorbed with the lesson or with individual students and forget that dismissal time is approaching, the student helpers become reminders when they start clean-up procedures. Carrying around the wastepaper basket, collecting materials, stacking materials, and placing the desks in order are done before dismissal in a well-managed classroom.

Remember reflection time. A few minutes before dismissal is an excellent time for students to reflect. A simple activity is to choose one learning from the lesson and share it with a learning buddy.

KEY POINTS

◆ The key to effective classroom management is establishing procedures.

◆ Structure activities or arrange the environment to reduce or eliminate conflict.

◆ Establish some prompt to regain attention when you want to address the class.

◆ When students enter the classroom, they should immediately become engaged in a meaningful learning experience.

◆ Taking attendance should not subtract from learning time. Take roll while students are engaged in a learning activity.

◆ Establish routines for supplies and materials as one of the first management decisions.

◆ Teach the term "collateral" and use it when lending pencils.

◆ The teacher, rather than an automated sound system, should dismiss students.

_____

Before reading the next section, please see Preliminary Note on page 38.

HOME ASSIGNMENTS

Showing how the home assignment is in the
students' own best interests
is the most effective approach.

Home assignments are an extension of instruction. They are related to teaching and learning, not to discipline in the sense of classroom disruptions or social irresponsibility.

PURPOSE

Home assignments provide opportunities to practice and improve skills or gain further knowledge or understanding. Home assignments also teach lessons that cannot be measured, such as self-discipline, perseverance, and time management. Home assignments teach how to begin a task, complete it, and be responsible for the outcome.

CONSIDERATIONS

Especially at the elementary grades, home assignments need to be tempered with considerations for other demands on young people's time. Home assignments have modest influence on achievement in the early grades. When the amount and number of assignments become overwhelming, negative attitudes about school and learning result. Assignments should be short, interesting, and easy to complete *by the students*. Leave the more demanding work for the classroom.

More than 100 studies have shown that it is not until middle school that home assignments really begin to pay off. (Begley, March 1998, p. 51)

ASSIGNING

In order to make home assignments attractive, offer the choice of two assignments. Be sure students understand the purpose of the assignments. Periodically, have a short discussion of the benefits. Ask for input from students. Explain what you believe students will learn or accomplish from an assignment, and then ask for suggestions.

Home assignments should be focused. For example, rather than asking students to write about an open-ended theme from a novel that the class is reading, ask them to pick one character and explain why that character behaved in a particular way.

SCAFFOLDING

Assigning a chapter to read before it is discussed in class is almost useless. The practice works only if the teacher does some pre-teaching by providing a cognitive map—an organizing scheme or scaffold. A scaffold is a frame built before constructing something. Building a scaffold for students makes it easier for them to make sense of what is being read. Give them clues about the chapter. Then, when they are motivated enough to read, they will enjoy the satisfaction of discovery.

Another approach is to teach students to preview or "multipass" by passing through the chapter looking for organizers before reading it. This scanning includes headings, subheadings, bold print and italics, chapter summary, pictures and graphs, objectives, chapter questions, and vocabulary words that are listed.

REDUCING THE CORRECTION OF HOME ASSIGNMENTS

Since we learn best by teaching, have students become teachers. For example, before the teacher checks any essay, at least two other people should check it. When final papers are submitted, they will be of higher quality and more enjoyable to read. Also, when papers are submitted, refrain from correcting them. Instead, make a comment such as, "You have a spelling error in this paragraph." "Check for noun-verb agreement in this sentence." Using abbreviations will save time: "✓ SP" and "✓ n-v agr." This "grappling" by the student encourages self-evaluation and self-correction.

Save time with arithmetic by selecting only five problems to correct, rather than checking all answers. The problems may be the last five or any five problems. When students submit their papers, correct only these pre-selected problems. Looking at only these will give you enough indication of whether or not more time needs to be invested in a review lesson with selected students.

Review *Collaborative Evaluation*, the last topic in the section *Collaboration—Rather than Competition—for Quality Learning* in Chapter 4.

KEY POINTS

◆ Home assignments are an extension of instruction. They are related to teaching and learning, not to discipline as it applies to inappropriate behavior.

◆ Evaluate the importance and necessity of each home assignment.

◆ Hold a quick discussion of what will be gained by the assignment.

◆ Point out what key things to look for before giving a reading assignment.

CONCLUSION

Anyone can lead one to the classroom,
but only a teacher can lead one to learn.

Curriculum, instruction, classroom management, and discipline are four separate entities. Curriculum has to do with *what* is taught, instruction with *how* the curriculum is taught and learned, and classroom management with how instruction is made *efficient.* Discipline has to do with *student* behavior. Whereas curriculum, instruction, and classroom management are the teacher's responsibility, *discipline is the student's responsibility.*

When a student disrupts the lesson, the teacher must determine from which category the problem emanates. Is the *curriculum* lacking in interest, relevancy, enjoyment, or usefulness? Is the *instruction* interactive and engaging to students? Is *classroom management* efficient? Or, is the student lacking *self-discipline?* Answers to these questions help point to the most effective resolution of the problem.

6
PARENTING

TIPS FOR PARENTS

An acorn is capable of becoming a mighty oak,
but it will never become a giant redwood—
no matter how much you push it.
Discover your child's nature and then nurture that nature.
–Jim Cathcart

Being a parent can be as frustrating and stressful as it is rewarding and joyful. Parenting is often fraught with emotional baggage and habits left over from our own childhoods. Yet, it is possible to break free of such habits and offer our children guidance without guilt or blame. When we plant flowers and they do not grow as we would like, we don't blame them, we look for reasons why the flowers are not doing well. Yet, when we have problems with our children, we too often blame them—along with criticizing and nagging them. But if we know how to influence them, they will mature, which is what we want. This does not mean we can change their nature, but we can certainly nourish them to become responsible and contributing members of society. The challenge for many parents today is one of being neither overly strict nor overly permissive. This chapter focuses on how to accomplish both.

PRACTICE POSITIVITY

One of the most effective ways to influence and to reduce stress for both parent and child is to communicate using positive messages. Just think for a moment of your reaction when someone made a positive statement about you. On the other hand, think about your emotions when someone said something that you interpreted as criticism or blame. People do better when they feel better, not worse. Yet, we often ignore this common-sense approach and send negative messages because we allow our impulses to direct what we do.

The first step to reducing stress is simply to become aware of the number of times you state something negatively that could be stated positively. For example, suppose you have an adolescent who would like to visit her friend on a school night. You are concerned that home assignments be completed first. When your child asks, "Can I go to Hillary's house?" your response may likely be, "Not until you finish your home assignments." If you practice the mental habit of positivity, your response would be something like, "Sure, you can go—as soon as your assignments are finished" or simply, "When you are satisfied with your assignments." Two very important principles are at work here. In the latter two statements, the responsibility is clearly on the young person, where it belongs, and, in addition, you have conveyed a message of trust. Notice that the responses, whether stated negatively or positively, are basically the same. That is, the home assignments will be completed before the youngster visits the friend. However, how the message is received is dramatically different.

Here is another example where positivity is used and where the responsibility is placed on the youngster. It is natural for a parent to admonish a young child before the child leaves for school. The parent may say, "Don't forget your lunch," or "Don't forget to take your key." A more effective approach to accomplish the same objective is to say, "Check your list." This approach not only eliminates nagging, but it puts the responsibility on the youngster, who has made the list perhaps with your assistance. Lists can be made for school-related assignments and materials, appropriate dress pertaining to inclement weather, or other situations that the child can check before leaving.

Stating ideas in positive terms not only reduces stress, it also builds trust, avoids conflicts in interactions, and increases the amount of satisfaction and contentment. Consider the woman who reduced her aggravation every time her husband or two children dropped their dirty clothes on the floor instead of putting them in the hamper. The situation became unfair to the others as well because the sight of the dropped clothes so bothered her that she indiscriminately blew up at all members of the family. She then asked herself, "How could I turn this into a positive situation for me as well as for them?" She told her family that whenever any clothes were found on the floor, she would pick them up, as she would do anyway, but the culprit owed her a five-minute backrub, collectable whenever she wanted it and done lovingly. The result not only freed the air of a lot of negativity, but she received a number of loving backrubs. Also, fewer clothes began appearing on the floor.

John Goddard, perhaps the world's most famous lecturer on travel adventures, relates how his father handled situations. When John was eight years old, he told his father he wanted to be a fireman. His father did not tell him that he could fall off the fire truck as it turned around a corner or how dangerous fire fighting is. When John was ten, he told his father that he wanted to be a policeman. His father did not tell him that police work is a dangerous profession, that he might get hurt, and that it required rigorous training. Instead, his father told him that he would look fine in a blue uniform with copper buttons. His parents never fed him any negatives. The lesson Goddard makes is that when parents look at and talk to children, they should *empower them, rather than instill fears.*

Another way to communicate in a positive manner is to comment on the youngster's action, rather than on the youngster himself. Separating the deed from the doer is one of the most important attributes of *The Raise Responsibility System.* The adult does not identify the young person's action; instead, the youngster himself identifies a level of social development. Doing so automatically separates the act from the actor and prompts the young person to reflect and accept responsibility. No embarrassment is involved and no dignity is lost. A major advantage of the approach is total acceptance from the parent, rather than conditional acceptance. The message communicated is that the child is always accepted, but collaboration is necessary so everyone can be satisfied with the child's actions.

This concept of separating the person from an action, that is, separating love from behavior, applies well to giving a money allowance. A prime purpose for giving an allowance is to engage youngsters in making decisions regarding saving, spending, and charity. This is totally different from family obligations. If a parent is not satisfied with behavior or how chores are done, these should be dealt with separately, rather than by turning the allowance into a reward that is contingent on pleasing the parent.

Focusing on stating thoughts and desires in positive terms is challenging, but it is also fun. When people become aware of how often they state something negatively, they become amazed at the frequency. Just a little practice can turn what would have been a negative statement into a more positive one.

Chapter 1, *Reducing Stress,* offers additional suggestions on this topic.

OFFER CHOICES

Choices are a critical component of fostering responsibility and influencing behavior. The reason is that choice brings ownership; it fosters a sense of independence and also empowers. Offering options engages a youngster in cooperation and is much more effective than giving commands.

The choices can be limited, but the sooner a young person starts to make choices, to exercise decision making, the more responsible the youngster becomes. Of course, the choices must be ones that satisfy both parties. Suppose a youngster is asked to suggest a chore he will do. If the chore the youngster offers is not satisfactory, then the parent asks, "What else?" The same two words "What else?" "What else?" are repeated until both parties agree. Offering options, rather than imposing the chores, gives the ownership to the youngster. Later, if the youngster does not fulfill the chosen chore, rather than imposing a consequence, the consequence is *elicited* from the youngster. The two friendly words "What else?" are again used until there is agreement. Another approach regarding chores is for the parent to *add* choices. For example, if a youngster has two chores to perform and is not doing them, *add* three more so that five choices are available; the youngster then chooses two from the five. Empowering by *adding to* is a positive approach and is much more effective than threatening to remove a privilege for noncompliance, which is a negative approach.

I remember refusing to eat what my mother had given me for dinner as a youngster. This is a common way for a child to assert a desire for power. Forcing a child to eat is rather difficult and often results in the child's becoming more obstinate. My mother simply diffused the situation by asking, "Which are you going to eat first, your carrots or your peas?" Notice that in the process, the responsibility was placed on me, where it belonged.

A perennial challenge for parents has to do with the desire to be obeyed, in large part because we think that what we want is better for the youngster than what the youngster wants. Often, especially with older adolescents, parents would be well served to make the choice of *being kind, rather than of being right.* A father was seeking advice because he felt that he could not communicate with his seventeen-year-old son. The counselor asked, "Whose fault is that? Do you expect your son to communicate with you if you don't successfully communicate with him?" The counselor suggested that when the father gets home to go up to his son and say, "Son, I realize that I have not communicated the best that I can. Is it possible that you could be doing the same?" The counselor then challenged the man, "But I don't think you would have the courage to do it." Two months later, the man called and said that he had been trying to reach out, trying to communicate with his son, but had not been successful. Then came a Sunday morning when the son was in the kitchen chewing on a sandwich, and the father was in the bedroom chewing on his nails. Suddenly, the father walked into the kitchen and said, "Son, I realize that I have not communicated with you the best that I can. Is it possible that you could be doing the same?" The boy suddenly felt about ten feet tall; he lifted his father up and hugged him.

As adults can make choices to change behaviors, so can young people. Change is a product of a decision, and decisions are possible only when there are choices. Therefore, offering choices paves the way to change behavior. Remember that young people exercise choice without parents' permission. A powerful choice is to do nothing. Adults call this defiance. The most effective way to avoid this is for the adult to offer choices.

We have been brought up to believe that power corrupts and that absolute power corrupts absolutely. However, *powerlessness* also corrupts. When people feel a lack of power, the mission becomes one of gaining it. Even children have a natural desire to feel empowered. Offering options is an easy way to accomplish this. As long as a young person has a choice, the youngster does not lose— and not losing is more important than winning.

Chapter 1 offers additional suggestions on this topic.

ENCOURAGE REFLECTION

The underlying theory behind every strategy in this book is geared toward reflection. Reflection is simply the act of thinking about our relationships, our desires, and our behaviors. The purpose of reflection is to stimulate *internal motivation,* which is far more effective in changing behavior than anything that is imposed externally. Even though we may temporarily control others, we don't change them. Besides, controlling others is counterproductive to the very thing we want, which is having them *want* to change. The question then becomes one of how to influence others to change themselves. The most effective and powerful approach is to have them reflect.

My wife and I visited our cousins, and we accompanied them when they picked up their daughters. One was at a babysitter's while the other was at a friend's home. Before the children were picked up, the parents described their daughters. The six-year-old was a parent's dream. The three-and-a-half-year-old was a real challenge. The parents told us that the younger daughter had a difficult time sharing. In preschool, she would express her unhappiness by screaming out if she did not get what she wanted. The parents described her as being very manipulative.

When both girls were in the car, my wife and I announced that we had a gift for them but that the store only had one Versatile set left. (Versatiles are manipulatives that come in a long narrow container. They are tiles of different shapes with numbers on the reverse sides. The object is to match the designs to make certain patterns. When the tiles are turned over, the numbers appear in a certain order.) I asked the girls if they would mind sharing. They assured me that there would be no problem.

At the house, after showing the girls how the Versatiles were used, it was agreed that the younger daughter would have the first turn. It was also agreed that each would have two turns before sharing. The younger sister, after her allotted two turns, did not want to give the set to her sister. I reminded her of the agreement wherein each player was to receive two turns. She ignored my comment.

I asked myself, "What can I *ask,* not tell, to have her reflect on the agreement in order to have her take responsibility?" As she was playing with the set for the third time, I asked, "Was this your second try at your second game?" The youngster looked at me and then gave the set to her sister. Asking a reflective question was more successful than using coercive persuasion in any of its various forms.

Later, I shared some questioning techniques with the parents, ones that would prompt the challenging child to reflect and think about her actions. When I spoke to the father months later, he told me that his younger daughter was still very clever at winning but that she had stopped her outbursts when she did not get her way.

Sometimes we need to be happy with only a single step in the right direction. A single is not a home run, but it gets the player to first base and going in the desired direction. In the situation with my cousin's daughter, the child was not pleased that she gave up the set when she still wanted to play with it. I was not pleased that she did not share after her allotted second try. However, progress was made. I was satisfied with a step in the right direction.

Criticizing, complaining, and nagging are coercive, external approaches and are often stress-inducing. In addition, such approaches engender resistance rather than responsibility. Forcing responsibility is difficult and perhaps even impossible because, although responsibility can be assigned, it only becomes effective when voluntarily taken. *Awareness* and *ownership* always precede taking responsibility. That is the reason why asking effective questions is so successful in changing behavior. Questions direct the other person's thinking. It is the questioning process that starts the thinking process, both for the questioner as well as for the person answering. This is the reason why smart communicators ask smart questions. They not only hear the answers, but also the person asked hears his own answers. The person answering gains clarity.

Furthermore, the answers that are most effective for people are their own. People don't argue with their own statements. There is immediate ownership, and ownership is a critical component to self-evaluation and change.

It is because effective questioning directs thinking to self-evaluation that it is one of the most valuable skills to be cultivated when working with anyone, especially young people.

USE EFFECTIVE QUESTIONS

Here is an invaluable set of four questions that leads to a change in behavior:

    (1) "What do you *want?*"

        Asking this question stimulates thinking and leads to reflection.

(2) "Is what you are *choosing to do* helping you get what you want?"

This question leads to evaluation of one's behavior.

(3) "If what you are choosing to do is not getting you what you want, then what is your *plan*?"

This question encourages the making of a plan. The plan may be made solely by the young person or with assistance, but it must be the youngster's plan, not the adult's.

(4) "What are your *procedures* to implement your plan?" Or, for a younger child, "What steps will you take to make your plan work?"

This question leads to mental imaging and specific steps that will be taken to carry out the plan. These implementation ideas can come about with the assistance of the parent, but, as with the previous question, should be elicited from the young person before the adult makes a suggestion. *"What else?"* is a good follow-up question to encourage more specificity.

A question that has a positive focus is more effective than one that invites a negative response. For example, "What is the best thing that happened today?" elicits a more positive response than, "What happened today?"

As emphasized in Chapter 1 in the section *The Importance of Reflection and Self-Evaluation,* the quality of the answers depends on the quality of the questions. The parents spent $500 to send the youngster to summer camp. Upon return, the parents ask, "How was camp?" The youngster responds, "O.K." That is all the parents receive for their camp expenditure. However, the youngster's response would have been completely different had the parents asked a more specific question: "What was the most enjoyable experience you had at camp?" This question leads the youngster to reflect and relive an enjoyable experience.

Persistence may be necessary, especially with adolescents. Be persistent and patient, as was done with a fifteen-year-old girl who had low self-esteem and a bad attitude. The parent knew about asking effective questions, so instead of the normal evening greeting, "How was your day?" the parent asked, "What was the best thing that happened to you today." The youngster replied, "Nothing. Get off my back!" The parent did not give up. The same question was asked several times over a period of weeks, getting the same negative response. Weeks later, the daughter came in for breakfast and said, "I already know what is the best thing that will happen to me today." The parent was startled by this uncharacteristic expression but asked, "What is it?" The teenager replied with a big smile, "I woke up thinking about the best thing that will happen to me today."

Following are some questions particularly effective with young people:

- What have you done to get what you want?
- What can you do to improve the situation?
- What are you doing that is working?
- How would you describe the way you want it to turn out?
- What were you able to do today better than in the past?
- To what do you attribute your doing better today?
- What did you learn about doing it that you can apply to other areas?
- What was special for you about what you did?
- What was most pleasing for you today?
- What would you like to look forward to for tomorrow?
- What do you most appreciate?
- What plans do you have for the future?
- What would motivate you to use your plan?
- What do you see as your next step?
- How can I help you?
- On a scale of 1 to 10, how have things been in the past 3 days? What would it take to make a 10?

I was seated on an airplane next to an active young boy whose mother was having a challenging time with him. During the course of the flight, the young boy took the phone out of its security case from the back of the seat in front of him and started to play with it. I leaned over to him and asked, "What would happen if you broke the phone?" Without a moment's hesitation, the youngster replaced the phone. The question that I asked led to quick reflection. Rather than aiming at obedience by telling the youngster what to do, I aimed at responsibility. Telling the boy what to do may have led to the same result, but I doubt if it would have been nearly so effective or have led to such a rapid response.

Asking effective questions is a skill and requires practice. Thinking about a skill is not practicing the skill. Thinking is necessary for focus, but only the actual asking of questions in real situations is practicing the skill. We learn to do something by doing it—not by *thinking* it or *trying* to do it. Trying to stand is not standing. You either stand or you don't. Asking a person to try to take a $5.00 bill from your hand will result in this awareness. If the person takes the bill, the person did not *try*; the person actually did it. If the person just *tried* to take the money, it would still be in your hand.

It is almost impossible to raise a child without criticizing. One way to reduce criticism is to turn it into questions. Asking, "If you were to do that over again, what would you do differently?" will get the message across without bringing aggravation to the parent and negative feelings to the child.

As parents, we can also reflect by the questions we ask ourselves, such as, "Am I proud of the way I interacted with my child?" "Would I be offended if someone interacted with me as I interacted with my child?" "What is my plan for next time?"

LISTEN TO LEARN

If I were limited to one recommendation that would improve relationships between parent and child, especially with teenagers, it would be *listen to learn.* Listening and valuing young people's feelings and ideas is what promotes the ability of parents to effectively communicate with them.

Listen to learn means not inserting one's opinion and not judging what the youngster says *while the youngster is speaking.* Parents have a natural tendency to approve or disapprove of young people's statements. Parents' first reaction is to evaluate from their own point of view and then approve or disapprove of what the youngster says. This is listening autobiographically. The tendency to make evaluations is common in almost all conversations, but it is much more intense when feelings are involved. An easy strategy for replacing this tendency of listening autobiographically is to cultivate the habit of listening to learn.

Listening in anticipation of what a child will say is also a habit to be broken. Listening in anticipation encourages interruptions. A child wants to be acknowledged and does not wish to feel that you know what he is about to say. A parent who listens well acknowledges the youngster's feelings and opinions. In addition, listening well can be a model for adolescents, who often do not listen well.

"Zip the lip" is extremely difficult for a parent, but it is the surest way to improve communication and understanding. *No great insight ever enters the mind through an open mouth.* It is important to let young people know that a parent is willing to listen, even though it may not result in agreement. A simple, "Talk to me about it" is an effective start toward dialogue. Just use the most effective sales principle: *Inquiry precedes advocacy.*

LIMIT LECTURING AND TELLING

Parents fear that children will not make responsible decisions, so lecturing begins. This implies that the parents do not have faith in their children's decision-making abilities. After awhile, children lose faith in themselves, in their own inner knowing. If young people do not have faith in themselves, then the parents' faith in them decreases even more, and the lecturing begins again.

Even well-intentioned lectures convey the subtle, negative message that what the youngster has done is wrong or not good enough. This often results in defensiveness and resistance, especially with adolescents. If telling worked, young people would do exactly what they were told. Trying to persuade adolescents by using reason often has little effect; they know they are right. In addition, the youngster sees this as, "My parents are trying to control me again!" An adage when dealing with young people is not to say more than thirteen words at a time, and with a teenager, make it twelve.

Since young people are sensitive about being told what to do, yet parental help is perfectly appropriate, think of suggestions as questions: "What do you think about…?" "Have you thought of…?" "Would you consider…?"

A habit is most easily changed by replacing it with another. When there is a temptation to tell, redirect it by thinking of the question, "Will the results be better if I tell or ask?" Another approach is to follow Harry S Truman's approach: "I have found the best way to give advice to your children is to find out what they want, and then advise them to do it."

CHECK ASSUMPTIONS

Some of the decisions we make are based on inaccurate assumptions. We may know exactly what we are thinking and what we mean, but the child may have a completely different perspective.

In a Calvin and Hobbs comic strip, Calvin says to his mom, "I'm hungry. Can I have a snack?" His mom says, "Sure. Help yourself." In the next scene, Calvin is walking through the living room carrying a big cookie jar, one cookie in his hand and another cookie in his mouth. He hears his mom say, "You can have an apple or an orange from the fridge." Calvin stands there and thinks, "Even though we are both speaking English, we are not speaking the same language." Calvin's definition of a snack is a cookie. His mother's definition of a snack is an apple or orange.

A father is walking through the forest with his three-year-old daughter. As they are walking, he repeatedly tells her to stay on the path. The little girl is walking all around. She looks at this tree, that bush, meanders here and there. He continually says, "Stay on the path. I told you to stay on the path." Eventually, he gets so angry with her that he pulls her over, shakes her a bit, and shouts, "I told you to stay on the path!" The little girl looks up at him with tears in her eyes and says, "Daddy, what's a path?"

FOCUS ON THE IMPORTANT

Choose your battles. While clashes may be unavoidable, it is not necessary to get pulled into every skirmish. An effective strategy here is to ponder the answer to the question, "Will this matter a week from now?"

Youngsters explore and try out different roles. These can be irritating and bewildering. As painful as it may be to watch, it is one way that young people learn to function on their own. As a rule of thumb, *only make a fuss about those issues that are harmful to the youngster or others, or are irreversible.* Wearing baggy pants or an "outrageous" hat at thirteen may not be very serious; getting a large tatoo on your arm with controversial language is serious. Situations that involve safety or that are illegal or immoral are non-negotiable.

ASK FOR ASSISTANCE

As no one can place knowledge or wisdom into the head of another, so no one can make another person responsible. Although responsibility can be delegated, it does not become effective until taken. A much-overlooked opportunity is for young people to help parents. In former generations, the parents were the center of the household and children were expected to assist in the running of that household. Very often in today's family, the emphasis is on giving to children, rather than on the children doing the giving.

An effective way for parents to gain respect and assistance is to refrain from doing some favors for their youngsters and let their youngsters perform services for them. A simple way to do this is for the parent to express a need, giving the child an opportunity to help. Children (and adults) grow by giving. Some examples are, "I need quiet time," "I need you to help me put the groceries away," or "I need your help with dinner." Machiavelli made the point: *People are by nature as much bound by the benefits they confer as by those they receive.*

A request for assistance is easy to hear. This approach is proactive and is more effective than a reactive approach that criticizes, blames, or complains, such as, "You should have helped me with the groceries."

RECOGNIZE IMPLICIT MESSAGES

Parents deliver explicit messages unaware of sending implicit ones. "Explicit" refers to the actual words stated. "Implicit" refers to what is learned by inference. For example, tickets for a movie theater are more expensive for a thirteen-year-old than for a twelve-year-old. The parent wants to save money so the thirteen-year-old daughter is told to state her age as twelve. The explicit message is that saving money is desirable; however, the implicit message is that being dishonest is acceptable.

The teenager tells the parent, "I'm going out tonight; I may be late and I may drink at the party." The parent says, "You're grounded!" The explicit message to the offspring is very clear; yet, so is the implicit message: "I don't trust you."

Here is another instance of the parent's sending one message, but the result from the implicit message is counterproductive. The eighteen-year-old calls her parent and says she drank a little too much and she wants to be picked up. This is a very responsible thing to do. However, the parent becomes angry with the daughter. On the drive home, the parent relentlessly chastises her daughter, who concludes, "I'm not going to tell my parent next time."

If parents get angry and forbid young people to do certain things, they can put their heads in the sand believing their prohibition is going to be effective. However, in more cases than we would like, offspring will do what they want anyway; they just won't talk about it to their parents. In such situations, the parents *have lost the opportunity to influence their children*—to tell them how they see the situation, to share what they did when younger, and to share their parental feelings about the situation.

Parents always need to be aware of implicit messages. When parents become upset and yell at children, the implicit message taught is that when upset, yelling is acceptable. The same goes for hitting. The parents, usually without realizing it, are teaching the youngster to deal with upsetting situations by losing control and even striking out.

FOSTER RESPONSIBILITY

Fostering responsibility should start at a very young age. A young child sits in the highchair and drinks his milk. When he is finished, he throws the bottle away. He hears the "thump" sound and likes it. He enjoys flexing his muscles. When the mother picks up the bottle, the infant is getting a message that he, to a certain extent, can control his mother. The mother decides that she is not going to let her child behave this way. The mother does not threaten or punish; she simply makes sure her hand is ready when the baby finishes the milk. She then removes the bottle and cleans his face while talking to him. The mother begins to teach her son responsible behavior at a very young age.

Very young people cannot be left to their own devices. It is a parent's responsibility to protect the child. For example, if a child runs into the street, a parent can pick up the child and put her on the sidewalk. The parent can talk to the child about the dangers of cars but needs not make the child feel blameworthy for her innocent act. Rather than focusing on what the child did wrong, a wiser approach is to have the youngster develop a plan and procedure to prevent a reoccurrence.

As children grow older, parents often resort to rules. Especially with teenagers, this invites a problem because when rules and prohibitions are established, they are seen as restrictions. Teenagers, who are asserting their independence, view restrictions as controlling. Rebellion is not their focus; rather, their focus is on finding and asserting their identity. Instead of establishing restrictions, parents can help by communicating expectations, which are much more positive. Using self-evaluative questions and entering into dialogue with teenagers is much more effective than imposing restrictions.

The media plays a significant role in the lives of youth. Young people have rights, know them, and articulate them in their parents' faces. However, rights need not be at the expense of responsibility. Treating young people with respect and dignity fosters responsibility. This is especially important during the adolescent years when parents (and youth) are under such stress. By these years, much of what parents want can only be negotiated. Parents can no longer physically control youngsters, just as they can no longer control their children's exposure to outside influences or what their children do when not in their presence.

When responsibility has been fostered, parents are always "with" young people. "What is the right thing to do?" "Do I really want this?" "Am I being manipulated?" "What would my parents think?" are constantly thoughts on their children's minds. When parents have been negotiating with children, and the children understand the difference between internal and external motivation (a prime focus of *The Raise Responsibility System*), young people find it much easier to make responsible choices.

EXHIBIT PERSONAL RESPONSIBILITY

As explained in the discussion on motivation earlier in this book, we act and communicate from the beliefs we hold. These beliefs are often not clear to us. For example, the parent praises the youngster by saying, "I am so proud of you." The implicit message the parent sends is that if the child really loved the parent, the child would always do things that make the parent proud. To a certain extent, the parent is saying that the youngster is responsible for the parent's feelings. The message sent is, "If you really loved me you would make me happy." The same message is implied when the parent makes comments like, "You're making me angry," "You're making me upset," or "You're making me sick." Comments like these place the responsibility for how the parent feels on the child. (This logic was discussed more fully in Chapter 1 in the section *The Empowerment of Choice* in the topic *Choice-Response Thinking*.)

When a parent gets upset, stimulated by a child's action, the thinking process often appears to be, "I am upset, and it is the child's fault." In these cases, the parent is not taking personal responsibility for his or her own response. The parent should be thinking, "I'm upset; how can I best handle the situation?" Instead, the parent is putting the responsibility for his or her feelings on the youngster.

Similarly, it is easy to turn this around and believe that if other people are responsible for our feelings, then we are responsible for other people's feelings. For instance, the parent feels the caretaker role and accepts responsibility for making the child happy and puts his or her own desires aside. This approach is neither good for the parent nor for the growing child. For example, when the child asks the parent to do something and the parent gives herself or himself up to do it, the parent, sooner or later, feels some anger or resentment. Just as important is the implicit learning. It teaches that the child need not value what the parent wants—that the child comes first.

The child not only learns to be manipulative *but also becomes more demanding of the parent's time.* It would be better for the parent sometimes to say, "I'll do that with you later," or "I need some time alone. You need to play by yourself now." Children learn that they can indeed make themselves happy. Of course, any parent will often put his or her child first—but not to the point of dependency, and less and less as the child grows more able to take responsibility.

It is the nature of childhood to test during this transition period between being cared for and caring for oneself. A youngster will attempt to manipulate by yelling and screaming. If the parent always gives in to the manipulation, the implicit message is that the child should use the approach again because of its success. Young people can become very good at having others take responsibility for them.

The approach of demonstrating personal responsibility is one of the hardest to implement, but the benefit is most worthwhile because the parent is role-modeling personal, responsible behavior. Needless to say, at first a child will not like it. But after a while, the youngster realizes more satisfaction by taking personal responsibility than by relying on someone else for his or her happiness. When the parent says to the child, "I have to take care of you because you can't do it for yourself," and the child goes along with it, the child's self-esteem is compromised. However, when the parent says, "I am here for you if you need me, but I have faith that you can make yourself happy," the child learns to behave in a more autonomous, responsible way.

MAINTAIN STANDARDS

The British poet Samuel Taylor Coleridge was visited by an admirer one day. During the conversation, the subject came around to children. The visitor stated that he believed children should be given free rein to think and act and learn at an early age to make their own decisions—the only way they can grow into their full potential. Coleridge invited the visitor outside to see his flower garden. The visitor took one look and exclaimed that it was nothing but a yard full of weeds. Coleridge retorted that the garden used to be filled with roses, but this year he thought that he would let the garden grow as it willed without tending to it, and that this mess was the result.

At times children, and especially adolescents, will not like what is required of them and will act as if they do not like their parents. During this time in youngsters' lives, being a parent takes precedence over being a friend. Remarks such as, "You don't understand," or "I'm the only one who has to," or "I'll die if you don't let me," are attempts to have the parent relent and say, "Yes," when the parent knows it is really best to say, "No." In these situations, the parent should focus on what is best for the youngster *in the long run.* However, in the process, the child needs to understand the reasons for the decision. A simple technique to employ when a "No" needs to be given is to place the challenge on the youngster by simply saying, "Convince me." The challenge encourages reflection and responsible thinking. This is especially important with teenagers, who want to feel right even when they are wrong.

Just as our democratic system of government needs to be learned by each generation, so do the morals, values, and ethics upon which democracy rests. In a practical sense, this means that *behaviors take precedence over feelings.* The young boy in the park goes up to a smaller boy and pushes him down, hurting the smaller boy. The mother runs to the pusher, her son, and asks, "What made you feel so bad to do a thing like that?" Even if the boy could articulate the reason, it is no excuse for what he did. Rather than feelings or excuses, *the behavior should be addressed.* Developing a sense of right and wrong takes precedence over natural impulses.

Treating young people with respect and dignity is the most effective way for a parent to receive respect in return. Parents get offended when children treat them discourteously but often fail to recognize when they themselves are not respecting their children. For example, a parent who goes through a teenager's possessions without permission is showing disrespect. Parents would get angry if the teenager went through their possessions without permission. Of course, teens owe parents the courtesy of informing them as to their whereabouts and how they can be reached. If respect and courtesy are linked and applied, much of the rule making that our children believe is the parents' way of controlling them can be eliminated.

USE AUTHORITY WITHOUT BEING PUNITIVE

The keys to the success of using authority without being punitive are in using positive communications, empowerment of choice, and reflection. These practices instill the mindset that the objective is to raise responsibility, rather than to punish. Punishment fosters evasion of responsibility and also has the disadvantage of increasing the distance between parents and children. A far more effective approach than punishment is to treat the situation as a teaching and learning opportunity. *Elicit* from the youngster what the youngster can do to ensure that the situation will not be repeated. In this way, the young person creates and maintains ownership. The implicit message is that a person is responsible for his actions and that inappropriate action is being remedied. This approach uses irresponsible behavior as an opportunity for growth.

If an elicited consequence is not appropriate or acceptable, "What else?" is asked until there is agreement on the consequence. Any consequence should fulfill three requirements:

1. The consequence should be related to the incident.
2. The consequence should be reasonable.
3. The consequence should be related to growth.

The teenage girl slams her bedroom door repeatedly. The father tells the daughter that the slamming really bothers him. The daughter agrees not to slam the door, but the behavior continues. The father tells his daughter that if she develops a procedure it would be easier for her to direct her impulse, and he communicates that he has confidence she can do this. He attempts to assist: "When walking into the bedroom," he says, "pause, turn around, then close the door." The daughter visualizes the procedure. The father invites her to suggest a better procedure or to alter his. After a few moments, they agree. However, the father now wants to be prepared to use authority, just in case the situation is repeated. So the father asks, "What could be done if it occurs again?" "What else?" "What else?" The daughter understands that the door will be removed if the slamming continues. It does. The father takes a hammer and screwdriver, taps the hinge bolts upward, removes them and the door, and puts the door in the garage. The father informs his daughter that he knows how much she desires her privacy and that he prefers to leave the door on its hinges. He tells his daughter that the door will be replaced as soon as she comes up with a more effective plan for not slamming it.

While using authority, the father approached the situation with a strategy. First, he was positive by showing faith in her and even helping her establish a procedure. Second, he helped her become aware of her choices. Third, he encouraged reflection just in case the situation was to be repeated. Finally, he followed through but still invited his daughter to make a new plan.

LET THE YOUNGSTER LEAD

If a youngster is critical of the way a parent does things, a good strategy is to let the youngster plan an activity. Assistance can be given by providing a few guidelines and a budget. This strategy will not necessarily ensure that everyone has a great time, but it eliminates much of the complaining.

A forgetful or unreliable child can also lead by being in charge of a message center, such as a "Things to Remember" board (on or near the refrigerator, of course). Things that are important, such as appointments and activities, are on the board and are read each day. "I didn't know" is not an acceptable excuse. The youngster can post messages on the board. The strategy also ensures that the youngster in charge of the board will not "forget" what is on it.

TEACH PROCEDURES TO DEAL WITH IMPULSES

Impulses, emotions, and even behavior reflexes emanate from within ourselves, even though something outside of us may have caused the stimulation. As with dreams, emanations may "pop up" without any deliberate thinking. Although the bad news is that these eruptions cannot be entirely prevented, the good news is that they can be diminished by our response to them—even to the point that they no longer direct our behavior. Our choice of how we respond to the impulse, urge, or reflex affects its frequency and strength. For example, a youngster gets angry. Unless the youngster consciously chooses to respond to the anger in a constructive way, the emotion will continue to erupt and may even increase in frequency and duration. Learning a *procedure* is the most practical way to deal with destructive thoughts, negative emotions, or inappropriate behaviors.

The most effective approach is to first recognize and teach that, *whatever the internal emanation,* the person still has a choice of responses. Here is a simple strategy for younger children. A small drawing of a traffic signal is made or purchased and the colors of the signal filled in. With older children, just a mental image of a traffic signal will do.

The RED on the top indicates to STOP and breathe *out.* When in a highly emotional state, breathing is shallow. Exhale the remaining breath. Then while slowly inhaling *with a long gasping breath,* the youngster visualizes the YELLOW of the traffic signal. During this *gasping* breathing, the jaw is opened—releasing tension—and the person is prevented from becoming emotionally hijacked. During this second phase, options are considered by asking, "What is the smartest way to handle this situation?" The GREEN of the signal indicates to go with the wisest decision. (A longer discussion of this approach is found in Chapter 4 in the section *Challenges: Impulse and Anger Management.*)

This procedure must be continually practiced until it becomes habitual. The next time the youngster allows emotions to direct his behavior, the first action should be to hold up a signal. (A few signals can be scattered around in various places for quick grabbing.)

Consequences mean nothing to a person in a highly emotional state. Using a prompt is more successful than threatening or punishing—and is less stressful on both parties.

Even very young people can learn that, although emotions and thoughts cannot be stopped from erupting, *growth and maturation come according to how people respond to them.* The more an emanation like anger is responded to with a procedure such as described above, the less its frequency and intensity become.

INTERVENE IN SIBLING SQUABBLES

Positive sibling relationships can be a source of strength for life, whereas unresolved early conflicts can create wounds that never quite heal.

When an older child is hitting his baby sister, of course the parent needs to intervene immediately and make it clear that hurting others is not acceptable. The same is true for verbal abuse between siblings, which leaves one or both constantly angry or with depleted confidence. Treating the word "hate" like a forbidden swear word and not allowing "shut up" between siblings are simple examples. Without access to this sort of incendiary language, fighting becomes less frequent. A "no hitting, no hurting" expectation can be established so the youngsters will know that they are to work out their problems peacefully.

Parents need not intervene in every children's quarrel. However, parents should intervene directly whenever an argument turns violent or threatens to do so. Most children hate fighting—even when they are winning. They do it because they do not have the tools for dealing with their frustrations. Fighters should be separated to cool off. An effective technique is to have them sit down until each gives the other permission to get up. *This technique diminishes anger more speedily than if the children are separated completely.* Parents can then listen to both parties while the youngsters come up with a solution.

Another approach is to have each sibling write down his or her side of the story. This will provide for a cooling-off period. When the parent looks at the two stories, each will be different. The charge is then given for the siblings to present an ending that both can live with. A variation is to have them write their individual stories and then read each other's. Then have them create a plan they both can agree on, even an impractical one. Anger dissipates even more as they come up with zany endings.

The strategy in Chapter 4 in the section *Conflict Resolution: Solving Circles* definitely should be reviewed.

BE AWARE OF GENDER DIFFERENCES

One of the most important parental teachings is that being different is not being wrong. Understanding differences is crucial in our diverse, civil society. Understanding differences includes how males and females operate.

Generally, girls will sit and discuss feelings rather easily. Boys usually will not. In order to get boys to express feelings, engage them in some activity, such as throwing a baseball, playing basketball, or taking a walk.

Boys have a very strong desire to feel competent. Telling a boy what to do interferes with his desire for competency, which is why boys so often react negatively even when they know a parent is correct.

Understanding the differences between parents is also helpful. Whereas a mother has a desire to protect a boy and prevent him from doing something because he may get hurt, a father may say, "Let him do it. That is how he will learn." A father is more likely to think that as long as an activity is *not life-threatening, unhealthy,* or *morally wrong,* it should be allowed. For example, a father is more willing to allow boys to engage in rough and tumble play.

This "boy-play" is natural and different from what we normally think of as negatively aggressive behavior, such as bullying. The sooner the parent intervenes when a youngster bullies, the better. Bullies tend to grow into, not out of, their behavior.

USE ACKNOWLEDGMENTS MORE THAN PRAISE

After conducting a seminar in Washington, D.C., I received a letter from one of the participants, a principal in Alexandria, Virginia. She wrote:

> Your comment about acknowledgments versus praise really hit a chord with me. My eleven-year-old daughter had done something terrific and I launched into my usual, "Oh, Honey, Mommy's so proud of you." Well, she stopped me mid-gush, put her hand on her hips and implored, "Mom, please stop!

> Whenever you do that, you make me feel like you're surprised that I can do things—like I'm not capable!"

The mother was using praise in an attempt to reward her daughter. Although the mother's intentions were honorable, the complimentary message was not congruent with the implicit message, which questioned the child's competency.

Praise, such as the kind the mother used, has its price. With older children, it can be demeaning. With young children, it encourages them to do what parents want them to do in order to make the adult happy. A statement like, "I'm so proud of you because you're such a good boy" implies that the boy is O.K. only when he is good, and that when the boy is not good, he is not O.K. Praise is also like candy; once you start giving it, stopping is difficult because the child wants it constantly.

The Virginia mother has since started to acknowledge her daughter's actions *without* constant reference to her own motherly pride. Acknowledgment simply identifies ownership and responsibility for the achievement, which has a more powerful effect for developing self-esteem.

Self-esteem has to do with (internal) feelings of competency. In this sense, people empower themselves. When the focus is on the action, then reflection and feelings of competency thrive because of the satisfaction engendered. Much of the flawed self-esteem movement is based upon an external approach, as if someone else can pass out self-esteem.

My concern with the self-esteem movement is that it encourages approaches that address the *person*, rather than the *action*. For example, rather than saying, "I'm proud of you for getting such a good grade," simply saying, "Well done!" is more meaningful and sends a more empowering message. Saying, "I see you made your bed" fosters feelings of self-competence. In contrast, saying, "I'm so proud of you for making your bed," encourages making decisions to please the parent.

Acknowledgment accomplishes the intent of praise but without the disadvantages. It fosters feelings of being worthwhile, without relying on the approval of others. The long-range effect is to engender self-confidence and self-reliance, rather than dependence on others for feelings of one's self-worth.

Young children generally want to behave in ways that please their parents. However, we really want our children to learn to do the right thing, not because someone is dangling a carrot in front of them, but because it is the right thing to do. When people do the right thing—when they make good decisions, when they behave in a responsible manner—they feel good. They learn to value themselves. Developing responsibility—rather than obedience to please—is more advantageous for both children and parents. The children gain confidence and the parents promote responsibility. Parents who foster this approach give children a precious gift that is treasured for a lifetime.

An easy way to distinguish between praise and acknowledgment is to consider whether the comment would be made to an adult. If the comment would not be made to an adult, then it is probably patronizing praise.

As Ralph Waldo Emerson so aptly put it, "The reward for a thing well done is to have done it."

HONOR HOME ASSIGNMENTS

Home assignments teach two lessons. The most obvious reason for home assignments is to provide opportunities to practice and improve skills or to gain further knowledge or understanding. Practice is essential for skill mastery. Gaining knowledge and understanding is not limited to class time.

Home assignments also teach other lessons: responsibility, self-discipline, independence, perseverance, and time management. Home assignments teach how to begin a task, complete it, and be responsible for the outcome.

When a home assignment is difficult and the young person begins to struggle, parents want to help, and they should—up to a point. When the helping has reached the point where the youngster knows how to do the assignment, then the parent should back away; otherwise, the rescuing and over-involvement result in a gradual dependence on others.

Home assignments should be something done on a regular basis. A time that can be used regularly is most effective. Selecting a time that is earlier is preferable to a time that is later. Young people are generally fresher and more alert in the late afternoon or early evening than they are later on.

We choose our attitude when doing any activity, and this includes home assignments. Assuming that the parent will also be involved in some worthwhile activity while the youngster tends to home assignments, the parent can make a positive comment that both have responsibilities. Also, an encouraging comment, such as, "What do you expect to learn or reinforce from this assignment?" is preferable to one that is negative or nagging, such as "Have you finished your assignment?" Negative comments only encourage doing the assignment in order to get away from the negativity. This often results in the youngster's doing the assignment but then forgetting to take it to school. The motivation in such cases is not the assignment, but rather getting away from the nagging.

WORK SMARTER RATHER THAN HARDER

Do not do things for young people that they can do for themselves. Performing tasks engenders responsibility.

Once a task has been performed, the objective should be to focus on progress—rather than on perfection. If the activity does not meet parental expectations, something positive can be found on which to comment. This is far more effective than comments that foster guilt or a sense of failure. A positive approach prompts an incentive for the task—in contrast to criticizing, which provides a disincentive.

A specific time of day for required activities should be chosen. When structured and organized, tasks are more easily undertaken. When establishing routines, timing should be considered, such as whether or not the child is tired or hungry.

Offering help to start an activity is a good technique. Younger children prefer starting tasks with others rather than in isolation. After the youngster is involved, then withdraw, saying something like, "I'm sure you have the skills to do the rest without my help."

Any task should be age appropriate. "Tidy your desk," is more manageable and not as discouraging as, "Clean your room." In addition, once the desk is cleaned, the other may naturally follow.

It is important to recognize when a child is overtired, ill, or overwhelmed by expectations. These may be causes for being cranky or uncooperative. Similarly, if a child's favorite activity or television program is interrupted, the youngster should not be expected to be very cooperative.

Especially with an adolescent, the "state of mind" needs to be considered. A typical example is a parent's demand on a youngster's time. The son has not taken out the trash or completed some other chore. He is watching television. The parent gets after him. The poor timing is met with a negative reaction. A more successful approach would be to ask to see the son at the end of the television program or wait until he is upright, preferably in motion. Once on his feet and moving, the young man will be in a state of mind much more receptive to taking out the trash. In addition, the implicit message will not be that what the parent wants is more important than what the youngster wants. A key phrase to remember is "Under duress, they do less."

NURTURE YOUR CHILD'S NATURE

If an acorn is planted in good soil, is fertilized, and receives adequate water, the acorn will grow and may wind up becoming a giant oak tree. However, if a giant redwood is desired but an acorn is germinated and planted, that acorn will still grow up to be an oak.

Young people are not clones of their parents. Some are continually engaging in thought, while others are driven by how they feel. Some are constantly engaged in activities, while others are constantly looking for relationships. Being mindful of the child's nature can have a dramatic effect on relationships. The key consideration here is to work with youngsters according to *their* make-up. Simply remembering that each child is different, and not a duplicate of parents, can reduce stress and enhance relationships.

REAP THE JOY

A joy of parenting is watching a child develop and mature. Possessiveness has been a hallmark of parenting for hundreds of generations. Today, parents can no longer consider children their possessions. Children have rights and are watched over by the general society. An indication of this is the fine line drawn between punishment and child abuse.

Perhaps the paramount desire of parents has to do with simultaneously giving roots and wings. Parents model, foster values, and teach by what they say and do. They provide the shelter, clothing, affection, and security so necessary for a healthy environment. All of these provide roots. Parents also give wings and hope that the direction of flight will be toward responsible living. Perhaps the combination of roots and wings was most eloquently expressed in 1932 by Kahlil Gibran in *The Prophet*.

> *Your children are not your children.*
> *They are the sons and daughters of Life's longing*
>   *for itself.*
> *They come through you but not from you,*
> *And though they are with you yet they belong not to*
>   *you.*
>
> *You may give them your love but not your thoughts,*
> *For they have their own thoughts.*
> *You may house their bodies but not their souls,*
> *For their souls dwell in the house of tomorrow, which*
>   *you cannot visit, not even in your dreams.*
> *You may strive to be like them, but seek not to make*
>   *them like you.*
> *For life goes not backward nor tarries with yesterday.*
>
> *You are the bows from which your children as living*
>   *arrows are sent forth.*
> *The archer sees the mark upon the path of the*
>   *infinite, and He bends you with His might that*
> *His arrows may go swift and far.*
> *Let your bending in the archer's hand be for*
>   *gladness;*
> *For even as He loves the arrow that flies, so He loves also*
>   *the bow that is stable.*

KEY POINTS

◆ Practice positivity. One of the most effective ways to influence children and reduce stress is to communicate using positive messages.

◆ Offer choices. Choice brings ownership and empowers. Offering options engages a youngster in cooperation and is much more effective than giving commands.

◆ Encourage reflection. The purpose of reflection is to stimulate internal motivation.

◆ Use effective questions. Effective questions direct thinking to self-evaluation. This process brings awareness and clarity, both for the questioner and for the person answering.

◆ Listen to learn. Listening to and valuing young people's feelings and ideas are what promote the ability of parents to effectively communicate with them.

◆ Limit lecturing and telling. Although the intention may be to share and save youngsters from a frustrating experience, the message is often perceived as criticism. Lectures convey the message that what the youngster has done is wrong or not good enough. This often results in defensiveness and resistance.

◆ Check assumptions. We may know exactly what we are thinking and what we mean, but the child may have a completely different perspective.

◆ Focus on the important. Choose your battles. While clashes may be unavoidable, it is not necessary to get pulled into every skirmish.

◆ Ask for assistance. People become responsible by giving and putting forth effort; give young people opportunities to help you.

◆ Recognize implicit messages. "Implicit" refers to what is learned without our intentions. When parents become upset and yell at children, the implicit message is that when upset, yelling is acceptable.

◆ Foster responsibility. Parents can best view the adolescent years as a quest for identity. Conflicts can be avoided by using reflective questions and negotiating through dialogue, rather than by using coercion.

◆ Demonstrate personal responsibility. Accept responsibility for allowing a situation or stimulus to upset you; do not blame the child. The parent should be thinking, "I'm upset; how can I best handle the situation?"

◆ Maintain standards. Sometimes maintaining standards takes a higher priority than that of parental popularity.

◆ Use authority without being punitive. Rather than imposing a punishment, a much more effective approach to changing behavior is to *elicit* a consequence from the youngster. Then the young person has ownership of it.

◆ Let the youngster lead. Have the youngster plan an activity. Assistance can be given by providing a few guidelines and a budget.

◆ Teach procedures for dealing with impulses. Recognize that people have choices regarding their responses to impulses.

◆ Intervene in sibling squabbles. Parents need not intervene in every children's quarrel, but should intervene whenever an argument turns violent or threatens to do so.

◆ Be aware of gender differences. Engage boys in an activity before expecting them to express their feelings. Boys have strong desires to feel competent, and "telling" a boy what to do interferes with this.

◆ Use acknowledgments more than praise. Acknowledgment simply identifies ownership and responsibility for the achievement.

◆ Honor home assignments. They provide opportunities to practice and improve skills and teach other lessons such as responsibility, self-discipline, independence, perseverance, and time management. Assist only to the point where the youngster can do the assignment himself.

◆ Work smarter rather than harder. Do not do things for young people that they can do for themselves. Focus on progress, rather than on perfection.

◆ Nurture your child's nature. Simply remembering that each child is different, and not a duplicate of parents, can reduce stress and enhance relationships.

◆ Reap the joy. A joy of parenting is watching a child develop and mature while simultaneously giving the child roots and wings.

SUMMARY

The world is a looking glass
and gives to every man the reflection of his own face.
Frown at it and it, in turn, will look sourly at you;
laugh at it, and with it, and it is a jolly, kind companion.
   –William Makepeace Thackeray

As emphasized throughout this book, optimism pays. Listen to your self-talk. As you can upset yourself with negative self-talk, so you have the capability to talk yourself into a positive state. Be kind to yourself. Be like the monkey who eats only the healthy part of the banana.

No empowerment is more effective than self-empowerment. Because being positive is so enabling, it is best to displace thoughts and communications that are destructive. Continually ask how what you want to communicate can be put in a positive way. For example, saying, "You are bad tempered," has the same meaning as, "You need to work on controlling your temper." However, the first *labels* the person, whereas the second *enables* the person.

People change more by building on their strengths and aptitudes than by working on their weaknesses. This does not mean that an area of weakness should not be worked on, but it does mean that a parent's emphasis should be on what the child can do, rather than what the child cannot do. The simple belief that something can be done is the spark that ignites the brain to act.

Listen to how you communicate with your children. Listen to the tone of your voice. It communicates your emotions. Be aware of your body language. Facial expressions, body stance, and gestures communicate your message as much as the words you actually say.

Separate the young person from the behavior. If a child is not acting responsibly, acknowledge the action, but do not call the child irresponsible. Label the behavior, rather than the person. "Do you consider that the responsible thing to do?" or "That was not worthy of you," are better than "You are irresponsible." Of course, having the child do the labeling is even more effective.

The whole problem with *telling*, rather than *asking*, must be kept in mind constantly because so often parents tell a youngster what the parent would do in a similar situation. Unfortunately, a common message is that what the youngster does is not good enough, or certainly not as good as what the parent suggests. A simple solution to this dilemma is for the parent to ask the youngster reflective questions.

Three ways to impair relationships are to criticize, blame, and complain. Rather than using these negative approaches, ask a self-evaluative, reflective question in order to involve the child in a non-threatening way.

No one likes to be cornered, literally or figuratively. Having no choices encourages resistance because of the feeling of being trapped. When a child has no options, the result is not only resistance but also resentment.

Refrain from arguing. It only fuels hostility and diminishes healthy communications. Arguments rarely focus on solutions, and reasoning with someone who is upset is futile. One approach is to simply hold up your hand, palm out, making the "stop" sign, or signal "time out" with hands overhead like a referee. Also, avoid attempting to talk young people out of their feelings. Young people have the right to feel hurt, upset, and disappointed. Their reactions should be acknowledged without being condoned. The acknowledgment itself can diffuse anger mightily.

Deal in the present. The past cannot be changed. When it is re-lived, it becomes the present and builds frustration.

Avoid doing things for young people that they can do themselves. Accept the fact that growth comes through struggle. Babying children keeps them dependent and hinders their development.

Focus on treating children as if they are who, how, and what you would like them to be. Treating people as if they are responsible increases the chances of their becoming so.

EPILOGUE

BUSINESS:
A POOR MODEL FOR LEARNING

There is no such thing as an immaculate perception.
What you see depends upon what you thought before you looked.
—Myron Tribus

Government, business, and even education leaders often compare schooling to business. Schools are referred to as workplaces, students are referred to as customers, and performance is measured by accountability. Equating young people's learning with what adults do to make money is a false equation. Using a business model for learning is a practice that has been described by the comic strip character Dagwood Bumstead: "You know, that makes a lot of sense if you don't think about it."

THE PURPOSES OF SCHOOL AND BUSINESS
ARE DIFFERENT

The basic purpose of business is to survive. Even in graduate business courses that teach that one purpose of business is to serve, the fact remains that if there is no profit, the business will eventually fail.

Survival is not a factor in schooling. Society finds ways—be they public, private, or a combination thereof—to educate its young. The purpose of schooling is to promote understanding, make meaning, and perpetuate and improve society. Preparing students to live successful lives certainly includes some of the necessary skills and characteristics essential in business. However, the fact that some of the same skills are used does not mean that the skills taught in school are taught *for* purposes of business.

THE PRODUCT IS DIFFERENT

Businesses produce *products*. The product may be tangible or intangible and in the form of information, services, or goods.

Learning is a *process*, not a product. Even if students were to be considered products, the product would be their education. Schools educate and businesses train. The term "training" is not often used when referring to K–12 education. Schools do not train for specific information dissemination as do businesses, nor are students trained to provide services to others, nor are they trained to produce goods for use or for consumption. Training is used for areas that are vocational in nature.

In a business transaction, the customer is clearly identified. This is not the case in education. The customer consists of parents (especially in this age of school choice), the society at large (since students are members), other institutions of learning (where students often need to qualify), and future employers. In business, *only* the customer needs *live with the product*; however, the people who live with the results of schooling are the parents and others with whom the learner interacts.

Business can control the components of its product—what will go into making a product. Schools do not have this luxury; they (at least the public schools) have no discretionary power to determine or control the "raw materials." Besides, students are not assembled according to well-established specifications. Schools must individualize education for many students.

Business has the opportunity and even the obligation for recalls. No such possibility exists for schools. Clearly, comparing the building of people to building products is a faulty comparison.

THE PEOPLE ARE DIFFERENT

Students are young people and, as such, are different from adults. When juvenile courts were established, the legal system acknowledged that childhood is different from adulthood. Vast amounts of psychological, social, developmental, medical, and brain research have demonstrated that children and youth are different from adults. Few parents—whether in government, business, or education—would ever consider treating their own eight-year-old as an eighteen-year-old.

THE TASKS ARE DIFFERENT

The nature of the work differs. Business has to do with providing a product or service to others. Schooling has to do with personal and social growth. A review of the chapter on teaching clearly demonstrates that the nature of learning differs from the nature of producing.

FUNDING AND COMPENSATION ARE DIFFERENT

In business, the person who pays derives the benefit. This is not the case in education. The person who is most directly involved—the learner—does not pay for education. In addition, even though businesses and other agencies contribute to the support of schools, the primary revenue source for public education is the general society—not private funds.

Also, and this may not be apparent to those who equate learning with business, *money is a satisfier—not a motivator.* Giving a person more money rarely produces more work. Money does not usually make a person work harder. Take yourself as an example. If you were given more money, would you work harder than you work now? If a chief executive officer (CEO) of a business were given more compensation, do you think he or she would work harder? Money is compensation, and unless a person is being paid by piecework or is on commission, money will not often motivate him to work harder.

Students do not receive money for learning. Besides, giving money for learning would be a mistake. External rewards alter motivation and diminish creativity, two of the most powerful incentives for learning.

In business, if a worker does not perform satisfactorily, the employment, along with the compensation, is removed. Public schools do not fire students or prevent their continued attendance.

THE SUCCESS FACTOR IS DIFFERENT

In business, success on the job often requires initiative, flexibility, and teamwork. No defense is given here for not employing similar approaches in schools. However, that is not currently the case in most schools. Schooling is administered in a competitive manner. Grades, rankings, and other evaluation techniques are largely based on pitting students against each other and militate against initiative, flexibility, and teamwork.

Outcomes in the business world can be objectively measured. Units manufactured and sold, the number of customers returning, and the number of retained clients can all be objectively measured. This is not the case in learning; outcomes cannot be objectively measured. Even if they could be, the evaluation instruments currently available could indicate only an insignificant amount of learning that had been acquired—either in quality or quantity.

In this regard, businesses do not set up evaluation instruments that mandate only a fifty percent (50%) success factor. It is interesting to note that educational leaders follow the ideas of business and government leaders. But these leaders would never consider evaluating the success of workers on any kind of an instrument where, by design, half would fall below the average. Yet, this is what schools do when standardized tests are administered. Not only do half of the students fall below the average, so do half of the schools. No other institution would operate in this way—a poignant, and unfortunate, further differentiation.

THE PROCEDURES AND TIME FACTORS ARE DIFFERENT

A manager who oversees employees, an administrator who is accountable for a project or department, or a business executive who is responsible for the success and survival of the business operate differently from a teacher. The teacher's charge is to impart information, foster comprehension, develop communication skills, and build behavior to promote a civil society. Therefore, a slow learner is treated differently from a fast learner. Various activities are assigned according to the students' skills and abilities. Because schools aim at attending to students' needs, flexibility of time is incorporated. In contrast to schools, business uses procedures that focus on production and are usually under strict time constraints.

Finally, business primarily deals in the present. Schools deal primarily with the future.

CONCLUSION

Learning is learning; it is not business. Comparing learning to business is not only a poor metaphor, it is a false one. Just because business and learning share attributes of efforts and skills, it is unwise to compare them for the reasons listed. We would be well served to call attention to and refute the comparison whenever made.

BIBLIOGRAPHY

Alessandra, Tony, and Michael O'Connor. *The Platinum Rule.* New York: Warner Books, 1996.

Alexander, F. M. *The Use of the Self.* Great Britain: Guernsey, Channel Islands: Guernsey Press, Ltd., 1985.

Armstrong, Thomas. *ADD/ADHD Alternatives in the Classroom.* Alexandria, VA: Association for Supervision and Curriculum Development, 1999.

_____. *Awakening Genius in the Classroom.* Alexandria, VA: Association for Supervision and Curriculum Development, 1998.

_____. *Multiple Intelligences in the Classroom.* Alexandria, VA: Association for Supervision and Curriculum Development, 1994.

_____. *The Best Schools.* Alexandria, VA: Association for Supervision and Curriculum Development, 2006.

Begley, Sharon. "Homework Doesn't Help," *Newsweek* (March 30, 1998).

_____. "Mind: Living Hand to Mouth: New Research Shows that Gestures Often Help Speakers Access Words from Their Memory Bank," *Newsweek* (November 2, 1998).

Bellanca, James. "Teaching for Intelligence: In Search of Best Practices," *Phi Delta Kappan* (May 1998).

Bloom, Benjamin S., and others, eds. *Taxonomy of Educational Objectives: Cognitive Domain.* New York: David McKay Co. Inc., 1956.

Bluestein, Jane. *21st Century Discipline: Teaching Students Responsibility and Self-Control.* Jefferson City, MO: Scholastic, Inc., 1988.

Bracey, Gerald W. *Setting the Record Straight: Responses to Misconceptions about Public Education in the United States.* Alexandria, VA: Association for Supervision and Curriculum Development, 1977.

Bromley, Karen, Linda Irwin-DeVitis, and Marcia Modlo. *Graphic Organizers: Visual Strategies for Active Learning.* New York: Scholastic Professional Books, 1995.

Brooks, David and Patricia Freedman. *Implementing Character Education.* San Diego, CA: Education Assessment Publishing, 2002.

Bruner, Jerome. *Going Beyond the Information Given.* New York: Norton, 1973.

_____. *The Process of Education.* Cambridge: Harvard University Press, 1961.

California State Department of Education. *Toward A State Of Esteem: The Final Report of the California Task Force to Promote Self-esteem and Personal and Social Responsibility.* Sacramento, CA: California State Department of Education, 1990.

California State Department of Education, Sacramento County Office of Education, and California Partnership in Character Education. *Building Communities & Schools of Character.* Mechanism for Change Conference: Character Education, March 11, 1999.

Canfield, Jack, and Harold Wells. *100 Ways to Enhance Self-Concept in the Classroom.* Boston: Allyn and Beacon, 1994.

Canfield, Jack, and Mark Victor Hansen. *The Aladdin Factor.* New York: Berkley Books, 1995.

Capell, Dianne. Personal correspondence to Marvin Marshall. January 7, 1999.

Carnegie, Dale. *How to Win Friends & Influence People.* NY: HarperCollins, 1999.

Cathcart, Jim. *The Acorn Principle.* New York: St. Martin's Griffin, 1999.

Charles, C.M. *Building Classroom Discipline.* Eighth edition. Boston: Pearson Education, 2005.

Chase, Bob. "Trial by Fire: Are We Setting Up New Teachers to Fail?" *Education Week* (November 18, 1998): 17.

_____. "Stigmatizing Success," *Education Week* (January 20, 1999): 37.

Clark, Richard E. Personal correspondence to Marvin Marshall. September 3, 1995.

Clark, Ron. *The Essential 55*. New York: Hyperion, 2003.

Coleman, James S. *The Adolescent Society: The Social Life of the Teenager and Its Impact on Education.* New York: Free Press of Glencoe, 1961.

Covey, Stephen. *The Seven Habits of Highly Effective People.* New York: Simon & Schuster, 1990.

Crawford, Donna, Richard Bodine, and Robert Hoglund. *The School for Quality Learning.* Champagne, IL: Research Press, 1993.

Cummings, Carol. *Winning Strategies for Classroom Management.* Alexandria, VA: Association for Supervision and Curriculum Development, 2000.

Damasio, Antonio. *Descartes' Error - Emotion, Reason, and the Human Brain.* New York: Quil, HarperCollins, 2000.

Danzig, Robert. *Cooperating School Districts 2000 Character Education Conference.* St. Louis, MO: July 13, 2000. (Available on audio cassette tape CE0002)

Deci, Edward L., and Richard Flaste. *Why We Do What We Do: Understanding Self-Motivation.* New York: Penguin Books, 1995.

Deming, W. Edwards. "A Day with Dr. Deming," sponsored by the Chief of Naval Operations, December 21, 1991, and published by the Chief of Naval Operations, The Pentagon, Room 4E522, Washington, D.C. 20350-2000.

_____. *Out of the Crisis.* Cambridge: Massachusetts Institute of Technology, 1986.

_____. *The New Economics for Industry, Government, and Education.* Cambridge: Massachusetts Institute of Technology, 1993.

Dewey, John. *Experience & Education.* New York: Macmillan, 1958.

Dickinson, Amy. "Bully Pulpit," *Time* (August 30, 1999): 76.

Dill, Vicky Schreiber. *A Peaceable School: Cultivating a Culture of Nonviolence.* Bloomington, IN: Phi Delta Kappa Educational Foundation, 1998.

Dougherty, John W. *Four Philosophies that Shape the Middle School.* Bloomington, IN: Phi Delta Kappa Educational Foundation, 1997.

DuFour, Rick. "Functioning as Learning Communities Enables Schools to Focus on Student Achievement," *Journal of Staff Development.* Oxford, OH: National Staff Development Council (Spring 1997).

Elam, Stanley. *How America Views Its Public Schools: The PDK/Gallop Polls, 1964–1994.* Bloomington, IN: Phi Delta Kappa International Foundation, 1995.

Elias, Marilyn. "3 Studies, 1 Result: School Bullying Worsening," *USA Today* (August 23, 1999).

Ellis, Albert. "Rational Emotive Behavior Therapy as an Integral Control of Psychology," *International Journal of Reality Therapy.* Boston, MA: Northeastern University (Fall 1999).

Ellis, Albert, and Catherine MacLaren. *Rational Emotive Behavior Therapy: A Therapist's Guide.* San Luis Obispo, CA: Impact Publishers, 1998.

Farivar, Sydney. "Research Review: Citizenship Education," *Social Studies Review.* Millbrae, CA: Journal of the California Council for the Social Studies (Spring 1996).

Fouse, Beth, and Suzanne Brians. *A Primer on Attention Deficit Disorder.* Bloomington, IN: Phi Delta Kappa Educational Foundation, 1993.

Frankl, Viktor E. *Man's Search for Meaning.* New York: Washington Square Press, 1968.

Fuetsch, Michele. "Program Aims to Keep Teachers from Quitting," *Los Angeles Times* (June 3, 1993): J1.

Fulghum, Robert. *All I Really Need to Know I Learned in Kindergarten.* New York: Villard Books, 1989.

Gardner, Howard. "A Prescription for Peace," *Time* (January 25, 1999): 62–63.

———. *Frames of Mind: The Theory of Multiple Intelligences.* New York:

Basic Books, 1993.

Gauld, Joseph. "Why American Education is Failing: A Plea for Intrinsic, Rather than Extrinsic Forms of Motivation," *Education Week* (April 29, 1997): 41.

Gaustad, Joan. "Characteristics Associated with Student Discipline Problems," *ERIC Digest* 78. Reported in *Thrust for Educational Leadership*. Burlingame, CA: The Association of California School Administrators (October 1994).

Gelb, Michael J. *Body Learning*. New York: Henry Holt and Company, 1994.

_____. *Thinking for a Change*. New York: Harmony Books, 1995.

Gibran, Kahlil. *The Prophet*. New York: Alfred A. Knopf, 1996.

Gladwell, Malcolm. *Blink - The Power of Thinking without Thinking*. New York: Little, Brown and Company, 2005.

Glasser, William. "A New Look at School Failure and School Success," *Phi Delta Kappan* (April 1997).

_____. *Choice Theory: A New Psychology of Personal Freedom*. New York: HarperCollins, 1998.

_____. *Choice Theory in the Classroom*. New York: Harper & Row, 1998.

_____. *Every Student Can Succeed*. San Diego, CA: Black Forest Press, 2000.

_____. *The Quality School*. New York: HarperCollins, 1992, 1998.

_____. *The Quality School Teacher*. New York: HarperCollins, 1993, 1998.

_____. *Schools without Failure*. New York: Harper & Row, 1969.

_____. *The Identity Society*. New York: Harper & Row, 1975.

Goldstein, Sam, and Michael Goldstein. *A Teacher's Guide: Attention-Deficit Hyperactivity Disorder in Children*. Salt Lake City: Neurology Learning and Behavior Center, 1995.

Goleman, Daniel. *Emotional Intelligence*. New York: Bantam Books, 1995.

Gootman, Marilyn. *The Caring Teacher's Guide to Discipline: Helping Young Students Learn Self-Control, Responsibility, and Respect.* Thousand Oaks, CA: Corwin Press, 1997.

Gray, John. *Men Are from Mars, Women Are from Venus.* New York: HarperCollins, 1992.

Grote, Richard C. *Discipline without Punishment.* Kansas City, MO: American Management Association, 1995.

Harris, Judith Rich. *The Nurture Assumption: Why Children Turn Out the Way They Do – Parents Matter Less than You Think and Peers Matter More.* New York: The Free Press, 1998.

Healy, Jane M. "The 'Meme' That Ate Childhood," *Education Week* (October 7, 1998): 56.

Helmstetter, Shad. *Choices.* New York: Simon & Schuster, 1989.

Hicks, Jerry. *Los Angeles Times* (October 30, 1997).

Hill, Napoleon. *Think and Grow Rich.* North Hollywood, CA: Wilshire Book Co., 1996.

Hunter, Madeline. *Discipline That Develops Self-Discipline.* Thousand Oaks, CA: Corwin Press, 1967.

_____. *Motivation Theory for Teachers.* Thousand Oaks, CA: Corwin Press, 1990.

Jameson, Marnell. "Bully for Them," *Los Angeles Times* (March 9, 1997).

Jamison, Kaleel. *The Nibble Theory and the Kernel of Power.* Mahwah, NJ: Paulist Press, 1989.

Jenkins, Lee. *Permission to Forget - And Nine Other Root Causes of America's Frustration with Education.* Milwaukee, Wisconsin: American Society for Quality, Quality Press, 2004.

Jensen, Eric. *Completing the Puzzle: A Brain-Based Approach to Learning.* Del Mar, CA: Turning Point Publishing, 1996.

_____. *SuperTeaching.* Del Mar, CA: Turning Point Publishing, 1995.

_____. *Teaching with the Brain in Mind.* Alexandria, VA: Association for Supervision and Curriculum Development, 1998.

Johnson, LouAnne. *The Queen of Education - Rules for Making School*

Work. San Francisco: Jossey-Bass, 2004.

Kennedy, John F. *Profiles in Courage*. New York: Black Dog & Leventhal, 1955, 1984.

Kohn, Alfie. *Beyond Discipline: From Compliance to Community*. Alexandria, VA: Association for Supervision and Curriculum Development, 1996.

_____. "How Not to Teach Values: A Critical Look at Character Education," *Phi Delta Kappan* (February 1997).

_____. *Punished by Rewards*. Boston: Houghton Mifflin, 1993.

_____. "Students Don't 'Work'—They Learn," *Education Week* (September 3, 1997).

_____. "The Author Responds," *Phi Delta Kappan* (May 1997).

_____. *What to Look for in a Classroom*. San Francisco: Jossey-Bass, 1998.

Langdon, Carol. "The Third Phi Delta Kappa Poll of Teachers' Attitudes Toward the Public Schools," *Phi Delta Kappan* (November 1996).

Lickona, Thomas. *Educating for Character: How Our Schools Can Teach Respect and Responsibility*. New York: Bantam Books, 1991.

MacDonald, Glynn. *Alexander Technique*. Great Britain: Hodder & Stoughton, 1994.

McGregor, Douglas. *The Human Side of Enterprise*. New York: McGraw-Hill, 1960.

Margulies, Nancy. *Mapping Inner Space: Learning and Teaching Mindmapping*. Tucson, AZ: Zephyr, 1991.

Marshall, Marvin. "Discipline without Stress, Punishments, or Rewards." *The Clearing House*, Washington, D.C.: Heldref Publications (September/October 2005).

_____. "Ensuring Social Responsibility," *Thrust for Educational Leadership*. Burlingame, CA: The Association of California School Administrators (January 1994).

_____. "Better Classroom Behavior By Raising Responsibility." *The Journal of the New England League of Middle Schools*. Topfield: MA

New England League of Middle Schools (September 2003).

_____. "Evaluation: A Tool for Better Relationships," *Thrust for Educational Leadership*. Burlingame, CA: The Association of California School Administrators (November/December 1997).

_____. "Fostering Social Responsibility and Handling Disruptive Classroom Behavior," *NASSP Bulletin*. Reston, VA: The National Association of Secondary School Principals (March 1998).

_____. *Fostering Social Responsibility*. Bloomington, IN: Phi Delta Kappa Educational Foundation, 1998.

_____. "How to Discipline without Stress, Punishments, or Rewards and Raise Responsibility." *Texas Study of Secondary Education*. Austin, TX (Spring 2001).

_____. "Promoting Positivity, Choice and Reflection: Three simple practices can make school a place where teachers and students want to be." *Leadership*. Burlingame, CA (May/June 2005).

_____. "Rethinking Our Thinking on Discipline: Empower—Rather than Overpower," *Education Week* (May 27, 1998): 32, 36.

_____. "Using Teacher Evaluation to Change School Culture," *NASSP Bulletin*. Reston, VA: The National Association of Secondary School Principals (October 1998).

Marshall, Marvin and Kerry Weisner. "Using A Discipline System to Promote Learning." *Phi Delta Kappa Kappan*. Bloomington, IN: Phi Delta Kappa International (March 2004).

Marshall, Marvin, and Sherry Posnick-Goodwin. "Behaving for All the Right Reasons," *California Educator*. Burlingame, CA: California Teachers Association (April 1998).

Maslow, Abraham H. *Motivation and Personality*. New York: Addison Wesley Longman, Third Edition, 1987.

Maurer, Robert. *One Small Step Can Change Your Life - The Kaizen Way*. New York: Workman Publishing, 2004.

McCormack, Patricia M. Student *Self-Discipline in the Classroom & Beyond*. Washington, D.C.: National Catholic Educational Association, 2003.

McGregor, Douglas. *The Human Side of Enterprise*. New York; McGraw-Hill, 1960.

Mendler, Allen. *Motivating Students Who Don't Care*. Bloomington, IN: National Education Service, 2000.

Mulrine, Anna. "A Common Thread? Once Bullied, Now Bullies—with Guns," *U.S. News & World Report* (May 3, 1999).

National Association of Secondary School Principals (NASSP). *Breaking Ranks: Changing an American Institution*. Reston, VA: National Association of Secondary School Principals, 1996.

National PTA. *Discipline: A Parent's Guide*. Chicago: National Congress of Parents and Teachers, 1993.

Nelsen, Jane, Lynn Lott, and Stephen Glenn. *Positive Discipline in the Classroom: How to Effectively Use Class Meetings*. Rocklin, CA: Prima Publishing, 1993.

Oakley, Ed, and Doug Krug. *Enlightened Leadership*. New York: Simon & Schuster, 1993.

Page, Bill. *At-Risk Students*. Nashville, TN: Educational Dynamics, 2006.

Payne, Ruby. *A Framework for Understanding Poverty*. Highlands Texas: Aha Press, 2001.

Peale, Norman Vincent. *The Power of Positive Thinking*. Pawling, NY: Peale Center for Christian Living, 1978.

Phi Delta Kappa. *Handbook for Developing Schools with Good Discipline*. Bloomington, IN: Phi Delta Kappa, 1982.

Pike, Robert W. *Creative Training Techniques Handbook*. Minneapolis, MN: Lakewood Books, 1994.

Prager, Dennis. *Happiness Is a Serious Problem*. New York: Regan Books (HarperCollins), 1998.

Pryer, Karen. *Don't Shoot the Dog*. New York: Simon & Schuster, 1984.

Raffini, James P. *150 Ways to Increase Intrinsic Motivation in the Classroom*. Boston: Allyn & Bacon, 1996.

Raywid, Mary Anne, and Libby Oshiyama. "Musings in the Wake of

Columbine: What Can Schools Do?" *Phi Delta Kappan* (February 2000): 444–449.

Reavis, George H., and Carter V. Good Lee. *An Educational Platform for the Public Schools*. Bloomington, IN: Phi Delta Kappa Educational Foundation, Facsimile Edition, 1996.

Reynolds, Gardner. "Some Thoughts on Peer Pressure." Paper submitted to Marvin Marshall. Loredo, Texas (October 1996).

Roberts, Monty. *Horse Sense for People*. NY: Viking, 2001.

Sagor, Richard. *At-Risk Students: Reaching and Teaching Them*. Swampscott, MA: Watersun Publishing Company, 1993.

_____.*Motivating Students and Teachers in an Era of Standards*. Alexandria, VA: Association for Supervision and Curriculum Development, 2003.

Salk, Lee. *Familyhood: Nurturing the Values that Matter*. New York: Simon & Schuster, 1992.

Sansone, Carol and Judith Harackiewicz (Eds). *Intrinsic and Extrinsic Motivation*. NY: Academic Press, 2000.

Scoresby, A. Lynn. *Teaching Moral Development*. Oram, UT: Knowledge Gain Publications, 1996.

Secretary's Commission on Achieving Necessary Skills. *Teaching the SCANS Competencies*. Washington, D.C.: United States Department of Labor, 1993.

Senge, Peter M. *The Fifth Discipline: The Art and Practice of the Learning Organization*. New York: Doubleday, 1990.

Shore, Rebecca. *Creating a Positive School Climate*. Mt. Kisco, NY: Plan for Social Excellence, 1997.

Simmons, Rachel. *Odd Girl Out - The Hidden Culture of Aggression in Girls*. NY: Harcourt, 2002.

Simon, Sidney B. *Negative Criticism*. Chesterfield, PA: Values Press, 1978.

Sousa, David A. *How the Brain Learns*. Reston, VA: National Association of Secondary School Principals, 1995.

Sprenger, Marilee. *Learning and Memory: The Brain in Action.* Alexandria, VA: Association for Supervision and Curriculum Development, 1999.

Sullo, Robert A. *Inspiring Quality in Your School: From Theory to Practice.* Washington, D.C.: National Education Association, 1997.

Sutton, James D. *If My Kid's So Nice…Why's He Driving ME Crazy?* Pleasanton, TX: Friendly Oaks Publications, 1997.

Sylwester, Robert. *A Celebration of Neurons: An Educator's Guide to the Brain.* Alexandria, VA: Association for Supervision and Curriculum Development, 1995.

Tamara, Henry. "Principals Urge Broad Changes in High Schools," *USA Today* (February 22, 1996).

Time Magazine (November 2, 1992): 57.

Time Magazine (April 28, 1997): 28.

Tracy, Louise Felton. *Grounded for Life?! Stop Blowing Your Fuse and Start Communicating with Your Teenager.* Seattle, WA: Parenting Press, 1994.

Tribus, Myron. Personal communication to Marvin Marshall. June 27, 1997.

Urban, Hal. *Life's Greatest Lessons: 20 Things I Want My Kids to Know.* Redwood City, CA: Great Lessons Press, 2000.

Van der Meer, and Ad Dudink. *The Brain Pack: An Interactive, Three-Dimensional Exploration of the Mysteries of the Mind.* Philadelphia, PA: Running Press Book Publishers, 1996.

Van Ness, Ross. *Raising Self-Esteem of Learners.* Bloomington, IN: Phi Delta Kappa Educational Foundation, 1995.

Viadero, Debra. "Research: Bullies Beware," *Education Week* (May 26, 1997): 19–21. www.charactercounts.org/backgrnd.htm

Wolfe, Patricia. *Brain Matters: Translating Research into Classroom Practice.* Alexandria, VA: Association for Supervision and Curriculum Development, 2001.

Wong, Harry K., and Rosemary Wong. *How to be an Effective Teacher—The First Days of School.* Mountain View, CA: Harry K. Wong Publications, 2004.

Wubbolding, Robert. *Employee Motivation.* Knoxville, TN: SPC Press, 1995.

_____. *Understanding Reality Therapy: A Metaphorical Approach.* New York: Harper Perennial, 1991.

_____. *Reality Therapy for the 21st Century.* Philadelphia: Brunner-Routledge, 2000.

Wycoff, Joyce. *Mindmapping: Your Personal Guide to Exploring Creativity and Problem Solving.* New York: Berkley Books, 1991.

Zahorik, John A. *Constructivist Teaching.* Bloomington, IN: Phi Delta Kappa Educational Foundation, 1995.

APPENDIX

SUGGESTIONS FOR MOTIVATION

The aphorism states, "When the student is ready,
the teacher will appear." But we can speed up the process.

Create curiosity.
Curiosity is perhaps the greatest of all motivators. In Japanese schools, students are first introduced to a problem or challenge. They *grapple* with it. Curiosity thereby is naturally engendered. By contrast, in American schools the information to be learned or the skill to be practiced is generally presented *without first creating interest.*

Share the "Why?" of the lesson to create interest.
Ask yourself why the lesson will be taught. Since people today are tuned to radio station WII-FM ("What's In It For Me"), spend a little time at the beginning of a lesson to talk about how the lesson benefits students in their current stage of life. Start by sharing how students can use the information. When you find this difficult, put the discussion on the table for students to grapple with. You will be amazed at (1) how resourceful they will be and (2) how it helps them to buy into the lesson.

Structure experiences to apply to life outside of school.
Interest will increase the more you tie the lesson into showing long-term benefits and how the learning will make life easier and better. Share how the lesson will help students make better decisions, solve more problems, get along better with others, and/or make them more effective. Share the following wisdom: "Wise people think long-term, not just for today."

Teach students to ask themselves questions.
The questioning process starts the thinking process. When students

begin to ask themselves "Why?" and "How?" questions, both alertness and interest increase. This process also assists in developing metacognition skills.

Use students' knowledge of themselves.
After sharing *what* you will be teaching, ask students how *they* believe they can best learn. See the example in *Differentiated Instruction*.

Develop a sense of personal responsibility.
Remember the fundamental principle of motivation: consciously or nonconsciously people motivate themselves. Each individual is responsible for learning, but it is the teacher's responsibility to create the best possible climate in which that learning can take place. An effective way to do this is to give students an opportunity at the beginning of a lesson to indicate:

The expectations *they* have,

The outcomes *they* expect, and

What *they* are willing to do to achieve those results.

Use acknowledgments.
Acknowledgment/recognition/validation affirm. Saying, "I think you know you did that well," fosters reflection and feelings of competence. Consider repeating a comment you have heard or that someone has told you. "Evelyn made an interesting comment, one that applies to what we've been exploring. I think it bears repeating." You not only encouraged Evelyn but you encouraged others to become more involved. You also demonstrated that you are open to feedback and that students' comments contribute to their own learning.

Encourage.
One of the most effective techniques is to let the student know that you believe the student can accomplish the task. A word of encouragement during a frustration is worth more than a whole lot of praise after a success.

Focus on Growth.
Emphasize that learning is a process and that no one can learn and be perfect at the same time. Doing something one way and not being successful is another thing learned. It is not to be considered a failure. Failure only arrives when trying stops.

Reduce competition and increase collaboration for improved learning.

Competition improves *performance*—but not learning. Some students will practice for hours spurred on by the competitive spirit in music competition, athletics, or speech contests. These students are motivated to compete. Competition can be fun, as witnessed by the hours youth invest in such activities. However, competition is devastating for the youngster who never finds himself/herself in the winner's circle. Rather than compete, that student drops out by giving up.

Every time a teacher has students raise a hand to answer a question, students are competing for the teacher's attention. Since only one person is called on, only one person wins. Move from competition to *collaboration* by posing a question. Posing opens the possibility of several approaches. It invites thinking. Have students discuss possible answers with each other. In cases where there is only one correct answer, still have students share with each other—rather than compete for the attention of the teacher. Sharing with each other involves all students. Even a shy student will talk with one other person. Most importantly, when students know the correct answer, their satisfaction is enhanced *from their learning*—rather than from recognition by the teacher. *(Having all students participate requires an attention management procedure so that the teacher can obtain students' attention immediately. An example follows these suggestions.)*

Encourage self-comparison.

Comparing oneself to others is a natural human characteristic. However, its foundation is competitiveness. The more that one learns that growth emanates from measuring one's own progress/growth (self-comparison), the greater the satisfaction. Comparing oneself with others too often engenders dissatisfaction with oneself and prompts negative feelings. Since people are more apt to persevere when they feel good, success is enhanced when measurement is with oneself, rather than against others. A critical understanding for youth is the recognition that every person is different. Comparing oneself with others is like comparing palm trees with oak trees.

Build on strengths.

Students who are at risk will become less so when they find and feel success. This is accomplished by building on what is successful, rather than on focusing on what needs to improve. Too often, teachers focus on perfection. "Implement now; perfect later" should be the motto. When perceptions of negative feedback come before feelings of competence, it is too often counterproductive. The reason is that feelings of discouragement work against persevering. After young people feel some competence, they are more willing to accept feedback for improvement. A simple approach to start is by marking correct answers in yellow, rather than marking incorrect responses in red.

Plan for improved interpersonal relationships.
Relationships are extremely important to youth. This is especially true for teenagers who come from poverty. Teacher-student relationships will be significantly enhanced when the three principles of positivity, choice, and reflection are practiced.

Also, in addition to the teacher's connecting with the students on a one-on-one basis, helping students connect with one another can be valuable. Periodically, give students an opportunity to socialize for short periods.

Offer choices.
Regardless of age, everyone likes to feel control over one's own life. When we make choices, we feel we have that control. Therefore, offer a choice of activities. By providing two or three options (or even more activities as in the example of *Differentiated Instruction*), students feel ownership of their decisions and thereby a sense of control. This feeling of control is a prime differentiation between a pessimistic attitude and an optimistic one. Giving students a choice from among two or three options also applies to home assignments. *Notes*: (1) Offering *three* options is more effective than offering two. This is particularly the case in relationships where having a third choice eliminates all perceptions of coercion. (2) Logic prompts people to think, but emotions (feelings) prompt them to act.

Use variety.
A myriad of visual techniques can be employed including charts, bright colors, cartoons, selected parts of films, videocassettes and/ or digital versatile discs (DVD's), overhead transparencies, and power point creations. Dressing the part of a character (teacher

and/or student) qualifies. Audio techniques—such as playing music, rapping, or anything that has rhythm—add to both fun and retention. Remember how you learned your ABC's? "Twinkle, Twinkle Little Star" is the tune for "The Alphabet Song." A myriad of kinesthetic techniques can be used. Examples include (1) using a hand to draw the spelling of a word in the air, (2) sitting in a small group rocking back and forth together to feel seasick on the boat crossing the Atlantic Ocean as early 20th century immigrants, and (3) students' expressing a true or false response to a question by a thumbs up or down. Other approaches include relating personal experiences to a learning buddy on the topic. A technique with older students is to give them a partially completed worksheet that they fill out during the presentation. This activity keeps them involved and also gives them something they can refer to later.

Get yourself excited.
You shouldn't expect others to get excited about what you are teaching if you are not excited yourself. Telling a story, creating analogies and metaphors, showing how the lesson is meaningful or relevant, relating new information to previous leanings and/or to different situations is fun and engenders enthusiasm for both teacher and learner.

Use a student's perspective.
Think of yourself as a student while planning and teaching the lesson. Continually reflect on how you would react to the lesson if you were the student.
   Ask yourself, "If I were a student, would I want me as a teacher?"

Conclusion.
It's a wonderful experience to have classrooms of students who are there because they *want* to be, rather than because they are obliged to be. Using these motivational techniques promotes this endeavor.

Attention Management

PROMPT

FOCUS on the teacher

SIGNAL others

DISCIPLINE without STRESS®

A NONCOERCIVE APPROACH
(BUT NOT PERMISIVE)

KEY CHARACTERISTICS

1. *Discipline without Stress®* focuses on *promoting responsibility*—rather than on obedience, which too often results in resistance, resentment, and even rebellion. Obedience does not create desire. However, when responsibility is promoted, obedience becomes a natural by-product.

2. When implemented in an individual classroom, a *learning culture* is established. When implemented school-wide, a *learning community* is created.

3. The program can be used in *any grade level*, subject area, school, or home setting.

4. The *principles are universal* in that they can be used in one's *personal life* as well as in one's *professional life* to increase effectiveness and enhance relationships.

5. The approach uses a *comprehensive teaching model*, rather than a series of techniques.

6. The approach is *totally noncoercive*, thereby eliminating power struggles and adversarial relationships; however, it is *not permissive.*

7. A *positive learning environment* is maintained at all times—even when irresponsible behavior is demonstrated.

8. The program is *proactive*. The stage is set for dealing with disruptive behaviors *before* they occur. This is in contrast to the reactive strategy of dealing with disruptive behaviors after they occur.

9. When handling irresponsible behaviors, a *stress-reducing mode is used*, in contrast to the usual stress-inducing mode.

10. *Brain compatible strategies* that actuate desired behaviors are implemented.

11. Motivation is engendered so young people develop a *desire to be responsible* and a *desire to put forth effort to learn.*

12. Since our choices direct our lives, the use of *choice-response thinking* is continually employed.

13. The approach empowers young people to *resist victimhood thinking.*

14. A *deductive* approach is used. Four hierarchical concepts are taught at the outset. Individual situations are categorized into one of these four levels. This is in contrast to the usual inductive approach of first teaching specifics in order to arrive at general concepts, such as listing rules in order to arrive at desired behaviors.

15. A *constructivist* approach is used. Students create their own examples to make the four levels of the hierarchy meaningful and relevant to them. This approach is most effective when emphasizing thinking, understanding, and self-control.

16. Rather than limiting acceptable levels to only one, the hierarchy of development has two such levels, thereby *increasing propensity for success.*

17. The system *separates the person from the person's behavior*—the deed from the doer, the act from the actor. This eliminates a natural tendency for the student to be self-defensive, a major block for acknowledging responsibility of one's action.

18. Inappropriate behavior is viewed as a response to an impulse, rather than as a deliberate disruption. The situation becomes a *teachable moment*—as when a student makes a mistake, commits an error, or does poorly in a subject area.

19. The approach systematically *prompts reflection* and evaluation of one's actions.

20. *Dignity* is retained at all times with all involved.

21. *Impulse management* to redirect inappropriate decisions and behaviors is an integral part of the approach.

22. A *guiding* and empowering mode is employed, in contrast to the more common *telling* and *overpowering* approach.

23. *Class time is not wasted* when the teacher attends to a disruption. During the short guidance interchange, the entire class is reinforcing the hierarchy of the levels of development.

24. Disruptive behavior is usually most effectively dealt with privately, but this strategy also allows the guidance to take place in a *whole-class setting.*

25. Students gain an understanding between *internal* and *external motivation,* when each is appropriate, and ways to *resist irresponsible peer influence.*

26. The system *promotes quality* learning because it sets the stage for evaluation before instruction begins.

27. The program *promotes character development* without using external approaches, such as adult monitoring.

28. The program *fosters internal motivation* to be responsible and act appropriately. This is in contrast to an approach where the motivation is designed for using external sources, such as rewards and punishments.

29. *External approaches* of giving rewards for expected behavior and using threats *are not used* because they (a) foster obedience rather than commitment, (b) require an adult presence for monitoring, (c) prompt students to be dependent upon external agents, and (d) do not foster long-term motivation for responsibility.

30. *Authority is used <u>without</u> being punitive* because punishments are based on the false premise that a youngster has to be harmed in order to learn. In addition, punishments for young people are counterproductive because they adversely affect relationships.

The following principles are incorporated:

(1) Positivity is a more constructive teacher than negativity.

(2) Choice empowers.

(3) Self-evaluation is essential for lasting improvement.

(4) People choose their own behaviors.

(5) Self-correction is the most effective approach to change behavior.

(6) Acting responsibly is the most satisfying of rewards.

(7) Growth is greater when authority is used without punishment.

Instructional Model
The Raise Responsibility System

The system is based on the following instructional model:
> **(1) <u>Teaching the levels</u>** *(Teaching)*
> **(2) <u>Checking for understanding</u>** *(Asking)*
> **(3) <u>Guided choices</u>** *(Eliciting)*

(1) <u>Teaching the levels</u> *(Teaching)*

Four levels of development are taught:
> **(D)** *Democracy* (develops self-discipline and demonstrates responsibility)
> > <u>**In**</u>*ternal motivation*–Takes initiative to do what is expected

> **(C)** *Cooperation/Conformity* (complies to what is expected/ conforms to peer influence)
> > <u>**Ex**</u>*ternal motivation*

> **(B)** *Boss<u>ing</u>/Bully<u>ing</u>* (breaks laws and makes own standards)
> > *[Note verb form.] Obeys only when enforcer shows more authority*

> **(A)** *Anarchy* (absence of order-aimless-chaotic)

(2) <u>Checking for understanding</u> *(Asking)*

Disruptions are handled by <u>checking for understanding</u>.

> The purpose is for the disrupting student to *recognize* and *acknowledge* the developmental level of the action.

> Recognizing the level is necessary in order to accept responsibility.

> **The key to raising responsibility is (1) <u>teaching the levels</u> and (2) <u>checking for understanding</u>.**

> The vast majority of situations are handled using this basic learning approach of teaching and then checking.

(3) <u>Guided choices</u> *(Eliciting)*

> <u>Guided choices</u> are used for students who have acknowledged disruptive behavior and continue their irresponsibility.

> *Authority without being punitive is used in these situations.*

> <u>Guided choices</u> elicits a procedure to redirect future impulses.

Using a Butterfly Analogy to Explain the Hierarchy

From a post at
http://groups.yahoo.com/group/DisciplineWithoutStress/

I began by reminding the students of their study in third grade of the life cycle of a butterfly. They recalled that there are four stages of development in the life cycle of a butterfly: egg, caterpillar, pupa, and butterfly. We talked about how all butterflies are in some stage of this process, but they have no control over their movement through this process.

We then moved on to comparing the butterfly's life cycle to that of humans. We decided that humans go through four basic stages as well. We called them: baby/infant, child/youth, adolescence/teen, and adult/grown-up. Again we agreed that humans had little control over the stage of physical development in which they found themselves.

Then we began to look at the four stages of social development in which one human and/or a society could operate. We talked about what a human and a society in anarchy would look like and how such a situation was so hopeless. Then we talked about what would likely occur to remedy the problems of an anarchy-based society. We decided that someone would rise up and take control of the situation (thereby becoming a boss) and that this may or may not be a good thing. We looked at countries around the world where we thought this might have happened.

Next we moved on to looking at the level of control or power in a group of friends. We decided that a group of friends works together to share control based on what they agree is their mission and that oftentimes this mission and the group control is not ever discussed; it is more or less just understood among the group members. From here a discussion of blind conformity developed and how this type of cooperation is not necessarily good. We went on to look at how being considerate of others and cooperating for the right reasons resulted in a democratic society like the United States.

We decided that doing what is right because we know it is the best thing to do is a much higher level of development than doing what is right as a result of peer pressure. Finally, we talked about how we had more control over our stage of social development than we did over our stage of physical development. The thought of being in control over something about themselves heightened their interest in the Raise Responsibility System.

FORMS

Levels of Development

D *Democracy*

<> **Highest level of development**

- Develops self-discipline
- Demonstrates Initiative
- Does good because it is the right thing to do
- <u>Demonstrates responsibility because it is essential for democracy</u>

The motivation is <u>internal</u>.

C *Cooperation/Conformity*

<> **Appropriate and acceptable level of behavior**

- Considerate
- Complies
- Conforms to peer pressure

The motivation is <u>external</u>.

B *Bossing/Bullying*

<> **Neither appropriate nor acceptable level of classroom behavior**

- Bothers others
- Bullies others
- Breaks laws and makes own rules and standards

Must be bossed to behave

A *Anarchy*

<> **Lowest level of behavior**

- Absence of order
- Aimless and chaotic
- Absence of government

Anarchy is the fundamental enemy of civilization.

> **The difference between levels C and D is often in the *<u>motivation</u>*, rather than the action.**

Sample Letter to Parents
The Raise Responsibility System

Dear Parents:

Our classroom houses a small society. Each student is a citizen who acts in accordance with expected standards of behavior.

With this in mind, rewards are not given for expected behavior—just as society does not give rewards for behaving properly. Also, irresponsible behavior is seen as an opportunity for growth, rather than for punishment.

Our approach encourages students to exercise self-discipline through reflection and self-evaluation. Students learn to control their own behavior, rather than always relying on the teacher for control.

We want our classroom to be encouraging and conducive to learning at all times. In this way, young people develop positive attitudes and behavioral skills that are so necessary for successful lives.

Sincerely,

Teacher

Essay

The Raise Responsibility System

<u>Describe clearly and fully</u>:

1. What **<u>did</u>** I do? *(acknowledgment)*

2. What **<u>can</u>** I do to prevent it from happening again? *(choice)*

3. What **<u>will</u>** I do? *(commitment)*

- -

Note: The purpose of the essay is to:

   (1) isolate the disrupting student, and

   (2) give the student a responsibility-producing activity to have the student think about his/her disruption.

The key is for the student to describe—not for the teacher to tell.

Before the student leaves the classroom, two questions are asked:

   Do you know why this form was given to you?

   Do you think it is personal?

Self-Diagnostic Referral – Upper Elementary
The Raise Responsibility System

Name _____

Date _____

1. What happened?

2. On what level did you act?

3. Explain this level.

4. When you act on this level, how must the teacher treat you?

5. Is this how you want to be treated? Why or why not?

6. On what level should you act?

7. List at least one solution to the problem you could have used if
    you had acted more responsibly.

Self-Diagnostic Referral
The Raise Responsibility System

Name (Print) _____

Date _____ Period _____

1. Define the problem you created that resulted in your getting this assignment.

2. Tell on what developmental level you acted.

3. Explain this level.

4. Explain why you see yourself at this level.

5. When you act at this level, on what level must the teacher react to you ?

6. How must the teacher treat you on this level?

7. Is this how you want to be treated in the classroom?

8. Why or why not?

9. On what level should you have acted?

10. If you had acted on this level, how would the situation have been different?

11. **On the back** of this Self-Diagnostic Referral, list three (3) solutions to the problem you could have used if you would have acted more responsibly.

Parent Note
The Raise Responsibility System

Re: Period:

Dear Parent:

Self-Diagnostic Referrals are enclosed. The purpose of this type of referral is to help students understand their self-chosen behavior level and to become more socially responsible. The **first** referral is <u>handled between the teacher and the student</u>.

If a **second** referral is necessary, a copy of the **first** and **second** are sent home.

Please note that your child has chosen to act on a level that is not acceptable in my classroom. <u>Please have your child explain this level to you</u>.

If a **third** referral is necessary, a copy of all three are sent home, and future socially irresponsible behavior will be referred to the school office.

Please sign this note and have your child return it to me. Thank you.

_____

Teacher

_____

Parent Signature

Date:

Date due back:

Problem:

Grades 5–8 Sample Schedule of Implementation
The Raise Responsibility System

Day 1 (15 minutes)
Introduce levels A and B.

Day 2 (45 minutes)
Sponge – Students create examples of levels A and B.

Pass out the **Levels of Development** (form describing levels A, B, C, D).

Review levels A and B.

Discuss level C and <u>external motivation</u> (**especially peer pressure**).

Discuss level D and <u>internal motivation</u> (**especially responsibility and initiative**).

Divide students into groups.

-Groups create three (3) **examples** of **classroom behavior** for each level (A, B, C, D).

-Inform students that on the next day all members of the group will stand together during their presentation.

-Each group chooses a leader who is responsible for coordinating the presentation/report of that group.

Groups then create three examples for each level.

<u>**HOME ASSIGNMENT:**</u> Students copy the following on the **reverse** side of the *Levels of Development* form for parent signature.

(Student's name)_____ has explained the *Levels of Development* to me and that levels A and B are not acceptable levels of classroom behavior.

_____
Parent signature

Day 3 (15 minutes)
Groups meet and choose <u>one</u> of their three examples from each level to report.
Groups share the one example from each level.

Substitute/Guest Teacher Information

The Raise Responsibility System

READ TO EACH CLASS AT THE START OF THE PERIOD.

This class understands levels of development. It is the basis of discipline in this classroom. A substitute teacher does not have to be versed in the system to use it.

It is the responsibility of the class members to maintain their own discipline. Students know that they choose the level of behavior they want.

If students behave and do the given assignment, they are on *Level C* or *Level D* and should not present a problem.

Level B students are the ones who defy your authority. My students know that they alone choose their level of behavior and that they must accept the responsibility for their choice. I need a list of the defiant students so they can carry out the assignment that goes along with their choice of behavior.

Please leave me a list of students *who chose to act on Level B.*

INDEX

NOTES